Lecture Notes in Computer Science   11982

More information about this series at http://www.springer.com/series/7410

Jaideep Vaidya · Xiao Zhang ·
Jin Li (Eds.)

Cyberspace Safety
and Security

11th International Symposium, CSS 2019
Guangzhou, China, December 1–3, 2019
Proceedings, Part I

Springer

Editors
Jaideep Vaidya
Rutgers University
Newark, NJ, USA

Xiao Zhang
Beihang University
Beijing, China

Jin Li
Guangzhou University
Guangzhou, China

ISSN 0302-9743 ISSN 1611-3349 (electronic)
Lecture Notes in Computer Science
ISBN 978-3-030-37336-8 ISBN 978-3-030-37337-5 (eBook)
https://doi.org/10.1007/978-3-030-37337-5

LNCS Sublibrary: SL4 – Security and Cryptology

This Springer imprint is published by the registered company Springer Nature Switzerland AG
The registered company address is: Gewerbestrasse 11, 6330 Cham, Switzerland

Preface

Welcome to the proceedings of the 11th International Symposium on Cyberspace Safety and Security (CSS 2019), which was organized by Guangzhou University and held in Guangzhou, China, during December 1–3, 2019.

CSS 2019 was the 11th event in a series of international symposiums devoted to research on cyberspace safety and security. Previous iterations of the symposium include CSS 2018 (Amalfi, Italy), CSS 2017 (Xi'an, China), CSS 2016 (Granada, Spain), CSS 2015 (New York, USA), CSS 2014 (Paris, France), CSS 2013 (Zhangjiajie, China), CSS 2012 (Melbourne, Australia), CSS 2011 (Milan, Italy), CSS 2009 (Chengdu, China), and CSS 2008 (Sydney, Australia).

The CSS symposium aims to provide a leading-edge forum to foster interaction between researchers and developers with the cyberspace safety and security communities, and to give attendees an opportunity to network with experts in this area. It focuses on cyberspace safety and security, such as authentication, access control, availability, integrity, privacy, confidentiality, dependability, and sustainability issues of cyberspace.

CSS 2019 attracted 235 high-quality research papers highlighting the foundational work that strives to push beyond the limits of existing technologies, including experimental efforts, innovative systems, and investigations that identify weaknesses in existing cyber technology. Each submission was reviewed by at least three experts in the relevant areas, on the basis of their significance, novelty, technical quality, presentation, and practical impact. According to this stringent peer-review process involving about 65 Program Committee members and several additional reviewers, 61 full papers were selected to be presented at the conference, giving an acceptance rate of 26%. Additionally, we also accepted 40 short papers.

CSS 2019 was made possible by the behind-the-scene effort of selfless individuals and organizations who volunteered their time and energy to ensure the success of this conference. We would like thank all authors for submitting and presenting their papers. We also greatly appreciated the support of the Program Committee members and the reviewers. We sincerely thank all the chairs–without their hard work, the success of CSS 2019 would not have been possible.

Last but not least, we would like to thank all the contributing authors and all conference attendees, as well as the great team at Springer that assisted in producing the conference proceedings, and the developers and maintainers of EasyChair.

December 2019

Jaideep Vaidya
Xiao Zhang
Jin Li

Organization

Honorary General Chair

Binxing Fang   Guangzhou University, China

General Chairs

Jin Li   Guangzhou University, China
Zhihong Tian   Guangzhou University, China

Program Chairs

Jaideep Vaidya   Rutgers University, USA
Xiao Zhang   Beihang University, China

Publication Chair

Yu Wang   Guangzhou University, China

Publicity Chairs

Xiaochun Cheng   Middlesex University, UK
Nan Jiang   East China Jiaotong University, China
Zheli Liu   Nankai University, China
Weizhi Meng   Technical University of Denmark, Denmark

Track Chairs

Xu Ma   Qufu Normal University, China
Hui Tian   National Huaqiao University, China

Steering Committee Chair

Yang Xiang   Swinburne University of Technology, Australia

Program Committee

Andrea Abate   University of Salerno, Italy
Silvio Barra   University of Cagliari, Italy
Carlo Blundo   University of Salerno, Italy
Yiqiao Cai   Huaqiao University, China
Luigi Catuogno   University of Salerno, Italy

Lorenzo Cavallario	Royal Holloway, University of London, UK
Fei Chen	Shenzhen University, China
Laizhong Cui	Shenzhen University, China
Frederic Cuppens	Enst Bretagne, France
Massimo Ficco	Second University of Naples, Italy
Dieter Gollmann	Hamburg University of Technology, Germany
Lorena Gonzalez	Carlos III University of Madrid, Spain
Zhitao Guan	North China Electric Power University, China
Jinguang Han	Nanjing University of Finance and Economics, China
Saeid Hosseini	Singapore University of Technology and Design, Singapore
Xinyi Huang	Fujian Normal University, China
Shuyuan Jin	Sun Yat-sen University, China
Lutful Karim	Seneca College of Applied Arts and Technology, Canada
Sokratis Katsikas	University of Piraeus, Greece
Xuejun Li	Anhui University, China
Kaitai Liang	Manchester Metropolitan University, UK
Jay Ligatti	University of South Florida, USA
Huiting Liu	Anhui University, China
Xiapu Luo	Hong Kong Polytechnic University, Hong Kong, China
Liangfu Lv	Tianjin University, China
Xiaobo Ma	Xi'an Jiaotong University, China
Fabio Martinelli	IIT-CNR, Italy
Mehrnoosh Monshizadeh	Nokia Bell Labs, Finland
Vincenzo Moscato	University of Naples, Italy
Francesco Moscato	Second University of Naples, Italy
Richard Overill	King's College London, UK
Umberto Ferraro Petrillo	Sapienza University of Rome, Italy
Florin Pop	University Politehnica of Bucharest, Romania
Jianzhong Qi	The University of Melbourne, Australia
Lianyong Qi	Qufu Normal University, China
Alim Al Islam Razi	Bangladesh University of Engineering and Technology, Bangladesh
Dharmendra Sharma	University of Canberra, Australia
Willy Susilo	University of Wollogon, Australia
Zhiyuan Tan	Edinburgh Napier University, UK
Donghai Tian	Beijing Institute of Technology, China
Ding Wang	Peking University, China
Hua Wang	Victoria University, Australia
Jianfeng Wang	Xidian University, China
Wei Wang	Beijing Jiaotong University, China
Lingyu Wang	Concordia University, Canada
Bing Wu	Fayetteville State University, USA
Tao Xiang	Chongqing University, China
Ping Xiong	Zhongnan University of Economics and Law, China

Contents – Part I

Machine Learning and Security

Cyberspace Safety

Big Data and Security

Cloud and Security

Contents – Part II

Information Security

Machine Learning and Security

Cyberspace Safety

Network Security

Research and Application of Anomaly Detection of Industrial Control System Based on Improved Zoe Algorithm

Xin Xie, Bin Wang$^{(\boxtimes)}$, Tiancheng Wan, Xunyi Jiang, Weiru Wang, and WenLiang Tang

East China Jiaotong University, Nanchang 330013, China
wangbin199702@163.com

Abstract. Due to the complexity of components and the diversity of protocols in industrial control systems, it is difficult to simply use content-based anomaly detection system with the background. This paper proposes an improved Zoe algorithm. In the algorithm, the similarity between traffics is calculated through sequence coverage. And we use Count-Mean-Min Sketch to store and count the sub-strings. Finally, we utilize clustering to achieve the anomaly detection of the industrial control system. The experimental results show that this algorithm can achieve higher detection rate and lower false positive rate of anomaly detection in industrial control systems.

Keywords: Zoe algorithm · Sequence coverage · Industrial control system · Anomaly detection

1 Introduction

Anomaly detection is a key component of network security defense in industrial control systems (ICS). One of the methods is matching known anomalous traffic models by collecting and analyzing network traffic in ICS. If the match fails, it is regarded as unknown abnormal traffic, which is analyzed to determine whether there is suspicious intrusion and attack behavior [1]. The early ICS security solutions proposed are mainly transplanting traditional active defense solutions [2, 3], while the components in industrial control systems usually come from different vendors and use specific non-standardized protocols, therefore, the traditional intrusion detection methods are not universal for ICS, and that's why the network of industrial control systems become more vulnerable to hacking [4, 5].

Some papers proposed to predict data currently by using flow-based methods or modelling basic physical processes to achieve anomaly detection. YingXu [6] et al. presented an novel approach to build a traffic model based on structural time series model. They proposed a basic structural model based on the analysis of industrial traffic to decomposes time series into four factors, which improves detection accuracy and the effectiveness of detecting abnormal data positioning significantly. Arévalo [7] et al. proposed using information fusion method and different architectures with applying the combination rules to the fusion classification method prediction to improve the overall

© Springer Nature Switzerland AG 2019
J. Vaidya et al. (Eds.): CSS 2019, LNCS 11982, pp. 3–12, 2019.
https://doi.org/10.1007/978-3-030-37337-5_1

effect of fault detection and evaluation. Tsai [8] et al. used identity-based signature and encryption to propose a new anonymous key distribution scheme for the smart grid environment. This scheme requires only a small amount of calculation and is safe under the random prediction model. Liu [9] et al. proposed a new method for the fusion of network and physical processes to detect bad data injection (BDI) of smart grid by combining traffic characteristics in the information network and physical process laws in power system. The forecast data is compared to actual data to determine if an abnormality has occurred. Although these methods can greatly increase the accuracy of anomaly detection, the scope of application is limited. On the other hand, it can only be used to detect flood attacks or incremental attacks [10] in most cases, and constructing models is also difficult. Also, some scholars use optimization models to solve such problems [11, 12].

With the development of machine learning and neural networks, deep learning has gradually combined with the intrusion detection of industrial control systems [13], and has achieved considerable results. Yu [14] et al. proposed to use long short term memory (LSTM) to model industrial control intrusion detection process and used cross-validation to select the relatively optimal LSTM model, which achieved higher accuracy rate than the traditional intrusion detection method. Due to the widespread use of proprietary binary protocols in industrial control networks, the use of content-based methods for anomaly detection [15] can achieve better results in some cases. Wressnegger et al. [16] proposed an algorithm called Zoe to detect intrusions, it effectively utilizes the content-based anomaly detection framework to improve the accuracy of anomaly detection. However, the use of cosine similarity [17] to calculate the similarity between any pair of traffics results in the loss of traffic characteristics and leads to dimensional explosion when the amount of data is large, which will result in certain impact on the accuracy of the clustering.

In order to avoid the problems, this paper proposes an improved Zoe algorithm, using sequence coverage [18] to calculate the similarity between any pair of traffics and Count-Mean-Min Sketch [19] is used to count the traffic contained in each cluster, which further improves the accuracy and speed of the detection.

2 The Analysis of Zoe Algorithm

The Zoe algorithm is a content-based anomaly detector that can handle the problems generated by binary and text-based protocols, it uses clustering [20] to implement anomaly detection. For the message m, all sub-string of length n are extracted from m by using the n-gram. Each sub-string is corresponding to a dimension of the feature space, so the message m is mapped to the corresponding feature vector:

$$x = \phi(m) \tag{1}$$

The mapping ϕ is defined as follows:

$$\phi : m \rightarrow (\phi_s(m))_{s \in S}, \phi_s(m) = occ(s, m) \tag{2}$$

where the set S represents all sub-strings of length n, and the function $occ(s,m)$ represents the occurrence of the sub-string s in the input message m.

Using this mapping, a set of messages can be translated to a set of vectors to build the input dataset X. Then, k samples are drawn from the input data to initialize clusters $C_1, C_2, \ldots, C_k$. For each following sample x, the similarity is measured to each cluster and assign x to the cluster C_j that has the closest proximity:

$$j = \arg\max_{i\in[1,k]} \text{prox}(x, C_i) \tag{3}$$

$$\text{prox} : x, C \rightarrow \frac{1}{|C|} \sum_{y\in C} \text{sim}(x, y) \tag{4}$$

where $\text{sim}(x, y) = \frac{x \cdot y}{\|x\|_2 \|y\|_2}$, $|C| = \sum_{y\in C_i} y$ and the value is obtained by Count-Min Sketch [21].

By introducing a threshold, features are pruned that occur in less than the threshold after input samples have been associated with a cluster and thereby depends effectively discard noise from the training data.

The minimum score value from model is defined to determine the nature of the messages:

$$\text{score} : m, M \rightarrow \min_i d(m, M_i) \tag{5}$$

$$d : m, M \rightarrow \text{cov}(m, M) \tag{6}$$

The function $\text{cov}(m, M)$ returns the number of bytes in m covered by feature vectors M.

In accordance to d and using an overall threshold T, a message is considered malicious for $\text{score}(m, M) \geq T$ and benign otherwise.

For the process, after the sub-string is extracted by the n-gram, the frequency of each sub-string is taken as the value corresponding to each dimension in the feature vector, but the message is essentially divided into isolated units by n-gram and converted into discrete one-hot vector, which cannot consider the inherent connectivity. And the value of n is critical, the constraint information appears for the next symbol is more and greater discrimination when n increased, the sub-string appears more times and more reliable statistics of message when n is reduced. On the other hand, the dimensionality of the generated vector space is very high, and if there is no enough training data, it will affect the detection accuracy [22].

3 The Sequence Coverage Similarity Algorithm

Let $\sum$ be a finite alphabet and $\sum^*$ be the set of all sequences defined over. ε is noted as the empty sequence.

$S \subset \sum^*$ is noted as any set of sequences, and S_{sub} is the set of all subsequences that extracted from any element of $S \cup \sum$. Let $M(S_{sub})$ be the set of all the multisets that composed from the elements of S_{sub}.

$C \in M(S_{sub})$ is called a partial covering of sequence $s \in \sum^*$ if and only if

(1) all the subsequences of C are also subsequences of s.
(2) indistinguishable copies of a particular element in C correspond to distinct occurrences of the same subsequence in s.

$C_S^*(s)$ is noted as the S-optimal covering of s.

Define the covering similarity measure between any nonempty sequence s and any set $S \subset \sum^*$ as

$$\varphi(s, S) = \frac{|s| - |C_S^*(s)| + 1}{|s|} \tag{7}$$

where $|C_S^*(s)|$ is the number of subsequences composing a S-optimal covering of s, and $|s|$ is the length of sequence s.

Note that the covering similarity between a sequence and a set of sequences as defined in Eq. 7 enables the definition of a covering similarity measure on the sequence set itself. For any pair of sequences s_1, s_2, this measure is defined as follows:

$$\varphi_{seq}(s_1, s_2) = \frac{1}{2}(\varphi(s_1, \{s_2\}) + \varphi(s_2, \{s_1\})) \tag{8}$$

where the larger the value of φ_{seq}, the more similar the sequence is.

4 ICS Anomaly Detection Based on Improved Zoe Algorithm

The Zoe algorithm is an extensional anomaly detection method which based on content. Clustering the messages with sequence coverage similarity algorithm through this method framework and combining with Count-Mean-Min Sketch data structure to identify unknown abnormal traffics.

The schematic diagram of the anomaly detection process based on the improved Zoe algorithm is as follows (Fig. 1):

We use the above coverage similarity to calculate which cluster the input traffic belongs to. By performing sequence coverage similarity calculation on the original traffic, we avoid the problem of setting the value of n in n-gram feature extraction stage and avoid the problem of dimension explosion.

In order to obtain the similarity between the input traffic and any cluster, it is necessary to calculate the similarity between any traffic y in the cluster C and the input traffic m first.

$$\varphi_{seq}(y, m) = \frac{1}{2}(\varphi(y, \{m\}) + \varphi(m, \{y\})) \tag{12}$$

$$\varphi(y, \{m\}) = \frac{|y| - |C_{\{m\}}^*(y)| + 1}{|y|} \tag{13}$$

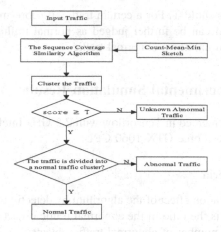

Fig. 1. Schematic diagram of the algorithm flow

$$\varphi(m, \{y\}) = \frac{|m| - \left|C^*_{\{y\}}(m)\right| + 1}{|m|} \tag{14}$$

where $\{m\}$ and $\{y\}$ represent the set of all possible binary sub-sequences of traffic m and y respectively. The larger the value of $\varphi_{seq}(y, m)$, the more similar between the traffic m and y is.

We select k traffic in the training set to initialize k clusters $C_1, C_2,...,C_k$ randomly.

For each traffic in C, the above calculation is performed with the input traffic m, and the similarity between the traffic m and the cluster C is calculated:

$$new - prox : m, C \rightarrow \frac{1}{|C|} \sum_{y \in C} \varphi_{seq}(y, m) \tag{15}$$

where $|C|$ is obtained by the Count-Mean-Min Sketch data structure.

We calculate the similarity between each cluster and the traffic in turn, and select the cluster j with the greatest similarity to the traffic, and classify the traffic into the cluster.

$$j = \underset{i \in [1,k]}{\arg \max} \, new - prox(m, C_i) \tag{16}$$

Then we define the maximum value of the similarity between the traffic m and all clusters as the basis of the model's judgment of the nature of the traffic.

$$score : m, C \rightarrow \max_i new - prox(m, C_i) \tag{17}$$

Finally, we set a threshold T. For a certain traffic, if $score(m, C) \geq T$, it is divided into known clusters and can be further judged as normal traffic or known abnormal traffic, otherwise it is an unknown abnormal traffic.

5   Analysis of Experimental Simulation Results

Our experiment is implemented in Tensorflow with 2.5 GHz Intel Core I7-4710 M, 8G memory and NVIDIA GeForce GTX 1060 GPU.

5.1   Evaluation Criteria

We evaluated the application effect of the algorithm by detection rate and false positive rate. The detection rate is the ratio of the abnormal traffic object correctly identified in the data set to the total number of abnormal traffic objects:

$$ DRate = \frac{TP}{TP + FN} \tag{18} $$

The false positive rate indicates the ratio of the number of the normal traffic object which is marked as abnormal traffic to all normal numbers:

$$ FRate = \frac{FP}{FP + TN} \tag{19} $$

where TP (True Positive) is the number of abnormal traffic that is correctly detected. FN (False Negative) is the number of abnormal traffic that has occurred but has not been detected. FP (False Positive) is the amount of normal traffic that is incorrectly marked as abnormal. TN (True Negative) is the amount of normal traffic that has been correctly identified.

5.2   Datasets

In order to validate the improved Zoe algorithm, we used the industrial control intrusion detection standard data set [23] established by Mississippi State University (MSU) in 2014 and three public data sets [24, 25] to test the algorithm. These data sets contain the original records of the process parameter values and associated tags, which indicate the traffic is normal or abnormal.

The data set established by MSU is the network layer data of the natural gas pipeline control system. All data have been numerically processed and can be divided into four types of attack data: detection attack, command injection attack (MSCI, MPCI and MFCI), denial of service attack, response injection attacks (NMRI and CMRI). Two of the three public datasets called Single-hop Outdoor Real-time Data (SORD) and Multi-hop Outdoor Real-time Data (MORD), these were collected from an outdoor real wireless sensor network, using a single-hop and multi-hop topology with a duration of 6 h, they contains two process parameters (temperature and humidity) and each data set has a tiny partition that marks the dangerous state [26]. Each of these two dataset is further divided into two parts: the part containing the abnormal traffic and the normal flow part. The fourth data set comes from the DUWWTP (Data of Urban Waste Water Treatment Plant), which consists 38 process parameters.

5.3   Experimental Results and Analysis

The improved Zoe algorithm and Zoe algorithm are applied to the same four data volume sets respectively, and 70% of the traffic in the data set is used as the training set, 30% of the data is used as the test set. The detection rate and the false positive rate are shown in Table 1.

Table 1. Comparison of results

Dataset	Zoe algorithm		The improved Zoe algorithm in this paper	
	Detection rate	False positive rate	Detection rate	False positive rate
MSU	0.94438	0.01013	0.95472	0.00904
SORD	0.96839	0.01923	0.97347	0.00946
MORD	0.92938	0.00595	0.94731	0.00347
DUWWTP	0.98561	0.02031	0.98845	0.00850

We can see that on the MSU dataset with diverse data types, the improved Zoe algorithm improves the detection rate of abnormal data without increasing the false positive rate compared with the original algorithm, and the detection rate is close to 0.96. On other datasets, the improved Zoe algorithm in this paper has also achieved a certain improvement in detection rate and reduced the false positive rate. In addition, in order to reflect the sensitivity of the algorithm to abnormal traffic, we also used the risk degree score [27] to compare the Zoe algorithm with the improved Zoe algorithm. The accuracy of the hazard scoring technique is defined as a criterion: The degree of danger of a data point can be regarded as the distance with the dangerous data point. Thus the smaller the distance, the higher the degree of danger and the sensitivity to abnormal traffic, the faster the response to anomalies; conversely, the greater the distance, the lower the risk and the sensitivity to abnormal traffic, and the slower the response to anomalies.

$$\text{precision} = \frac{p}{n} \qquad (20)$$

where n is the number of dangerous data points in the data set, and p is the number of dangerous data points in the first n data points of the risk score.

We sorted the degree of danger obtained by the Zoe algorithm and the improved Zoe algorithm, and found the number of the previous dangerous data points respectively. The comparison results as shown in Table 2.

Table 2. Comparison of the results of the risk degree scoring technique

Dataset	Zoe algorithm	The improved Zoe algorithm in this paper
	Precision	Precision
MSU	0.9623	0.9764
SORD	0.9688	0.9812
MORD	0.9532	0.9723
DUWWTP	0.9235	0.9447

In the experiment, we used the Zoe algorithm and the improved Zoe algorithm to calculate the risk degree score for each data point in the data set. Since the training data has been marked whether the data is in a normal state or an abnormal state, so it can be seen that the improved Zoe algorithm scores in the normal traffic is densely at a lower score, while the abnormal traffic is generally at a higher score. We can see that the improved Zoe algorithm improves the sensitivity to abnormal traffic compared with the Zoe algorithm, and enhances the response speed to abnormal traffic when anomalies occur.

6   Summary and Outlook

In this paper, we analyzed the Zoe algorithm in detail, and improved it. The similarity between any two flows in the industrial control system is calculated by using the sequence coverage similarity and is used as the basis of clustering. Then, for the Count-Min Sketch used in the Zoe algorithm, we used Count-Mean-Min Sketch to further improve the accuracy of the anomaly detection. The improved Zoe algorithm improves the detection rate on the four datasets of the experiment, and the false positive rate also decreases. On these data sets, the improved Zoe algorithm is more sensitive to the abnormal traffic in the industrial control system than the Zoe algorithm. However, some methods should be adopted to reduce the computational complexity when calculating the sequence coverage similarity without affecting the detection accuracy, so as to further improve the efficiency of the algorithm.

Acknowledgements. This work is supported by the National Natural Science Foundation of China, under Grant No. 61762037. Science and Technology Key Research and Development Program of Jiangxi Province, under Grant No. 20192ACB50027.

References

1. Sun, Z., Liang, G., Bai, Y.: A hierarchical intrusion detection model in wireless sensor networks. Inf. Control **42**(6), 670–676 (2013)
2. Shn, S., Kwon, T., Jo, G.Y.: An experimental study of hierarchical intrusion detection for wireless industrial sensor networks. IEEE Trans. Industr. Inf. **6**(4), 744–757 (2010)
3. Jones, R.A., Horowitz, B.: A system-aware cyber security architecture. Syst. Eng. **15**(2), 225–240 (2012)

4. Cherepanov, A.: Win32/industroyer – a new threat for industrial control systems. Technical report, ESET (2017)
5. K. Lab: The DUQU 2.0 – technical details. Technical report, Kaspersky Lab (2015)
6. Yingxu, L., Jiao, J., Jing, L.: Analysis of industrial control systems traffic based on time series. In: 2015 IEEE Twelfth International Symposium on Autonomous Decentralized Systems, pp. 123–129. IEEE Press, Taichung (2015)
7. Arévalo, F., Rernentería, J., Schwung, A.: Fault detection assessment architectures based on classification methods and information fusion. In: 2018 IEEE 23rd International Conference on Emerging Technologies and Factory Automation (ETFA), pp. 1343–1350. IEEE Press, Turin (2018)
8. Tsai, J., Lo, N.: Secure anonymous key distribution scheme for smart grid. IEEE Trans. Smart Grid 7(2), 906–914 (2016)
9. Liu, T., Sun, Y., Liu, Y., et al.: Abnormal traffic-indexed state estimation: a cyber-physical fusion approach for smart grid attack detection. Future Gener. Comput. Syst. 49, 94–103 (2015)
10. Kurt, M.N., Yılmaz, Y., Wang, X.: Distributed quickest detection of cyber-attacks in smart grid. IEEE Trans. Inf. Forensics Secur. 13(8), 1 (2018)
11. Jiang, N., Li, B., Wan, T., Liu, L.: C-POEM: comprehensive performance optimization evaluation model for wireless sensor networks. Soft. Comput. 21(12), 3377–3385 (2017)
12. Jiang, N., Xiao, X., Liu, L.: Localization scheme for wireless sensor networks based on "shortcut" constraint. Ad Hoc Sens. Wirel. Netw. 26(1–4), 1–19 (2015)
13. Lai, Y.X., Liu, Z.H., Cai, X.T., et al.: Research on intrusion detection of industrial control system. J. Commun. 38(2), 143–156 (2017)
14. Yu, B.B., Wang, H.Z., Yan, B.Y.: Intrusion detection of industrial control systems based on long and short time memory networks. Inf. Control 47(01), 54–59 (2018)
15. Song, L.K., Fei, C.W., Bai, G.C., et al.: Dynamic neural network method-based improved PSO and BR algorithms for transient probabilistic analysis of flexible mechanism. Adv. Eng. Inform. 33, 144–153 (2017)
16. Hadžiosmanović, D., Simionato, L., Bolzoni, D., Zambon, E., Etalle, S.: N-gram against the machine: on the feasibility of the N-gram network analysis for binary protocols. In: Balzarotti, D., Stolfo, S.J., Cova, M. (eds.) RAID 2012. LNCS, vol. 7462, pp. 354–373. Springer, Heidelberg (2012). https://doi.org/10.1007/978-3-642-33338-5_18
17. Huang, Y.W., Chen, G., Ye, J.F.: Weighted K-nearest neighbor indoor positioning algorithm based on cosine similarity. Comput. Appl. Softw. 36(02), 159–162 (2019)
18. Wressnegger, C., Kellner, A., Rieck, K.: Zoe: content-based anomaly detection for industrial control systems. In: 2018 48th Annual IEEE/IFIP International Conference on Dependable Systems and Networks, pp. 127–138. IEEE Press, Luxembourg City (2018)
19. Marteau, P.-F.: Sequence covering for efficient host-based intrusion detection. IEEE Trans. Inf. Forensics Secur. 14(4), 994–1006 (2019)
20. Coates, A., Ng, Andrew Y.: Learning feature representations with K-means. In: Montavon, G., Orr, G.B., Müller, K.-R. (eds.) Neural Networks: Tricks of the Trade. LNCS, vol. 7700, pp. 561–580. Springer, Heidelberg (2012). https://doi.org/10.1007/978-3-642-35289-8_30
21. Cormode, G., Muthukrishnan, M.: Approximating data with the count-min sketch. IEEE Softw. 29(1), 64–69 (2012)
22. Creech, G., Hu, J.: A semantic approach to host-based intrusion detection systems using contiguous and discontiguous system call patterns. IEEE Trans. Comput. 63(4), 807–819 (2014)
23. Deng, F., Rafiei, D.: New estimation algorithms for streaming data: Count-min can do more. http://www.cs.ualberta.ca/~fandeng/paper/cmm.pdf

24. Nader, P., Honeine, P., Beauseroy, P.: One-class classification for intrusion detection in SCADA systems. IEEE Trans. Industr. Inf. **10**(4), 2308–2317 (2014)
25. Frank, A., Asuncion, A.: UCI machine learning repository. School Information and Computer Science, University of California, Irvine, CA, USA. http://archive.ics.uci.edu/ml. Accessed 10 2018
26. Suthaharan, S., Alzahrani, M., Rajasegarar, S., et al.: Labelled data collection for anomaly detection in wireless sensor networks. In: Sixth International Conference on Intelligent Sensors, pp. 269–274. IEEE Press, Brisbane (2010)
27. Almalawi, A., Fahad, A., Tari, Z., et al.: An efficient data-driven clustering technique to detect attacks in SCADA systems. IEEE Trans. Inf. Forensics Secur. **11**(5), 893–906 (2016)

An Intrusion Detection Method Based on Hierarchical Feature Learning and Its Application

Xin Xie[1], Xunyi Jiang[1(✉)], Weiru Wang[1], Bin Wang[1],
Tiancheng Wan[1], and Hao Yang[2]

[1] East China Jiaotong University, Nanchang 330013,
People's Republic of China
johnson_jyang@163.com
[2] State Grid Jiangxi Electric Power Research Institute, Nanchang 330096,
People's Republic of China

Abstract. Network traffic classification, which generally adopts traditional machine learning methods, is one of the most important methods in intrusion detection. However, how to design a feature set that accurately characterizes network traffic is still a problem. This paper proposes an intrusion detection method based on hierarchical feature learning, which first learns the byte-level features of network traffic through deep convolutional neural networks and then learns session-level features using Stacked Denoising Autoencoder. Experiments show that this method can obtain very important characteristics in network traffic, whose precision and false alarm rate are optimized by 0.41% compared to the CNN-only approach, so as to effectively improve the precision of network traffic classification and reduce the false alarm rate. The method can meet the requirements of network intrusion detection.

Keywords: Intrusion detection · Deep learning · Hierarchical learning of features

1 Introduction

In the traditional machine learning intrusion detection, usually, feature engineering [1] is used to construct features that reflect intrusion semantics. The features will no longer be valid when new complex attack types appear in practical applications, which cannot meet the need for flexibility and adaptability of network intrusion detection systems [2]. Some scholars deal with such problems by optimizing models [3, 4]. Meanwhile, Deep learning algorithm is a research hotspot and trend in the field of network intrusion detection, and it can find complex, potential structures or features at an abstract level. The deep learning algorithms are mainly divided into unsupervised learning, supervised learning and hybrid learning. Unsupervised deep learning methods include Sparse Auto-Encoder (SRAE) [5], Restricted Boltzmann Machine (RBM) [6], Deep Belief Network (DBN) [7] and Recurrent Neural Network (RNN) [8]. SRAE is an improved algorithm for autoencoders, Niyaz et al. [9] performed classification tasks in the NSL-KDD [10] dataset using SRAE and softmax classifiers. In the experiment, the

© Springer Nature Switzerland AG 2019
J. Vaidya et al. (Eds.): CSS 2019, LNCS 11982, pp. 13–20, 2019.
https://doi.org/10.1007/978-3-030-37337-5_2

result of SRAE and softmax regression algorithm were compared, but SRAE was not compared with other deep learning algorithms to illustrate the superiority of SRAE over other deep learning algorithms. Moreover, although the NSL-KDD dataset is an improved version of the KDD dataset [11], it still has defects and is not applicable to the current network. Yuan et al. [12] used DBN to classify and detect Android malware. Although the test results reached a maximum of 96.76%, the author extracted 192 features for each software through manual analysis, which was very complicated and time-consuming. Yin et al. [13] proposed a deep learning method for intrusion detection using RNN, which compared with other machine learning methods and showed superior performance. But data preprocessing will consume a lot of time and manpower. In addition, Li et al. [14] proposed an improved Stacked Auto-Encoder (SKAE) that has high performance in traffic identification. The supervised deep learning methods are mainly based on Convolutional Neural Network (CNN) and its improved algorithm. CNN reduce the number of parameters through sparse connectivity and shared weights, so as to improve the architecture of common neural networks, but CNN for supervised learning needs features are used as the input labeled data as input. Yao et al. [15] proposed a model combining CNN and Multi-Layer Perceptron (MLP) for intrusion detection, the 35 features in the KDD data set were manually selected as inputs to the neural network model, but the types of selected features were not specifically indicated in the paper. Hybrid learning algorithm organically combines deep learning with classical machine learning algorithms. Erfani et al. [16] combined DBN and One-Class Support Vector Machine (One-Class SVM) for network anomaly detection, but the used dataset is not common and has not been specified. Besides, each feature set in the experiment contains artificial features of different dimensions. All the above studies follow the same research model: the artificially constructed features are used as the input, which is used in unsupervised deep learning algorithm and supervised deep learning algorithm, to complete the classification task. The disadvantage of this model is that there are many problems with the artificially constructed features. The structure of network packets and network flows is similar to the structure of natural language processing (i.e. characters, sentences and segments), as shown in Fig. 1. In the intrusion detection study based on raw traffic data, Eesa et al. [17] demonstrated that we can improve the detection rate and reduce the false alarm rate (FAR) by using a better traffic feature set. Wang et al. [18] further proposed a deep learning method based on the hierarchical spatial-temporal structure, which achieved a high detection rate of intrusion detection.

In view of the above problems, this paper proposes an intrusion detection method based on hierarchical feature learning. Following the natural language processing method, we use the One-hot encoding (OHE) to extract features of the raw traffic. Then we combine CNN with Stacked Denoising Autoencoder (SDA) [19] to perform hierarchical feature learning. The method learns a better feature set to improve the accuracy and reduce the FAR of network intrusion detection.

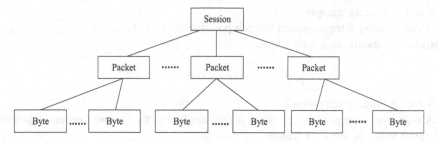

Fig. 1. Hierarchy of network traffic

2 Overview of CNN-Based Intrusion Detection Algorithms

At the network traffic packet level, each network packet is converted to a two-dimensional image whose internal byte-level spatial features are learned by CNN. The spatial features is used to classify traffic as normal or malware.

Step1: Preprocessing

During this process, OHE is used to convert the first n traffic bytes of the network flow. If the OHE vector is m-dimensional, the entire network flow can be transformed into an $m * n$ two-dimensional image. Let $x_i \in R$ be the k-dimensional vector corresponding to the i-th traffic byte in a packet or flow. A packet or flow of length n can be encoded according to the following formula, where $\oplus$ is the concatenation operator. In general, $x_{i:i+j}$ denotes the concatenation of traffic bytes $x_i, \ldots, x_{i+j}$.

$$x_{1:n} = x_1 \oplus \ldots \oplus x_n \tag{1}$$

Step2: Cross-validation

The dataset is randomly divided into k equal parts. In each iteration, one part is selected as the verification dataset, and all other k-1 parts are treated as the training dataset [20].

Step3: Spatial feature learning at the byte level

CNNs are used to learn the spatial features of the two-dimensional traffic images. The spatial features of the entire image flow are learned from a single $m * n$ image, and the output is a single flow vector. The specific process of convolution operation, feature mapping and pool operation is as follows:

Step3.1: Convolution

A convolution operation involves a filter $w \in R$, which is applied to a window of h traffic bytes to produce a new feature. For example, a feature c_i is generated using this formula, where $b \in R$ is a bias term, and f denotes Rectified Linear Unit (ReLU) activation function [21].

$$c_i = f(w \cdot x_{i:i+h-1} + b) \tag{2}$$

Step3.2: Feature mapping

A convolution filter is applied to each possible window $\{x_{1:h}, x_{2:h+1}, \ldots, x_{n-h+1:n}\}$ to produce a feature map with $c \in R$

$$c = [c_1, c_2, \ldots, c_{n-h+1}] \tag{3}$$

Step3.3: Pooling operation

A max-over-time pooling operation is then applied to the feature map and takes the maximum value as the final feature.

$$\hat{c} = \max\{c\} \tag{4}$$

Step4: Softmax classifier

The softmax classifier is used to determine whether the input traffic is normal or malware based on the flow vector.

The method adopts the OHE method to extract the features of the bytes in the application layer load, and convert them into grayscale images. Then the CNN captures the spatial features of the byte level, and finally the traffic is classified by the softmax classifier. On the one hand, CNN can extract deep features between different locations of traffic bytes. Due to the duration of the invasion, intrusion behavior can be better detected by detecting changes in the traffic bytes over a period of time. On the other hand, SDA has superior performance in feature learning of the session level.

3   Intrusion Detection Method Based on Hierarchical Feature Learning

The main ideas are as follows: At the network packet level, each network packet is transformed into a one-hot feature vector, and its internal byte-level features are learned by CNN. At the network flow level, SDA further learns the session-level features. Finally, the traffic is classified into the normal or the malicious by the generated traffic features.

CNN learns the feature vector which is transformed into a one-hot feature vector, and output the packet flow vector. Then, the session-based data preprocessing module extracts few simple features from packets' header portion and selects payloads of the network application layer within a session as features. The header features and payloads within a session together form a record. First preprocess the data and preprocessed data is used as input to SDA.

The input is first randomly corrupted by a random mapping $\tilde{x} \sim qD(\tilde{x}|x)$, and the corruption method randomly set some input units to zero. A deterministic map is then used to map the corrupted input vector $\tilde{x}$ to a hidden representation h called code:

$$h = f(W\tilde{x} + b) \tag{5}$$

Where W is a weight matrix and b is a bias vector, and the mapping $f(\cdot)$ called the encoder is a sigmoid function (i.e. $f(z) = \frac{1}{1+e^{-z}}$) in our model. The code h then is transformed back into an n-dimensional vector $x = \hat{x}$ called the reconstruction of input x. The transformation is implemented by the same mapping called decoder:

$$\hat{x} = f(W'h + b') \tag{6}$$

Where W' is set to tied weighs. SDA attempts to reconstruct the raw input from corrupted version of the input. In order to minimize the reconstruction error of the input and the output, the cross-entropy loss function:

$$L(x, \hat{x}) = -\sum_{j=1}^{n} \left[x_j \log \hat{x}_j + (1 - x_j) \log(1 - \hat{x}_j) \right] \tag{7}$$

In the first stage, the deep learning structure is trained through minimizing reconstruction error of the input and output. The second denoising autoencoder is then trained by taking the hidden-layer output of the first autoencoder as input. Thus, the denoising autoencoders are stacked into a deep neural network through training a number of denoising autoencoders. In the second stage, the output of the last hidden layer of SDA is used as input to the softmax classifier. The entire neural network is then trained as a multilayer perceptron and optimize all the parameters using labeled samples.

4   Experimental Results and Performance Analysis

The experimental environment is as follows: TensorFlow, which is run on the Ubuntu 16.04 64-bit OS, is used as the software frameworks. The CPU is Intel Core i5-3230M 2.6 GHz, the RAM is 8G, and the GPU is GeForce GT 750M. CTU-UNB was used to evaluate the performance of the intrusion detection method by comparing with the method based CNN-only.

4.1   Data Sets and Evaluation Indicators

Majority of intrusion detection datasets, such as NSL-KDD, do not contain raw traffic data. From among the few public datasets that contain raw traffic data, we choose CTU-UNB [22, 23] as our dataset. The sample distribution of the CTU-UNB dataset is shown in Table 1.

The proportion of the training set and testing set is 5:1 in CTU-UNB dataset. There were three hidden layers in the SDA neural network. The number of hidden units was all simply set to 1000 and the corruption level for training each denoising autoencoder was separately set to 10%, 20%, and 30%. The corruption level in our experiments means how many input units of a denoising autoencoder are randomly set to 0. The performance analysis of the experiment was indicated by four indicators: Accuracy (AC), Precision (P), Recall (R), F-Mean (F).

AC indicates the percentage of the correct sample in all samples, P describes the percentage of correctly identified attacks and all detected attacks, R describes the percentage of correctly identified attacks versus all actual attacks, F represents the weighted

Table 1. The sample distribution of the CTU-UNB dataset

Dataset	Training		Test	
	Count	Percentage	Count	Percentage
Normal	41480	51.11%	8177	51.11%
Neris	8039	9.90%	1584	9.90%
Rbot	6073	7.48%	1197	7.48%
Virut	18914	23.30%	3728	23.30%
Menti	217	0.27%	43	0.27%
Sogou	34	0.04%	7	0.04%
Murlo	2013	2.48%	397	2.48%
NSIS.ay	4395	5.42%	867	5.42%
Total	81165		16000	

average of the AC and R. True Positive (TP) is a positive class that is predicted to be a positive class, True Negative (TN) is a negative class that is predicted to be a negative class, and a false positive (False Positive, FP) is a negative class that is predicted to be a positive class. False Negative (FN) is a positive class that is predicted to be negative. AC, P, R, and F can be respectively obtained by Eqs. (8), (9), (10), and (11).

$$AC = (TP + TN)/(TP + TN + FP + FN) \tag{8}$$

$$P = TP/(TP + FP) \tag{9}$$

$$R = TP/(TP + FN) \tag{10}$$

$$F = 2PR/(P + R) \tag{11}$$

4.2 Experimental Results

Experiment: In the binary classification and multivariate classification, the algorithm proposed in this paper is compared with the CNN method in Sect. 2. As shown in Table 2, the proposed method and the CNN-based intrusion detection method are used for binary classification and multivariate classification in the CTU-UNB dataset. In the binary classification, the method proposed in this paper produces more than 99% of all evaluation indicators, and the AC and R are slightly higher than the CNN-based detection method; In the multivariate classification, the value of the evaluation index is slightly lower than the value in the binary classification, and the AC can reach 98.40%.

Table 2. The indicators binary classification and multivariate classification

Type	Method	AC	P	R	F
Binary classification	CNN	99.68	98.98	98.98	98.98
	Proposed method	99.48	99.39	99.39	99.39
Multivariate classification	CNN	98.04	97.66	95.74	96.69
	Proposed method	98.40	98.44	98.40	98.41

5 Conclusions and Future Work

In this paper, the OHE is used to the extracted raw traffic data. Based on CNN feature learning, SDA further learns the features and representative features are obtained. Compared with the method based CNN-only, this method effectively improves the precision, while reduce the FAR. In some cases, many published studies have shown that some artificially designed traffic features are useful for improving intrusion detection. In order to improve the detection performance, these traffic features can be integrated into the framework of intrusion detection, and its feasibility is worthy of further research.

Acknowledgements. This work is supported by the National Natural Science Foundation of China, under Grant No. 61762037.

References

1. Yu, Y., Long, J., Liu, F., Cai, Z.: Machine learning combining with visualization for intrusion detection: a survey. In: Torra, V., Narukawa, Y., Navarro-Arribas, G., Yañez, C. (eds.) MDAI 2016. LNCS (LNAI), vol. 9880, pp. 239–249. Springer, Cham (2016). https://doi.org/10.1007/978-3-319-45656-0_20
2. Sommer, R., Paxson, V.: Outside the closed world: on using machine learning for network intrusion detection. In: 2010 IEEE Symposium on Security and Privacy, Berkeley/Oakland, CA, USA, pp. 305–316. IEEE Press (2010)
3. Jiang, N., Li, B., Wan, T., Liu, L.: C-POEM: comprehensive performance optimization evaluation model for wireless sensor networks. Soft. Comput. 21(12), 3377–3385 (2017)
4. Jiang, N., Xiao, X., Liu, L.: Localization scheme for wireless sensor networks based on "shortcut" constraint. Ad Hoc Sens. Wirel. Netw. 26(1–4), 1–19 (2015)
5. Chen, J., Qi, Y.: Intrusion detection method based on deep learning. J. Jiangsu Univ. Sci. Technol. (Natural Science Edition) 31(06), 795–800 (2017)
6. Seo, S., Park, S., Kim, J.: Improvement of network intrusion detection accuracy by using restricted Boltzmann machine. In: 2016 8th International Conference on Computational Intelligence and Communication Networks, Tehri, India, pp. 413–417. IEEE Press (2016)
7. Yang, X., Gao, L., Wang, H., et al.: A cooperative deep belief network for intrusion detection. In: 2018 Sixth International Conference on Advanced Cloud and Big Data, Lanzhou, China, pp. 230–236. IEEE Press (2018)
8. Naseer, S., Saleem, Y., Khalid, S., et al.: Enhanced network anomaly detection based on deep neural networks. IEEE Access 6(99), 48231–48246 (2018)

9. Javaid, A., Niyaz, Q., Sun, W., et al.: A deep learning approach for network intrusion detection system. In: Proceedings of the 9th EAI International Conference on Bio-inspired Information and Communications Technologies, New York City, United States, pp. 21–26. Institute for Computer Sciences, Social-Informatics and Telecommunications Engineering (2016)
10. Tavallaee, M., Bagheri, E., Lu, W., et al.: A detailed analysis of the KDD CUP 99 data set. In: 2009 IEEE Symposium on Computational Intelligence for Security and Defense Applications, Ottawa, ON, Canada, pp. 1–6. IEEE Press (2009)
11. Verma, A., Ranga, V.: Statistical analysis of CIDDS-001 dataset for network intrusion detection systems using distance-based machine learning. Procedia Comput. Sci. **125**, 709–716 (2018)
12. Yuan, Z., Lu, Y., Xue, Y.: Droiddetector: android malware characterization and detection using deep learning. Tsinghua Sci. Technol. **21**(1), 114–123 (2016)
13. Yin, C., Zhu, Y., Fei, J., et al.: A deep learning approach for intrusion detection using recurrent neural networks. IEEE Access **5**, 21954–21961 (2017)
14. Li, P., Chen, Z., et al.: An improved stacked auto-encoder for network traffic flow classification. IEEE Netw. **32**, 22–27 (2018)
15. Yao, Y., Wei, Y., Gao, F., et al.: Anomaly intrusion detection approach using hybrid MLP/CNN neural network. In: 6th International Conference on Intelligent Systems Design and Applications, Jinan, China, pp. 1095–1102. IEEE Press (2006)
16. Erfani, S., Rajasegarar, S., Karunasekera, S., et al.: High-dimensional and large-scale anomaly detection using a linear one-class SVM with deep learning. Pattern Recogn. **58**, 121–134 (2016)
17. Eesa, A., Orman, Z., Brifcani, A.: A novel feature-selection approach based on the cuttlefish optimization algorithm for intrusion detection systems. Expert Syst. Appl. **42**(5), 2670–2679 (2015)
18. Wang, W., Sheng, Y., Wang, J., et al.: HAST-IDS: learning hierarchical spatial-temporal features using deep neural networks to improve intrusion detection. IEEE Access **6**, 1792–1806 (2018)
19. Yu, Y., Long, J., Cai, Z.: Session-based network intrusion detection using a deep learning architecture. In: Torra, V., Narukawa, Y., Honda, A., Inoue, S. (eds.) MDAI 2017. LNCS (LNAI), vol. 10571, pp. 144–155. Springer, Cham (2017). https://doi.org/10.1007/978-3-319-67422-3_13
20. Rodriguez, J., Perez, A., Lozano, J.: Sensitivity analysis of k-fold cross validation in prediction error estimation. IEEE Trans. Pattern Anal. Mach. Intell. **32**(3), 569–575 (2010)
21. Nair, V., Hinton, G.E.: Stacked denoising autoencoders: rectified linear units improve restricted Boltzmann machines. In: Proceedings of the 27th International Conference on International Conference on Machine Learning, Haifa, Israel, pp. 807–814. Omnipress (2010)
22. The CTU-13 Dataset: A Labeled Dataset with Botnet, Normal and Background traffic. https://www.stratosphereips.org/datasets-ctu13
23. Ali, S., Hadi, S., Mahbod, T., et al.: Toward developing a systematic approach to generate benchmark datasets for intrusion detection. Comput. Secur. **31**(3), 357–374 (2012)

Spoofing Attack Detection for Radar Network System State Estimation

Tianqi Huang[✉], Buhong Wang, and Dong Lin

Information and Navigation College, Air Force Engineering University,
Xi'an 710077, China
hl37250827@outlook.com

Abstract. The residue-based traditional chi-square detector cannot effectively detect the falsified data during radar state estimation, and propose a spoofing attack detection method for radar network system state estimation. Firstly, the model of radar measurement and state estimation in the radar network system is established and the spoofing attack is described on this basis. Then, in the process of Kalman filter based data fusion and confirmation, the distribution difference of the updated innovation before and after the spoofing attack is studied. A detection method for dealing with spoofing attacks is proposed and the error covariance of state estimation corresponding to different detection results is analyzed. Finally, the simulation verifies the universal validity of the detection method.

Keywords: Radar network · State estimation · Spoofing attack · Attack detection

1 Introduction

With the development of modern information technology, radar as the main means of detecting targets has not only been limited to the role of a single radar, but is increasingly associated with the system [1]. The radar network system refers to an organic whole formed by a plurality of different systems, different frequency bands, different working modes, and different polarization modes of the radar, and connected by means of communication means, and integrated by the central station [2]. After radar networking, the coverage of space, time and frequency is expanded, the spatial resolution and target discovery probability in the overlap region are improved, and the observation accuracy is improved [3]. The radar network has greatly improved the overall performance of the radar [4].

However, as a typical cyber physics system, radar network systems can easily be attacked by cyber attacks in wireless or wired networks connected to radar and fusion centers [5]. Its security issues are receiving increasing attention [6]. Most of the existing research work focuses on the cooperative anti-spoofing interference of radar network systems [7–9], and pays little attention to the impact of network attacks on the communication network between radar and fusion center [10]. One form of such an attack is a spoofing attack, that is, tampering with information in a transmitted data

© Springer Nature Switzerland AG 2019
J. Vaidya et al. (Eds.): CSS 2019, LNCS 11982, pp. 21–33, 2019.
https://doi.org/10.1007/978-3-030-37337-5_3

packet [11], loss of information reduces the performance of state estimation, and misleading information makes detection more difficult [12].

Although the residual-based chi-square detector is widely used to detect the received data, it cannot detect the carefully forged data. The literature [13] derives the residual constraints of attack vector avoiding bad data detection in state estimation based on the linear state estimation model. Therefore, in order to improve the detection ability of the radar network system for spoofing attacks, we has studied the distribution difference of the updated innovation in the state estimation process before and after the spoofing attack, and, proposes the spoofing attack detection method of the state estimation in the radar network system on this basis.

2   Preliminaries

2.1   Radar Measurement and State Estimation

Consider a radar network system with some radars and a data fusion center, the process by which the radar $i \in N = \{1, 2, \cdots, N\}$ measures the position of the target is as follows:

$$x(k+1) = Ax(k) + \omega(k) \tag{1}$$

$$y_i(k) = C_i x(k) + v_i(k) \tag{2}$$

Where $k \in N$ is a time series; $x(k) \in R^{n_x}$ is a state vector; A is the target position state transition matrix; $y_i(k) \in R^{n_{y_i}}$ is the radar's measurement; C is the measurement matrix; $\omega(k)$ and $v_i(k)$ are zero mean Gaussian white noise, and for $\forall j, k \in N, i = 1, 2, \cdots, N$, they satisfy: $E[\omega(k)\omega(j)^T] = \delta_{kj}Q(Q \geq 0)$, $E[\omega(k)v_i(j)^T] = 0$ and $E[v_i(p)v_j(q)^T] = \delta_{ij}\delta_{pq}R_i(R_i > 0)$.

The initial state $x(0)$ is a zero mean Gaussian random vector whose covariance is non-negative. For convenience of study, it is assumed that the measurement noise of each radar is irrelevant.

The radar network system needs to integrate all radar measurements at the same time, and the measurement set at time k is denoted by $Y_k = \{y_1(k), y_2(k), \cdots, y_N(k)\} = \{y_{1:N}(k)\}$. We define the following two equations as state estimates and corresponding error covariances:

$$\hat{x}_k = E[x(k)|Y_{1:k}] \tag{3}$$

$$P_k = E[(x(k) - \hat{x}_k)(x(k) - \hat{x}_k)^T|Y_{1:k}] \tag{4}$$

In order to reduce the communication bandwidth and meet the security requirements, each radar first processes the original measurement data locally, and then transmits the innovation of measurement to the data fusion center. However, in a multiradar network system, each radar cannot calculate a priori estimate $\hat{x}_{k|k-1}$ based on local measurements. Therefore, the data fusion center will broadcast its $\hat{x}_{k|k-1}$ at every moment, so that each radar sends the innovation defined as:

$$z_{k,i} = y_i(k) - C_i\hat{x}_{k|k-1} \tag{5}$$

It is easy to prove that the innovation also obeys the Gaussian distribution of zero mean, and the covariance [14] is:

$$Cov(z_i) = C_i P_{k|k-1} C_i^T + R_i \tag{6}$$

In the absence of spoofing attacks, the general fusion algorithm can obtain the minimum mean square error state estimation based on multiple radar measurements [15]. However, as described below, the performance of a general fusion algorithm will be greatly affected by spoofing attacks.

2.2 Spoofing Attacks

In the radar network system, the data fusion center generally uses a residual-based chi-square detector to check the statistical characteristics of the innovation data. A typical chi-square detector for the innovation z_k uses the following hypothesis test:

$$\begin{cases} a_k = \sum\limits_{i=k-J+1}^{k} z_k^T Cov^{-1}(z)z_k < \eta_1 & H_0 \\ a_k = \sum\limits_{i=k-J+1}^{k} z_k^T Cov^{-1}(z)z_k \geq \eta_1 & H_1 \end{cases} \tag{7}$$

Among them, the null hypothesis H_0 represents that the received data is normal, hypothesis H_1 is the opposite. J is the detection window size and η_1 is the defined threshold. Since z_k obeys a Gaussian distribution, a_k obeys χ^2 distribution with a degree of freedom $J\eta_1$. If the value of a_k exceeds the determined threshold η_1 it will alarm and the current innovation data will be discarded.

At time k, the data fusion center will receive the innovation data, which can be recorded as two innovation matrices $z_{k,s}$ and $\tilde{z}_{k,a}$, in which the innovation data from the attacked radar will be falsified by spoofing attack:

$$\tilde{z}_{k,a} = T_k z_{k,s} + b_k \tag{8}$$

Where b_k is subject to a Gaussian distribution of zero mean, covariance is $Cov(b)$, and is independent of z_k. Obviously $\tilde{z}_{k,a}$ still obeys the Gaussian distribution of zero mean, and the covariance is:

$$Cov(\tilde{z}_{k,a}) = T_k Cov(z_{k,s}) T_k^T + Cov(b) \tag{9}$$

Although the chi-square detection in Eq. (7) can effectively detect bad data, when the falsified innovation $\tilde{z}_{k,a}$ has the same statistical characteristics as the innovation $z_{k,s}$, the detection rate of the above spoofing attack is the same as when there is no attack, and at this time attacker can avoid the residual constraint condition of bad data detection in the state estimation [13]. The falsified innovation $\tilde{z}_{k,a}$ needs to have the same distribution $N(0, Cov(z_{k,s}))$ as the innovation $z_{k,s}$, which is $Cov(\tilde{z}_{k,a}) = T_k Cov(z_{k,s}) T_k^T + Cov(b)$.

Therefore, if the matrix T_k chosen by the attacker satisfies:

$$Cov(\tilde{z}_{k,a}) - T_k Cov(z_{k,s}) T_k^T = Cov(b) \geq 0$$

Then a spoofing attack is successfully launched, which is not detected.

3   Attack Detection Principles and Methods

If the data fusion center needs to fuse all the data, then after obtaining a one-step estimate $\hat{x}_{k,s}$, since the innovation $\tilde{z}_{k,a}$ comes from $\tilde{z}_{k,a} = y_a(k) - C_a \hat{x}_{k|k-1}$,

The fusion center needs to update the innovation $z_{k,a}$ to $\bar{z}_{k,a}$:

$$
\begin{aligned}
\bar{z}_{k,a} &= y_a(k) - C_a \hat{x}_{k,s} \\
&= \tilde{z}_{k,a} + C_a \hat{x}_{k|k-1} - C_a \hat{x}_{k,s} \\
&= \tilde{z}_{k,a} - C_a K_{k,s} z_{k,s}
\end{aligned}
\tag{10}
$$

Then calculate the second step estimate based on malicious data:

$$\hat{x}_{k,a} = \hat{x}_{k,s} + K_{k,a} \bar{z}_{k,a} \tag{11}$$

Where,

$$K_{k,a} = P_{k,s} C_a^T [C_a P_{k,s} C_a^T + R_a]^{-1} \tag{12}$$

Since both $\tilde{z}_{k,a}$ and $z_{k,s}$ obey the zero means Gaussian distribution, $\bar{z}_{k,a}$ is also a zero means Gaussian random variable.

So the following inference can be obtained:

$$
\begin{aligned}
E\left[\tilde{z}_{k,a}\tilde{z}_{k,a}^T|P_{k|k-1}\right] &= E\left[(\tilde{z}_{k,a} - C_aK_{k,s}z_{k,s})(\tilde{z}_{k,a} - C_aK_{k,s}z_{k,s})^T|P_{k|k-1}\right] \\
&= E\left[\tilde{z}_{k,a}\tilde{z}_{k,a}^T|P_{k|k-1}\right] + C_aK_{k,s}E\left[z_{k,s}z_{k,s}^T|P_{k|k-1}\right]K_{k,s}^TC_a^T - C_aK_{k,s}E\left[z_{k,s}\tilde{z}_{k,a}^T|P_{k|k-1}\right] \\
&\quad - E\left[\tilde{z}_{k,a}z_{k,s}^T|P_{k|k-1}\right]K_{k,s}^TC_a^T \\
&= Cov(z_a) + C_aK_{k,s}Cov(z_a)K_{k,s}^TC_a^T - C_aK_{k,s}E[z_{k,s}\tilde{z}_{k,a}^T|P_{k|k-1}] - E[\tilde{z}_{k,a}z_{k,s}^T|P_{k|k-1}]K_{k,s}^TC_a^T \\
&= Cov(z_a) + C_aK_{k,s}(C_sP_{k|k-1}C_s^T + R_s)K_{k,s}^TC_a^T - C_aK_{k,s}E[z_{k,s}\tilde{z}_{k,a}^T|P_{k|k-1}] - E[\tilde{z}_{k,a}z_{k,s}^T|P_{k|k-1}]K_{k,s}^TC_a^T \\
&= Cov(z_a) + C_aP_{k|k-1}C_s^TK_{k,s}^TC_a^T - C_aK_{k,s}E[z_{k,s}\tilde{z}_{k,a}^T|P_{k|k-1}] - E[\tilde{z}_{k,a}z_{k,s}^T|P_{k|k-1}]K_{k,s}^TC_a^T
\end{aligned}
$$

When $\tilde{z}_{k,a}$ has not been falsified, there is:

$$
\begin{aligned}
E[z_{k,s}\tilde{z}_{k,a}^T|P_{k|k-1}] &= E[z_{k,s}z_{k,a}^T|P_{k|k-1}] \\
&= E[(y_s(k) - C_s\hat{x}_{k|k-1})(y_a(k) - C_a\hat{x}_{k|k-1})^T|P_{k|k-1}] \\
&= E[[C_s(x(k) - \hat{x}_{k|k-1}) + v_s(k)][C_a(x(k) - \hat{x}_{k|k-1}) + v_a(k)]^T|P_{k|k-1}] \\
&= C_sP_{k|k-1}C_a^T
\end{aligned}
$$

So $E[\tilde{z}_{k,a}z_{k,s}^T|P_{k|k-1}] = C_aP_{k|k-1}C_s^T$

Similarly, when $\tilde{z}_{k,a}$ is under spoofing attack, $\tilde{z}_{k,a} = T_kz_{k,a} + b_k$, there is

$$
\begin{aligned}
E[z_{k,s}\tilde{z}_{k,a}^T|P_{k|k-1}] &= E[z_{k,s}(T_kz_{k,a} + b_k)^T|P_{k|k-1}] \\
&= E[(y_s(k) - C_s\hat{x}_{k|k-1})(y_a(k) - C_a\hat{x}_{k|k-1})^T|P_{k|k-1}]T_k^T + E[(y_s(k) - C_s\hat{x}_{k|k-1})b_k^T|P_{k|k-1}] \\
&= C_sP_{k|k-1}C_a^TT_k^T
\end{aligned}
$$

and $E[\tilde{z}_{k,a}z_{k,s}^T|P_{k|k-1}] = T_kC_aP_{k|k-1}C_s^T$.

Based on the above results, when there is no spoofing attack, the updated innovation Covariance is:

$$
\begin{aligned}
Cov(II_0) &= Cov(z_a) + C_uP_{k|k-1}C_s^TK_{k,s}^TC_u^T - C_aK_{k,s}C_sP_{k|k-1}C_a^T - C_aP_{k|k-1}C_s^TK_{k,s}^TC_a^T \\
&= Cov(z_a) - C_aK_{k,s}C_sP_{k|k-1}C_a^T \\
&= C_a(I - K_{k,s}C_s)P_{k|k-1}C_a^T + R_a \\
&= C_aP_{k,s}C_a^T + R_a
\end{aligned}
$$

Similarly, when a spoofing attack occurs, the updated innovation covariance is:

$$
\begin{aligned}
Cov(H_1) &= Cov(z_a) + C_a P_{k|k-1} C_s^T K_{k,s}^T C_a^T - T_k C_a P_{k|k-1} C_s^T K_{k,s}^T C_a^T - C_a K_{k,s} C_s P_{k|k-1} C_a^T T_k^T \\
&= Cov(H_0) + (I - T_k) C_a P_{k|k-1} C_s^T K_{k,s}^T C_a^T + C_a K_{k,s} C_s P_{k|k-1} C_a^T (I - T_k^T)
\end{aligned}
$$

In summary, the spoofing attack caused the change of distribution of the updated innovation. Specifically, when the attacker has not falsified the data, $T_k = I$, there are: $Cov(H_1) = Cov(H_0)$.

Otherwise, the two are not equal.

Based on the above conclusions, the following detection method is proposed:

$$
\begin{cases}
a_{k,a} = \sum_{i=k-J+1}^{k} \bar{z}_{i,a}^T Cov^{-1}(\bar{z}) \bar{z}_{i,a} \leq \eta_2 & H_0 \\
a_{k,a} = \sum_{i=k-J+1}^{k} \bar{z}_{i,a}^T Cov^{-1}(\bar{z}) \bar{z}_{i,a} > \eta_2 & H_1
\end{cases}
\tag{13}
$$

The threshold η_2 is a pre-designed parameter. If the condition $a_{k,a} < \eta_2$ is met, the received data $\bar{z}_{k,a}$ will be used to update the estimate, otherwise it will be discarded.

Since the updated innovation covariance $Cov(H_1)$ after the data has been falsified depends on the attacker's choice of the attack mode, and the detector cannot obtain the relevant information, the detection method can only detect whether the received data is original or falsified.

Although the distribution of updated innovation $\bar{z}_{k,a}$ depends on whether they are attacked, the Gaussian distribution of zero mean must be met. Therefore, based on the detection method in Eq. (13), the data fusion center needs to adjust the threshold to balance the damage caused by false alarms and missed alarms.

4   Data Fusion

In order to deal with some malicious data that may have been falsified, we proposes a data fusion algorithm based on Kalman filtering: $\hat{x}_k$, P_k and the corresponding Kalman gain are continuously updated until the minimum mean square error state estimation of the trusted measurement is generated. The algorithm process pseudo code is as follows:

Algorithm 1. data fusion
1. $\hat{x}_0 = 0$; $P_0 = Cov(0)$; // State initialization
2. For $k = 1:T$
3. $\hat{x}_{k\|k-1} = A\hat{x}_{k-1}$;
4. $P_{k\|k-1} = AP_{k-1}A^T + Q$;
5. $\hat{x}_{k,0} = \hat{x}_{k\|k-1}$; $P_{k,0} = P_{k\|k-1}$;
6. $a_{k,a} = \sum_{i=k-J+1}^{k} \bar{z}_{i,a}^T Cov^{-1}(\bar{z})\bar{z}_{i,a}$;
7.   If $a_{k,a} \leq \eta_2$ // Attack detection
7. $K_{k,s} = P_{k\|k-1}C_s^T[C_s P_{k\|k-1}C_s^T + R_s]^{-1}$;
8. $\hat{x}_{k,s} = \hat{x}_{k\|k-1} + K_{k,s}z_{k,s}$;
9. $P_{k,s} = (I - K_{k,s})C_s P_{k\|k-1}$;
10. $K_{k,a} = P_{k,s}C_a^T[C_a P_{k,s}C_a^T + R_a]^{-1}$;
11. $\hat{x}_{k,a} = \hat{x}_{k,s} + K_{k,a}(\bar{z}_{k,a} - C_a K_{k,s}z_{k,s})$;
12. $P_{k,a} = (I - K_{k,a})C_a P_{k,s}$;
13      $\hat{x}_k = \hat{x}_{k,a}$; $P_k = P_{k,a}$;
14.   Else
15. $K_{k,s} = P_{k\|k-1}C_s^T[C_s P_{k\|k-1}C_s^T + R_s]^{-1}$;
16. $\hat{x}_{k,s} = \hat{x}_{k\|k-1} + K_{k,s}z_{k,s}$;
17. $P_{k,s} = (I - K_{k,s})C_s P_{k\|k-1}$;
18. $\hat{x}_k = \hat{x}_{k,s}$; $P_k = P_{k,s}$;
19.   EndIf
20.   End

In the above algorithm, the data fusion center first processes the innovation of measurement $z_{k,s}$ through the detection, and we can obtain:

$$\hat{x}_{k,s} = \hat{x}_{k|k-1} + K_{k,s}z_{k,s} \tag{14}$$

Where,

$$K_{k,s} = P_{k|k-1}C_s^T[C_s P_{k|k-1}C_s^T + R_s]^{-1} \tag{15}$$

The corresponding error covariance is:

$$P_{k,s} = (I - K_{k,s})C_s P_{k|k-1} \tag{16}$$

It is assumed that the state estimation of the data fusion center has been integrated by the measurements: $\hat{x}_{k,s}$ and $P_{k,s}$. Based on the decision conditions and data fusion process in Eq. (13), there are:

$$\hat{x}_k = \begin{cases} \hat{x}_{k,s} & a_{k,a} > \eta \\ \hat{x}_{k,s} + K_{k,a}\bar{z}_{k,a} & a_{k,a} \leq \eta \end{cases} \tag{17}$$

Next, the influence of the four cases corresponding to different detection results on the state estimation performance of the updated iteration in Eq. (17) is analyzed.

When the data has not been falsified and $a_{k,a} \leq \eta$ the data fusion center will fuse $z_{k,s}$ and $z_{k,a}$ based on Eqs. (15) and (16), then the corresponding error covariance is: $P(a) = P_{k,a} = P_{k,s} - K_{k,a}C_a P_{k,s}$.

When $a_{k,a} > \eta$, regardless of whether the data has been falsified, the fusion center will only fuse the data which passed the detection, so the error covariance is: $P(b) = P(d) = P_{k,s}$.

When the data is falsified and $a_{k,a} \leq \eta$, the estimator will merge the falsified data $\tilde{z}_{k,a}$, which will result in

$$\hat{x}_k = \hat{x}_{k,s} + K_{k,a}\bar{z}_{k,a} = \hat{x}_{k,s} + K_{k,a}(\tilde{z}_{k,a} - C_a K_{k,s}z_{k,s})$$

Therefore the corresponding error covariance is:

$$
\begin{aligned}
P(c) =& E[(x(k) - \hat{x}_k)(x(k) - \hat{x}_k)^T | P_{k,s}, a_{k,a} \leq \eta] \\
=& E[(x(k) - \hat{x}_{k,s} - K_{k,a}\bar{z}_{k,a})(x(k) - \hat{x}_{k,s} - K_{k,a}\bar{z}_{k,a})^T | P_{k,s}, a_{k,a} \leq \eta] \\
=& E[(x(k) - \hat{x}_{k,s})(x(k) - \hat{x}_{k,s})^T | P_{k,s}, a_{k,a} \leq \eta] + K_{k,a}E[\bar{z}_{k,a}\bar{z}_{k,a}^T | P_{k,s}, a_{k,a} \leq \eta]K_{k,a}^T \\
& - E[(x(k) - \hat{x}_{k,s})\bar{z}_{k,a}^T | P_{k,s}, a_{k,a} \leq \eta]K_{k,a}^T - K_{k,a}E[\bar{z}_{k,a}(x(k) - \hat{x}_{k,s})^T | P_{k,s}, a_{k,a} \leq \eta] \\
=& P_{k,s} + K_{k,a}Cov(H_1)K_{k,a}^T - E[(x(k) - \hat{x}_{k,s})(\tilde{z}_{k,a} - C_a K_{k,s}z_{k,s})^T | P_{k,s}, a_{k,a} \leq \eta]K_{k,a}^T \\
& - K_{k,a}E[(\tilde{z}_{k,a} - C_a K_{k,s}z_{k,s})(x(k) - \hat{x}_{k,s})^T | P_{k,s}, a_{k,a} \leq \eta] \\
=& P_{k,s} + K_{k,a}Cov(H_1)K_{k,a}^T - E[(x(k) - \hat{x}_{k,s})\tilde{z}_{k,a}^T | P_{k,s}, a_{k,a} \leq \eta]K_{k,a}^T + E[(x(k) - \hat{x}_{k,s})\tilde{z}_{k,s}^T | P_{k,s}, a_{k,a} \leq \eta]K_{k,s}^T C_a^T K_{k,a}^T \\
& - K_{k,a}E[\tilde{z}_{k,a}(x(k) - \hat{x}_{k,s})^T | P_{k,s}, a_{k,a} \leq \eta] + K_{k,a}C_a K_{k,s}E[z_{k,s}(x(k) - \hat{x}_{k,s})^T | P_{k,s}, a_{k,a} \leq \eta]
\end{aligned}
$$

In summary, the error covariance in the four cases corresponding to different test results is:

$$P_k = \begin{cases} p(a) & a_{k,a} \leq \eta \wedge H_0 \\ p(b) & a_{k,a} > \eta \wedge H_0 \\ p(c) & a_{k,a} \leq \eta \wedge H_1 \\ p(d) & a_{k,a} > \eta \wedge H_1 \end{cases}$$

Where, $P(a) = P_{k,a} = P_{k,s} - K_{k,a}C_a P_{k,s}$, $P(b) = P(d) = P_{k,s}$,

$$P(c) \approx P_{k,s} - K_{k,a}T_k C_a P_{k,s} + P_{k,s}C_a^T(I - T_k^T)K_{k,a}^T + K_{k,a}(I - T_k)C_a P_{k|k-1}C_s^T K_{k,s}^T C_a^T K_{k,a}^T$$
$$+ K_{k,a}C_a K_{k,s}C_s P_{k|k-1}C_a^T(I - T_k^T)K_{k,a}^T$$

5 Simulation

We assumed that the radar networking system is arranged in a regular hexagonal circle within a circle with a radius of 200 km, and a data fusion central station is provided at the center for fraud detection. Each station radar scans synchronously, performs filtering and state estimation at the end of each scanning period, and then sends the estimated information to the data fusion center for processing. The tracking target motion process lasts for 100 s; the radar sampling interval is 1 s, the ranging error is 50 m, and the angle measurement error is 0.02 rad;

Firstly, the detection performance of the proposed spoofing attack detection method is verified. It is assumed that only one radar in the radar network system is attacked by false data injection. And the size of the attack parameter b is continuously adjusted. The number of successful detections is counted in 1000 Monte Carlo simulations. The results are as follows:

It can be seen from the above figure that as the attack parameter b gradually increases from zero, the detection rate of the detection method quickly reaches an ideal probability, and the sensitivity is high (Fig. 1).

The state estimation process in the four cases corresponding to different detection results is simulated separately. The state estimation error results are shown in the following four figures (Fig. 2):

In the absence of spoofing attacks, the system's detection index is less than the threshold, that is, the data is not falsified. At this time, no alarm occurs, and the fusion center will fuse data from all radars. Compared to systems using traditional spoofing attack detection, the mean of the estimated errors is approximately equal, but the corresponding error covariance is reduced (Fig. 3).

In the absence of a spoofing attack, the detection index of the system is greater than the threshold, that is, the data is considered to be falsified, and a false alarm occurs at this time, and the fusion center will only fuse the data that passes the detection. Compared to systems using traditional spoofing attack detection, the mean of the estimated errors is reduced and the corresponding covariances are approximately equal (Fig. 4).

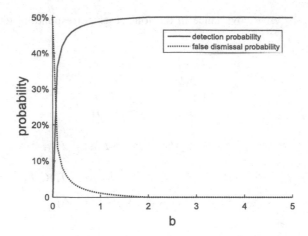

Fig. 1. Impact of attack parameter b on detection performance

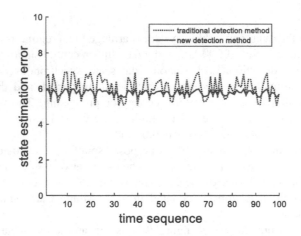

Fig. 2. The detection index is less than the threshold and there is no spoofing attack.

In the case of a spoofing attack, the system's detection index is less than the threshold, that is, the data is not falsified. At this time, a false dismissal alarm occurs, and the fusion center will fuse data from all radars. Compared with the system using traditional spoofing attack detection, the mean of the estimation error is roughly equal to the corresponding error covariance.

In the case of a spoofing attack, the detection index of the system is greater than the threshold, that is, the detected data is falsified, and the correct alarm occurs at this time, and the fusion center will only fuse the data that passes the detection. The mean of the estimated errors is reduced compared to systems using traditional spoofing attack detection, but the corresponding error covariances are approximately equal (Fig. 5).

Based on the detection method in Eq. (13), the size of the threshold will determine whether a correct alarm, false alarm, and missed alarm occur. To this end, the average value of the estimated error corresponding to the system when the threshold values are different is simulated. The result is shown in the following figure (Fig. 6):

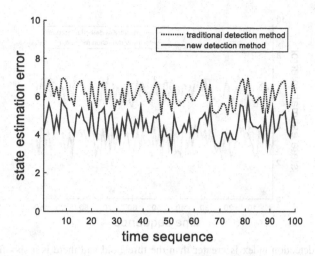

Fig. 3. The detection index is greater than the threshold and there is no spoofing attack

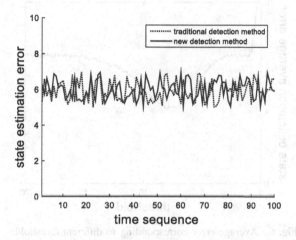

Fig. 4. The detection index is less than the threshold and there is a spoofing attack.

It can be observed from the figure that when the threshold value is small, the state estimation average error is large, because the system will treat most of the received data as falsified data and discard it, resulting in fused very few data and the large error. When the threshold value changes from small to large, the state estimation average error undergoes a process of decreasing first and then increasing, because as the threshold increases, the system will fuse more reliable data, so that the error gradually reaches the smallest. Until the threshold is too large, the system will fuse all the data including the falsified, so that the error increases again to a gentle level. There is a moderate optimal value for the visible threshold.

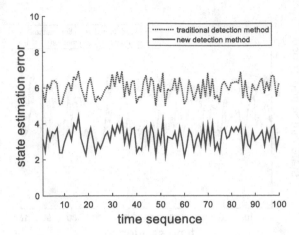

Fig. 5. The detection index is greater than the threshold and there is a spoofing attack.

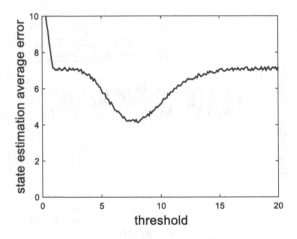

Fig. 6. Average error corresponding to different thresholds

6 Conclusion

For the traditional residual-based chi-square detector can not effectively detect the falsified data in the radar state estimation process, we proposed the spoofing attack detection method in radar network system state estimation. In order to deal with some malicious data that may have been falsified, we proposed a data fusion algorithm based on Kalman filtering: $\hat{x}_k, P_k$ and the corresponding Kalman gain are continuously updated until the minimum mean square error state estimation of the trusted measurement is generated. Finally, the simulation verifies the universal validity of the detection method in the case of different detection results.

References

1. Ma, M.: Research on Standard System of Radar Network System. J. Natl. Def. Technol. Found. **5**, 18–19 (2009)
2. Cai, W.: Research on optimized networking method of radar networking system, pp. 1–3. Jiangsu University of Science and Technology (2010)
3. Fan, J.: Modeling simulation and effectiveness evaluation of networked radar system, pp. 1–2. Xidian University (2011)
4. Yang, S., Hua, L.: Research on functional model of networked radar countermeasure system. J. Electron. Inf. Countermeasure Technol. **28**, 59–60 (2013)
5. Lestriandoko, N., Juhana, H., Munir, R.: Security system for surveillance radar network communication using chaos algorithm. In: Proceedings of IEEE International Conference on Telecommunication Systems Services and Applications, Kuta, Indonesia, October, pp. 1–6 (2014)
6. Tahmoush, D.: Securing radars using secure wireless sensor networking. In: Proceedings of SPIE 9097, Cyber Sensing, 90970B, 18 June, pp. 1–5 (2014)
7. Xu, J.: Characteristics of radar networking system and its anti-interference design. J. Electron. Sci. Technol. **04**(02), 65–68 (2017)
8. Jiang, W.: Research on anti-interference measures in radar networking system. J. Digit. Technol. Appl. (11), 117 (2016)
9. Zhang, L., Zhao, S., Zhou, Y., L, N., Zhang, J.: Research progress of networked radar cooperative anti-spoofing interference technology. J. Data Acquis. Process. **29**(04), 516–525 (2014)
10. Chen, H., Himed, B.: Analyzing and improving MIMO radar detection performance in the presence of cybersecurity attacks. In: 2016 50th Asilomar Conference on Signals, Systems and Computers, Pacific Grove, CA, pp. 1135–1138 (2016)
11. Icriverzi, G., Cristea, V.: A security model for system track radar data. **74**, 3–14 (2012)
12. He, Y., Zhou, C., Zheng, L., et al.: False data attack detection method based on extended Kalman filter. J. China Electric Power **50**(10), 35–40 (2017)
13. Guo, Z., Shi, D., Johansson, K.H., Shi, L.: Optimal linear cyber-attack on remote state estimation. IEEE Trans. Control. Netw. Syst. **4**(1), 4–13 (2017)
14. Zhang, Q., Sun, H., Hu, Z.: Research on maneuvering target trajectory estimation algorithm based on the innovation covariance. J. J. Inf. Eng. Univ. **13**(06), 729–733 (2012)
15. Ding, W.: Multi-sensor information fusion theory and its application in maneuvering target tracking, pp. 8–18. Northwestern Polytechnical University (2007)
16. Yang, R.: Research on detection method of false data injection attack in networked control system, pp. 28–29. North China University of Technology (2017)

Survey of Network Security Situational Awareness

Jiayu Yao[1](✉), Xiani Fan[1], and Ning Cao[2]

[1] School of Information, Beijing Wuzi University, Beijing, China
1127893733@qq.com, fxn0517@163.com
[2] School of Internet of Things, Wuxi Commercial Vocational
and Technical College, Wuxi, China
ning.cao2008@hotmail.com

Abstract. With the increasing importance of cyberspace security, more attention is being paid to the research and application of network security situation awareness (NSSA). NSSA realizes behavior identification, intention understanding and impact assessment of various activities in the network to support reasonable security response decisions. It is a means of quantitative analysis of network security. Network security management system can grasp the security situation of the whole network and analyze the intentions of attackers with the help of network security management system. It provides an important basis for management decision-making. Then, it summarizes network security from three aspects: extraction of elements of network security situation, evaluation of network security situation and prediction of network security situation. Research status and development trend of situational awareness.

Keywords: Network security · Situation awareness · Development trend · Overview

1 Introduction

With the continuous development of Internet infrastructure and the emergence of new applications, the scale of network is gradually expanding, the topology structure is increasingly complex, and the difficulty of network security management is increasing. In order to deal with increasingly complex and hidden network threats, various detection technologies have emerged, such as vulnerability detection technology, malicious code detection technology, intrusion detection technology and so on. These technologies attempt to use different angles. In recent years, the concept of network security situational awareness has gradually aroused the interest of researchers, hoping to use it to identify the network from a large number of noisy data. In order to reduce the loss caused by the attack as much as possible, we should grasp the security situation of the whole network macroscopically and respond reasonably and effectively. This has a positive effect

Supported by organization x.

on improving the monitoring ability and emergency response ability of the network system. However, at present, the research of network security situational awareness is still in the exploratory stage and has not formed a consensus.

Facing more and more serious and complex cyberspace security threat situation, major countries in the world pay more and more attention to the research and development of Cyberspace Security Situational Awareness technology and project construction. Developed countries led by the United States have invested a lot of resources in this field, formed a reasonable overall strategic layout and development process, are gradually grasping the current overall Cyberspace Security situation, and have achieved the network. Strategic advantages in space.

2 Overview of Network Security Situational Awareness

In 1988, Endsley put forward the definition of situational awareness for the first time. Situational Awareness (SA) refers to "recognizing and understanding environmental factors within a certain time and space, and predicting the future development trend" [1]. The conceptual model of the definition is shown in Fig. 1. However, the traditional concept of situational awareness is mainly applied to the consideration of human factors in the field of aviation, and has not been introduced into the field of network security.

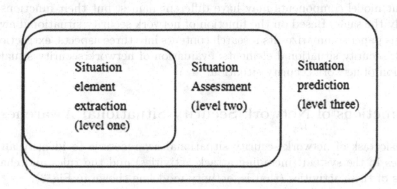

Fig. 1. Conceptual model of situational awareness

In 1999, Bass et al. [2] pointed out that "the next generation network intrusion detection system should integrate data collected from a large number of heterogeneous distributed network sensors to achieve cyberspace situational awareness". Based on JDL (Joint Directors of Laboratories) model of data fusion, a network situational sense based on multi-sensor data fusion was proposed. Knowledge function model. As shown in Fig. 2.

Although network posture can be divided into security posture, topology posture and transmission posture according to different application fields, the current research on network posture is centered on network security posture.

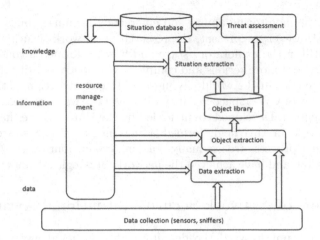

Fig. 2. Functional model of network situational awareness

Endsley [1] and Bass [2] lay the foundation for the research of network security situational awareness. Based on the conceptual model of Endsley [1] situational awareness and the functional model of Bass [2], more than a dozen network security situational awareness models have been proposed by later researchers. Different model components may have different names, but their functions are basically the same. Based on the function of network security situational awareness, this paper summarizes its research contents into three aspects: extraction of network security situational elements; evaluation of network security situation; prediction of network security situation.

3   Functions of Network Security Situational Awareness

The basic task of network security situational awareness is to identify all the activities in the system (including attack activities) and the rules and characteristics of these activities (that is, activity modeling shown in Fig. 3).

The general model of network security situational awareness includes three functions: extraction, evaluation and prediction of network security situation, as shown in Fig. 3. On the basis of acquiring massive network security data information, the macro network security situation can be obtained by analyzing the correlation between the information and evaluating it. Situational awareness is a learning process, so there is a feedback relationship between activity modeling and perception results.

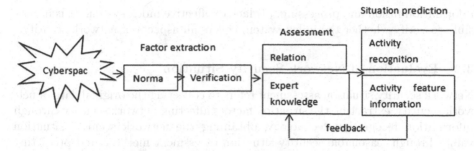

Fig. 3. Security situation awareness model

3.1 Extraction of Network Security Situation Elements

Accurate and comprehensive extraction of network security situational factors is the basis of network security situational awareness research. However, as the network has developed into a huge non-linear complex system with strong flexibility, it is very difficult to extract network security situation elements.

At present, the elements of network security situation mainly include static configuration information, dynamic operation information and network traffic information. Among them: static configuration information includes basic environment configuration information such as network topology information, vulnerability information and status information; dynamic operation information includes basic operation information such as threat information obtained from log collection and analysis technology of various protective measures.

Foreign scholars generally evaluate the security situation of the network by extracting the situation elements from a certain angle. For example, Jajodia et al. [3] and Wang et al. [4,5] collected network vulnerability information to assess network vulnerability situation; Ning et al. [6,7] collected network alert information to assess network threat situation; Barford et al. [8] and Dacier et al. [9] used data information collected by Honeynet to assess network attack situation.

Domestic scholars generally take into account all aspects of the network information, and describe the network security situation hierarchically from multiple perspectives. For example, Wang et al. [10] proposed a network security index system. According to different levels, different information sources and different needs, four secondary comprehensive indicators representing the nature of macro-network were extracted, and more than 20 primary indicators were drawn up to construct the network security index system. All the network security situation elements that need to be extracted were defined by the network security index system.

To sum up, there are the following problems in extracting network security situation elements: (1) foreign research collects information from a single point of view, and can not obtain comprehensive information; (2) domestic research, although trying to obtain comprehensive information, does not consider the correlation among the factors in the index system, will lead to great difficulties in information fusion and processing; (3) lack of effective index system. It is impossible to verify whether the index system covers all aspects of network security.

3.2   Evaluation of Network Security Situation

Network security situation assessment refers to collecting the original data of network security, extracting the situation factors affecting network security through information recognition technology, obtaining the network security situation value through reasonable security situation assessment method, and predicting the network security situation. There are many methods for network security situation assessment, including machine learning, artificial neural network, evidence theory and probability theory. These methods can be classified into the following categories:

(1) Network security situation assessment method based on mathematical model. The network security situation assessment methods used earlier are basically based on mathematical models. The network security situation assessment method based on mathematical model collects the situation factors which cause the network security state to change, constructs the evaluation function, and aggregates several situation factors to get the situation results through the evaluation function. Because there are many factors that cause the change of network security state and there are complex dynamic relationships, it is very important to construct an evaluation function based on mathematical model. Typical network security situation assessment methods based on mathematical model include network security situation assessment methods based on analytic hierarchy process [11], deviation method, score method, fuzzy comprehensive evaluation method and set pair analysis method.

(2) Network security situation assessment method based on knowledge reasoning. The method of network security situation assessment based on knowledge reasoning refers to the establishment of network security situation assessment model according to certain rules and existing experience knowledge, and the application of logical reasoning theory to network security situation assessment. By reasonably selecting and applying effective prior knowledge, this method can deal with some difficult situations in mathematical models. Compared with the method of network security situation assessment based on mathematical model, the method of network security situation assessment based on knowledge reasoning has a certain degree of artificial intelligence, avoiding the subjective opinions of experts. Typical knowledge-based reasoning methods include Bayesian-based reasoning, DS-based evidence theory, probability-based reasoning, graphbased reasoning, Markov-based reasoning, etc. [12].

Although the network security situation assessment method based on knowledge reasoning has certain artificial intelligence, the difficulty of acquiring reasoning rules and prior knowledge becomes the bottleneck of this method.

(3) Network security situation assessment method based on pattern recognition. With the development of machine learning technology, pattern recognition technology has been promoted and applied to network security situation assessment. This method mainly refers to machine learning theory, but does not rely too much on the knowledge and experience of experts, and has strong learning ability. It can be divided into two stages: sample pattern establishment and target pattern matching. Sample pattern establishment, as its name implies, is to identify all possible security states in training samples, in order to establish a security assessment model. In the target pattern matching stage, the real-time monitoring data is correlated with the training sample pattern data. If the correlation calculation results reach the predetermined threshold, the matching is considered successful, and the real-time monitoring data is considered as a safe state. Typical network security situation assessment methods based on pattern recognition include network security situation assessment methods based on neural network, grey relational degree, rough set and support vector machine.

The network security situation assessment method based on pattern recognition has high accuracy, but the training sample of this method is time-consuming and computational intensive, and the training speed is affected by the scale of training set, which can not meet the real-time requirements of the real network application environment.

3.3 Prediction of Network Security Situation

The prediction of network security situation refers to the prediction of the development trend of network in the future according to the historical information and current status of network security situation. Prediction of security situation is a basic goal of situational awareness.

Because of the randomness and uncertainty of network attack, the security situation change based on it is a complex non-linear process, which limits the use of traditional prediction model. At present, the network security situation prediction generally adopts the methods of neural network, time series prediction and support vector machine.

Neural network is the most commonly used network situation prediction method at present. Firstly, the algorithm takes some input and output data as training samples, adjusts the weights through the self-learning ability of the network, and constructs a situation prediction model. Then, it uses the model to realize the non-linear mapping from the input state to the output state space. Ren et al. [13] and Lai et al. [14] of Shanghai Jiaotong University used the neural network method to forecast the situation respectively, and achieved some results.

Neural network has the advantages of self-learning, self-adaptability and non-linear processing. In addition, the complex connection and variable connection weight matrix between neurons in the neural network make the model operation highly redundant, so the network has good fault tolerance and robustness.

However, the following problems exist in the neural network, such as difficulty in providing credible explanations, long training time, over-fitting or insufficient training, etc.

Time series forecasting method reveals the law of situation changing with time by historical data of time series, and extends this law to the future, so as to predict the future of situation. In network security situation prediction, the network security situation value x obtained from situation assessment is abstracted as a function of time series t, $i.e.\, x = f(t)$, which has the characteristics of non-linearity. Network security situation value can be regarded as a time series, assuming that the time series with network security situation value $x = \{x_i | x_i \in R, i = 1, 2, ..., L\}$. The process of forecasting is to predict the post M situation values by the situation values of the first N moments of the sequence.

The time series forecasting method is more convenient and operable in practical application. However, in order to establish a time series model with high accuracy, not only the best estimation of model parameters, but also the appropriate order of the model are required. The modeling process is quite complex.

Support Vector Machine (SVM) is a pattern recognition method based on statistical learning theory. The basic principle of SVM is to map the input space vector to a high-dimensional feature space by a non-linear mapping, and carry out linear regression in this space, so as to transform the nonlinear regression problem in low-dimensional feature space into the linear regression problem in high-dimensional feature space. Zhang et al. [15] According to the network attack data provided by intrusion detection system in recent period, the network attack situation was predicted by using support vector machine.

In summary, the neural network algorithm mainly relies on the principle of empirical risk minimization, which easily leads to the decline of generalization ability and the difficulty of determining the model structure. When the number of learning samples is limited, the learning process error is easy to converge to the local minimum, and the learning accuracy is difficult to guarantee; when the number of learning samples is large, it falls into the disaster of dimensionality and the generalization performance is not high. However, the time series prediction method is not ideal when dealing with time series data formed by macro network situation values with nonlinear relationship and non-normal distribution characteristics. Support Vector Machine (SVM) effectively avoids the problems faced by the above-mentioned algorithms, has small prediction absolute error, guarantees the correct trend rate of prediction, and can accurately predict the development trend of network situation. Support Vector Machine (SVM) is a research hotspot in network security situation prediction.

4   Development Trend of Network Security Situational Awareness

Based on the understanding of the basic concepts of network security situational awareness and the previous research progress in this field, there are still some key problems to be solved in this field.

(1) Fusion processing of massive heterogeneous measurement Data
   The original measurement data of network security situational awareness can come from different models, different implementation technologies, different development and producers'network operation management system, network security management system, host management system and application management system. These systems generate heterogeneous operation monitoring data and log data, and need to adopt streaming data processing mode in different time windows. At present, the research in this area is obviously insufficient. Although the existing large data analysis technology can provide some support and reference, the applicability of these methods to situation awareness still needs targeted research.

(2) Activity identification under incomplete information
   This problem refers to how to identify the activities in the network as accurately as possible under the premise that there are omissions, false positives and lack of information in the measurement system. This kind of research can be considered to originate from the field of network intrusion detection, but it has been given a broader meaning in the field of network security situational awareness. Internet traffic has a heavy tail. Traditional research often pays attention to typical and main parts of traffic behavior, such as traffic classification. But in situation awareness, not only these parts need attention, but also sporadic behavior of small traffic needs attention, such as APT detection, and identification of such activities under incomplete information conditions is more difficult. More elaborate methods of correlation analysis of measurement data are needed.

(3) Semantic computing of network activities
   From the current practice, the intention recognition of network attack is basically done by hand, that is, it needs to rely on the judgment of human experience. In view of human capacity constraints and the shortage of related human resources, this manual implementation mode brings great limitations to the large-scale application of network security situational awareness. Therefore, it is necessary to study the machine processing method of network activity feature extraction and intention recognition to improve the autonomy of network security situational awareness system. Although the work in the field of IPS can provide a certain basis, it is far from enough to realize network security situational awareness with different time granularity to meet the different needs from the automatic response of millisecond attacks to APT detection.

(4) Visualization of Network Situation
   The massive heterogeneous measurement data processed by network security situational awareness and their processing results need to be expressed and applied in an appropriate way. Visualization technology is recognized as a feasible support. HSARPA also mentioned in its strategic research plan the need to study scalable visualization methods to support the use of situational awareness data, including visualization with accurate location. Method, visual analysis method supporting Drill-down and visualization technology suitable for different users to use and express different content.

(5) Synergy of network security situational awareness

Cyberspace security requires global cooperation, at least at the national level, requiring collaborative network security situational awareness systems to have synergistic capabilities, as required by HSARPA planning. If we refer to the relevant research in the field of network intrusion detection, the requirements for cooperation mechanisms include at least configuration interoperability (i.e., the ability of information exchange among cooperating parties), and a similar S is needed. Standard protocols such as NMP and IPFIX; the grammatical interoperability of shared information requires standard data structures similar to IDMEF; and semantic interoperability, such as the standard measures for describing network security situation and their values, is still blank in the field of network intrusion detection. In addition, due to the possible restrictions on access to information, how to achieve a balanced grasp of information sharing and privacy protection is a problem that needs to be studied.

(6) More perfect situation projection method

Current situation projection methods are basically static, which can not meet the needs of the process of network security situational awareness. Therefore, it is necessary to study the corresponding dynamic situation projection methods, such as the situation projection method with early warning capability based on non-cooperative incomplete information dynamic game theory.

5   Conclusion

Network security situational awareness includes the extraction of network security situational elements, the assessment of network security situation and the prediction of network security situation. It is a complete cognitive process. It is not only a simple summary and superposition of the security elements in the network, but also a series of models with theoretical support based on different user needs to find out the intrinsic relationship between these security elements and real-time analysis of the security situation of the network.

Network security situational awareness is a research hotspot in the field of network security. Although it has been concerned for a long time, it has not yet formed a complete system and a clear and consistent goal. In the existing research of network security situational awareness, it is regarded as a summary of the application of large data processing and visualization technology to network security events and as a fusion calculation based on network security events. The viewpoints expressed quantitatively about network security state do not fully reflect its goals and tasks; the viewpoint that it is regarded as the realization form of network security monitoring is inaccurate.

At present, the research of network security situational awareness is a developing subject. Most of the research focuses on reconstructing attack activities, which is an extension of the research in the field of network intrusion detection. There are already good foundations, but there are many problems to be studied and solved. On the other hand, it includes network measurement, network traffic behavior, network management technology, large data processing technology, etc. The development of other related fields, such as streaming data processing technology and visualization technology, has also provided positive support for the research of network security situational awareness. Although the research of network security situational awareness is still in its infancy, with the continuous improvement of various related technologies and research, network security situational awareness technology will become mature and practical, and play a more and more important role in ensuring network security. More and more important role.

Acknowledgement. This work was supported in part by the Beijing Great Wall Scholars' Program under Grant CIT and TCD20170317, in part by the Beijing Tongzhou Canal Plan "Leading Talent Plan", in part by the Beijing Collaborative Innovation Center and in part by the Management Science and Engineering High-precision Project.

References

1. Endsley, M.R.: Design and evaluation for situation awareness enhancement. In: Proceeding of the 32nd Human Factors Society Annual Meeting, pp. 97–101. Human Factors and Ergonomics Society, Location (1988)
2. Bass, T.: Multisensor data fusion for next generation distributed intrusion detection systems. In: Proceeding of IRIS National Symposium on Sensor and Data Fusion, pp. 24–27. Laurel, Ann Arbor (1999)
3. Jajodia, S., Noel, S., O'Berry, B.: Topological Analysis of Network Attack Vulnerability, pp. 247–266. Kluwer Academic Publisher, Dordrecht (2005)
4. Wang, L., Singhal, A., Jajodia, S.: Measuring network security using attack graphs. In: Proceedings of the 2007 ACM Workshop on Quality of Protection, pp. 49–54. New York, Location (2007)
5. Wang, L., Singhal, A., Jajodia, S.: Measuring the overall security of network configurations using attack graphs. In: Barker, S., Ahn, G.-J. (eds.) DBSec 2007. LNCS, vol. 4602, pp. 98–112. Springer, Heidelberg (2007). https://doi.org/10.1007/978-3-540-73538-0_9
6. Ning, P., Cui, Y., Reeves, D.S., et al.: Techniques and tools for analyzing intrusion alerts. Trans. Inf. Syst. Secur. **7**(2), 274–318 (2004)
7. Xu, D., Ning, P.: Alert correlation though trigger event and common resource. In: Proceedings of the 20th Annual Computer Security Applications Conference, pp. 360–369. IEEE Computer Society, Location (2004)
8. Barford, P., Chen, Y., Goyal, A., et al.: Employing honeynets for network situational awareness. In: Proceedings of the Fourth Workshop on Hot Topics in Networks, pp. 71–102. Springer-Verlag, Berlin (2005)
9. Thonnard, O., Dacier, M.: A framework for attack patterns' discovery in honeynet data. In: Proceeding of the 8th Digital Forensics Research Conference, pp. S128–S139. Baltimore, Location (2008)
10. Wang, J., Zhang, F., Fu, Y., et al.: Research on the index system of network situational awareness. Comput. Appl. **27**(8), 1907–1909 (2007)
11. Li, F., Yang, S., Zhu, J.: An improved network security situation assessment method based on fuzzy hierarchy method. Comput. Appl. **34**(9), 2622–2626 (2014)

12. Xie, R., Yun, X., Zhang, Y.: An improved quantitative evaluation method of network security situation. J. Comput. Sci. **38**(4), 749–758 (2015)
13. Ren, W., Jiang, X., Sun, Z.: Network security situation prediction method based on RBF neural network. Comput. Eng. Appl. **42**(31), 136–138 (2016)
14. Lai, J., Wang, H., Liu, X., et al.: A quantitative prediction method of network security situation based on wavelet neural network. In: Proceedings of the First International Symposium on Data, pp. 197–202. IEEE Computer Society, DC (2017)
15. Zhang, X., Hu, C., Liu, S., et al.: Research on network attack situation prediction technology based on support vector machine. Comput. Eng. **33**(11), 10–12 (2017)

Encrypting VoLTE Communication
via Baseband Firmware Extension

Yao Wang[1], Wencong Han[1], Lianfang Wang[1], Lu Liu[1(✉)],
and Xiao Yu[2(✉)]

[1] School of Computer Science and Technology, Beijing Institute of Technology,
Beijing 100081, China
{874832628,457361448,775494199}@qq.com,
liulu@bit.edu.cn
[2] Department of Computer Science and Technology,
Shandong University of Technology, Zibo 255022, China
yuxiao8907118@163.com

Abstract. VoLTE is a technology carried on 4G network by RTP, and realizes
the unification of data and voice communication. At the same time, it also faces
the vulnerability of wireless communication. This paper proposes a HOOK-
based method to modify the mobile phone baseband to implement end-to-end
encrypted VoLTE calls. The experiment first builds a framework with assembly
code, which can hook the process functions for sending and receiving packet, in
order to capture the RTP data packet and inject the encryption and decryption
patch function. Then through the analysis of the data packet, the key agreement
and extension using the packet header is completed by C language. The automatic voice data encryption with AES 256 algorithm is realized through the
library functions in the baseband. In conclusion, the experiment implements a
one-time pad encryption mechanism to ensure VoLTE communication security,
so that even if a third party intercepts the data packet, the information cannot be
leaked.

Keywords: Android · Communication encryption · Baseband firmware · RTP

1 Introduction

VoLTE (Voice over Long-Term Evolution) is a communication scheme based on all-IP
conditions over the 4G network [1]. Unfortunately, VoLTE is threatened by various
attacks due to the dependence on wireless communication technology. Unencrypted
voice data is monitored and captured easily during transmission. Therefore, we propose
an end-to-end encryption scheme to perform data encryption and decryption at both
sides of the call, so that the security of data can be guaranteed even if the packet
intercepted by a third party such as a network operator or an attacker.

VoLTE deals with RTP packets mainly through the baseband processor of mobile
device. The baseband processor can perform a large number of scientific computing in
the physical layer and realize various digital signal processing algorithms in real time
[2], which can meet the requirements of VoLTE communication. The baseband

© Springer Nature Switzerland AG 2019
J. Vaidya et al. (Eds.): CSS 2019, LNCS 11982, pp. 45–56, 2019.
https://doi.org/10.1007/978-3-030-37337-5_5

environment is relatively closed and independent, with sophisticated process functions such as sending and receiving communication data, as well as, most library functions required by our patch functions, which can facilitate the implementation of the encryption VoLTE communication.

The remainder of this article mainly contains the following sections. The second chapter introduces the related researches on HOOK and VoLTE technology. The encryption design is described in the third chapter. The fourth chapter proposes a hooking and patching framework and the fifth chapter describes the implementation of encryption VoLTE communication with the framework in detail. We analyze the experimental results in the sixth chapter and show conclusion and future work in the last.

2   Related Works

2.1   HOOK

HOOK technology originally is a platform of message process mechanism on Windows operating system. It can monitor various event messages in the process, as well as intercept and process the messages sent to the target window [3]. Now, HOOK technology is no longer limited to Windows and becomes an important technology for attack and defense. For example, the file virus infects all standard DOS executable files through hooking INT 21, and the boot virus infects the boot sector by hooking INT 13 [4].

Essentially, HOOK technology is a way to change the control flow of program by hijacking function calls. So that we can implement encrypted VoLTE call only through hooking the processes of sending and receiving RTP packet in the baseband, and then patching our added encryption code, without the third party participation. For system based on Linux, there are two key points to the implementation of HOOK technology: one is how to inject patch code, the other is how to determine the address of the target function [5].

2.2   VoLTE and RTP

VoLTE is a high-speed wireless communication standard for voice and data terminals [6]. VoLTE is carried on the IP multimedia subsystem, so that voice data can be transmitted as a data stream on the LTE network without relying on the traditional circuit-switched voice network [7]. Today wireless communication is often attacked, and the security issues have received widespread attention [8]. VoLTE based on wireless communication also faces the attacks. Nowadays, LTE only encrypts data at the air interface, while the signal and user data will be transmitted in plaintext on the core network [9].

There are a few latest researches on how to attack VoLTE. A covert channel is proposed via adjusting silence periods, and covert message is modulated by the postponing or extending silence periods in VoLTE traffic [10]. Because the device OS and chipset fail to prohibit non-VoLTE apps from accessing and injecting packets into VOLIT7, while the network infrastructure also lacks proper access control and runtime check mechanism, the adversary can easily gain free data access to disrupt both data and voice in operational networks [11]. In the latest VoLTE, an attacker can manipulate the radio resource states of the victim's device in a silent call attack, thereby draining the victim's battery 5–8 times faster [12]. On the other hand, there are also researches on the VoLTE protection. A data encryption algorithm based MDEA for wireless network mobile communication is proposed to achieve high-precision detection of intrusion data [13]. A new approach for securing End-to-End (e2e) VoLTE media based the Ethereum Blockchain is suggested to solve the creation and storage of public and private keypairs [14].

VoLTE adopts the RTP/RTCP protocol for real-time voice data transmission [15]. The RTP header structure is shown in Fig. 1. The sequence number is used to mark the data packet, whose initial value is random and each time increased by 1. Based on this field, the packet receiving side can detect packet loss, and reassemble the data in order [16]. The timestamp is generated by the sampling time of the first byte of the RTP packet, and the receiver detects delay and jitter through this field to control synchronization between the two sides [17]. The SSRC (Synchronization source) field is used to identify the source of the packet. Because it is random value but unique and fixed in a call, we can use the randomization and variability of these fields for encryption [18].

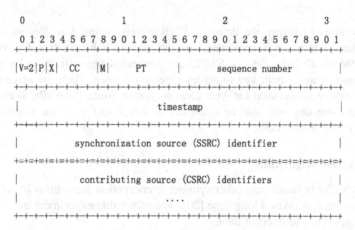

Fig. 1. Structure of the RTP header specified in RFC 3550.

3 Encryption Design

In order to realize one-time pad encrypted VoLTE call, a dynamic key generation mechanism was designed to avoid the risk of fixed key. Since the first 12 bytes of the RTP header are needed to use for encryption, the voice data is only encrypted from the 13th byte.

3.1 Key Agreement

If the RTP packet is encrypted with the fixed key, the plaintext or the data regulation can be analyzed when captured by a third party [19]. So that, in each call, different keys should be used to avoid this risk.

Algorithm 1 Key agreement with the SSRCs of both sides

---

function SET_AGREEMENT_KEY (*SSRC_A, SSRC_B, UserKey, encryptx_key*) ▷
SSRC_A: the 4-byte string of sent packet. *SSRC_B*: the 4-byte string of received packet. *UserKey*: a 32-byte fixed string as the original key. *encryptx_key*: key extension function.
  if *SSRC_A*[3] > *SSRC_B*[3] **then**
    UserKey[8]:[15]⟵ Concatenate *SSRC_A* and *SSRC_B* ▷ *SSRC_A* in front of *SSRC_B* concatenated to 8-byte string then assigned to *UserKey* from the ninth byte.
  else
    UserKey[8]:[15]⟵ Concatenate *SSRC_B* and *SSRC_A*
  endif
  e_Key⟵Run *encryptx_key* (*UserKey*, 256, *e_Key*) ▷ *e_Key*: a variable contains the extended *UserKey* through key extension function *encryptx_key*.
end function

As Algorithm 1 shown, we define a 32-byte fixed string *UserKey* as the initial agreement key, then make it associated with the random value SSRCs. By comparing the size of the fourth byte, the two SSRCs are connected sequentially to be an 8-byte string as a part of agreement key to achieve the consistence. Then the agreement key needs to be extended and used for AES 256 encryption. Since the SSRC is changed in different calls, the key will also be changed, so that it can meet the requirement of different key in different calls.

3.2 Encryption Algorithm

Because AES 256 is faster than other symmetric encryption algorithms in calculating, and for brute force, it takes a long time [20]. Therefore, this experiment uses AES 256 encryption algorithm to encrypt data.

The *e_Key* is used to encrypt 48-byte fixed *plaintext* through the encryption function, then a 48-byte *ciphertext* is obtained. In order to make the *ciphertext* different in each data packet, we change the encryption vector *IV*. We take a 16-byte string as the initial *IV* and then make the packet's timestamp as the first four bytes of the *IV* for each packet. Since timestamp is changed as packet being sent, *IV* is also changed, making the ciphertexts different from each other. Finally, the voice data is cyclically XOR with the *ciphertext* in 48 bytes to encrypt. The data encryption process is described in Algorithm 2. After the data packet received, the same process will perform: extending the agreement key, obtaining *IV* through timestamp, encrypting the same 48-byte *plaintext* and getting the same *ciphertext*. Then the encrypted voice data is decrypted by XOR with the *ciphertext*.

Algorithm 2 Voice data encryption

---

function ENCRYPT_VOICE_DATA (*rtp, rtp_len, AES256, plaintext, IV, e_Key*) ▷
rtp: the RTP packet and the voice data is from the thirteenth byte. *rtp_len*: length of
rtp. *AES256*: AES_CBC 256 encryption function. *IV*: a 16-byte fixed vector for AES
256. *plaintext*: a 48-byte fixed string.

$IV[0]:[3]$ ←*rtp_timestamp*   ▷*rtp_timestamp*: the 4-byte string from the fifth
to the eighth byte of the rtp and assigned to the first 4 bytes of *IV*.

ciphertext←Run *AES*256 (*plaintext, ciphertext*, 48, *e_Key, IV*) ▷*ciphertext*: a
48-byte string contains encrypted plaintext.

for each *i* from 12 to *rtp_len* **do**

$rtp[i]$ ←$rtp[i] \wedge ciphertext[i \%48]$

end for

end function

The reason why the experiment dose not choose to encrypt the voice data directly is
that the length of the data packet is not fixed, and may not meet the 16-integer-multiple
plaintext requirement for AES [21]. Therefore, directly encrypting the 48-byte string
can solve this problem.

4 Hooking and Patching Framework

Our experiment was carried out on a Samsung A5, whose Android version is Android
5.1.1 and baseband version is A5108ZMU1APAF. First, we obtain the original baseband from the experimental device, which includes process functions, library functions,
and their corresponding addresses required for the experiment.

The *a5-mk.c* file is the interface between the baseband and the experimental
designed program. In the file, the structure *_pachl* saves the address of each original
needed function and the address of added patch function. The hook function is
implemented with assembler in the *entry.S* file. For each hooked function, the
parameters stored in the registers are obtained then passed to the corresponding patch
function in *main.c* file, then the data is pushed onto the stack. After the called patch
function has been executed, it will return to the original function according to the
address and variables saved in the stack. The *main.c* contains all patch functions written
in C language. It includes the concrete implementation of the key agreement and data
encryption. The *entry.S* and *main.c* file is compiled by the arm-elf-gcc compiler
respectively, and the generated *entry.o* and *main.o* files are compiled and combined to
generate *main.elf*. Finally, all files are integrated into the original modem by the GCC
script. Through this framework, we can hook and rewrite any modem functions we are
interested in. The hooking and patching workflow is illustrated in Fig. 2.

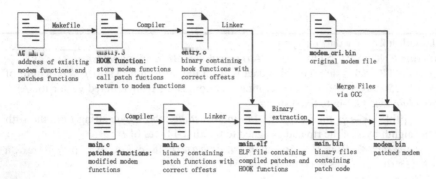

Fig. 2. The A5 modem hooking and patching framework allows to write modem hooks and patches code then compiles them into binary files that can be integrated into existing modem functions.

5   Implement

5.1   Hook Packet Sending and Receiving Functions

VoLTE transmits data mainly through the RTP protocol. The RTP packet sending process adds the frame header to the data then transmits the packets to the upper layer for UDP socket transmission, while the RTP packet receiving process can parse the RTP data from the received UDP packet [22]. So, we try to search for the keyword "send_socket" in IDA, then the x_socket_send_sub_401C3C38 was found from several searched results. Based on its specific implementation and parameters shown in Fig. 3, we verified this address should be the socket sending function.

```
ROM:401C3C38 x_socket_send_sub_401C3C38        ; CODE XREF: x_DAL_SENDTO_sub_401C3DE4+22↓p
ROM:401C3C38                                    ; ROM:401C3E32↓p
ROM:401C3C38
ROM:401C3C38              PUSH.W     {R4-R11,LR}                          socket sending function
ROM:401C3C3C              MOV.W      R8, #0
ROM:401C3C40              SUB        SP, SP, #0x64          signed int __fastcall x_socket_send_sub_401C3C38(int a1, int a2, int a3)
ROM:401C3C42              MOV.W      R9, #0xFFFFFFFF   pseudocode  {
ROM:401C3C46              MOV        R10, R2                              v4 = a2;
ROM:401C3C48              MOV        R4, R1                               v11 = *(v4 + 8);
ROM:401C3C4E              STR.W      R8, [SP,#0x88+var_2C]                v12 = *(v4 + 12);
ROM:401C3C4E              MOV        R5, R0                               *av14 = *(v4 + 8);
ROM:401C3C50              STRD.W     R9, R8, [SP,#0x54]                   if ( v15 > 0 )
ROM:401C3C54              MOVS       R2, #0x44                            {
ROM:401C3C56              MOV        R1, R8                                 while ( 1 )
ROM:401C3C58              ADD        R0, SP, #0x88+var_78                   {
ROM:401C3C5A              BL.W       sub_406FEE2C                            v34 += *(v14 + 4);
ROM:401C3C5E              LDR        R0, =unk_41F3BA9C                       v15 = v34;
ROM:401C3C60              MOV        R1, R5                                  if ( v34 >= 0x80050000 )
ROM:401C3C62              LDR        R2, =0xFECDBA98                           break;
ROM:401C3C64              STR        R0, [SP,#0x88+var_88]                   ++v13;
ROM:401C3C66              MOVW       R0, #0x1A62                             v14 += 3;
ROM:401C3C6A              STR        R0, [SP,#0x88+var_84]     hooked address   if ( *(v4 + 12) <= v13 )
ROM:401C3C6C              MOV        R0, SP                                     goto LAB66_17;
ROM:401C3C6E              BL         x_dbt_sub_40018A20                      }
ROM:401C3C72              ADD        R2, SP, #0x88+var_34                   *(v40 + 64) = 21;
ROM:401C3C74              ADD        R1, SP, #0x88+var_30     calling other function
ROM:401C3C76              MOV        R0, R5
```

Fig. 3. The socket sending function implementation at 0x401C3C38 address.

Because the sending function would call others on 0x401C3C6E, and we needed to process the data before it was passed out, to make sure that the following processed data had been encrypted. As a result, we chosen 0x401C3C64 to hook.

A function needs to be saved the scene before calling other function, therefore all the data such as parameters and address is pushed onto the stack which is needed for the function return. As shown in Fig. 4, in the entry.S file, firstly the parameters of the sending function stored in registers R0–R7 were pushed onto the stack, and the parameter in R4 was copied to R1 then passed to the corresponding patch function, finally the patch function named as ex_socket_send was called by BL command. When the patch function had been finished, the data saved in the stack was popped out, and the program execution returned to the address stored in R7. At last, the program re-entered the normal processing flow.

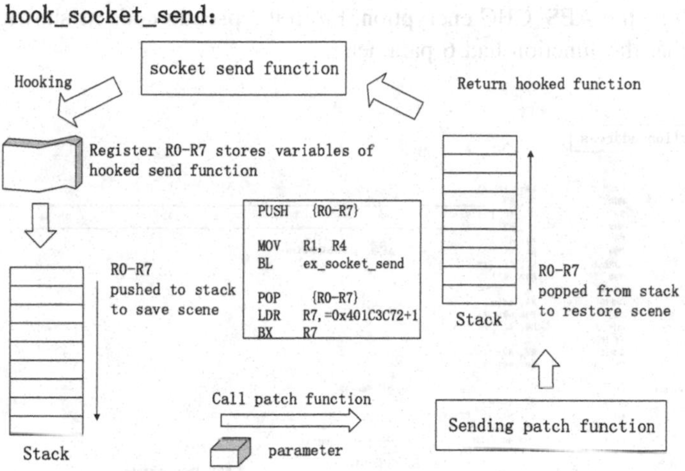

Fig. 4. The code in the *entry.S* file implements hooking 0x401C3C64 address function and calling *ex_socket_send* patch function then returning back.

The concrete implementation of the *ex_socket_send* patch function was completed in the *main.c* file. According to the pseudo code shown in Fig. 3, it could be found that the original function had three parameters, and the second was mostly used to take the offset value, so it should be the pointer. As shown in Fig. 5, the parameter of *ex_socket_send* function needed to correspond to the parameter of the hooked function one by one: 3 parameters and the second parameter was a pointer. The printed log revealed that in the second parameter, the string from the ninth element started with 0x80 which was the RTP characteristic, while the tenth value was the all bytes contained in the RTP packet, thus it should be the length.

In summary, we can prove that the address we have found was correct and we can successfully obtain the RTP data packet from the sending socket function. The same method was used to find the receiving socket function at 0x401C401C address, and hook the 0x401C4042 address then patch the required function to the baseband through the above framework.

send patch function ex_socket_send:

```
void ex_socket_send(int r0, unsigned int * r1, int r2)
```

unsigned char *rtp = (unsigned char *)r1[8]
int len = (int)r1[9]

Fig. 5. Parameter passed to the *ex_socket_send* patch function.

5.2 Encryption and Decryption

Since the baseband ROM has encapsulated the implementation of the AES_CBC 256 encryption, we can directly use it. Similar to the method to get above function, we first searched for the keyword "AES", and found the 0x401FBFD8 address, then judged that it should be the AES_CBC encryption. From the pseudo code as shown in Fig. 6, we can see that the function had 6 parameters.

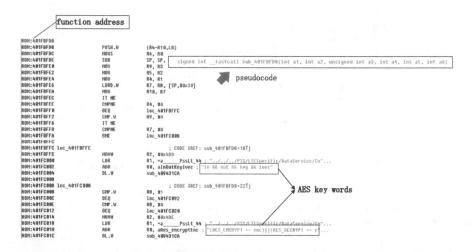

Fig. 6. 0x401FBFD8 address function.

As shown in Table 1, referring to the AES_CBC function prototype in Openssl, we made variables correspond to these parameters one by one. The *AES_func* function pointer was defined in *main.c* pointed to six parameters, while the function return type was void. Then we defined the *AES_func* type variable *aesx*, and the 0x401FBFD8 address was mandatory converted to *AES_func* type and assigned to the *aesx* variable.

So, we can directly call *aesx*(input, *out_cipher*, 48, *e_Key*, *IV*, 1) to get the 48-byte ciphertext to XOR with the voice data to encrypt. After the other side received the packet, it used the same *UserKey* to perform the same process to restore the original voice data.

Table 1. Defined function pointer to call *AES_cbc_encrypt* function.

	Function
AES_CBC prototype in Openssl	*void AES_cbc_encrypt(const unsigned char *in, unsigned char *out, size_t length, const AES_KEY *key, unsigned char *ivec, const int enc)*
Function pointer to call 0x401FBFD8	*void (*AES_func) (void *in, void *out, unsigned int len, void *key, void *iv, int enc)* *AES_func aesx = (AES_func) (0x401FBFD8)*

6 Results and Analysis

In order to observe the real-time log while VoLTE calling, we chose the serial debugging tool SSCOM. We verified key agreement and voice data encryption respectively through the characteristics of the RTP data packet.

6.1 Agreement Key

Taking the log of one side as an example, the 32-byte fixed string was used as the initial *UserKey*, and the eight bytes from the eighth byte were the combination of the two sides' SSRCs while the remaining bytes are fixed. As can be seen from Table 2, the SSRC of the one side was f7 01 01 f6, and the other was 92 e7 82 75. By comparing the size of the fourth byte, the two SSRCs were stitched in order and generated a new 32-byte string as the *UserKey* for this call. The key required for AES 256 encryption was obtained through the key extension function with the *UserKey*, and remained unchanged during a call.

Table 2. An example of the key agreement.

Process	SSRC	UserKey
initialize	–	81 ac 9b 38 1c 02 c5 c8 1d 7c a0 3f 87 be f2 c6
		04 cc 42 5e 84 8e fe a9 c5 49 00 9f 30 55 94 c0
send	f7 01 01 f6	
receive	92 e7 82 75	81 ac 9b 38 1c 02 c5 c8 **f7 01 01 f6 92 e7 82 75**
		04 cc 42 5e 84 8e fe a9 c5 49 00 9f 30 55 94 c0

6.2 Data Encryption and Decryption

As show in the Fig. 7, we found the transmitted data according to the log, and got the original data in the right image. The voice data from the first 12 byte XOR with the obtained *out_cipher* byte by byte.

```
0c1b1ee5 00000049 socket_receive encrypted data          07d534f6 00000049 socket_send original and unencrypted data
[00] 80 74 5a db 1f ff 03 65 - f7 01 01 f6 2c 34 8e c2    [00] 80 74 5a db 1f ff 03 65 - f7 01 01 f6 f4 60 43 1a
[10] b9 cd 96 a3 9e 6f 5f e5 - d5 f0 5b 00 d0 b5 14 d0    [10] d4 90 ce 9b 64 82 ea 27 - 1b 87 43 45 09 fd f7 58
[20] 72 1f a4 9e f6 e8 be 04 - 05 d6 00 a5 9f e2 d5 c2    [20] 1b f6 ab 16 a6 9d b3 b9 - 2d 73 01 bc 81 c5 ad 5c
[30] 98 68 19 51 57 e8 2a 43 - 5b 11 67 0a 6e ce 63 60    [30] 9d 27 bf 52 84 fa 56 d5 - 81 34 fa 7f b6 9a ae b8
[09] b6 0d 33 ca 5e 4b f2 03 - e8 00 00 00 00 00 00 00    [09] db d0 6b f2 a4 a6 47 c1 - 26 00 00 00 00 00 00 00
0c1b1ee5 00000002 socket_receive out_ciphers              07d534f6 00000002 socket_send out_ciphers
[00] d8 54 cd d8 6d 5d 58 38 - fa ed b5 c2 ce 77 18 45    [00] d8 54 cd d8 6d 5d 58 38 - fa ed b5 c2 ce 77 18 45
[10] d9 48 e3 88 69 e9 0f 88 - 50 75 0d bd 28 a5 01 19    [10] d9 48 e3 88 69 e9 0f 88 - 50 75 0d bd 28 a5 01 19
[20] 1e 27 78 9e 05 4f a6 03 - d3 12 7c 96 da 25 9d 75    [20] 1e 27 78 9e 05 4f a6 03 - d3 12 7c 96 da 25 9d 75
0c1b1ee5 00000049 socket_receive decrypted and original data  07d534f6 00000049 socket_send encrypted data
[00] 80 74 5a db 1f ff 03 65 - f7 01 01 f6 f4 60 43 1a    [00] 80 74 5a db 1f ff 03 65 - f7 01 01 f6 2c 34 8e c2
[10] d4 90 ce 9b 64 82 ea 27 - 1b 87 43 45 09 fd f7 58    [10] b9 cd 96 a3 9e 6f 5f e5 - d5 f0 5b 00 d0 b5 14 d0
[20] 1b f6 ab 16 a6 9d b3 b9 - 2d 73 01 bc 81 c5 ad 5c    [20] 72 1f a4 9e f6 e8 be 04 - 05 d6 00 a5 9f e2 d5 c2
[30] 9d 27 bf 52 84 fa 56 d5 - 81 34 fa 7f b6 9a ae b8    [30] 98 68 19 51 57 e8 2a 43 - 5b 11 67 0a 6e ce 63 60
[09] db d0 6b f2 a4 a6 47 c1 - 26 00 00 00 00 00 00 00    [09] b6 8d 33 ca 5e 4b f2 03 - e8 00 00 00 00 00 00 00
```

Fig. 7. The right image shows the sent packet's original data, ciphertext used for XOR, and encryption result whose sequence number is 03 65, and the left shows this encrypted packet is received by the other side and restored the original voice data with the same key.

The left image showed the received data, and according to the sequence number, it can be judged that this received packet was the sent packet mentioned above. We performed the same encryption to obtain the same *out_cipher*, which was used to perform XOR with the encrypted data to decrypt. Since *out_cipher* is a 48-byte irregular string resulted from AES encryption, so that in the absence of valid information, brute force needs to try $2^{(48 * 8)}$ times for one packet.

6.3   Performance Evaluation

A comparative experiment was conducted to verify the effect of our encryption process on normal call. In tests, call time was set 30 s, 60 s, 120 s, 180 s, 240 s and 300 s respectively, and each call time was performed 3 times to calculate the average value. In the same time group of experiments, the same piece of music was played each time, and all the received and sent packets number were recorded by the added flag variables in the patch function. Then the average RTP packets number in each group was taken, and the number of RTP packets transmitted per second was calculated. As shown in Fig. 8, in unencrypted call, packets number transmitted per second was relatively stable at 49.60, while the encrypted call's average number were 49.59. The variances of encrypted and unencrypted VoLTE calls were 0.04 and 0.03 respectively. Therefore, we thought the encryption processing had little effect on VoLTE communication performance.

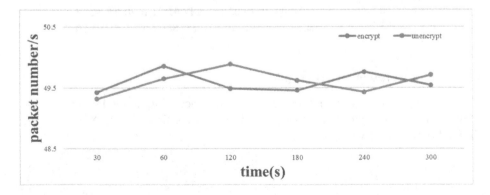

Fig. 8. The number of RTP packets transmitted per second in encrypted and unencrypted calls.

7 Conclusions

VoLTE is the ultimate voice solution for 4G networks, and the voice data of both sides is transmitted through RTP packets, which is easily intercepted by hackers and third parties. Therefore, end-to-end encrypted VoLTE calls are required to ensure data security. We mainly hook the RTP packet sending function and receiving function at the 0x401C3C64 and 0x401C4042 address in baseband respectively, in order to get the RTP data packet and patch encryption/decryption process. First, SSRCs of both sides are used to perform key agreement, then the key is extended by the baseband encapsulation function. After that, the 48-byte fixed plaintext is encrypted by the AES 256 function at the 0x401FBFD8 address to obtain a 48-byte ciphertext which will XOR with the voice data. Since the *IV* is related to the timestamp of the packet, the ciphertext of each packet is always different, thus guaranteeing one-time pad. When the RTP packet from the other side is received, the same operation as the encryption is performed, thereby obtain the original voice data through decryption.

In order to overcome the problem that the agreement keys of both sides may not always be synchronized due to the packet loss, we make the random variables used for encryption are related to the information carried by the packet header. In the future, it is necessary to find the method to generate more random keys to make encrypted data more secure.

Acknowledgment. This work is supported by National Natural Science Foundation of China (No. 61876019 & U1636213).

References

1. Mohseni, M., Banani, S.A., Eckford, A.W., Adve, R.S.: Scheduling for VoLTE: resource allocation optimization and low-complexity algorithms. IEEE Trans. Wireless Commun. **18**(3), 1534–1547 (2019)
2. Zhang, X.Y., Gao, S.Q., Jiang, H.J.: Baseband circuit design for wireless speech acquisition transmitter based on G.726 coding. Microelectron. Comput. **35**(1), 31–35, 40 (2018)
3. Dick, S., Volmar, D.: DLL hell: software dependencies, failure, and the maintenance of microsoft windows. IEEE Ann. Hist. Comput. **40**(4), 28–51 (2018)
4. Shin, K., Won, Y.: Study on malicious code behavior detection using windows filter driver and API call sequence. In: Park, James J., Loia, V., Yi, G., Sung, Y. (eds.) CUTE/CSA - 2017. LNEE, vol. 474, pp. 938–943. Springer, Singapore (2018). https://doi.org/10.1007/978-981-10-7605-3_149
5. Zhan, D.Y., Ye, L., Zhang, H.L.: A high-performance virtual machine filesystem monitor in cloud-assisted cognitive IoT. Futur. Gener. Comput. Syst. Int. J. Escience **88**, 209–219 (2018)
6. Natarajan, H., Diggi, S., Kanagarathinam, MR.: D-VoWiFi - a guaranteed bit rate scheduling for VoWiFi in non dedicated channel. In: 16th IEEE Annual Consumer Communications and Networking Conference (CCNC), pp. 1–6. IEEE, Las Vegas, NV (2019)
7. Sung, Y.C., Ho, Y.S., Lin, Y.B.: Voice/Video quality measurement for LTE services. IEEE Wirel. Commun. **25**(4), 96–103 (2018)

8. Yang, H.J., Shi, M., Xia, Y.Q.: Security research on wireless networked control systems subject to jamming attacks. IEEE Trans. Cybern. **49**(6), 2022–2031 (2019)
9. Kim, H., Kim, D., Kwon, M.: Breaking and fixing VoLTE: exploiting hidden data channels and mis-implementations. In: 22nd ACM SIGSAC Conference on Computer and Communications Security (CCS), pp. 328–339. Assoc Comp Machinery, Denver, CO (2015)
10. Zhang, X.S., Tan, Y.A., Liang, C., Li, Y.Z.: A covert channel over VoLTE via adjusting silence periods. IEEE Access **6**, 9292–9302 (2018)
11. Li, C.Y., Tu, G.H., Peng, C.Y.: Insecurity of voice solution VoLTE in LTE mobile networks. In: 22nd ACM SIGSAC Conference on Computer and Communications Security (CCS), pp. 316–327. Assoc Comp Machinery, Denver, CO (2015)
12. Tu, G.H., Li, C.Y., Peng, C.Y.: How voice call technology poses security threats in 4G LTE networks. In: 2015 IEEE Conference on Communications and Network Security (CNS), pp. 442–450. Springer, Florence, Italy (2015)
13. Fan, A.W., Wang, Q.M., Debnath, J.: A high precision data encryption algorithm in wireless network mobile communication. Discret. Continuous Dyn. Syst.-S **12**(4–5), 1327–1340 (2019)
14. Kfoury, E.F., Khoury, D.J.: Secure end-to-end VoLTE based on ethereum blockchain. In: 41st International Conference on Telecommunications and Signal Processing (TSP), pp. 128–132. IEEE, Athens, Greece (2018)
15. Zhang, Q.X., Gong, H.X., Zhang, X.S.: A sensitive network jitter measurement for covert timing channels over interactive traffic. Multimed. Tools Appl. **78**(3), 3493–3509 (2019)
16. Zhao, M., Jia, B., Wang, J.: Performance optimization on dynamic adaptive streaming over HTTP in multi-user MIMO LTE networks. IEEE Trans. Mob. Comput. **17**(12), 2853–2867 (2018)
17. Li, J., Hao, Z.h., Gao, Q.: Implementation of a multimedia communication system over IP network. In: IEEE 2nd Information Technology, Networking, Electronic and Automation Control Conference (ITNEC), pp. 141–145. IEEE, Chengdu, Peoples of China (2017)
18. Wenger, S.: H.264/AVC over IP. IEEE Trans. Circuits Syst. Video Technol. **13**(7), 645–656 (2003)
19. Bachtiar, M., Wasista, S., Ditanaya, T.: Security enhancement of AES based encryption using dynamic salt algorithm. In: International Conference on Applied Engineering (ICAE). IEEE, Batam, Indonesia (2018)
20. Rao, M., Kaknjo, A., Omerdic, E.: An efficient high speed AES implementation using traditional FPGA and LabVIEW FPGA platforms. In: 10th International Conference on Cyber-Enabled Distributed Computing and Knowledge Discovery (CyberC), pp. 93–100. IEEE, Zhengzhou, Peoples of China (2018)
21. Long, X., Wang, J., Zhao, G.: Forward security research of key management scheme in wireless sensor networks. Comput. Eng. Appl. **47**(25), 68–70, 88, 136 (2011)
22. Ahmed, A.A., Ali, W.: A lightweight reliability mechanism proposed for datagram congestion control protocol over wireless multimedia sensor networks. Trans. Emerg. Telecommun. Technol. **29**(3), 1–17 (2018)

Mitigating Link-Flooding Attack with Segment Rerouting in SDN

Lixia Xie$^{(\boxtimes)}$, Ying Ding, and Hongyu Yang

School of Computer Science and Technology,
Civil Aviation University of China, Tianjin 300300, China
lxxie@126.com, dingy136@163.com, yhyxlx@hotmail.com

Abstract. Link-flooding attack (LFA) is a new type of DDoS attack used to flood and congest the crucial network links, which has severely damaged enterprise networks. LFA can be launched by large-scale low-rate legitimate data flows with quite a low cost and is difficult to detect. While target areas in a network can be easily isolated since the crucial links are unavailable. SDN architecture provides new opportunities to address this critical network security problem with its global view of traffic monitoring enabled by the separation of data plane and control plane. Recently, segment routing (SR), which is an evolution of source routing, has been viewed as a promising technique for flow rerouting and failure recovery. Segment routing is a lightweight easy-deployed scheme known for its flexibility, scalability, and applicability. Therefore, in this paper, we try to mitigate LFA with segment rerouting within the SDN architecture. With the comprehensive network-wide view of the data flows and links, we first design a monitoring mechanism to detect LFA based on the availability of the crucial links. Then we use segment routing to detour the congested flows and alleviate the burden on the crucial links. Finally, the LFA bots will be identified and the malicious traffic will be blocked. Sufficient evaluations demonstrate that our LFA defense can efficiently detect LFA and preserve the network services, while only introduce a little signaling overhead between the controllers and data plane.

Keywords: Link-flooding attack · Segment routing · Rerouting · SDN

1 Introduction

The Internet is threatened by a new type of DDoS attack called link-flooding attack (LFA). LFA is usually launched by large-scale botnets using low-rate data flows which pretend to be legitimate. Network services can be disrupted or even broken off since the critical links are congested and then the target network areas are isolated from the visitors. Recently LFAs have been both described in academia and observed in real networks. For example, in the Coremelt attack [1], core network links can be flooded by bot-to-bot flows crossing these links. In the Crossfire attack [2], the connectivity of chosen end-point servers publicly can be

© Springer Nature Switzerland AG 2019
J. Vaidya et al. (Eds.): CSS 2019, LNCS 11982, pp. 57–69, 2019.
https://doi.org/10.1007/978-3-030-37337-5_6

severely degraded by flooding a small number of selected links with low-rate flows from bots to publicly accessible servers. Both put a challenge on the network service providers since *(i)* they use non-spoofed source IP addresses which is difficult to filter, *(ii)* they flood indirectly by sending packets to seemingly non-target nodes such as publicly accessible decoy servers, and *(iii)* they use low-rate legitimate flows which are difficult to detect.

SDN is an innovative architectural technique which enables a centralized network control by separating the data plane and control plane. LFA is difficult to be handled in traditional network architecture but SDN makes a breakthrough. In the SDN architecture, we can deploy a network-wide traffic monitoring mechanism that periodically reports the congested links. Once a link is congested by the flooding flows, the SDN controller can immediately react to the LFA attack and detour the data flows through flow rerouting. Segment routing (SR), an evolution of source routing, is a promising approach for routing control in SDN. We consider an OpenFlow-based Segment routing (SR) scheme for the routing control and the rerouting operation due to its flexibility, scalability, and applicability. To completely block the malicious flows from the bots, we also devise a detection mechanism based on the ICMP packets. Since the botnets need to rebuild the route map to relaunch new attacks, if they do not give up the attacks, they will send tremendous traceroute packets. Once the SDN controller detects the drastically increased traceroute packets, the bots will be exposed and the malicious flows sent by the bots will be filtered.

The main contributions of this paper are summarized as follows:

- This paper investigates the mitigation of LFA based on the SDN architecture. Providing the network-wide control enabled by the SDN, we design a global traffic monitoring mechanism to periodically report the congested links and achieve an immediate reaction to the flooding traffic.
- This paper implements an OpenFlow-based Segment Rerouting scheme to detour the data flows congested at the critical network links. By exploiting the flexibility, scalability, and applicability of SR, we try to alleviate the congested links and preserve the network connectivity through a lightweight approach with a little overhead imposing on the SDN controller. Network services can thus be restored from the disruption caused by the botnets.
- This paper also devises a bot detection mechanism based on the monitoring of ICMP packets. After the traffic rerouting, the bots either give up the attacks or relaunch new attacks by sending tremendous traceroute packets to rebuild the route map. Once we detect the abnormal increase on the number of ICMP packets, the bots can be easily detected coming with the malicious flows blocked.

The remainder of this paper is organized as follows. Section 2 introduces the background of LFA, SDN, and SR, lists the related work and compares the previous research with ours. Section 3 presents the system model and the overview of our LFA defense. Section 4 proposes the detailed approaches and scheduling procedures in our LFA defense. Section 5 carries out the numerical experiment and the simulation results are comprehensively analyzed and discussed. Section 6 concludes this paper.

2   Background and Related Work

2.1   Link-Flooding Attack

LFA is a new type of DDoS attack draw great attention from both academia and industries. The Coremelt attack [1] and Crossfire attack [2] are viewed as the most threatening LFAs. The Coremelt attack is launched in three steps: *(i)* select a targeted link in the core network; *(ii)* select the pairs of bots that the traffic within each pair will traverse the target link; and *(iii)* generate traffic to overload the target link. Crossfire is an evolution of Coremelt with new concepts of decoy servers, flow density, and rolling attacks. Crossfire attacks do not need cooperative bot pairs deployed in the target network area and are usually launched by four steps: *(i)* construct link map; *(ii)* compute flow density and select the target link; *(iii)* coordinate the botnets; and *(iv)* launch the rolling attack.

LFAs have several remarkable features making LFAs different from traditional DDoS attacks and difficult to detect and defend. Rather than send a large amount of unexpected traffic directly to the target server, LFA attackers usually organize a large-scale botnet to generate low-rate data flows to flood the critical network links. Traditional DDoS attacks aim to render one server unavailable, but LFAs can isolate a target network area from visitors, which means all the servers within the area are prevented from accessing the Internet. Current DDoS defense systems usually attempt to filter the unwanted traffic sent by the botnet owned by the DDoS attackers, however, bots in LFAs can use legitimate traffic. Furthermore, LFA attackers can assign valid IP source IP addresses to their bots, and the traffic flows cannot be blocked by the anti-spoofing filers.

2.2   SDN and Segment Routing

Software-defined networking (SDN) [3–5] is a revolutionary architectural technique for next-generation Internet which can flexibly define the flow forwarding capabilities of network devices by operating flow tables. OpenFlow [5,6] protocol is usually used for communication between SDN switches and SDN controllers. SDN provides a novel network architecture migrating the control plane from the physical network devices to off-device remote controllers. This architecture has been proved to be manageable, cost-effective and adaptive, which is deemed to be suitable for the high-bandwidth and dynamic conditions of today's networks. Therefore, more unparalleled opportunities for innovation and customization for network applications and services are created with the abstraction of underlying network infrastructure.

Segment routing (SR) [7], on the other hand, is an innovative routing paradigm. SR has emerged as an update of source routing methodology aiming to handle the challenges in current routing schemes or routing control policies. SR has a great advantage on flexibility, scalability, and applicability, especially in software defined networks [8]. The source node steers an incoming packet by an ordered list of instructions (prefixes) called segment list which represent a performance engineered path. Usually, the prefixes are encoded as a multi-protocol label switching (MPLS) label stack or an IPv6 addresses in the packet header. SR has already been used to optimize network performances on load balance [9] and link failure recovery or restoration [10].

2.3 Previous Studies on LFA Defense

LFA defense has been researched by several previous works, however, most of the defense schemes or systems, especially those based on traditional network architecture, are inefficient and costly. Several studies try to exploit SDN to improve network security. FRESCO [11] is an OpenFlow-based security framework designed to facilitate the rapid design, and modular composition of detection and mitigation modules. Avant-Guard [12] implements the connection migration and actuating trigger, making SDN-based security applications more scalable and responsive to dynamic network threats. FlowGuard [13] is a comprehensive framework which accurately detects and effectively resolves violations on firewall policies in dynamic OpenFlow networks. Based on SDN and NFV, Bohatei [14] is designed for flexible and elastic DDoS defense.

For LFA detecting and mitigating, Linkscope [15] employs both end-to-end and hop-by-hop network measurement to capture abnormal link performance degradation. Codef [16] distinguishes low-rate malicious flows from legitimate flows on modified routers, and at the same time protects legitimate traffic from LFAs. Spiffy [17] leverages the SDN traffic engineering to logically increase link bandwidth and then forces the attackers to either allow bots detection or accept an increase on attacking cost. Virtual node (VN) migration approach proposed by [18] significantly increases the uncertainty about critical links of multiple virtual nodes with the expense of migrating the target area network and servers. [19] proposes an SDN-based MTD mechanism to mitigate LFAs. [20] defenses LFA by the incremental deployment of SDN. [21] proposes a framework to detect suspicious bots and target areas in LFA by continuously rerouting traffic to reveal the presence of bots based on traffic engineering. [22] tries to design an LFADefender containing two modules, the LFA detection through target link selection and link congestion monitoring as well as the LFA mitigation through traffic rerouting and malicious traffic blocking.

3 System Model

System model is shown in Fig. 1. This model adopts the OpenFlow protocol to coordinate three interrelated SDN application modules and SDN controller, dynamically adjusting the network configuration. The collaborative operation process of the three modules in the model is designed as:

(1) The ICMP monitoring module continuously monitors ICMP packets and reports the information to the SDN controller. When excessive route tracking packets are detected, it indicates that the bots are preparing for an LFA.

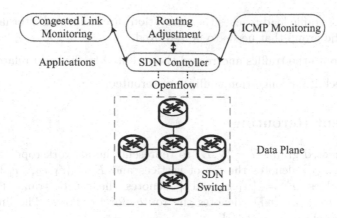

Fig. 1. System model.

(2) The congestion monitoring module periodically measures the link bandwidth utilization in case of link failure. When the utilization rate of a link reaches 50%, it should be particularly paid attention to. When the link utilization rate reaches 75%, congestion is likely to occur and this link cannot take more burden. 100% link bandwidth utilization means this link fails under an LFA.

(3) The route adjustment module performs rerouting operation based on the network-wide route map and congestion situations.

The rerouting control procedures are designed as follows:

Step 1. Select the potential target links that may be attacked. This is done by comparing the flow density of each link. The flow density of each link can be calculated by traversing the paths of all the flows hop by hop from the boundary switch. Generally links with top-k highest flow densities are likely to be attacked and in this system model k is assumed to be 3. This selection complexity is determined by the number of flows and links.

Step 2. Compute the link load and select the congestion flows need to be rerouted. A suspect level parameter x_k is set to determine the suspicious level of a source address for a given period. x_k is defined as follows:

$$x_k = n_k/w \tag{1}$$

where w denotes the number of the rerouting rounds, f_k denotes the number of occurrences of the source address a_k during w rounds of rerouting. If x_k is over than 75%, the source address k is considered to be suspicious and added to a suspicious address set A. The suspicious address set A_m for each round of LFA is recorded and after M rounds of LFAs the bot host can be calculated by:

$$B = A_1 \cap A_2 \cap ... \cap A_M \tag{2}$$

Step 3. If the traffic load reaches the congestion threshold, find alternate routes for each traffic group that needs to be rerouted.

Step 4. Reroute the traffics and record the rerouted traffics and related links.

Step 5. Check if all congestion traffics are rerouted.

4   Segment Rerouting

We use a directed graph $G = (V, E)$ to represent the network topology, where $V = \{v_1, v_2, ...v_u\}$ denotes the set of vertices and $E = \{e_1, e_2, ...e_n\}$ denotes the set of edges. $F = \{\alpha_1, \alpha_2, ...\alpha_f\}$ denotes the set of traffic flows and $R = \{r(\alpha_1), r(\alpha_2), ...r(\alpha_f)\}$ denotes the routes for the flows. The link capacity is $C = \{c(e_1), c(e_2), ..., c(e_n)\}$.

When a link congestion or failure takes place, we need to first calculate the link load and figure out the related data flows. Given a link e, the link load is calculated by:

$$P(e) = \sum_{e \in r(\alpha)} \alpha, \ \alpha \in F \tag{3}$$

and obviously if e is under an LFA, then $P(e) > c(e)$. Data flows passing this link is considered to be related with the congestion. Rerouting aims to detour the link load and need to guarantee the reserved link load is lower than the threshold which is 50% set in the system model. The rerouted data flows are selected based on the suspicious level, i.e., higher suspicious level means high priority of rerouting. For data flows with the same suspicious level, the selection is done randomly.

Given the flows selected to be rerouted, the rerouting scheme needs to guarantee that the links chosen to offload the rerouting traffic have sufficient available bandwidth. The rerouting traffic offloading from link e to e' is calculated by:

$$T(e, e') = \sum_{e \in r(\alpha), e' \in r'(\alpha)} \alpha, \alpha \in F \tag{4}$$

The constraint is that for all e', the sum of the primary link load and the rerouted load cannot be greater than the link bandwidth, which is represented by:

$$P'(e') = P(e') + T(e, e') < c(e'), \forall e' \in E \tag{5}$$

To make the new traffic load distribution more robust to link failure, the optimization of the rerouting scheme is done by solving the mathematical problem:

$$\Pi = arg \min \lambda \tag{6}$$

$$\lambda = \max\{P'(e')/c(e')\}, \forall e' \in E \tag{7}$$

The main idea of segment routing is to divide a route of a flow into several segments. Within each segment, the path is calculated by Dijkstra or other shortest-path algorithms based on the IGP link weights. Given a route $r = \{sou(\alpha) = v_s \cap$

des(α) = v_d} with v_s as the source node and v_d as the destination node. Suppose r fails under an LFA. The segment rerouting routing algorithm can be divided into the following two cases according to whether the segments i.e., prefixes in packet header need to be changed for accessibility or optimality.

Considering the computation and signaling overhead of a global rerouting operation, the segment rerouting scheme first tries to locally solve the link congestion or failure. This is done by updating the link graph G while deleting the failed link. Then new path for the failed segment can be calculated by Dijkstra algorithm. If there is a new path available (as the example in Fig. 2), there is no need to change the segments and the rerouting is locally handled without a global reconfiguration. In Fig. 2, the primary route between i and j is unaccessible due to a link failure over this route. However, a restoration route can still be found and the primary traffic load on the failed link can be offloaded to alternative links. This is done through Algorithm 1.

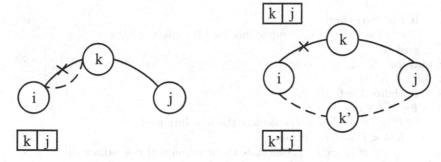

Fig. 2. New path available for a segment.   **Fig. 3.** Updating on segments.

The another case is that the SR header needs to be changed for each flow related with the failure link. On the one hand, if the failed segment has no alternative path for the data flows, the segments need to be reconfigured (as the example shown in Fig. 3). In Fig. 3, a link failure over the route between node i and k result in the isolation of the intermediate node k. Therefore, a new intermediate node k' needs to be selected and then k is replaced by k'. On the other hand, even there is an alternative path, the whole route may not be optimal since the sum of IGP link weight may increase. According to [10], 2-segment routing can be implemented with only on extra prefix and achieves excellent performance while the generalization to more segments is straightforward and just involves more computation. Therefore, we focus on the scenario of 2-segment rerouting and try to find the new intermediate node for this case. This is done through Algorithm 2.

The complexity of the algorithms depend on the number of the failed flows. Since the cause of the failure LFA, it is assumed that the hardware facilities is sufficient. Considering that the attackers' resources are limited, it is assumed that the link failure doesn't occur densely in a large scale, and most links can operate normally. Therefore the total bandwidth of the normal operating links are sufficient to support rerouting.

Algorithm 1. Rerouting within a segment

Input:
SR header i, j; Failed flow α; Failed link e; Network topology G
Output:
New routing path r' for flow α within segment $S(i, j)$

1: Get topology G' by removing e from G
2: Get the set of alternative shortest paths R' from i to j through Dijkstra algorithm
3: Initialize $\lambda' = 1$.
4: **for** $e' \in E$ **do**
5:    **if** $e' \in r(\alpha)$ **then**
6:        $P(e') = P(e') - \alpha$ //Update link load for affected links
7:    **end if**
8: **end for**
9: **for** $r \in R$ **do**
10:    Initialize $\lambda = 0$
11:    **for** $e' \in r$ **do**
12:        $P'(e') = P(e') + \alpha$ //Calculate the new link load
13:        **if** $\lambda < P'(e')/c(e')$ **then**
14:            $\lambda = P'(e')/c(e')$ //Calculate the maximum of link utilization
15:        **end if**
16:    **end for**
17:    **if** $\lambda' > \lambda$ **then**
18:        $\lambda' = \lambda$
19:        $r' = r$ //Update r' with r whose links have more available bandwidth
20:    **end if**
21: **end for**
22: **return** r'

Algorithm 2. Segment update algorithm for rerouting

Input:
SR header i, j; Failed link e; Network topology G
Output:
k' //New intermediate node
1: Get topology G' by removing e from G
2: Get the set of nodes N between i and j
3: **for** $k \in N$ **do**
4:     Check the accessibility from i to k and k to j
5:     **if** (i,k) or (k,j) is unaccesible **then**
6:         Remove k from N; //Guarantee accessibility of the intermediate node
7:     **end if**
8: **end for**
9: Initialize $\lambda' = 1$
10: **for** $k \in N$ **do**
11:     Initialize $\lambda = 0$
12:     **for** $e' \in (i, k) \cup (k, j)$ **do**
13:         **if** $P(e')/c(e') > \lambda$ **then**
14:             $\lambda = P(e')/c(e')$ //Get the max utilization of intermediate link
15:         **end if**
16:     **end for**
17:     **if** $\lambda' > \lambda$ **then**
18:         $\lambda' = \lambda$
19:         $k' = k$ // Intermediate node needs to maximize the available bandwidth of intermediate links
20:     **end if**
21: **end for**
22: Call **Algorithm 1** to reroute flow α in segment (i, k') and (k', j)
23: **return** k'

---

5 Performance Evaluation

This experiment considers a network topology shown in Fig. 4. The link bandwidth used in the simulation is set as 20 Mbps and the data flow rate is set as 0.5 Mbps. We deploy 40 virtual machine to serve as bots while 20 virtual machine as normal hosts. The numerical experiment is carried on Mininet, which is an open source network emulator, and this paper adopts OpenFlow protocol for SDN deployment. Switch-1 and Switch-3 serve as the gateway. The link between Switch-2 and Switch-5 is chosen as the target link while there are several backup links available to visit the target area e.g., the link between Switch-2 and Switch-4 and the link between Switch-4 and Switch-5.

The experiment evaluates the network performance and the bot detection accuracy. We compare the network throughput and packet loss between segment rerouting mechanism with other two approaches, i.e., the data rate control and traditional rerouting control through flow tables. The former approach lower the source data rate to avoid link congestion and guarantee the link availability in the expense of network throughput. The latter needs to re-configure the routing policy over the whole network which may introduce more latency on the reaction.

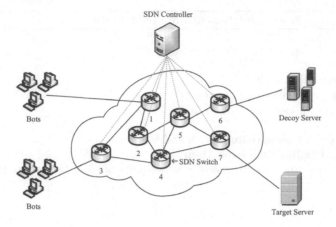

Fig. 4. Network topology in the simulation.

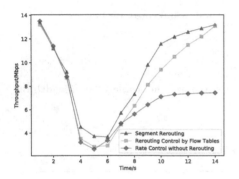
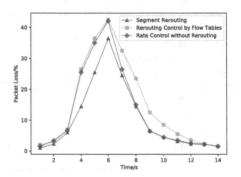

Fig. 5. Network throughput.   **Fig. 6.** Packet loss.

Figures 5, 6 and 7 show the network performance on packet delay, network throughput and packet loss. The network performance during a period of 15 s are evaluated. At the beginning, the target link is flooded by the malicious data flows and then the three approaches react to the attack and try to alleviate the congestion. All the three figures demonstrate the advantage of the segment rerouting mechanism much because segment rerouting enables an immediate reaction and introduce quite a little overhead, while efficiently utilizing the bandwidth resources.

Figure 8 shows the bot detection accuracy based on the rerouted flow IP addresses as well as the number of traceroute packets calculated by the ICMP monitoring. After the segment rerouting, as long as the botnets try to relaunch new attacks, they have to rebuild the route map through the route trace. Each bot need to send at least 6 traceroute packets to get the link-map and an LFA requires a large-scale botnet. This means the bots are easily to get revealed as illustrated that over 90% of the bots are detected after 7 attack rounds.

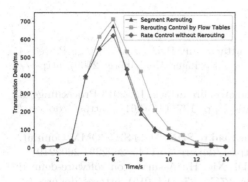

Fig. 7. Transmission delay.

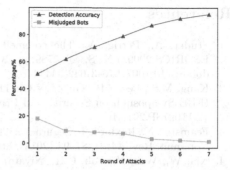

Fig. 8. Bot detection accuracy.

6 Conclusion

This paper investigates the mitigation of a new type of DDoS attack i.e., LFA. LFA aims to disrupt or even break off the network services by congesting the critical network links and isolating targeted network area from the visitors. LFA severely threatens the network connectivity and the availability of network services but is difficult to detect or defend. The SDN architecture provides new opportunities to mitigate LFAs with its network-wide view of network conditions and global traffic monitoring. To alleviate the congested links and guarantee the network connectivity, this paper proposes a segment rerouting scheme to detour the data flows. As segment routing is a lightweight mechanism and only introduce a little communication overhead between the control plane and data plane, this rerouting scheme is feasible for large-scale deployment. Based on the distribution of rerouted traffic flows, it is much easier to detect the malicious flows since the bots need to launch new attacks but gets revealed due to the drastically increased traceroute packets. Otherwise, the bots can only conform to the detection test and give up the attacks, which means the malicious data flows are blocked. Sufficient simulation results demonstrate that our LFA defense can protect the network services from disruption and preserve the network availability while only causes a little overhead.

This paper considers a scenario within an SDN architecture which enabled a centralized control over the whole network. However, in real networks, especially cross-domain scenarios, things will be quite different since the widely-used BGP protocols work in a distributed manner and the interactions between routing controllers of different ASes may take quite a long time. In that case, we need to consider the extension of SDN architecture coming with the modification of our LFA defense, which will be included in our future work.

Acknowledgement. This work is funded by the Civil Aviation Joint Research Fund Project of National Natural Science Foundation of China under granted number U1833107.

References

1. Studer, A., Perrig, A.: The coremelt attack. In: Backes, M., Ning, P. (eds.) ESORICS 2009. LNCS, vol. 5789, pp. 37–52. Springer, Heidelberg (2009). https://doi.org/10.1007/978-3-642-04444-1_3

2. Kang, M.S., Lee, S.B., Gligor, V.G.: The crossfire attack. In: 2013 Proceedings of IEEE Symposium on Security and Privacy, pp. 127–141 (2013). https://doi.org/10.1109/SP.2013.19

3. Feamster, N., Rexford, J., Zegura, E.: The road to SDN. ACM SIGCOMM Comput. Commun. Rev. **44**(2), 87–98 (2014). https://doi.org/10.1145/2602204.2602219

4. Xia, W., Wen, Y., Foh, C.H., Niyato, D., Xie, H.: A survey on software-defined networking. IEEE Commun. Surv. Tutor. **17**(1), 27–51 (2015). https://doi.org/10.1109/COMST.2014.2330903

5. Mckeown, N., Anderson, T., Balakrishnan, H., Parulkar, G.M., Turner, J.S.: OpenFlow: enabling innovation in campus networks. ACM SIGCOMM Comput. Commun. Rev. **38**(2), 69–74 (2008). https://doi.org/10.1145/2602204.2602219

6. OpenFlow: Openflow. http://archive.openflow.org/

7. Filsfils, C., Nainar, N.K., Pignataro, C., Cardona, J.C., Francois, P.: The segment routing architecture. In: Proceedings of 2015 IEEE Global Communications Conference, GLOBECOM, pp. 1–6 (2015). https://doi.org/10.1109/GLOCOM.2014.7417124

8. Abdullah, Z.N., Ahmad, I., Hussain, I.: Segment routing in software defined networks: a survey. IEEE Commun. Surv. Tutor. **21**(1), 464–486 (2019). https://doi.org/10.1109/COMST.2018.2869754

9. Desmouceaux, Y., Pfister, P., Tollet, J., Townsley, M., Clausen, T.: 6LB: scalable and application-aware load balancing with segment routing. IEEE/ACM Trans. Netw. **26**(2), 819–834 (2018). https://doi.org/10.1109/TNET.2018.2799242

10. Hao, F., Kodialam, M., Lakshman, T.V.: Optimizing restoration with segment routing. In: Proceedings of IEEE INFOCOM, pp. 1–9, July 2016. https://doi.org/10.1109/INFOCOM.2016.7524551

11. Shin, S., Porras, P.A., Yegneswaran, V., Fong, M.W., Gu, G., Fresco, M.T.: Modular composable security services for software-defined networks. In: Proceedings of Distributed System Security Symposium (NDSS) (2013)

12. Shin, S., Yegneswaran, V., Porras, P., Gu, G.: AVANT-GUARD: scalable and vigilant switch flow management in software-defined networks. In: Proceedings of the 2013 ACM SIGSAC Conference on Computer and Communications Security, pp. 413–424. ACM (2013)

13. Hu, H., Han, W., Ahn, G.J., Zhao, Z.: FLOWGUARD: building robust firewalls for software-defined networks. In: Proceedings of the Workshop on Hot Topics in Software Defined Networking, pp. 97–102 (2014)

14. Fayaz, S.K., Tobioka, Y., Sekar, V., Bailey, M.: Bohatei: flexible and elastic DDoS defense. In: Proceedings of 24th USENIX Security Symposium (USENIX Security 15), pp. 817–832 (2015)

15. Xue, L., Luo, X., Chan, E.W., Zhan, X.: Towards detecting target link flooding attack. In: Proceedings of the 28th Large Installation System Administration Conference (LISA14), pp. 90–105 (2014)

16. Lee, S.B., Kang, M.S., Gligor, V.D.: CoDef: collaborative defense against large-scale link-flooding attacks. In: Proceedings of the 9th ACM Conference on Emerging Networking Experiments and Technologies, pp. 417–428. ACM (2013)

17. Kang, M.S., Gligor, V.D., Sekar, V.: SPIFFY: inducing cost-detectability tradeoffs for persistent link-flooding attacks. In: Proceedings of Network and Distributed System Security Symposium (NDSS) (2016)
18. Gillani, F., Al-Shaer, E., Lo, S., Duan, Q., Ammar, M., Zegura, E.: Agile virtualized infrastructure to proactively defend against cyber attacks. In: Proceedings of 2015 IEEE Conference on Computer Communications (INFOCOM), pp. 729–737. IEEE (2015)
19. Aydeger, A., Saputro, N., Akkaya, K., Rahman, M.: Mitigating crossfire attacks using SDN-based moving target defense. In: Proceedings of IEEE Conference on Local Computer Networks (LCN), pp. 627–630 (2016)
20. Wang, L., Li, Q., Jiang, Y., Wu, J.: Towards mitigating link flooding attack via incremental SDN deployment. In: Proceedings of IEEE Symposium on Computers and Communication (ISCC), pp. 397–402 (2016)
21. Liaskos, C.K., Kotronis, V., Dimitropoulos, X.: A novel framework for modeling and mitigating distributed link flooding attacks. In: Proceedings of 2015 IEEE Conference on Computer Communications (INFOCOM) (2016)
22. Wang, J., Wen, R., Li, J., Yan, F., Zhao, B., Yu, F.: Detecting and mitigating target link-flooding attacks using SDN. IEEE Trans. Dependable Secur. Comput. **5971**(c), 1–13 (2018). https://doi.org/10.1109/TDSC.2018.2822275

System Security

BQSV: Protecting SDN Controller Cluster's Network Topology View Based on Byzantine Quorum System with Verification Function

Yifang Zhi[1], Li Yang[2(✉)], Shui Yu[3], and Jianfeng Ma[1]

[1] School of Cyber Engineering, Xidian University, Xi'an, China
[2] School of Computer Science and Technology, Xidian University, Xi'an, China
yangli@xidian.edu.cn
[3] School of Computer Science, University of Technology Sydney, Sydney, Australia

Abstract. In Software-defined network (SDN), SDN applications and administrators rely on the logically centralized view of the network topology to make management decisions. Therefore, the correctness of SDN controller cluster's network topology view becomes critical. However, the lack of security mechanism in SDN controller cluster makes the network topology view easy to be tampered with. In this paper, we argue that malicious controllers in a cluster can easily damage the network view of the cluster through the east-west bound interfaces. We present a scheme based on Byzantine Quorum System with verification function (BQSV) to prevent malicious controllers from manipulating the cluster's network view through east-west bound interface and providing wrong topology information to SDN applications and administrators. Moreover, we implement the prototype of our scheme and extensive experiments to show that the proposed scheme can prevent malicious controllers from damaging the topology information of the cluster with trivial overheads.

Keywords: Software-defined network (SDN) · Byzantine Quorum System · Cluster · Security

1 Introduction

In Software-defined network (SDN), the control layer must ensure the accuracy of the network topology view because the topology information is adopted to most controllers' core services and upper-layer applications [14].

Several attempts have been made to ensure that SDN controller provides accurate topology information, such as using a stealthy probing-based verification approach [1], relying on behavioral profiling and invariant checking [5,11], using an anomaly-detection approach [2] and detecting malicious manipulations on topology information by observing the control channel [10], while they all focus on the accuracy of the topology information provided by a single controller. However, few researchers have been able to pay attention to the

© Springer Nature Switzerland AG 2019
J. Vaidya et al. (Eds.): CSS 2019, LNCS 11982, pp. 73–88, 2019.
https://doi.org/10.1007/978-3-030-37337-5_7

correctness of the SDN controller cluster's network topology view. Directly utilizing prior approaches based on a single controller in a cluster environment
may make sense in some cases, but there exists a new threat in a cluster: what
if the malicious controllers in a cluster damage the cluster's network topology
view through east-west bound interfaces or provide wrong topology information
when applications and administrators are requesting? In this paper, to deal with
this threat, we propose a method to prevent malicious controllers from writing
wrong information into the cluster and providing tampered topology information
to SDN applications and administrators. The overall method is described in the
following.

In our framework, we realize the verification function for topology update
messages on controllers. Each controller's status is equivalent, and each controller can verify the topology update messages sent by peers. Moreover, we
build Byzantine Quorum System [8] with verification function (BQSV) on the
cluster to ensure the security of the cluster's network topology view when malicious controllers exist. Reading and writing of the cluster's topology information
needs to be completed by a quorum. Furthermore, our method can provide traces
of each controller to locate malicious controllers.

The main contributions of this paper are summarized below.

- We analyze the security of the east-west bound interface in SDN. We then
  exploit the messages provided by OpenFlow protocol to realize the verification
  function for topology update messages on the east-west bound interface.
- We propose a scheme that combines functionalities provided by OpenFlow
  and traditional Byzantine Quorum System to realize Byzantine Quorum System with verification function, which is designed to resist malicious controllers' manipulation on the cluster's network topology view and locate malicious controllers.
- We implement the prototype of our scheme and extensive experiments to show
  that our scheme can prevent malicious controllers from damaging topology
  information of the cluster with trivial overheads.

The rest of this paper is organized as follows. Section 2 introduces the
background information and threat model. Section 3 details our methodology.
Section 4 gives the implementation and experiment. Section 5 offers related work.
Finally, we conclude this paper in Sect. 6.

2 Preliminaries

This section reviews the background knowledge and discusses our threat model.

2.1 Background

SDN and OpenFlow. In general there are three layers in SDN: the data layer,
the control layer and the application layer [4]. On the control layer, multiple

controllers communicate with each other through the east-west bound interface to form a cluster [7]. The functions of east-west bound interfaces include import/export data between controllers, algorithms for data consistency models, and monitoring/notification capabilities. The OpenFlow protocol is a foundational element for building SDN solutions [6]. It was the original south bound interface and has become the de facto standard protocol. This protocol enables the controller to discover the topology, defines forwarding rules in the flow tables and collects statistics from the switches.

Topology Management in SDN. Generally, in an SDN/OpenFlow network, topology management includes three parts: (1) switch discovery, (2) host discovery, (3) internal link (i.e., switch-to-switch link) discovery [5]. The switch discovery can be realized when a switch establishes a connection to the SDN controller. In an SDN/OpenFlow network, a switch receives any packet from a host, and if it does not match any flow rule in the flow table, a *Packet in* message encapsulating the packet is sent to the SDN controller. The SDN controller then learns the information about the host and its location (i.e., the corresponding attached switch port) according to the *Packet in* message to realize host discovery. For internal link discovery, most SDN controller implementations follow OpenFlow Discovery Protocol (OFDP) to send LLDP packets to discover links.

Byzantine Quorum System. Quorum systems serve as a basic tool providing a uniform and reliable way to achieve coordination between processors in a distributed system. The definition of Quorum System is as follows: Given a set $S = \{s_1, s_2...s_n\}(n \geq 1)$ a set system QS is a quorum system over S, if and only if $\forall Q_1, Q_2 \in QS$: $Q_1 \cap Q_2 \neq \emptyset$ [13]. Each set Q_i is referred to as a quorum. When using the quorum system, the client arbitrarily selects a quorum to write data. The written data can be read from any quorum because there is an intersection between any two quorums. Byzantine Quorum System is designed to solve the problem that there exist Byzantine faulty nodes in the system [8]. Masking Quorum System is a kind of Byzantine Quorum System that is used to cope with the situation where faulty servers can tamper the data.

2.2   Threat Model

We assume a set C of SDN controllers, $|C| = n$, and a set F of malicious controllers, where $F \subsetneq C$ and $|F| = f$. In our model, we focus on the process of updating the cluster's network topology view through east-west bound interface triggered by a member in the cluster. The topology update messages contains the following: (1) switch information update (i.e., add/remove a switch), (2) host information update (i.e., add/remove a host), and (3) internal link information update (i.e., add/remove a link).

There are two kinds of controllers in the cluster: benign controllers and malicious controllers. Controllers that obey their specifications are benign controllers. Malicious controllers can send wrong topology update messages to peers and deviate from their specifications arbitrarily when processing received messages. In this paper, we focus on how to defend the network topology view from these malicious controllers' behaviors. We imply these behaviors as follows.

- **Deceive:** Malicious controllers send wrong topology update messages to peers in the cluster.
- **Drop:** Malicious controllers drop normal topology update messages.
- **Frame up:** Malicious controllers treat correct topology update messages as wrong topology update messages.
- **Team up:** Malicious controllers treat wrong topology update messages as correct topology update messages.

Each controller in the cluster has its own unique key-pair. The message sent by each controller should be signed by itself. We assume that malicious nodes only exist in the control plane, that is, the devices on the data plane should provide precise information.

3   Byzantine Quorum System with Verification Function

In this section, we will discuss how to realize the verification function for topology update messages and the effectiveness of BQSV.

3.1   Verification Function

We try to exploit the abundant messages provided by OpenFlow protocol to realize the verification function on each controller for the three kinds of topology update messages in Sect. 2.2. The detailed methods of verifying three kinds of topology update messages are proposed below.

Switch Information Update: In OpenFlow protocol, *Echo request/reply* messages are used to verify the aliveness of a controller-switch connection. Therefore, a controller can send *Echo request* message to the target switch to confirm if there is such a switch when receives switch information update message.

Internal Link Information Update: In general, we can confirm the connectivity of a link through the LLDP packets. However, this method begets additional time overhead for transforming LLDP packet between two switches. Another lightweight method is based on our observations. In our experiment, we found that the ports states at the ends of a link become *Down* when the link is disconnected and become *Up* when a link connects them. Therefore, the conditions of a controller verifying a link information update message of removing a link are as follows: (1) there is such a link in the previous network topology and (2) the ports states at the ends of the link become *Down*. Moreover, the conditions of a controller verifying the message about newly added link are as follows: (1) there is no link between the ports in the original network topology, (2) the ports states become *Up* and (3) the amount of the port's transmitted packets at one end equals the amount of the port's received packets at the other end with a value greater than zero. Condition (3) is a unique feature of a link in an ideal network environment and the reason why the numbers of transmitted/received packets are greater than zero is that there must be at least one LLDP packet transmitted in the link; otherwise, the link cannot be discovered by the controller. The port state and the numbers of a port's transmitted/received packets can be collected by *Port status request/reply*. This method avoids time overhead for transmitting LLDP packet between two switches.

Host Information Update: In SDN, we found that if a host leaves the network, the original port's state of the switch to which the host is connected becomes *Down*. Motivated by this, we propose the conditions for checking the correctness of the message that a host leaves the network: (1) the specified location (i.e., the corresponding attached switch port) originally had a host and (2) the state of the switch port becomes *Down*. The conditions for verifying a message about a host joining the network are the following: (1) the specified switch port is not connected to any device before, (2) the state of the switch port becomes *Up* and (3) the amount of the switch port's received packets is greater than zero. The condition (3) is vital because a host must proactively send packets to trigger *Packet in* messages, so that it can be discovered by a controller. However, a new switch joining the network has the same phenomenon as a new host joining the network. To address such a problem, we add an extra condition that the controller cannot obtain the *Echo reply* message from the newly joined device's address. This is because *Echo request/reply* messages are only identified by OpenFlow devices, while a host does not support OpenFlow protocol.

3.2   The Effectiveness of BQSV

This section enumerates all the attack scenarios based on the behaviors of malicious controllers mentioned in Sect. 2.2 to demonstrate that Byzantine Quorum System with verification function can defend all the malicious behaviors.

We construct the controller cluster based on the role mechanism in distributed SDN controller [3] and assign each switch with a master controller based on controller assignment algorithms (which is out of this paper's scope). When the topology of a certain area changes, the master controller of this area will send a topology update message to peers. As shown in Fig. 1, there is a controller in the cluster whose nature is unknown (benign/malicious). In *Process A*, if the controller is malicious, it may send wrong topology update messages, such as *Switch1 is down*, *Link a is down* or *Host1 is offline* to peers through east-west bound interface to **deceive** peers. The malicious controller should first send the message to a random quorum. The controllers in the quorum need to determine if the message is correct after performing the verification process, the benign controllers will conclude that the message is wrong so the message cannot cause any change in their topology information, while the malicious controllers in the quorum can **team up** with the malicious controller and mark the message as correct, changing their topology into the wrong status. Then, if an application or administrator request this quorum for topology information, the requester will receive different replies. The reader needs to determine which controllers provide correct topology information based on the numbers of replies. This yields the first condition of our system.

$$\forall b \in F \; \forall Q \in QS : |Q \setminus (F \setminus \{b\})| > |Q \cap (F \setminus \{b\})| \tag{1}$$

Condition 1 can guarantee that the number of correct topology messages is more than the number of wrong topology messages in every quorum. However, it will be more complex if the malicious controllers are in the intersection of two quorums. As shown in Fig. 1 *Process B*, the wrong message is sent to Q_1 and an administrator or application requests topology information from Q_2. The malicious controllers in the intersection of Q_1 and Q_2 can **team up** with the sender. Now, Q_2 is divided into three subsets: the expired value subset, wrong value subset and correct value subset. The requester will discard the values that come from the expired value subset and will read the information from the wrong value subset and correct value subset. To obtain the correct information, we can employ the second condition of our system.

$$\forall b \in F \; \forall Q_1, Q_2 \in QS : |(Q_1 \cap Q_2) \setminus (F \setminus \{b\})| > |(Q_1 \cap Q_2) \cap (F \setminus \{b\})| \tag{2}$$

Condition 2 can guarantee that the elements in the correct value subset are more than the elements in the wrong value subset. If the controller is benign, it will send correct topology update messages to peers when topology changes in the data plane. In *Process A*, suppose that the benign controller detects some changes in the data layer and sends correct topology update messages to peers through east-west bound interface to update the cluster's network view. It will also randomly choose a quorum to send the topology update message and the controllers in the chosen quorum will perform verification process. However, malicious controllers may **drop** the messages. To handle this problem, we can employ the third condition of our system.

$$\forall Q \in QS : Q \nsubseteq F \tag{3}$$

Condition 3 can ensure that there is at least one benign controller in each quorum so that the topology update message can be delivered to the cluster by any quorum. What's worse, malicious controllers can mark the topology update message as wrong after the verification process to **frame up** the benign one. In this case, an application or administrator requesting this quorum for topology information will also obtain different replies. To solve this problem, we conclude our fourth condition.

$$\forall Q \in QS : |Q \setminus F| > |Q \cap F| \tag{4}$$

Condition 4 can guarantee that the reader can obtain more correct replies than wrong replies from any quorum. There is also a more complex situation, as shown in Fig. 1 *Process B*, where malicious controllers are in the intersection of this quorum and another one. The update message is sent to Q_1, and a reader requests the topology information from Q_2. Malicious controllers can **drop** the update message to prevent the latest topology information from being propagated to Q_2. To handle this problem, we can employ our fifth condition.

$$\forall Q_1, Q_2 \in QS : |Q_1 \cap Q_2| \not\subseteq F \tag{5}$$

Condition 5 can ensure that the correct messages can be propagated to each quorum so that administrators or applications can obtain the latest network view. However, malicious controllers can record the correct update messages as wrong to **frame up** benign controllers. Now Q_2 is also divided into three subsets: the expired value subset, wrong value subset and correct value subset. To obtain the correct information, we can design our system to meet the sixth condition.

$$\forall Q_1, Q_2 \in QS : |(Q_1 \cap Q_2) \setminus F| > |(Q_1 \cap Q_2) \cap F| \tag{6}$$

We can clearly find that all conditions can be derived from Conditions 4 and 6. However, the distribution of the malicious controllers is unknown. They may all exist in one quorum, or they may all exist in the intersection of two quorums. Therefore, Condition 4 should be denoted as $\forall Q \in QS : |Q| \geq 2f + 1$, and Condition 6 should be denoted as $\forall Q_1, Q_2 \in QS : |Q_1 \cap Q_2| \geq 2f + 1$ and these two conditions can also be simplified to Condition 7.

$$\forall Q_1, Q_2 \in QS : |Q_1 \cap Q_2| \geq 2f + 1 \tag{7}$$

Therefore, if BQSV meets Condition 7, all malicious behaviors in Sect. 2.2 can be defended and Condition 7 is the requirement of Masking Quorum System [9], so that we can utilize Masking Quorum System to build BQSV.

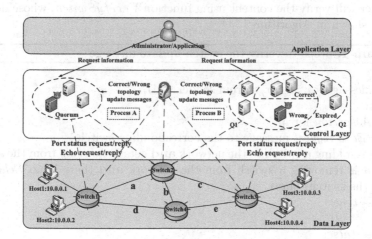

Fig. 1. A controller sends topology update messages to peers.

3.3 Detail Process Steps

In this section, we will discuss the detailed process steps of BQSV. There are three roles in BQSV: sender, verifier and reader. Sender refers to the controllers in cluster who attempts to send topology update messages to peers. Verifier refers to the controllers in the selected quorum who are responsible for verifying messages sent by the sender. Reader refers to the administrator or application who wants to request the topology information from the control plane.

The Sender: A sender who attempts to send messages should first construct a message $<i, m, t, \sigma_i>$, where i refers to the ID of the sender, m is the content of this message which can be tree kinds of topology update messages, t refers to the current time of the cluster and σ_i is the signature of the message signed by the sender's private key. After generating the message, the sender will randomly select a quorum to send the constructed message. If the sender itself is in the selected quorum, it reselects a quorum until it is not in the selected quorum. This action occurs because that if a sender can send a message to its own quorum, the sender can also be a verifier and the reader only considers the latest messages obtained from a quorum. In this case, a malicious controller can arbitrarily generate the latest topology update message and provide the verification result for the message arbitrarily without accessing other controllers.

The Verifier: The verifier will first confirm that the message is from another quorum, verify the signature and confirm that the timestamp of the message is larger than the timestamp of the last processed message and smaller than the current system time of the cluster. The verifier will verify the content of the message according to the type. If the content is the switch information update, the verifier will verify the content using function $VerifySwitch$, whose detailed steps are shown in Algorithm 1.

Algorithm 1. Steps to verify the switch update message

Input:
  The message $<i, m, t, \sigma_j>$ from sender i: M_i
Output:
  The *Assertion* for M_i
1: Send *Echo request* message to the corresponding switch;
2: **if** (m is adding a switch to the network **and** gets *Echo reply* from the switch)
   or (m is removing a switch from the network **and** there is no *Echo reply*
   from the switch) **then**
3:    $r \leftarrow true$;
4: **else**
5:    $r \leftarrow false$;
6: **end if**
7: **return** Assertion $<j, M_i, t, r, \sigma_j>$;

If the content is the host information update, the verifier will verify the content using function *VerifyHost*. The detailed steps of function *VerifyHost* are shown in Algorithm 2.

Algorithm 2. Steps to verify the host update message

Input:

The message $<i, m, t, \sigma_j>$ from sender i: M_i

Output:

The *Assertion* for M_i

1: Send *Port status request* to the corresponding switch;
2: **if** m is adding a host to the network **then**
3:     **if** the switch port is *Down* in the previous topology **and** the switch port is *Up* in *Port status reply* **and** the amount of the switch port's received packets > 0 **and** no reply when sending *Echo request* message to the host's address **then**
4:         $r \leftarrow true$;
5:     **else**
6:         $r \leftarrow false$;
7:     **end if**
8: **end if**
9: **if** m is removing a host from the network **then**
10:     **if** the host is connected to the switch port in the previous topology **and** the switch port become *Down* in *Port status reply* **then**
11:         $r \leftarrow true$;
12:     **else**
13:         $r \leftarrow false$;
14:     **end if**
15: **end if**
16: **return** *Assertion* $<j, M_i, t, r, \sigma_j>$;

If the content is link information update, the verifier will verify the content using function *VerifyLink* whose detailed code is shown in Algorithm 3.

Algorithm 3. Steps to verify the link update message

Input:

The message $<i, m, t, \sigma_j>$ from sender i: M_i

Output:

The *Assertion* for M_i

1: Send *Port status requests* to the corresponding switches;
2: **if** m is adding a link to the network **then**
3:     **if** there is no such a link in the previous topology **and** both switch ports are *Up* in *Port status replies* **and** the amount of the port's transmitted packets at one end = the amount of the port's received packets at the other end > 0 **then**
4:         $r \leftarrow true$;
5:     **else**

6:      $r \leftarrow false$;
7:   **end if**
8: **end if**
9: **if** m is removing a link from the network **then**
10:    **if** there is such a link in the previous topology **and** both switch ports are
       Down in *Port status replies* **then**
11:      $r \leftarrow true$;
12:    **else**
13:      $r \leftarrow false$;
14:    **end if**
15: **end if**
16: **return** $Assertion <j, M_i, t, r, \sigma_j>$;

After performing the verification process, the verifier will store the *Assertion*, where j is the identifier of the verifier, t is current system time and σ_j is the signature for the *Assertion*. The verifier will modify the network topology view if the result of the *Assertion* is true. The changes of the topology information that cannot find corresponding assertions will be considered invalid.

The Reader: The detailed steps for the reader to obtain the topology information and locate malicious controllers are shown in Algorithm 4. The reader first randomly choose a quorum to access the cluster and the process to find malicious senders is shown in line 8 to line 12.

Algorithm 4. Steps to obtain the topology information

Output:
     Topology information and malicious controllers
1: Discard the out-of-date messages;
2: **if** the topology messages are consistent **then**
3:    $Result \leftarrow$ topology messages, $MaliciousList \leftarrow \emptyset$;
4: **else**
5:    $Result \leftarrow$ numerous topology messages;
6:    $BenignList \leftarrow$ Controllers who provide correct topology messages;
7:    $MaliciousList \leftarrow$ Controllers who provide wrong topology messages;
8:    **for** each *Assertion* in a benign controller's assertions **do**
9:       **if** r of *Assertion* $= false$ **then**
10:         Add the sender of the *Assertion*'s message to $MacliciousList$
11:      **end if**
12:    **end for**
13: **end if**
14: **return** $Result, MacliciousList$

Now we can see that in BQSV, the status of each controller is equivalent and the verifier and the sender are separate. For a controller, only its peers can change its topology information and its peers cannot arbitrarily change the topology information unless the messages have been verified. Moreover, controllers cannot arbitrarily modify the messages they have received because the messages are all signed by peers' private keys and the assertions are important evidence to locate malicious controllers.

4 Implementation and Experiment

In this section, we describe the implementation details about how to build BQSV. Then, we conduct experiments to prove that our system is feasible and efficient.

4.1 Implementation

Quorum System. In the implementation process, we use Grid [8] to establish our proposed quorum system. Suppose that the universe of controllers is of size $n = k^2$ for some integer k and the universe of malicious controllers is of size f. Then arrange them into a $k \times k$ grid. Denote the rows and columns of the grid by R_i and C_i, respectively, where $1 \leq i \leq k$. Then the quorum system is

$$Q = \left\{ C_j \cup \bigcup_{i \in I} R_i : I, \{j\} \subseteq \{1...k\}, |I| = \left\lceil \frac{2f+1}{2} \right\rceil \right\}.$$

We also use the multi-grid (denoted M-Grid) structure [9] to construct our quorum system. Also arrange the universe into a $k \times k$ grid. Denote the rows and columns of the grid by R_i and C_i, respectively, where $1 \leq i \leq k$. Then the quorum system is

$$Q = \left\{ \bigcup_{j \in J} C_j \cup \bigcup_{i \in I} R_i : J, I \subseteq \{1...k\}, |J| = |I| = \left\lceil \sqrt{f+1} \right\rceil \right\}.$$

SDN. In our experiments, we developed applications based on Opendaylight (version Carbon) to realized the detail process steps proposed in Sect. 3.3, and we assign a unique key-pair to each controller before joining the cluster. We store the assertions of each controller to the Datastore, a distributed database provided by Opendaylight. To simulate malicious senders, we expose RESTful API to input wrong topology update messages so that we can let controllers send wrong topology update messages through the interfaces. Besides, we also expose interface to set the natures of controllers to simulate malicious verifiers. The natures include *Benign*, *Evil* (**team up** with malicious senders and **frame up** with benign ones) and *Silence* (**drop** all topology update messages without assertions). The default natures of the controllers are *Benign* and we then randomly choose some controllers to change their natures according to our experimental needs.

4.2 Experiments

In our experiments, we choose Mininet (version 2.3.0d4) to create different scales of tree topology (size n contains $2^n - 1$ switches and 2^n hosts). We use Docker containers to build controller cluster on a workstation (24 CPU cores and 128 GB of RAM). We first implement experiments to show the feasibility of our scheme, and we randomly choose some controllers as *Evil* or *Silence* controllers. We use controllers' interface to send wrong topology information to peers. Our experiments show that the scheme can successfully defend all malicious behaviors proposed in Sect. 2.2.

We also evaluate the performance of our scheme. We first test the time consumption of the verification of the three kinds of topology update messages for one controller. In our experiment, we create a tree topology with size 7 and construct a cluster with 49 controllers for which the size of one quorum is 19. We use Mininet's API to shutdown/open a link, shutdown/open a switch or shutdown/open a host to trigger a controller to send topology update messages to peers and record the maximum time consumption for one controller in the cluster. As shown in Fig. 4, after many times of experiments, we find that the overhead is small.

We next test how many extra OpenFlow packets are introduced to in BQSV. We construct a cluster with 49 controllers for which one quorum's size is 19 and create different scales of tree topology by Mininet. We record the number of *Echo request* and *Port status request* messages in different durations in normal case to calculate the growth rate of these messages. We use a script to randomly change the topology 10 times in each experiment. From Fig. 2 we can find that the growth rates are less than 10%, which illustrate that BQSV does not introduce excessive OpenFlow messages. We then test how much impact on the communication delay of the control channel. We test the average communication delay between switches and controllers in different scales of tree topology. We compared the average communication delay in normal case and different topological change frequencies. From Fig. 3, we can find there is no significant growth of communication delay in different topological change frequencies.

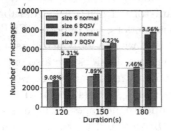

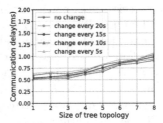

Fig. 2. Results of extra OpenFlow messages test.

Fig. 3. Communication delay comparison of control channel.

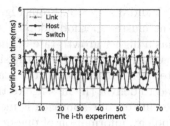

Fig. 4. Time consumption of the verification.

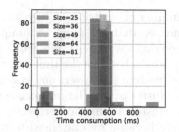

Fig. 5. Time overhead distribution.

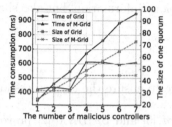

Fig. 6. Effectiveness comparison in updating topology.

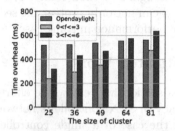

Fig. 7. Effectiveness comparison with Opendaylight's cluster method.

To compare the effectiveness between the two Byzantine Quorum System's construct methods in Sect. 4.1, we test the time overheads of updating topology information through these two methods in different sizes of clusters. In the process of measuring time overheads, we test 10 times in each case and calculate the average as the final result. Figure 6 shows the experimental results with a cluster size of 81. As the number of malicious controllers increases, the size of one quorum increases, but the growth rate of M-Grid is smaller. In our system prototype, we send the topology update messages to each member of the quorum individually so the time consumption has the same growth trend with the size of one quorum.

Turning now to the experimental evidence on the overhead comparison between our proposed solution and Opendaylight's cluster method, we implement this experiment in a benign environment, changing the network topology with Mininet APIs. We record the time consumption of updating topology information based on Opendaylight's cluster method and the time consumption of our solution. In our experiment, we found that the time overhead of the Opendaylight's cluster method varies widely, so we performed 100 tests on clusters of different sizes. Figure 5 shows the distribution of time overhead. We can find that approximately 80% of the time overheads are distributed between 400 ms and 800 ms. Therefore, we use the values between 400 ms and 800 ms to calculate the average as the final result. The comparison result is shown in Fig. 7. We use M-Grid construction to record the time consumption in two situations, where the number of malicious controllers are $0 < f \leq 3$ and $3 < f \leq 6$. From Fig. 7, we can see that the time consumption of current cluster method adopted by Opendaylight is more stable, while our scheme has a higher growth rate of time consumption because the time consumption is positively correlated with the size of one quorum. However, our system shows better performance when the scale of the cluster isn't so large because we do not need to deliver the message to the entire cluster. From the perspective of the entire cluster, our approach is more effective because we only need to update the topology information of one quorum to achieve consensus and if we apply concurrent technology in the process of accessing one quorum, our method will have better performance. Moreover, Opendaylight's method cannot defend controllers' malicious behavior, while our method can not only protect the security of topology information, but also show better performance in some cases.

5   Related Work

In this section, we review the efforts being made to ensure the correctness and accuracy of SDN controller's network topology view.

In the case of a single controller, *TopoGuard* [5] and *SPHINX* [2] prevent topology tampering attacks via monitoring of switch-based sensors and packets sent to the SDN controller. Skowyra et al. [11] analyze these two defenses and present two new attacks which can successfully bypass them. They then develop and present extensions to *TopoGuard* to make it resilient to such attacks. Compared with *TopoGuard* and *SPHINX*, *SPV* [1] uses active approach of sending probing packets in a stealthy manner to detect fake links in network topology view regardless of the attacking methods used to fabricate them. In the case of multiple controllers, Yuan et al. [15] utilize Byzantine model to automatically tolerate faulty switches to ensure the correctness of topology information. However, few writers have been able to pay attention to the correctness of controller's input from east-west bound interface in the case of multiple controllers. Therefore, these works cannot tackle the problem we attempt to solve.

In order to avoid the controller providing incorrect topology information to the application, works [12] and [10] present approaches to compare the controller's view which is from the SDN controller's north bound interface and the network's view which is generated by observing the control channel to detect the malicious SDN applications' manipulations on network topology view. However, their methods cannot be applied on controller cluster because we cannot obtain precise controller messages from every controller's control channel for the role mechanism in distributed SDN controller [3]. Our method combines SDN cluster with Byzantine Quorum System to ensure that the cluster can provide correct network topology view even when malicious controllers exist.

6   Conclusion

In this paper, based on the security problem of topology information of cluster that can be caused by malicious controllers, we propose a method on controller cluster based on Byzantine Quorum System with verification function (BQSV), where each update operation of cluster's network topology information needs to be verified by a quorum. The experiments show that the method can protect the network view of the cluster from malicious controllers' arbitrary behaviors with trivial overheads.

Acknowledgments. We would like to thank the anonymous reviewers for their careful reading and useful comments. This work was supported by the National Key Research and Development Project (2017YFB0801805), the National Natural Science Foundation of China (61671360, 61672415, 61672413), the Key Program of NSFC-Tongyong Union Foundation under Grant (U1636209), the Key Program of NSFC Grant (U1405255).

References

1. Alimohammadifar, A., et al.: Stealthy probing-based verification (SPV): an active approach to defending software defined networks against topology poisoning attacks. In: Lopez, J., Zhou, J., Soriano, M. (eds.) ESORICS 2018. LNCS, vol. 11099, pp. 463–484. Springer, Cham (2018). https://doi.org/10.1007/978-3-319-98989-1_23
2. Dhawan, M., Poddar, R., Mahajan, K., Mann, V.: SPHINX: detecting security attacks in software-defined networks. In: 22nd Annual Network and Distributed System Security Symposium, NDSS 2015, San Diego, pp. 8–11 (2015)
3. Dixit, A., Hao, F., Mukherjee, S., Lakshman, T.V., Kompella, R.: Towards an elastic distributed SDN controller. Comput. Commun. Rev. **43**(4), 7–12 (2013)
4. Feamster, N., Rexford, J., Zegura, E.W.: The road to SDN: an intellectual history of programmable networks. Comput. Commun. Rev. **44**(2), 87–98 (2014)
5. Hong, S., Xu, L., Wang, H., Gu, G.: Poisoning network visibility in software-defined networks: new attacks and countermeasures. In: 22nd Annual Network and Distributed System Security Symposium, NDSS 2015, San Diego, pp. 8–11 (2015)
6. Kim, H., Feamster, N.: Improving network management with software defined networking. IEEE Commun. Mag. **51**(2), 114–119 (2013)
7. Kreutz, D., Ramos, F.M.V., Veríssimo, P.J.E., Rothenberg, C.E., Azodolmolky, S., Uhlig, S.: Software-defined networking: a comprehensive survey. Proc. IEEE **103**(1), 14–76 (2015)
8. Malkhi, D., Reiter, M.K.: Byzantine quorum systems. Distrib. Comput. **11**(4), 203–213 (1998)
9. Malkhi, D., Reiter, M.K., Wool, A.: The load and availability of byzantine quorum systems. SIAM J. Comput. **29**(6), 1889–1906 (2000)
10. Röpke, C., Holz, T.: Preventing malicious SDN applications from hiding adverse network manipulations. In: Proceedings of the 2018 Workshop on Security in Softwarized Networks: Prospects and Challenges, SecSoN@SIGCOMM 2018, Budapest, pp. 40–45 (2018)
11. Skowyra, R., et al.: Effective topology tampering attacks and defenses in software-defined networks. In: 2018 48th Annual IEEE/IFIP International Conference on Dependable Systems and Networks (DSN), pp. 374–385 (2018)
12. Tatang, D., Quinkert, F., Frank, J., Röpke, C., Holz, T.: SDN-guard: protecting SDN controllers against SDN rootkits. In: 2017 IEEE Conference on Network Function Virtualization and Software Defined Networks, NFV-SDN 2017, Berlin, 6–8 November 2017, pp. 297–302 (2017)

13. Vukolic, M.: Quorum Systems: With Applications to Storage and Consensus. Synthesis Lectures on Distributed Computing Theory. Morgan & Claypool Publishers, San Rafael (2012)
14. Yoon, C., et al.: Flow wars: systemizing the attack surface and defenses in software-defined networks. IEEE/ACM Trans. Netw. 25(6), 3514–3530 (2017)
15. Yuan, B., Jin, H., Zou, D., Yang, L.T., Yu, S.: A practical byzantine-based approach for faulty switch tolerance in software-defined networks. IEEE Trans. Netw. Serv. Manag. 15(2), 825–839 (2018)

A Data Protection Scheme via Isolating Android Partitions

Kai Yang, Xiaoya Ma, Hongwei Jiang, Yuan Xue, Wencong Han,
Lianfang Wang, and Lu Liu$^{(\boxtimes)}$

School of Computer Science and Technology, Beijing Institute of Technology,
Beijing 100081, China
1406996437@qq.com, mxy950907@163.com,
1411038349@qq.com, xueyuan_1007@163.com,
775494199@qq.com, 457361448@qq.com, liulu@bit.edu.cn

Abstract. With the continuous development of Android devices, the sensitive data of users have been leaked and maliciously deleted. In this article, a data security protection scheme based on TF card is designed to meet the security requirements of the physical isolation of data in different scenarios for users. The advantage of the scheme is that the data protection is not achieved by using chips or other peripheral devices. In order to achieve this goal, the scheme builds an ecosystem exactly like the normal system on the TF card. This article introduces the design and implementation of the private zone. The prototype of the private zone is realized on the Android related mobile phones and can be easily transplanted to other Android embedded devices. At the same time, in order to illustrate the usage and security of the private zone, this article makes some experiments to evaluate the performance cost between the normal system and the private zone. Experimental results show that this method has reasonable performance and can effectively reduce the risk of sensitive information leakage.

Keywords: Data protection · Android security · TF card · Privacy data

1 Introduction

With the development of society, the number of smart phone users is increasing. According to the GSMA report [1], the total number of mobile users reached 5.1 billion by the end of 2018, accounting for about one-third of the world's population. According to the market share data of March 2019 released by StatCounter, the traffic monitoring agency [2], Android ranked first with a market share of 38%, higher than Windows (37.47%) and IOS (13.78%). Due to the huge market share of the Android system with smart phones, it has become the main target of malicious attacks [3]. At the same time, with the development of the mobile terminal market, and the continuous improvement of the mobile network and performance of hardware and software, the safety problem of intelligent terminal equipment is becoming more and more important [4]. Since individual users tend to put important pictures, working documents and bank accounts, etc. into mobile phones, which brings great security threats to users' privacy

© Springer Nature Switzerland AG 2019
J. Vaidya et al. (Eds.): CSS 2019, LNCS 11982, pp. 89–101, 2019.
https://doi.org/10.1007/978-3-030-37337-5_8

[5, 6]. Therefore, the protection of mobile phone users' privacy data emerges in the background of this demand [7].

In today's increasingly complex application environment, protecting the privacy data of enterprises or individuals from being stolen is an important aspect of data security [4]. Data security protection refers to the measures which protect user's sensitive data. Privacy protection is built on the basis of data security protection which protects the privacy of individuals on a deeper level of security needs. Nowadays, the loss of mobile phones, the connection of insecure WiFi hotspots, the scanning of malicious QR codes, the click of malicious network links [8] and other behaviors, as well as the cross-border access of Android mobile APP to obtain permissions [9] and other issues have brought severe challenges to privacy data protection.

In this scheme, the red-green system is realized by means of physical partition [10], and individual developers can manually implement the data protection technology. The advantages of this scheme are better security isolation, more choices for users [11], less consumption of resources, no interface between the normal system and the private zone, and the security of the private zone is guaranteed.

The contribution of this article is as follows:

- We introduce the TF card-based private zone on mobile devices. The TF card is used to realize two separate systems and the private zone is deployed on the TF card.
- We evaluate several key indicators of private zone, and defines the stable private zone.

The rest of this article is organized as follows: Sect. 2 introduces the relevant work and the involved techniques. Section 3 introduces the design scheme of the private zone. Sections 4 and 5 describes the details of implementation and then evaluates the performance of the prototype. Section 6 introduces the limitations and future work, and Sect. 7 is the final conclusion.

2   Related Works

In this section, we first summarize the previous work and clarify the advantages and disadvantages of the existing methods. There are two main ideas for data security protection: one way is to encrypt the user's privacy application data without affecting the user experience. Another way is to provide a secure and trusted space for users to store private information. Up to now, the relevant research of privacy data protection is as follows:

2.1   Encryption Solution

Android4.4 and Android7.0 introduce full encryption and file-level encryption respectively, so that user-created data are automatically encrypted before it is written to the disk, and all reads are automatically decrypted before it is returned to the calling process [12]. WeiFang [13] proposed a method of smali-based cryptographic application security analysis for financial applications, which establishes an application security rule library to ensure the security of applications and data. Rachmat et al. [14] proved that Serpent has a higher encryption and decryption performance compared with Rijndael and Twofish, it occupies a relatively small CPU performance and is more suitable for encrypting private data. However, due to the user's wrong operation, the encrypted data may be cracked by malicious programs or users, meanwhile, encryption technology may cause unnecessary burden on system performance [15].

2.2 Security Domain Solution

Samsung's Knox Workspace Container [16] is a dual-container platform with a high level of protection that keeps data in and out of the workspace isolated from each other [17]. Applications in and out of the workspace cannot communicate via android process or data sharing, thus protecting sensitive data from hackers and viruses. Guan et al. [18] proposed TrustShadow, which allows unmodified applications to run in the security domain. Under the security environment, the kernel does not deal with the protected applications. Rubinov et al. [19] put forward the way of automatic partition of Android. The application program is divided into the code part that runs normally and the confidential data part that processes the security zone [20].

The methods above are implemented in the framework layer or application layer, while the method in this article is protecting the security through TF card, which can realize data isolation at the hardware level [21, 22].

3 Design

In this section, we will introduce the design idea of private zone according to the difficulties and indicators in the implementation process.

3.1 Summary

Private zone provides users with a private space, it is isolated from the ordinary user space, and on this basis, the private data space achieves the needs of data security protection. To create this execution environment, our solution is to generate a mirror image of a system that performs the same function as the ordinary user space within the TF card, and can switch between the private system and the ordinary user space freely and securely.

In addition, we also consider putting the relevant partitions into the TF space. Considering the security, it is suggested to encrypt the external SD card.

3.2 Performance Overhead

If the performance overhead of private zone is too large, it will affect the normal use of users. In order to minimize the impact of private zone on terminal performance, this article adopts the following two optimization methods:

On the one hand, each partition should be simplified as much as possible, they only need to complete the functions required by the security requirements, need not to consider other relatively complex functions to make the private zone as perfect as ordinary user space. So partitions should be blank and implement only the most basic functions of the original partition.

On the other hand, the partitions associated with this article need to be implemented, and other partitions which are important, but less relevant to the isolation goals can be implemented in a shared manner, such as/Misc partitions. This approach maximizes consistency with normal system state and is important for the user experience. According to the partition structure, we decides to load the system and cache partitions.

3.3   The Isolation Between Normal and Private Zone

The new operating environment is installed on different partitions of SD card external on smart mobile devices, so that the data in each space is completely isolated. The specific implementation is shown in Fig. 1.

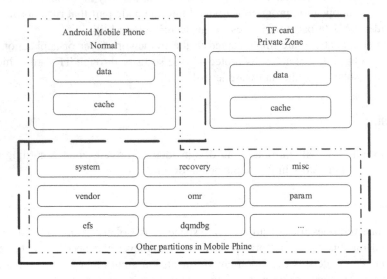

Fig. 1. The structure of normal user space and private zone.

As shown in Fig. 1, in the private zone, we should arrange data partition and cache partition on the external TF card. As for the rest of the partitions, we choose to share with normal user space. In this way, we can effectively protect the security and reliability of data generated by applications or user themselves.

As shown in Fig. 1, in the private zone, the relevant partitions – data partition, cache partition – should be deployed on the external TF card, and the rest partition should be shared with ordinary user space. This method can effectively guarantee the security of user data, app data and cache data.

3.4   The Switch Between Normal and Private Zone

We consider the use of multi-boot technology to realize quick transitions between two environments.

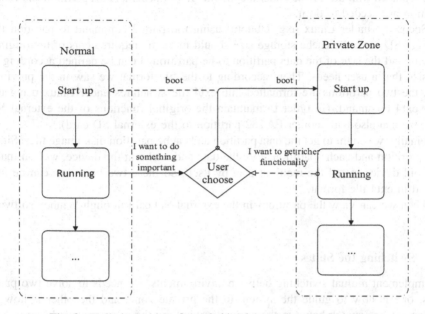

Fig. 2. Preliminary ideas for switching between two environments.

The method is similar to the dual-system selection method on a PC. When dual systems are installed, the two systems are installed on different partitions, and the latter system will not overwrite the former system. And each individual system has its own partition format without causing conflicts. After installing the dual system, when the device is started, the multiple boot menu will appear, and you can choose which operating system to enter. In the current state, only one system is running and cannot be switched at will. If you want to get into another one, you have to restart and re-select.

As shown in Fig. 2, after the device is turned on, the boot program runs first, which enables the user to operate the normal operating system and use the phone as usual. If you need to switch to a private zone to restart the device, you can select the environment to enter. In this way, users can switch between app scenarios freely.

4   Implementation

In order to implement the private zone, we need to modify ramdisk, cache partition and data partition, etc., re-mount the other operations. The implementation details are covered in this section.

4.1 Configuration of TF Card

There are three steps to configure TF card partitions:

Firstly, cat command is necessary to gain the size and file format of each partition to be replaced with the device under the mobile. In our scheme, data partition and cache partition are needed to do it.

Secondly, under Linux (e.g. Ubuntu) using the parted command to partition the external SD card, the cache storage size should meet the requirements of the original system, and the size of the data partition to be partitioned can be defined according to the size that a user needs. Then, according to the file format we saw in the previous step, the two partitions are formatted into ext4 file structures under Linux using the mkfs.ext4 command. (In order to maintain the original functions of the external SD card, we can also add another FAT32 partition to the external SD card).

Finally, we ought to get the data partition and cache partition disk image files. Since data partition and cache partition store the data and cache in the device, we can make Android device install the required data by itself, so these two partitions can be formatted in ext4 file format.

Then we can view the partitions in the external SD card through Winhex software on PC.

4.2 Switching the States

To implement mutual switching between environments, we needs to solve two problems: one is how to guide the system to the private zone, and the other is how to implement free switch between the normal system and the private zone. According to Sect. 3.2, the init process is the first user-space process after the kernel starts and waits for the user process to execute. Many important daemons are started during the init initialization process, which includes mounting each partition to a context of use, so we needs to modify the partition's mount table and redirect the partition to mount to the partition corresponding to the private zone on the external SD card. According to the analysis of the start-up process, the identification of the external TF card is prior to partition mounted. Therefore, the first problem can be solved by modifying the partition. Boot partition is responsible for the operating system kernel and the guidance process, so the implementation of the guide involved changes of boot partition: to decompress the boot.img by mkboot tools under Ubuntu system, and modify the ramdisk partition table, replace the data partition and cache partition path of the normal system with the corresponding path of the private zone in the external SD card, and finally repackage and flush into the phone. Refer to Fig. 3 for the specific process.

To solve the second problem, we developed an Android application to switch. When the ordinary user space switches to the private zone, the modified boot.img needs to be brushed into the boot partition. Similarly, if the private zone switches back to the ordinary user space, the normal boot.img needs to be brushed in. Thus, when the Android phone is started, it will have the function of a private zone dual system.

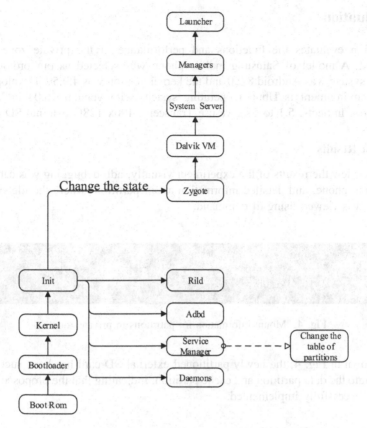

Fig. 3. The boot process when entering private zone.

4.3 Encryption of Private Zone

We can make use of the function of encrypting internal SD card on internal phone to encrypt the external SD card transparently. The encrypted external SD card can only be read on the encrypted Android device, and in other devices or using the device reader to read the encrypted external SD card, only get the result of garbled code. Since the external SD card is completely encrypted, the plain text of the encrypted data cannot be obtained even with the use of professional data decryption software. By this way, we can prevent the loss of the encrypted SD card caused by data leakage. We can also use the third party encryption software to encrypt external SD card to achieve the purpose of effective protection of sensitive data.

5 Evaluation

This section evaluates the functions and performance of the private zone. In the experiment, A model of Samsung mobile phone was selected as our prototype. Its operating system was Android 8.0.0 and the kernel version was 4.9.59. Developing the software environment is Ubuntu operating system with version 16.04 in VMware Workstation. In Sects. 5.1 to 5.4, we use Transcend 400x 128G external SD card.

5.1 Test Results

In order to view the results of the experiment visually, adb debugging was carried out on Samsung phone, and detailed information about partition (where the file system is mounted) was viewed using df command.

```
tmpfs                    1735204          0    1735204    0% /mnt/secure
tmpfs                    1735204          0    1735204    0% /mnt/secure/asec
/dev/block/mmcblk0p3     1998672       3096    1995576    1% /cache
/dev/block/mmcblk0p2    14833680    1698700   13134980   12% /data
/dev/block/sda3            16048       3196      12852   20% /efs
/dev/block/sda17           12016         12      12004    1% /dqmdbg
/dev/block/sda23           46288         12      46276    1% /omr
```

Fig. 4. Mount information for partitions in private zone.

As shown in Fig. 4, the newly partitioned external SD card has been successfully mounted into the data partition and cache partition, indicating that the proposed scheme has been successfully implemented.

5.2 Performance Evaluation

In order to test the performance of the private zone, we compile an APP to test the influence of the private zone on the speed of reading and writing files.

Table 1. Comparison of normal and private zone partitions.

Size	Normal		Private zone	
	Write	Read	Write	Read
5M	0.10 s	0.08 s	0.05 s	0.07 s
10M	0.20 s	0.13 s	0.08 s	0.17 s
64M	1.30 s	0.21 s	0.15 s	1.53 s
128M	2.44 s	0.30 s	0.19 s	3.7 s
256M	4.92 s	0.52 s	4.34 s	8.67 s
512M	9.80 s	1.74 s	9.90 s	20.80 s
1G	19.51 s	4.24 s	44.61 s	25.10 s

Table 2. Comparison of various properties with Antutu software.

Parameter	Normal	Private zone
CPU arithmetic-single core	23434	23168
Common CPU algorithms-single core	12751	11375
CPUMulti-Core PerformanceMulti-Core	53655	53922
GPU-OpenGL ES3.0	19839	19870
GPU-OpenGL ES3.0	30735	30794
GPU-OpenGL ES3.1+AEP	41204	40933
UX data security-hash, secure testing	9557	9556
UX data processing-XML and JSON processing	14335	14565
UX image processing-fisheye, blur, JPG decoding	13348	13743
UX usage experience - list, HTML5, two-dimensional code	16774	17002
RAM memory performance-memory read-write speed	3714	4029
ROM storage performance- read-write speed	4802	1140

As shown in Table 1, the performance of private zone compared with that of ordinary user space, when the data which is read and written is less than 1 GB, the difference in reading and writing time for users is only within 30%, and the difference is relatively small. When the data which is read and written is more than 1 GB, the reading and writing time will grow indirect proportion to the size of the data. So it is recommended to process relatively small data in the private zone.

In order to understand the performance difference between the private zone and user space more macroscopically, this section uses an official authoritative test software to evaluate the performance. As shown in Table 2, it is found that the score of ordinary user space is 244,148 and the score of private zone is 240097 after the test. Therefore, the performance of private zone is within the acceptable range.

5.3 The Speed of Switching Evaluation

The speed of switching between the two environments is also an aspect concerned by users. As shown in Fig. 5, we can see the comparison of switch time between the them.

As shown in Fig. 5, the start up time of the private zone is slower than the normal start up time, but the waiting time is not very long, which is acceptable.

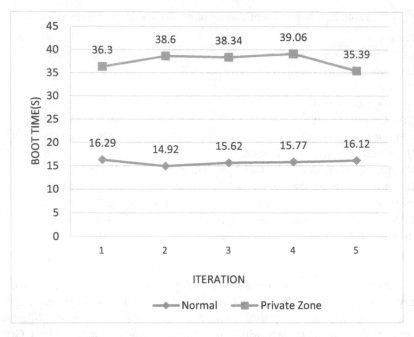

Fig. 5. Comparison of switching speeds.

5.4 Security Evaluation

The main function of private zone is implementing mutual isolation from the ordinary user space. The main feature of the two regions is their respective resources. As shown in Table 3, application, sound recording, picture, video, cache, contact, message and other relevant information are respectively stored in the ordinary user space. However, after entering the private zone, this information is no longer existing. When re-entering the ordinary user space, these information will reappear. It can be seen that the experimental results are same with the expected results, confirming the reliability of the system further.

Table 3. View the isolation of private zones.

Parameter	Normal	Private zone	Normal	Private zone
APPs	√	×	×	√
Recordings	√	×	×	√
Pictures	√	×	×	√
Videos	√	×	×	√
Caches	√	×	×	√
Contacts	√	×	×	√
Messages	√	×	×	√
Calls recording	√	×	×	√

√ represents the existence of files and × represents the absence of files.

5.5 Performance Evaluation of Different TF Cards

In this part, we compare with two different external SD cards, their speed is 300X and 400X individually. We still tests them according to the above methods.

In Fig. 6, we tested the start up time of mobile phones equipped with external SD cards with different performances. In this experiment, the starting time is the time when we press the boot button, and the ending time is the time when the Android system is fully loaded. The difference between the two is the test result. It can be seen from the above experiments that external SD cards with different performance have an impact on the experimental results. Therefore, in practical applications, we suggest using external SD cards with faster reading and writing speed and better performance.

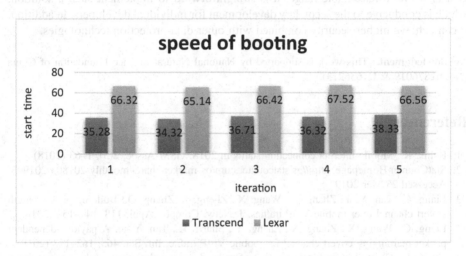

Fig. 6. Boot speed of TF cards with different performance in private zone.

6 Limitation and Future Work

This section highlights the shortcomings of the proposed scheme and put forward suggestions for improvement. It can be concluded from the experimental results in the previous section that the user experience of this scheme is good and safe and reliable. But there are the following shortcomings:

Firstly, private zone consumes more time when reading and writing larger data. Secondly, with the increasing number of file, the time consumption will increase linearly at the same time, which is not conducive to the processing of users' big private data. It is suggested to use external SD card with better performance.

Secondly, it is suggested to encrypt TF card with stronger encryption algorithm, so as to improve the security of private zone and increase the strength of security protection. In addition, it is recommended to use other data protection methods for better protection of mobile devices.

Thirdly, there is no in-depth test on various types of attack methods. The next step is testing the various types of attack methods in this scheme and improving the scheme according to the experimental results.

7 Conclusions

We propose a novel defense-level secure, trusted space technology that uses the some space capacity of TF cards as a secure space based on an in-depth understanding of the Android system architecture and start up process. Experiments show that the scheme can effectively meet the security and privacy protection requirements, and the performance cost is within a reasonable range. It is straightforward to implement such a solution, which is conducive to the secondary development for individual developers. In addition, it can achieve higher security combined with other data protection technologies.

Acknowledgment. This work is supported by National Natural Science Foundation of China (No. 61876019 & U1636213).

References

1. Bahis, K.: Mobile internet connection status in 2018. GSM Assoc. **2**(5), 1–63 (2018)
2. StatCounter Homepage. http://gs.statcounter.com/os-market-share#monthly-201803-201903. Accessed 25 Mar 2019
3. Liang, C., Tan, Y.-a., Zhang, X., Wang, X., Zheng, J., Zhang, Q.: Building packet length covert channel over mobile VoIP traffics. J. Netw. Comput. Appl. **118**, 144–153 (2018)
4. Liang, C., Wang, X., Zhang, X., Zhang, Y., Sharif, K., Tan, Y.-a.: A payload-dependent packet rearranging covert channel for mobile VoIP traffic. Inf. Sci. **465**, 162–173 (2018)
5. Gu, J., Li, C., et al.: Combination attack of android apps analysis scheme based on privacy leak. In: Proceedings of 2016 4th IEEE International Conference on Cloud Computing and Intelligence Systems, CCIS 2016, pp. 62–66 (2016)
6. Short, A., Li, F.: Android smartphone third party advertising library data leak analysis. In: Proceedings - 11th IEEE International Conference on Mobile Ad Hoc and Sensor Systems, MASS 2014, pp. 749–754 (2015)
7. Tan, Y.-a., Zhang, X., Sharif, K., Liang, C., Zhang, Q., Li, Y.: Covert timing channels for IoT over mobile networks. IEEE Wircl. Commun. **25**(6), 38–44 (2018)
8. Yoon, S., Jeon, Y.: Security threat analysis for Android based Mobile Device. In: 2014 International Conference on Information and Communication Technology Convergence (ICTC), pp. 775–776 (2014)
9. Maier, D., Protsenko, M., et al.: A game of Droid and Mouse: the threat of split-personality malware on Android. Comput. Secur. **54**, 2–15 (2015)
10. StatCounter Homepage. https://blog.cSDn.net/luoshengyang/article/details/35392905. Accessed 15 Dec 2018
11. Wu, Q., Zhao, C., Guo, Y.: Android Security Mechanism Analysis and App Practice, 2nd edn. The China Machine Press, Beijing (2013)
12. Zhang, Q., et al.: A self-certified cross-cluster asymmetric group key agreement for wireless sensor networks. Chin. J. Electron. **28**(2), 280–287 (2019)

13. Fanjiao, M., et al.: A high efficiency encryption scheme of dual data partitions for android devices. In: Proceedings - 2017 IEEE International Conference on Computational Science and Engineering and IEEE/IFIP International Conference on Embedded and Ubiquitous Computing, CSE and EUC 2017, vol. 1, pp. 823–828 (2017)
14. Rachmat, N.: Performance analysis of 256-bit AES encryption algorithm on android smartphone. J. Phys. Conf. Ser. **1196**, 012049 (2019). 6 pp.
15. Tan, Y.-a., et al.: A root privilege management scheme with revocable authorization for Android devices. J. Netw. Comput. Appl. **107**, 69–82 (2018)
16. SAMSUNG: Samsung Knox Technology White article (2018)
17. Zhang, X., Liang, C., Zhang, Q., Li, Y., Zheng, J., Tan, Y.-a.: Building covert timing channels by packet rearrangement over mobile networks. Inf. Sci. **445–446**, 66–78 (2018)
18. Guan, L., et al.: TrustShadow: secure execution of unmodified apps with ARM TrustZone. In: Proceedings of the 15th Annual International Conference on Mobile Systems, Applications, and Services. ACM (2017)
19. Rubinov, K., et al.: Automated partitioning of android apps for trusted execution environments. In: ICSE (2016)
20. Guan, Z., et al.: Privacy-preserving and efficient aggregation based on blockchain for power grid communications in smart communities. IEEE Commun. Mag. **56**(7), 82–88 (2018)
21. Guan, Z., Zhang, Y., Zhu, L., Wu, L., Yu, S.: EFFECT: an efficient flexible privacy-preserving data aggregation scheme with authentication in smart grid. Sci. China Inf. Sci. **62**, 1–14 (2019)
22. Xue, Y., Tan, Y.-a., Liang, C., Li, Y., Zheng, J., Zhang, Q.: RootAgency: a digital signature-based root privilege management agency for cloud terminal devices. Inf. Sci. **444**, 36–50 (2018)

A Code Protection Scheme via Inline Hooking for Android Applications

Hongwei Jiang, Kai Yang, Lianfang Wang, Jinbao Gao,
and Sikang Hu(✉)

School of Computer Science and Technology, Beijing Institute of Technology,
Beijing 100081, China
1411038349@qq.com, 1406996437@qq.com,
457361448@qq.com, 2537907878@qq.com, skhu@163.com

Abstract. In recent years, more and more criminals tamper with APKs (Android Package) of Android phones by reverse engineering, which brings great threat to the interests of developers and users. Therefore, it is necessary to strengthen the protection of APK code. But with the continuous evolution of the Android system compilation mode, the protection of APK code has encountered more and more difficulties. Main code protection schemes are just for applications based on Interpretation or AOT (Ahead of Time) compilation mode, but the new hybrid compilation mode used in Android 8.0 makes it difficult for the code protection schemes to protect APK code. So we refer to the Android system source code to study the hybrid compilation process of Android 8.0. By analyzing the loading, compiling and executing flow of programs in Android 8.0, we find a way to control the compilation mode. Combined with inline hook technology, our code protection scheme effectively avoids the impact of the complicated hybrid compilation mode, restores the instructions successfully and achieves the purpose of protecting APK code.

Keywords: Android · Code protection · Inline hooking · Hybrid compilation

1 Introduction

At present, the control of downloading and installing applications is not strict enough in Android system and users can download APKs from unofficial channels. On the one hand, some APKs may be tampered with to make malicious deductions or obtain user's private information [1] illegally. On the other hand, APKs may be easily analyzed by crackers through reverse engineering to get the key algorithms of the application, and someone may even directly obtain the source code of the application. In addition, some applications need to be paid in order to provide a service, if cracked by reverse means, it will cause economic loss to the copyright owner of the program. So it is necessary to protect the code of APKs.

To protect the code of APKs, Android Studio (the official integrated development environment for Android operating system) has provided the ProGuard tool, which can help to confuse the code to make the decompiled names of functions and variables hard to understand. But code obfuscation can only improve the difficulty of reversing, and

J. Vaidya et al. (Eds.): CSS 2019, LNCS 11982, pp. 102–116, 2019.
https://doi.org/10.1007/978-3-030-37337-5_9

the processed APKs can still be cracked by tampers. In 2011, Ramesh Shrestha proposed a way to protect Android applications based on dynamic loading technology at the ICIS conference by analyzing the structure of the dex file and the loading mechanism of Dalvik, which has been adopted by later researchers. In the method, the bytecodes will be protected with AES algorithm, the original dex file will be restored after the protected bytecodes being decrypted [2], and the original dex will be loaded into memory then. In 2014, Zhou et al. proposed a method to extract, encrypt and protect core methods in ACM Conference on Data and Application Security and Privacy. In the scheme, the protected method will only be decrypted and run at the moment of execution, which will prevent the application from being cracked by static reversing means [3], and main code protection schemes later are most based on this scheme. Prior to Android 4.4, the compiler mainly interpreted bytecodes through Dalvik and since Android 5.0, ART (Android Runtime) completely replaced Dalvik. At present, open schemes are mainly designed based on scheme above applying to either Dalvik mode or ART mode. But since Android 7.0, the system starts to combine AOT, Interpretation and JIT [5] three kinds of runtimes. The change in the compilation process makes the protection of the code more difficult. To achieve the effect of instructions recovery, we have to consider a variety of situations to perform the code restore operation. In our scheme, we control the compilation mode by analyzing the compilation and execution process of the program, and realize the purpose of replacing the protected instructions dynamically.

2 Background

2.1 Dex File Structure

The dex file that stores the core code of the program is compressed and packaged in the APK. When the program is running, the dex file will be loaded into memory for execution. The dex format is a compression format specially designed for Dalvik and the format consists of three parts [6]: the Header section records some basic information of the dex file; the table section records the storage location of various types of data such as strings and types in the file; the Data Section stores data and code information for classes and methods. Method instructions to be protected are just stored in the Data Section (Fig. 1).

2.2 Android Hook Framework

Hooking techniques enables a function to "integrate" its own code, in the process of being hooked, and the code inserted becomes part of the target process. So with Android hook framework, we can just make the Android API to execute our specified instructions. According to the level of the APIs hooked in the Android platform, Android hooking techniques are divided into Java level hook and Native level hook [8]. In our project, we need to hook the Native level functions to change the compilation process, so we use the Native level hooking techniques. The Native level hooking techniques are further divided into PLT [9] hooking technique and inline hooking technique. Though inline hooking

Fig. 1. Structure of dex file

framework is more difficult to implement than PLT hooking framework, but the functions of inline hooking are not limited to functions in PLT tables, and nearly all executable code in target method can be hooked, which is necessary for our project.

3   Scheme

We will extract the instructions of the target method (the method we want to protect) from the dex file of the APK and clear the original instructions in the dex file, then we will encrypt instructions extracted from the dex file and insert the encrypted instructions into the .so file in our project, and finally the instructions can be decrypted and restored into memory when the method we protected is executed. We summarize the entire code protection scheme into three steps: instructions extraction, instructions storage and instructions restoration.

3.1   Instructions Extraction

There are two steps to get the instructions of the target method from the dex file [10], as follows (Fig. 2):

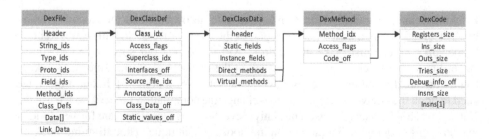

Fig. 2. Basic process of extracting dalvik bytecodes from dex file

First, we need to find the relevant information of the class of the method instructions we want to protect by the class name. The basic flow is: calculate the position of *DexClassDef* through the field *Class_Defs* (stores the classdefitem array) of the dex file; traverse the classdefitem array, get the name of the class from the *string_Ids* array with the *class_Idx* in each classdefitem and get the classdefitem structure of the target class; then obtain the *DexClassData* structure (stores the information of the entire class) of the corresponding class from the *classDataOff* field in the classdefitem structure.

Next, we should find the target method from the obtained class structure (*DexClassData*). The basic process is: traverse the *DexMethod* structure of all methods (includes *direct_Methods* and *virtual_Methods*) through the class's *DexClassData* structure, where the *DexMethod* structure stores information about the method; determine the target method (the method that we want to protect) according to the *method_idx*, and find the *DexMethod* struct of the method through the *codeOff* field. In the *DexClassData* struct, the *insnsSize* field is the instruction number of the method, and the field *insns* is the offset of the specific instructions (dalvik bytecodes).

After the above process, we extract the instructions of the target method from the dex file and we just need to clear the instructions in the dex file. It should be noted that after we clear the corresponding instructions in the dex file, we should recalculate the *Signature* with SHA-1 algorithm and *Checksum* with Adler-32 algorithm in the *Header* struct to ensure that the dex file can pass the system verification during the loading process.

3.2 Instructions Storage

To store the extracted instructions in the APK, we insert the instructions and other related information of target methods into the .so file of the APK. So we design a structure to store the method as follows: "*0xffffffff*" is the start flag of the first protected method; "*length of first struct*" represents the total length from "*length of the class-name*" to "*method instructions*"; "*......*" represents the structures of next methods to be protected immediately after the first structure; "*key flag*" is used to verify the AES [13] key entered by the user, and it is encrypted with MD5. The white part below should all be encrypted with AES algorithm (Fig. 3).

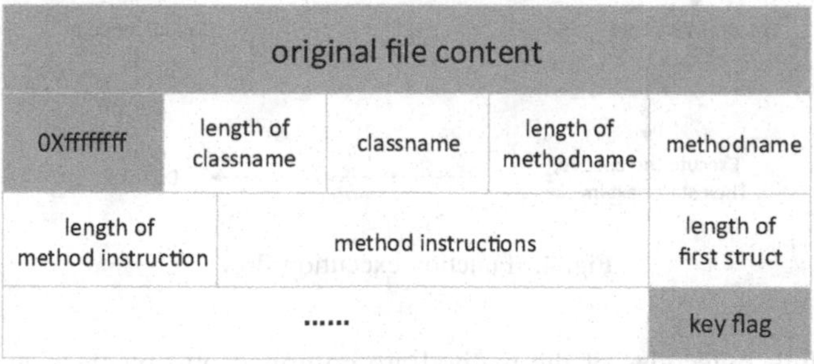

original file content				
0Xffffffff	length of classname	classname	length of methodname	methodname
length of method instruction	method instructions			length of first struct
......				key flag

Fig. 3. Structure of the file hiding instructions

After the above process, we will repack the APK with the two processed files. After the APK is installed and the program starts to run, the program will verify if the user's password typed is correct by calculating the MD5 hash value of the user's password and comparing the hash value with the *"key flag"* stored at the end of the .so file. If correct, the password will be used to decrypt the instructions and related information of target methods stored in the .so file for future restoration operations.

3.3   Instructions Restoration

To restore the instructions, we should focus on three main aspects: force the application to use the interpretation mode, replace protected instructions and get the dexcode address during the class loading process.

a. Force the application to use the Interpretation mode

In the hybrid compilation mode, the flow of function execution generally has three cases: first, determine whether the program function exists in the *jit codecache* [14], if the function exists in the *jit codecache*, the instructions in the *jit codecache* will be executed; if not in the *jit codecache*, it starts to determine whether the function precompiled (AOT) has been loaded into memory, if the function precompiled has been loaded, the precompiled function will be executed; if the function is not compiled into machine instructions, the dalvik bytecodes will be directly executed in Interpretation mode (Fig. 4).

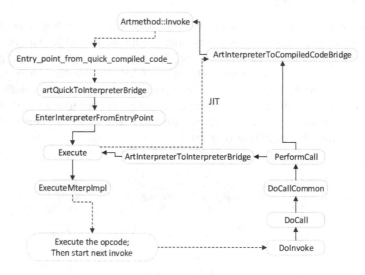

Fig. 4. Function execution flow

If the Dalvik bytecodes of the method are compiled into machine instructions in AOT or JIT compilation mode, it is hard for us to judge the time to restore the target method. So we consider to force the application to use Interpretation mode only.

We study the Android source code, analyze the execution flow of a function, and find that when a function is called, the system function *AddSamples* will be called [15], as shown (Fig. 5):

```
void Jit::AddSamples(Thread* self, ArtMethod* method, uint16_t count, bool with_backedges) {
  if (thread_pool_ == nullptr) {
    // Should only see this when shutting down.
    DCHECK(Runtime::Current()->IsShuttingDown(self));
    return;
  }

  if (method->IsClassInitializer() || method->IsNative() || !method->IsCompilable()) {
    // We do not want to compile such methods.
    return;
  }
  DCHECK(thread_pool_ != nullptr);
  DCHECK_GT(warm_method_threshold_, 0);
  DCHECK_GT(hot_method_threshold_, warm_method_threshold_);
  DCHECK_GT(osr_method_threshold_, hot_method_threshold_);
  DCHECK_GE(priority_thread_weight_, 1);
  DCHECK_LE(priority_thread_weight_, hot_method_threshold_);

  int32_t starting_count = method->GetCounter();
  if (Jit::ShouldUsePriorityThreadWeight()) {
    count *= priority_thread_weight_;
  }
  int32_t new_count = starting_count + count;    // int32 here to avoid wrap-around;
  if (starting_count < warm_method_threshold_) {
    if ((new_count >= warm_method_threshold_) &&
        (method->GetProfilingInfo(kRuntimePointerSize) == nullptr)) {
      bool success = ProfilingInfo::Create(self, method, /* retry_allocation */ false);
      if (success) {
        VLOG(jit) << "Start profiling " << method->PrettyMethod();
      }
```

Fig. 5. Definition of the function *AddSamples*

The parameter *hotness_count_* is used to record the hotness of the method. Once called, the function *Addsamples* will increase the value of *hotness_count_*. When *hotness_count_* is higher than *warm_method_threshold* (a specific threshold), the method will be profiled for AOT compilation when the mobile phone is idle and charging, and when the application starts next time, the precompiled code during AOT compilation will be directly loaded into memory; when *hotness_count_* is higher than *hot_method_threshold_*, this method will be asynchronously added to the JIT compilation task and compiled into machine instructions to be cached in the *jit codecache*.

Based on the above analysis, we consider zeroing the method's *hotness_count_* field, which will make the method not compiled in JIT or AOT compilation mode, so that the method will only be executed in Interpretation mode. So we hook the function *AddSamples* and change the increment (the parameter *count*) of the *hotness_count_* to 0, which ensures that the method's *hotness_count_* is always 0, thus we only need to consider the Interpretation compilation when we perform the restoration operation.

b. Replace instructions

Next we just need to consider replacing instructions. When the target method is called, the function *PerformCall* will be executed and it will determine whether the parameter *use_interpreter_entrypoint* is true. After our hooking operation to the function *AddSamples*, the parameter *use_interpreter_entrypoint* must will be true, so the execution flow will only jump to the function *ArtInterpreterToInterpreterBridge* to interpret the method. The function *ArtInterpreterToInterpreterBridge* is defined in the Android system source as follows:

```
ArtInterpreterToInterpreterBridge (void *thread,
                            DexCode const *dexCode,
                            void *shadow_frame,
                            void *jValue)
```

Among the parameters of the function *ArtInterpreterToInterpreterBridge*, the parameter *dexCode* stores the method instructions to be interpreted. So we should just hook the function *ArtInterpreterToInterpreterBridge* and replace the instructions in the parameter *dexCode* with the instructions decrypted from the .so file. But the function *ArtInterpreterToInterpreterBridge* is called during the execution process of every method. So we should ensure the instructions to be replaced belong to the target method that we protected. We should consider of some way to determine whether the method to be executed is the target method. Because after the class is loaded into memory when the application starts, the address of the instructions will not change any more, we can determine that by comparing the *dexCode* address of the target method at the start of the dex file with the *dexCode* address in the function *ArtInterpreterToInterpreterBridge*. This replacing operation can be realized in the hooking framework. So we should try to get the *dexCode* address in the class loading process in advance.

c. Get the dexcode address in the class loading process

According to the Android source code, the class loading process in the system is mainly divided into two steps: load the dex file and find classes [16]. At the start of the APK, the class *ClassLoader* loads the dex file and generates the element array (storing all dex file instances) in memory. Then the function *Findclass* traverses all dex file instances in the element array. In the traversing process, we find that the function *FindClassDef* will be called.

```
const Dexfile::ClassDef* OatFile::OatDexFile::
FindClassDef ( const DexFile& dex_file,
              const char* descriptor,
              size_t hash)
```

The parameters of the function *FindClassDef* include the dexfile object, the descriptor of the class and the hash value, and the return value of the function is a *ClassDef* class pointer. So we can hook the function *FindClassDef*, compare the parameter descriptor of the function *FindClassDef* with the target class's descriptor and find the target *ClassDef* struct. With the target *ClassDef* struct, we can search for the target method and finally get the dexcode struct of the target method.

The main algorithm of our scheme is concluded as follows:

Algorithm 1 Restore Instructions

1: //Recover the decrypted instructions to Vector<Methodstruct*>Methodstructs
2: DumpCodeTo(Methodstructs)
3: //Hook function *FindClassDef()* to get the dexcode address of target method while loading classes
4: **for** methodstruct **in** Methodstructs
5:    **if** descripter == methodstruct->classname
6:    **then** classdataitem←getclassdataitem(*dex_file, descripter*)
7:    **for** dexmethod **in** classdataitem
8:      **if** dexmethod->fullname == methodstruct->fullname
9:      **then** methodstruct->pdexcode←getdexcode(dexmethod)
10:     **end if**
11:    **end for**
12:   **end if**
13: **end for**
14: //Hook function *ArtInterpreterToInterpreterBridge()* to restore decrypted instructions before execution
15: **for** methodstruct **in** methodstructs
16:    **if** methodstruct->pdexcode == *dexCode*//it means the target method will be excuted now
17: **then** replace the dexcode with a new dexcode pointed to decrypted instructions
18:   **end if**
19: **end for**

---

4   Experiment

4.1   Configure and Use Hooking Framework in the Project

We will build our project using the open source Android-Inline Hook framework of ele7enxxh [22] and JNI [23] technology should be used to implement the hook framework. The name of the function we defined for testing is *Printlog*. Let's take the function *ArtInterpreterToInterpreterBridge* as an example to illustrate how to hook native functions.

First we need to decompile *libart.so* and find the exported function symbol of the function in the file. From the */system/lib/* directory of the mobile phone, we pull the *libart.so* file, open it with IDA Pro [25], search for the function in the Exports table and find the exported symbol of the function (Fig. 6).

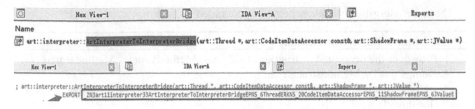

Fig. 6. Exported symbol of *ArtInterpreterToInterpreterBridge*

Then we define the hooking registration function as follows:

```
void* getDexProtectClass(void *funclib, const char* func_name)
{
    void* func = ndk_dlsym(funclib, func_name);
    if(func == NULL)
    {
        LOGD("unable to find the symbol %s", func_name);
        return NULL;
    }
    if(registerInlineHook((uint32_t)func,
(uint32_t)NArtInterpreterToInterpreterBridge,
(uint32_t**)&OArtInterpreterToInterpreterBridge) != ELE7EN_OK)
    {
        LOGD("registerInlineHook interpreterTointerpreter error");
        return NULL;
    }else{
        LOGD("registerInlineHook interpreterTointerpreter ok");
    }
    return func;
}
```

In this registration function, the parameter *func_name* is the export symbol of the function and the parameter *funclib* is the dynamic link library (here, *libart.so*) reference. We register the hooking operation on the function *ArtInterpreterToInterpreterBridge* by the function *registerInlineHook*, where the function *NArtInterpreterToInterpreterBridge* is the new function that we defined to replace the original function *OArtInterpreterToInterpreterBridge*.

We can do the hooking operation on the other two functions *AddSamples* and *FindClassdef*, just in similar process as above.

4.2   Process and Install APK

After we build the project to generate the APK, we need to process the APK: decompress the APK, extract instructions of the target method from *classes.dex*, clear the corresponding instructions, store the instructions in *libnative-lib.so* file, and repackage the APK (Fig. 7).

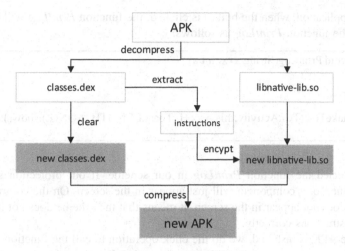

Fig. 7. Process APK

The above operation is implemented by using Python program. Before processing, we should configure the config.ini file to control the processing flowing. The parameters are that: the parameter *targetfile* is the location of the APK to be protected in the computer, the parameter *functionsignature* is composed according to class name + '#' + method name + parameter list + return value type, the parameter *libpath* is the relative path of .so file we store target instructions after we install the APK, the parameter *libname* is the name of the .so file, and the parameter *password* is used to perform AES encryption (Fig. 8).

```
[global]
targetfile = E:\8.0\protectcode\clickButton\app\build\outputs\apk\debug\app-debug.apk
functionsignature =Lcom/example/administrator/clickbutton/TestActivity;#PrintLog(Ljava/lang/String;I)V
libpath = lib\armeabi-v7a\
libname = libnative-lib.so
password = 123
```

Fig. 8. Config.ini

After the APK is processed as above, we will test the APK in the Android phone.

4.3   Evaluation

After the processing, we will install and test the APK in the Android phone *Samsung Galaxy S9*.

a. Usability test

We test our scheme with methods of four different access control modifiers: public, private, protected and static.

In our application, when the button is clicked, the function *PrintLog* will be called. We define the function *PrintLog* as follows:

```
protected void PrintLog(String xxx, int a)
{
    int i=0;
    i=i+1;
    Toast.makeText(TestActivity.this, xxx+i, Toast.LENGTH_LONG ).show();
}
```

We protected the function *PrintLog* in our scheme. If our protection scheme is successful, the Toast component will just appear in the screen. On the contrary, if the component does not appear in the screen, it means that the scheme does not restore the protected instructions correctly.

After the APK is installed, we do the click operation to call the function *PrintLog*, the Toast component appears normally; we repeat the click operation for more than 25 times, the Toast component appears normally; after the above repeated operation, we will exit the program and idle the mobile phone for 24 h, and then repeat the above click test, the Toast component still appears normally (Table 1).

Table 1. Usability on different methods.

Method type	Click 1 times	Click 25 times	Click after 24 h of idle
Public	✓	✓	✓
Private	✓	✓	✓
Protected	✓	✓	✓
Static	✓	✓	✓

The above results show that we have successfully implemented the control of the compilation mode of the target function, and successfully achieved the purpose of dynamic restoration of the target instructions.

b. Safety test

We use apktool to decompress classes.dex and view it with 010editer to compare the original APK and the processed APK. We analyze the dex in the original APK as follows (Fig. 9):

We analyze the *classes.dex* in the APK we have processed, as follows (Fig. 10):

It can be seen that the instructions of the target method in *classes.dex* after being processed are replaced by our instructions, and the original instructions are no longer present in classes.dex.

After the APK is installed, we execute command *"oatdump --oat-file=base.odex -- output=dumpfile"* in the application installation directory with ADB (Android Debug Bridge), to get the dex code in the APK.

Name	
struct encoded_method method[0]	public void com.example.administrator.clickbutton.TestActivity.PrintLog'
int p	0
> struct uleb128 method_idx_diff	0x3CA4
> struct uleb128 access_flags	(0x1) ACC_PUBLIC
> struct uleb128 code_off	0x127624
int64 pos	2093129
∨ struct code_item code	7 registers, 3 in arguments, 3 out arguments, 0 tries, 33 instructions
ushort registers_size	7
ushort ins_size	3
ushort outs_size	3
ushort tries_size	0
uint debug_info_off	1434904
int64 pos	1209904
> struct debug_info_item debug_info	
uint insns_size	33
∨ ushort insns[33]	
ushort insns[0]	28690
ushort insns[1]	4370
ushort insns[2]	4272
ushort insns[3]	538
ushort insns[4]	21266
ushort insns[5]	794
ushort insns[6]	6890
ushort insns[7]	8305
ushort insns[8]	13638
ushort insns[9]	50
ushort insns[10]	546

Fig. 9. Instructions of *Printlog* in original dex

Name	
struct encoded_method method[0]	public void com.example.administrator.clickbutton.TestActivity.PrintLog
int p	0
> struct uleb128 method_idx_diff	0x3CA4
> struct uleb128 access_flags	(0x1) ACC_PUBLIC
> struct uleb128 code_off	0x127624
int64 pos	2093129
∨ struct code_item code	7 registers, 3 in arguments, 3 out arguments, 0 tries, 33 instructions
ushort registers_size	7
ushort ins_size	3
ushort outs_size	3
ushort tries_size	0
uint debug_info_off	1434904
int64 pos	1209904
> struct debug_info_item debug_info	
uint insns_size	33
∨ ushort insns[33]	
ushort insns[0]	4114
ushort insns[1]	14
ushort insns[2]	0
ushort insns[3]	0
ushort insns[4]	0
ushort insns[5]	0
ushort insns[6]	0
ushort insns[7]	0
ushort insns[8]	0
ushort insns[9]	0
ushort insns[10]	0

Fig. 10. Instructions of *Printlog* in processed dex

We install the original APK, and after the command is executed, the dumpfile is as follows (Fig. 11):

```
3: void com.example.administrator.clickbutton.TestActivity.PrintLog
   DEX CODE:
      0x0000: 1270                     | const/4 v0, #+7
      0x0001: 1211                     | const/4 v1, #+1
      0x0002: b010                     | add-int/2addr v0, v1
      0x0003: 1a02 1253                | const-string v2, "xxf" // s
      0x0005: 1a03 ea1a                | const-string v3, "Test" //
      0x0007: 7120 4635 3200           | invoke-static {v2, v3}, int
      0x000a: 2202 c207                | new-instance v2, java.lang.
      0x000c: 7010 a23d 0200           | invoke-direct {v2}, void ja
      0x000f: 6e20 ac3d 5200           | invoke-virtual {v2, v5}, ja
   method@15788
      0x0012: 6e20 a83d 0200           | invoke-virtual {v2, v0}, ja
```

Fig. 11. Dex code of *Printlog* in original application

We install the APK we have processed, and the dumpfile is as follows (Fig. 12):

```
3: void com.example.administrator.clickbutton.TestActivity.PrintLog
   DEX CODE:
      0x0000: 1210                     | const/4 v0, #+1
      0x0001: 0e00                     | return-void
      0x0002: 0000                     | nop
      0x0003: 0000                     | nop
      0x0004: 0000                     | nop
      0x0005: 0000                     | nop
      0x0006: 0000                     | nop
      0x0007: 0000                     | nop
      0x0008: 0000                     | nop
      0x0009: 0000                     | nop
      0x000a: 0000                     | nop
      0x000b: 0000                     | nop
      0x000c: 0000                     | nop
      0x000d: 0000                     | nop
      0x000e: 0000                     | nop
```

Fig. 12. Dex code of *Printlog* in processed application

By comparison, we can see that the dexcode instructions of the target method is replaced by our specified invalid instructions.

c. Performance test

In addition, we calculate the APK scale and method time consuming of the scheme, when we protect four different kinds of methods. The performances of our code protection scheme are shown as follows (Table 2):

Table 2. Performances on different methods

Method type	Original APK scale (/Byte)	New APK scale (/Byte)	Original time consuming (/s)	New time consuming (/s)
Public	1,654,157	1,681,312	0.045	0.068
Private	1,653,256	1,680,368	0.046	0.069
Protected	1,655,359	1,681,825	0.051	0.073
Static	1,653,296	1,680,137	0.042	0.060

The data show that our protection scheme has little effect on the scale of the APK, but it has a greater impact on the speed of the program.

5 Conclusion

In our paper, at first, the basic structure of the dex format is analyzed, the process of searching for the corresponding instructions of the specific method is sorted out, and a specific file structure for encrypting and decrypting multiple methods is designed. Then we study the basic principle of Android hybrid compilation modes, and combined with the hook framework, we hook the Android native function to modify the execution mode of the specific function. In addition, we analyze the loading process of the function and extract the mapped address of the target function instructions in memory. Finally, we implement a code dynamic restoration method based on the uniqueness of the dexcode address in memory.

There are still some aspects that can be improved. After the dynamic restoration, the decrypted instructions already exist in the memory, which may be extracted by the debugging tool. So we can further clear the corresponding position in the memory after the instructions are run to improve the safety. In addition, our scheme only focuses on the protection of java code and the protection of native code should be studied in the future.

Acknowledgment. This work is supported by National Natural Science Foundation of China (No. 61876019 & U1636213).

References

1. Mulliner, C., Oberheide, J., Robertson, W., Kirda, E.: PatchDroid: scalable third-party security patches for Android device. In: Computer Security Applications Conference (2013)
2. Shreshtha, R.: A systemic code-protection methodology for the dex file on Android platform. In: Proceedings of 2012 IEEE International Conference on Computer Science and Automation Engineering (2012)
3. Zhou, W., Wang, Z., Zhou, Y., Jiang, X.: DILIVAR: diversifying intermediate language for anti-repackaging on Android platform. In: ACM Conference on Data & Application Security & Privacy (2014)

4. Portokalidis, G., Homburg, P., Anagnostakis, K., Bos, H.: Paranoid Android: versatile protection for smartphones. In: Proceedings of the 26th Annual Computer Security Applications Conference (2010)
5. https://source.android.com/devices/tech/dalvik/jit-compiler
6. https://wladimir-tm4pda.github.io/porting/dalvik.html
7. Chen, Q., Jia, L.-f., Zhang, W.: Research of software protection methods based on the interaction between code and shell. Comput. Eng. Sci. **12** (2006). 011
8. GToad, 05 July 2018. https://gtoad.github.io/2018/07/05/Android-Native-Hook/
9. Bryant, R.E., O'Hallaran, D.R.: Computer Systems: A Programmer's Perspective. Pearson, London (2015)
10. Zhang, Y., Luo, X., Yin, H.: The terminator to Android hardening services. In: DEFCON 25 Hacker Conference (2017)
11. Xue, Y., Tan, Y., Liang, C., Li, Y., Zheng, J., Zhang, Q.: RootAgency: a digital signature-based root privilege management agency for cloud terminal devices. Inf. Sci. **444**, 36–50 (2018)
12. https://androidxref.com/8.0.0_r4/xref/art/runtime/interpreter/interpreter.cc
13. Daemen, J., Rijmen, V.: The Design of Rijndael: AES - The Advanced Encryption Standard. Springer, Heidelberg (2013)
14. Codecache Tuning. https://docs.oracle.com/javase/8/embedded/develop-apps-platforms/codecache.htm
15. rk700, 30 June 2017. http://rk700.github.io/2017/06/30/hook-on-android-n/?tdsourcetag=s_pcqq_aiomsg
16. Mai ke, 02 August 2018. https://blog.csdn.net/u013394527/article/details/80980340
17. Yang, Z., et al.: Appintent: analyzing sensitive data transmission in Android for privacy leakage detection. In: Proceedings of the 2013 ACM SIGSAC Conference on Computer & Communications Security (2013)
18. Grassi, M.: Reverse engineering, pentesting, and hardening of Android apps. DroidCon (2014)
19. Hexo, 25 September 2018. https://ansgarlin.github.io/zh-tw/news/2018/09/25/about_art_1_compilation/
20. Tsai, K.-Y., Chiu, Y.-H., Wu, T.-C.: Android App copy protection mechanism based on dynamic loading. In: International Symposium on Consumer Electronics (2014)
21. Wißfeld, M.: ArtHook Callee-side method hook injection on the new Android runtime ART. Information Security and Cryptography (2015)
22. ele7enxxh (2018). https://github.com/ele7enxxh/Android-Inline-Hook
23. Liang, S.: The Java Native Interface – Programmer's Guide and Specification. Addison-Wesley Professional, Boston (1999)
24. Drake, J.J., Lanier, Z., Mulliner, C., Fora, P.O., Ridley, S.A., Wicherski, G.: Android Hacker's Handbook. Wiley, Hoboken (2014)
25. Eagle, C.: The IDA Pro Book. No Starch Press, San Francisco (2011)
26. Martelli, A., Ravenscroft, A., Ascher, D.: Python Cookbook. O'Reilly Media, Sebastopol (2005)
27. Chen, H.: Privacy and Security Enhancements for Android Application. University of California, Los Angeles (2012)
28. Levin, J.: Dalvik and ART. In: Andevcon (2015)
29. Nolan, G.: Decompiling Android. Apress, New York (2012)
30. Park, Y.: We can still crack you! general unpacking method for Android packer (no root). In: Blackhat Asia (2015)

Log-Based Control Flow Attestation for Embedded Devices

Jingbin Liu[1,2]($\boxtimes$), Qin Yu[2], Wei Liu[4], Shijun Zhao[2],
Dengguo Feng[2,3], and Weifeng Luo[4]

[1] University of Chinese Academy of Sciences, Beijing, China
[2] TCA, Institute of Software, Chinese Academy of Sciences, Beijing, China
{liujingbin,qin_yu,zhaosj,feng}@tca.iscas.ac.cn
[3] SKLCS, Institute of Software, Chinese Academy of Sciences, Beijing, China
[4] Shenzhen Power Supply Bureau Co., Ltd., Shenzhen, China
{liuwei,luoweifeng}@sz.csg.cn

Abstract. Remote attestation is a very important mechanism helping a trusted party to get the status of a remote embedded device. Most remote attestation schemes aim at checking the code integrity and leave devices vulnerable to runtime attacks. Recently a new kind of attestation called control flow attestation has been proposed to get rid of this limitation. However, previous studies on control flow attestation cannot verify the attestation result efficiently and lack secure storage.

In this paper, we present a log-based attestation scheme that not only can attest the control flow path of programs on embedded devices but also can verify the attestation result very efficiently. We use a lightweight root of trust in our attestation. We implement our system on Hikey board using ARM TrustZone security extension. We evaluate the performance using a popular embedded device benchmark Mibench and demonstrate that our scheme has a high security assurance and a good performance.

Keywords: Embedded system security · Remote attestation · Trusted execution environment

1 Introduction

Embedded systems are applied widely in our everyday life. Some of them are deployed in security-critical environments and their vulnerability may incur serious security issues. For example, it may threaten our life if automobile control systems or cardiac pacemaker are compromised. So it is urgent to secure embedded devices.

Remote attestation is an effective way to verify the state of a remote entity. It usually contains two entities, a verifier who wants to know the state and one or more provers who present the report of the status of them. Most often, it is realized as a protocol between the verifier and the prover. The verifier accepts the report sent by the prover and checks it to decide whether to trust

© Springer Nature Switzerland AG 2019
J. Vaidya et al. (Eds.): CSS 2019, LNCS 11982, pp. 117–132, 2019.
https://doi.org/10.1007/978-3-030-37337-5_10

the prover or not. Remote attestation usually requires a basic trusted component that is called the trust anchor. The trust anchor cannot be compromised by the attacker and hence can provide a secure region to build trust. The trust anchor has many implementations, e.g. Trusted Platform Module (TPM), SMART [1], TrustLite [2]. Unfortunately, they all have some disadvantages, either is too expensive or are not be commercially used. A promising implementation is Trust-Zone technique provided on ARM platforms. It is lightweight and widely used.

Most attestation schemes use a static method to measure the state of a program. In this way, the prover collects the static measurement that typically is a hash of the program code, computes a signature or a MAC and sends them to the verifier. However, static attestation cannot detect the control flow attacks, such as Return-oriented Programming [3], Jump-oriented Programming [4]. These attacks aim at corrupting the control data to direct the control flow to a specific location and make the program do some malicious behaviour. Current control flow attacks use code-reuse technique and do not need to inject malicious instructions. So the measurement remains unchanged and the verifier cannot detect the attacks on the prover. In order to overcome these challenges, some new techniques have been proposed, such as control-flow integrity (CFI) [5], and code-pointer integrity (CPI) [6]. However, simply combining these with the remote attestation can only tell the verifier whether a control-flow attack happened.

Recently a new kind of attestation, control flow attestation [7,8], was proposed. They use software or hardware solutions to report the control flow path to the verifier. But these solutions encounter problems when verifying the report. If the verifier does not have all concrete information (e.g., input, state information of the device) of the prover or the program is complex, it would lead to the state explosion verifying the result with an aggregated authenticator of the control flow.

In this paper, we propose a log-based control flow attestation. Our solution allows the prover to produce a program state log to record the control flow. Leveraging the information in the log, the verifier can efficiently verify whether the prover has been compromised. Previous schemes [7,8] have to record measurements of all paths. In our scheme, we only need to store the analysis result of the program and it will preserve space and time in the verifier side. Furthermore, the verifier can find out which part of the program has been corrupted. Due to the lack of secure storage in TrustZone technique, we use a lightweight root of Trust based on the on-chip SRAM Physical Unclonable Functions (PUFs) [9] in our attestation. A prototype of our solution is implemented on a commonly used platforms and can be easily transplanted to other platforms. The main contributions are listed as follows:

1. We propose a log-based control flow attestation scheme. Our solution uses a log to record the control flow events that can be used to detect control flow attacks and avoids the state explosion problem in verifying the result.
2. We provide a method that can check which part of the program has been attacked. The verifier can use the log to analyse the program control flow

and get the detailed execution status and find the vulnerability based on the attack.

3. We use a lightweight trust anchor for the attestation. We use the on-chip SRAM Physical Unclonable Functions (PUFs) as the root of trust. We do not need any specific persistent secure key storage.
4. We implement a proof-of-concept prototype of our solution including log analysis tool, program instrumentation tool, and attestation service.
5. We evaluate the performance of our scheme systematically using an open-source embedded device benchmark Mibench and demonstrate the security against the control flow attacks.

In the rest of the paper, we will introduce the background and related work (Sect. 2), present the threat model (Sect. 3) and the system (Sect. 4), introduce the implementation (Sect. 5), evaluate our approach (Sects. 6 and 7) and conclude (Sect. 8).

2   Background and Related Work

2.1   Remote Attestation

Remote attestation mechanism is used by an entity to verify the software status of another remote entity. Static remote attestation only concentrates on the code integrity but dynamic remote attestation pays attention to the integrity of control flow. Recent studies include C-FLAT [7] and LO-FAT [8]. C-FLAT first proposes a control flow attestation scheme that measures the control flow path and LO-FAT provides a hardware-based control flow attestation. They both use a hash chain of control flow transitions as the proof. However, if a program has a lot of transitions, it will bring unacceptable expenses storing a measurement for each path. Hence, our mechanism uses a control flow log to attest. It costs little time to verify the result and get the control flow path of the program.

2.2   ARM Architecture

ARM architecture is a type of reduced instruction set computing (RISC) architectures. In this paper, we only talk about 32-bit ARM processors. 32-bit ARM processors have 16 general-purpose registers including the program counter (pc). The 16 general-purpose registers are labeled r0-r15 or R0-R15 and have different usages. We use the lower case in this paper and represent an unknown register in r0-r15 as rx. Table 1 lists these registers and their usage.

To make compiler resolve subroutine calls and returns in an interchangeable manner, ARM provides ARM Architecture Procedure Call Standard (AAPCS). Programs confirming to this standard use Branch with Link (bl) or Branch with Link and eXchange (blx) instruction to perform subroutine calls. These two functions load the address of the subroutine to the program counter (pc) and the return address to the link register (lr). The ARM processors do not provide a return instruction like Intel processors, so a subroutine usually leverages *bx lr*

Table 1. ARM core registers

Register	Special	Usage
r0 - r1		Argument/result/scratch register
r2 - r3		Argument/scratch register
r4 - r8		Variable register
r9		Platform register
r10 - r11		Variable register
r12	IP	The intra-procedure-call scratch
r13	SP	The stack pointer
r14	LR	The link register
r15	PC	The program counter

and *pop* $\{..., pc\}$ to return back to the calling program. The *bx lr* instruction is used if subroutine does not call other subroutines. The *pop* $\{..., pc\}$ instruction is used in other subroutines. These subroutines first perform a *push* $\{..., lr\}$ instruction and store the return address on the stack. At the end of these subroutines, they perform *pop* $\{..., pc\}$ instruction to jump to the return address on the stack. Other branch instructions, such as Branch *b* and Branch and eXchange *bx*, are used in a program to jump to a dedicated address or an address in the register.

2.3   TrustZone

TrustZone [10] is a hardware-based security extension of ARM System on Chip. It provides a secure execution environment by separating the secure and non-secure world and blocking accesses from the non-secure world to secure world. People can put trusted programs and a secure operating system, such as OP-TEE [11] and QSEE [12], into the secure world to provide secure services. Non-secure world usually contains the services we use to provide the function, such as the service code and some mobile operating systems, such as iOS, Android. Recently, ARM provides TrustZone feature on its embedded processor Cortex-M series and gives more security assurance to embedded platforms. In our schemes, we leverage TrustZone to provide a trusted environment to execute the secure log preservation and attestation service.

2.4   Physical Unclonable Functions

Physical Unclonable Functions (PUF) are physical one-way functions that are introduced by Pappu et al. [9]. They are such hardware components that output a response with noises depending on the manufacturing process when given a challenge. PUFs have two properties, robustness and uniqueness. Robustness means a PUF should produce outputs with little noise when it is challenged with the same input. Uniqueness means different PUFs should produce independent responses when they are evaluated with the same challenge. These properties make PUF a potential technique to extract keys by applying a fuzzy extractor [13]. Zhao et al. [14] built a lightweight root of trust scheme based on SRAM PUF in ARM Trustzone environment. This method does not need to store keys on secure non-volatile memory and resists hardware attacks such as directly reading the disk. Furthermore, this method can resist clone attacks because of the physically unclonable property.

3 Threat Model and Assumption

Our solution concerns about control flow attacks, in which the attacker is given the ability to control the instruction pointer (IP). In control flow attacks, the attacker can instrument the control flow to execute malicious programs. Based on the method tampering the control flow, these attacks can be divided into several types. One type is code injection attack. In this type of attack, the attacker first injects some malicious codes and then instruments a program to jump to this location. Another type is code reuse attack, such as ROP [3] and JOP [4]. This type of attack uses existing codes instead of injected codes by creating a chain of small code pieces and fulfil the function. Besides these two attacks, non-control-data-attack is also a real threat. It does not change the control data on the stack like the former two attacks, it tampers the control flow by changing the non-control-data like loop counters, variables used in the judgement. In this paper, the attacker can carry out control flow attacks including all these three types of attacks, but the attacker cannot perform other attacks like data-only attacks and physical attacks.

We assume the attacker has some limitations and the platform has some security features. We assume the adversary can have full control over the process memory, but has no ability to modify the code segment. We also assume the attacker can access arbitrary memory except for the secure world memory.

4 Design

We first present our high-level design, then describe each component in detail.

4.1 Design Overview

The architecture of our scheme is depicted in Fig. 1. At first the verifier instruments the target program, generates the control flow graph (CFG) and sends the program to the prover. Then the prover hooks the target program and collects the control flow information. Upon resuming the program, the prover records the information needed in the control flow log. When the verifier sends a challenge to the prover, the prover generates an attestation report using the key derived from the SRAM PUF and response. The prover is divided into a normal world

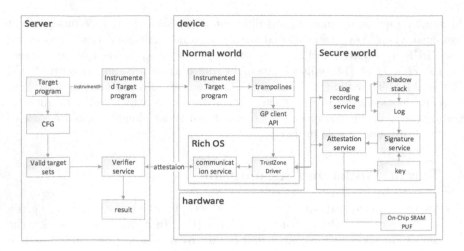

Fig. 1. Architecture

and a secure world. Most of the operations are done in the secure world. At last the verifier verifies the response using the CFG generated before and checks whether the program is executed as expected.

Our scheme records the values of specific pointers, such as the values of the return addresses and function pointers in the log. Figure 2 shows a simple test program. When we use a function pointer to call a function, our scheme records the value of the function pointer and puts some extra information into the log. As illustrated in Fig. 2, our scheme records the address of function call instruction when calling function fptr. When the function returns, our scheme records the target address of the return instruction. Our scheme can check whether the function returns as expected and can prove whether the program suffers control flow attacks. In the test program, our scheme records the return address when foo1 and foo2 return. We call function pointers and return addresses code pointers here for convenience. When the verifier sends a challenge, the prover first gets a record, responses to the verifier. Due to the imprecision of static analysis, we propose using a shadow stack to help verify return addresses. In order to check which part of the program is attacked, we propose a new structure of log which can be used to recover the function call sequence.

4.2 Design Details

Hook Function. In our scheme, we instrument five types of instructions $bx\ lr$, $pop\ pc\ rx$, $blx\ rx$, $bl\ rx$ and $bx\ rx$. We leave b instruction uninstrumented because we assume the code segment cannot be changed by the attacker and the target address is written in the code explicitly. The other five types of instructions direct the control flow to an address in the register and may leave a chance to attack. We do not instrument some instructions like $mov\ pc, X$ because these

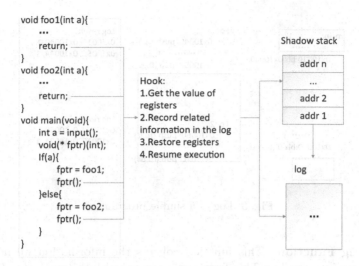

Fig. 2. Sample program

instructions mostly lie in the operating system and we only focus on user mode application.

We instrument them to the corresponding hook functions. These functions have both four procedures. The first three procedures are nearly the same. The first is to save registers in case of changing some registers and affecting later execution. For return instruction, register 0 should be saved because it contains the return value. For function call instruction, register 0–3 should be saved because they contain the function parameters. The second is to call the log saving function, which will be described in later sections. The third is to restore registers that were saved in the first step. The final step is to return to the original program execution. For return instructions, our hook function pops pc and other registers in the stack and direct control flow to the caller function. For the other instructions, our hook function gets the value of the original target register, jumps to the target address and continues execution.

Log Architecture. Figure 3 shows the function calling procedure of the example program and its log. In this figure, we can see we record the address of the *blx* and *pop* instruction and the target address of them. In each line of the record, we record some helper data beyond the two addresses we mentioned above. One usage of helper data is to help the verifier get more information to decide whether the program executes in the right way. Another usage is to shorten the log. If the log is too big, transmitting the data will be a big problem. Further description is shown in later sections. We only record the necessary information in our scheme and in this example we put only three values in our log: source address, target address and function level.

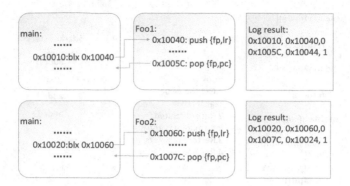

Fig. 3. Log of a simple program

Log Saving Function. This function collects the information we need and records them into the log. This function is separated into two parts. The first part collects control flow information. It gets the source address from the register lr. Because we rewrite the target instruction to branch and link instruction, the source address is the value of register lr minus 4. The target address and helper data are collected from the shadow stack, which will be described in detail in the next section. The second part save the log. After collecting control flow data, the program records them into the log and then returns back. This function lies in the secure world because we must guarantee the integrity of the log and protect it from the malicious program. The log is stored in the secure world.

Shadow Stack. In the first invoking of log saving function, we initiate a shadow stack. During the execution of a program, we produce a shadow stack different from the program stack. We only record return addresses into the shadow stack. In the log saving function of function calling instructions, we push the source address into the stack. Then in the log saving function of return instructions, we pop the address from the shadow stack and check whether the target address is the same as the address stored in the shadow stack.

We use a shadow stack due to the imprecision of backward control flow when verifying the targets of return instruction. Otherwise, we must check the call return matching in the verifier side and it will bring extra expenses. To make shadow stack immune to attacks from other applications in the normal world, we put shadow stack in the secure world.

Key Generation and Reproduction. We use SRAM puf as our root of trust for attestation. We use it in key generation and reproducing procedures. The procedures are shown in Fig. 4. Before the device is deployed in the environment, the server collects a set of on chip SRAM startup values. On the device, the on chip SRAM startup value is measured and transferred by the BootROM after powered on. In Fig. 4, PS stands for a primary seed that is a random

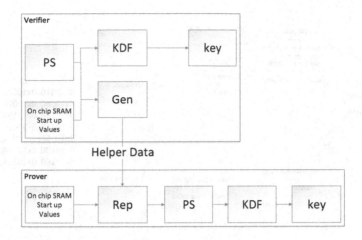

Fig. 4. Key generate and reproduce

number selected by the server. Gen and rep stand for the generate and reproduce procedure in the fuzzy extractor. KDF stands for the key derivation functions. The server first generates PS and select a SRAM startup value, then get a helper data and a key pair after the generate procedure and KDF. When the server wants to do attestation with the device, it sends the helper data to the device. The device then reproduces the PS based on the on chip start up value and the helper data. After that, the device can get a secure key for attestation. All these procedures on the device are processed in the secure world.

Verification. We firstly use points to analysis to get all targets of every code pointer, each pointer has a set that includes all its targets. We put all possible addresses to the sets of the return address just to check if it is lawful but do not consider if it matches with the calling instruction because it is checked in the previous steps. When we get the log, we compare the real target of code pointers to the pointer in the set we get in the beginning. If we find they are not in the sets, we are sure the program has been corrupted. When all addresses in the log are within the sets of the code pointers, we can say the program has executed correctly.

Previous schemes [7,8] have to record measurement for each path. It is feasible when the program is not complex. If the program is complex and has a lot of paths, it will cost much space to store all measurements. In our scheme, we only need to store the analysis result of the program. For example, there are 3 code pointers with 4 possible target addresses each in a program. This program must go through all these 3 code pointers. The count of all paths is 81 but the analysis result only has 12 items. Another advantage is that it will cost less time to check. Using the example above, previous schemes must compare the received

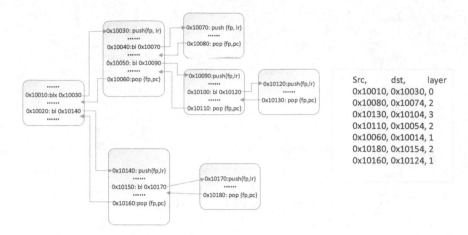

Fig. 5. Restore function calling procedure

measurement with the 81 measurements. In our scheme, we only need to compare each pointer to 4 items and compare 12 times in sum. It will save a lot of time.

Restoring Function Calling Procedure. The log architecture we designed contains the helper data. At present, the helper data only contains the layer of the code pointer in the shadow stack. Firstly we can use the address of the instruction to get the type of the instruction. We search the address in the binary file and get whether this instruction is a function call instruction or a return instruction. Then we use the type and the layer of the stack to restore function calling procedure. Figure 5 is an example.

Firstly we verify the function pointers to make sure that all indirect jumps go to the start of a function. Next we leverage the address of the return instruction and the result from the analysis of the program to get the start of corresponding function. Then we use the layer to get the function calling sequence. For example, instruction at 0×10080 is at layer 2. It means it is called by a function at layer 1 and returns to layer 1. The next instruction is at layer 3, that means the function at layer 1 calls another function at layer 2, the function at layer 2 calls its sub-function at layer 3 and the function at layer 3 returns to layer 2. In this way, we can restore all function calling procedure step by step. If we find one function returns to a place that it is not allowed to jump to, we can tell this function has a weakness and is compromised by an attacker.

5   Implementation

This section presents our detailed architecture and discusses some problems we faced in implementation.

5.1   Architecture

To test our design, we implement it on an embedded platform. In our experiment, we choose HiKey (LeMaker version) as our platform because Trustzone is available on this platform. In our experiment, we use Linux in our normal world and OP-TEE [11] in our secure world. These can give us more security assurance to provide the service.

Our implementation is mainly divided into two parts. One part is at the verifier. We develop a program analyzer that can compute the legal targets of every indirect jump instruction and a verify program to verify the log. We also develop a binary rewriting tool to instrument the binaries in order to instrument all indirect jump instructions. Another part is at the prover, that mainly contains log recording service, attestation service, PUF device key derivation and signature service.

5.2   Instrumentation

After the compilation, we get the binaries and use our binary analysis tool to get all indirect jump instructions and compute all legal targets and store them into a database in the server. For bl instruction, we create a function table that contains the source and target address of bl instruction and passes it to the device. The device will use it in *hook_bl* for searching the target address. Then we instrument the instructions to the corresponding trampolines, the blx instruction to the *hook_blx* function, bl instruction to the *hook_bl* and the pop instruction to the *hook_pop* function. We search for all these instructions and replace these instructions with bl instructions and the target address is the address of corresponding hook functions.

When a program faces a control flow instruction, the program will pass its control to the trampolines and trampoline will call GP client API to use services in the secure world. For example, the return instruction will call log recording service, and then pop address from the shadow stack, checks the address and at last put a record into the log.

5.3   Optimization

We mainly make two optimizations. The first optimization is using helper data to shorten log size. When a loop contains a function call, the same return instruction may repeat several times in our log. To avoid this, we propose putting repeat times into the helper data. When we find two same log lines that are next to each other, we delete one and add the repeat times of the last log lines with 1. Only the repeated lines use this helper data, so we only record the repeated times in the repeated lines. Another optimization is using the offset of the address to represent the address in the log. When the program is not big, for example, the program is smaller than 64k, we can only record the offset between the start address and the real address. The start address is selected as the begin address of the program and any address in the code region is no more than 2^{16} distance from the start. As a consequence, we can only use 16 bits to record the address instead of using 32 bits. The only thing we should do additionally is to put the start address at the start of the log and send it to the server for verification. As for verification, it is easy to restore the real address by adding the start address and the offset. In this way, we can shorten our log to nearly one half.

5.4   OP-TEE Integration

We choose OP-TEE as our trusted OS because we need multiple trusted applications to support our service. We also need to communicate with the server and multitask management so we use Linux as the normal world OS. We faced some problems when implementing our design on this platform. One problem is how to access the normal world memory from the secure world. In OP-TEE, it is forbidden to access any normal world memory from the secure world. Because OP-TEE does not map the memory in normal world to secure world for security reason, in case of some attacks such as BOOMAGANG vulnerability [15]. But when a trusted application (TA) wants to access some memory, we must change its mechanism. We first use static TA rather than the dynamic TA that is loaded when needed. Static TA lies in the kernel of the secure OS, so it can invoke some system call in the kernel. In OP-TEE, only dynamic TA can access part of the normal world. Then we invoke *core_mmu_add_mapping()* to map the memory address in the normal world to the secure world. At last, when we access the address, we use *phys_to_virt()* to transfer the physics address passed by the normal world to the corresponding virtual address in the secure world. We detailly check the pointer used and make sure we leave no BOOMAGANG vulnerability in our program.

6   Evaluation

6.1   Experimental Setup

We use HiKey board as our prover. HiKey (LeMaker version) is powered by the Kirin 620 SoC with octa core ARM Cortex-A53 64-bit CPU up to 1.2 GHz and high performance Mali450-MP4 GPU. It also has 1 GB LPDDR3 DRAM (800 MHz) and 8 GB eMMC storage on board. HiKey is also a board that satisfies the Linaro LCG 96boards design specification. We run Linux kernel 4.5 in the normal world and OP-TEE 2.5 in the secure world.

We mainly evaluate our scheme using an embedded device benchmark Mibench. Mibench is a free, commercially representative embedded benchmark suite. It is divided into six suites. Each suite represents one kind of embedded applications in the real world. We pick one application from each category and use these applications to evaluate the performance of our prototype.

Table 2. Log size comparation

Program	Control flow events	Log size (KB)	Verify time (ms)
basicmath	140481	1264	192
jpeg	263758	2374	331
dijkstra	273610	2462	349
stringsearch	2781	25	2
sha	111681	1005	160
crc32	2	0.018	0.04

6.2   Log Length

We test the log length of six applications in the benchmark, basicmath, jpeg, Dijkstra, string search, sha and crc32. Table 2 shows the result. In Table 2, we can see the logs of four programs are about 1 MB or 2 MB and string search and crc32 have smaller logs. In the benchmark, each program is repeated several times. As for some programs, if they have little control flow events like string search and crc32, we can see that it costs little space to save the log.

We test the optimization method and it significantly decreases the size of our log in basicmath and sha. The log length of basicmath is reduced to 299 bytes and sha is reduced to 104 bytes. The log length of the other three programs does not reduce significantly. The reason is that basicmath and sha have function call in the loop. Due to the optimization of recoding the iteration times, we only need a very little log to record the whole control flow events. The other three programs do not have such features so our optimization does not work. Another situation is that we can not resolve the problem that several function calls lies in the same iteration. We can reduce the log size by checking the last n logs, but we do not add this feature in our scheme and we will do this in the future.

6.3   Performance

We use a pc with Intel Core i3-4170 3.70 GHz running Linux Ubuntu 4.4.0 x64 as our verifier. We measure the time used to verify the logs. The verify time of five programs is 192 ms, 331 ms, 349 ms, 2 ms, 160 ms, 0.04 ms. We can see that the verify time of applications we tested is about several hundred milliseconds. It is very time-saving when verifying the logs. The verify time of dijkstra and crc32 is even less because their control flow events are less than other programs. The results prove our scheme can efficiently verify the result. For C-flat, the verify time can reach 2^n in theory where n denotes the number of control flow events. In practical applications, the verify time is decided by the space of the target program parameters. We do not give a comparison here due to C-flat cannot verify the result in polynomial time if we define all the inputs as lawful inputs.

7 Security

7.1 Code Injection Attack

Traditional control-flow attacks need code injection as the first step of the attack. An attacker cannot inject the code into the code space because the code space is marked as read-only. So the attacker can only inject the malicious code into the data space. But it also does not make sense. One reason is that most of the devices are equipped with DEP mechanism [16], that marks the data space as non-executable. Even the attacker has injected the code into the data space, the code cannot execute. Another reason is that when attacker wants to redirect the control flow to the injected code, he or she must corrupt a code pointer and change its value to the address of the code. However, our scheme records all values of code pointers and will detect this attack.

7.2 Code Reuse Attack

Code reuse attacks do not need extra code like code injection attacks. They only combine code sequences to fulfil malicious functions. They firstly scan the program and search for available snippets. Then they find a sequence to chain these snippets and indirect the control flow to these sequences. In this way, they can attack a program without injecting extra codes.

The most representative example of code reuse attack is called return-oriented programming [3]. They firstly put the address of snippets onto the stack and then exploit the return address to jump to the start of the sequences. The start of the sequences may lie in the middle of the function or the start of the function. If it lies in the middle of the function, then we can detect this attack by verifying the target address of the return address. If it lies in the start of the function, we can detect this attack in two places. When the attacker first uses return function to jump to the start of the sequence, we can detect it by comparing the target address of the return function to the address poped from the shadow stack. We can also detect it by verifying if the target address of the return function is a valid target. A challenging case is that the start of the function is the right address of the return instruction. In this case, we cannot distinguish whether the program has been attacked at this time. But we can detect the attack when comparing the result with the target address sets in the verifier side because the return address of the snippets cannot be the right address.

8 Conclusion

In this paper, we propose a log-based control flow attestation scheme. We solve the problem of the state explosion problem. We use a lightweight root of trust in our attestation and do not need a secure storage. Our scheme instruments the target program and monitors the control-flow events. We also prove our scheme has a good performance on testing benchmarks. In the future, we will add support for variable length instructions and TrustZone-M.

Acknowledgements. The research presented in this paper is supported by the National Key Research and Development Program of China under Grant No. 2018YFB0904900, 2018YFB0904903 and the National Natural Science Foundation of China under Grant No. 61872343, 61802375, 61602455.

References

1. Eldefrawy, K., Tsudik, G., Francillon, A., Perito, D.: SMART: secure and minimal architecture for (establishing dynamic) root of trust. In: NDSS, vol. 12, pp. 1–15 (2012)
2. Koeberl, P., Schulz, S., Sadeghi, A.-R., Varadharajan, V.: TrustLite: a security architecture for tiny embedded devices. In: Proceedings of the Ninth European Conference on Computer Systems, EuroSys 2014, pp. 10:1–10:14. ACM, New York (2014)
3. Buchanan, E., Roemer, R., Shacham, H., Savage, S.: When good instructions go bad: generalizing return-oriented programming to RISC. In: Proceedings of the 15th ACM Conference on Computer and Communications Security, pp. 27–38. ACM (2008)
4. Bletsch, T., Jiang, X., Freeh, V.W., Liang, Z.: Jump-oriented programming: a new class of code-reuse attack. In: Proceedings of the 6th ACM Symposium on Information, Computer and Communications Security, ASIACCS 2011, pp. 30–40. ACM, New York (2011)
5. Abadi, M., Budiu, M., Erlingsson, Ú., Ligatti, J.: Control-flow integrity. In: Proceedings of the 12th ACM Conference on Computer and Communications Security, CCS 2005, pp. 340–353. ACM, New York (2005)
6. Kuznetsov, V., Szekeres, L., Payer, M., Candea, G., Sekar, R., Song, D.: Code-pointer integrity. In: Proceedings of the 11th USENIX Conference on Operating Systems Design and Implementation, OSDI 2014, pp. 147–163. USENIX Association, Berkeley (2014)
7. Abera, T., et al.: C-FLAT: control-flow attestation for embedded systems software. In: Proceedings of the 2016 ACM SIGSAC Conference on Computer and Communications Security, CCS 2016, pp. 743–754. ACM, New York (2016)
8. Dessouky, G., et al.: Lo-fat: low-overhead control flow attestation in hardware. In: Proceedings of the 54th Annual Design Automation Conference 2017, DAC 2017, pp. 24:1–24:6. ACM, New York (2017)
9. Pappu, R., Recht, B., Taylor, J., Gershenfeld, N.: Physical one-way functions. Science **297**(5589), 2026–2030 (2002)
10. ARM Information Center, 11 July 2017. http://infocenter.arm.com/help/index.jsp
11. OP-TEE Trusted OS. https://github.com/OP-TEE/optee_os
12. Qualcomm Security Platform. https://www.qualcomm.com/solutions/mobile-computing/features/security
13. Linnartz, J.-P., Tuyls, P.: New shielding functions to enhance privacy and prevent misuse of biometric templates. In: Kittler, J., Nixon, M.S. (eds.) AVBPA 2003. LNCS, vol. 2688, pp. 393–402. Springer, Heidelberg (2003). https://doi.org/10.1007/3-540-44887-X_47
14. Zhao, S., Zhang, Q., Hu, G., Qin, Y., Feng, D.: Providing root of trust for ARM TrustZone using on-chip SRAM. In: Proceedings of the 4th International Workshop on Trustworthy Embedded Devices, TrustED 2014, pp. 25–36. ACM, New York (2014)

15. Machiry, A., et al.: Boomerang: exploiting the semantic gap in trusted execution environments (2017)
16. Data Execution Prevention. https://msdn.microsoft.com/zh-cn/library/aa366553 (vs.85).aspx

A New Algorithm for Retrieving Diffuse Attenuation Coefficient Based on Big LiDAR Bathymetry Data

Kai Ding[1(✉)] [ID], Chisheng Wang[2] [ID], Ming Tao[1] [ID],
and Peican Huang[1] [ID]

[1] School of Computer Science and Technology, Dongguan University
of Technology, Dongguan 523808, People's Republic of China
{dingkai,huangpc}@dgut.edu.cn,
ming.tao@mail.scut.edu.cn
[2] Department of Urban Spatial Smart Sensing, Shenzhen University,
518060 Shenzhen, People's Republic of China
wangchisheng@szu.edu.cn

Abstract. The diffuse attenuation coefficient, K_d, is an inherent optical parameter of water. It is an important hydrologic index for both oceanography and biology. We proposed a new method to retrieve the diffuse attenuation coefficient from airborne LiDAR bathymetry data in this paper. Firstly, a formula was derived for calculating the values of K_d by using waveform from single laser shot. An algorithm was then deduced from the formula. K_d values could be retrieved from this algorithm. A case study on Wuzhizhou island in China was carried out to validate the method, it using a big Optech Aquarius bathymetry data. The results show well agreement with the MODIS products. Compared with other previous algorithms, this new algorithm could obtain the value of K_d from single laser shot, and the method could be applied to laser shots without bottom response even in deep or turbid water area.

Keywords: LiDAR bathymetry data · Diffuse attenuation coefficient

1 Introduction

The diffuse attenuation coefficient, K_d, is an index of water clarity or ocean turbidity of the Earth, it could be used to analyze the water quality, classify the ocean water types, compute available photosynthetically radiation and estimate the chlorophyll concentration [1]. It is the key index to describe ocean color, and therefore, important to synoptically assessing ocean productivity [2]. For airborne bathymetric LiDAR, K_d is a very important parameter to determine the bottom reflected signal amplitude and receive power to the airborne LiDAR sensor [3].

There are many different and usual methods to acquire the accurate value of K_d. Implement an in-situ measurement by instruments such as secchi disk [4] or reflective tube absorption meter [5] belongs to the traditional K_d capture method. The in-situ measurement results always own relatively high accuracy, however, it is time-costing,

© Springer Nature Switzerland AG 2019
J. Vaidya et al. (Eds.): CSS 2019, LNCS 11982, pp. 133–142, 2019.
https://doi.org/10.1007/978-3-030-37337-5_11

labor-consuming, expensive, and limited to the navigable area. Rapid and inexpensive remote sensing measurement provides a better option to solve the disadvantages of traditional K_d acquisition methods. Previous studies have been done for estimating the global scale maps with low spatial resolutions by satellite observation data. Empirical or semi-analytical formulas for estimation have been proposed by researchers [6–8].

However, dataset applied in this study all come from passive sensors, which is difficult to operate at night and also easily affected by the weather conditions such as fog or an overcast sky. Furthermore, the low-resolution satellite image is incapable to provide the high-resolution distribution. In contrast, by applying LiDAR technique, the data can be obtained from waveform measurements of received LiDAR pulse. It can provide a rapid operation with acceptable accuracy and a high spatial density [9, 10]. But until now, little attention has been paid to study the algorithms for retrieving inherent optical properties from the single-wavelength airborne LiDAR bathymetry data. Several previous studies apply exponential fitting method to compute it from LiDAR bathymetric data by measuring the slope of a linear regression of the log irradiance versus depth data over different range of depth [3, 9, 10]. But this method requires the bottom response from LiDAR pulse, and the calculated value will be affected by irrelevant factors such as the bottom reflectivity.

In this paper, an Optech Aquarius dataset were used to detect and estimate the value. We propose a new algorithm which calculate the K_d based on the volume backscattering return. It can acquire the value from single laser shot without the requirement of bottom return, and avoid of the effects of bottom. Although the algorithm is only applied to the Optech Aquarius in this study, it can also work in other similar bathymetric systems recording full waveform data.

2   Theory of Retrieving K_d from ALB Dataset

Airborne LiDAR equation is described below:

$$P_{i=b,w} = \frac{P_T R \eta F_p A_r M(\theta_i) N(\theta_i) \cos^2 \theta_i}{(n_w H + D)^2} e^{-2K_d D} e^{-2\tau} \tag{1}$$

$$R = \begin{cases} \frac{\rho}{\pi} i = b \\ \frac{c\tau}{2n} \beta(\pi) i = w \end{cases} \tag{2}$$

where P_b is the received peak power from the bottom return, P_w is the received power from the volume backscattering return, P_T is the peak power of the emit laser pulse, ρ is the reflectivity of the bottom, η is the combined optical loss factor for the transmitter and receiver optics, F_p is the field of view factor, n_w is the refractive index of water, A_r is the aperture area of the receiver telescope, θ is nadir angle, $M(\theta_i)$ is the hot spot affection, $N(\theta_i)$ is the pulse stretching affection, H is altitude of the aircraft, D is the bottom depth, τ is the optical thickness of the air, β is volume backscattering coefficient [3, 11]. Figure 1 shows a general sample of bathymetric LiDAR received waveform, which is composed of the surface return, bottom return and volume backscattering. The water volume backscattering return can be simply described as:

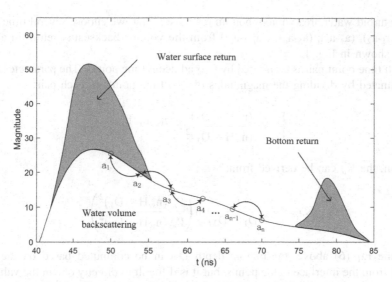

Fig. 1. The sample of bathymetric LiDAR received waveform.

$$P_{i=b,w} = \frac{S * P_T}{(n_w H + D)^2} e^{-2K_d D} \qquad (3)$$

$$\text{where } S = R\eta F_p A_r M(\theta_i) N(\theta_i) \cos^2 \theta_i e^{-2\tau} \qquad (4)$$

Since the unknown parameter S in equation above cannot be determined directly, therefore, the value of K_d cannot be obtained as well. Prior studies considered the unknown parameter S as a constant number in the exponential fitting method, it is based on the relationship between received peak power (P_b) and water depth (D). The received peak power P_b is exhibit approximately an exponential decay with the increase of (D). As revealed in Eq. (5), the degree of decay is related to K_d. After fitting the observed received peak power (P_b) with an exponential function of water depth (D), the averaged value of K_d could be calculated correspondingly [3, 9]. However, there are several disadvantages for this method. First of all, it is unable to work in turbid or deep water area where no bottom response can be detected. Without the bottom response, the water depth (D) and the received peak power (P_b) cannot be obtained, and therefore the K_d cannot be derived. Furthermore, the exponential fitting method require large numbers of laser points with different water depths. It is impossible to obtain the K_d for single point by using the exponential fitting method. Finally, it is very possible that the water quality and parameter S (ρ, θ, $M(\theta_i)$, $N(\theta_i)$) differ a lot among the laser points. The calculated K_d may be biased due to such diversity. In this study, we proposed an algorithm to compensate these disadvantages and obtain the value of K_d from single point.

This algorithm adopts the volume backscatter return (P_w) to calculate the value of K_d. Unlike the bottom return, the volume backscatter return exists in all waveforms even if the laser cannot penetrate into the bottom. So it would obtain K_d value even in deep or turbid water area without bottom response. First, we choose several time point pairs $((a_1-a_2), (a_3-a_4), (a_5-a_6)...(a_{n-1}-a_n))$ from the volume backscatter return in a laser shot as shown in Fig. 1.

Each time point pair is composed by two adjacent time points. The parameter S can be eliminated by dividing the magnitudes of two time points in each pair:

$$\frac{P_{a_1}}{P_{a_2}} = \frac{(n_wH+D_2)^2}{(n_wH+D_1)^2}e^{-2K_d(D_1-D_2)} \tag{5}$$

Then, the K_d can be derived from:

$$K_d = -\frac{1}{2(D_1-D_2)}\ln\left(\frac{P_{a_1}(n_wH+D_1)^2}{P_{a_2}(n_wH+D_2)^2}\right) \tag{6}$$

In the Eq. (6) above, the bottom depth D can be computed based on the time interval from the interface to the points, but it is difficult to directly obtain the values of P_w from received return waveform. Because pulse amplitude was recorded once a nanosecond as one time point in the Optech Aquarius system, and the received return pulse signal are recorded for 288 time points. The surface return, volume backscatter return and bottom return are mixed together in some time points.

Second, we retrieve volume backscatter return amplitude by using the Gaussian decomposition (GD) algorithm, which is widely applied for decomposing waveforms [12]. It uses a series of Gaussian functions to approximate the return waveform. GD method assumes that the scattering cross section is a superposition of Gaussians. The unknown parameters for these Gaussian functions can be obtained by minimizing the cost function, given by:

$$f_c(t) = \frac{1}{N}W_R(t) - \sum_{i=1}^{N}\alpha_i e^{-\frac{(t-\mu_i)^2}{2\delta_i^2}} \tag{7}$$

where N is the number of Gaussian components used for fitting, and it can be selected through an iterative process [12]. W_R, α_i, μ_i, and δ_i are the received return amplitude, amplitude, location, and half-width of the i th Gaussian components. However, since the bathymetric LiDAR waveform is mainly composed of a surface return and a bottom return, therefore, we follow a previous study that using two Gaussian functions (N = 2) to fit the received waveform [13].

The surface and bottom returns were considered as Gaussian functions. Then we can obtain volume backscattering power from equation below:

$$f_q(t) = W_R(t) - f_s(t) - f_b(t) \tag{8}$$

Each laser shot contains several point pairs, multiple K_d values will be generated from them. We then average these values to obtain a final K_d. The flowchart of the proposed method is illustrated in Fig. 2.

The proposed algorithm process is list below:

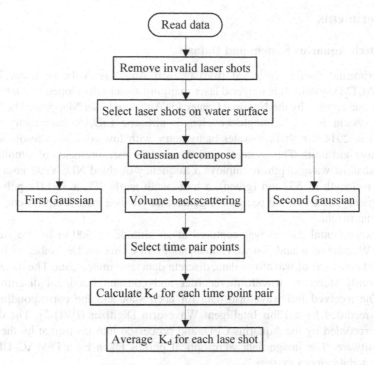

Fig. 2. Flowchart of the proposed method.

1) Remove invalid laser shots.
2) Select the discrete points under water.
3) Retrieve the volume backscatter return by using Gaussian decomposition method.
4) Choose several time point pairs from the volume backscatter return waveform.
5) Divide the magnitudes of two points in each pair by following Eq. (5) and calculate K_d as Eq. (6).
6) Compute the averaged value of K_d of the test area.

We removed ineffective shots which the amplitude values of waveform data were recorded as zero. Meanwhile, the discrete points under water were selected while the z-coordinate value was below a threshold value. The volume backscatter return can be retrieved by using Gaussian decomposition method, whether two Gaussian functions or one would be obtained after decomposing. The time interval between two points of a time point pair can be determined at least one nanosecond, and the number of time point pairs depend on the time interval between the peak and valley value of volume backscattering amplitude.

3   Experiments

3.1   Optech Aquarius System and Dataset

The experimental data is collected from Optech Aquarius Airborne Laser Terrain Mapper (ALTM) system. It is a hybrid laser mapping system developed by Optech Inc. of Canada and applied by the National Center for Airborne Laser Mapping. The Optech Aquarius system is a new single-wavelength airborne LiDAR bathymetry system developed in 2011 for shallow-water bathymetry with low-cost, high-resolution and small lightweight units. This system is capable to take measurements of simultaneous land and shallow water depth. It employs a frequency-doubled ND: YAG laser with a single- wavelength of 532 nm (green), a half-swath angle 20°, a 33 kHz pulse repetition frequency, and 1 m rad beam divergence that yields a laser footprint one 1000th of the flying height.

The experimental dataset was captured at an altitude of 300 m by the Aquarius system at Wuzhizhou island, Sanya, Hainan, southern China, on December 19th, 2012. The dataset consisted of waveform data, discrete data, and image data. The dataset was simultaneously stored in waveform recorder and constant fractional discrimination (CFD). The received full waveform data for each shot and the corresponding GPS times are recorded by a 12bit Intelligent Waveform Digitizer (IWD-2). The discrete data were recorded by the Aquarius CFD, and processed into las format by the use of Optech software. The image data were optical photos taken by a DiMAC ULTRA-LIGHT + aerial camera system.

The Aquarius waveform data consists of time-series amplitude data of numerous laser shots. For each laser shot, both the transmitted and returned amplitude waveform are recorded. To organize the large number of laser shots, a certain amount of sequential shots are grouped into a frame. In this experiment, the Aquarius waveform data contains 6290 frames and 86766800 shots.

Each frame has a unique frame number and a GPS time. The GPS time is defined as the acquired time for the first shot in the frame. With the GPS time of frames and the number of shots in each frame, the interval time between two neighboring laser shots can be calculated. Correspondingly, the GPS time of each shot in the frame can be determined. The GPS time for the shots are then used to synchronize with positioning data collected by the ALTM.

3.2   Calculation

For comparison purposes, we apply the exponential fitting method and the proposed method at same time in order to calculate the K_d values around the Wuzhizhou island. 3000 data points with bottom response has been collected from the test area in order to running the exponential fitting. The result suggests a K_d value of $0.0908(m^{-1})$. The R-square for the fitting is 0.514.

After that, we used the proposed method to calculate the K_d values. The first step is Gaussian decomposition method. As shown in Fig. 3, a volume backscattering return can be obtained whether the bottom response can be retrieved or not. The optimization of the cost function can be carried out by a nonlinear least squares fitting based on the

Levenberg Marquardt method [14]. By the use of a peak detection algorithm, the initial parameters for the Gaussian functions are set according to the detected target responses so that meaningless results can be avoided [15, 16].

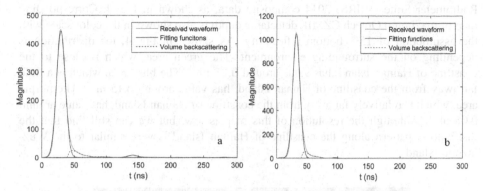

Fig. 3. Examples of the Gaussian decomposition method. (a) The bottom response can be retrieved. (b) The bottom response cannot be retrieved.

Next, according to the Eqs. (5) and (6), we selected three point pairs with one nanosecond time interval from volume backscattering return and compute the value of K_d. In order to reduce the computational burden, we sample the waveform data at a periodic interval (once every 200 shots). After the sampling, there were together 116815 shots left for this experiment (Table 1).

Table 1. The averaged value of K_d of the test area.

Number of laser shots	K_d Value (m^{-1})
116815	0.0835

3.3 Validation

In this case, the flight experiment was performed in 2014, and the in-situ measurements for the test sea area have not been obtained from a surface vessel simultaneously at that time. Therefore, it is difficult to validate the results with the simultaneous in situ observations. However, we can obtain the averaged diffuse attenuation coefficient at 490 nm of the test area from the MODIS data using KD2 algorithm [17].

In order to be consistent with the acquired time of LiDAR data, we choose Aqua and Terra MODIS month composite data on Dec, 2014. The diffused attenuation coefficient at 490 nm was calculated using KD2 algorithm with resolution of 4 km. The LiDAR-derived data will cover an irregular butterfly-shape region with size of 1.48 km^2, and coastline of 5.7 km. This district is 1.4 km across from east to west and 1.1 km from north to south. The values were retrieved from MODIS products will cover the whole test area.

Firstly, we convert the big data at 490 nm to 532 nm following a previous study [18]. We can see that the average value of the whole test area calculated using this new algorithm are consistent with the MODIS products.

Moreover, we obtain a K_d map of the test area using Visible Infrared Imaging Radiometer Suite (VIIRS) 2014 composite data, as shown in Fig. 4. Corresponding map of maximum Optech CZMIL detectable depth is also shown in the color scale with the assumption of 15% bottom reflectivity. As shown in Fig. 4, the distribution is depending on the surrounding environment. The green area, which is close to the coastline of Hainan Island, has value around 0.25 m^{-1}. The blue area, which is a little far away from the coastline of Hainan Island, has value around 0.15 m^{-1}. The purple area, which is relatively far away from the coastline of Hainan Island, has value around 0.06 m^{-1}. Although the resolution of this map is low, but we can still find that the distribution pattern along the coastline of Hainan Island is very similar to the Wuzhizhou island.

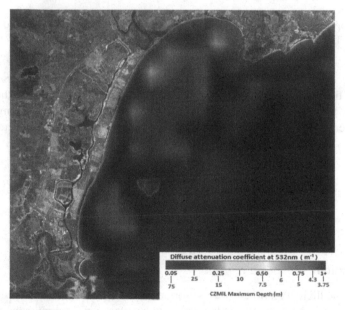

Fig. 4. K_d map for Wuzhizhou island using VIIRS data, December.2014. (Color figure online)

4   Conclusion

The previous algorithm applying a fitting curve to calculate the value of diffused attenuation coefficient.It sometimes may not work when there is no or weak bottom response.We have derived a new formula to estimate the value of of seawater from big LiDAR full waveform data. Since no bottom response information is used in the formula, the calculation will not be affected by the factors of bottom reflectivity, retro-reflectance, and pulse stretching effects. Based on the formula, we propose an algorithm to retrieve the value from single laser shot. The experiment shows that the results from the proposed algorithm fits well with the MODIS products. There is a similar spatial distribution feature in the maps derived from LiDAR and VIIRS datasets, where the value decreases along with the distance from shoreline. This proposed algorithm may be used for the purpose of quick and detailed water quality mapping.

Acknowledgments. This work was supported in part by the Shenzhen Future Industry Development Funding program (No. 201507211219247860), the Shenzhen Scientific Research and Development Funding Program (No. JCYJ20170302144002028), and the Social Science and Technology Development (Key) Project of Dongguan City (No.20185071401606).

References

1. Baker, K.S., Smith, R.C.: Quasi-inherent characteristics of the diffuse attenuation coefficient for irradiance. In: Ocean Optics VI, pp. 60–63 (1980)
2. Smith, R.C., Baker, K.S.: The bio-optical state of ocean waters and remote sensing. Limnol. Oceanogr. **23**, 247–259 (1978)
3. Guenther, G.C.: Airborne laser hydrography: System design and performance factors. National Ocean Service 1, National Oceanic and Atmospheric Administration, Rockville, MD (1985)
4. Mankovsky, V.I.: Relation between the diffuse attenuation coefficient and the Secchi depth. Oceanology **54**, 32–37 (2014)
5. Zaneveld, J.R.V.: A reflectivetube absorption meter. In: Proceedings Spie, vol. 1302, pp. 124–136 (1990)
6. Lee, Z.P., Darecki, M., Carder, K.L., et al.: Diffuse attenuation coefficient of downwelling irradiance: An evaluation of remote sensing methods. J. Geophys. Res.-Oceans, vol. 110 (2005)
7. Jamet, C., Loisel, H., Dessailly, D.: Estimation of the Diffuse Attenuation Coefficient Kd (Lambda) with a Neural Network Inversion. In: IEEE International Geoscience and Remote Sensing Symposium (Igarss), pp. 114–117 (2011)
8. Yu, X., Salama, M.S., Shen, F., et al.: Retrieval of the diffuse attenuation coefficient from GOCI images using the 2SeaColor model: a case study in the Yangtze Estuary. Remote Sens. Environ. **175**, 109–119 (2016)
9. Billard, B., Abbot, R.H., Penny, M.F.: Airborne estimation of sea turbidity parameters from the WRELADS laser airborne depth sounder. Appl. Opt. **25**, 2080–2088 (1986)
10. Smart, J.H, Kang, H.K.K.: Comparisons between in-situ and remote sensing estimates of diffuse attenuation profiles. In: Proceedings of SPIE - The International Society for Optical Engineering, vol. 2964 (1996)
11. Wang, C.-K., Philpot, W.D.: Using airborne bathymetric lidar to detect bottom type variation in shallow waters. Remote Sens. Environ. **106**, 123–135 (2007)
12. Hofton, M.A., Minster, J.B., Blair, J.B.: Decomposition of laser altimeter waveforms. IEEE Trans. Geosci. Remote Sens. **38**, 1989–1996 (2000)
13. Allouis, T., Bailly, J.-S., Pastol, Y., et al.: Comparison of LiDAR waveform processing methods for very shallow water bathymetry using Raman, near-infrared and green signals. Earth Surface Processes and Landforms (2010)
14. Marquardt, D.W.: An algorithm for least square estimation of non-linear parameters. J. Soc. Ind. Appl. Math. **11**, 431–441 (1963)

15. Wang, C., Li, Q., Liu, Y., et al.: A comparison of waveform processing algorithms for single-wavelength LiDAR bathymetry. ISPRS J. Photogrammetry Remote Sens. **101**, 22–35 (2015)
16. Ding, K., Li, Q., Zhu, J., et al.: An improved quadrilateral fitting algorithm for the water column contribution in airborne Bathymetric Lidar waveforms. Sensors **18**(2), 552 (2018)
17. NASA. http://oceancolor.gsfc.nasa.gov/cgi/l3. Accessed 27 Dec 2018
18. Li, K., Tong, X., Zhang, Y., et al.: Inversion of diffuse attenuation coefficient spectral in the Yellow Sea/East China Sea and evaluation of laser bathymetric performance. J. Remote Sens. **19**, 761–769 (2015)

Shuffle Dense Networks for Biometric Authentication

Huaijuan Zang, Qiuyu Li, Ailian Chen, Jinlong Chen, and Shu Zhan[(✉)]

School of Computer Science and Information Engineering,
Hefei University of Technology, Hefei, Anhui, China
shu_zhan@hfut.edu.cn

Abstract. In recent years, with the continuous development of artificial intelligence technology, biometric authentication based on computer vision technology have also been developed rapidly. In this paper, we propose a novel Shuffle dense networks (SDN) with combining ShuffleNet and DenseNet for biometric authentication. ShuffleNet is an extremely computation-efficient structure that can obtain more channels information. DenseNet makes full use of all hierarchical features, which can facilitate the flow of information. Specifically, dense skip connections is adopted for combining the low-level features and the high-level features to enhance the performance of the reconstruction and residual learning is applied for easing the difficulty of training the deep neural network. In addition, the grouped convolutions are introduced for reducing computational complexity and the number of parameters. What's more, the shuffle dense connections are proposed for mitigating the grouped convolutions problem of lacking information exchange between the groups. The proposed method is evaluated quantitatively and qualitatively on four benchmark datasets, and the experimental results of super-resolution illustrated that our SDN achieves great performance over the state-of-the-art frameworks.

Keywords: Biometric authentication · Deep learning · Dense network · Shuffle network · Super-resolution

1 Introduction

Recently, with the increase of high-tech crimes, cyberspace safety and security issues have been paid attention to in many cases. Security has become an important part of privacy protection with the development of artificial intelligence technology. As a security authentication method, biometric authentication has been widely used in many fields [1–6], such as: fingerprint authentication, iris authentication, vein pattern authentication, voice authentication and so on. Due to the improvement of computer hardware and network structure, deep learning technology has obtained explosive development in the world. In the field of

Supported by organization National Nature Science Foundation of China Grand No: 61371156.

computer vision research, convolutional neural network (CNNs) has become the mainstream method and achieved great success.

Data and network security are increasingly important, the clear image can obtain higher security, so it is necessary to reconstruct the biometric image with super-resolution. Single image super-resolution is a computer vision research with extensively studied, which aims to reconstruct a high resolution (HR) image from a single low resolution (LR) image. Because of the image super-resolution assumption of the LR image which is obtained by subsampling the HR image, the loss of high frequency information that occurs during the subsampling operations is a highly ill-posed problem. A key assumption of SISR is that much of the high frequency components is redundant and thus can be restored from low frequency information accurately [7–11].

Early methods for reconstruct the HR image include interpolation, statistical image priors or internal patch recurrence. Huang et al. [12] expanded the internal patch search space to adapt the affine transform and perspective distortion. Timofte et al. [13] anchored to the dictionary atoms for fast super-resolution. Owing to the powerful learning ability, the convolutional neural networks are extensively adopted for SISR problem in recent years. Dong et al. [14] successfully proposed a three layer convolutional neural network, named SRCNN, for the SISR problem and achieved significantly performance over conventional methods. Wang et al. [15] used Cascaded Sparse Coding Network (CSCN) which combines the domain knowledge of sparse coding with the deep network to improve the reconstruction performance. Kim et al. [16] proposed a very deep convolutional network (VDSR) inspired by VGG net [17], which exploits the residual skip-connection and adjustable gradient clipping to ease the problem of the gradient explosion. Subsequently, they proposed a deeply-recursive convolutional network (DRCN) [18] with recursive-supervision and skip-connection. Deep Recursive Residual Network (DRRN) [19] was improved upon DRCN by adopting the residual structure and recursive learning to achieve better performance and keep model compact. Lai et al. [20] proposed a Laplacian pyramid super-resolution network (LapSRN) which utilizes a Laplacian pyramid structure for increasing the image size gradually. For providing rich information for the SR reconstruction, Tong et al. [21] employed dense connected structures which adopt the dense skip connections.

In this paper, we proposed a novel Shuffle dense networks (SDN) with dense connections for image super resolution (SDN). In this network, the dense connections are employed for fully utilizing the features from all the layers in the dense block and the residual connections are adopted for carrying the features from shallow layer into the deep layer. The grouped convolutions extend the transformations without increasing the complexity. For strengthen relationship between the groups, the shuffle dense connections are proposed. The performance of this network is assessed reasonably by a series of experiments on the widely used benchmark datasets. In summary, the contributions of this research can be summarized as:

- This network employs dense connections to fuse hierarchical features in the dense block which combines the low-level features and high-level features by concatenating the feature maps. The dense connections improve the flow of information through the network and help training of deep network architectures.
- Residual learning is introduced for easing the difficulty of training deep network through learning between LR and HR image from shortcut connection. Due to the high correlation between the input and output images, the input signal will be carried into deeper layers through the shortcut connection for improving the reconstruction performance.
- Grouped convolutions are employed for mapping the input data efficiently into independent channel-space segments. It increases the set of transformations in network without increasing the width and depth. The shuffle dense connections enhance the information exchanges between the input and output channels of group convolutional.

The remainder of the paper is organized as follows. In Sect. 2 we review related works. SDN architecture is analyzed in detail in Sect. 3. Section 4 demonstrates experimental results. At last, the conclusions of this research approach are followed in the Sect. 5.

2   Related Work

2.1   Dense Connections

Recently, Huang et al. proposed a novel CNN architecture, Densely Connected Convolutional Networks (DenseNets) [22], which has direct connections between any two layers for encouraging feature reuse. For all the layers in the dense block, they are easy to reuse the information from preceding layers. Owing to the dense connections, DenseNets are more efficient in the parameter usage for alleviating the vanishing-gradient problem. Tong et al. [21] proposed SRDenseNet which introduces the dense block from DenseNet for SISR and obtains the remarkable results.

2.2   Residual Learning

Since the deep convolutional network suffer from problem of vanishing or exploding gradients, the residual learning is introduced by He et al. [23] for easing the difficulty of training very deep networks. Denoting the input as x and the non-linear transformation as $H(x)$, the residual mapping is defined as $G(x) = H(x) - x$. So the original mapping is expressed as indicates and the structure of residual block is:

$$y = G(x, \{W_i\}) + x \tag{1}$$

Where y means the output of the residual block, w is a set of weights, i is the index of layer and the function $G(x, \{W_i\})$ indicates the residual mapping to be

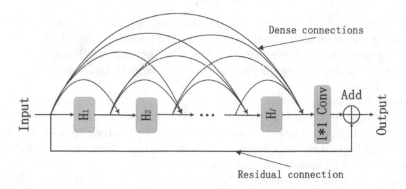

Fig. 1. Dense block with residual connection.

learned. In the neural network, this formulation of (1) can be realized by shortcut connections structure which skip several layers and add neither extra parameter nor computational complexity. The 152-layer deep network, ResNet [23], was constructed by the number of stacked residual connections and won the first place in the ILSVRC 2015 classification competition. The residual connections not only carry the details to the deeper layer but also make convergence easier.

2.3 Grouped Convolutions

The concept of grouped convolutions was first proposed in AlexNet [24] for distributing the model over two GPUs and the effectiveness of it has been illustrated in ResNeXt [25]. Xception [26] proposed depthwise separable convolution which is inspired by Inception modules. MobileNet [27] employs the depthwise separable convolutions and obtains state-of-the-art results. Because of changing the connectivity structure of the internal convolutional blocks, ShuffleNet [28] makes the input and output channels of group convolutional layer be fully related. Grouped convolutions could increase the set of transformations without making network deeper or wider and reduce computational complexity.

3   Method

In this section, the technical parts of the network proposed in this paper are described entirely.

3.1   Dense Connections with Residual Learning

Inspired from DenseNet [22] and SRDenseNet [21], the local dense connections are introduced into our network. For easing the difficulty of training the deep network, residual connections are introduced into our network. The residual branch connects the input and the output of the dense block and carries the input features to the deeper layer. For matching the number of the feature maps

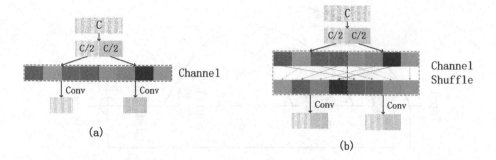

Fig. 2. Group convolution with channel shuffle operation.

between the input and the output of the dense block, a 1×1 convolutional layer is introduced for adaptively controlling the number of the feature maps. The dense block with residual connection is illustrated in Fig. 1.

Considering the feature maps F_0 that are the input of a dense block which comprises L layers, and denote a non-linear transformation as $H_l(\cdot)$, where l indexes the layer. $H_l(\cdot)$ can be a composite function of operations such as convolution (Conv) and rectified linear units (ReLU). The output of the lth layer is defined as F_l. The input of lth layer which receives the feature maps of all preceding layers in same dense block $F_0, \cdots, F_{l-l}$ is expressed as:

$$F_l = H_l([F_0, F_1, \cdots, F_{l-l}]) \tag{2}$$

Where $[F_0, F_1, \cdots, F_{l-l}]$ means the concatenation of the feature maps produced in all preceding layers. Consequently, the final output of the dense block with residual connection could be expressed as:

$$F_{output} = C([F_0, F_1, \cdots, F_l]) + F_0 \tag{3}$$

Where C denotes the 1×1 convolutional layer. As illustrated in Fig. 1, the input of this dense block and the output of the 1×1 convolutional layer are associated together by the residual connection.

3.2 Shuffle Dense Connections

The $H_l(\cdot)$ in Fig. 1 is a commonly used convolutional operation which requires a lot of parameters to be learnt. For reducing computational complexity and the number of parameters, the group convolutions are introduced into our network. Let K denotes the kernel size and C_{in}, C_{out} denote the number of input and output channels, respectively. The parameters of a base convolutional layer is given as:

$$K \cdot K \cdot C_{in} \cdot C_{out} \tag{4}$$

Let G be the group size, the parameters of a group convolutional layer is given as:

$$K \cdot K \cdot (\frac{C_{in}}{G}) \cdot (\frac{C_{out}}{G}) \cdot G = K \cdot K \cdot C_{in} \cdot C_{out}/G \tag{5}$$

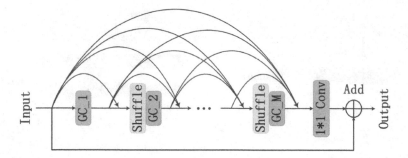

Fig. 3. The whole structure of the Shuffle Dense Block (SDB) with the dense connections and residual connection

It shows that the larger group size would reduce more parameters, but there is a trade-off between the group size G and the performance which is analyzed in the Sect. 5.

In all dense blocks, the group convolutional layers are utilized instead of the all base convolutional layers. When the multiple group convolutions stack together, the outputs from a certain channel only relate to a small fraction of input channels. The two stacked group convolutional layers are illustrated in Fig. 2(a). The different colors mean the different channel groups. It is clear that the same color output only relate to the same color input within the group. That could block information flow between channel groups. Therefore, ShuffleNet [28] employs the channel shuffle operation to make the input and output channels will be fully related. As shown in Fig. 2(b), the feature maps in each group are divided into two subgroups firstly. Then, the each group in the next layer is feed with different subgroups. It makes sure that the input of the each group are related to the every group of the previous layer output. The channel shuffle operation is helpful to build more powerful network with the multiple group convolutional layers. Although the dense structure mitigates a certain problem of the information exchange between the groups, shuffle operation would make the groups more relevant. Inspired by the channel shuffle operation, we propose a channel shuffle structure for dense connections, named Shuffle Dense Block (SDB).

As shown in Fig. 3, SDB is composed of group convolutional (GC), shuffle operation, dense connections and residual connection. M denotes the number of group convolutions. We further give a detailed explanation of SDB in Fig. 4. For illustration, the number of input feature maps is set to 4 and the group size G is set to 2. The different color means the different feature maps and Arabic numerals on feature maps represent the contained feature information. As is shown in Fig. 4, the input of the first group convolutional layer (GC_1) are divided into 2 subgroups. Meanwhile, the original input feature maps are passed backward by dense connection. Then, the two parts of feature maps are concatenated together into shuffle processing module. The output of shuffle are feed into the next group convolutional layer (GC_2). It is plain to see that each

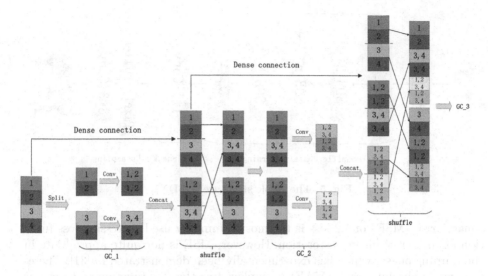

Fig. 4. The processing of dense connections and shuffle operations in SDB.

output feature map of GC_2 contains all the feature information of the original input. The subsequent layers in the block repeats this operation, therefore, we will not explain it in details.

3.3   Network Structure

The whole structure of SDN proposed in this paper is illustrated in Fig. 5. Overall, the SDN architecture includes four parts: a 3×3 convolutional layer, shuffle densely learning module, bottleneck and upsampling module. The first 3×3 convolutional layer is used for low-level feature extraction. The shuffle densely learning module includes N SDBs, meanwhile, the concatenation is introduced for adaptively fusing a range of features with different SDBs. Additionally, the number of channels to be processed keeps increasing. Therefore, a 1×1 convolutional layer is cascaded as "bottleneck" operation. The last module is upsampling module for reconstruction structure, which has one pixel-shuffler and one 3×3 convolutional layer for restoring the HR image. The last convolutional layer has the 1 output map for reconstructing the HR image, other base convolutional layers has the 128 output feature maps and every group convolutional layer in SDB has the 16 output feature maps. Our architecture includes 8 SDB (N = 8), and every SDB consists of 8 group convolutional layers (M = 8).

PReLU [29] layer which is omitted for clarity is used after each group convolutional layer and base convolutional layer. However, since EDSR [30] presented that batch normalization would get rid of range flexibility from networks, the batch normalization layers are removed from our network. The loss function is important for the performance of the network, which is used to measure the difference between the ground truth image Y and the network output $\hat{Y}$. Mean

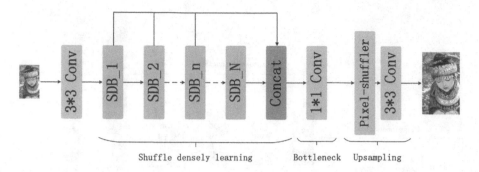

Fig. 5. The whole structure of SDN.

square error (MSE) or L2 loss is the most commonly used regression loss function for universal image restoration. However, MSE is not quite appropriate in the training phase, which has experimentally been demonstrated in [31]. Therefore, mean absolute error (MAE) is employed as the loss function to train our network, which is defined as follows

$$l_{MAE} = \frac{1}{n} \sum_{i=1}^{n} \|\hat{Y}_i - Y_i\|_1, \tag{6}$$

Where n is the number of training patches. The objective function is optimized via Adam [32] with back-propagation. In the following, we will evaluate our designed methodology.

4   Experiments

In this section, several widely used benchmark datasets and metrics are first introduced, followed by the description of the implementation details. Then the shuffle operation investigation is presented. Finally, we compare SDN with other methods on benchmark datasets.

4.1   Datasets and Metrics

DIV2K dataset [33] is a newly released high-quality image dataset for image restoration applications, which contains 1000 images of 2K-resolution, including 800 training images, 100 validation images, and 100 test images. By following [30], we train our network with 800 training images in DIV2K dataset. For testing, we carry experiment on the widely used datasets: Set5 [34], Set14 [35], BSD100 [36] and Urban100 [12], which contain 5, 14, 100 and 100 images respectively. We quantitatively evaluate the SR images with two commonly used image quality metrics: Peak Signal-to-Noise Ratio (PSNR) [37], Structural SIMilarity (SSIM) [38]. For fair comparison, we measure PSNR and SSIM only on the luminance channel (Y) and crop the same amount of pixels as scales from image boundary. Thus the average PSNR and SSIM are computed of the Y channel on four benchmark datasets.

4.2   Implementation Details

For training, original LR images are generated via bicubic downsampling operation on the corresponding HR images, using the function imresize of Matlab with the option bicubic. We randomly crop input patches from LR images with different scale factor of ×2, ×3 and ×4 to train the independent models. To take full advantage of the training data, inspired by [39], we augment the training data in two ways, which is by flipping horizontally or vertically and rotating 90°, 180° and 270° at random. For optimization, We exploited Adam optimizer [32] to optimize all the network by setting momentum parameter $\beta_1 = 0.9$ and $\beta_2 = 0.999$, and the initial learning rate is set to 10^{-4} and decreased by a factor of 10 after 600K update iterations. We set the mini-batch size to 16. All the input patches are preprocessed by subtracting the mean RGB value of the training datasets. For every convolutional layer, the operation of padding zeros around the boundaries is adopted for keeping the size of all feature maps the same as the input during training. We use MAE (L1 loss) instead of MSE (L2 loss) to train the proposed network. We implement our network with Pytorch, and run the entire network on a NVIDIA GTX 1080ti GPU.

Table 1. The study of the shuffle operation in set5 dataset for scaling factor ×3

Structure		$G = 0$	$G = 2$	$G = 4$	$G = 8$
Without shuffle	PSNR	34.12	33.86	33.75	33.62
	Parameters	2.2M	1.6M	1.3M	1.2M
With shuffle	PSNR	/	34.05	33.95	33.83
	Parameters	/	1.6M	1.3M	1.2M

4.3   Study of the Shuffle Operation

To investigate the contribution of the shuffle operation to the final performance, we compare two models which have different group size with and without shuffle operation. Table 1 shows the performance of our model which is easy to see the trade-off between the group size and the shuffle operation at eight dense blocks. From the results with scaling factor ×3 in Set5 [34], the larger group size that the network has, the more parameters will be reduced, but the worse performance will be obtained. However, the shuffle operation which could help the information flowing across group eases the information exchange problem of the group convolution. The group convolution with shuffle operation have better performance than without shuffle operation and the parameters would not increase. The shuffle operation is introduced to solve the problem of poor performance of using group convolution. Hence, When group convolution is added to the dense connections structure, the use structure of the shuffle dense connections (SDN) can further improve the performance of the network.

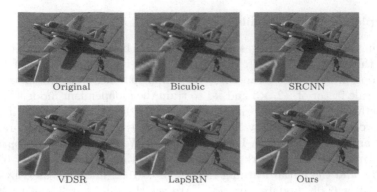

Fig. 6. The img37073 image from the BSD100 dataset with an upscaling factor 4. (*Zoom in for best view*)

4.4 Comparison with Other Methods

To demonstrate the ability of the suggested network, we conduct a comprehensive comparison between our proposed method with several SISR algorithms both deep learning and non-deep-learning based methods, including Bicubic [9], A+[13], [14], VDSR [16], DRCN [18] and LapSRN [20]. The quantitative results for three scale factors ($\times 2$, $\times 3$, $\times 4$) are showed in Table 2 on the four benchmark datasets. We employ the average PSNR and SSIM values to evaluate these approaches. For these existing methods, we utilize SR results publicly released by the authors. From Table 2 we can see our shuffle dense connections structure is superior to other methods in three scale factors ($\times 2$, $\times 3$, $\times 4$). In order to further illustrate the effectiveness of the proposed SDN, we compare our method against different SR approaches in a qualitative manner. Visual evaluation of different approaches on scale $\times 4$ are presented in Figs. 6, 7, 8 and 9. We can observe that our method has the sharper edges and more detailed textures in Fig. 6, and more

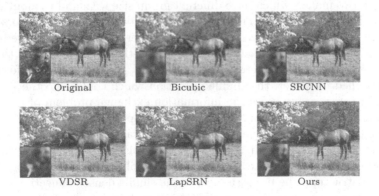

Fig. 7. The img291000 image from the BSD100 dataset with an upscaling factor 4. (*Zoom in for best view*)

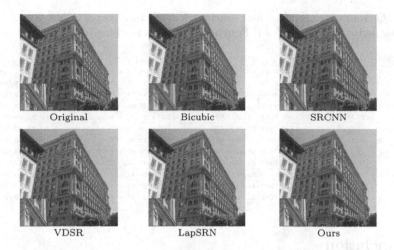

Fig. 8. The img014 image from the Urban100 dataset with an upscaling factor 4. (*Zoom in for best view*)

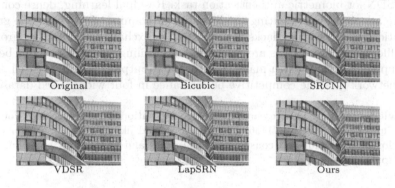

Fig. 9. The img052 image from the Urban100 dataset with an upscaling factor 4. (*Zoom in for best view*)

accurately reconstruct horse from BSD100 in Fig. 7 with the previous methods. In addition, from Figs. 8 and 9, the proposed method can recover fine the lines and the clearer contours while other approaches generate the blurred edge and different degrees of distortions. Therefore, our method has better visual effect. This is because our network employs shuffle dense connections which can solve the problem of lack of information exchange between groups in group convolution and improve the utilization efficiency of features for the improvement of our performance.

Table 2. Quantitative results on four benchmark datasets. Average PSNR/SSIM values for scaling factor ×2, ×3, and ×4. **Fontbold** indicates the best performance.

Dataset	Scale	Bicubic [9]	A^+ [13]	SRCNN [14]	VDSR [16]	LapSRN [20]	DRCN [18]	SDN (ours)
Set5	×2	33.66/0.9299	36.54/0.9544	36.66/0.9542	37.53/0.9587	37.52/0.9591	37.63/0.9588	**37.71/0.9589**
	×3	30.39/0.8682	32.58/0.9088	32.75/0.9090	33.66/0.9213	33.82/0.9227	33.82/0.9226	**34.05/0.9246**
	×4	28.42/0.8104	30.28/0.8603	30.48/0.8628	31.35/0.8838	31.54/0.8855	31.53/0.8854	**31.62/0.8871**
Set14	×2	30.24/0.8688	32.28/0.9056	32.42/0.9063	33.03/0.9124	33.08/0.9130	33.04/0.9118	**33.25/0.9139**
	×3	27.55/0.7742	29.13/0.8188	29.28/0.8209	29.77/0.8314	29.79/0.8320	29.76/0.8311	**29.99/0.8350**
	×4	26.00/0.7027	27.32/0.7491	27.49/0.7503	28.01/0.7674	28.19/0.7720	28.02/0.7670	**28.22/0.7722**
B100	×2	29.56/0.8431	31.21/0.8863	31.36/0.8879	31.90/0.8960	31.80/0.8950	31.85/0.8942	**32.03/0.8971**
	×3	27.21/0.7385	28.29/0.7835	28.41/0.7863	28.82/0.7976	28.82/0.7973	28.80/0.7963	**29.94/0.8003**
	×4	25.96/0.6675	26.82/0.7087	26.90/0.7101	27.29/0.7251	27.32/0.7280	27.23/0.7233	**27.37/0.7282**
Urban100	×2	26.88/0.8403	29.20/0.8938	29.50/0.8946	30.76/0.9140	30.41/0.9101	30.75/0.9133	**31.10/0.9168**
	×3	24.46/0.7349	26.03/0.7973	26.24/0.7989	27.14/0.8279	27.15/0.8276	27.53/0.8378	**27.49/0.8372**
	×4	23.14/0.6577	24.32/0.7183	24.52/0.7221	25.18/0.7524	25.21/0.7553	25.14/0.7510	**26.38/0.7589**

5   Conclusion

This research proposed a novel neural network with shuffle dense connections, named SDN for biometric authentication task. Residual learning, dense connections are adopted for mitigating the difficulty of training. For easing the group convolution problem which lacks the information exchange between the groups, the shuffle dense connections are proposed for shuffling the feature maps before the group convolution which make the input and output are fully related. This neural network gets the competitive performance in four widely used datasets.

Acknowledgements. This research supported by National Nature Science Foundation of China Grand No: 61371156. The authors would like to thank the anonymous reviews for their helpful and constructive comments and suggestions regarding this manuscript.

References

1. Li, J., Chen, X., Li, M., et al.: Secure deduplication with efficient and reliable convergent key management. IEEE Trans. Parallel Distrib. Syst. **25**(6), 1615–1625 (2014)
2. Li, J., Huang, X., Li, J., et al.: Securely outsourcing attribute-based encryption with checkability. IEEE Trans. Parallel Distrib. Syst. **25**(8), 2201–2210 (2014)
3. Li, J., Li, J., Chen, X., et al.: Identity-based encryption with outsourced revocation in cloud computing. IEEE Trans. Comput. **64**(2), 425–437 (2015)
4. Li, J., Li, Y., Chen, X., et al.: A hybrid cloud approach for secure authorized deduplication. IEEE Trans. Parallel Distrib. Syst. **25**(5), 1206–1216 (2015)
5. Li, J., Tan, X., Chen, X., Wong, D.S.: OPoR: enabling proof of retrievability in cloud computing with resource-constrained devices. IEEE Trans. Cloud Comput. **3**(2), 195–205 (2015)
6. Li, J., Zhang, F., Chen, X., et al.: Generic security-amplifying of ordinary digital signatures. Inf. Sci. **201**(2), 128–139 (2012)
7. Cheng, G., Matsune, A., Li, Q., Zhu, L., Zang, H., Zhan, S.: Encoder-decoder residual network for real super-resolution. In: CVPRW (2019)

8. Yang, W., Zhang, X., Tian, Y., et al.: Deep learning for single image super-resolution: a brief review. IEEE Trans. Multimed. (2019)
9. Liu, Z., Mu, H., Zhang, X., et al.: MetaPruning: meta learning for automatic neural network channel pruning. arXiv preprint arXiv:1903.10258 (2019)
10. Li, F., Bai, H., Zhao, Y.: Detail-preserving image super-resolution via recursively dilated residual network. Neurocomputing **358**, 285–293 (2019)
11. Li, F., Bai, H., Zhao, Y.: FilterNet: adaptive information filtering network for accurate and fast image super-resolution. IEEE Trans. Circuits Syst. Video Technol. (2019)
12. Huang, J.-B., Singh, A., Ahuja, N.: Single image super-resolution from transformed self-exemplars. In: Proceedings of the IEEE Conference on Computer Vision and Pattern Recognition (2015)
13. Timofte, R., De Smet, V., Van Gool, L.: A+: adjusted anchored neighborhood regression for fast super-resolution. In: Cremers, D., Reid, I., Saito, H., Yang, M.-H. (eds.) ACCV 2014. LNCS, vol. 9006, pp. 111–126. Springer, Cham (2015). https://doi.org/10.1007/978-3-319-16817-3_8
14. Dong, C., et al.: Image super-resolution using deep convolutional networks. IEEE Trans. Pattern Anal. Mach. Intell. **38**(2), 295–307 (2016)
15. Wang, Z., et al.: Deep networks for image super-resolution with sparse prior. In: Proceedings of the IEEE International Conference on Computer Vision (2015)
16. Kim, J., Lee, J.K., Lee, K.M.: Accurate image super-resolution using very deep convolutional networks. In: Proceedings of the IEEE Conference on Computer Vision and Pattern Recognition (2016)
17. Simonyan, K., Zisserman, A.: Very deep convolutional networks for large-scale image recognition. Comput. Sci. (2014)
18. Kim, J., Lee, J.K., Lee, K.M.: Deeply-recursive convolutional network for image super-resolution. In: Proceedings of the IEEE Conference on Computer Vision and Pattern Recognition (2016)
19. Tai, Y., Yang, J., Liu, X.: Image super-resolution via deep recursive residual network. In: IEEE Conference on Computer Vision and Pattern Recognition IEEE Computer Society, pp. 2790–2798 (2017)
20. Lai, W.S., Huang, J.B., Ahuja, N., et al.: Deep Laplacian pyramid networks for fast and accurate super-resolution. In: Proceedings of IEEE Conference on Computer Vision Pattern Recognition, pp. 624–632 (2017)
21. Tong, T., Li, G., Liu, X., et al.: Image super-resolution using dense skip connections. In: 2017 IEEE International Conference on Computer Vision (ICCV), pp. 4809–4817. IEEE (2017)
22. Huang, G., Liu, Z., Weinberger, K.Q., et al.: Densely connected convolutional networks. In: Proceedings of the IEEE Conference on Computer Vision and Pattern Recognition (2017)
23. He, K., et al.: Deep residual learning for image recognition. In: Proceedings of the IEEE Conference on Computer Vision and Pattern Recognition, pp. 1e–4 (2016)
24. Krizhevsky, A., Sutskever, I., Hinton, G.E.: ImageNet classification with deep convolutional neural networks. In: Advances in Neural Information Processing Systems (2012)
25. Xie, S., et al. Aggregated residual transformations for deep neural networks. In: 2017 IEEE Conference on Computer Vision and Pattern Recognition (CVPR). IEEE (2017)
26. Chollet, F.: Xception: deep learning with depthwise separable convolutions. arXiv preprint arXiv:1610.02357 (2016)

27. Howard, A.G., et al.: MobileNets: efficient convolutional neural networks for mobile vision applications. arXiv preprint arXiv:1704.04861 (2017)

28. Zhang, X., Zhou, X., Lin, M., et al.: ShuffleNet: an extremely efficient convolutional neural network for mobile devices. arXiv preprint arXiv:1707.01083 (2017)

29. He, K., Zhang, X., Ren, S., et al.: Delving deep into rectifiers: surpassing human-level performance on ImageNet classification. In: Proceedings of the IEEE International Conference on Computer Vision, pp. 1026–1034 (2015)

30. Lim, B., et al.: Enhanced deep residual networks for single image super-resolution. In: The IEEE Conference on Computer Vision and Pattern Recognition (CVPR) Workshops (2017)

31. Zhao, H., Gallo, O., Frosio, I., et al.: Loss functions for neural networks for image processing. Computer Science (2015)

32. Kingma, D., Ba, J.: Adam: a method for stochastic optimization. Computer Science (2014)

33. Timofte, R., Agustsson, E., Van Gool, L., et al.: NTIRE 2017 challenge on single image super-resolution: methods and results. In: 2017 IEEE Conference on Computer Vision and Pattern Recognition Workshops (CVPRW), pp. 1110–1121. IEEE (2017)

34. Bevilacqua, M., Roumy, A., Guillemot, C., Alberi-Morel, M.L.: Low-complexity single-image super-resolution based on nonnegative neighbor embedding. In: BMVC (2012)

35. Zeyde, R., Elad, M., Protter, M.: On single image scale-up using sparse-representations. In: Boissonnat, J.-D., et al. (eds.) Curves and Surfaces 2010. LNCS, vol. 6920, pp. 711–730. Springer, Heidelberg (2012). https://doi.org/10.1007/978-3-642-27413-8_47

36. Martin, D., et al.: A database of human segmented natural images and its application to evaluating segmentation algorithms and measuring ecological statistics. In: Proceedings of Eighth IEEE International Conference on Computer Vision (2001)

37. Szegedy, C., et al.: Going deeper with convolutions. In: Proceedings of the CVPR (2015)

38. Wang, Z., Bovik, A.C., Sheikh, H.R., Simoncelli, E.P.: Image quality assessment: from error visibility to structural similarity. IEEE Trans. Image Process. **13**(4), 600–612 (2004)

39. Timofte, R., Rothe, R., Van Gool, L.: Seven ways to improve example-based single image super resolution. In: Proceedings of the IEEE Conference on Computer Vision and Pattern Recognition (2016)

Information Security

An Efficient Attribute Based Encryption Scheme in Smart Grid

Wenti Yang and Zhitao Guan(✉)

School of Control and Computer Engineering,
North China Electric Power University, Beijing 102206, China
guan@ncepu.edu.cn

Abstract. To protect the smart grid data sharing, a flexible access control strategy, the Ciphertext Policy Attribute-Based Encryption (CP-ABE) can be adopted, which often cost huge computational overheads. Hence, how to balance the efficiency and the level of security provided is of considerable importance. In this paper, we propose Co-CPABE, a cooperative CP-ABE scheme for smart grid. In our scheme, the heavy encryption computation tasks are dispersed to several data owners. Concretely, the access tree can be computed independently and simultaneously. As a result, the encryption is implemented by the cooperation of data owners and the Central Authority (CA), in which the CA only performs simple calculations such as multiplication and division. Moreover, an enhanced scheme is introduced to further improve the encryption efficiency. Finally, Co-CPABE is proved to be secure as well as efficient.

Keywords: Smart grid · CP-ABE · Efficient · Encryption

1 Introduction

With the rapid development of technologies, people are having higher demands on economical and reliable electricity power supply. This requires intelligent energy management and distribution, as well as reliable communication and data aggregation, which cannot be satisfied by the traditional power grid. To cope with these problems, a new concept called smart grid has emerged into view. As the next generation power grid, it provides two-way flows of electricity and information, and builds a widely distributed energy delivery network [1, 2].

Smart grid encompasses a wide variety of network and communication technologies [3, 4], which means that some of the concerns involved in these technologies would be passed on to the smart grid. For instance, data confidentiality and system efficiency are both key factors in keeping the operation stable and developing in long-term period for smart grid [5, 6]. In smart grid, there are large quantities of data owners and data users. The data are collected from various applications running on the terminal devices of the data owners, and transferred to the outsourced servers; the data users, including the power grid staffs, government agencies, researchers, and other authorized users, may access and analyze the data. All parties have their own areas of expertise, sensitive information such as the energy transactions or bidding data, should only be

© Springer Nature Switzerland AG 2019
J. Vaidya et al. (Eds.): CSS 2019, LNCS 11982, pp. 159–172, 2019.
https://doi.org/10.1007/978-3-030-37337-5_13

sent to trusted data users for processing. Therefore, data access control is considered a critical issue in smart grid.

Public key encryption is considered as one of the most prevalent schemes to cope with diverse security issues in smart grid. A variety of public key encryption schemes have been developed and adopted. Identity-based encryption (IBE) is one kind of such schemes being widely used, such as [7–9]. Currently, there are several schemes adopting Attribute-based Encryption (ABE) [10–12] (or their variants) [13–15] to achieve fine-grained access control in smart grid. However, most of existing works focus on reducing the decryption cost, but seldomly take the encryption overhead into consideration [16, 17]. In smart grid, it is necessary to take advantage of end user collaboration to relieve the computation workload considering that the large number of end users will generate a huge amount of data [18, 19]. In this paper, we propose Co-CPABE, a cooperative efficient encryption scheme with verifiable outsourced decryption in smart grid, in which efficient encryption and decryption are achieved simultaneously. Co-CPABE can enhance the data encryption efficiency without using any external server (no sacrifice of data security and privacy). Meanwhile, Co-CPABE provides verifiability for the outsourced decryption computations. The main contributions of this paper can be summarized as follows: (1) Firstly, instead of hiring additional servers or devices to delegate the heavy computation overheads, we have the data owners to cooperate with their central authority to conduct the encryption using their smart devices, which improves the encryption efficiency dramatically. (2) Secondly, we set a *Seed* for each sub-tree. In certain scenarios, a *Seed* would grow into the corresponding access sub-tree. When the access structures are used repeatedly, data owners who own the seeds are able to perform encryption more efficiently than those who don't. (3) Finally, we show the security analysis and provide a detailed performance evaluation to demonstrate the advantages of our scheme.

The rest of this paper is organized as follows. We give the preliminaries and definitions in Sect. 2. We describe the system model and algorithm details in Sect. 3. The security analysis and the performance evaluation of our scheme are presented in Sects. 4 and 5 respectively.

2 Preliminaries

2.1 Bilinear Maps

Definition 1 (Bilinear Maps). Let $\mathbb{G}_0$ and $\mathbb{G}_1$ be two multiplicative cyclic groups of prime order p and g be the generator of $\mathbb{G}_0$. The bilinear map e is, $e : \mathbb{G}_0 \times \mathbb{G}_0 \rightarrow \mathbb{G}_1$, for all $a, b \in \mathbb{Z}_p$:

- Bilinearity: $\forall u, v \in \mathbb{G}_1, e(u^a, v^b) = e(u, v)^{ab}$.
- Non-degeneracy: $e(g, g) \neq 1$.
- Symmetric: $e(g^a, g^b) = e(g, g)^{ab} = e(g^b, g^a)$.

2.2 Complexity Assumptions

Definition 2 (Discrete Logarithm Problem). Let $\mathbb{G}$ be a multiplicative cyclic group of prime order p and g be its generator. Given a tuple $<g, g^x>$, where $g \in_R \mathbb{G}$ and $x \in \mathbb{Z}_P$ is chosen uniformly at random, as input. The DL problem is to recover x.

The Discrete Logarithm Problem (DL) assumption holds in $\mathbb{G}$ is that no probabilistic polynomial-time (PPT) algorithm can solve the DL problem with negligible advantage. We define the advantage of $\mathcal{A}$ as follows:

$$\Pr[\mathcal{A} < g, g^x> = x]$$

The probability is over the generator g, the randomly chosen x and the random bits consumed by $\mathcal{A}$.

2.3 Security Model

We now give the security model for CP-ABE. The game proceeds as follows:

Setup: The challenger $\mathcal{C}$ runs this algorithm. It gives the public parameters PK to the adversary $\mathcal{A}$ and keeps MK to himself.

Phase 1: $\mathcal{A}$ issues queries for private keys corresponding to the sets of attributes $S_1 \cdots S_{q_1}$ (q and q1 are integers randomly chosen by $\mathcal{A}$ and $1 < q_1 < q$). If any of the attributes $S_1 \cdots S_{q_1}$ satisfies the access structure AS*, then aborts. Otherwise, $\mathcal{C}$ generates the corresponding secret keys to the attribute sets for $\mathcal{A}$.

Challenge: $\mathcal{A}$ submits two equal length messages M_0 and M_1 to $\mathcal{C}$. The challenger $\mathcal{C}$ randomly flips a coin b, and encrypts M_b under the challenge access structure AS*. Then the generated ciphertext CT* is given to $\mathcal{A}$.

Phase 2: Repeat Phase 1, and the attributes are changed from $S_1 \cdots S_{q_1}$ to $S_{q_1+1} \cdots S_q$.

Guess: The adversary $\mathcal{A}$ outputs its guess $b' \in \{0, 1\}$ for b and wins the game if $b' = b$.

The advantage of an adversary $\mathcal{A}$ in this game is defined as:

$$Adv(\mathcal{A}) = |\Pr[b' = b] - 1/2|$$

where the probability is taken over the random bits used by the challenger and the adversary.

Definition 3. A CP-ABE scheme is CPA-secure if no probabilistic polynomial time (PPT) adversary $\mathcal{A}$ can win the above game with non-negligible advantage.

3 Description of Our System

3.1 System Model

In a certain smart community that has already deployed the smart grid facilities, it is seemingly reliable and promising to utilize the traditional CP-ABE scheme to preserve data security and user privacy. With limited computation ability, those original smart devices on the network edge cannot deal with heavy computation overheads introduced by CP-ABE. To balance the functionality and efficiency, some related works hire cloud services for the encryption computation.

Generally, most data owners in a smart community may share the same access structure. Depending on this feature, we propose the Co-CPABE scheme and give a description of our system model below.

The overview of our system model is shown in Fig. 1. Our system model includes four entities: DO, CA, DSP, and DR. In the smart grid scenario, CA defines the access policy for its subsidiary districts. DO denotes data collection and transmission devices of the same level in a given district, which share the same access policy and assist the encryption by generating cryptographic structures for the corresponding sub-access policy. After the ciphertexts are uploaded over the network, DR can request for the desired data in ciphertexts, and obtain the plaintexts by outsourcing for decryption.

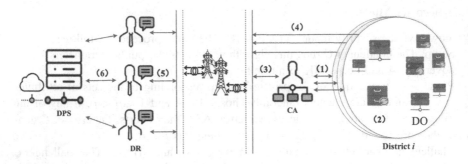

Fig. 1. System model

3.2 Basic Scheme

Setup(1^λ) →**PK, MK.** The CA runs this setup algorithm and generates a set of public parameters. $\mathbb{G}_0$ is a bilinear group of prime order p with generator g, several exponents: $\alpha, \beta, q, \delta \in \mathbb{Z}_p$ are chosen at random. $H_a : \{0,1\}^* \to \mathbb{G}_0$ and $H_m : \{0,1\}^* \to \mathbb{G}_0$ are collision-resistant hash functions. We set $MK = \{\alpha, \beta, \delta, q\}$. The public key is published as:

$$PK = \{\mathbb{G}_0, g, h = g^\beta, e(g,g)^\alpha, g^q,$$
$$k = g^\delta, K = g^{1/\delta}, H_a(), H_m(), h_0()\ldots h_{n-1}()\}.$$

SK_Gen(PK, MK, pk$_u$, S)→**SK.** Once a user joins the system, he/she chooses a random exponent $\lambda_u \in \mathbb{Z}_P$. Then the user's public and private key pair is given by $(pk_u = g^{\lambda_u}, sk_u = \lambda_u)$. The set of attributes S is the input and a corresponding key is the output. This algorithm first chooses $R_1, R_2, r_j \in \mathbb{Z}_P$, at random for each attribute $j \in S$ and sets $R_0 = R_1 + R_2$. Then it computes the key as:

$$SK = (D = g^{\lambda_u \frac{(\alpha + R_1)}{\beta}}, D_1 = g^{\frac{R_2}{\beta}}, \hat{D} = K^{\lambda_u R_0},$$

$$\forall j \in S : D_j = g^{R_0 \lambda_u} \cdot H_a(j)^{r_j}, D'_j = g^{r_j}).$$

Encrypt$_{DO}$(M$_i$, PK, AS$_i$) $\to$ **(E$_i$, st$_i$).** CA defines the access structure and assigns a distinct string $t_j \in \{0, 1\}^*$ to identify the sub-tree. CA defines a function *tparent*(t_j) to denote the upper level sub-tree of t_j.

Upon receiving a request from CA, for sub-tree t_i, this algorithm first randomly chooses $s_i, \theta_i \in \mathbb{Z}_p$. DO$_i$ generates a polynomial $f_i(x)$ and sets

$$f_i(x) = s_i + a_1 x + a_2 x^2 + \ldots a_{m-1} x^{m-1}.$$

For $\forall 1 \le j \le m, j \ne i,$:

$$G(ID_i) = f_1(ID_i) + \ldots f_i(ID_i) + \ldots f_m(ID_i)$$

Additionally, DO$_i$ securely share a secret parameter $\omega \in \mathbb{Z}_p$ with others in the local network. It computes $E_i = M_i \cdot e(g, g)^{\alpha \omega}$ and sets

$$\tilde{C}_i = e(g, g)^{\alpha \omega} \cdot e(g, g)^{\alpha G(ID_i) \prod_{j=1, j \ne i}^{m} \frac{ID_j}{ID_j - ID_i}}.$$

For the root node of sub-tree t_i, it sets $q_{i,R}(0) = \theta_i$. and computes

$$\hat{C}_{i,1} = h^{s_i}, \hat{C}_{i,2} = k^{s_i}, C'_i = k^{\theta_i}.$$

For attribute nodes $\forall x \in S_i$, it sets $C_x = g^{q_x(0)}$ and $C'_x = H(att(x))^{q_x(0)}$, where $q_x(0) = q_{i,R}(index(x))$.

For non-attribute nodes $\forall y \in S_{na}$, it sets $N_{i,y} = k^{q_y(0)}$, where $q_y(0) = q_{i,R}(index(t_j))$, and t_j denotes another sub-tree with *tparent*(t_j) = t_i. It computes the sub-ciphertext components as follows:

$$\forall y \in S_{na}, N_{i,y} = k^{q_y(0)},$$

$$\forall x \in S_a, \{C_x = g^{q_x(0)}, C'_x = H_a(att(x))^{q_x(0)}\}.$$

Finally, it outputs the sub-ciphertext as follows:

$$st_i : \ <t_i, \hat{C}_{i,1}, \hat{C}_{i,2}, \tilde{C}_i, C'_i,$$

$$\forall x \in S_a, \{C_x, C'_x\}, \forall y \in S_{na}, N_{i,y}> \ .$$

Encrypt$_{CA}$(st$_i$, PK)→T. CA receives all the sub-ciphertexts from these m sub-districts, it encapsulates them together. The computation is as follows:

$$s = \sum_{i=1}^{m} s_i,$$

$$C = \prod_{i=1}^{m} \hat{C}_{i,1} = \prod_{i=1}^{m} h^{s_i} = h^{\sum_{i=1}^{m} s_i} = h^s,$$

$$N_{R,1} = \prod_{i=1}^{m} \hat{C}_{i,2} = \prod_{i=1}^{m} k^{s_i} = k^{\sum_{i=1}^{m} s_i} = k^s,$$

$$C_1 = N_{R,1}/C_1' = k^{s-\theta_1}, \ldots, C_j = N_{tparent(j),y}/C_j' = k^{q_y(0)-\theta_j},$$

$$\tilde{C} = \prod_{i=1}^{m} \tilde{C}_i = e(g,g)^{\alpha m \omega} \cdot e(g,g)^{\alpha \sum_{i=1}^{m} .G(ID_i) \prod_{j \neq i}^{m} \frac{ID_j}{ID_j - ID_i}}$$

$$= e(g,g)^{\alpha m \omega} \cdot e(g,g)^{\alpha s}.$$

Thus, the algorithm outputs the complete access structure:

$$CT : \ <\tilde{C}, C, \forall x \in S, \{C_x, C_x'\}, \forall i \in S_{sub-tree}, E_i> \ .$$

Decrypt$_{DR}$(CT, SK, BF, sk$_u$)→M or ⊥. DR runs this algorithm to decrypt the ciphertext. DR can proceed to decryption. For each attribute a, let j = att(a), if $j \in S$, then,

$$F_a = DecryptLeafNode(CT, SK, a) = \frac{e(D_j, C_a)}{e(D_j', C_a')} = e(g,g)^{\lambda_u R_0 q_a(0)}.$$

Else, $DecryptLeafNode(CT, SK, a) = \perp$.

If a is an interior node, for all nodes a that are children of node b, according to the recovered threshold d_i of b, if the total number of F_a is less than d_i, it aborts and outputs ⊥ directly. Else, it computes

$$F_b' = \prod_{a \in S_b} F_a^{\Delta_{n,S_b'}(0)}, \ where \ \begin{cases} n = index(a) \\ S_b' = \{index(a) : a \in S_b\} \end{cases}$$

$$= \prod_{a \in S_b} \left(e(g,g)^{\lambda_u R_0 q_a(0)} \right)^{\Delta_{n,S_x'}(0)}$$

$$= \prod_{a \in S_b} \left(e(g,g)^{\lambda_u R_0 q_{parent(a)}(index(a))} \right)^{\Delta_{n,S_b'}(0)}$$

$$= \prod_{a \in S_b} \left(e(g,g)^{\lambda_u R_0 q_b(n)} \right)^{\Delta_{n,S_b'}(0)} = e(g,g)^{\lambda_u R_0 \theta_j},$$

$$F_b = F_b' \cdot e(K^r, C_j) = e(g,g)^{\lambda_u R_0 q_{ti}(0)}.$$

For the root node R of this access tree:

$$F_R = F_R' \cdot e(K^{\lambda_u R_0}, C_1) = e(g,g)^{\lambda_u R_0 \theta_1} e(K^{\lambda_u R_0}, C_1) = e(g,g)^{\lambda_u R_0 s}.$$

Then it computes:

$$e(g,g)^{\alpha \omega m} = \frac{\tilde{C} \cdot F_R}{e(D,C) \cdot e(D_1,C)^{sk_u}}$$

$$= \frac{e(g,g)^{\alpha \omega m} \cdot e(g,g)^{\alpha s} \cdot e(g,g)^{\lambda_u R_0 s}}{e\left(h^s, g^{\frac{(\alpha + \lambda_u R_1)}{\beta}}\right) e\left(h^s, g^{\frac{R_2}{\beta}}\right)^{\lambda_u}}$$

$$= \frac{e(g,g)^{\alpha \omega m} \cdot e(g,g)^{\alpha s} \cdot e(g,g)^{\lambda_u R_0 s}}{e(g,g)^{s(\alpha + \lambda_u R_1)} e(g,g)^{s \lambda_u R_2}}$$

$$= \frac{e(g,g)^{\alpha \omega m} \cdot e(g,g)^{(\alpha + \lambda_u R_0)s}}{e(g,g)^{s(\alpha + \lambda_u R_0)}}.$$

Then:

$$M_i = \frac{E_i}{(e(g,g)^{\alpha \omega m})^{1/m}}.$$

3.3   Enhanced Scheme

We consider a practical concern that the access policy would not be redefined each time. That is to say, the same access policy would be involved in multiple rounds of encryption within a period, we propose an enhanced scheme to further improve the encryption efficiency. The following are all the algorithm details and security analysis.

For each sub access structure AS_i, its information is contained in ct_i where,

$$ct_i : t_i, C_i' = k^{\theta_i}, \forall y \in S_{na}, N_{i,y} = k^{q_y(0)},$$

$$\forall x \in S_a, \{C_x = g^{q_x(0)}, C_x' = H_a(att(x))^{q_x(0)}\}.$$

The sub-district can record the access structure AS_i and consider it as an Encryption Seed. We define its Encryption Seed ES_i as follows:

$$ES_i : \ <t_i, B_{i,1} = C_i', \forall y \in S_{na}, \{B_{i,2,y} = N_{i,y}\},$$

$$\forall x \in S_a, \{B_{i,3,x} = C_x, B_{i,4,x} = C_x'\}> .$$

Once a certain sub-district requires to encrypt another new message M_j' with AS_i, it runs this encryption algorithm.

EncryptES(M_i, PK, ES_i)→ct_i. This algorithm encrypts the message only with ES_i rather than AS_i. At first, this algorithm selects $\theta_i', \varepsilon_i \in \mathbb{Z}_P$ at random. Set

$$\hat{\theta}_i = \theta_i + \theta_i', \hat{q}_y(0) = q_y(0) + \theta_i', \hat{q}_x(0) = q_x(0) + \theta_i',$$

$$C_i' = (B_{i,1} \cdot k^{\theta_i'})^\varepsilon = k^{\hat{\theta}_i \varepsilon_i},$$

$$\forall y \in S_{na}, N_{i,y} = (B_{i,2,y} \cdot k^{\theta_i'})^\varepsilon = k^{\hat{q}_y(0)\varepsilon_i},$$

$$\forall x \in S_a, \{C_x = (B_{i,3,x} \cdot g^{\theta_i'})^{\varepsilon_i} = g^{\hat{q}_x(0)\varepsilon_i},$$

$$C_x' = (B_{i,4,x} \cdot H_a(att(x))^{\theta_i'})^{\varepsilon_i} = H_a(att(x))^{\hat{q}_x(0)\varepsilon_i}\}.$$

Next, it re-selects the random $s_i', u_i \in \mathbb{Z}_P$ and encrypts the message as follows:

$$E_i = Enc_\kappa(M_i'),$$

$$\tilde{C}_i = \kappa e(g, g)^{\alpha s_i' \varepsilon_i},$$

$$\hat{C}_{i,1} = h^{s_i' \varepsilon_i}, \hat{C}_{i,2} = k^{s_i' \varepsilon_i},$$

Actually, the sub-ciphertext obtained by this algorithm is equivalent to one received directly from the algorithm Encrypt$_{DO}$.

Each sub-district can run this algorithm independently. In other words, it can generate ct_i by this algorithm while others use the algorithm Encrypt$_{DO}$.

4 Security Analysis

Theorem 1: The Co-CPABE scheme described above is selectively CPA-secure with respect to Definition 5.

In this proposed scheme, we introduce several hash functions to assist the encryption. We improve the encryption efficiency of traditional CP-ABE by generating the sub-trees independently, which means the way of encryption may affect the security of the proposed system.

Theorem 2: If the hash function H_a is collision resistant, our system can be proved to be secure and can resist chosen plaintext attacks in random oracle model.

Proof: The ciphertext and its components of the proposed scheme are shown as follows:

$$CT: \ <\tilde{C}, C, \forall i \in S_{sub-tree}, c_i, E_i, \forall x \in S, \{C_x, C'_x, c_x\}>.$$

where $\forall x \in S, \{C_x = g^{q_x(0)}, C'_x = H_a(att(x))^{q_x(0)}\}$.

Assume that there is a random function f that is able to replace the hash function H. Therefore, $\mathcal{A}$ can obtain that

$$\forall x \in S_a, \{C_x = g^{q_x(0)}, C'_x = f(att(x))^{q_x(0)}\}.$$

We call this scheme as the alternative scheme.

Finally, we define a game between the challenger $\mathcal{C}$ and the adversary $\mathcal{A}$ to simulate the chosen plaintext attack here.

Setup: $\mathcal{C}$ runs this algorithm. It gives the public parameters PK to $\mathcal{A}$ and keeps MK to himself.

Phase 1: $\mathcal{A}$ calls the encryption oracle and requests for a ciphertext for plaintext x_j in the probabilistic polynomial time. The challenger $\mathcal{C}$ runs the alternative scheme and returns $f(att(x_j))^{q_{x_j}(0)}$ to $\mathcal{A}$.

Phase 2: $\mathcal{A}$ first chooses two messages x_j^0, x_j^1 with equal length. Then $\mathcal{C}$ computes $f(att(x_j^0))^{q_{x_j^0}(0)}, f(att(x_j^1))^{q_{x_j^1}(0)}$.

Challenge: $\mathcal{A}$ asks for a challenge plaintext, $\mathcal{C}$ flips a coin and get a random number $b \in \{0, 1\}$ and sends $f(att(x_j^b))^{q_{x_j^b}(0)}$ to the adversary.

Phase 3: $\mathcal{A}$ continues to query some different plaintexts to $\mathcal{C}$, which is the same as the above steps.

Guess: $\mathcal{A}$ outputs his guess b', and wins the game when $b = b'$. Otherwise, he fails. $\mathcal{A}$ can win this game only by two ways:

(1) $g^{q_x(0)}, g^s$ can be broken and the powers can be recovered. However, this contradicts the DL problem.

(2) $\mathcal{A}$ designs two messages x, x' $(x \neq x')$ such that $f(att(x))^{q_x(0)} = f(att(x'))^{q_{x'}(0)}$. The probability is negligible as f is a random function.

The advantage of $\mathcal{A}$ in our scheme is defined as follows:

$$Adv(\mathcal{A}) = \Pr[H\ Collision] + \Pr[Recover\ secrets] + \Pr[D\ wins]$$

A function $negl_1[k]$ is defined that is negligible with the system security parameter k. The probability that collision occurs in hash function H is $\Pr[H\ Collision]$. Since H is collision resist, $negl_1[k]$ can be used to denote its probability. D is used to distinguish f with a random function. If D wins, it means that f is distinguished from a random function successfully. Since f is a pseudo random function, $\Pr[D\ wins]$ is $negl_2[k]$.

Additionally, though we adopt the independent and parallel encryption method when generating the access tree in this paper, the new ciphertext components are also in the form of $g^{\Delta C}(\Delta C \in \mathbb{Z}_p)$. Since it is computationally infeasible to solve DL problem, $\Pr[Recover\ secrets]$ is $negl_3[k]$.

Finally, $Adv(\mathcal{A}) \leq negl_1[k] + negl_2[k] + negl_3[k]$. We complete the proof.

Theorem 3: Suppose that the DL assumption holds in the prime order bilinear group system, the above Co-CPABE enhanced scheme is secure.

Proof: We prove this theorem with the following game. Suppose that an adversary $\mathcal{A}$ can attack the construction of ciphertexts in our scheme with non-negligible advantage. The game proceeds as follows:

Setup: The challenger $\mathcal{C}$ runs this algorithm. It gives the public parameters PK to $\mathcal{A}$ and keeps MK to himself.

Phase 1: $\mathcal{A}$ submits an access structure AS to $\mathcal{C}$.

Challenge: $\mathcal{C}$ first chooses $M \in \{0, 1\}^*$, $\kappa_{as}, \kappa_{es} \in \mathbb{G}_T$, and $s, \varepsilon, \theta \in \mathbb{Z}_p$. Then it encrypts twice (double check) under this challenge access structure. One of the ciphertexts is encrypted with the traditional method AS, while the other one is encrypted with ES.

Then $\mathcal{C}$ sends the two ciphertexts CT_{as}, CT_{es} to adversary $\mathcal{A}$. Where,

$$CT : \; <\tilde{C}, C, \forall i \in S_{sub-tree}, c_i, E_i, \forall x \in S, \{C_x, C'_x, c_x\}> .$$

$$\tilde{C}_{as} = \kappa_{as} e(g, g)^{\alpha s},$$

$$C_{as} = h^s,$$

$$E_{as} = Enc_{\kappa_{as}}(M),$$

$$V_{as} = u_{as}^{H_m(M_i)q},$$

$$\forall x \in S_a, \{C_{as,x} = g^{q_x(0)}, C'_{as,x} = H_a(att(x))^{q_x(0)}\}.$$

$$\tilde{C}_{es} = \kappa_{es} e(g, g)^{\alpha s' \varepsilon},$$

$$C_{es} = h^{s' \varepsilon},$$

$$E_{es} = Enc_{\kappa_{es}}(M),$$

$$V_{es} = u_{es}^{H_m(M_i)q},$$

$$\forall x \in S_a, \{C_{es,x} = g^{\hat{q}_x(0)\varepsilon}, C'_{es,x} = H_a(att(x))^{\hat{q}_x(0)\varepsilon}\}.$$

Note that:

$$s' = s + \theta', \hat{q}_y(0) = q_y(0) + \theta', \hat{q}_x(0) = q_x(0) + \theta'.$$

The strings that denote the different sub-trees will be changed each time.

Phase 2: $\mathcal{A}$ continues to query for different ciphertexts as in phase 1.

Output: $\mathcal{A}$ outputs his guess about the Encryption Seed ES^*.

If $\mathcal{A}$ wins the game, $\mathcal{C}$ obtains the ES^*, where $\kappa_{as} \neq \kappa_{es}$. However,

$$y_1 = \frac{g^{\hat{q}_x(0)\varepsilon}}{g^{q_x(0)}} = g^{(q_x(0)+\theta')\varepsilon - q_x(0)}$$

$$= g^{x_1},$$

$$y_2 = \frac{H_a(att(x))^{\hat{q}_x(0)\varepsilon}}{H_a(att(x))^{q_x(0)}} = H_a(att(x))^{(q_x(0)+\theta')\varepsilon - q_x(0)}$$

$$= H_a(att(x))^{x_2},$$

To recover $x_1 = x_2 = (q_x(0) + \theta')\varepsilon - q_x(0)$, he must solve the DL problem. Since it is computationally infeasible to solve the problem in G, $\mathcal{C}$ cannot attack the construction of ciphertext that is generated with ES in our scheme with non-negligible advantage.

5 Performance Evaluation

We give the efficiency analysis for the encryption process. The time cost in each step is shown in Table 1.

Table 1. The parameters in comparison of storage cost

Symbols	Description
m	Total number of sub-districts
TT_i	The i-th sub-tree generation time
Max()	The max value of its inputs
VT_m	Time for multiply operation
VT_p	Time for pairing operations

Each sub-district is responsible for generating one sub-tree, and handing in their sub-ciphertexts to CA. In the worst case (we denote it as case (1)), all these sub-ciphertexts are submitted one after another, this case is similar to that of the traditional scheme. Thus, we set $T_{w,0}$ to denote the total encryption time:

$$T_{w,0} \approx TT_1 + \ldots + TT_i + \ldots + TT_m = \sum_{i=1}^{m} TT_i.$$

This value is nearly identical to that of traditional scheme.

In the best case (we denote it as case (2)), all the sub-trees are generated in parallel, it means that no network latency exists. Thus, the total time $T_{b,0}$ equals to the longest generation time:

$$T_{b,0} \approx Max(TT_1, \ldots, TT_i, \ldots, TT_m).$$

Next, in case (1), if there is any sub-district performing the encryption with its Encryption *Seed*, the total encryption time differs from the above results. In the worst case, only one sub-tree is generated by its Encryption *Seed*, thus,

$$T_{w,1} \approx TT_1 + \ldots + ET_j + \ldots + TT_m = \sum_{i=1}^{m} TT_i - TT_j + ET_j.$$

Note that $ET_j \leq TT_j$. However, if all the sub-trees are generated by their own Encryption Seeds, the total time $T_{w,2}$ is showed as follows:

$$T_{w,2} \approx ET_1 + \ldots + ET_j + \ldots + ET_m = \sum_{i=1}^{m} ET_i.$$

Thus, in case (1), we can draw the following conclusions: $T_{w,2} < T_{w,1} < T_{w,0}$.

When it comes to case (2), if there is any sub-district performing the encryption with its *Encryption Seed*, the total encryption time may or may not change. We set $T_{b,1}$ to denote the total encryption time:

$$T_{b,1} \approx Max(TT_1, \ldots, ET_j, \ldots, TT_m).$$

If all the sub-trees are generated by their own *Encryption Seeds*, the encryption time $T_{b,2}$ is reduced significantly, as shown below:

$$T_{b,2} \approx Max(ET_1, \ldots, ET_j, \ldots, ET_m).$$

The relationship among the three of them depends on the value of $T_{b,0}$. If $T_{b,0} = TT_i, i \neq j$, $T_{b,2} < T_{b,1} = T_{b,0}$. Else,

$$T_{b,0} = TT_j, T_{b,2} < T_{b,1} < T_{b,0}.$$

If the batch operations are not available, users have to perform m pairing operations. The result is shown as follows:

$$T_{v,1} = m \cdot VT_p.$$

Generally, pairing operation takes much longer time than that of multiplication operation. We can obtain $T_{v,0} \geq T_{v,1}$ only when

$$VT_p \leq \frac{m}{m-1} VT_m.$$

Otherwise,

$$T_{v,0} < T_{v,1}.$$

Acknowledgment. This work is supported by Beijing Natural Science Foundation (4182060).

References

1. Fang, X., Misra, S., Xue, G., Yang, D.: Smart grid—the new and improved power grid: a survey. IEEE Commun. Surv. Tutorials **14**(4), 944–980 (2011)
2. Gungor, V.C., Sahin, D., Kocak, T., Ergut, S., Buccella, C.: Smart grid technologies: communication technologies and standards. IEEE Trans. Industr. Inf. **7**(4), 529–539 (2011)
3. Fouda, M.M., Fadlullah, Z.M., Kato, N., Lu, R., Shen, X.S.: A lightweight message authentication scheme for smart grid communications. IEEE Trans. Smart Grid **2**(4), 675–685 (2011)
4. Fadlullah, Z.M., Kato, N., Lu, R., Shen, X.: Toward secure targeted broadcast in smart grid. IEEE Commun. Mag. **50**(5), 150–156 (2012)
5. Bera, S., Misra, S., Rodrigues, J.J.P.C.: Cloud computing applications for smart grid: a survey. IEEE Trans. Parallel Distrib. Syst. **26**, 1477–1494 (2015)
6. Baek, J., Vu, Q.H., Liu, J.K., Huang, X., Xiang, Y.: A secure cloud computing based framework for big data information management of smart grid. IEEE Trans. Cloud Comput. **3**(2), 233–244 (2015)
7. Shamir, A.: Identity-based cryptosystems and signature schemes. In: Blakley, G.R., Chaum, D. (eds.) CRYPTO 1984. LNCS, vol. 196, pp. 47–53. Springer, Heidelberg (1985). https://doi.org/10.1007/3-540-39568-7_5
8. Boneh, D., Franklin, M.: Identity-based encryption from the weil pairing. In: Kilian, J. (ed.) CRYPTO 2001. LNCS, vol. 2139, pp. 213–229. Springer, Heidelberg (2001). https://doi.org/10.1007/3-540-44647-8_13
9. Waters, B.: Efficient identity-based encryption without random oracles. In: Cramer, R. (ed.) EUROCRYPT 2005. LNCS, vol. 3494, pp. 114–127. Springer, Heidelberg (2005). https://doi.org/10.1007/11426639_7
10. Sahai, A., Waters, B.: Fuzzy identity-based encryption. In: Cramer, R. (ed.) EUROCRYPT 2005. LNCS, vol. 3494, pp. 457–473. Springer, Heidelberg (2005). https://doi.org/10.1007/11426639_27
11. Goyal, V., Pandey, O., Sahai, A., Waters, B.: Attribute-based encryption for fine-grained access control of encrypted data. In: Proceedings ACM Conference on Computer & Communications Security, pp. 89–98 (2010)
12. Bethencourt, J., Sahai, A., Waters, B.: Ciphertext-policy attribute-based encryption. In: Proceedings IEEE Symposium on Security & Privacy, pp. 321–334 (2007)
13. Waters, B.: Ciphertext-policy attribute-based encryption: an expressive, efficient, and provably secure realization. In: Catalano, D., Fazio, N., Gennaro, R., Nicolosi, A. (eds.) PKC 2011. LNCS, vol. 6571, pp. 53–70. Springer, Heidelberg (2011). https://doi.org/10.1007/978-3-642-19379-8_4
14. Li, M., Yu, S., Zheng, Y., Ren, K., Lou, W.: Scalable and secure sharing of personal health records in cloud computing using attribute-based encryption. IEEE Trans. Parallel Distrib. Syst. **24**(1), 131–143 (2013)
15. Han, J., Susilo, W., Mu, Y., Zhou, J., Man, H.A.A.: Improving privacy and security in decentralized ciphertext-policy attribute-based encryption. IEEE Trans. Inf. Forensics Secur. **10**(3), 665–678 (2015)
16. Liu, D., Li, H., Yang, Y., Yang, H.: Achieving multi-authority access control with efficient attribute revocation in smart grid. In: Proceedings IEEE International Conference on Communications (ICC), pp. 634–649 (2014)
17. Ning, J., Dong, X., Cao, Z., Wei, L., Lin, X.: White-box traceable ciphertext-policy attribute-based encryption supporting flexible attributes. IEEE Trans. Inf. Forensics Secur. **10**(6), 1274–1288 (2015)

18. Rahulamathavan, Y., Veluru, S., Han, J., Li, F., Rajarajan, M., Lu, R.: User collusion avoidance scheme for privacy-preserving decentralized key-policy attribute-based encryption. IEEE Trans. Comput. **65**(9), 2939–2946 (2016)
19. Lee, K., Choi, S.G., Dong, H.L., Park, J.H., Yung, M.: Self-updatable encryption: time constrained access control with hidden attributes and better efficiency. Theoret. Comput. Sci. **667**, 51–92 (2017)
20. Shamir, A.: How to share a secret. Commun. ACM **22**(11), 612–613 (1979)
21. Blakley, G.R.: Safeguarding cryptographic keys. In: Proceedings Managing Requirements Knowledge, International Workshop, p. 313 (1979)
22. Green, M., Hohenberger, S., Waters, B.: Outsourcing the decryption of ABE ciphertexts. In: Proceedings USENIX Conference on Security, p. 34 (2011)
23. Dong, C., Chen, L., Wen, Z.: When private set intersection meets big data: an efficient and scalable protocol. In: Proceedings of CCS 2013, pp. 789–800. ACM (2013)

Attribute-Based Signatures
for Inner-Product Predicate from Lattices

Yanhua Zhang[1]([✉]), Ximeng Liu[2], Yupu Hu[3], Qikun Zhang[1], and Huiwen Jia[4]

[1] Zhengzhou University of Light Industry, Zhengzhou 450002, China
{yhzhang,qkzhang}@zzuli.edu.cn
[2] Fuzhou University, Fuzhou 350108, China
snbnix@gmail.com
[3] Xidian University, Xi'an 710071, China
yphu@mail.xidian.edu.cn
[4] Guangzhou University, Guangzhou 510006, China
hwjia@gzhu.edu.cn

Abstract. Attribute-based signature (ABS) is a versatile cryptographic primitive that allows a user possessing a set of attributes from the trusted authority to sign a message with fine-grained control over the identifying information, and the signature will reveal nothing no more than the fact that the attributes of the signer satisfy the predicate with respect to the message. In this paper, we introduce a fully secure and efficient attribute-based signature for inner-product (IP) predicate from lattice assumptions in the random oracle model, in which the admissible IP predicate is more general in contrast to those of the existing lattice-based constructions. More precisely, the proposed scheme is the first attribute-based signature from lattices to support conjunctions, disjunctions, threshold predicates, polynomial evaluations, and CNF/DNF formulas.

Keywords: Attribute-based signature · Inner-product predicate · Lattice-based cryptography · Random oracle model

1 Introduction

Attribute-based signatures (ABS), first introduced by Maji et al. in a preliminary version [21], allow a user possessing a set of attributes from a trusted authority to sign some message anonymously, while enjoying a fine-grained control over the identifying information, and the signature can convince the verifier that it was generated by some user with an attribute set satisfying the given signing policy which is usually expressed as a predicate, while the signature will reveal nothing else. As a consequence, ABS has a wide range of real-life applications, such as in attribute-based messaging systems, anonymous authentications, leaking secrets trust-negotiations, and much more (see [22] for more details).

In the past few years, there have been several attempts to realize ABS and its different variants according to the predicates it supports. Maji, Prabhakaran and

© Springer Nature Switzerland AG 2019
J. Vaidya et al. (Eds.): CSS 2019, LNCS 11982, pp. 173–185, 2019.
https://doi.org/10.1007/978-3-030-37337-5_14

Rosulek [21] provided an ABS scheme supporting any monotone access structure predicates, which cover AND, OR, and threshold gates, however, their construction can be only proven secure in the generic group model. Soon afterwards, ABS schemes proven secure in the standard model and supporting flexible threshold predicates were constructed in [6,10,17], then Okamoto and Takashima [24] presented a fully secure ABS scheme supporting non-monotone predicates in the standard model, which means the negation of attributes is allowed. To overcome the drawbacks of multi-authority ABS, Okamoto and Takashima [25] introduced decentralized multi-authority ABS in which no a central authority exists.

More recently, various other useful features have been added to ABS to meet the real-life requirements, such as the traceability [8,13], which allows the tracing authority to recover the identity of signer in the case of dispute; user-controlled linkability [11,12], which allows user to opt to make some signatures directed at the same verifier linkable without sacrificing anonymity; controllable-inkability [26], which means that the signatures can be anonymously linked if in possession of a linking key managed by a trusted entity called a linker; arithmetic branching programs [5], which are an expressive model of arithmetic model of computations between signers and signatures.

Lattice-based cryptography, believed to be the most promising candidate for post-quantum cryptography, has attracted significant interest by the research community, and a large number of schemes are constructed, such as lattice-based group signature schemes [9,18–20] $\cdots$ and attribute-based signature schemes [4, 14,27,28]. However, almost all of the existing lattice-based ABS schemes can only support AND, OR, threshold predicates, and unbounded circuits. To date, one of the central research themes on lattice-based ABS is to expand the expressiveness of the class of signing policies, and thus it remains an open problem to design efficient lattice-based ABS schemes which can support more general admissible predicates.

In this paper, we introduce an efficient ABS scheme for inner-product predicate from lattices to reply to the above problem positively, in which the attributes and predicates are expressed as two vectors $\mathbf{v}$ and $\mathbf{w}$, respectively, and we say that the attribute $\mathbf{v}$ satisfies a given predicate $\mathbf{w}$ if and only if $\langle \mathbf{v}, \mathbf{w} \rangle = c$, where c is some constant. Despite this apparently restrictive structure, while as it was discussed in [15], IP predicate can support conjunctions, disjunctions, hidden- vector predicates, as well as threshold predicates, polynomial evaluations, CNF/DNF formulas. Thus, our construction is believed to quantum-resistant, and in which the admissible predicate is more general in contrast to those of the existing ones. Moreover, it is proven to be fully secure, that is, adaptive-predicate unforgeable and perfectly private, under the hardness assumption of Short Integer Solution (SIS) problem for general lattice in the random oracle model.

2 Preliminaries

NOTATIONS. Assume that all vectors are in a column form. $\mathcal{S}_k$ denotes the set of all permutations of k elements, $\overset{\$}{\leftarrow}$ denotes that sampling elements from a given distribution uniformly at random. Let $\|\cdot\|$ and $\|\cdot\|_\infty$ denote the Euclidean norm (ℓ_2) and infinity norm (ℓ_∞) of a vector, respectively. Given $\mathbf{x} = (x_1, \cdots, x_n)$, and $\mathbf{y} = (y_1, \cdots, y_n) \in \mathbb{R}^n$, Parse$(\mathbf{x}, k_1, k_2)$ denotes $(x_{k_1}, x_{k_1+1}, \cdots, x_{k_2}) \in \mathbb{R}^{k_2-k_1+1}$ for $1 \leq k_1 \leq k_2 \leq n$, we define $\langle \mathbf{x}, \mathbf{y} \rangle = \sum_{i=1}^n x_i \cdot y_i$. $\log a$ denotes the logarithm of a with base 2. The acronym PPT stands for "probabilistic polynomial-time".

2.1 Attribute-Based Signatures for IP Predicate

An attribute-based signature for inner-product predicate (ABS-IP) consists of 4 polynomial-time algorithms.

Syntax of ABS-IP. Let P be an inner-product space over a field F, then four algorithms are described as follows:

Setup(1^λ): A PPT algorithm takes as input a security parameter λ, and outputs a set of public parameters pp and a master secret key msk.

KeyGen(pp, msk, $\mathbf{v}$): A PPT algorithm takes as input the parameters pp, master secret key msk, an attribute vector $\mathbf{v} \in$ P, and outputs a secret key sk$_\mathbf{v}$.

Sign(pp, sk$_\mathbf{v}$, $\mathbf{w}$, M, c): A PPT algorithm takes as input the public parameters pp, a secret key sk$_\mathbf{v}$, a predicate vector $\mathbf{w} \in$ P satisfying $\langle \mathbf{v}, \mathbf{w} \rangle = c$, where $c \in$ F, and a message $M \in \{0, 1\}^*$, and outputs a signature Σ.

Verify(pp, Σ, $\mathbf{w}$, c, M): A deterministic algorithm takes as inputs the public parameters pp, a signature Σ, a message $M \in \{0, 1\}^*$, a predicate vector $\mathbf{w} \in$ P, and outputs either '0' or '1'. The output '1' indicates that Σ is a valid signature on M with respect to $\mathbf{w}$ and c.

Correctness and Security of ABS-IP. As put forward by Maji, Prabhakaran and Rosulek [22], a conventional ABS should satisfies correctness, perfect privacy, and unforgeability. Thus for ABS-IP, these 3 requirements also should be satisfied.

1. Correctness: For all (pp, msk) outputted by Setup, any attribute vector $\mathbf{v} \in$ P, secret key sk$_\mathbf{v} \leftarrow$ KeyGen(pp, msk, $\mathbf{v}$), all claim-predicate vectors $\mathbf{w} \in$ P such that $\langle \mathbf{v}, \mathbf{w} \rangle = c \in$ F and $M \in \{0, 1\}^*$,

$$\text{Verify}(\text{pp}, \text{Sign}(\text{pp}, \text{sk}_\mathbf{v}, \mathbf{w}, M, c), \mathbf{w}, M, c) = 1.$$

2. Perfect privacy: In this game, the goal of adversary $\mathcal{A}$ is to determine which of the two adaptively chosen users with attribute vectors $\mathbf{v}_1 \in$ P and $\mathbf{v}_2 \in$ P, respectively, satisfying $\langle \mathbf{v}_1, \mathbf{w}^* \rangle = \langle \mathbf{v}_2, \mathbf{w}^* \rangle = c^* \in$ F, generated the signature Σ^*. $\mathcal{A}$ is allowed to give access to both secret keys.
   a. Setup: The challenger $\mathcal{C}$ runs Setup to get (pp, msk) and sends them to $\mathcal{A}$.
   b. Challenge: $\mathcal{A}$ outputs a message $M^* \in \{0, 1\}^*$, a predicate vector $\mathbf{w}^* \in$ P, two users with the attribute vectors $\mathbf{v}_1 \in$ P and $\mathbf{v}_2 \in$ P, respectively, both satisfying $\langle \mathbf{v}_1, \mathbf{w}^* \rangle = \langle \mathbf{v}_2, \mathbf{w}^* \rangle = c^* \in$ F. $\mathcal{C}$ chooses a bit $b \xleftarrow{\$} \{0, 1\}$, runs sk$_{\mathbf{v}_b} \leftarrow$ KeyGen(pp, msk, $\mathbf{v}_b$), and computes $\Sigma^* \leftarrow$ Sign(pp, sk$_{\mathbf{v}_b}$, M^*, $\mathbf{w}^*$, c^*) as a signature on M^*, and returns it to $\mathcal{A}$.
   c. Output: $\mathcal{A}$ outputs a bit $b' \in \{0, 1\}$, and wins if $b' = b$.

The advantage of $\mathcal{A}$ wins the above game is defined as $\mathsf{Adv}_{\mathcal{A}}^{\mathsf{priva}} = |\Pr(b' = b) - 1/2|$. Thus, an ABS-IP scheme satisfies the perfect privacy property if $\mathsf{Adv}_{\mathcal{A}}^{\mathsf{priva}}$ is negligible.

3. Unforgeability: In this game, $\mathcal{A}$'s goal is to forge a signature on a message $w.r.t.$ a predicate vector not satisfied by its attribute vector, even if $\mathcal{A}$ pools the coalition attribute vectors together which ensures resistance against collusion.
   a. Setup: $\mathcal{C}$ runs Setup to obtain $(\mathsf{pp}, \mathsf{msk})$, and provides pp to $\mathcal{A}$.
   b. Queries: $\mathcal{A}$ can adaptively make a polynomially bounded number of queries:
      - Corruption: Request for the secret key of user with an attribute vector $\mathbf{v} \in \mathsf{P}$, $\mathcal{C}$ returns $\mathsf{sk}_{\mathbf{v}}$.
      - Signing: Request for a signature on M of user with an attribute vector $\mathbf{v} \in \mathsf{P}$, which satisfies a predicate vector $\mathbf{w}$, $i.e.$, $\langle \mathbf{v}, \mathbf{w} \rangle = c$, here $c \in \mathsf{F}$, then $\mathcal{C}$ returns $\Sigma \leftarrow \mathsf{Sign}(\mathsf{pp}, \mathsf{sk}_{\mathbf{v}}, M, \mathbf{w}, c)$.
   c. Forgery: $\mathcal{A}$ outputs a message $M^* \in \{0, 1\}^*$, a predicate vector $\mathbf{w}^* \in \mathsf{P}$, a constant $c^* \in \mathsf{F}$, and a signature Σ^*. $\mathcal{A}$ wins the game if:
      - $\mathsf{Verify}(\mathsf{pp}, \Sigma^*, \mathbf{w}^*, M^*, c^*) = 1$.
      - $(M^*, \mathbf{w}^*, c^*)$ was never queried to the signing oracle by $\mathcal{A}$.
      - For all queries of $\mathcal{A}$ to the corruption oracle, $\langle \mathbf{v}, \mathbf{w}^* \rangle \neq c^*$.

The advantage of $\mathcal{A}$ is defined as its probability in wining the above game, denoted by $\mathsf{Adv}_{\mathcal{A}}^{\mathsf{unfor}} = \mathsf{SuccPT}_{\mathcal{A}}$. Thus, an ABS-IP scheme satisfies the unofrgeability if $\mathsf{Adv}_{\mathcal{A}}^{\mathsf{unfor}}$ is negligible.

2.2 Background on Lattices

Ajtai [2] first introduced how to obtain a statistically close to uniform matrix $\mathbf{A}$ together with a short trapdoor for $\Lambda_q^{\perp}(\mathbf{A}) = \{\mathbf{e} \in \mathbb{Z}^m \mid \mathbf{A} \cdot \mathbf{e} = \mathbf{0} \bmod q\}$, then two improved algorithms were investigated by [3,23].

Lemma 1 ([2,3,23]). *Let integers $n \geq 1$, $q \geq 2$, and $m = 2n\lceil \log q \rceil$. There exists a PPT algorithm $\mathsf{TrapGen}(q, n, m)$ that outputs $\mathbf{A}$ and $\mathbf{R_A}$, such that $\mathbf{A}$ is statistically close to a uniform matrix in $\mathbb{Z}_q^{n \times m}$ and $\mathbf{R_A}$ is a trapdoor for $\Lambda_q^{\perp}(\mathbf{A})$.*

Lemma 2 ([7,23]). *Let integers $n \geq 1$, $q \geq 2$, and $m = 2n\lceil \log q \rceil$, given $\mathbf{A} \in \mathbb{Z}_q^{n \times m}$, a trapdoor $\mathbf{R_A}$ for $\Lambda_q^{\perp}(\mathbf{A})$, a parameter $s = \omega(\sqrt{n \log q \log n})$ and a vector $\mathbf{u} \in \mathbb{Z}_q^n$, there is a PPT algorithm $\mathsf{SamplePre}(\mathbf{A}, \mathbf{R_A}, \mathbf{u}, s)$ that returns a short vector $\mathbf{e} \in \Lambda_q^{\mathbf{u}}(\mathbf{A})$ sampled from a distribution statistically close to $\mathcal{D}_{\Lambda_q^{\mathbf{u}}(\mathbf{A}), s}$.*

We recall the definition and hardness for short integer solution (SIS) problem.

Definition 1. *The $\mathsf{SIS}_{n,m,q,\beta}^{\infty}$ problem is: Given a uniformly random matrix $\mathbf{A} \in \mathbb{Z}_q^{n \times m}$ and a real $\beta > 0$, to find a short non-zero integer vector $\mathbf{e} \in \mathbb{Z}^m$ such that $\mathbf{A} \cdot \mathbf{e} = \mathbf{0} \bmod q$ and $\|\mathbf{e}\|_{\infty} \leq \beta$.*

Lemma 3 ([7]). *For m, $\beta = \mathsf{poly}(n)$, and $q \geq \beta \cdot \widetilde{\mathcal{O}}(\sqrt{n})$, the average-case $\mathsf{SIS}^\infty_{n,m,q,\beta}$ problem is at least as hard as the SIVP_γ problem in the worst-case to within $\gamma = \beta \cdot \widetilde{\mathcal{O}}(\sqrt{nm})$ factor.*

We recall a new sampling algorithm used in the security proofs of this work.

Lemma 4 ([1]). *Let $q \geq 3$, $m > n$, $\mathbf{A}, \mathbf{B} \in \mathbb{Z}_q^{n \times m}$ and a real $s \geq \|\widetilde{\mathbf{R_B}}\| \cdot \sqrt{m} \cdot \omega(\log m)$. There is a PPT algorithm $\mathsf{SampleRight}(\mathbf{A}, \mathbf{B}, \mathbf{R}, \mathbf{R_B}, \mathbf{u}, s)$ that given a trapdoor $\mathbf{R_B}$ for $\Lambda_q^\perp(\mathbf{B})$, a low-norm matrix $\mathbf{R} \in \mathbb{Z}_q^{m \times m}$, and a vector $\mathbf{u} \in \mathbb{Z}_q^n$, outputs $\mathbf{e} \in \mathbb{Z}^{2m}$ distributed statistically close to $\mathcal{D}_{\Lambda_q^\mathbf{u}([\mathbf{A}|\mathbf{AR}+\mathbf{B}]),s}$.*

3 The Underlying Interactive Protocol

In this section, we present an efficient proof of knowledge protocol (one main building block for our construction in Sect. 4), which allows the prover $\mathcal{P}$ to convince verifier $\mathcal{V}$ that $\mathcal{P}$ is a valid user who signed a message (*i.e.*, $\mathcal{P}$'s attribute vector satisfies the predicate vector, and $\mathcal{P}$ has a valid signing secret key).

3.1 Some Sets and Matrices

We define some sets and matrices as follows:

1. $\mathsf{B}_{2\ell}$: the set of all vectors in $\{0,1\}^{2\ell}$ having the Hamming weight ℓ.
2. B_{3m}: the set of all vectors in $\{-1,0,1\}^{3m}$ having the same number of -1, 0, and 1, namely, m coordinates -1, m coordinates 1 and m coordinates 0.
3. $\mathbf{G}_{n \times n\lceil \log q \rceil}$: a power-of-two matrix,

$$
\mathbf{G}_{n \times n\lceil \log q \rceil} = \begin{pmatrix} 1\,2\cdots 2^{\lceil \log q \rceil - 1} \\ \vdots \\ 1\,2\cdots 2^{\lceil \log q \rceil - 1} \end{pmatrix} \in \mathbb{Z}_q^{n \times n\lceil \log q \rceil}.
$$

Thus, for $\mathbf{e} = (e_1, e_2, \cdots, e_n) \in \mathbb{Z}_q^n$, $\mathbf{e} = \mathbf{G}_{n \times n|\log q\rceil} \cdot \mathsf{bin}(\mathbf{e})$, where $\mathsf{bin}(\mathbf{e}) \in \{0,1\}^{n\lceil \log q \rceil}$ denotes the binary representation of $\mathbf{e}$.

3.2 Some Techniques

As in [20], we introduce the **Decomposition-Extension** technique and **Matrix-Extension** technique.

For $\beta > 0$, let $k = \lfloor \log \beta \rfloor + 1$, $\beta_1 = \lceil \beta/2 \rceil$, $\beta_2 = \lceil (\beta - \beta_1)/2 \rceil$, $\cdots$, $\beta_k = 1$.

Extension: Given a vector $\mathbf{e} = (e_1, e_2, \cdots, e_m) \in \{0,1\}^m$, the goal is to extend it to $\mathbf{e}' \in \mathsf{B}_{2m}$. The procedure Ext_m proceeds as follows:

1. Denote the numbers of coordinates 0 and 1 in $\mathbf{e}$ are λ_0 and λ_1, respectively.
2. Pick a binary vector $\tilde{\mathbf{e}} \in \{0,1\}^m$, which has exactly $(m - \lambda_0)$ coordinates 0 and $(m - \lambda_1)$ coordinates 1.

3. Let $\mathbf{e}' = (\mathbf{e}, \tilde{\mathbf{e}})$. It is easy to see: for any permutation $\pi \in \mathcal{S}_{2m}$, $\mathbf{e}' \in \mathsf{B}_{2m} \Leftrightarrow \pi(\mathbf{e}') \in \mathsf{B}_{2m}$.

Decomposition-Extension: Given $\mathbf{e} = (e_1, e_2, \cdots, e_m) \in \mathbb{Z}^m$, $\|\mathbf{e}\|_\infty \leq \beta$, the goal is to represent it by k vectors in B_{3mk}. The procedure $\mathsf{Dec\text{-}Ext}_{m,\beta}$ proceeds as follows:

1. For $i \in \{1, 2, \cdots, m\}$, express e_i as $\sum_{j=1}^k \beta_j e_{i,j}$, where $e_{i,j} \in \{-1, 0, 1\}$.
2. For $i \in \{1, 2, \cdots, m\}$, define $\hat{\mathbf{e}}_i = (e_{i,1}, e_{i,2}, \cdots, e_{i,k})$ and denote the numbers of coordinates -1, 0 and 1 in $\hat{\mathbf{e}}_i$ are $\lambda_{i,-1}$, $\lambda_{i,0}$ and $\lambda_{i,1}$, respectively.
3. For $i \in \{1, 2, \cdots, m\}$, choose a vector $\tilde{\mathbf{e}}_i \in \{-1, 0, 1\}^{2k}$ which has $(k - \lambda_{i,-1})$ coordinates -1, $(k - \lambda_{i,0})$ coordinates 0 and $(k - \lambda_{i,1})$ coordinates 1.
4. Let $\mathbf{e}' = (\hat{\mathbf{e}}_1, \hat{\mathbf{e}}_2, \cdots, \hat{\mathbf{e}}_m, \tilde{\mathbf{e}}_1, \tilde{\mathbf{e}}_2, \cdots, \tilde{\mathbf{e}}_m) \in \mathsf{B}_{3mk}$, and we define a matrix,

$$\mathbf{K}_{m,\beta} = \begin{pmatrix} \beta_1 \beta_2 \cdots \beta_k & & \\ & \vdots & \\ & & \beta_1 \beta_2 \cdots \beta_k \end{pmatrix} \in \mathbb{Z}^{m \times mk}.$$

Then, we define an extension of $\mathbf{K}_{m,\beta}$ as $\mathbf{K}'_{m,\beta} = [\mathbf{K}_{m,\beta} | \mathbf{0}^{m \times 2mk}] \in \mathbb{Z}^{m \times 3mk}$. Thus we have that $\mathbf{e} = \mathbf{K}'_{m,\beta} \cdot \mathbf{e}'$, and observe that for any permutation $\varphi \in \mathcal{S}_{3mk}$, $\mathbf{e}' \in \mathsf{B}_{3mk} \Leftrightarrow \varphi(\mathbf{e}') \in \mathsf{B}_{3mk}$.

Matrix-Extension: Given $\mathbf{A}' = [\mathbf{A} | \mathbf{A}_0 | \mathbf{A}_1 | \cdots | \mathbf{A}_\ell]$, the goal is to extend it to $\mathbf{A}^* \in \mathbb{Z}_q^{n \times (2\ell+2)3mk}$. The procedure $\mathsf{Matrix\text{-}Ext}$ proceeds as follows:

1. Multiply each of component-matrices by $\mathbf{K}'_{m,\beta}$ and add ℓ blocks of $\mathbf{0}^{n \times 3mk}$.
2. Output $\mathbf{A}^* = [\mathbf{A} \cdot \mathbf{K}'_{m,\beta} | \mathbf{A}_0 \cdot \mathbf{K}'_{m,\beta} | \cdots | \mathbf{A}_\ell \cdot \mathbf{K}'_{m,\beta} | \mathbf{0}^{n \times 3\ell mk}] \in \mathbb{Z}_q^{n \times (6\ell+6)mk}$.

3.3   The Underlying Protocol

Let $m = 2n\lceil \log q \rceil$, the underlying protocol can be summarized as follows:

1. The public inputs are: $\mathbf{A}$, $\{\mathbf{A}_i\}_{i=0}^\ell$, $\mathbf{D} \in \mathbb{Z}_q^{n \times m}$, $\mathbf{D}_1, \mathbf{D}_2 \in \mathbb{Z}_q^{2n \times 2m}$, $\mathbf{u} \in \mathbb{Z}_q^n$, and a predicate vector $\mathbf{w} = (w_1, w_2, \cdots, w_{4n}) \in \mathbb{Z}_q^{4n}$ with a constant $c \in \mathbb{Z}_q$.
2. The witness are: $\mathbf{t} = (t_1, t_2, \cdots, t_\ell) \in \{0, 1\}^\ell$, $\mathbf{v} = (v_1, v_2, \cdots, v_{4n}) \in \mathbb{Z}_q^{4n}$, $\mathbf{s} \in \mathbb{Z}^{2m}$, and $\mathbf{e} = (\mathbf{e}_1, \mathbf{e}_2) \in \mathbb{Z}^m \times \mathbb{Z}^m$, where $\|\mathbf{s}\|_\infty, \|\mathbf{e}\|_\infty \leq \beta$.
3. The goal of $\mathcal{P}$ is to convince $\mathcal{V}$ in zero-knowledge that:
   a. $\mathbf{A} \cdot \mathbf{e}_1 + \mathbf{A}_0 \cdot \mathbf{e}_2 + \sum_{i=1}^\ell \mathbf{A}_i \cdot t_i \mathbf{e}_2 - \mathbf{D} \cdot \mathsf{bin}(\mathbf{D}_0 \cdot \mathbf{s} + \mathbf{D}_1 \cdot \mathsf{bin}(\mathbf{v})) = \mathbf{u} \bmod q$.
   b. $\langle \mathbf{v}, \mathbf{w} \rangle = c \bmod q$.

We now proceed in the following 3 steps:

1. To transform the equation in a to the form $\mathbf{P} \cdot \mathbf{z} = \mathbf{u}' \bmod q$, where $\|\mathbf{z}\|_\infty = 1$ and $\mathbf{z} \in \mathsf{Valid}$, where Valid is a specially set and defined in the next part.

Let $\mathbf{y} = \text{bin}(\mathbf{c}'_{\mathbf{v}} = \mathbf{D}_0 \cdot \mathbf{s} + \mathbf{D}_1 \cdot \text{bin}(\mathbf{v})) \in \{0,1\}^m$, and $\tilde{\mathbf{v}} = \text{bin}(\mathbf{v}) \in \{0,1\}^{2m}$, then we have $\mathbf{G}_{2n \times m} \cdot \mathbf{y} = \mathbf{D}_0 \cdot \mathbf{s} + \mathbf{D}_1 \cdot \tilde{\mathbf{v}} \bmod q$, and a can be rewritten as:

$$\mathbf{A} \cdot \mathbf{e}_1 + \mathbf{A}_0 \cdot \mathbf{e}_2 + \sum_{i=1}^{\ell} \mathbf{A}_i \cdot t_i \mathbf{e}_2 + \begin{pmatrix} -\mathbf{D} \\ -\mathbf{G}_{2n \times m} \end{pmatrix} \cdot \mathbf{y} + \mathbf{D}_0 \cdot \mathbf{s} + \mathbf{D}_1 \cdot \tilde{\mathbf{v}} = \mathbf{u} \bmod q. \quad (1)$$

Next, we transform (1) by using Ext, Dex-Ext, Matrix-Ext techniques from Sect. 3.2, and do the following:

$$\begin{cases} \mathbf{e}'_1 \in \mathsf{B}_{3mk} \leftarrow \text{Dec-Ext}_{m,\beta}(\mathbf{e}_1), \mathbf{e}'_2 \in \mathsf{B}_{3mk} \leftarrow \text{Dec-Ext}_{m,\beta}(\mathbf{e}_2), \\ \mathbf{y}' \in \mathsf{B}_{2m} \leftarrow \text{Ext}_m(\mathbf{y}), \mathbf{s}' \in \mathsf{B}_{6mk} \leftarrow \text{Dec-Ext}_{2m,\beta}(\mathbf{s}), \\ \mathbf{t}' = (t_1, t_2, \cdots, t_{2\ell}) \in \mathsf{B}_{2\ell} \leftarrow \text{Ext}_\ell(\mathbf{t}), \mathbf{v}' \in \mathsf{B}_{4m} \leftarrow \text{Ext}_{2m}(\tilde{\mathbf{v}}), \\ \mathbf{A}^* = [\mathbf{A} \cdot \mathbf{K}'_{m,\beta} | \mathbf{A}_0 \cdot \mathbf{K}'_{m,\beta} | \cdots | \mathbf{A}_\ell \cdot \mathbf{K}'_{m,\beta} | \mathbf{0}^{n \times 3\ell mk}] \in \mathbb{Z}_q^{n \times (6\ell+6)mk}, \\ \begin{pmatrix} -\mathbf{D}^* \\ -\mathbf{G}^*_{2n \times m} = \begin{pmatrix} -\mathbf{G}^{*0}_{2n \times m} \\ -\mathbf{G}^{*1}_{2n \times m} \end{pmatrix} \end{pmatrix} = \begin{pmatrix} -\mathbf{G}_{n \times n \lceil \log q \rceil} | \mathbf{0}^{n \times m} \\ -\mathbf{G}_{2n \times m} | \mathbf{0}^{2n \times m} \end{pmatrix} \in \mathbb{Z}_q^{3n \times 2m}, \\ \mathbf{D}_0^* = \mathbf{D}_0 \cdot \mathbf{K}'_{2m,\beta} \in \mathbb{Z}_q^{2n \times 6mk}, \mathbf{D}_1^* = (\mathbf{D}_1 | \mathbf{0}^{2n \times 2m}) \in \mathbb{Z}_q^{2n \times 4m}. \end{cases}$$

Let $d = 6m(\ell k + 2k + 1)$, and we construct a following matrix,

$$\mathbf{P} = \left(\begin{pmatrix} \mathbf{A}^* \\ \mathbf{0}^{n \times (6\ell+6)mk} \\ \mathbf{0}^{n \times (6\ell+6)mk} \end{pmatrix} \middle| \begin{pmatrix} -\mathbf{D}^* \\ -\mathbf{G}^{*0}_{2n \times m} \\ -\mathbf{G}^{*1}_{2n \times m} \end{pmatrix} \middle| \begin{array}{c} \mathbf{D}_0^* \\ \mathbf{0}^{n \times 6mk} \end{array} \middle| \begin{array}{c} \mathbf{D}_1^* \\ \mathbf{0}^{n \times 4m} \end{array} \right) \in \mathbb{Z}_q^{3n \times d},$$

two vectors $\mathbf{z} = (\mathbf{e}'_1, \mathbf{e}'_2, t_1 \mathbf{e}'_2, t_2 \mathbf{e}'_2 \cdots, t_{2\ell} \mathbf{e}'_2, \mathbf{y}', \mathbf{s}', \mathbf{v}')$ and $\mathbf{u}' = \begin{pmatrix} \mathbf{u} \\ \mathbf{0}^{2n} \end{pmatrix}$, thus, we have that $\mathbf{P} \cdot \mathbf{z} = \mathbf{u}' \bmod q$.

We now define Valid, a set owning the following form,

$$\mathbf{x} = (\mathbf{x}_1, \mathbf{x}_2, g_1 \mathbf{x}_2, \cdots, g_{2\ell} \mathbf{x}_2, \mathbf{x}_3, \mathbf{x}_4, \mathbf{x}_5) \in \{-1, 0, 1\}^d,$$

where $\mathbf{x}_1, \mathbf{x}_2 \in \mathsf{B}_{3mk}$, $\mathbf{g} = (y_1, y_2, \cdots, g_{2\ell}) \in \mathsf{B}_{2\ell}$, $\mathbf{x}_3 \in \mathsf{B}_{2m}$, $\mathbf{x}_4 \in \mathsf{B}_{6mk}$, and $\mathbf{x}_5 \in \mathsf{B}_{4m}$. So it is easy to check that: $\mathbf{z} \in$ Valid.
2. To specify a set $\mathcal{S}$ and a permutation $\mathcal{T}_\pi$ of d elements, where $\pi \in \mathcal{S}$.
   1. Define $\mathcal{S} = \mathcal{S}_{3mk} \times \mathcal{S}_{3mk} \times \mathcal{S}_{2\ell} \times \mathcal{S}_{2m} \times \mathcal{S}_{6mk} \times \mathcal{S}_{4m}$.
   2. For $\pi = (\phi, \varphi, \gamma, \rho, \psi, \eta) \in \mathcal{S}$, $\mathbf{e} = (\mathbf{e}_0, \mathbf{e}'_0, \mathbf{e}_1, \mathbf{e}_2, \cdots, \mathbf{e}_{2\ell}, \mathbf{k}_1, \mathbf{k}_2, \mathbf{k}_3) \in \mathbb{Z}_q^d$, $\mathbf{e}_0, \mathbf{e}'_0, \mathbf{e}_1, \mathbf{e}_2, \cdots, \mathbf{e}_{2\ell} \in \mathbb{Z}_q^{3mk}$, $\mathbf{k}_1 \in \mathbb{Z}_q^{2m}$, $\mathbf{k}_2 \in \mathbb{Z}_q^{6mk}$, $\mathbf{k}_3 \in \mathbb{Z}_q^{4m}$, define:

$$\mathcal{T}_\pi(\mathbf{e}) = (\phi(\mathbf{e}_0), \varphi(\mathbf{e}'_0), \varphi(\mathbf{e}_{\gamma(1)}), \cdots, \varphi(\mathbf{e}_{\gamma(2\ell)}), \rho(\mathbf{k}_1), \psi(\mathbf{k}_2), \eta(\mathbf{k}_3)).$$

Thus, it is easy to check that: $\mathbf{z} \in$ Valid $\Leftrightarrow \mathcal{T}_\pi(\mathbf{z}) \in$ Valid.
3. To prove the equation in b, i.e., the knowledge of $\mathbf{v} = (v_1, v_2, \cdots, v_{4n}) \in \mathbb{Z}_q^{4n}$. Let $\tilde{\mathbf{v}} = \text{bin}(\mathbf{v}) \in \{0,1\}^{2m}$, we have $\mathbf{v} = \mathbf{G}_{4n \times 2m} \cdot \tilde{\mathbf{v}}$, the equation in b can be equivalently rewritten as $\langle \mathbf{G}_{4n \times 2m} \cdot \tilde{\mathbf{v}}, \mathbf{w} \rangle = c \bmod q$. We further transform it as follows: $\mathbf{v}' \leftarrow \text{Ext}_{2m}(\tilde{\mathbf{v}})$, $\mathbf{G}^*_{4n \times 2m} = (\mathbf{G}_{4n \times 2m} | \mathbf{0}^{4n \times 2m}) \in \mathbb{Z}_q^{4n \times 4m}$. Now we have $\langle \mathbf{G}^*_{4n \times 2m} \cdot \mathbf{v}', \mathbf{w} \rangle = \langle \mathbf{v}, \mathbf{w} \rangle = c \bmod q$.

Putting the above techniques together, we can derive a Stern-type statistical zero-knowledge argument of knowledge (ZKAoK) for the relations a and b from the following combined interactive protocol.

In our ABS-IP construction, we utilize a statistically hiding, computationally blinding commitment scheme (COM) as proposed in [16]. For simplicity, we omit the randomness of the commitment and the details of the protocol are as follows:

1. **Commitments:** The prover $\mathcal{P}$ samples the following random objects:

$$\mathbf{r} \xleftarrow{\$} \mathbb{Z}_q^{6m(\ell k+2k+1)}; \phi, \varphi \xleftarrow{\$} S_{3mk}; \gamma \xleftarrow{\$} S_{2\ell}; \rho \xleftarrow{\$} S_{2m}; \psi \xleftarrow{\$} S_{6mk}; \eta \xleftarrow{\$} S_{4m}.$$

Let $\pi = (\phi, \varphi, \gamma, \rho, \psi, \eta)$, $\mathbf{r}' = \mathsf{Parse}(\mathbf{r}, 2m(3\ell k + 6k + 1), 6m(\ell k + 2k + 1))$. $\mathcal{P}$ sends the commitment $\mathsf{CMT} = (\mathbf{c}_1, \mathbf{c}_2, \mathbf{c}_3)$ to $\mathcal{V}$, where

$$\begin{cases} \mathbf{c}_1 = \mathsf{COM}(\pi, \mathbf{P} \cdot \mathbf{r} \bmod q, \langle \mathbf{G}^*_{4n \times 2m} \cdot \mathbf{r}', \mathbf{w} \rangle \bmod q), \\ \mathbf{c}_2 = \mathsf{COM}(\mathcal{T}_\pi(\mathbf{r})), \\ \mathbf{c}_3 = \mathsf{COM}(\mathcal{T}_\pi(\mathbf{r} + \mathbf{z})). \end{cases}$$

2. **Challenge:** $\mathcal{V}$ chooses a challenge $Ch \xleftarrow{\$} \{1, 2, 3\}$ and sends it to $\mathcal{P}$.
3. **Response:** Depending on the challenge Ch, $\mathcal{P}$ replies as follows:
   - $Ch = 1$. Let $\mathbf{t_z} = \mathcal{T}_\pi(\mathbf{z})$, $\mathbf{t_r} = \mathcal{T}_\pi(\mathbf{r})$, define:

$$\mathsf{RSP} = (\mathbf{t_z}, \mathbf{t_r}).$$

   - $Ch = 2$. Let $\pi_1 = \pi$, $\mathbf{y} = \mathbf{z} + \mathbf{r} \bmod q$, define:

$$\mathsf{RSP} = (\pi_1, \mathbf{y}).$$

   - $Ch = 3$. Let $\pi_2 = \pi$, $\mathbf{r}_1 = \mathbf{r}$, define:

$$\mathsf{RSP} = (\pi_2, \mathbf{r}_1).$$

4. **Verification:** Receiving the response RSP, $\mathcal{V}$ checks as follows:
   - $Ch = 1$. Parse $\mathsf{RSP} = (\mathbf{t_z}, \mathbf{t_r})$, and check that:

$$\mathbf{t_z} \in \mathsf{Valid}, \mathbf{c}_2 = \mathsf{COM}(\mathbf{t_r}), \mathbf{c}_3 = \mathsf{COM}(\mathbf{t_z} + \mathbf{t_r}).$$

   - $Ch = 2$. Parse $\mathsf{RSP} = (\pi_1, \mathbf{y})$, let $\mathbf{y}' = \mathsf{Parse}(\mathbf{y}, 2m(3\ell k + 6k + 1), 6m(\ell k + 2k + 1))$, and check that: $\mathbf{c}_3 = \mathsf{COM}(\mathcal{T}_{\pi_1}(\mathbf{y}))$,

$$\mathbf{c}_1 = \mathsf{COM}\left(\pi_1, \mathbf{P} \cdot \mathbf{y} - \begin{pmatrix} \mathbf{u} \\ \mathbf{0}^{2n} \end{pmatrix} \bmod q, \langle \mathbf{G}^*_{4n \times 2m} \cdot \mathbf{y}', \mathbf{w} \rangle - c \bmod q\right).$$

   - $Ch = 3$. Parse $\mathsf{RSP} = (\pi_2, \mathbf{r}_1)$, let $\mathbf{r}'_1 = \mathsf{Parse}(\mathbf{r}_1, 2m(3\ell k + 6k + 1), 6m(\ell k + 2k + 1))$, and check that: $\mathbf{c}_2 = \mathsf{COM}(\mathcal{T}_{\pi_2}(\mathbf{r}_1))$,

$$\mathbf{c}_1 = \mathsf{COM}(\pi_2, \mathbf{P} \cdot \mathbf{r}_1 \bmod q, \langle \mathbf{G}^*_{4n \times 2m} \cdot \mathbf{r}', \mathbf{w} \rangle \bmod q).$$

In its each case, $\mathcal{V}$ outputs '1' iff all the conditions hold, otherwise '0'. The following theorem gives a detailed analysis of the above protocol.

Theorem 1. *Let* COM *(as proposed in [16]) be a statistically hiding and computationally binding commitment scheme, for a given commitment* CMT, *3 valid responses* RSP_1, RSP_2, RSP_3 *with respect to 3 different values of challenge* Ch, *the proposed protocol is a statistical ZKAoK for the relations* a *and* b, *and its each round has perfect completeness, soundness error 2/3, argument of knowledge property and communication cost* $\mathcal{O}(\ell m \log \beta) \log q = \widetilde{\mathcal{O}}(\ell n \log \beta)$.

The proof employs a list of standard techniques for Stern-type protocol as in [16,20], and due to the limited space, the proof is omitted here, if any necessary, please contact the corresponding author for the full version.

4   The ABS-IP Scheme from Lattices

4.1   Description of the Scheme

– Setup(1^λ): Take input the security parameter λ, set $n = \mathcal{O}(\lambda)$, $m = 2n\lceil \log q \rceil$, $\ell = \mathcal{O}(\log \lambda)$, $q = \widetilde{\mathcal{O}}(\ell n^3)$, $s = \omega(\sqrt{n \log q \log n})$, and $\beta = s \cdot \omega(\log m)$. This algorithm specifies the following steps:
  1. Run TrapGen(q, n, m) to obtain $\mathbf{A} \in \mathbb{Z}_q^{n \times m}$ and a trapdoor $\mathbf{R_A}$ of $\Lambda_q^\perp(\mathbf{A})$.
  2. Sample $\ell + 1$ random matrices $\mathbf{A}_0, \mathbf{A}_1, \mathbf{A}_2, \cdots, \mathbf{A}_\ell \xleftarrow{\$} \mathbb{Z}_q^{n \times m}$.
  3. Sample 3 matrices $\mathbf{D} \xleftarrow{\$} \mathbb{Z}_q^{n \times m}$, $\mathbf{D}_0, \mathbf{D}_1 \xleftarrow{\$} \mathbb{Z}_q^{2n \times 2m}$, and a vector $\mathbf{u} \xleftarrow{\$} \mathbb{Z}_q^n$.
  4. Let $\mathcal{H} : \{0,1\}^* \to \{1,2,3\}^{k' = \omega(\log n)}$ be a hash function as a random oracle.
  5. Output $\mathsf{pp} = (\mathbf{A}, \{\mathbf{A}_i\}_{i=0}^\ell, \mathbf{D}, \mathbf{D}_0, \mathbf{D}_1, \mathbf{u}, \mathcal{H})$, and $\mathsf{msk} = \mathbf{R_A}$.

– KeyGen($\mathsf{pp}, \mathsf{msk}, \mathbf{v}$): Take input the public parameters pp, the master secret key msk, and an attribute vector $\mathbf{v} = (v_1, v_2, \cdots, v_{4n}) \in \mathbb{Z}_q^{4n}$. This algorithm specifies the following steps:
  1. Sample a random binary string $\mathbf{t} = (t_1, t_2, \cdots, t_\ell) \xleftarrow{\$} [0,1]^\ell$.
  2. Let $\mathbf{A_t} = [\mathbf{A} | \mathbf{A}_0 + \sum_{i=1}^\ell t_i \mathbf{A}_i]$, sample a Gaussian vector $\mathbf{s} \xleftarrow{\$} \mathcal{D}_{\mathbb{Z}^{2m}, s}$.
  4. Let $\mathbf{c_v} = \mathbf{D}_0 \cdot \mathbf{s} + \mathbf{D}_1 \cdot \mathsf{bin}(\mathbf{v}) \in \mathbb{Z}_q^{2n}$, and $\mathbf{u_v} = \mathbf{u} + \mathbf{D} \cdot \mathsf{bin}(\mathbf{c_v}) \in \mathbb{Z}_q^n$.
  5. Sample $\mathbf{e}_2 \xleftarrow{\$} \mathcal{D}_{\mathbb{Z}^m, s}$, and let $\mathbf{u}' = (\mathbf{A}_0 + \sum_{i=1}^\ell t_i \mathbf{A}_i) \cdot \mathbf{e}_2 \bmod q$. Then run SamplePre($\mathbf{A}, \mathbf{R_A}, \mathbf{u_v} - \mathbf{u}', s$) to obtain $\mathbf{e}_1 \in \mathbb{Z}^m$.
  6. Let $\mathbf{e} = (\mathbf{e}_1, \mathbf{e}_2) \in \mathbb{Z}^{2m}$, thus $\mathbf{A_t} \cdot \mathbf{e} = \mathbf{u_v} \bmod q$, and $0 < \|\mathbf{e}\|_\infty \leq \beta$.
  7. Output the secret key $\mathsf{sk_v} = (\mathbf{t}, \mathbf{e}, \mathbf{s}) \in \{0,1\}^\ell \times \mathbb{Z}^{2m} \times \mathbb{Z}^{2m}$.

– Sign($\mathsf{pp}, \mathsf{sk_v}, \mathbf{w}, M, c$): Take input the public parameters pp, the signing secret key $\mathsf{sk_v}$, a predicate vector $\mathbf{w} = (w_1, w_2, \cdots, w_{4n}) \in \mathbb{Z}_q^{4n}$, a constant $c \in \mathbb{Z}_q$ and a message $M \in \{0,1\}^*$. This algorithm specifies the following steps:
  1. If $\langle \mathbf{v}, \mathbf{w} \rangle \neq c \bmod q$, then output $\perp$ and abort.

2. Otherwise, generate a valid non-interactive zero-knowledge proofs protocol to show the possession of $(\mathbf{v}, \mathbf{t}, \mathbf{s}, \mathbf{e})$ satisfying:

$$\begin{cases} \mathbf{t} \in \{0,1\}^{\ell}, \mathbf{e} = (\mathbf{e}_1, \mathbf{e}_2) \in \mathbb{Z}^m \times \mathbb{Z}^m, \|\mathbf{e}\|_{\infty} \le \beta, \\ \mathrm{bin}(\mathbf{v}) \in \{0,1\}^{2m}, \mathbf{s} \in \mathbb{Z}^{2m}, \|\mathbf{s}\|_{\infty} \le \beta, \langle \mathbf{v}, \mathbf{w} \rangle = c \bmod q, \\ \mathbf{A} \cdot \mathbf{e}_1 + \mathbf{A}_0 \cdot \mathbf{e}_2 + \sum_{i=1}^{\ell} \mathbf{A}_i \cdot t_i \mathbf{e}_2 - \mathbf{D} \cdot \mathrm{bin}(\mathbf{D}_0 \mathbf{s} + \mathbf{D}_1 \mathrm{bin}(\mathbf{v})) = \mathbf{u} \bmod q. \end{cases}$$

This can be achieved by repeating $k' = \omega(\log n)$ times the interactive pro-
tocol as in Sect. 3.3 with the public inputs $(\mathbf{A}, \{\mathbf{A}_i\}_{i=0}^{\ell}, \mathbf{D}, \mathbf{D}_0, \mathbf{D}_1, \mathbf{u}, \mathbf{w}, c)$
and the witness $(\mathbf{v}, \mathbf{t}, \mathbf{s}, \mathbf{e})$, then it is made non-interactive via the Fiat-
Shamir heuristic as a tripe $\Pi = (\{\mathsf{CMT}_i\}_{i=1}^{k'}, \mathsf{CH}, \{\mathsf{RSP}_i\}_{i=1}^{k'})$, where
$\mathsf{CH} = \{Ch_i\}_{i=1}^{k'} = \mathcal{H}(M, \mathbf{A}, \{\mathbf{A}_i\}_{i=0}^{\ell}, \mathbf{D}, \mathbf{D}_0, \mathbf{D}_1, \mathbf{u}, \mathbf{w}, c, \{\mathsf{CMT}_i\}_{i=1}^{k'})$.
3. Output the signature $\Sigma = (M, \mathbf{w}, c, \Pi)$.

- Verify($\mathsf{pp}, M, \mathbf{w}, \Sigma, c$): Take input the parameters pp, a signature Σ on a message $M \in \{0,1\}^*$ with a predicate vector $\mathbf{w} = (w_1, w_2, \cdots, w_{4n}) \in \mathbb{Z}_q^{4n}$, and
  a constant $c \in \mathbb{Z}_q$, the verifier specifies the following steps:
  1. Parse the signature $\Sigma = (M, \mathbf{w}, c, \{\mathsf{CMT}_i\}_{i=1}^{k'}, \mathsf{CH}, \{\mathsf{RSP}_i\}_{i=1}^{k'})$.
  2. Check that if

$$\mathsf{CH} = \{Ch_i\}_{i=1}^{k'} = \mathcal{H}(M, \mathbf{A}, \{\mathbf{A}_i\}_{i=0}^{\ell}, \mathbf{D}, \mathbf{D}_0, \mathbf{D}_1, \mathbf{u}, \mathbf{w}, c, \{\mathsf{CMT}_i\}_{i=1}^{k'}).$$

  3. For $i \in \{1, 2, \cdots, k'\}$, run the verification step of the protocol from
     Sect. 3.3 to check the validity of RSP_i with respect to CMT_i and Ch_i.
  4. If the above are satisfied, output '1' and accept Σ, otherwise reject it.

4.2 Analysis of the Scheme

Efficiency and Correctness: The proposed ABS-IP scheme can be implemented in
polynomial time, we analyze its efficiency, with respect to security parameter λ.

- The public parameters pp has bit-size $\mathcal{O}(\ell n m \log q) = \ell \cdot \widetilde{\mathcal{O}}(\lambda^2)$.
- The signing secret key $\mathsf{sk_v}$ has bit-size $\mathcal{O}(\ell + m \log q) = \widetilde{\mathcal{O}}(\lambda)$.
- The bite-size of signature Σ is dominated by that of the Stern-type statistical
  ZKAoK Π, roughly $k' = \omega(\log n)$ time the communication cost of interactive
  protocol in Sect. 3.3, which is $\ell \cdot \widetilde{\mathcal{O}}(\lambda)$ for the chosen parameters. This is also
  the asymptotical bound on the size of the signature Σ.

The correctness of algorithm Verify follows from the facts that any user with a
valid signing secret key corresponding to an attribute vector satisfying the given
inner-product predicate is able to compute a satisfying witness for the relations
a and b, and the underlying argument system is perfectly complete.

Perfect privacy: For the Perfect privacy, we show the following theorem.

Theorem 2. *If* COM *is a statistically hiding commitment scheme, the proposed
scheme satisfies perfect privacy property in the random oracle model.*

Proof. To proof this theorem, we define two games as follows:

Game 0: It is the original privacy game, the challenger $\mathcal{C}$ honestly does as follows:

1. Run Setup to obtain $(\mathsf{pp}, \mathsf{msk})$, and send them to adversary $\mathcal{A}$.
2. $\mathcal{A}$ outputs a message $M^* \in \{0,1\}^*$, a predicate vector $\mathbf{w}^* \in \mathbb{Z}_q^{4n}$, and two users with the attribute vectors $\mathbf{v}_1, \mathbf{v}_2 \in \mathbb{Z}_q^{4n}$, respectively, both of which satisfying $\langle \mathbf{v}_1, \mathbf{w}^* \rangle = \langle \mathbf{v}_2, \mathbf{w}^* \rangle = c^* \bmod q$, where $c^* \in \mathbb{Z}_q$ is a constant.
3. $\mathcal{C}$ picks a random bit $b \xleftarrow{\$} \{0,1\}$, samples a random vector $\mathbf{t}_b \xleftarrow{\$} \{0,1\}^\ell$, computes $\mathsf{sk}_{\mathbf{v}_b} \leftarrow \mathsf{KeyGen}(\mathsf{pp}, \mathbf{v}_b, \mathsf{msk})$, and generates the signature $\Sigma^* = \mathsf{Sign}(\mathsf{pp}, \mathbf{w}^*, \mathsf{sk}_{\mathbf{v}_b}, M^*, c^*) = (M^*, \mathbf{w}^*, c^*, \Pi)$, and returns Σ^* to $\mathcal{A}$.
4. Finally, $\mathcal{A}$ outputs a bit $b' \in \{0,1\}$.

Game 1: $\mathcal{C}$ does as in Game 0, except that it simulates the signature generation in Step 3 of Game 0 by appropriately programming the random oracle:

1. The simulation algorithm does as in the proof of Theorem 1, and the underlying interactive protocol will be repeated $k' = \omega(\log n)$ times. $\mathcal{C}$ programs the random oracle $\mathcal{H}(M^*, \mathbf{A}, \{\mathbf{A}_i\}_{i=0}^\ell, \mathbf{D}, \mathbf{D}_0, \mathbf{D}_1, \mathbf{u}, \mathbf{w}^*, c^*, \{\mathsf{CMT}_i\}_{i=1}^{k'}) = (Ch_1, \cdots, Ch_{k'})$, and due to the statistically zero-knowledge of underlying argument of knowledge, the distribution of Π^* is statistically close to Π.
2. $\mathcal{C}$ outputs a simulated signature $\widehat{\Sigma}^* = (M^*, \Pi^*, \mathbf{w}^*, c^*)$.

According to the statistically hiding property of COM, for $i \in \{1, 2, \cdots, k'\}$, the distributions of CMT_i, Ch_i, and RSP_i are statistically close to those in the real interaction, which imply that $\widehat{\Sigma}^*$ is a valid signature and $\widehat{\Sigma}^*$ is statistically indistinguishable from the legitimate signature Σ^* in Game 0. Therefore Game 0 is statistically close to Game 1, and since $\widehat{\Sigma}^*$ is independent of b, the advantage $\mathsf{Adv}_{\mathcal{A}}^{\mathsf{priva}}$ in Game 1 is 0. Hence the advantage $\mathsf{Adv}_{\mathcal{A}}^{\mathsf{priva}}$ in Game 0 is negligible, *i.e.*, the proposed scheme satisfies the perfect privacy property.

Unforgeability: For the unforgeability, we show the following theorem.

Theorem 3. *If the* $\mathsf{SIS}_{n,2m,q,\mathcal{O}(\ell m \beta^2)}^\infty$ *problem is hard, then our construction is unforgeable in the random oracle model.*

Proof. Because of the page limitation, we omit the detailed discussion of proof, if any necessary, please contact the corresponding author for the full version.

Acknowledgments. The authors thank the anonymous reviewers of CSS 2019 for their helpful comments, San Ling, and Khoa Nguyen for helpful discussions. This research is supported by the National Natural Science Foundation of China under Grant 61772477.

References

1. Agrawal, S., Boneh, D., Boyen, X.: Efficient lattice (H)IBE in the standard model. In: Gilbert, H. (ed.) EUROCRYPT 2010. LNCS, vol. 6110, pp. 553–572. Springer, Heidelberg (2010). https://doi.org/10.1007/978-3-642-13190-5_28
2. Ajtai, M.: Generating hard instances of lattice problems (Extended Abstract). In: STOC 1996, pp. 99–108. ACM (1996). https://doi.org/10.1145/237814.237838
3. Alwen, J., Peikert, C.: Generating shorter bases for hard random lattices. Theory Comput. Syst. **48**(3), 535–553 (2011). https://doi.org/10.1007/s00224-010-9278-3
4. Bansarkhani, R., Kaafarani, A.: Post-Quantum Attribute-Based Signatures from Lattice Assumptions. Cryptology ePrint Archive. http://eprint.iacr.org/2016/823
5. Datta, P., Okamoto, T., Takashima, K.: Efficient attribute-based signatures for unbounded arithmetic branching programs. In: Lin, D., Sako, K. (eds.) PKC 2019. LNCS, vol. 11442, pp. 127–158. Springer, Cham (2019). https://doi.org/10.1007/978-3-030-17253-4_5
6. Ge, A., Ma, C., Zhang, Z.: Attribute-based signature scheme with constant size signature in the standard model. IET Inf. Secur. **6**(2), 47–54 (2012). https://doi.org/10.1049/iet-ifs.2011.0094
7. Gentry, C., Peikert, C., Vaikuntanathan, V.: Trapdoor for hard lattices and new cryptographic constructions. In: STOC 2008, pp. 197–206. ACM (2008). https://doi.org/10.1145/1374376.1374407
8. Ghadafi, E.: Stronger security notions for decentralized traceable attribute-based signatures and more efficient constructions. In: Nyberg, K. (ed.) CT-RSA 2015. LNCS, vol. 9048, pp. 391–409. Springer, Cham (2015). https://doi.org/10.1007/978-3-319-16715-2_21
9. Gordon, S.D., Katz, J., Vaikuntanathan, V.: A group signature scheme from lattice assumptions. In: Abe, M. (ed.) ASIACRYPT 2010. LNCS, vol. 6477, pp. 395–412. Springer, Heidelberg (2010). https://doi.org/10.1007/978-3-642-17373-8_23
10. Herranz, J., Laguillaumie, F., Libert, B., Ràfols, C.: Short attribute-based signatures for threshold predicates. In: Dunkelman, O. (ed.) CT-RSA 2012. LNCS, vol. 7178, pp. 51–67. Springer, Heidelberg (2012). https://doi.org/10.1007/978-3-642-27954-6_4
11. El Kaafarani, A., Chen, L., Ghadafi, E., Davenport, J.: Attribute-based signatures with user-controlled linkability. In: Gritzalis, D., Kiayias, A., Askoxylakis, I. (eds.) CANS 2014. LNCS, vol. 8813, pp. 256–269. Springer, Cham (2014). https://doi.org/10.1007/978-3-319-12280-9_17
12. El Kaafarani, A., Ghadafi, E.: Attribute-based signatures with user-controlled linkability without random oracles. In: O'Neill, M. (ed.) IMACC 2017. LNCS, vol. 10655, pp. 161–184. Springer, Cham (2017). https://doi.org/10.1007/978-3-319-71045-7_9
13. El Kaafarani, A., Ghadafi, E., Khader, D.: Decentralized traceable attribute-based signatures. In: Benaloh, J. (ed.) CT-RSA 2014. LNCS, vol. 8366, pp. 327–348. Springer, Cham (2014). https://doi.org/10.1007/978-3-319-04852-9_17
14. El Kaafarani, A., Katsumata, S.: Attribute-based signatures for unbounded circuits in the ROM and efficient instantiations from lattices. In: Abdalla, M., Dahab, R. (eds.) PKC 2018. LNCS, vol. 10770, pp. 89–119. Springer, Cham (2018). https://doi.org/10.1007/978-3-319-76581-5_4
15. Katz, J., Sahai, A., Waters, B.: Predicate encryption supporting disjunctions, polynomial equations, and inner products. In: Smart, N. (ed.) EUROCRYPT 2008. LNCS, vol. 4965, pp. 146–162. Springer, Heidelberg (2008). https://doi.org/10.1007/978-3-540-78967-3_9

16. Kawachi, A., Tanaka, K., Xagawa, K.: Concurrently secure identification schemes based on the worst-case hardness of lattice problems. In: Pieprzyk, J. (ed.) ASIACRYPT 2008. LNCS, vol. 5350, pp. 372–389. Springer, Heidelberg (2008). https://doi.org/10.1007/978-3-540-89255-7_23

17. Li, J., Au, M., Susilo, W., Xie, D., Ren, H.: Attribute-based signature and its applications. In: ASIACCS 2010, pp. 60–69. ACM (2010). https://doi.org/10.1145/1755688.1755697

18. Ling, S., Nguyen, K., Wang, H., Xu, Y.: Lattice-based group signatures: achieving full dynamicity with ease. In: Gollmann, D., Miyaji, A., Kikuchi, H. (eds.) ACNS 2017. LNCS, vol. 10355, pp. 293–312. Springer, Cham (2017). https://doi.org/10.1007/978-3-319-61204-1_15

19. Ling, S., Nguyen, K., Wang, H., Xu, Y.: Constant-size group signatures from lattices. In: Abdalla, M., Dahab, R. (eds.) PKC 2018. LNCS, vol. 10770, pp. 58–88. Springer, Cham (2018). https://doi.org/10.1007/978-3-319-76581-5_3

20. Ling, S., Nguyen, K., Roux-Langlois, A., Wang, H.: A lattice-based group signature scheme with verifier-local revocation. Theor. Comput. Sci. **730**, 1–20 (2018). https://doi.org/10.1016/j.tcs.2018.03.027

21. Maji, H., Prabhakaran, M., Rosulek, M.: Attribute-Based Signatures: Achieving Attribute-Privacy and Collusion-Resistance. IACR Cryptology ePrint Archive. http://eprint.iacr.org/2008/328

22. Maji, H.K., Prabhakaran, M., Rosulek, M.: Attribute-based signatures. In: Kiayias, A. (ed.) CT-RSA 2011. LNCS, vol. 6558, pp. 376–392. Springer, Heidelberg (2011). https://doi.org/10.1007/978-3-642-19074-2_24

23. Micciancio, D., Peikert, C.: Trapdoors for lattices: simpler, tighter, faster, smaller. In: Pointcheval, D., Johansson, T. (eds.) EUROCRYPT 2012. LNCS, vol. 7237, pp. 700–718. Springer, Heidelberg (2012). https://doi.org/10.1007/978-3-642-29011-4_41

24. Okamoto, T., Takashima, K.: Efficient attribute-based signatures for non-monotone predicates in the standard model. In: Catalano, D., Fazio, N., Gennaro, R., Nicolosi, A. (eds.) PKC 2011. LNCS, vol. 6571, pp. 35–52. Springer, Heidelberg (2011). https://doi.org/10.1007/978-3-642-19379-8_3

25. Okamoto, T., Takashima, K.: Decentralized attribute-based signatures. In: Kurosawa, K., Hanaoka, G. (eds.) PKC 2013. LNCS, vol. 7778, pp. 125–142. Springer, Heidelberg (2013). https://doi.org/10.1007/978-3-642-36362-7_9

26. Urquidi, M., Khader, D., Lancrenon, J., Chen, L.: Attribute-based signatures with controllable linkability. In: Yung, M., Zhang, J., Yang, Z. (eds.) INTRUST 2015. LNCS, vol. 9565, pp. 114–129. Springer, Cham (2016). https://doi.org/10.1007/978-3-319-31550-8_8

27. Wang, Q., Chen, S.: Attribute-based signature for threshold predicates from lattices. Secur. Commun. Netw. **8**(5), 811–821 (2015). https://doi.org/10.1002/sec.1038

28. Wang, Q., Chen, S., Ge, A.: A new lattice-based threshold attribute-based signature scheme. In: Lopez, J., Wu, Y. (eds.) ISPEC 2015. LNCS, vol. 9065, pp. 406–420. Springer, Cham (2015). https://doi.org/10.1007/978-3-319-17533-1_28

Efficient and Secure Three-Factor User Authentication and Key Agreement Using Chaotic Maps

Jiaxi Hu[1,2], Zhiqiang Xu[1], Debiao He[1,2(✉)], Sherali Zeadally[3], and Kim-Kwang Raymond Choo[4]

[1] School of Cyber Science and Engineering, Wuhan University, Wuhan, China
hedebiao@163.com
[2] Cyberspace Security Research Center, Peng Cheng Laboratory, Shenzhen, China
[3] College of Communication and Information,
University of Kentucky, Lexington, USA
[4] The University of Texas at San Antonio, San Antonio, USA

Abstract. User authentication and key agreement are essential for implementing secure wireless communication, especially in mobile devices. Many authentication and key agreement schemes are based on both the smart card and the password. Unfortunately, most of these schemes are vulnerable, such as password guessing attack and smart card loss attack. Recently, Han et al. proposed a three-factor key agreement and authentication scheme by using fuzzy extractor and chaotic maps. However, it is proved that Han et al.'s scheme can not protect user anonymity and involves some redundant operations. To address the security defects, we proposed an improved user authentication and key agreement scheme. Although our scheme incurs slightly delay than others, it can resist various attacks. Moreover, our scheme is efficient for practical application deployments compared with other previously proposed user authentication schemes.

Keywords: Authentication · Chaotic maps · Security · Smart card

1 Introduction

To ensure secure communication between a remote client and a server, many authentication protocols [8,9,11,14] have been proposed. Initially, password-based authentication schemes are used widely, because the password is simple and short. In order to transmit data over an insecure channel, Lamport [12] proposed the first password-based authentication scheme which used one-way hash function. However, it could not withstand attacks such as the password guessing attack and smart card loss attack. Based on Lamport et al.'s research work,

---

The original version of this chapter was revised: the affiliation of the fourth author was corrected. The correction to this chapter is available at https://doi.org/10.1007/978-3-030-37337-5_49

many authentication protocols that based on password have been proposed to enhance the protocol's security.

To improve the communication security between the remote client and the server in the telecare medical information system, Wu et al. [19] proposed a discrete logarithm problem-based secure authentication scheme. However, He et al. [4] showed that their scheme has security weaknesses because it can not resist impersonation attack and insider attack. To enhance the security of medical information systems, Chen et al. [3] proposed an efficient and secure dynamic authentication scheme based on Identifiers (ID). However, Lin [15] demonstrated that their protocol can not protect user privacy and resist off-line password guessing attack. To address the user's anonymity problem, Lin [15] proposed a chaotic map-based key agreement scheme. Han *et al.* proposed a three-factor key agreement and authentication scheme, nevertheless, it is showed that their scheme is in lack of user's privacy protection. To improve the above problem between remote clients and servers, we proposed a noval and efficient scheme.

1.1 Related Work

Many traditional authentication schemes are based on discrete logarithm problems or factoring problems. These schemes require modular exponential and elliptic curve point multiplication operations. To improve the computation efficiency, researchers use Chebyshev chaotic map to design user authentication schemes. Guo and Chang [5] proposed a chaotic maps-based key agreement and authentication scheme.

However, Hao et al. [7] proved that the scheme [5] cannot protect user privacy and requires the usage of two secret keys. Hao et al. proposed a new authentication scheme which can solve these problems. Unfortunately, Jiang et al. [10] demonstrated that their scheme can not resist the stolen smart card attack. Wang et al. [18] proposed a dynamic identity-based authentication scheme using chaotic maps to enhance the security of telecare medical information systems. However, Han et al. [6] showed that their scheme can not resist denial of service attacks.

1.2 Our Contributions

We propose a key agreement and user authentication scheme based on chaotic maps and fuzzy extraction. Our major contributions are summarized as follows:

- First, we analyze Han et al.'s scheme [6] and prove it cannot protect user privacy.
- Second, we propose a key agreement and user authentication scheme using chaotic maps and fuzzy extraction that is based on biometric. The new scheme can protect user privacy and withstand various attacks.
- Finally, we analyze the security of our proposed scheme and demonstrate that the scheme is provably secure. Moreover, the proposed scheme can satisfy the security requirements of key agreement and user authentication.

Table 1. Notations

Notation	Description
U	The user/patient
S	The telecare server
s	Private key
SK	Session key
$\parallel, \oplus$	Concatenation operation and Exclusive-or operation
$h\,(.)$	One-way hash function
$Enc_s\,(.)$	Symmetric encryption
$DEc_s\,(.)$	Symmetric decryption
$Gen\,(BIO)$	Generation of biometric algorithm
$Rep\,(BIO)$	Reproduction of biometric algorithm

1.3   Organization

The rest of the paper is organized as follows. Section 2 presents some preliminaries used in this paper. Section 3 reviews Han et al.'s authentication scheme. Sections 4 and 5 analyze the security weaknesses of Han et al.'s protocol and propose an efficient and secure three-factor key agreement and user authentication scheme using chaotic maps. Section 6 elaborates the security of the new scheme briefly. Section 7 compares the proposed scheme with a few previous authentication schemes in terms of efficiency and security. Finally, we make some concluding remarks.

2   Preliminaries

We present the notations used in this work along including basic concepts of fuzzy extractor of biometric, and chaotic maps along with some hard problems.

2.1   Notations

We list the notations that are used in Han et al.'s protocol in Table 1.

2.2   Fuzzy Extractor

The traditional hash function is very sensitive and it will return different outputs only if the inputs are not the same. Since the biometric information is very easy to be mixed up with various noises, reproducing the actual biometrics, therefore, using the traditional hash function is impossible. We can use the fuzzy extractor method to solve the problem [17,20]. With the help of an auxiliary string, the fuzzy extractor can extract a uniformly-random string from biometric input. Only if the input is very close to the original biometric, the fuzzy extractor can recover the original biometric data with a helper string. The fuzzy extractor includes generate(Gen) and reproduce(Rep).

- $Gen\,(BIO) = (R, P)$. We input a biometric input BIO, the probabilistic algorithm of Gen will output a random biometric string R and an auxiliary string P.
- $Rep\,(BIO', P) = (R)$. As long as the distance between BIO' and BIO satisfies the given verification threshold, the deterministic algorithm of Rep can recover R from the biometric data BIO' with an auxiliary string P.

2.3   Chebyshev Chaotic Map

Next, we describe the Chebyshev chaotic map and its properties.

1. **Definition of Chebyshev polynomials:** Referring to Mason and Handscomb [2,13,16], Chebyshev polynomial $T_m\,(y) : [-1, 1] \longrightarrow [-1, 1]$ is a polynomial, where $y \in [-1, 1]$. With $T_m\,(y) = cos\,(m \cdot cos^{-1}\,(y))$, the recurring relation is:
   $T_m\,(y) = 2yT_{m-1}\,(y) - T_{m-2}\,(y), m >= 2,$
   $T_0\,(y) = 1,$
   $T_1\,(y) = y.$
2. **Properties of Chebyshev polynomials:** At least one element $S \in G_1$ makes $e(S, S) \neq 1_{G_2}$ hold.

   Semigroup property. $T_u\,(T_v\,(y)) = T_v\,(T_u\,(y))$, holds for $u, v \in N$ and $x \in (-\infty, +\infty)$.

Computational problems of Chebyshev polynomials
   Discrete Logarithm Problem (DLP): Given p, x and y, it is infeasible to find an integer r such that $x = T_r(y) \bmod p$.
   Computational Diffie Hellman (CDH) problem: Given three numbers y, $T_u\,(y)$ and $T_v\,(y)$, it is impossible to compute $T_{uv}\,(y)$.

2.4   Network Model

- U: In order to get the service from server S, user U needs to validate the server. The smart card that the user owns is not tamper-resistant and it can be lost or stolen by the adversary.
- S: After the user U successfully authenticates with the server S, the server S provides services to it. Because of cost constraints, we do not need to equip the server with tamper-resistant hardware. An adversary can get the keying materials stored in the server's memory.

2.5   Requirements

A security authentication scheme should meet the following security requirements:

- Mutual authentication: By using gateway network (GWN), S and U can authenticate each other.

- Anonymity: The user's identity cannot be obtained by the adversary.
- Session key: After S and U authenticate each other, a session key should be generated.
- Unconstrained by GWN: User registered information can not be computed by GWN.
- Attack resistance: A security scheme can withstand various attacks.
- Efficient password change: Without the GWN, the user's password can be changed.

3   Review of Han et al.'s Scheme

We review Han et al.'s scheme [6] briefly, including registration, login, authentication, and password change.

3.1   Registration Phase

U selects ID, PW and B(biometric). The server registers the user who can get a Smart Card SC from GWN. The details of the registration process are given below.

- U selects his/her identity ID, password PW. For his/her biometric B, he/she executes the fuzzy extractor of $\langle R, P \rangle = Gen\,(B)$. Then U can calculate $A = h\,(PW \,\|\, R) \oplus r$ where r is a random number.
- U sends $\{ID, A\}$ to S.
- S calculates $AID = h\,(ID \,\|\, s)$ with private s, $\mathrm{K} = h\,(AID)$, $V' = AID \oplus A$. SC is stored by $\{K, V', CID; h\,(.)\}$.
- U calculates $V = V' \oplus A \oplus h\,(ID \,\|\, PW \,\|\, R)$, and replaces V' with V and stores P into SC.

3.2   Login and Authentication Phase

After the card reader reads the information from the smart card, the user inputs the ID, PW and B' (B' is similar to B).

The card reader reads the login information, then SC runs the following steps:

- SC calculates $R = Rep\,(B', P)$, calculates $AID = V \oplus h\,(ID \,\|\, PW \,\|\, R)$. SC checks whether $h\,(AID) \overset{?}{=} K$. If the verification is correct, SC executes the next step.
- The smart card selects a digital u where u is a random nonce, then calculates $X = T_u\,(AID)$ and $V_1 = h\,(ID \,\|\, X \,\|\, CID \,\|\, T_1)$. The smart card sends $\{CID, X, V_1, T_1\}$ to S.

After S receives the information of the login request, it executes the following steps:

- The server checks whether $|T_c - T_1| < \Delta T$, where T_c is the current time. If the verification is correct, S decrypts the CID with his/her private key s to extract the ID. Then, S calculates $AID = h(ID \| s)$.
- S checks $V_1 = h(ID \| X \| CID \| T_1)$. If the equation holds, S selects two random nonces a' and v.
- The server calculates $CID' = Enc_s\left(ID \| a'\right), SK = h(T_v(X)), Y = T_v(AID)$, and $V_2 = h\left(CID' \| Y \| SK \| T_2\right)$, where T_2 is the current time.
- The server transmits $\left\{CID', Y, V_2, T_2\right\}$ to U.

After SC receives the information, it executes the following steps:

- It checks whether $|T_c - T_1| < \Delta T$. If so, U computes $SK = h(T_u(Y))$.
- It checks whether $V_2 = h\left(CID' \| Y \| SK \| T_2\right)$. If the equation holds, the smart card updates the CID with CID'.
- It calculates $V_3 = h(SK \| T_3)$. In the end the smart card transmits $\{V_3, T_3\}$ to the server.

After S receives the message $\{V_3, T_3\}$, it executes the following steps:

- It checks whether $|T_c - T_3| < \Delta T$ and $V_3 = h(SK | T_3|)$.
- If the server authenticates U successfully, SK becomes their session key.

3.3 Password and Biometric Change Phase

- U inputs $\left\{ID, PW, B'\right\}$, SC first computes $R = Rep\left(B', P\right)$ where P is stored in SC, $AID = V \oplus h(ID \| PW \| R)$. Then SC checks whether $K = h(AID)$. If so, it accepts the request.
- U inputs $\{PW^{new}, B^{new}\}$. SC computes $\langle R^{new}, P^{new}\rangle = Gen(B^{new})$ and $V^{new} = V \oplus h(ID \| PW \| R) \oplus h(ID \| PW^{new} \| R^{new})$. Then it puts V with V^{new}.

4   Security Weaknesses of Han et al.'s Scheme

In this section, we show that Han et al.'s scheme can not protect user's privacy during the authentication phase. We also indicate that their protocol involves redundant operations.

4.1   Lack of Protection of User Anonymity

It is worth noting that the adversary could eavesdrop on the messages $\{CID, X, V_1, T_1\}$ and $\left\{CID', Y, V_2, T_2\right\}$, where $CID' = Enc_s\left(ID \| a'\right)$. CID' is probably encrypted ciphertexts of the user's identity ID using the server's private key. Although the adversary can not decrypt CID and CID' to get the user's identity, the adversary could eavesdrop on the message CID' and save it. The adversary could then compare it with the information of each transmission and keep track of CID'. Therefore, their scheme cannot protect the anonymity of the user.

4.2 Flaws in the Validation of Timestamp

First, due to the existence of network delays, a lot of information does not arrive at the destination in time. When network delay occurs, the information may become invalid. Furthermore, the verification of timestamp is redundant to guarantee the frashment of the random number in authentication phase. The random numbers can completely withstand replay attack because each time the random number that is selected is different, and the session secret key is not the same.

5 Proposed Scheme

To improve the user's privacy in Han et al.'s scheme, we propose an efficient and secure three-factor key agreement and user authentication scheme. Our scheme can protect user privacy during the authentication phase. Our scheme is composed of four phases:

1. The registration phase.
2. The login phase.
3. The authentication phase.
4. The password change phase.

5.1 Registration Phase

U selects ID, PW and biometric B, and then registers ID with S. The server registers the user who can get a smart card SC from GWN. The registration process includes the following steps.

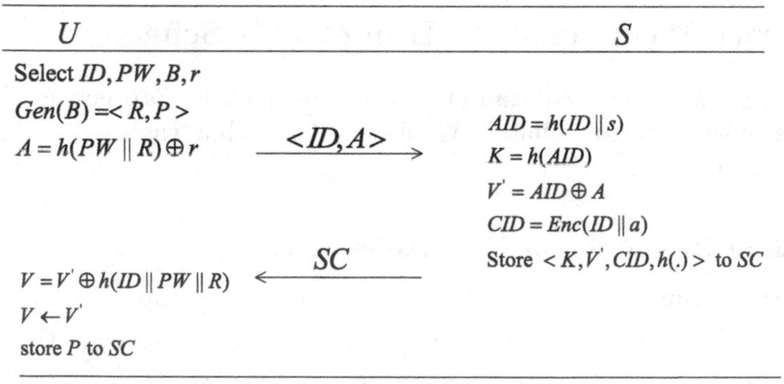

U		S
Select ID, PW, B, r		
$Gen(B) = < R, P >$		$AID = h(ID \parallel s)$
$A = h(PW \parallel R) \oplus r$	$\xrightarrow{\ <ID,A>\ }$	$K = h(AID)$
		$V^{'} = AID \oplus A$
		$CID = Enc(ID \parallel a)$
	$\xleftarrow{\ SC\ }$	Store $< K, V^{'}, CID, h(.) >$ to SC
$V = V^{'} \oplus h(ID \parallel PW \parallel R)$		
$V \leftarrow V^{'}$		
store P to SC		

Fig. 1. Registration phase

(1) U selects ID, PW and imprints biometric B. U computes $\langle R, P \rangle = Gen\,(B)$ with the fuzzy extractor. U chooses a random number r and calculates $A = h\,(PW \,\|\, R) \oplus r$ and sends $\{ID, A\}$ to S.

(2) S computes $AID = h\,(ID \,\|\, s)$, where s is its private key. Then, S calculates $K = h\,(AID)$, $V' = AID \oplus A$ and $CID = Enc_s\,(ID \,\|\, a)$, where a is a random number. Finally, S stores the message $\left\{ K, V', CID, h\,(.) \right\}$ in SC and issues SC to U.

(3) After receiving SC, U computes $V = V' \oplus A \oplus h\,(ID \,\|\, PW \,\|\, R)$ and replaces V' with V and stores P in SC.

Figure 1 shows the steps of the registration phase.

5.2   Login and Authentication Phase

The steps of the login and the authentication process are:

(1) SC first computes $R = Rep\left(B', P\right)$ and $AID = V \oplus h\,(ID \,\|\, PW \,\|\, R)$. Then, SC checks whether $K = h\,(AID)$. If true, SC calculates $X = T_u\,(AID)$ and $V_1 = h\,(ID \,\|\, X \,\|\, CID)$. SC sends $\{CID, X, V_1\}$ to the server.

(2) Upon receiving $\{CID, X, V_1\}$, S first computes $ID \,\|\, a = Dec_s\,(CID)$, where s is the private key of S. Then, S calculates $AID = h\,(ID \,\|\, s)$ and checks whether $V_1 = h\,(ID \,\|\, X \,\|\, CID)$ is correct. If holds, S selects a' and v randomly and computes $CID' = Enc_s\,(ID \,\|\, a')$, $SK = h\,(T_v\,(X))$, $Y = T_v\,(AID)$, $V_2 = h\,(CID' \,\|\, Y \,\|\, SK)$ and $CID'' = CID' \oplus h\,("0", SK)$. Finally, S sends $\left\{ CID'', Y, V_2 \right\}$ to U.

(3) After receiving the response message $\left\{ CID'', Y, V_2 \right\}$, U first calculates $SK = h\,(T_u\,(Y))$, $CID' = CID'' \oplus h\,("0", SK)$. Then, U verifies whether $V_2 = h\,(CID' \,\|\, Y \,\|\, SK)$ is correct. If holds, SC replaces CID with CID' and computes $V_3 = h\,("1", SK)$. SC sends $\{V_3\}$ to the server S.

(4) S checks whether the equation $V_3 = h\,("1", SK)$ holds. If so, authentication is complete. U and S take SK as their session key.

Figure 2 shows the steps of the registration phase.

5.3   Password and Biometric Change Phase

As shown in Fig. 3, the steps for the password and biometric change are presented below.

(1) U inputs the message $\{ID, PW, B'\}$.

(2) SC computes $R = Rep\,(B', P)$ and $AID = V \oplus h\,(ID \,\|\, PW \,\|\, R)$. Then, SC verifies whether $K = h\,(AID)$ holds. If so, SC accepts the request.

(3) U inputs $\{PW^{new}, B^{new}\}$. SC computes $\langle R^{new}, P^{new} \rangle = Gen\,(B^{new})$ and $V^{new} = V \oplus h\,(ID \,\|\, PW \,\|\, R) \oplus h\,(ID \,\|\, PW^{new} \,\|\, R^{new})$, then replaces V with V^{new}.

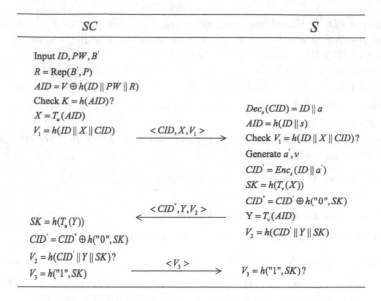

Fig. 2. Login and authentication phase

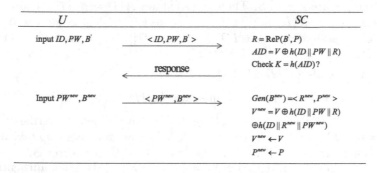

Fig. 3. Password change phase

6 Analysis

6.1 Proof of Authentication and Key Agreement Using BAN Logic

We demonstrate the security of our authentication scheme using BAN logic [1]. The notations related to BAN logic are shown in Table 2.

(1) Logical postulates:
  – Message meaning rule
$$\frac{P\,believes\,Q\xleftrightarrow{K}P,\,P\,sees\,\{X\}_K}{P\,believes\,Q\,said\,X}$$
  – Nonce-verification rule
$$\frac{P\,believes\,fresh(X),\,P\,believes\,Q\,said\,X}{P\,believes\,Q\,believes\,X}$$

- Jurisdiction rule

$$\frac{P\,believes\,Q\,controls\,X,\, P\,believes\,Q\,believes\,X}{P\,believes\,X}$$

- Freshness-conjuncatenation rule

$$\frac{P\,believes\,fresh(X)}{P\,believes\,fresh(X,Y)}$$

(2) Security goals:

- $Goal_1$:

$$U| \equiv U \xleftrightarrow{SK} S$$

- $Goal_2$:

$$S| \equiv U \xleftrightarrow{SK} S$$

- $Goal_3$:

$$U| \equiv S| \equiv U \xleftrightarrow{SK} S$$

- $Goal_4$:

$$S| \equiv U| \equiv U \xleftrightarrow{SK} S$$

(3) Idealized scheme:

- Mesg 1:

$$U \longrightarrow S : \left(ID, X, \left(U \xleftrightarrow{V_i} S\right)\right)_{h(ID||s)}$$

- Mesg 2:

$$S \longrightarrow U : \left(ID, a', \left(U \xleftrightarrow{CID'} S\right), \left(U \xleftrightarrow{V_i} S\right)\right)_{h(ID||s)}$$

- Mesg 3:

$$U \longrightarrow S : \left(ID, V_i, Y, CID', \left(U \xleftrightarrow{sk=SK} S\right)\right)_{SK}$$

- Mesg 4:

$$U \longrightarrow S : \left(V_i, \left(U \xleftrightarrow{sk=SK} S\right)\right)_{SK}$$

(4) Initial state assumptions: $p_1 S| \equiv \#(v)$ $p_2 U| \equiv \#(u)$ $p_3 U| \equiv \#(a')$ $p_4 U| \equiv$
$\left(U \xleftrightarrow{h(ID||s)} S\right)$ $p_5 S| \equiv \left(U \xleftrightarrow{h(ID||s)} S\right)$ $p_6 U| \equiv S| \leftrightarrow \left(U \xleftrightarrow{Ksr} S\right)$ $p_7 S| \equiv$
$U| \leftrightarrow \left(U \xleftrightarrow{Ksr} S\right)$

Table 2. Notations of BAN logic

Notation	Description
$P| \equiv X$	P believes X
$P \lhd X$	P sees X
$P| X$	P once said X
$P \Rightarrow X$	P has jurisdiction over X
$\#(X)$	Denotes freshness of X
$P \xleftrightarrow{K} Q$	P and Q may use the shared key K
$sk = SK$	The session key used in the current authentication session
$\langle X \rangle_{iY}$	X combined with the formula Y
$(X)_K$	X hashed under the key K
$\{X\}_K$	X encrypted under the key K

Security Analysis of the Idealized Form of the Proposed Scheme

- According to Msg 1, we have:

$$S \triangleleft \left(ID, X, \left(U \xleftrightarrow{V_i} S \right) \right)_{h(ID\|s)} \tag{1}$$

- From (1) & p_5 and the message meaning rule

$$S| \equiv U| \left(ID, X, \left(U \xleftrightarrow{V_i} S \right) \right) \tag{2}$$

- From p_1, and the freshness-conjuncatenation rule

$$S| \equiv \# \left(ID, X, \left(U \xleftrightarrow{V_i} S \right) \right) \tag{3}$$

- From (2) *and* (3), and the nonce-verification rule

$$S| \equiv U| \equiv \left(ID, X, \left(U \xleftrightarrow{V_i} S \right) \right) \tag{4}$$

- From (4) and the believe rule

$$S| \equiv U| \equiv \left(U \xleftrightarrow{V_i} S \right) \tag{5}$$

- From A 6 & (5), and the jurisdiction rule

$$S| \equiv \left(U \xleftrightarrow{V_i} S \right) \tag{6}$$

- According to $T_{uv}\,(AID) \bmod p = sk = T_{vu}\,(AID) \bmod p$, we obtain

$$S| \equiv \left(U \xleftrightarrow{SK} S \right) Goal_3$$

- From Mesg 2, we have

$$U \triangleleft \left\langle ID, a', \left(U \xleftrightarrow{CID'} S \right), \left(U \xleftrightarrow{V_i} S \right) \right\rangle_{h(ID\|s)} \tag{7}$$

- From (7) & p_4 and the message meaning rule

$$U| \equiv S| \left(ID, a', \left(U \xleftrightarrow{CID'} S \right), \left(U \xleftrightarrow{V_i} S \right) \right) \tag{8}$$

- From p_3 and the freshness-conjuncatenation rule

$$U| \equiv \# \left(ID, a', \left(U \xleftrightarrow{CID'} S \right), \left(U \xleftrightarrow{V_i} S \right) \right) \tag{9}$$

- From (8) and (9) and the nonce-verification rule

$$U| \equiv S| \equiv \left(ID, a', \left(U \xleftrightarrow{CID'} S \right), \left(U \xleftrightarrow{V_i} S \right) \right) \tag{10}$$

- From (10) and the believe rule

$$U| \equiv S| \equiv \left(U \xleftrightarrow{CID'} S \right) \tag{11}$$

- From p_7 and (11) and the jurisdiction rule

$$U| \equiv \left(U \xleftrightarrow{V_i} S \right) \tag{12}$$

- According to $T_{uv}(AID) \bmod p = sk = SK = T_{vu}(AID) \bmod p$, we obtain

$$U| \equiv \left(U \xleftrightarrow{SK} S \right) Goad_1$$

- From Mesg 3, we have

$$U \triangleleft \left(ID, V_i, Y, CID', \left(U \xleftrightarrow{sk=SK} S \right) \right)_{SK} \tag{13}$$

- From (13) and Goal 1 and the message meaning rule

$$U| \equiv S| \left(ID, V_i, Y, CID', \left(U \xleftrightarrow{sk=SK} S \right) \right) \tag{14}$$

- From p_2 and the freshness-conjuncatenation rule

$$U| \equiv \# \left(ID, V_i, Y, CID', \left(U \xleftrightarrow{sk=SK} S \right) \right) \tag{15}$$

- From (14) and (15) and the nonce-verification rule

$$U| \equiv S| \equiv \left(ID, V_i, Y, CID', \left(U \xleftrightarrow{sk=SK} S \right) \right) \tag{16}$$

- From (16) and the believe rule

$$U| \equiv S| \equiv \left(U \xleftrightarrow{sk=SK} S \right) Goad_2$$

- From Mesg 4, we have

$$S \triangleleft \left(V_i, \left(U \xleftrightarrow{sk=SK} \right) \right)_{SK} \tag{17}$$

- From (17), $Goal_3$ and the message meaning rule

$$S| \equiv U| \left(V_i, \left(U \xleftrightarrow{sk=SK} \right) \right) \tag{18}$$

- According to P_1 and the freshness-conjuncatenation rule

$$S| \equiv \# \left(V_i, \left(U \xleftrightarrow{sk=SK} \right) \right) \tag{19}$$

- According to (18), (19) and the nonce-verification rule

$$S| \equiv U| \equiv \left(V_i, \left(U \xleftrightarrow{sk=SK} \right) \right) \tag{20}$$

- According to (20) and the believe rule

$$S| \equiv U| \equiv \left(U \xleftrightarrow{sk=SK} S \right) Goal_4$$

According to $Goal_1$, $Goal_2$, $Goal_3$ and $Goal_4$, SK will become the session key between U and S.

6.2 Security Analysis Against Various Attacks

(1) User untraceability and anonymity

The proposed scheme preserves the anonymity of users. In our scheme, taking the situation where an adversary can get the message $\{V, K, CID, P\}$ from the smart card, where $K = h(AID), V = AID \oplus h(ID \| PW \| R), CID = Enc_s(ID \| a)$. The adversary may also eavesdrop the information $\{CID, X, V_1\}$ and $\{CID', Y, V_2\}$, where only V, CID, CID' are related to the user's identity. As CID, CID' cannot be decrypted by anyone other than the server, it is impossible to get the ID of user from CID or CID'. As the random and AID cannot be known by the adversary, it is impossible to get the user's identity from V. Thus, an adversary cannot obtain the user's identity.

Provides Strong User Un-traceability

Since $SC = \{K, V, CID, h(.)\}$ and it does not store ID in clear form. The adversary cannot get the identity of the user even if the latter has lost his/her smart card. Moreover, various authentication messages belonging to a specific user do not involve any common value. During the login and authentication phase of our scheme, the adversary cannot trace the behavior of a user by CID'', because $CID'' = CID' \oplus h("0", SK)$.

Thus, neither an attacker can guess/obtain a user's identity nor can he/she trace the user. Therefore, our scheme provides strong user anonymity and untraceability.

(2) Perfect forward secrecy

We can compute the session key SK as $h(T_u(T_v(AID)))$, where u is selected randomly by the user U and v is chosen randomly by the server in each session. The attacker only knows $T_u(AID)$ and $T_v(AID)$. Computing $T_u(T_v(AID))$ is hard because it is a computational Diffie Hellman problem in Chebyshev chaotic maps. Thus, the attacker cannot compute previous session keys even if he/she owns the long-term private keys. So our scheme can provide forward secrecy

(3) Mutual authentication

In the proposed scheme, user U and server S must authenticate each other. U authenticates S by checking whether $V_2 = h(CID' \| Y \| SK)$ is true. S authenticates U by checking $V_1 = h(ID \| X \| CID)$ and $V_3 = h(SK)$. We conclude that the proposed scheme can provide proper mutual authentication.

(4) Off-line password guessing attack

SC can be extracted by the attacker who may try to guess PW by using the values of SC. Only if the attacker computes the correct B with guessing passwords and generates many correct equations, then, the attacker can guess correctly. As the biometric of the user cannot be forged, it is impossible to guess the password of user correctly in the proposed scheme.

(5) Smart card loss attack

Suppose an adversary obtains the SC of the user and extracts the stored values $\{V, K, CID, P\}$, where $K = h(AID)$, $V = AID \oplus h(ID \| PW \| R)$, $CID = Enc_s(ID \| a)$. The adversary cannot get any useful information with these values. Furthermore, without the correct ID, PW and B, the adversary cannot generate a valid login request message. We therefore conclude that our scheme can withstand smart card loss attack.

(6) User impersonation attack

The values of smart card can be extracted by the attacker who wants to get the service from S. The attacker must generate and send a valid login request message $\{CID, X, V_1\}$ to S. However, the attacker needs to compute a valid $X = T_v(AID)$, where v is a random number and AID is unknown to the adversary. So the attacker cannot send a legal login request message. If the adversary eavesdrops on $\{CID, X, V_1\}$ and sends the same message to S, then S returns the response message $\{CID', Y, V_2\}$. Upon receiving the response message, the adversary must send the message $\{V_3\}$ to S, where $V_3 = h(SK)$. Since the adversary is unable to compute the value of SK, the adversary cannot generate a valid message. Thus, we conclude that the proposed scheme is secure enough to withstand the user impersonation attack.

(7) Server Spoofing Attack

To impersonate as a legal server, the adversary should be able to answer the authentication message sent by U. He must generate a valid response message $\{CID'', Y, V_2\}$, $CID' = Enc_s(ID \| a')$, $SK = h(T_v(X))$, $Y = T_v(AID)$, $V_2 = h(CID' \| Y \| SK)$, $CID'' = CID' \oplus h("0", SK)$. Since the adversary cannot get the value of AID and the server's secret key s, the adversary cannot compute the value Y, V_2. Hence, the scheme is secure enough to withstand impersonation attacks.

7   Comparison of Our Scheme with Related and Recently Proposed Schemes

Next, we compare our proposed scheme with recent authentication and key agreement schemes proposed in terms of security and performance (as shown in Table 3). $\sqrt{}$ denotes that it can provide the property; $\times$ denotes that it cannot provide the property;

From Table 2, Han et al.'s scheme [6] fails to protect user anonymity and untraceability. In contrast, our proposed scheme can withstand these attacks.

In Table 4, we compare the computational cost of our proposed scheme with recently proposed schemes. T_h denotes the running time of one-way hash function; T_{sym} denotes the running time for symmetric encryption/decryption; T_M

Table 3. Comparison of security

Security attributes and schemes	[6]	Our Scheme
Provides user anonymity and untraceability	×	√
Off-line password guessing attack	√	√
Stolen smart card attack	√	√
Impersonation attack	√	√
Replay attack	√	√
Denial of service attack	√	√
Strong forward secrecy	√	√
Insider attack	√	√
Session key verification	√	√
Efficient password change	√	√

Table 4. Comparison of performance at the user side and the server side

Schemes	User computation	Server computation
[6]	$6T_h + 2T_C$	$2T_{sym} + 5T_h + 2T_C$
Our scheme	$7T_h + 2T_C$	$2T_{sym} + 5T_h + 2T_C$

denotes the execution time for a modular exponentiation; T_{ECC} denotes the execution time for an elliptic curve point multiplication; T_C denotes the execution time for a Chebyshev chaotic map operation.

According to [15], the running time of these aforementioned operations are 0.32, 5.6, 19.2, 17.1 and 32.2 ms respectively. To conclude, Table 3 presents the computational costs at the user side and the server side during the login and authentication phase of several recent schemes. Although our proposed scheme incurs slightly higher computation costs than most of these schemes in Table 3, the scheme is still fast for practical implementations and deployments in smart cards.

8 Conclusion

In this paper, we analyzed the security of Han et al.'s scheme and show that their scheme can not protect user's privacy. Moreover, we proposed a three-factor based authentication and key agreement scheme to protect user privacy. The new scheme is secure and can resist various attacks such as password guessing attack, replay attack, user impersonation attack, server spoofing attack and denial of service attack. In our proposed scheme, we employ a fuzzy extractor and Chebyshev chaotic maps to implement the authentication scheme. Our proposed scheme is suitable for deployment in various low-power smart cards, and in particular for mobile computing networks.

Acknowledgements. The work was supported in part by the National Key Research and Development Program of China (No. 2018YFC1315404) and the National Natural Science Foundation of China (Nos. 61572370, 61572379).

References

1. Burrows, M., Abadi, M., Needham, R.: A logic of authentication. In: Twelfth ACM Symposium on Operating Systems Principles, pp. 1–13 (1989)
2. Chatterjee, S., Roy, S., Das, A.K., Chattopadhyay, S., Kumar, N., Vasilakos, A.V.: Secure biometric-based authentication scheme using Chebyshev chaotic map for multi-server environment. IEEE Trans. Dependable Secur. Comput. **15**(5), 824–839 (2016)
3. Chen, H.M., Lo, J.W., Yeh, C.K.: An efficient and secure dynamic id-based authentication scheme for telecare medical information systems. J. Med. Syst. **36**(6), 3907–3915 (2012)
4. Debiao, H., Jianhua, C., Rui, Z.: A more secure authentication scheme for telecare medicine information systems. J. Med. Syst. **36**(3), 1989–1995 (2012)
5. Guo, C., Chang, C.C.: Chaotic maps-based password-authenticated key agreement using smart cards. Commun. Nonlinear Sci. Numer. Simul. **18**(6), 1433–1440 (2013)
6. Han, L., Xie, Q., Liu, W., Wang, S.: A new efficient chaotic maps based three factor user authentication and key agreement scheme. Wirel. Pers. Commun. **95**, 3391–3406 (2017)
7. Hao, X., Wang, J., Yang, Q., Yan, X., Li, P.: A chaotic map-based authentication scheme for telecare medicine information systems. J. Med. Syst. **37**(2), 1–7 (2013)
8. He, D., Kumar, N., Khan, M.K., Wang, L., Shen, J.: Efficient privacy-aware authentication scheme for mobile cloud computing services. IEEE Syst. J. **12**(12), 1621–1631 (2018)
9. He, D., Zeadally, S., Xu, B., Huang, X.: An efficient identity-based conditional privacy-preserving authentication scheme for vehicular ad hoc networks. IEEE Trans. Inf. Forensics Secur. **10**(12), 2681–2691 (2015)
10. Jiang, Q., Ma, J., Lu, X., Tian, Y.: Robust chaotic map-based authentication and key agreement scheme with strong anonymity for telecare medicine information systems. J. Med. Syst. **38**(2), 1–8 (2014)
11. Jiang, Q., Ma, J., Lu, X., Tian, Y.: An efficient two-factor user authentication scheme with unlinkability for wireless sensor networks. Peer-To-Peer Netw. Appl. **8**(6), 1070–1081 (2015)
12. Lamport, L.: Password authentication with insecure communication. Commun. ACM **24**(11), 770–772 (1981)
13. Lee, C.C., Hsu, C.W.: A secure biometric-based remote user authentication with key agreement scheme using extended chaotic maps. Nonlinear Dyn. **71**(1–2), 201–211 (2013)
14. Li, X., Niu, J., Kumari, S., Wu, F., Sangaiah, A.K., Choo, K.K.R.: A three-factor anonymous authentication scheme for wireless sensor networks in internet of things environments. J. Netw. Comput. Appl. **103**(1), 194–204 (2018)
15. Lin, H.Y.: Chaotic map based mobile dynamic ID authenticated key agreement scheme. Wirel. Pers. Commun. **78**(2), 1487–1494 (2014)
16. Mason, J.C., Handscomb, D.: Chebyshev polynomials **c**(8-9), pp. 855–857 (2002)
17. Sebé, F., Domingo-Ferrer, J., Martinez-Balleste, A., Deswarte, Y., Quisquater, J.J.: Efficient remote data possession checking in critical information infrastructures. IEEE Trans. Knowl. Data Eng. **20**(8), 1034–1038 (2007)

18. Wang, Z., Huo, Z., Shi, W.: A dynamic identity based authentication scheme using chaotic maps for telecare medicine information systems. J. Med. Syst. **39**(1), 158 (2015)
19. Wu, Z.Y., Lee, Y.C., Lai, F., Lee, H.C., Chung, Y.: A secure authentication scheme for telecare medicine information systems. J. Med. Syst. **36**(3), 1529–1535 (2012)
20. Zhang, L., Zhu, S., Tang, S.: Privacy protection for telecare medicine information systems using a chaotic map-based three-factor authenticated key agreement scheme. IEEE J. Biomed. Health Inform. **21**(2), 465–475 (2017)

Achieving Data Security, Access Control and Authentication of Controllers in Hierarchical Software Defined Networking with Attribute Based Encryption

YuHua Xu[1,2] and ZhiXin Sun[1,2]([✉])

[1] Nanjing University of Posts and Telecommunications, Nanjing 210003, China
sunzx@njupt.edu.cn
[2] Key Lab of Broadband Wireless Communication and
Sensor Network Technology, Nanjing 210003, China

Abstract. Software defined networking (SDN) separates the data layer and the control layer to achieve logical centralization, scalability and programmability. In hierarchical software defined networking (HSDN), controllers are classified into the upper controller- Root Controller (RC) and the lower controller- Local Controller (LC) to improve the scalability of the network. HSDN effectively relieve the workload of controllers. However, the features of HSDN puts forward higher requirements of data privacy protection and access control. Because RC stores global network data, it must ensure authorized access and prevent the forged data. The attribute-based encryption scheme can provide fine-grained data access control and data privacy protection of controllers at the same time. When LC accesses data in RC, the algorithm of ciphertext-policy attribute-based encryption with identity authentication (CP-ABE-IA) is presented to protect the data privacy of RC and guarantee the legitimate access of LC. When LC sends message to RC, we propose an algorithm of key-policy attribute based signcryption for multi-access structures (KP-ABSC-MAS). KP-ABSC-MAS provides data privacy protection and verification as well as the authentication of LC.

Keywords: Hierarchical software defined networking · Attribute-based encryption · Signcryption

1 Introduction

Software defined networking (SDN) decouples the traditional network into data plane, control plane and application plane. It logically realizes centralized man-

Supported by the National Natural Science Foundation of China (61672299, 61972208, 61702281, and 61802200), The Natural Science Foundation of the Jiangsu Higher Education Institutions of China (16KJB520033), and in part by Postgraduate Research & Practice Innovation Program of Jiangsu Province.

© Springer Nature Switzerland AG 2019
J. Vaidya et al. (Eds.): CSS 2019, LNCS 11982, pp. 203–213, 2019.
https://doi.org/10.1007/978-3-030-37337-5_16

agement of the network. SDN shows great advantages in flexibility, scalability, and many other aspects. However, with the rapid expansion of networks, the controller of SDN becomes the network bottleneck, due to its limited computing and storage capabilities. In large scale networks, hierarchical software defined networking (HSDN) can effectively extend the control plane to achieve distributed control of networks. HSDN divides the control plane into two layers [1]. In the upper layer, Root Controllers (RC) are deployed in the backbone network. In the lower layer, Local Controllers (LC) are deployed in local area networks with no interconnection. LC controls one or a handful of switches by running local control applications. It collects physical device information and link information, and sends the information to RC [2]. RC maintains global abstracted network view and management information of networks, and reassigns different flow setups to proper controllers [3]. HSDN reduces the workload of controllers and achieves global optimization of distributed network communication by centralized management.

With the development of HSDN, issues of access control and security have become major challenges. The communication between RC and LC in plaintext may cause the data theft. Attackers can further damage the network, according to the stolen data. A security scheme is needed for the data privacy protection of controllers. What's more, RC stores global network data and various application data, an attacker may masquerade as a LC to access the data in RC, or transmit forged data to RC to destroy the network.

Existing SDN access control schemes can be divided into two categories: One is to assign access rights to users based on users' access flow and service request [4]; the other is based on the host's identity credentials [5]. Both of these solutions require complex authentication and privilege assignments for users, and separate SDN access control from data privacy protection resulting in low efficiency. On the other hand, the protection of SDN data privacy is mainly based on a traditional public key cryptosystem such as the SSL/TLS protocol [6]. But traditional public key cryptosystems cannot achieve fine-grained access control. To the best of our knowledge, the scheme of controller data privacy protection, anti-counterfeiting, and fine-grained access control has not been proposed for HSDN.

Attribute-based encryption algorithm encrypts the message with attribute set or attribute access structure. Attribute-based signcryption combines attribute-based encryption with attribute-based signature. It can provide fine-grained data access and confidentiality simultaneously. According to the characteristics of HSDN network, we improve the attribute-based encryption scheme to guarantee data confidentiality and integrity, and realize the identity authentication of lower controllers.

The main contributions are summarized as follows:

(1) When LC accesses data in RC, we present ciphertext-policy attribute-based encryption with identity authentication (CP-ABE-IA) to achieve fine-grained and illegal data access.

(2) When RC accesses data in LC, we propose key-policy attribute based sign-cryption for multi-access structures (KP-ABSC-MAS) to search the access structure for decryption, provide data security and authentication of LC, as well as verify the integrity of the data.
(3) Our scheme can provide data privacy protection of controllers, aim at the network architecture of HSDN. And when the number of controllers increases, our scheme is scalable.

The remainder of this paper is structured as follows: The related work of attribute-based encryption and signcryption is introduced in Sect. 2. The scheme model is designed in Sect. 3. In Sect. 4, the attribute-based access control and privacy-preserving algorithm for HSDN is described. The conclusion is provided in Sect. 5.

2   Related Work

Attribute-based encryption algorithm is one of the primary methods for achieving fine-grained control access. In 2005, Sahai and Waters [7] introduced the concept of attribute-based encryption (ABE). ABE regards the attribute set as the identity of the user. It makes the identity information descriptive, and implements various access strategies [8]. It can be divided into: Key-Policy Attribute-Based Encryption (KP-ABE) and Ciphertext-Policy Attribute-Based Encryption (CP-ABE) [9]. In the KP-ABE [10] mechanism, the ciphertext is labeled with a set of attributes, while the private decryption key is associated with an access structure in the form of a tree. The leaves of the tree represent the descriptive attributes. A user can be able to make a decryption, if and only if the access structure matches the attribute set, in the system of KP-ABE. The CP-ABE system [11] encrypts the plaintext with an attribute access structure, and the decryption key corresponds to a set of attributes, and the ciphertext can be decrypted if and only if the attribute set fits the access structure. CP-ABE is widely used to achieve different access rights according to users' attribute set [12].

Signcryption can complete both signing and encryption as a single logical primitive. It is first introduced by Zheng [13]. Signcryption has smaller cost than traditional method of encrypting and signing. Attribute-based signcryption (ABSC) [14] implements confidentiality, fine-grained access control and unforge-ability simultaneously. The key-policy attribute-based signcryption (KP-ABSC) system encrypts and signs the plaintext with the attribute set, only the users who have the matching access structure can obtain and verify plaintext. Rao [15] proposes an attribute-based signcryption scheme for LSSS-realizable access structures with the constant size ciphertext. Traceable attribute-based signcryption is presented [16], it uses non-interactive witness indistinguishable proofs to enjoy traceability. Liu [17] presents a key-policy attribute-based signcryption scheme with delegated computation and efficient key updating. However, the existing KP-ABSC cannot distinguish multiple access structures.

Attribute-based encryption has been applied in SDN to protect network data security. Armando et al. [18] take an advantage of CP-ABE to guarantee authorized terminals to receive and route packets in SDN. In the industrial internet of things environment, Chaudhary et al. [19] use CP-ABE algorithm to implement secure communication between the data requesters and the master controller of a hierarchical SDN network. He et al. [20] propose the hierarchical attribute-based encryption method to implement data privacy protection of the controller and provide the authentication protocol for HSDN. However, the existing schemes mainly focus on the usage of CP-ABE to protect the data security and fine-grained access control in the upper controller- RC, but do not consider the communication security when LC transmits data to RC.

Based on the above research, when LC accesses the data in RC, CP-ABE can be extended to achieve fine-grained data access control and authentication of LC to guarantee the legal access. When LC sends information to RC, KP-ABSC can be improved to verify the authenticity and integrity of the received data. RC stores multiple access structures according to network service demands, the access structure for decryption needs to be confirmed. What's more, RC needs to verify the identity of the LC to prevent attackers from uploading fake messages. Therefore, we propose a key-policy attribute based signcryption for multi-access structures (KP-ABSC-MAS).

3   System Model

The hierarchical SDN network privacy protection scheme mainly involves three entities: Local Controller (LC), Root Controller (RC) and Key Authority (KA).

RC: RC stores global network topology data and various application data. Different types of data have different access rights. This results in various access structures. RC generates a list $\mathcal{L}$ that associates the IP address of LC with the identity number.

LC: LC stores the topology and application data of the regional network and needs to upload the data to RC to build global network data. Each LC has a separate attribute set based on its characteristics.

KA: It is responsible for generating various types of keys, including master key (MK), system public key (PK), private key (SK), signature key K_{sign} and verification key K_{ver}. (MK) is stored in KA. PK is sent to the data owner for encryption. KA generates SK, and transmit it to the visitor through the secure channel. K_{sign} is delivered to the data owner, and K_{ver} is sent to the decipherer to verify the authenticity of the data.

3.1   The Model of LC Accessing RC

In order to prevent the attacker from controlling LC, RC needs to authenticate LC, while LC is accessing RC. As shown in Fig. 1, KA generates $MK_{LC \to RC}$ and $PK_{LC \to RC}$, and sends $PK_{LC \to RC}$ to RC for encryption via the ordinary channel. LC transmits the attribute set to the KA via the secure channel, and KA returns

$SK_{LC \to RC}$. $SK_{LC \to RC}$ is generated with the attribute set and $MK_{LC \to RC}$. After LC sends access request to RC, RC looks up LC's IP address in the list $\mathcal{L}$. If there is no LC's IP address, the access request will be denied. If the IP is found, RC will use $PK_{LC \to RC}$ and the access structure to encrypt the network data file and identity number ID_j, and send the ciphertext to LC. ID_j is associated with LC's IP address. Each LC has a separate attribute set. Only when LC's attribute set satisfies the access structure of the encrypted data file, LC can obtain the plaintext and ID_j. (LC's ID_j has to be encrypted, because LC needs to generate the access structure index for RC. Once the ID_j is stolen, the private key of RC may be destroyed).

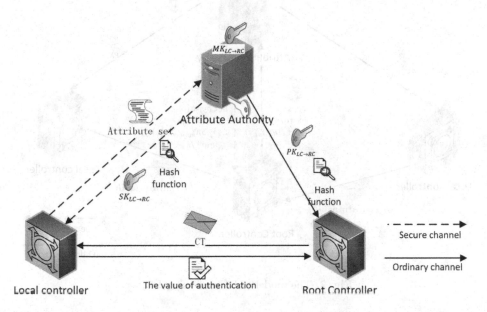

Fig. 1. The model of LC accessing RC.

Then LC automatically returns the hash value of ID_j. By verifying the hash value, RC can confirm whether LC has successfully made decryption and obtained the correct identity number. In other words, access right of LC can be detected with encrypted identity number. If the verification value is correct, RC will associate the access structure γ_d of the data file with ID_j and the IP address of LC in the list $\mathcal{L}\{ID_j, \gamma_d\}$. If the verification value is incorrect or LC does not return the verification value, it means LC's decryption key is incorrect or LC has a security problem. Then RC notifies the network administrator to isolate LC and take security measures, and removes the related information of LC in the list $\mathcal{L}\{ID_j, \gamma_d\}$. After the recovery, LC registers with RC. And RC re-records the IP address in the list and assigns a new ID to LC. Although the illegal LC may obtain the ciphertext, the security of the data and the identity number can be protected by attribute based encryption.

3.2   The Model of RC Accessing LC

Since the attacker may distort and forge the data of LC, RC needs to verify the integrity of the data and identity of LC, while RC is accessing LC. As depicted in Fig. 2, RC sends its own identity number ID_0 and the access structure list $\mathcal{L}\{ID_j, \gamma_d\}$ to KA via a secure channel at first. The access structure index value V_j can be obtained by the hash transformation of ID_j.

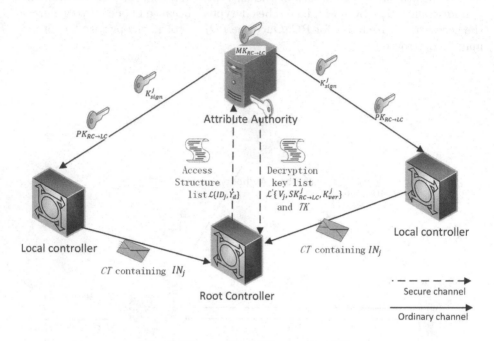

Fig. 2. The model of RC accessing LC.

KA generates master key $MK_{RC \rightarrow LC}$, public key $PK_{RC \rightarrow LC}$, and sign key K_{sign}^j, verification key K_{ver}^j of LC. $PK_{RC \rightarrow LC}$ and K_{sign}^j are sent to LC for encryption and signature via an ordinary channel. Then KA calculates all the private keys $SK_{RC \rightarrow LC}^j$ according to the list $\mathcal{L}\{ID_j, \gamma_d\}$, computes the trapdoor TK of V_j with ID_0, and generates the decryption key list $\mathcal{L}'\{V_j, SK_{RC \rightarrow LC}^j, K_{ver}^j\}$ which associates $SK_{RC \rightarrow LC}^j$ and K_{ver}^j with V_j. TK and $\mathcal{L}'\{V_j, SK_{RC \rightarrow LC}^j, K_{ver}^j\}$ are transmitted to RC via a secure channel. When LC sends a message to RC, LC generates IN_j the ciphertext of index value to inform RC of the information of the decryption access structure and its identity, and calculates CT_{sign}^j the ciphertext of the message with $PK_{RC \rightarrow LC}$ and K_{sign}^j. After receiving the ciphertext including IN_j and CT_{sign}^j, RC decrypts IN_j to get V_j with TK. According to V_j, RC searches for the correct decryption key and the verification key in the list $\mathcal{L}'\{V_j, SK_{RC \rightarrow LC}^j, K_{ver}^j\}$ to decrypt and verify the message. And the ciphertext can be decrypted if and only if the access structure of the key can match the attribute set of LC.

4   Construction of Our Proposed Scheme for Controllers in HSDN

4.1   Algorithm Model of CP-ABE-IA

In order to achieve fine-grained data access in RC, the data files are encrypted by CP-ABE with different access structures. LC can access the data if and only if LC's attribute set suits with the access structure. A generic algorithm model of access control in RC consists of the following algorithms:

(1) **Setup:** KA takes a security parameter as input, outputs the system public key $PK_{LC \to RC}$, the master key $MK_{LC \to RC}$ and a hash function $H(x)$, and transmits $PK_{LC \to RC}$ and $H(x)$ to RC.

(2) **KeyGenerate** $(MK_{LC \to RC}, A_j)$: KA takes $MK_{LC \to RC}$ and attribute set of LC as input, computes the corresponding private key $SK_{LC \to RC}$ and transmits $SK_{LC \to RC}$ and $H(x)$ to LC.

(3) **Encrypt** $(PK_{LC \to RC}, \gamma_d, M, ID_0, ID_j)$: RC encrypts the message M, ID_0, ID_j and a random number r with $PK_{LC \to RC}$ and the access structure γ_d, outputs the ciphertext $CT(M \parallel ID_0 \parallel ID_j)$ and transmits CT to LC.

(4) **Decrypt** $(CT, SK_{LC \to RC})$: LC decrypts CT using $SK_{LC \to RC}$ and gets M', ID'_0, ID'_j and r'.

(5) **Authenticate** (ID'_0, ID'_j, r'): LC computes $Z' = H(ID'_0 \parallel ID'_j \parallel r')$ and sends Z' to the RC.

(6) **Verify** (Z', ID_0, ID_j, r): RC computes $Z = H(ID_0 \parallel ID_j \parallel r)$ after receiving Z', and judges if Z is equal to Z'.

1–4 algorithms of the model make use of CP-ABE, which is specified in [14,15]. 5–6 algorithms carry out the authentication of LC. ID_0, ID_j and r are hidden in the ciphertext, thus attackers can not get the information of identifiers. If the authentication is correct, it means LC performs legal access. If LC does not perform hash calculation or the authentication fails, it means the LC performs illegal access.

4.2   Algorithm Model of KP-ABSC MAS

There are multiple access structures in RC. When RC accesses LC, the access structure for decryption has to be determined. Moreover, the identity of LC and the ciphertext integrity have to be verified. Thus we propose the algorithm of key-policy attribute based signcryption for multi-access structures (KP-ABSC-MAS).

KP-ABSC-MA consists of the following four algorithms:

(1) **Setup** $(\mathcal{L}\{ID_j, \gamma_d\})$: After receiving $\mathcal{L}\{ID_j, \gamma_d\}$ from RC, KA executes the algorithm as follows:

(1) Select a bilinear group $\mathbb{G}_1$ of prime order p with the generator g and let $e : \mathbb{G}_1 \times \mathbb{G}_1 \to \mathbb{G}_2$. Choose $y, w \in Z_p^*$, $g_2 \in \mathbb{G}_1$, and set $Y = e(g,g)^y$, $L = g^w$. For each attribute $att_i \in A_j$, select $t_i \in Z_p^*$ and compute $R_i = g^{t_i}$. Define three functions $f_1 : \{0,1\}^* \to Z_p^*$, $f_2 : \{0,1\}^* \to \mathbb{G}_1$, $f_3 : \{0,1\}^* \to Z_p^*$. The system master key is:

$$MK : \{t_i, y, w, x\} \tag{1}$$

And the system public key is

$$PK : \{\mathbb{G}_1, \mathbb{G}_2, p, g, g_2, e, R_i, L, Y, f_1, f_2, f_3\} \tag{2}$$

(2) Calculate the index value of each access structure with $\mathcal{L}\{ID_j, \gamma_d\}$:

$$V_j = f_1(ID_j) \tag{3}$$

(3) Select $k \in Z_p^*$, and set signature key and verification key with $\mathcal{L}\{ID_j, \gamma_d\}$:

$$K_{sign}^j = g^{(\frac{y+f_1(ID_j)}{w})k} \tag{4}$$

$$K_{ver}^j = g^{kf_1(ID_j)} \tag{5}$$

KA sends $PK_{RC \to LC}$ and K_{sign}^j to LC.

(2) **KeyGenerate** ($PK_{RC \to LC}$, $MK_{RC \to LC}$, ID_0, $\mathcal{L}\{ID_j, \gamma_d\}$): KA generates the trapdoor of the index value of the access structure and computes the private key of each LC for RC as follows:

(1) Select $d \in Z_p^*$, and compute $T_1 = g_2^w$, $T_2 = g^d$, $T_3 = g^{f_2(ID_0)d}$. The trapdoor of the index value of the access structure is:

$$TK = (T_1, T_2, T_3) \tag{6}$$

(2) Select polynomial q_x for each node in the access structure γ_d, set $q_{root}(0) = y$ for the root node, and $q_x(0) = q_{parent(x)}(index(x))$ for the child nodes. Select $h \in Z_p^*$, and compute $D_1 = g^{\frac{q_x(0)}{w}}$, $H_i = g^{t_i}$. The private key of the encrypted data of LC is

$$SK_{RC \to LC}^j = D_1, D_2, H_i, i \in \gamma_i \tag{7}$$

TK and $\mathcal{L}'\{V_j, SK_{RC \to LC}^j, K_{ver}^j\}$ are sent to RC in a secure channel.

(3) **SignCrypt** ($PK_{RC \to LC}$, M, A_j, K_{sign}^j, ID_0, ID_j): LC encrypts the message and the index value of the access structure as follows:

(1) Select $\alpha, \beta \in Z_p^*$, for each attribute $i \in A_j$, compute $C_{0,i} = R_i^\alpha = g^{t_i \alpha}$, $C_1 = f_2(ID_j)^\alpha$, $C_2 = Y^\beta = e(g,g)^{y\beta}$, $C_3 = L^\alpha = g^{w\alpha}$, $C_4 = L^{\alpha+\beta} = g^{w(\alpha+\beta)}$, $C_5 = g^\alpha$. Select $\zeta \in Z_p^*$, compute $\phi = g^\zeta \cdot K_{sign}^j = g^\zeta \cdot g^{(\frac{y+f_1(ID_j)}{w})k}$, $\mu = e(L^\alpha, g^\zeta) = e(g,g)^{w\alpha\zeta}$, $\pi = f_3(\mu/M) = f_3(e(g,g)^{w\alpha\zeta}/M)$. The signcryption is

$$CT_{sign}^j = (\forall i \in A_i C_{o,i}, C_1, C_2, C_3, C_4, C_5, \phi, \pi) \tag{8}$$

(2) Choose $s \in Z_p^*$, and compute $N_1 = e(L, g_2^s) \cdot f1(ID_j) = e(g^w, g_2^s) \cdot f_1(ID_j)$, $N_2 = g^s$, $N_3 = g^{f_2(ID_0)s}$. The encryption of the index value of the access structure is

$$IN_j = (N_1, N_2, N_3) \tag{9}$$

The encryption which is sent to RC is $CT^j_{RC \to LC}\{CT^j_{sign}, IN_j\}$.

(4) **Designcrypt** $(CT^j_{RC \to LC}\{CT^j_{sign}, IN_j\}, \mathcal{L}'\{V_j, SK^j_{RC \to LC}, K^j_{ver}\}, TK)$:
RC decrypts and verifies the message as follows:

(1) Calculate the index value of the access structure:

$$V_j = N_1 \cdot \frac{e(T_2, N_3)}{e(N_2, T_1 \cdot T_3)} = f_1(ID_j) \tag{10}$$

Search the decryption key and the verification key in the list
$\mathcal{L}'\{V_j, SK^j_{RC \to LC}, K^j_{ver}\}$ according to V_j.
(2) Compute the message:

$$A = \frac{e(C_1, H_i) \cdot e(D_2, C_4)}{e(C_{0,i}, D_1)}, M' = \frac{C_2}{A} \tag{11}$$

(3) Verify the message:

$$\tilde{A} = \frac{e(C_{0,i}, D_1)}{e(C_1, H_i)}, \mu' = \frac{e(C_3, \phi)}{e(C_5, K^j_{ver}) \cdot \tilde{A}}, \pi' = f_3(\mu'/M') \tag{12}$$

If $\pi' = \pi$, output M, otherwise output $\perp$.

5 Conclusion

In this paper, we presents an attribute-based access control and privacy preserving scheme for HSDN. When LC accesses data in RC, CP-ABE algorithm is combined with authentication to protect the security of the data in RC and ensure the legitimate access right of LC. When LC sends data to RC, we proposes KP-ABSC-MAS algorithm to achieve distinguishability of the decrypting access structure and confidentiality, unforgeability of the data. The scheme is scalable aim at the network structure features of HSDN. When the number of controllers increases, the solution is still applicable without additional calculations. Due to the page limit, the security proof and performance evaluation will be given in the extended version.

References

1. Jingjing, Z., Di, C., Weiming, W., Rong, J., Xiaochun, W.: The deployment of routing protocols in distributed control plane of SDN. Sci. World J. **2014**, 1–8 (2014)
2. Fu, Y., Bi, J., Gao, K., Chen, Z., Wu, J., Hao, B.: Orion: a hybrid hierarchical control plane of software-defined networking for large-scale networks. In: 2014 IEEE 22nd International Conference on Network Protocols, pp. 569–576. IEEE (2014)
3. Hassas Yeganeh, S., Ganjali, Y.: Kandoo: a framework for efficient and scalable offloading of control applications. In: Proceedings of the First Workshop on Hot Topics in Software Defined Networks, pp. 19–24. ACM (2012)

4. Klaedtke, F., Karame, G. O., Bifulco, R., Cui, H.: Access control for SDN controllers. In: Proceedings of the Third Workshop on Hot Topics in Software Defined Networking, pp. 219–220. Citeseer (2014)
5. Mattos, D.M.F., Duarte, O.C.M.B.: AuthFlow: authentication and access control mechanism for software defined networking. Ann. Telecommun. **71**(11–12), 607–615 (2016)
6. Ranjbar, A., Komu, M., Salmela, P., Aura, T.: An SDN-based approach to enhance the end-to-end security: SSL/TLS case study. In: NOMS 2016–2016 IEEE/IFIP Network Operations and Management Symposium, pp. 281–288. IEEE (2016)
7. Sahai, A., Waters, B.: Fuzzy identity-based encryption. In: Cramer, R. (ed.) EURO-CRYPT 2005. LNCS, vol. 3494, pp. 457–473. Springer, Heidelberg (2005). https://doi.org/10.1007/11426639_27
8. Boneh, D., Franklin, M.: Identity-based encryption from the weil pairing. In: Kilian, J. (ed.) CRYPTO 2001. LNCS, vol. 2139, pp. 213–229. Springer, Heidelberg (2001). https://doi.org/10.1007/3-540-44647-8_13
9. Goyal, V., Pandey, O., Sahai, A., Waters, B.: Attribute-based encryption for fine-grained access control of encrypted data. In: Proceedings of the 13th ACM Conference on Computer and Communications Security, pp. 89–98. ACM (2006)
10. Kim, J., Susilo, W., Guo, F., Au, M. H., Nepal, S.: An efficient KP-ABE with short ciphertexts in prime ordergroups under standard assumption. In: Proceedings of the 2017 ACM on Asia Conference on Computer and Communications Security, pp. 823–834. ACM (2017)
11. Guo, F., Mu, Y., Susilo, W., Wong, D.S., Varadharajan, V.: CP-ABE with constant-size keys for lightweight devices. IEEE Trans. Inf. Forensics Secur. **9**(5), 763–771 (2014)
12. Yang, K., Jia, X.: Expressive, efficient, and revocable data access control for multi-authority cloud storage. IEEE Trans. Parallel Distrib. Syst. **25**(7), 1735–1744 (2013)
13. Zheng, Y.: Signcryption and its applications in efficient public key solutions. In: Okamoto, E., Davida, G., Mambo, M. (eds.) ISW 1997. LNCS, vol. 1396, pp. 291–312. Springer, Heidelberg (1998). https://doi.org/10.1007/BFb0030430
14. Xu, Q., Tan, C., Fan, Z., Zhu, W., Xiao, Y., Cheng, F.: Secure data access control for fog computing based on multi-authority attribute-based signcryption with computation outsourcing and attribute revocation. Sensors **18**(5), 1609 (2018)
15. Rao, Y.S., Dutta, R.: *Expressive* bandwidth-efficient attribute based signature and signcryption in standard model. In: Susilo, W., Mu, Y. (eds.) ACISP 2014. LNCS, vol. 8544, pp. 209–225. Springer, Cham (2014). https://doi.org/10.1007/978-3-319-08344-5_14
16. Wei, J., Hu, X., Liu, W.: Traceable attribute-based signcryption. Secur. Commun. Netw. **7**(12), 2302–2317 (2014)
17. Liu, X., Xia, Y., Sun, Z.: Provably secure attribute based signcryption with delegated computation and efficient key updating. KSII Trans. Internet Inf. Syst. **11**(5), 2646–2659 (2017)
18. Armando, A., Ranise, S., Traverso, R., Wrona, K.: Compiling NATO authorization policies for enforcement in the cloud and SDNs. In: 2015 IEEE Conference on Communications and Network Security (CNS), pp. 741–742. IEEE (2015)

19. Chaudhary, R., Aujla, G.S., Garg, S., Kumar, N., Rodrigues, J.J.: SDN-enabled multi-attribute-based secure communication for smart grid in IIoT environment. IEEE Trans. Ind. Inform. **14**(6), 2629–2640 (2018)
20. Riad, K.: Multi-authority trust access control for cloud storage. In: 2016 4th International Conference on Cloud Computing and Intelligence Systems (CCIS), pp. 429–433. IEEE (2016)

ECC²: Error Correcting Code and Elliptic Curve Based Cryptosystem

Fangguo Zhang[1,2(✉)] and Zhuoran Zhang[1,2]

[1] School of Data and Computer Science,
Sun Yat-sen University, Guangzhou 510006, China
isszhfg@mail.sysu.edu.cn

[2] Guangdong Key Laboratory of Information Security, Guangzhou 510006, China

Abstract. With the fast development of quantum computation, code-based cryptography arises public concern as a candidate for post quantum cryptography. However, the large key-size becomes a drawback such that the code-based schemes seldom become practical. Algebraic geometry codes was considered to be a good solution to reduce the size of keys, but its special structure results in lots of attacks. In this paper, we propose a public key encryption scheme based on elliptic codes which can resist the known attacks. By choosing the rational points carefully, we build elliptic codes that can resist Minder's attack. We apply the list decoding algorithm to decryption thus more errors beyond half of the minimum distance of the code could be correct, which is the key point to resist other known attacks for AG code based cryptosystems.

Keywords: Code-based cryptography, Post quantum cryptography, Elliptic codes, List decoding

1 Introduction

Since the introduction of public key cryptography in 1976 [6], many cryptosystems have been proposed. However, with the discovering of Shor Algorithm [29] and the rapid development of quantum computers, most of the commonly used public key cryptosystems who based on the hardness of factoring or the discrete logarithm problem, become unsafe anymore. Thus, how to build cryptosystems that can resist the attack from quantum computers, i.e. post-quantum cryptosystems, raises the researchers concern.

The code-based McEliece system [17] was proposed in 1978. Its security relies on the hardness of decoding a random linear code, and it is a very strong candidate for the future post-quantum standards for public-key encryption. Niederreiter [23] gave a variant of McEliece system, and a significant amount of research went into analysing and improving them.

Algebraic geometry (AG) code was proposed by Goppa [8] in 1977 and was introduced into cryptography in 1996 by Janwa and Moreno [14]. Their original idea to use AG codes was to decrease the so large public key of McEliece scheme,

© Springer Nature Switzerland AG 2019
J. Vaidya et al. (Eds.): CSS 2019, LNCS 11982, pp. 214–229, 2019.
https://doi.org/10.1007/978-3-030-37337-5_17

since AG codes have structure that can be constructed by the divisor and the rational point set other than the generator matrix. Meanwhile, AG codes also give immense choice, allowing people to vary the field, the curves, and the divisors generating the codes.

Unfortunately, their special structure becomes a drawback as well, and results in many attacks towards it. In 1992, Sidelnikov and Shestakov [30] discovered a structural attack against Niederreiter's proposal using Reed-Solomon codes, i.e. AG codes with genus $g = 0$. In 2007, Minder [20] claimed the codes defined on elliptic curve whose genus $g = 1$ are broken. Minder and Faure [7] then generalized this work into hyperelliptic curve with $g = 2$. In 2014, Márquez-Corbella et al. proved that the structure of the curve can be recovered from the only knowledge of a generator matrix of the code [15,16], but the corresponding decoding algorithm is lacked. Recently, Pellikaan et al. [5] proposed a decoding attack using Error-Correct-Pairing (ECP) decoding algorithm which is efficient on codes from curves of arbitrary genus based on their previous work [12,25]. These attacks seem to warning us, AG code is not a good choice to construct cryptosystem.

However, after studying all the attacks above, we found that except Minder's attack, they all hold on the assumption that no more than $(d-1)/2$ errors occur, where d denotes the minimum distance of the code. This may arise from that most decoding algorithms used in building cryptosystem is unique decoding, whose error correcting bounding is less than $(d-1)/2$. In 1999, Guruswami and Sudan [10] proposed a list decoding algorithm for both RS and AG codes which can correct more than $(d-1)/2$ errors in polynomial time. When it comes to Minder's attack, we found it relies on the assumption that the minimum weight codeword can be sampled easily and the evaluated point set is large enough. Thus, as long as we choose suitable parameters, especially the number of error weights, we can build a security elliptic code based cryptosystem.

Our Contributions: In this paper, we reconsider the application of algebraic geometry codes, especially elliptic codes, in cryptography, and propose a public-key encryption scheme based on elliptic codes. We prove that under the elliptic codes syndrome decoding assumption, our scheme is IND-CPA secure. We choose evaluated points set carefully and introduce list decoding of elliptic codes into our scheme to prevent it from the known attacks.

Organization: In Sect. 2, we review some preliminaries that will be used later. In Sect. 3, we present our cryptosystem based on elliptic code. In Sect. 4, we show the security analysis together with the parameters we recognized. In Sect. 5, we analyse the efficiency of our scheme. Last but not least, Sect. 6 draws the conclusion to this paper.

2   Preliminaries

In this section, we present the notions of coding theory that are prerequisite for the following chapters as well as basic knowledge about code-based cryptography.

2.1 Linear Codes and Code-Based Cryptography

An $[n,k]_q$ linear error-correcting code $\mathcal{C}$ is a linear subspace of a vector space $\mathbb{F}_q^n$, where $\mathbb{F}_q$ denotes the finite field of q elements, and k denotes the dimension of the subspace. The generator matrix for a linear code is a $k \times n$ matrix with rank k which defines a linear mapping from $\mathbb{F}_q^k$ to $\mathbb{F}_q^n$. Namely, the code $\mathcal{C}$ is $\mathcal{C} = \mathcal{C}(\mathsf{G}) = \{\boldsymbol{x}\mathsf{G} \mid \boldsymbol{x} \in \mathbb{F}_q^k\}$. We call a vector in $\mathcal{C}$ a codeword.

Given a codeword $\boldsymbol{c} = (c_1, c_2, \ldots, c_n) \in \mathbb{F}_q^n$, its Hamming weight $\mathsf{wt}(\boldsymbol{c})$ is defined to be the number of non-zero coordinates, i.e. $\mathsf{wt}(\boldsymbol{c}) = |\{i \mid c_i \neq 0, 1 \le i \le n\}|$. The distance of two codewords $\boldsymbol{c}_1, \boldsymbol{c}_2$, denoted by $d(\boldsymbol{c}_1, \boldsymbol{c}_2)$ counts the number of coordinates they differ. The minimum distance $d(\mathcal{C})$ of code $\mathcal{C}$ is the minimal value of the distance between any two different codewords. If a linear $[n,k]_q$ code has d as the minimum distance, $\mathcal{C}$ is called a $[n,k,d]_q$ linear code.

If $\boldsymbol{c}$ is a codeword and $\boldsymbol{c} + \boldsymbol{e}$ is the received word, then we call $\boldsymbol{e}$ the error vector and $\{i|e_i \neq 0\}$ the set of error positions and $\mathsf{wt}(\boldsymbol{e})$ is the number of errors of the received word. If $\boldsymbol{r}$ is the received word and the distance from $\boldsymbol{r}$ to the code $\mathcal{C}$ is t', then there exists a codeword $\boldsymbol{c}'$ and an error vector $\boldsymbol{e}'$ such that $\boldsymbol{r} = \boldsymbol{c}' + \boldsymbol{e}'$ and $\mathsf{wt}(\boldsymbol{e}') = t'$. If the number of errors is at most $(d-1)/2$, then it is sure that $\boldsymbol{c} = \boldsymbol{c}'$ and $\boldsymbol{e} = \boldsymbol{e}'$. In other words, the nearest codeword to $\boldsymbol{r}$ is unique when $\boldsymbol{r}$ has distance at most $(d-1)/2$ to $\mathcal{C}$.

Nowadays, most code-based cryptography are variants of either McEliece [17] system or Niederreiter [23]. McEliece public-key encryption system was proposed in 1978. Figure 1 shows the McEliece PKE scheme. Niederreiter's cryptosystem [23] can be seen as the dual variant of the McEliece's. Instead of representing the message as a codeword, Niederreiter proposed to encode it into the error vector. The advantage of this dual variant is the smaller public key size since it is sufficient to store the redundant part of the matrix H^{pub}. The disadvantage is the fact that the mapping $\phi_{n,t}$ slows down encryption and decryption.

Key Generation:	**Encryption:**
G: $k \times n$ generator matrix of code $\mathcal{C}$	plaintext $\boldsymbol{m} \in \mathbb{F}^k$
with error correcting capability t	$\boldsymbol{e} \leftarrow_{\$} \mathbb{F}^n$ of weight t
S: $k \times k$ random non-singular matrix	$\boldsymbol{c} \leftarrow \boldsymbol{m}\mathsf{G}^{pub} \oplus \boldsymbol{e}$
P: $n \times n$ random permutation matrix	
$\mathsf{G}^{pub} \leftarrow \mathsf{SGP}$	**Decryption:**
C.Decode: decoding algorithm for $\mathcal{C}$	$\boldsymbol{c}\mathsf{P}^{-1} = (\boldsymbol{m}\mathsf{S})\mathsf{G} \oplus \boldsymbol{e}\mathsf{P}^{-1}$
$pk \leftarrow <\mathsf{G}^{pub}, t>$	$\boldsymbol{m}\mathsf{SG} = \mathsf{C.Decode}(\boldsymbol{c}\mathsf{P}^{-1})$
$sk \leftarrow <\mathsf{S}, \mathsf{P}, \mathsf{C.Decode}>$	$\boldsymbol{m} = \mathsf{C.Decode}(\boldsymbol{c}\mathsf{P}^{-1})\mathsf{S}^{-1}\mathsf{G}^{-1}$

Fig. 1. McEliece public-key encryption scheme

2.2 Algebraic Geometry Codes and List Decoding Algorithms

Let $\mathcal{X}$ be an irreducible curve over a finite field $\mathbb{F}_q$ of genus g. The function field of $\mathcal{X}$ is denoted by $\mathbb{F}_q(\mathcal{X})$. A divisor D on a curve $\mathcal{X}$ is a formal sum of points P on curve $\mathcal{X}$, i.e. $D = \Sigma_P n_P P$ where $n_P \in \mathbb{Z} \setminus \{0\}$ for a finite number of points on $\mathcal{X}$. The degree of a divisor D is defined as the sum of n_P, i.e., $deg(D) = \Sigma_P n_P$. The support of a divisor $supp(D)$ is the set of points with non-zero coefficients.

For each point $P \in \mathcal{X}$ and any $f \in \mathbb{F}_q(\mathcal{X}) \setminus \{0\}$, we can abstract the notion of evaluation of f at P by $v_P : \mathbb{F}_q(\mathcal{X}) \to \mathbb{Z} \cup \{\infty\}$. Any function $f \in \mathbb{F}_q(\mathcal{X}) \setminus \{0\}$ can be associated with a principal divisor. The principle divisor of $f \in \mathbb{F}_q(\mathcal{X})$ is defined as $div(f) = \Sigma_P v_P(f)P$. Let $G = \Sigma_P n_P P$ be any divisor of degree k on $\mathcal{X}$. Denote by $\mathcal{L}(G)$ all rational functions $f \in \mathbb{F}_q(\mathcal{X})$ such that the divisor $div(f)+G$ is effective, together with the zero function, i.e., $\mathcal{L}(G) = \{f \mid div(f) + G \succeq 0\} \cup \{0\}$. By the Riemann-Roch theorem, $\mathcal{L}(G)$ is a vector space over $\mathbb{F}_q$ of finite dimension $dim(\mathcal{L}(G)) = k - g + 1$, where g is the genus of $\mathcal{X}$. Given an irreducible curve $\mathcal{X}$ and the function field $\mathbb{F}_q(\mathcal{X})$ defined over $\mathcal{X}$, let $P_1, P_2, \ldots, P_n$ be distinct rational points on $\mathcal{X}$. These n points determine a divisor $D = \Sigma_{i=1}^n P_i$. Let G be an arbitrary divisor on $\mathcal{X}$ such that $\{P_1, \ldots, P_n\} \cap supp(G) = \emptyset$. An AG code $\mathcal{C}(D, G)$ is defined by the following injective mapping ev $: \mathcal{L}(G) \to \mathbb{F}_q^n$ with $\mathsf{ev}(f) = (f(P_1), f(P_2), \ldots, f(P_n))$. Hence $\mathcal{C}(D, G) = \mathsf{image}(\mathsf{ev})$. If $G = \Sigma_P n_P P$ is a divisor of degree k, then $\mathcal{C}(D, G)$ is an $[n, k - g + 1, d]_q$ code and $d \geq n - k + 1 - g$. The basic properties of AG codes can be found in [13].

List decoding is a powerful decoding algorithm with a long history. For any $[n, k, d]$ linear code, a well-known fact is that if the number of errors t satisfies $t \leq \lceil (d-1)/2 \rceil$, then there must exist a unique codeword within distance $\lceil (d-1)/2 \rceil$ from the received vector.

Sudan [32] proposed a list decoding algorithm for RS codes based on factorization of bivariate polynomials. The algorithm is able to efficiently output a list of codewords which lie in the sphere of radius up to $t = n - \sqrt{2n(n - d)}$ centered around the received vector. Immediately, Shokrollahi and Wasserman [28] generalized this results to AG codes, and can correct $n - \beta - 1$ errors with an output list of size b where $\beta = \lceil (n + 1)/(b + 1) + bk/2 + g - 1 \rceil$. In 1999, Guruswami and Sudan [9] proposed another list decoding algorithm for both RS and AG codes, and improve the error-bounding to $n - \sqrt{n(n - d)}$. Then Wu presented an efficient root finding algorithm in [33]. More precisely, the list decoding algorithm C.ListDecode takes as input a linear $[n, k]$ code $\mathcal{C}$, a received vector $\boldsymbol{r}$ and a parameter $t \leq n - \sqrt{n(n - d)}$, and it outputs a list of codewords whose Hamming distances to $\boldsymbol{r}$ are at most t. Up to now, the list decoding algorithm is one of the most powerful decoding methods for AG codes, and is widely used in communication engineering. Researchers also make use of it to reduce the key size for McEliece cryptosystems [21] or to solve ECDLP [34].

2.3   Hard Problems on Elliptic Codes

Consider the curve defined by the Weierstrass equation $\mathcal{E} : y^2 + a_1 xy + a_3 y = x^3 + a_2 x^2 + a_4 x + a_6$. If the parameters a_i are such that the curve is smooth, then it is an elliptic curve. If $char(\mathbb{F}_q) \neq 2, 3$, the Weierstrass equation can be taken in the form $\mathcal{E} : y^2 = x^3 + ax + b$ up to a coordinate transformation. Let $\mathcal{E}$ be an elliptic curve over $\mathbb{F}_q$ and $\mathbb{F}_q(\mathcal{E})$ be the elliptic function field, then there exists an additive abelian group $\mathcal{E}(\mathbb{F}_q)$ with the group operation defined by the "chord-and-tangent" rule on $\mathcal{E}$. More details in [31].

Let $P_1, P_2, \ldots, P_n \in \mathcal{E}(\mathbb{F}_q)$. Define $D = P_1 + \cdots + P_n$ be a divisor on $\mathcal{E}$. Let G be another divisor on $\mathcal{E}$ such that $0 < deg(G) = k < n$ and $supp(D) \cap supp(G) = \emptyset$. The elliptic code $\mathcal{C}(D, G)$ defined by G and D is

$$\mathcal{C}(D, G) = \{(f(P_1), \ldots, f(P_n)) \mid f \in \mathcal{L}(G)\} \subseteq \mathbb{F}_q^n.$$

Cheng [4] reduced the subset sum problem to the problem of computing minimum distance of elliptic codes and then come to the conclusion that deciding whether an AG code is maximum distance separable is NP-hard. An instance of minimum distance of elliptic codes (ECMD) problem is as follows.

Instance 1 (ECMD Problem). *Given an elliptic code $\mathcal{C}$. The ECMD problem ask for distinguish whether the minimum distance $d(\mathcal{C})$ of $\mathcal{C}$ is $n - k$ or $n - k + 1$.*

Syndrome Decoding (SD) Problem is one of the well-known hard problems in coding theory, and has been proved to be NP-hard for general linear codes in [2]. However, elliptic codes can be distinguished from random code by Schur production and SD problem for elliptic code has not been proved to be NP-hard. Instance 2 shows a computating elliptic code syndrome decoding (CECSD) problem. The corresponding deciding problem asks for a distinguish between the distribution of a real syndrome and a random one and is shown in Instance 3.

Instance 2 (CECSD Problem). *Given a parity check matrix H of elliptic code $\mathcal{C}$, a syndrome $\boldsymbol{y}$. The CECSD problem ask for a vector $\boldsymbol{x}$, whose weight $\mathsf{wt}(\boldsymbol{x}) \leq t$, s.t. $\mathsf{H}\boldsymbol{x} = \boldsymbol{y}$.*

Instance 3 (DECSD Problem). *Given a parity check matrix H of elliptic code $\mathcal{C}$, a vector $\boldsymbol{y}$. The DECSD problem ask for distinguish whether $\boldsymbol{y}$ is a syndrome given by $\mathsf{H}\boldsymbol{x} = \boldsymbol{y}$ for some $\boldsymbol{x}$ or a random vector.*

We can find that ECSD problem connect tightly with ECMD problem. If we set the syndrome $\boldsymbol{y} = 0$ and weight $t = n - k$, then the answer of this DECSD problem leads to an answer to the ECMD problem. Based on this fact, we make an assumption that DECSD problem is hard.

3   McEliece Based Cryptosystem from Elliptic Codes

In this section, we will propose our scheme based on elliptic codes and McEliece encryption scheme. At the beginning, we show an algorithm to generating elliptic codes, which will be used as a subroutine in the following schemes. Next, we first give the construction of a basic scheme, and then give a more efficient scheme with key-encapsulation mechanism. Last but not least, we show how to transform the basic scheme into the dual Niederriter version.

3.1 Generate Elliptic Codes

Inspired by [4], we first show a construction of elliptic code, whose complexity of finding minimum distance codeword can be reduced to a sub set sum problem.

A secure elliptic code generation algorithm:ECGen

Input: The finite field $\mathbb{F}_q$, an elliptic curve $\mathcal{E} : y^2 = x^3 + ax + b$ whose order is prime p, the code parameters n, k.
Output: An elliptic code defined on $\mathcal{E}$ with minimum distance $n - k$.

- Define $B = 2 * (n - k)$. Randomly choose $S_1 = \{s_1, s_2, \ldots, s_k\}$ with $s_i > B$ for $1 \leq i \leq k$ and $\Sigma_{i=1}^k = p$. Randomly choose $L_2 = \{l_1, l_2, \ldots, l_{n-k}\}$ with $l_i < B$ for $1 \leq i \leq n - k$.
- $R = S_1 \cup L_2$, and do a random permutation for elements in R. After the permutation, support $R = \{r_1, r_2, \ldots, r_n\}$.
- Randomly choose a rational point P on $\mathcal{E}$. Set divisor $D = r_1 P + r_2 P + \cdots + r_n P$ and $G = k\mathcal{O}$.
- $\mathcal{C}(D, G) = \{(f(P_1), \ldots, f(P_n)) \mid f \in \mathcal{L}(G)\} \subset \mathbb{F}_q^n$.

This algorithm will be used as a subroutine in our cryptosystem.

3.2 The Basic Scheme: ECC^2

Our public-key encryption scheme based on elliptic codes is shown as follows:

- **Set up(1^λ):** Generates the global parameters **param** $= (q, n, k, t)$, where q is the size of the finite field, n is the length of the code and k is the dimension of the code. Denote t as the number of errors that are add to the codeword, such that C.ListDecode can correct t errors.
- **KeyGen(param):** Take **param** as input, and output the key pair (pk, sk). Firstly construct a finite field $\mathbb{F}_q$ with q elements. Then randomly choose $u, b \in \mathbb{F}_q$, such that the elliptic curve $\mathcal{E} : y^2 = x^3 + ax + b$ has p rational points where p is prime.
  Secondly, run ECGen to get the set R, point P, and code $\mathcal{C}$.
  Let $G = [I|G^{pub}]$ be a generator matrix of $\mathcal{C}$ in systematic form, I is an identity matrix.
  $$\text{pk} \leftarrow (G^{pub}), \text{sk} \leftarrow (a, P, R)$$
- **Encrypt(pk, m):** Take pk and message $m \in \mathbb{F}_q^k$ as input, and output the cipher-text c.
  Firstly, randomly choose a vector $r \in \mathbb{F}_q^k$, and another random vector e in $\mathbb{F}_q^n$ of weight t. Set $G = [I|G^{pub}]$.
  Then calculate $c_1 \leftarrow rG + e$, $c_2 \leftarrow m + r$, and the cipher-text is

$$c \leftarrow c_1 \| c_2$$

- **Decrypt**(sk, c): Take the secret key sk and cipher-text c as input, and output the message m.
  Once get the cipher-text, depart it into two parts with length n and k respectively to get c_1 and c_2.
  Then run the list decoding algorithm to calculate $r \leftarrow$ C.ListDecode(c_1).
  And finally we get

$$m \leftarrow c_2 - r$$

Correctness: Notice that the correctness of our scheme relies on the success of list decoding algorithm about C. To avoid the situation that there are more than one codeword are returned in the list, we can add some redundancies to the original message. There are many analysis about the number of codeword in the output list, like [18] for Reed-Solomon codes and [34] for elliptic codes etc. Acutually, as showed in [3], in CCA2-secure variants of McElieces system there is no difficulty in identifying which codeword is a valid message. Once the decoding algorithm success and a unique codeword is decided, then for a given message m and its corresponding ciphertext c, we have $c_2 -$ C.ListDecode(c_1) $= c_2 - r = m + r - r = m$, i.e.

$$\mathbf{Decrypt}(\mathsf{sk}, (\mathbf{Encrypt}(\mathsf{pk}, m))) = m,$$

which shows the correctness of our scheme.

The systematic form of the generator matrix of the underlying code can be stored in a brief form, which leads to a smaller size of the public key. Here we use list decoding algorithm as a subroutine in the decryption algorithm, because the traditional unique decoding algorithm is impossible to correct more than $(d-1)/2$ errors. Our basic scheme is IND-CPA and can be transformed into a CCA2-secure version by the universal method as mentioned in [11].

3.3   Transform to Key Encapsulation Mechanism

To make our scheme more practical, we propose the corresponding key encapsulation mechanism (KEM) by *Fujisaki-Okamoto* transformation [11] as follows.

Alice and Bob want to share a common session secret key K. Bob publishes his public key pk $= (G^{pub}, t)$, and his secret key is denoted as sk $= (\mathcal{E}, P_D, \sigma)$. Besides, choose secure hash functions $\mathcal{H}, \mathcal{K}, \mathcal{F}$.

- **Encap:** Alice randomly chooses a vector $m \in \mathbb{F}_q^n$. Then run the **Encrypt** algorithm with Bob's public key pk and $(m||\mathcal{H}(m))$. The output cipher-text is denoted as c. Set $d \leftarrow \mathcal{F}(m)$. Alice sends (c, d) to Bob.
  The session key is defined as $K \leftarrow \mathcal{K}(m||c)$.
- **Decap:** Bob receives (c, d). Then run the **Decrypt** algorithm with his secret key pk and c. Denote the output as $(m^*, \mathcal{H}(m^*))$. Bob computes $c^* \leftarrow \mathbf{Encrypt}(\mathsf{pk}, m^*||\mathcal{H}(m^*))$ and $d^* \leftarrow \mathcal{F}(m^*)$.
  If $c^* = c$ and $d^* = d$, Bob computes the session key $K \leftarrow \mathcal{K}(m^*||c^*)$.
  Else return *false*.

According to [11], the above KEM version of our scheme is IND-CCA2.

4 Security and Efficiency

In this section, we first prove the IND-CPA security of our encryption scheme. The security of the KEM version is provided by the transformation described in [11]. Then we analyse how our scheme can resist the known attacks. The two most important types of attacks against code-based cryptosystems are structural attacks and decoding attacks. Structural attacks exploit structural weaknesses in the construction and then attempt to recover the secret key. Decoding attacks are used to decrypt a given ciphertext. In this section, we will show how our system resists the known attacks and then give our parameters.

4.1 IND-CPA

Theorem 1. *The scheme presented above is IND-CPA under the DECSD assumption, i.e., if there exists an adversary $\mathcal{A}$ that can break the IND-CPA of ECC^2, then we can build an algorithm that solves the ECMD problem and DECSD problem.*

Proof. To prove the security of ECC^2, we are going to build a sequence of games transitioning from an adversary receiving an encryption of message m_0 to an adversary receiving an encryption of a message m_1 and show that if the adversary manages to distinguish one from the other, then we can build a simulator breaking the DECSD assumption.

Game G_0: This is the real game.

Game G_1: In this game we started by forgetting the secret key sk, and taking G^{pub} at random, and then proceed honestly.

The adversary has access to pk and c^*. As he has access to pk and the Encrypt function, anything that is computed from pk and c^* can also be computed from just pk. Moreover, the distribution of c^* is independent of the game we are in, and therefore we can suppose the only input of the adversary is pk.

Game G_2: In this game we started by taking error vector e at random, i.e. we lift restriction on the weight of e.

Suppose he has an algorithm $\mathcal{D}_\lambda$, taking pk as input, and distinguishes **Game G_0** and **Game G_1** for some security parameter λ. Then we can build an algorithm $\mathcal{D}_{0,1}$ which solves the ECMD problem, when given as input a challenge $\mathsf{G} \in \mathbb{F}_q^{n \times k}$.

As we mentioned before, the minimum distance problem of elliptic codes can be reduced to a subset sum problem. Our parameter in ECGen make sure that the number of rational points on the curve is much larger than the evaluated points we used to generate the code, which means to solve the corresponding subset sum problem is difficult, and thus to decide the minimum distance of the code is whether $n - k$ or $n - k + 1$ is hard.

Suppose he has an algorithm $\mathcal{D}_\lambda$, taking c^* as input, and distinguishes Game $\mathbf{G}_1$ and $\mathbf{G}_2$ with advantage ϵ, for some security parameter λ. Then we can build an algorithm $\mathcal{D}_{1,2}$ which solves the **DECSD** problem with the same advantage, when given as input a challenge $(\mathsf{H}, y) \in \mathbb{F}_q^{(n-k) \times k} \times \mathbb{F}_q^n$. And we have

$$\Pr[\mathcal{D}_{1,2}(\mathsf{H}, \boldsymbol{y}) = \mathrm{ECSD} \mid (\mathsf{H}, \boldsymbol{y}) \leftarrow \mathrm{ECSD}]$$
$$= \Pr[\mathcal{D}_{\lambda}(\boldsymbol{c}^*) = 0 \mid \boldsymbol{c}^* \leftarrow \mathbf{Game}^1_{\mathcal{A}}(\lambda)]$$
$$\Pr[\mathcal{D}_{1,2}(\mathsf{H}, \boldsymbol{y}) = \mathrm{UNIFORM} \mid (\mathsf{H}, \boldsymbol{y}) \leftarrow \mathrm{ECSD}]$$
$$= \Pr[\mathcal{D}_{\lambda}(\boldsymbol{c}^*) = 1 \mid \boldsymbol{c}^* \leftarrow \mathbf{Game}^1_{\mathcal{A}}(\lambda)]$$

Similarly when $(\mathsf{H}, \boldsymbol{y})$ is uniform the probabilities of outputs match those of $\mathcal{D}_{\lambda}$ when $\boldsymbol{c}^*$ is from $\mathbf{Game}^1_{\mathcal{A}}(\lambda)$. Therefore the advantage of $\mathcal{D}_{1,2}(\mathsf{H}, \boldsymbol{y})$ is ϵ, equalling to the advantage of $\mathcal{D}_{\lambda}$.

Game G_3: In this game we started by taking the first part of ciphertext $\boldsymbol{c}_1$ at random, i.e. there is no relationship between two part of the ciphertext now.

In Game $\mathbf{G}_2$ and $\mathbf{G}_3$, the distribution of $\boldsymbol{c}_1$ are both uniform, thus definitely are indistinguishable from an information-theoretic point of view.

Game G_4: Now we encrypt the other plaintext. The other part remains the same with $\mathbf{G}_3$.

The outputs from $\mathbf{G}_3$ and $\mathbf{G}_4$ are all uniformed vectors in $\mathbb{F}_q^{n+k}$, and therefore the two games are indistinguishable from the information theory knowledge.

Game G_5: In this game, $\boldsymbol{c}_1^* \leftarrow \boldsymbol{r}_1 \mathsf{G} + \boldsymbol{r}_2$, i.e. the only difference compared with $\mathbf{G}_2$ is different plaintext is encrypted.

Game G_6: In this game, $\boldsymbol{c}_1^* \leftarrow \boldsymbol{r}_1 \mathsf{G} + \boldsymbol{e}$ and $\mathsf{wt}(\boldsymbol{e}) = t$, i.e. the only difference compared with $\mathbf{G}_1$ is different plaintext is encrypted.

Game G_7: This is the real game in which we encrypt $\boldsymbol{m}_1$, i.e. the only difference compared with $\mathbf{G}_0$ is different plaintext is encrypted.

The indistinguishable between Game $\mathbf{G}_5$ and $\mathbf{G}_6$ is the same to Game $\mathbf{G}_1$ and $\mathbf{G}_2$, and between Game $\mathbf{G}_6$ and $\mathbf{G}_7$ is the same to Game $\mathbf{G}_1$ and $\mathbf{G}_0$.

4.2   Known Attacks

Information-Set-Decoding. Information-Set-Decoding is an approach introduced by Prange [27]. The idea is to find a set of coordinates of a garbled vector which are error-free and such that the restriction of the codes generator matrix to these positions is invertible. Then, the original message can be computed by multiplying the encrypted vector by the inverse of the submatrix. Peters [26] generalised the ISD algorithm over $\mathbb{F}_2$ to $\mathbb{F}_q$, afterwards Niebuhr et al. [22] optimized it and show a lower bound for their ISD algorithm.

Let $\mathcal{C}$ be a $[n, k]_q$ code and r be the co-dimension. To correct t errors, the lower bound for the expected cost in the binary operation of the algorithm is

$$WF_{qISD}(n, k, t, q) = min_p \frac{1}{\sqrt{q-1}} \cdot \frac{2l \min\left(\binom{n}{t}(q-1)^t, q^r\right)}{\lambda_q \binom{r-l}{t-p}\binom{k+l}{p}(q-1)^t} \cdot \sqrt{\binom{k+l}{p}(q-1)^p}$$

with $l = \log_q \left(K_q \lambda_q \sqrt{\binom{k}{p}(q-1)^{p-1}} \cdot \ln(q)/2\right)$ and $\lambda_q = 1 - \exp(-1) \approx 0.63$. Noticing the functions above is associated with n, k and t very tightly. Thus so long as we choose appropriate parameters such that the complexity of the above algorithm is beyond the security level, our scheme will reach the security level.

Minder's Attack. Minder [20] claimed that they devised an effective structural attack against the McEliece cryptosystem based on algebraic geometry codes defined over elliptic curves. This attack is inspired by an algorithm due to Sidelnikov and Shestakov [30] which solves the corresponding problem for Reed-Solomon codes.

Minder's attack has four steps. In the first step, using the knowledge of minimum weight codeword to recover the group structure of elliptic curves. Secondly, finding an elliptic curve $\mathcal{E}$ passing through a set of points. Afterwards, attackers can compute all the rational points on $\mathcal{E}$ as well as the isomorphism that maps $z_i \mapsto P_i$. In the last step, attackers already gotten $\mathcal{C}_0 = \text{AGC}(\mathcal{E}, kO, (P_1, \ldots, P_n))$ and then can seek the unknowns $c_1, \ldots, c_n$ such that $(x_1, \ldots, x_n) \in \mathcal{C}_0 \leftrightarrow (c_1 x_1, \ldots, c_n x_n) \in \mathcal{C}$.

This algorithm is built on several assumptions: (1). Minimum weight codeword can be efficiently sampled. (2). The evaluated point set is large enough, i.e. the code length n is not much smaller than $|\mathcal{E}| = p$. (3). The linear systems do not have any undesired, systematic wrong solutions for the guesses.

Thus, as long as we can break any assumptions above, Minder's attack will not work on our scheme. Remind that we proposed an algorithm ECGen in Sect. 3.1. Now we claim that our construction generates an elliptic code whose minimum weight codeword is hard to sample.

Claim 1. *The probability of sample a minimum weight codeword in elliptic codes generate from* ECGen *is* $1/\binom{n}{k}$.

Proof. First, we show that in the integer set R, for an index set $I = \{i_1, \ldots, i_k\}$, $\Sigma_{i \in I} r_i = p$ iff $\{r_i \mid i \in I\} = S_1$. If there exists $l_j \in \{r_i \mid i \in I\}$ s.t. $\Sigma_{i \in I} r_i = p = \Sigma_{i=1}^{k} s_i$, then $\Sigma_{i=1}^{k} s_i - \Sigma_{i \in I} r_i = l_j - s_r = 0$ for some $r \in \{1, \ldots, k\}$. However, since $l_j < B$ and $s_r > B$, i.e. $l_j - s_r < 0$, which causes contradiction. Morcover, we have $\mathcal{O} = \Sigma_{i \in I} P_i - \Sigma_{i \in R}(r_i P) = (\Sigma_{i \in R} r_i) P$ iff $\{r_i \mid i \in I\} = S_1$.

Next, we prove that the probability of finding a minimum weight codeword (FMC) in $\mathcal{C}(D, G)$ is $Prob[\text{FMW}] = 1/\binom{n}{k}$.

Defining a principal divisor $div(f) = P_{i_1} + \cdots + P_{i_k} - G$, then $div(f) \in \mathcal{L}(G)$ Hence, $c = (f(P_1), \ldots, f(P_n))$ is a codeword of $\mathcal{C}(G, D)$, and $f(P_i) = 0$ iff $i \in \{i_1, \ldots, i_k\}$. Conversely, given $I = \{i_1, \ldots, i_k\}$, defining a divisor as $D' = \Sigma_{i \in I} P_i - G$. If D' is a principal divisor, then there exists a function $f \in \mathcal{L}(G)$ such that $D' = div(f)$ due to the fact that $D' + G$ is effective. For such an $f \in \mathcal{L}(G)$, we have $f(P_{i_j}) = 0$ with $1 \leq j \leq k$. Consequently, the Hamming weight of the codeword $c = (f(P_{i_1}), \ldots, f(P_{i_n}))$ is $n - k$. Since there is only one subset I such that $\Sigma_{i \in I} P_j - G$ is a principal divisor, i.e. $\{P_i \mid i \in I\} = \{P_j \mid P_j = s_j P, s_j \in S_1\}$, we know the probability of finding a minimum weight codeword is equal to that of sampling a specific subset $I \subset \{1, \ldots, n\}$ and $|I| = k$, then

$$Prob[\text{FMW}] = \frac{1}{\binom{n}{k}}.$$

As a result, when applying this attack to our scheme, the first step, i.e. recovering the group structure, whose idea is to use the fact that minimum weight codewords correspond to functions whose divisor is exactly known, is unlikely to be done. Moreover, we chose only a small part of rational points to evaluate, which breaks the second assumption. Thus, their attack is not efficient enough to break ECC^2.

Error Correcting Pair (ECP) Decoding. The attack with Error-Correcting-Pair was proposed by Pellikaan et al. in [5]. The ECP finding algorithm is able to be computed in $O(n^4)$ operations in $\mathbb{F}_q$, which allows the attacker to decrypt any encrypted message in $O(n^3)$ under the assumption that the users also use error correcting pairs.

For a public matrix of AG code $\mathcal{C}_\mathcal{L}(D, G)^\perp$, suppose $D = P_1 + \cdots + P_n$, one can compute an ECP for $\mathcal{C}_\mathcal{L}(D - P, G - P)$, where $P \in \{P_1, \ldots, P_n\}$, i.e. an ECP for $\mathcal{C}_\mathcal{L}(D, G)^\perp$ punctured at one position. Thus the attack can be can be performed by first correcting errors on the punctured code and then correcting an erasure, with the help of P-Filtrations technique.

The decoding algorithm comes from [24]. Its main idea is to use pair (A, B) to locating the error positions, and then recover the error vector. More precisely, one sets up a system of linear equations with the help of the vector space A and B. The set of zeros of a non-zero solution of these equation contains the error positions. Solving a set of linear equations involving the syndrome of the received word gives the error values. However, as claimed by the author, ECP decoding is a unique decoding algorithm, i.e.

Fact 1 *([24], Corollary 2.15.). If a linear code $\mathcal{C}$ has a t-error correcting pair, then $t \leq \lfloor (d(\mathcal{C}) - 1)/2 \rfloor$, where d^* is the design distance for the code.*

Thus, a t-error correcting pair can correct at most t errors, which means that if there are more than $(d^* - 1)/2$ errors added to the codeword, the ECP decoding algorithm will fail because the dimension of A is exactly the maximum number of errors, and $dim(A) = t + g < n - k - t$ by definition. Having noticed that, we add more than $(d^* - 1)/2$ random errors in the encryption algorithm to defence the ECP attack, and use list decoding algorithm in the decryption algorithm to recover the codewords.

Then there comes another combined attack that first exhaustive search for the added errors, then use ECP-attack, i.e. split the error e into e_1 and e_2 such that $e_1 + e_2 = e$ and $\mathsf{wt}(e_1) = \frac{d^*-1}{2} = t_0$. Denote the weight of e_2 by $t_1 = t - t_0$. The random errors may happen on any position, then there are $\binom{n}{t_1}$ possibilities for the error position, and $(q - 1)^{t_1}$ possibilities for the error value. Thus the cost of this attack is

$$\binom{n}{t_1}(q - 1)^{t_1}.$$

Other Attacks. Exhaustive search to recover the structure of codes: There are 3 parameters are needed to recover the code, i.e. b and P for the elliptic curve, and D for elliptic code. Another divisor $G = k\mathcal{O}$ is actually public. The elliptic curve has two parameters in $\mathbb{F}_q$, and at least $1 + q - 2\sqrt{q}$ points on a curve over $\mathbb{F}_q$. Hence to recover the elliptic code, the total cost is

$$q^2 \binom{1 + q - 2\sqrt{q}}{n}.$$

Other attacks against AG codes: In [16] and [15], Márquze-Corbella *et al.* showed an attack which can recover an equivalent algebraic geometry code with the underlying one. They proved that the structure of the code can be recovered from the only knowledge of a generator matrix of the code. Although they showed an efficient computational approach to the rational points and divisor finding algorithm, decoding algorithm from the obtained code's representation is still lacking. Thus, this result does not lead to an efficient attack.

4.3 Proposition of Parameters

We give our suggested parameters in **Table** 1, where

q: the prime to generate the finite field;
n: length of the elliptic code;
k: dimension of the elliptic code;
t_0: $t_0 = (d - 1)/2$ is the basic weight of error vector;
t_1: the added weight of error vector;
t: the total weight of error vector, which can be correct by a list decoding algorithm;

Table 1. Parameters for ECC^2

		q	n	k	t_0	t_1	t
2^{128}	ECC^2.GS	86753	360	153	103	17	120
	ECC^2.SW	134807	521	150	185	11	196
2^{192}	ECC^2.GS	203641	540	227	156	27	183
	ECC^2.SW	301831	781	225	277	17	294
2^{256}	ECC^2.GS	363841	700	331	184	28	212
	ECC^2.SW	561307	1031	322	354	10	364

As we mentioned before, Guruswami-Sudan list decoding algorithm needs to calculate the pole basis, the zero basis, and transition matrices from each zero basis to pole basis, which requires a tremendous storage area. Hence we make an alternative choice by using the Shokrollahi-Wasserman list decoding algorithm introduced in [28]. This algorithm can correct $n - \beta - 1$ errors and output a list of codeword with size less than b, where $\beta = \lceil (n+1)/(b+1) - bk/2 \rceil$ for elliptic codes. We set $b = 2$ to make sure the size of output is not too large.

5 Efficiency Analysis

Now we show how the proposed scheme preforms in the size of key pairs, and the complexity of encryption and decryption.

The size of public key can be calculated as the size of the generator matrix of elliptic code $\mathcal{C}$. Each element of the matrix is an element of $\mathbb{F}_q$ with $\log q$ bits, and the size of matrix is $(n-k) \times k$, thus we need $((n-k) \cdot k) \cdot \log q$ bits to save the public key. The secret key is a triple of (a, P, R). $a \in \mathbb{F}_q$ is a parameter for elliptic curve and needs $\log q$ bits. $P = (x_P, y_P)$ is a point on curve and $x_P, y_P \in \mathbb{F}_q$, thus $2 \log q$ bits is required. R is a set of n random numbers $r < q$, which leads to size of R is $n \log q$ bits. Therefore, the size of secret key is $(n + 3) \log q$ bits.

Thanks to the special structure of elliptic codes, we reduce the secret key size a lot compare to other variants of McEliece cryptosystem. Here we compare the key size of our scheme with HQC [19] and NTS-KEM [1] in **Table** 2.

Table 2. Key-size (bytes) for ECC^2

1^λ	Scheme	Public-key	Secret-key	KEM message
2^{128}	ECC^2.GS	67302	817	1123
	ECC^2.SW	125214	1179	1543
	HQC	5558	252	5622
	NTS-KEM	319488	9216	128
2^{192}	ECC^2.GS	159866	1270	1759
	ECC^2.SW	297114	1862	2422
	HQC	10150	404	10214
	NTS-KEM	929760	17524	162
2^{256}	ECC^2.GS	290081	1721	2482
	ECC^2.SW	570745	2585	3416
	HQC	14754	532	14818
	NTS-KEM	1419704	19890	253

HQC scheme does not hide any structure in their public generator matrix, then the code is published as a part of public parameters, which leads to its good performance in key-sizes. However, in order to get a more efficient decoding algorithm, the rate of the codes have to be lower. As a result, its KEM message is the longest. NTS-KEM performs like the classic McEliece scheme, the main drawback is its huge key-size, but the KEM message is very short. Our scheme ECC^2 seems to be a good balance between the key-size and KEM message.

Now let us focus on the computational costs of ECC^2. For **KeyGen**, the main cost is the Gaussian elimination for G^{pub}, whose complexity is $\mathcal{O}(n^3)$. Moreover, we also need to sample two sets with cost $\mathcal{O}(n)$. For **Encrypt**, the only cost is the multiplication of a vector and a matrix in $\mathcal{O}(n^2)$ and two vector addition. Then the cost is $\mathcal{O}(n^2)$. For **Decrypt**, there is always the cost of a vector addition in $\mathcal{O}(n)$, plus the cost of decoding. The complexity for Guruswami-Sudan list decoding is $\mathcal{O}(n^5)$ and for Shokrollahi-Wasserman list decoding is $\mathcal{O}(n^3)$. To sum up, ECC^2.GS performs better in key-size and ECC^2.SW performs better in decryption speed.

6 Conclusion

We construct a public-key encryption system based on elliptic codes, which can resist all attacks against AG codes as far as we know. The special structure of AG codes helps us to decrease the size of secret key. Minder's attack built on several assumptions such as the minimum weight codeword can be efficiently sampled and the evaluated points set is large enough. We construct elliptic codes that break the above assumptions to resist this attack. To resist other attacks, we add errors beyond the half of the minimum distance of the code, and then use list decoding algorithm as a subroutine to decrypt the ciphertext. Meanwhile, more errors and large prime field enables us to choose codes with less length, which leads to shorter kem cipher-text. Our cryptosystem performs well on the storage size and encryption speed, but the decrypt speed is sacrificed to ensure the security. With the development of list decoding algorithm, especially list decoding algorithm towards elliptic codes, the decryption speed will be accelerated.

Acknowledgements. This work is supported by the National Natural Science Foundation of China (No. 61672550) and the National Key R&D Program of China(2017YFB0802503).

References

1. Albrecht, M., Cid, C., et al.: NTS-KEM, NIST Submission (2017). https://nts-kem.io
2. Berlekamp, E.R., Mceliece, R.J., Tilborg, H.C.A.V,: On the inherent intractability of certain coding problems. IEEE Trans. Inform. Theory **24**(3), 384–386 (1978)
3. Bernstein, D.J., Lange, T., Peters, C.: Attacking and defending the McEliece cryptosystem. In: Buchmann, J., Ding, J. (eds.) PQCrypto 2008. LNCS, vol. 5299, pp. 31–46. Springer, Heidelberg (2008). https://doi.org/10.1007/978-3-540-88403-3_3
4. Cheng, Q.: Hard problems of algebraic geometry codes. IEEE Trans. Inform. Theory **54**(1), 402–406 (2008)
5. Couvreur, A., Márquez-Corbella, I., Pellikaan, R.: Cryptanalysis of McEliece cryptosystem based on algebraic geometry codes and their subcodes. IEEE Trans. Inform. Theory **63**(8), 5404–5418 (2017)
6. Diffie, W., Hellman, M.: New directions in cryptography. IEEE Trans. Inform. Theory **22**(6), 644–654 (1976)
7. Faure, C., Minder, L.: Cryptanalysis of the McEliece cryptosystem over hyperelliptic codes. The 11th ACCT, pp. 99–107 (2008)
8. Goppa, V.D.: Codes associated with divisors. Problemy Peredachi Informatsii. **13**(1), 33–39 (1977)

9. Guruswami, V., Sudan, M.: Improved decoding of reed-solomon and algebraic-geometry codes. IEEE Trans. Inform. Theory **45**(6), 1757–1767 (1999)
10. Guruswami, V., Sudan, M.: On representations of algebraic-geometric codes for list decoding, pp. 244–255. Springer, Berlin (2000)
11. Hofheinz, D., Hövelmanns, K., Kiltz, E.: A modular analysis of the Fujisaki-Okamoto transformation. In: Kalai, Y., Reyzin, L. (eds.) TCC 2017. LNCS, vol. 10677, pp. 341–371. Springer, Cham (2017). https://doi.org/10.1007/978-3-319-70500-2_12
12. Hoholdt, T., Pellikaan, R.: On the decoding of algebraic-geometric codes. IEEE Trans. Inform. Theory **41**(6), 1589–1614 (1995)
13. Hoholdt, T., Van Lint, J.H., Pellikaan, R.: Handbook of Coding Theory: Part 1: Algebraic Geometry Codes, pp. 871–961. Elsevier Science Inc., Amsterdam (1998)
14. Janwa, H., Moreno, O.: McEliece public key cryptosystems using algebraic-geometric codes. Des. Codes Cryptogr. **8**(3), 293–307 (1996)
15. Márquez-Corbella, I., Martínez-Moro, E., et al.: Computational aspects of retrieving a representation of an algebraic geometry code. J. Symbolic Computation. **64**, 67–87 (2014)
16. Márquez-Corbella, I., Martínez-Moro, E., Pellikaan, R.: On the unique representation of very strong algebraic geometry codes. Des. Codes Cryptogr. **70**(1–2), 215–230 (2014)
17. Mceliece, R.J.: A public-key cryptosystem based on algebraic. Coding Thv. **4244**, 114–116 (1978)
18. McEliece, R.J.: The Guruswami-Sudan Decoding Algorithm for Reed-Solomon Codes. JPL progress report. **42–153** (2003)
19. Melchor, C.A., Aragon, N., Bettaieb, S., et al.: Hamming Quasi-Cyclic (HQC) (2017). https://pqc-hqc.org
20. Minder, L.: Cryptography based on Error Correcting Codes. PhD thesis, EPFL, Lausanne (2007)
21. Misoczki, R., Barreto, P.S.L.M.: Key reduction of McEliece's cryptosystem using list decoding. 2011 IEEE ISIT, pp. 2681–2685 (2011)
22. Niebuhr, R., Cayrel, P.L., Bulygin, S., et al.: On lower bounds for information set decoding over Fq. The 2nd SCC, 10, pp. 143–157 (2010)
23. Niederreiter, H.: Knapsack-type cryptosystems and algebraic coding theory. Prob. Control and Inf. Theory **15**(2), 159–166 (1986)
24. Pellikaan, R.: On decoding by error location and dependent sets of error positions. Discrete Math. **106**, 369–381 (1992)
25. Pellikaan, R.: On the efficient decoding of algebraic-geometric codes. In: Camion, P., Charpin, P., Harari, S. (eds.) Eurocode 1992. ICMS, vol. 339, pp. 231–253. Springer, Vienna (1993). https://doi.org/10.1007/978-3-7091-2786-5_20
26. Peters, C.: Information-set decoding for linear codes over $\mathbf{F}_q$. In: Sendrier, N. (ed.) PQCrypto 2010. LNCS, vol. 6061, pp. 81–94. Springer, Heidelberg (2010). https://doi.org/10.1007/978-3-642-12929-2_7
27. Prange, E.: The use of information sets in decoding cyclic codes. IEEE Trans. Inform. Theory **8**(5), 5–9 (1962)
28. Shokrollahi, M.A., Wasserman, H.: List decoding of algebraic-geometric codes. IEEE Trans. Inform. Theory **45**(2), 432–437 (1999)
29. Shor, P.W.: Algorithms for quantum computation: discrete logarithms and factoring. IEEE Symposium on Foundations of Computer Science, pp. 124–134 (1994)
30. Sidelnikov, V.M., Shestakov, S.O.: On insecurity of cryptosystems based on generalized Reed-Solomon codes. Discrete Math. Appl. **2**(4), 439–444 (1992)

31. Silverman, J.H.: The arithmetic of elliptic curves. Inventiones Math. **23**(3–4), 179–206 (1974)
32. Sudan, M.: Decoding of reed solomon codes beyond the error-correction bound. J. Complex. **13**(1), 180–193 (1997)
33. Wu, X., Siegel, P.H.: Efficient root-finding algorithm with application to list decoding of algebraic-geometric codes. IEEE Trans. Inform. Theory **47**(6), 2579–2587 (2001)
34. Zhang, F., Liu, S.: Solving ECDLP via list decoding. IACR Cryptology ePrint Archive, Report 2018/795 (2018). https://eprint.iacr.org/2018/795.pdf

A New Provably Secure Identity-Based Multi-proxy Signature Scheme

Qunshan Chen[1,4(✉)] (iD), Zhenjie Huang[2], Yong Ding[3],
Yuping Zhou[1,4], and Hui Huang[1,5]

[1] College of Computer, Minnan Normal University,
Zhangzhou 363000, People's Republic of China
xiamensam@163.com, hhui323@163.com,
yp_zhou@mnnu.edu.cn
[2] Lab of Granular Computing, Minnan Normal University,
Zhangzhou 363000, People's Republic of China
zjhuang@mnnu.edu.cn
[3] School of Computer Science and Information Security,
Guilin University of Electronic Technology,
Guilin 541004, People's Republic of China
stone_dingy@126.com
[4] Key Laboratory of Data Science and Intelligence Application,
Fujian Province University, Zhangzhou 363000, People's Republic of China
[5] Key Laboratory of Financial Mathematics (Putian University), Fujian Province
University, Putian 351100, People's Republic of China

Abstract. In a multi-proxy signature scheme, an original signer could delegate his signing power to a designated proxy group. Only the cooperation of all proxy signers in the proxy group could generate a legitimate proxy signature on behalf of the original signer. In this paper, we formalize the definition and security model of the identity-based multi-proxy signature, and we construct a new identity-based multi-proxy signature scheme using bilinear pairings. We show the security of our scheme in the random oracle model, and the security of our scheme is based on the hardness of the computational Diffie-Hellman problem.

Keywords: Identity-based signature · Multi-proxy signature · Computational Diffie-Hellman problem · Provable security

1 Introduction

The concept of an identity-based (ID-based) cryptosystem was first introduced by Shamir [20] in 1984. In an ID-based cryptosystem, the user does not generate his key pairs by himself. The system needs a trusted third authority named the private key generator (PKG) to compute the user's private key, and the user's public key can be derived as an arbitrary string that indicates the user's identity information, such as the user's e-mail address, IP address, and social security number. An ID-based cryptosystem simplifies the problem of key management in traditional public-key cryptography. Due to this advantage, many ID-based cryptosystems have been proposed [1, 3, 5, 12, 21].

© Springer Nature Switzerland AG 2019
J. Vaidya et al. (Eds.): CSS 2019, LNCS 11982, pp. 230–242, 2019.
https://doi.org/10.1007/978-3-030-37337-5_18

In 1996, Mambo et al. [14, 15] introduced the concept of the proxy signature, which solved the problem of the authorization of the signing capability. In a proxy signature scheme, an original signer is allowed to delegate his signing power to a designated person named a proxy signer. Provided with the proxy delegation, the proxy signer could sign a message on behalf of the original signer. Any verifier could be convinced of both the original signer's authorization and the proxy signer's signature. Proxy signatures could be used in many situations, especially in applications where the delegation of rights is highly common, such as distributed computing and mobile communications. To date, many proxy signature schemes have been proposed [2, 7, 9, 18, 19, 23].

The primitive of the multi-proxy signature was first introduced by Hwang and Shi in 2000 [8]. In a multi-proxy signature scheme, an original signer can delegate his signing power to a designated proxy group. Only the cooperation of all proxy signers in the proxy group could generate a legitimate proxy signature on behalf of the original signer. The multi-proxy signature scheme can be regarded as a special threshold proxy signature scheme [24]. Since that work, some multi-proxy signature schemes have been successfully proposed [10, 11, 16, 17], but they lacked provable security, and their securities were only heuristically analyzed. In 2009, Cao and Cao [4] gave the first formal definition and security model of an ID-based multi-proxy signature and then proposed an ID-based multi-proxy signature scheme using bilinear pairings. However, Xiong et al. [22] showed that Cao-Cao's scheme was not secure under their security model. These researchers proposed an improved scheme, but they did not give the formal security proof of the improved scheme. Moreover, some provably secure multi-proxy signature schemes in the standard model have been proposed [6, 13].

In this paper, based on the work of Bellare et al. [1] and Cao and Cao [4], we give a formal definition and security model of an ID-based multi-proxy signature scheme. Then, we present a concrete ID-based multi-proxy signature scheme that meets our definition. Our scheme is provably secure in the random oracle model, and the security of our scheme is based on the hardness of computational Diffie-Hellman problem. To the best of our knowledge, to date, our scheme is the only ID-based multi-proxy signature scheme using bilinear pairings that is proved to be secure in the random oracle model.

The rest of this paper is organized as follows. In Sect. 2, we introduce some preliminaries. In Sect. 3, we give a formal definition and security model of the ID-based multi-proxy signature scheme. In Sect. 4, we propose a new ID-based multi-proxy signature scheme. In Sect. 5, we prove our scheme's security and compare the efficiency of our scheme with some similar schemes. The final section is the conclusion.

2 Preliminaries

In this section, we introduce some concepts for bilinear pairings and the computational Diffie-Hellman problem.

2.1 Bilinear Pairings

Let $(G_1, +)$ and $(G_2, \cdot)$ be two groups of prime order q. We call a map $e : G_1 \times G_1 \to G_2$ a bilinear pairing if it satisfies the following properties:

- **Bilinear:** For any $P, Q \in G_1$, and any $\alpha, \beta \in Z_q$, we have $e(\alpha P, \beta Q) = e(P, Q)^{\alpha\beta}$;
- **Nondegenerate:** Their exists $P, Q \in G_1$, such that $e(P, Q) \neq 1$;
- **Computable:** For any $P, Q \in G_1$, there is an efficient algorithm to compute $e(P, Q)$.

2.2   Computational Assumption

The security of our scheme is based on the hardness of the computational Diffie-Hellman problem.

Definition 1. Computational Diffie-Hellman (CDH) problem. Let G_1 be a group of prime order q with generator P. Given $aP, bP \in G_1$, where $a, b \in Z_q^*$, compute abP.

Definition 2. CDH Assumption. We say that the (t, ε)-CDH assumption holds in group G_1 if no probabilistic algorithm can solve the CDH problem in G_1 with a non-negligible probability of at least ε within polynomial time t.

3   Definition and Security Model of Identity-Based Multi-proxy Signature

In this section, we give a formal definition and security model for our ID-based multi-proxy signature scheme.

3.1   Definition of Identity-Based Multi-proxy Signature

We give the definition of the ID-based multi-proxy signature scheme as follows. More details can be found in [4].

Definition 3. An identity-based multi-proxy signature scheme consists of the following algorithms: Setup, User-Key-Gen, Delegation-Gen, Multi-Proxy-Sign, and Multi-Proxy-Verify. It is composed of the following entities: the key generation center KGC, the original signer U_0, the proxy signers $U_i(i = 1, 2, \cdots, n)$, and the verifier.

- **Setup:** This algorithm is run by the KGC on the input security parameter 1^k, and it generates the system's master key s and public parameters *params*.
- **User-Key-Gen:** This algorithm is run by the KGC. It takes as inputs the *params*, the identity ID_0 of the original signer U_0, or the identity ID_i of the proxy signer $U_i(i = 1, 2, \cdots, n)$, and then returns the corresponding private key $S_{ID_i}(i = 0, 1, 2, \cdots, n)$.
- **Delegation-Gen:** This algorithm is run by the original signer U_0. It takes as inputs the *params*, his private key S_{ID_0}, the identity ID_i of the proxy signer $U_i(i = 1, 2, \cdots, n)$, and a warrant message w, and it outputs a proxy delegation σ_0.
- **Multi-Proxy-Sign:** This algorithm is run by every proxy signer U_i. It takes as inputs the *params*, the private key S_{ID_i}, the delegation σ_0 and the message m, and it outputs a partial proxy signature S_i $(i = 1, 2, \cdots, n)$. Then, U_i sends S_i to a clerk who is a designated proxy signer in the proxy group. The clerk verifies the validity of S_i, and it returns the multi-proxy signature S if all of S_i are accepted; otherwise, the algorithm stops.

- **Multi-Proxy-Verify**: It takes as inputs the *params*, the identities ID_0 and $ID_i(i = 1, 2, \cdots, n)$, the message m and the multi-proxy signature S. The algorithm outputs 1 if S is a valid multi-proxy signature, and it outputs 0 otherwise.

3.2 Security Model of Identity-Based Multi-proxy Signature

According to the security model of the proxy signature that is proposed in [14, 15], the security of the proxy signature is mainly considered based on the unforgeability of the delegation and the proxy signature. The unforgeability of the delegation means that an adversary could not forge an efficient delegation on behalf of the original signer, and the proxy signer could not generate a valid proxy signature without the delegation. The unforgeability of the proxy signature means that nobody (including the original signer) could generate a legitimate proxy signature without the proxy signer's private key.

In our model, we consider the adversary who can adaptively choose an identity ID_0 for an original signer or an identity ID_i for a proxy signer, and then acts as a user with the identity of ID_0 or ID_i when executing the multi-proxy signature scheme with other users. Therefore, we can divide the potential adversaries into the following two kinds:

Type I: Adversary A_I attempts to forge a multi-proxy signature without the delegation. For the adversary A_I, we mainly model the malicious proxy signer. Moreover, adversary A_I can be considered as a collusion attack from multiple proxy signers.

Type II: Adversary A_{II} attempts to forge a multi-proxy signature without the proxy signer's private key. For the adversary A_{II}, we mainly model the malicious original signer.

According to the work of [4], we define the security model of an ID-based multi-proxy signature as follows.

Definition 4. Let A_I and A_{II} be adversaries that act as the malicious proxy signer and the original signer, respectively. The security of an ID-based multi-proxy signature scheme is modeled by the following games between a challenger C and A_I and A_{II}, respectively.

Game 1

The challenger C inputs a security parameter 1^k, performs the Setup algorithm, generates the system parameters *params*, and then C sends *params* to A_I. A_I can carry out the following queries in polynomial bounded times.

- **Hash query**: A_I can query the value of all Hash functions in the scheme.
- **User-Key query**: A_I can input an arbitrary user's identity ID_i to query the private key S_{ID_i}. C performs the User-Key-Gen algorithm to generate S_{ID_i} and returns the result to A_I.
- **Delegation query**: A_I can query the proxy delegation certificate σ_0 of a chosen warrant message w. C performs the Delegation-Gen algorithm and then returns the result to A_I.
- **Multi-Proxy-Sign query**: A_I can input the original signer's identity ID_0, the proxy signer's identity $ID_i(i = 1, 2, \cdots, n)$, the warrant message w and the message m, and queries the multi-proxy signature on m. C performs the Multi-Proxy-Sign algorithm to generate a multi-proxy signature S and then returns the result to A_I.

Finally, A_I outputs a multi-proxy signature S^* on message m using the proxy signers $U_i(i = 1, 2, \cdots, n)$ with the warrant message w. We say that A_I wins the game if and only if the multi-proxy signature S^* is accepted by the verifier, the warrant message w has not been queried in the Delegation query, and (w, m) has not been queried in the Multi-Proxy-Sign query.

Game 2

The challenger C inputs a security parameter 1^k, performs the Setup algorithm, generates the system parameters *params*, and then C sends *params* to A_{II}. A_{II} can perform the same queries as *Game 1* in polynomial bounded times.

Finally, A_{II} outputs a multi-proxy signature S^* on message m using the proxy signers $U_i(i = 1, 2, \cdots, n)$ with the warrant message w. We say that A_{II} wins the game if and only if the multi-proxy signature S^* is accepted by the verifier, there is at least one $ID_I \in \{ID_1, ID_2, \cdots, ID_n\}$ that has not been queried in the User-Key query, and (w, m) has not been queried in the Multi-Proxy-Sign query.

Definition 5. An identity-based multi-proxy signature scheme is existentially unforgeable against the chosen massage attack and chosen warrant attack if and only if there is no probabilistic polynomial-time (PPT) adversary that could win the above games with a non-negligible probability.

4 Identity-Based Multi-proxy Signature Scheme

In this section, we propose a new ID-based multi-proxy signature scheme based on the ID-based signature scheme that was constructed by Sakai-Ogishi-Kasahara [1, 12].

Setup: Given a security parameter 1^k, let G_1 be an additive group of prime order q with a generator P, G_2 is a multiplicative group with the same prime order, and $e : G_1 \times G_1 \rightarrow G_2$ is a bilinear map. The KGC chooses the hash functions $H_1 : \{0, 1\}^* \rightarrow G_1$, $H_2 : \{0, 1\}^* \times G_1 \rightarrow G_1$ and $H_3 : \{0, 1\}^* \times G_1 \times G_1 \rightarrow Z_q^*$. The KGC randomly chooses $s \in Z_q^*$ as the master key, computes the system public key $P_{pub} = sP$, and then publishes the system parameters $params = (G_1, G_2, q, e, P, P_{pub}, H_1, H_2, H_3)$.

User-Key-Gen: Given the identity ID_0 of the original signer U_0 or the identity ID_i of the proxy signer U_i, where $1 \leq i \leq n$, the KGC computes $Q_{ID_i} = H_1(ID_i)$ and $S_{ID_i} = sQ_{ID_i}$, and then it sends S_{ID_i} to $U_i(i = 0, 1, 2, \cdots, n)$ via a secure channel.

Delegation-Gen: The original signer U_0 generates the proxy warrant message w, which includes the identity information of the original signer and proxy signers, the scope of the proxy authority, and the delegation period.

1. U_0 randomly chooses $r_0 \in Z_q^*$, and computes $R_0 = r_0 P$.
2. U_0 computes $h_0 = H_2(w, R_0)$, $V_0 = r_0 h_0 + S_{ID_0}$.
3. U_0 sends a proxy warrant message w and its signature $\sigma_0 = (R_0, V_0)$ to the proxy signers $U_i(i = 1, 2, \cdots, n)$ via a secure channel.

The proxy signer U_i computes $h_0 = H_2(w, R_0)$, and then checks the following equation:

$$e(P, V_0) = e(P_{pub}, Q_{ID_0})e(R_0, h_0).$$

If the equality holds, U_i accepts σ_0 as a valid delegation.

Multi-Proxy-Sign: Given a message m to be signed, for $1 \leq i \leq n$, the proxy signer U_i can sign the message m as follows:

1. U_i randomly chooses $r_i \in Z_q^*$, computes $R_i = r_iP$, and broadcasts R_i to the other proxy signers.

2. U_i computes $R = \sum_{i=1}^{n} R_i$, $h_0 = H_2(w, R_0)$, $h = H_3(m, R_0, R)$, and $V_i = r_ih_0 + hS_{ID_i} + V_0$.

3. U_i sends the partial proxy signature $\sigma_i = (w, R_0, R_i, V_i)$ to the clerk who is a designated proxy signer in the proxy group.

4. The clerk computes $R = \sum_{i=1}^{n} R_i$, $h_0 = H_2(w, R_0)$, $h = H_3(m, R_0, R)$, then verifies the validity of σ_i using the following equation:

$$e(P, V_i) = e(P_{pub}, hQ_{ID_i} + Q_{ID_0})e(R_i + R_0, h_0), \ i = 1, 2, \cdots, n$$

If all of the equalities hold, the clerk computes $V = \sum_{i=1}^{n} V_i$, and then the multi-proxy signature on message m is $\sigma = (w, R_0, R, V)$.

Multi-Proxy-Verify: To verify a multi-proxy signature $\sigma = (w, R_0, R, V)$, the verifier computes $h_0 = H_2(w, R_0)$, $h = H_3(m, R_0, R)$, and accepts the signature if and only if the following equation holds:

$$e(P, V) = e(P_{pub}, nQ_{ID_0} + h\sum_{i=1}^{n} Q_{ID_i})e(nR_0 + R, h_0).$$

5 Analysis of Our Scheme

5.1 Correctness

The correctness of a partial proxy signature can be proved by the following:

$$\begin{aligned}
e(P, V_i) &= e(P, r_ih_0 + hS_{ID_i} + V_0) \\
&= e(P, r_ih_0)e(P, hS_{ID_i})e(P, r_0h_0)e(P, S_{ID_0}) \\
&= e(r_iP, h_0)e(P_{Pub}, hQ_{ID_i})e(r_0P, h_0)e(P_{Pub}, Q_{ID_0}) \\
&= e(P_{pub}, hQ_{ID_i} + Q_{ID_0})e(R_i + R_0, h_0).
\end{aligned}$$

The proposed ID-based multi-proxy signature scheme is correct according to the following:

$$e(P, V) = e(P, \sum_{i=1}^{n} (r_i h_0 + h S_{ID_i} + V_0))$$

$$= e(P, \sum_{i=1}^{n} r_i h_0) e(P, h \sum_{i=1}^{n} S_{ID_i}) e(P, n r_0 h_0) e(P, n S_{ID_0})$$

$$= e(\sum_{i=1}^{n} r_i P, h_0) e(P_{Pub}, h \sum_{i=1}^{n} Q_{ID_i}) e(n r_0 P, h_0) e(P_{Pub}, n Q_{ID_0})$$

$$= e(P_{pub}, n Q_{ID_0} + h \sum_{i=1}^{n} Q_{ID_i}) e(n R_0 + R, h_0).$$

5.2 Security Proof of Our Scheme

In this section, we will prove that our scheme is secure in the random oracle model. The Delegation-Gen algorithm in our scheme is the ID-based signature scheme that was constructed by Sakai-Ogishi-Kasahara [1, 12], which was proved to be secure, such that an adversary could not forge a valid delegation certificate without the original signer's private key.

Theorem 1. In the random oracle model, let A_I be a PPT adversary with the non-negligible probability ε to win *Game* 1 in time t. Assume that A_I makes at most q_{H_i} queries to the hash functions $H_i(i = 1, 2, 3)$, at most q_K queries to the User-Key-Gen oracle, at most q_D queries to the Delegation-Gen oracle, and at most q_P queries to the Multi-Proxy-Sign oracle. Then, there exists an algorithm C with the probability $\varepsilon' \geq \varepsilon \frac{1}{(q_K + q_D + n + 1)e}$ to solve the CDH problem in time $t' < t + (q_{H_1} + q_K + q_{H_2} + 3q_D + 3nq_P + n + 4)t_s + t_i$, where t_i is the time of an inversion computation in Z_q^*, and t_s is the time of a scalar multiplication in G_1.

Proof: Let (P, aP, bP) be a random instance of the CDH problem in G_1 acting as a challenger of A_I. C could compute abP via *Game* 1 as follows.

C runs the setup algorithm, sets the system public key $P_{Pub} = aP$, and generates the system parameters *params*. Then, it gives *params* to A_I. C maintains an H_1-list $(ID_i, Q_{ID_i}, t_i, c_i)$ to hold the value of hash function H_1, a UK-list (ID_i, S_{ID_i}) to hold the user's private key, an H_2-list (w, R_0, h_0, d_0) to hold the value of hash function H_2, a Del-list (ID_0, w, r_0, R_0, V_0) to hold the delegation certificate, and a H_3-list (m, R_0, R, h) to hold the value of hash function H_3.

A_I can conduct queries as follows.

H_1 Query: When A_I makes H_1 query $ID_i(i = 0, 1, 2, \cdots, n)$, ID_0 is the identity of the original signer, and $ID_i(i = 1, 2, \cdots, n)$ are the identities of the proxy signers. C responds as follows.

(1) For $0 \leq i \leq n$, if ID_i has been queried, C returns Q_{ID_i} from the H_1-list.
(2) Otherwise, C randomly chooses $t_i \in Z_q^*$, and generates a random coin $c_i \in \{0, 1\}$ such that $\Pr[c_i = 0] = \delta$ and $\Pr[c_i = 1] = 1 - \delta$, where $0 < \delta < 1$.

Then, C sets $Q_{ID_i} = H_1(ID_i) = t_iP$ if $c_i = 0$, and sets $Q_{ID_i} = t_i(bP)$ if $c_i = 1$. Finally, C adds $(ID_i, Q_{ID_i}, t_i, c_i)$ into the H_1-list, and returns Q_{ID_i} to A_I.

User-Key Query: When A_I queries the private key of ID_i, C responds as follows.

(1) C searches the UK-list. If ID_i has been queried, then C returns the corresponding private key S_{ID_i} to A_I.
(2) Otherwise, C searches the H_1-list to get $(ID_i, Q_{ID_i}, t_i, c_i)$. When there is no record of ID_i in the H_1-list, C will create $(ID_i, Q_{ID_i}, t_i, c_i)$ according to the H_1 query.

If $c_i = 0$, C computes $S_{ID_i} = t_i(aP)$, returns S_{ID_i} to A_I and adds (ID_i, S_{ID_i}) into the UK-list. If $c_i = 1$, C outputs "failure" and terminates the simulation.

H_2 Query: When A_I makes an H_2 query on (w, R_0), C responds as follows.

(1) If (w, R_0) has been queried, C returns h_0 from the H_2-list;
(2) Otherwise, C randomly chooses $d_0 \in Z_q^*$, and d_0 has not been in the H_2-list. C computes $h_0 = d_0P$ and returns h_0 to A_I. Then, C adds (w, R_0, h_0, d_0) into the H_2-list.

H_3 Query: When A_I makes an H_3 query on (m, R_0, R), C responds as follows.

(1) If (m, R_0, R) has been queried, C returns h from the H_3-list;
(2) Otherwise, C randomly chooses $h \in Z_q^*$, and h has not been in H_3-list. Then, C returns h to A_I and adds (m, R_0, R, h) into the H_3-list.

Delegation Query: A_I can query the proxy delegation certificate σ_0 of a chosen warrant message w from ID_0, and C responds as follows.

(1) If (ID_0, w) has been queried, C returns $\sigma_0 = (R_0, V_0)$ from the Del-list.
(2) Otherwise, C searches the UK-list to get $(ID_0, Q_{ID_0}, t_0, c_0)$.

If $c_0 = 0$, C randomly chooses $r_0 \in Z_q^*$ and computes $R_0 = r_0P$. Then, C searches the H_2-list to get (w, R_0, h_0, d_0), computes $V_0 = r_0h_0 + t_0(aP)$, returns $\sigma_0 = (R_0, V_0)$ to A_I, and adds (ID_0, w, r_0, R_0, V_0) to the Del-list.
If $c_i = 1$, C outputs "failure" and terminates the simulation.
When there are no records of ID_i or (w, R_0) in the UK-list and the H_2-list, C will create the corresponding values according to the User-Key query and H_2 query.

Multi-Proxy-Sign Query: A_I can input a proxy signer's identity $ID_i (i = 1, 2, \cdots, n)$, an original signer's identity ID_0, a warrant message w and a message m, and it then queries the multi-proxy signature. C responds as follows.

(1) C searches the H_1-list to get $(ID_i, Q_{ID_i}, t_i, c_i)$, where $i = 0, 1, 2, \cdots, n$. If $c_0 = 1$ or $c_i = 1$, C outputs "failure" and terminates the simulation.

(2) Otherwise, for $1 \leq i \leq n$, C randomly chooses $r_i \in Z_q^*$, and computes $R_i = r_iP$,

$$R = \sum_{i=1}^{n} R_i.$$

C searches the UK-list to get $(ID_i, S_{ID_i})(i = 0, 1, 2, \cdots, n)$, and then searches the Del-list, H_2-list and H_3-list to get the records (ID_0, w, r_0, R_0, V_0), (w, R_0, h_0, d_0) and (m, R_0, R, h), respectively. If there are no corresponding records in the lists, C generates the corresponding values according to the above queries.

For $1 \leq i \leq n$, C computes $V_i = r_ih_0 + hS_{ID_i} + V_0 = r_ih_0 + ht_i(aP) + r_0h_0 + t_0(aP)$, $V = \sum_{i=1}^{n} V_i$, and then returns $\sigma = (w, R_0, R, V)$ to A_I.

Finally, A_I stops the simulation, and outputs a multi-proxy signature tuple $\{ID_0, ID_i, m, \sigma^* = (w, R_0, R, V)\}$. C searches the H_1-list to get $(ID_i, Q_{ID_i}, t_i, c_i)$ $(0 \leq i \leq n)$. If $c_0 = 0$ or $c_i = 1$ $(1 \leq i \leq n)$, C outputs "failure" and terminates the simulation. Otherwise, $c_0 = 1$ and $c_i = 0$ $(1 \leq i \leq n)$, C gets (w, R_0, h_0, d_0) and (m, R_0, R, h) in the H_2-list and H_3-list, respectively. The forged multi-proxy signature satisfies the following equation.

$$e(P, V) = e(P_{pub}, h\sum_{i=1}^{n} Q_{ID_i} + nQ_{ID_0})e(R + nR_0, h_0)$$

$$= e(aP, h\sum_{i=1}^{n} t_iP + nt_0bP)e(R + nR_0, d_0P)$$

$$= e(P, h\sum_{i=1}^{n} t_iaP + nt_0abP + d_0(R + nR_0))$$

Then, C computes $abP = (nt_0)^{-1}(V - h\sum_{i=1}^{n} t_iP_{Pub} - d_0(R + nR_0))$. Therefore, C can solve the CDH problem.

To analyze the probability of C succeeding in the above game, we define the following five events, which are needed for C to succeed.

E_1: C does not abort in the User-Key query.
E_2: C does not abort in the Delegation-Gen query.
E_3: C does not abort in the Multi-Proxy-Sign query.
E_4: A_I succeeds to forge a valid multi-proxy signature.
E_5: Event E_4 occurs, $c_0 = 1$, and $c_i = 0(1 \leq i \leq n)$. Here, c_0 and c_i are the c-components of the tuple on the H_1-list.

Therefore, the probability that C can solve the instance of CDH problem is

$$\Pr[E_1 \wedge E_2 \wedge E_3 \wedge E_4 \wedge E_5]$$
$$= \Pr[E_1]\Pr[E_2|E_1]\Pr[E_3|E_1 \wedge E_2]\Pr[E_4|E_1 \wedge E_2 \wedge E_3]\Pr[E_5|E_1 \wedge E_2 \wedge E_3 \wedge E_4].$$

From the simulation, we have the following results.
$\Pr[E_1] \geq \delta^{q_K}$,
$\Pr[E_2|E_1] \geq \delta^{q_D}$,

$\Pr[E_3|E_1 \wedge E_2] = 1$,

$\Pr[E_4|E_1 \wedge E_2 \wedge E_3] \geq \varepsilon$, and

$\Pr[E_5|E_1 \wedge E_2 \wedge E_3 \wedge E_4] \geq (1 - \delta)\delta^n$.

Thus, we have $\Pr[E_1 \wedge E_2 \wedge E_3 \wedge E_4 \wedge E_5] \geq \varepsilon(1 - \delta)\delta^{q_K + q_D + n}$.

When $\delta = \frac{q_K + q_D + n}{q_K + q_D + n + 1}$, $(1 - \delta)\delta^{q_K + q_D + n}$ obtains the minimum value $\frac{1}{(q_K + q_D + n + 1)e}$. Then, the probability that C succeeds is $\varepsilon' \geq \varepsilon\frac{1}{(q_K + q_D + n + 1)e}$.

The total running time of C is $t' < t + (q_{H_1} + q_K + q_{H_2} + 3q_D + 3nq_P + n + 4)t_s + t_i$.

Theorem 2. In the random oracle model, let A_{II} be a PPT adversary with a non-negligible probability ε to win *Game* 2 in time t. Assume that A_{II} makes at most q_{H_i} queries to hash functions $H_i(i = 1, 2, 3)$, at most q_K queries to the User-Key-Gen oracle, at most q_D queries to the Delegation-Gen oracle, and at most q_P queries to the Multi-Proxy-Sign oracle. Then, there exists an algorithm C with the probability $\varepsilon' \geq \varepsilon\frac{n}{(q_K + q_D + n + 1)e}$ to solve the CDH problem in time $t' < t + (q_{H_1} + q_K + q_{H_2} + 3q_D + 3nq_P + n + 4)t_s + t_i$, where t_i is the time of an inversion computation in Z_q^*, and t_s is the time of a scalar multiplication in G_1.

Proof: Let (P, aP, bP) be a random instance of the CDH problem in G_1. C could conduct the same computation as in Theorem 1, and A_{II} could also conduct the same queries as in Theorem 1.

Finally, A_{II} stops the simulation, and outputs a multi-proxy signature tuple $\{ID_0, ID_i, m, \sigma^* = (w, R_0, R, V)\}$. C searches the H_1-list to get $(ID_i, Q_{ID_i}, t_i, c_i)$ $(0 \leq i \leq n)$. If $c_0 = 1$ or $c_i = 0(1 \leq i \leq n)$, C outputs "failure" and terminates the simulation. Otherwise, $c_0 = 0$ and at least one $c_i = 1$. Without the loss of generality, we assume that $c_1 = 1$, and C gets (w, R_0, h_0, d_0) and (m, R_0, R, h) in the H_2-list and H_3-list, respectively. The forged multi-proxy signature satisfies the following equation.

$$e(P, V) = e(P_{pub}, h\sum_{i=1}^{n} Q_{ID_i} + nQ_{ID_0})e(R + nR_0, h_0)$$

$$= e(aP, h\sum_{i=2}^{n} t_iP + ht_1bP + nt_0P)e(R + nR_0, d_0P)$$

$$= e(P, h\sum_{i=2}^{n} t_iaP + ht_1abP + nt_0aP + d_0(R + nR_0)).$$

Then, C computes $abP = (ht_1)^{-1}(V - h\sum_{i=2}^{n} t_iP_{Pub} - nt_0P_{Pub} - d_0(R + nR_0))$.

Therefore, C can solve the CDH problem. As with the proof in Theorem 1, the probability that C succeeds in the game is $\varepsilon' \geq \varepsilon\frac{n}{(q_K + q_D + n + 1)e}$.

The total running time of C is $t' < t + (q_{H_1} + q_K + q_{H_2} + 3q_D + 3nq_P + n + 4)t_s + t_i$.

5.3   Efficiency Comparison

We compare the efficiency of our scheme with some ID-based multi-proxy signature schemes based on bilinear pairings in Table 1. We only consider the computational costs for a single user and compare the algorithmic efficiency of delegation-gen, multi-proxy-sign and multi-proxy-verify, respectively. In Table 1, M denotes the point scalar multiplication operation in G_1, E denotes the exponentiation operation in G_2, and P denotes the pairing operation. We ignore other operations, such as hashing, in all the schemes.

Table 1. Comparison of efficiency for similar schemes

Schemes	Delegation-gen	Multi-proxy-sign	Multi-proxy-verify	Provable security
Scheme [4]	$2M + 3P$	$3M + 5P + 1E$	$3M + 4P$	Yes
Scheme [11]	$3M + 3P + 1E$	$5M + 3P + 1E$	$nM + 3P + 1E$	No
Scheme [16]	$1M + 1P + 3E$	$2M + 1P + 3E$	$1P + 2E$	No
Scheme [17]	$2M + 3P + 2E$	$4M + 4P + 3E$	$3P + 3E$	No
Scheme [22]	$2M + 3P$	$3M + 5P + 1E$	$3M + 4P$	No
Our scheme	$2M + 3P$	$4M + 3P$	$3M + 3P$	Yes

As shown in Table 1, we can see that our scheme is more efficient than the scheme in [4] which is provable secure. Moreover, we proved that our scheme was secure under the computational Diffie-Hellman problem. Although the scheme in [16] is more efficient than ours, there was no formal security proof in the scheme, and the schemes in [11, 17, 22] lacked provable security, as well. Meanwhile, it was proved that scheme [4] was not secure in [22]. Therefore, to the best of our knowledge, our scheme is the only ID-based multi-proxy signature scheme using bilinear pairings that is proved to be secure in the random oracle model.

6   Conclusion

In this paper, we describe the definition and security model of an identity-based multi-proxy signature scheme and propose a new identity-based multi-proxy signature scheme. Based on the hardness of the computational Diffie-Hellman problem, our scheme was proven to be secure in the random oracle model. Moreover, compared with previous ID-based multi-proxy signature schemes based on bilinear pairings, our scheme is provably secure and more efficient.

Acknowledgements. The authors would like to thank the anonymous reviewers for their helpful comments. This work is supported in part by the National Natural Science Foundation of China under Grant No. 61772150 and No. 61862012; the Natural Science Foundation of Fujian Province of China under Grant No. 2019J01750 and No. 2015J01662; the Research Project of Fujian Provincial Education Department of China under Grant No. JAT170345, No. JAT170346, and No. JK2017031; the Guangxi Key R&D Program under Grant No. AB17195025, the Guangxi Natural Science Foundation under Grant No. 2018GXNSFDA281054 and No. 2018GXNSFAA 281232, the National Cryptography Development Fund of China under Grant No. MMJJ2017 0217, and the Project of Key Laboratory of Financial Mathematics of Fujian Province University (Putian University) under Grant No. JR201806.

References

1. Bellare, M., Namprempre, C., Neven, G.: Security proofs for identity-based identification and signature schemes. In: Cachin, C., Camenisch, J.L. (eds.) EUROCRYPT 2004. LNCS, vol. 3027, pp. 268–286. Springer, Heidelberg (2004). https://doi.org/10.1007/978-3-540-24676-3_17
2. Boldyreva, A., Palacio, A., Warinschi, B.: Secure proxy signature schemes for delegation of signing rights. J. Cryptol. **25**(1), 57–115 (2012)
3. Boneh, D., Franklin, M.: Identity-based encryption from the Weil pairing. In: Kilian, J. (ed.) CRYPTO 2001. LNCS, vol. 2139, pp. 213–229. Springer, Heidelberg (2001). https://doi.org/10.1007/3-540-44647-8_13
4. Cao, F., Cao, Z.: A secure identity-based multi-proxy signature scheme. Comput. Electr. Eng. **35**(1), 86–95 (2009)
5. Choon, J.C., Hee Cheon, J.: An identity-based signature from gap Diffie-Hellman groups. In: Desmedt, Y.G. (ed.) PKC 2003. LNCS, vol. 2567, pp. 18–30. Springer, Heidelberg (2003). https://doi.org/10.1007/3-540-36288-6_2
6. Gu, K., Jia, W., Deng, Y., Nie, X.: Secure and efficient multi-proxy signature scheme in the standard model. Chin. J. Electron. **25**(1), 93–99 (2016)
7. Huang, X., Susilo, W., Mu, Y., Wu, W.: Proxy signature without random oracles. In: Cao, J., Stojmenovic, I., Jia, X., Das, S.K. (eds.) MSN 2006. LNCS, vol. 4325, pp. 473–484. Springer, Heidelberg (2006). https://doi.org/10.1007/11943952_40
8. Hwang, S., Shi, C.: A simple multi-proxy signature scheme. In: Proceedings of the 10th National Conference on Information Security, Hualien, Taiwan, ROC, pp. 134–138 (2000)
9. Li, J., Xu, L., Zhang, Y.: Provably secure certificate-based proxy signature schemes. J. Comput. **4**(6), 444–452 (2009)
10. Li, S., Zhang, F.: A new multi-proxy signature from bilinear pairing. Chin. J. Electron. **24**(1), 90–94 (2007)
11. Li, X., Chen, K.: ID-based multi-proxy signature, proxy multi-signature and multi-proxy multi-signature schemes from bilinear pairings. Appl. Math. Comput. **169**(1), 437–450 (2005)
12. Libert, B., Quisquater, J.J.: The exact security of an identity based signature and its applications. Cryptology ePrint Archive, Report 2004/102 (2004). http://eprint.iacr.org/2004/102
13. Liu, Z., Hu, Y., Zhang, X., Ma, H.: Provably secure multi-proxy signature scheme with revocation in the standard model. Comput. Commun. **34**(3), 494–501 (2011)
14. Mambo, M., Usuda, K., Okamoto, E.: Proxy signature: delegation of the power to sign messages. IEICE Trans. Fundamentals **E79-A**(9), 1338–1353 (1996)
15. Mambo, M., Usuda, K., Okamoto, E.: Proxy signature for delegating signing operation. In: Proceedings of the 3rd ACM Conference on Computer and Communications Security, pp. 48–57. ACM, New York (1996)
16. Mishra, S., Sahu, R.A., Padhye, S., Yadav, R.S.: Efficient ID-based multi-proxy signature scheme from bilinear pairing based on *k-plus* problem. In: Hruschka, E.R., Watada, J., do Carmo Nicoletti, M. (eds.) INTECH 2011. CCIS, vol. 165, pp. 113–122. Springer, Heidelberg (2011). https://doi.org/10.1007/978-3-642-22247-4_10
17. Rao, B.U., Reddy, P.V.: ID-based directed multi-proxy signature scheme from bilinear pairings. Int. J. Comput. Sci. Secur. **5**(1), 717–727 (2011)
18. Seo, S., Choi, K., Hwang, J., Kim, S.: Efficient certificateless proxy signature scheme with provable security. Inf. Sci. **188**, 322–337 (2012)

19. Singh, H., Verma, G.: ID-based proxy signature scheme with message recovery. J. Syst. Softw. **85**(1), 209–214 (2012)
20. Shamir, A.: Identity-based cryptosystems and signature schemes. In: Blakley, G.R., Chaum, D. (eds.) CRYPTO 1984. LNCS, vol. 196, pp. 47–53. Springer, Heidelberg (1985). https://doi.org/10.1007/3-540-39568-7_5
21. Waters, B.: Efficient identity-based encryption without random oracles. In: Cramer, R. (ed.) EUROCRYPT 2005. LNCS, vol. 3494, pp. 114–127. Springer, Heidelberg (2005). https://doi.org/10.1007/11426639_7
22. Xiong, H., Hu, J., Chen, Z., Li, F.: On the security of an identity based multi-proxy signature scheme. Comput. Electr. Eng. **37**(1), 129–135 (2011)
23. Zhang, F., Kim, K.: Efficient ID-based blind signature and proxy signature from bilinear pairings. In: Safavi-Naini, R., Seberry, J. (eds.) ACISP 2003. LNCS, vol. 2727, pp. 312–323. Springer, Heidelberg (2003). https://doi.org/10.1007/3-540-45067-X_27
24. Zhang, K.: Threshold proxy signature schemes. In: Okamoto, E., Davida, G., Mambo, M. (eds.) ISW 1997. LNCS, vol. 1396, pp. 282–290. Springer, Heidelberg (1998). https://doi.org/10.1007/BFb0030429

Privacy Preservation

A Differentially Private Trajectory Publishing Mechanism Based on Stay Points

Ying Xia[✉], Yao Lin, and Hao Wang

School of Computer Science and Technology, Chongqing University of Posts and Telecommunications, Chongqing 400065, China
{xiaying,haowang}@cqupt.edu.cn, linyao.cqupt@gmail.com

Abstract. Trajectory data contains abundant of spatiotemporal information, publishing unprotected trajectories may disclose individual privacy. Recently, researchers have proposed differential privacy to protect users' privacy when publishing trajectory. However, existing works tend to introduce additional noise when add Laplacian noise. To solve this problem, we propose a differentially private trajectory mechanism publishing based on stay points. Firstly, TF-IDF is used to estimate the importance of each stay point and applied to exponential mechanism as a utility function. Additionally, important stay points can be selected by exponential mechanism and assigned corresponding privacy budget based on the value of TF-IDF. Furthermore, noise which added to each protected stay point, is generated from two-dimensional Laplacian via sampling distance and angle between adjacent points. Experiments on two real trajectory data sets show that our proposed mechanism has high data availability while satisfying the privacy protection level.

Keywords: Differential privacy · Two-dimensional Laplacian noise · Stay points · Trajectory publication

1 Introduction

With the rapid development of mobile Internet and location technology, enormous trajectory data has been generated in our life. Trajectory data contains a large amount of spatiotemporal information. For service operators, trajectory data can be analyzed to support varieties of application requirements related to mobile objects, such as personalized information recommendation. City manager can analyze current traffic flow through trajectory data to provide appropriate traffic control solution. However, trajectory data may exist users' sensitive information which can be obtained by the attacker through data mining, such as behavior patterns, living habits or interests. Therefore, how to protect users' privacy when releasing trajectory data with high data availability is an important issue should be solved.

© Springer Nature Switzerland AG 2019
J. Vaidya et al. (Eds.): CSS 2019, LNCS 11982, pp. 245–257, 2019.
https://doi.org/10.1007/978-3-030-37337-5_19

The current trajectory publishing methods with privacy protection mainly include generalization method [6,14], fake data method [17] and suppression method [13]. But these methods are all need to assume the background knowledge of attackers, and are difficult to measure with a unified metric. Differential privacy can well solve the shortcomings of the above methods and has become a research hots pot in recent years. Chen et al. [4,5] first carried out the research work of combining trajectory release and differential privacy. They proposed a trajectory publishing mechanism named STM-Full which based on prefix tree. In their research, the original trajectory can be represented by a prefix tree, and the purpose of privacy protection is achieved by adding noise to the counting result on the leaf node. However, as the number of positions increases, the prefix tree has a problem of insufficient common prefix. In addition, the prefix tree cannot store the time information of each position. Thus, more researchers try to solve these privacy issues from the definition of differential privacy and the spatiotemporal properties of the trajectory sequence. Bordenabe et al. [2,3] proposed the concept of Geo-indistinguishability, which assigns the same privacy level to areas within the same radius to achieve user's positional information, and introducing two-dimensional Laplacian noise to disturb the actual position. Fang et al. [8] extended the concept of neighboring data sets in differential privacy and proposed the δ-neighborhood to emphasize the difference of spatiotemporal relation-ship between two adjacent data sets.

However, the above researches more consider protecting the location at a single moment. Trajectory is a kind of time-series data, even if every position of single moment is protected, continuous trajectories still possibly expose user's privacy. Xiong et al. [18] proposed an attack scheme to separate Laplacian noise from published data. Laplacian noise obeys independent and identical distribution, thus this scheme can filter data effectively and get relatively pure raw data by using the characteristics of noise. To resist filtering attack, Wang et al. [10,19] proposed a trajectory publishing mechanism CLM that uses correlation Laplacian noise and original sequence superposition to generate correlated Gaussian noise sequences through Gaussian white noise, and superimposes autocorrelation into time series to achieve the effect of privacy protection. Gu et al. [9] extracted the historical appearance frequency of the users' positions and added noise to the centroid of the sensitive position which defined by users. Shao et al. [15] proposed sampling and difference strategies to synthesize trajectory data, but only implemented a relatively weak differential privacy definition. Jiang et al. [12] proposed the SSD algorithm, which samples the direction and distance of each moment, and uses the exponential mechanism to publish the possible positions at the next moment. However, protects trajectory points at each moment in above methods is easy to introduce additional noise and reduce the availability of published data. At the same time, in actual situation, plenty of location information is useless to analysers.

In this paper, a differentially private trajectory publication mechanism based on stay points (DPTPSP) is proposed, so that to gain high data availability under the same privacy protection level. Main contributions of our work include:

(1) Exponential mechanism is used to select important stay points from trajectory. Furthermore, TF-IDF value is used as a utility function to indicate the importance of stay points for each user, and to allocate appropriate privacy budget for each stay point.
(2) To improve existing two-dimensional Laplacian noise-adding method by sampling the direction and distance among adjacent points in the process of adding noise, and the noise can be controlled to increase the data availability.

2 Preliminaries

2.1 Trajectory and Stay Points

Trajectory is a spatiotemporal sequence composed of time and position generated by the user in the process of continuous movement [22]. In this paper, a trajectory is defined below:

Definition 1 (Trajectory). A trajectory is a set of points sorted according to a time series: $T = \{(t_1, l_1), (t_2, l_2), \ldots, (t_{|T|}, l_{|T|})\}$, where $|T|$ represents the length of a trajectory, l_i $(1 \le i \le |T|)$ is the latitude and longitude coordinates of position at timestamp t_i.

User's trajectory can usually be divided into two states which are walking and stay, and the stay state is expressed as "Move a short distance over a long time" [16]. In order to facilitate the representation, the map is divided into grids according to latitude and longitude, and the user's moving range is expressed as the size of the grid.

Definition 2 (Stay Points Set). Given a time threshold ST, trajectory T and a subset T_i of T, where $T_i = \{(t_1, l_1), (t_2, l_2), \ldots, (t_i, l_i)\}$. If T_i appears in a single grid G, then T_i is a stay points set only when $ST \le (t_i - t_1)$.

2.2 Differential Privacy

The idea of differential privacy is to add random noise to original data or its query function, so that inserting or deleting a certain record in the data set does not affect the output result, thus implementing privacy protection.

Definition 3 (ϵ-Differential Privacy). Given a data set D and a neighboring data set D' which contains at most one different record compared with D, a random algorithm A satisfies differential privacy for any output R in D and D':

$$\Pr[A(D) = R] \le e^\epsilon \times \Pr[A(D') = R]$$

where ϵ is privacy budget. Obviously, a smaller ϵ means a higher degree of privacy protection.

Laplace mechanism and exponential mechanism are two basic implementation mechanisms in differential privacy. The Laplace mechanism is often used to protect numerical type results, and the exponential mechanism is used to protect non-numeric type results.

Definition 4 (Laplace Mechanism [7]). Given a data set D, for query $f : D \rightarrow R^d$, the sensitivity of the query function is Δf, random algorithm $A(D) = f(D) + Y$ provides ϵ-differential, where Y obeys the Laplace distribution of scale $\frac{\Delta f}{\epsilon}$.

Definition 5 (Exponential Mechanism [7]). Given a data set D, for any function $u : (D \times \tau) \rightarrow R$, algorithm M can choose an entity output $r \in R$ with probability $e^{\left(\frac{\epsilon u(D,r)}{2\Delta u}\right)}$ which ensures ϵ-differential privacy, where Δu is the sensitivity of the utility function u.

To solve a complex privacy protection problem, it is usually required multiple applications of differential privacy protection algorithms. The sequence combination feature of differential privacy can control the privacy protection level of the entire process within a given budget ϵ.

Definition 6 (Sequence Composition [7]). Suppose each algorithms A provides ϵ-Differential Privacy. A sequence of A_n over a database D provides $\left(\sum\limits_{i=1}^{n} \epsilon_i\right)$-differential privacy.

2.3   TF-IDF

TF-IDF (term frequency–inverse document frequency) is a weighting technique commonly used for information retrieval. TF indicates the frequency at which a word x appears in the document. IDF represents the frequency of occurrence where documents containing the word x.

A trajectory consists of multiple stay points, and each point has different important level for users. It is not suitable to measure the importance of stay points by frequency alone. Some points appear multiple times in a single trajectory, such as a user in a mall or park. On the contrary, some points appear only once or twice in a single trajectory, but regularly appear in other trajectories, such as user's workplace. It is obviously that TF-IDF can handle the above situation well.

Assuming the existing trajectory data set D and trajectory $T_d \in D$, the score of position l_i can be expressed as

$$Tf(l_i) = \frac{T_d(l_i)}{\sum\limits_{s_j \in T_d} T_d(l_j)} \times \log\left(\frac{|D|}{|\{T_d | T_d(l_i) \geq ST, T_d \in D\}|}\right) \tag{1}$$

where $T_d(l_i)$ represents the sum of time when l_i appears in T_d.

2.4   Data Availability

In this paper, data availability is measured by calculating RMSE [11] and query distortion [1]. Suppose the position published at time t is p_t, its true position is r_t, and the distance between two position is

$$dis(p_t, r_t) = \|p_t - r_t\|_2.$$

For a trajectory sequence of length L, RMSE is defined below

$$RMSE = \frac{1}{L} \sum_{t=1}^{L} dis(p_t, r_t). \tag{2}$$

The query distortion is mainly used to measure data availability in the query application, which is defined as $\frac{|Q(D) - Q(D')|}{max(Q(D), Q(D'))}$, where $Q(D)$ and $Q(D')$ represent the results of the query on data sets D and D'. Moreover, the query Q is defined as

$$Q : select\ count(*)\ from\ D\ where\ PSI(T \in D, R, t_b, t_e).$$

The function PSI indicates that the user has appeared in radius within the range of R at time $t(t_b, t_e)$, and R is replaced by the grid in this paper.

3   Differentially Private Trajectory Publication Mechanism Based on Stay Points

In this section, we present the design of the proposed DPTPSP mechanism. Specially, we first present how to select important stay points by exponential mechanism. Then we elaborate on the noise disturbance mechanism, and prove that the proposed mechanism satisfies ϵ-differential privacy.

3.1   Differentially Private Stay Points Selection

Protecting every stay point of each trajectory introduces excessive noise and destroys trajectory's original features. Thus, the exponential mechanism is used to select the appropriate stay point for protection according to probability. Assuming each user has k stay points to protect, stay points $s_i (i \in [1, k])$ can be chosen with utility function described in Sect. 2.3 following probability:

$$\Pr(s_i) = \frac{e^{(\frac{\epsilon}{2\Delta T_f} \times Tf(s_i))}}{\sum_{i=1}^{k} e^{(\frac{\epsilon}{2\Delta T_f} \times Tf(s_i))}}, \tag{3}$$

where ΔT_f is the sensitivity of the utility function, when a point is changed, the maximum effect on the function equals 1. To control the amount of noise introduced to each stay point, the privacy budget ϵ_i is assigned according to the probability

$$\epsilon_i = \epsilon \times (1 - \frac{\Pr(s_i)}{\sum\limits_{i=1}^{k} \Pr(s_i)}). \tag{4}$$

The main steps of selecting stay points by the exponential mechanism are given in Algorithm 1.

Algorithm 1. Differentially Private Stay Points Selection

Input: Trajectory set D, stay point set S, number of protected stay points k, privacy budget ϵ;
Output: Protected stay point set NS and privacy budget ϵ_i;
1: $NS = \{\}$;
2: $\Delta T_f \leftarrow 1$;
3: **for** each $T_k \in D$ **do**
4:    **for** each $s_i \in S$ **do**
5:        **if** $s_i \in T_k$ **then**
6:            Get Tf_i by Eq. 1;
7:            Get $Pr(s_i)$ by Eq. 3;
8:        **end if**
9:    **end for**
10:    $s_k \leftarrow$ random sample k-points from s_i followed $Pr(s_i)$;
11:    Get ϵ_i by Eq. 4;
12:    $NS = NS \cup \{s_k\}$;
13: **end for**
14: **return** NS, ϵ_i;

3.2 Two-Dimensional Laplacian-Based Trajectory Publication

Compared with existing works of adding noise independently for each dimension, two-dimensional probability density can effectively reduce the noise level under the same privacy protection intensity [2]. Position is a kind of two-dimensional point, according to Definition 4, the two-dimensional Laplacian probability density function can be obtained as

$$D_\epsilon(x) = \frac{\epsilon^2}{2\pi} e^{-\epsilon x}, \tag{5}$$

where x represents the Euclidean distance between the real position and the published position. In order to facilitate the calculation, Eq. 5 can be converted into the polar coordinate system form. The new density is:

$$D_\epsilon(r, \theta) = \frac{\epsilon^2}{2\pi} r e^{-\epsilon r}. \tag{6}$$

In Eq. 6, r ranges from 0 to ∞. When r becomes larger, the distance between published position and real position farther away, which is not reality in actual situation. Therefore, distance is limited by analyzed user's speed and time interval to ensure that user can reach published position within certain time. Assuming that the set of points $st_i = \{(x_1, y_1), (x_2, y_2), \ldots, (x_n, y_n)\}$ belongs to the stay points set S, then the maximum distance $R_{\max}$ is set to

$$R_{\max} = dis((x_n, y_n), (x_{n+1}, y_{n+1})),$$

where (x_n, y_n) denotes position's coordinate and $dis(\cdot)$ denotes the distance between two positions, the new radius range r' can be expressed as

$$r' = r \bmod R_{\max}.$$

Similarly, according to the direction of adjacent positions, θ is limited to (θ_n, θ_{n+1}), where θ_n denotes position's angle in polar coordinate. According to Eq. 6, marginal probability density distribution of r' and θ are denoted as:

$$D_\epsilon(r') = \int_{\theta_n}^{\theta_{n+1}} D(r', \theta)d\theta = \frac{(\theta_{n+1} - \theta_n)\epsilon^2}{2\pi} r' e^{-\epsilon r'}, \tag{7}$$

$$D_\epsilon(\theta) = \int_0^{r'} D(r', \theta)dr' = \frac{1}{2\pi}. \tag{8}$$

By respectively calculating the sum of the probability densities of Eqs. 7 and 8, noise can be added to points' coordinates. The research [12] pointed out that it is better to add different noise to each point rather than to add the same noise to a point set. Therefore, we add noise to each position of the stay point in the trajectory. The last published trajectory consists of two parts: one is the sequence of staying points after noise addition, and the other is the sequence of non-stay points that remain unchanged. The specific publishing mechanism is shown in Algorithm 2.

Algorithm 2. Two-dimensional Laplacian-based Trajectory Publication

Input: Trajectory T_k, set of protected stay points NS, privacy budget ϵ_i;
Output: Published trajectory sequence T';
  1: $NS = \{\}$;
  2: **for** each $point \in T_k$ **do**
  3:   **for** each $point \in T_k$ **do**
  4:     **if** $point_i \in NS$ **then**
  5:       $R_{\max} \leftarrow dis(point_i, point_{i+1})$;
  6:       Get r by Eq. 7 with ϵ_i;
  7:       Get θ by Eq. 8 with ϵ_i;
  8:       $r' = r \bmod R_{max}$;
  9:       $dp_i = point_i + < r\cos(\theta), r\sin(\theta) >$;
 10:       $T' = T' \cup \{dp_i\}$;
 11:     **else**
 12:       $T' = T' \cup \{point_i\}$;
 13:     **end if**
 14:   **end for**
 15: **end for**
 16: **return** T';

3.3   Algorithm Analysis

This section mainly analyzes the privacy protection and time complexity of DPTPSP. DPTPSP is processed for each stay point of each trajectory, so the time complexity of DPTPSP is $O(|D| * |S|)$, $|D|$ and $|S|$ represent the number of trajectories and stay points respectively. DPTPSP satisfies ϵ-differential privacy is proved next, as shown in Theorem 1. Since DPTPSP consists of the selection of stay points (see Algorithm 1) and the trajectory release (see Algorithm 2), according to the sequence properties of differential privacy, DPTPSP satisfies differential privacy if and only if Algorithm 1 and Algorithm 2 respectively satisfy differential privacy.

Theorem 1. *If the privacy budgets for Algorithm 1 and Algorithm 2 are assigned ϵ_1 and ϵ_2, DPTPSP guarantees $(\epsilon_1 + \epsilon_2)$-differential privacy.*

Proof. Algorithm 1 uses the exponential mechanism of differential privacy to extract the stay points. According to Definition 5, Algorithm 1 guarantees ϵ_1-differential privacy.

Algorithm 2 adds noise with ϵ_i and obeys a two-dimensional Laplacian distribution for coordinates in each stay point. It has proved that this noise-adding process satisfies ϵ_i-differential privacy in [2], according to Eq. 4, it can be calculated that $\epsilon_2 = \sum_{i=1}^{k} \epsilon_i$. Thus, according to Definition 6, Algorithm 2 guarantees the ϵ_2-differential privacy.

4   Experiments

4.1   Experiment Setup

Experiment is performed in Python language, Windows10 with 3.30 GHz CPU and 8.00 GB RAM. Two real trajectory databases are accessed, Geolife [21] and T-driver [20]. GeoLife contains 182 users' trajectories collected by Microsoft Research Asia from April 2007 to August 2012. Each trajectory has a series of time-ordered points which contains information such as latitude, longitude and timestamp. T-Drive a GPS trajectory data set of Beijing taxis from February 2, 2008 to February 8, 2008. The sampling frequency of the trajectories ranged from 30s to 300s. Ten users per data set are selected for testing and the scope of each trajectory is limited to the Sixth Ring in Beijing. According to the scope, the map is divided into grids with a size of 0.5 km $\times$ 0.5 km. The time threshold of stay points is set to 600s. After data pre-processing, the number of stay points included in each trajectory of users is shown in Fig. 1. It demonstrates that the number of trajectories extracted by Geolife and T-drive is 653 and 89. Considering that choosing too many stay points is not very helpful to the experimental results, and the distribution of Fig. 1 shows that the number of stay points of each trajectory is mostly between 1 and 4. Thus, this paper mainly discusses the effect of stay points $k(k \in [1,2,3,4])$ and privacy budget $\epsilon(\epsilon \in [0.2, 0.4, 0.6, 0.8, 1.0])$ on data availability.

4.2 Availability Evaluation

We first tested the effect of the number k of stay points on data availability in two data sets. Each user's experiment was run 10 times. The experimental results are shown in Fig. 2. It can be seen that as the k value increases, the RMSE value also increases, indicating that the increase of stay point introduces much noise to ensure that the privacy achieves the requirements. At the same time, as ϵ increases, the degree of privacy protection is smaller, so the introduced noise is also reduced. For Geolife users, when $\epsilon = 0.2$, $k = 4$, the RMSE value of the published data is 0.239, while the T-drive user has an RMSE value of 0.136 under the same conditions, which is slightly smaller than the value of the Geolife user. Similarly, this trend is also shown when k takes other values. The reason is that compared with the T-drive data set, Geolife selects more time spans of user data, and much noise is required to achieve the same privacy protection standards.

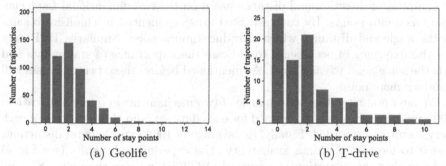

(a) Geolife

(b) T-drive

Fig. 1. Distribution of user stay points

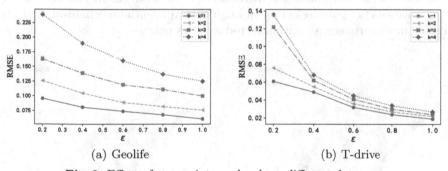

(a) Geolife

(b) T-drive

Fig. 2. Effect of stay point number k on different data sets

In order to verify data availability of the algorithm, we compared the proposed DPTPSP with SSD [12] and mechanism proposed by Gu et al. [9]. The SSD is a classical protection method that randomly takes values by exponential mechanism after sampling the distance and direction among positions, and it is suitable for local feature perturbation of the trajectory. The mechanism of Gu et al. is mainly to record the position around the stay points and draw polygons through historical data. The original stay point is replaced by adding noise to the center of mass of the polygon. In order to facilitate the later description, we abbreviate the mechanism proposed by Gu et al. as differential privacy polygons (DPP). The experimental results are shown in Fig. 3. It can be found that DPTPSP's data availability is better than SSD and DPP under different k values. This is because DPTPSP uses the exponential mechanism to select stay points which need to be protected, and assigns appropriate privacy budget to each stay point based on the score value. Thus, DPTPSP introduces less noise than assigning the same privacy budget to each point. At the same time, we add the sampling of direction and distance based on the two-dimensional Laplacian mechanism into points. By contrast, SSD uses exponential mechanism to sample the angle and distance, which introduces much noise. Similarly, DPP only uses the frequency of occurrence to indicate the importance of stay points and adds the same noise to each point. As mentioned before, these two processes will introduce more noise.

We next evaluated the performance of two mechanisms in query application. 1000 random queries were performed for each data set, and the distortion of each query result was recorded. Finally, the average of 1000 experimental distortions is used to measure the data availability. The experimental results (see Fig. 4) illustrate that the distortion of proposed DPTPSP is lower than the SSD and DPP under different k and ϵ. This is because DPTPSP mainly deals with the disturbance of the stay point. The disturbance mechanism ensures the rationality of the selected stay point selection through the exponential mechanism, and the subsequent disturbance algorithm introduces less noise.

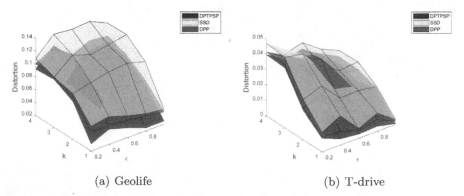

(a) Geolife   (b) T-drive

Fig. 3. Impact of stay point number k on different mechanisms

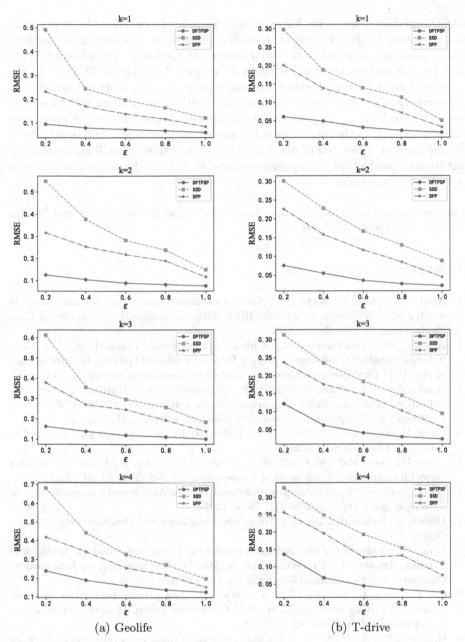

(a) Geolife   (b) T-drive

Fig. 4. Distortion of query Q

5   Conclusion

In this paper, a differentially private trajectory publication mechanism based on stay points is proposed. This mechanism first uses exponential mechanism to select important stay points for each user. In order to measure the importance of stay points, TF-IDF is used as the utility function of exponential mechanism. Then, noise is generated from two-dimensional Laplacian probability density with private budget which is distributed followed the value of TF-IDF. In the process of adding noise, distance and angle between two points are sampled to represent time information. Experimental results show that for the trajectory data, this mechanism can guarantee high data availability under the premise of ensuring privacy. In the future, we will consider the practicality and scalability of our mechanism in the case of big data. At the same time, we will optimize noise disturbance mechanism to improve the data availability based on the fusion of more time information.

Acknowledgement. This work was financially supported by the Natural Science Foundation of China (41571401).

References

1. Abul, O., Bonchi, F., Nanni, M.: Never walk alone: uncertainty for anonymity in moving objects databases. In: 2008 IEEE 24th International Conference on Data Engineering, pp. 376–385 (2008)
2. Andrés, M., Bordenabe, N., Chatzikokolakis, K., Palamidessi, C.: Geo-indistinguishability: differential privacy for location-based systems. In: Proceedings of the ACM Conference on Computer and Communications Security (2013)
3. Bordenabe, N.E., Chatzikokolakis, K., Palamidessi, C.: Optimal geo-indistinguishable mechanisms for location privacy. In: Proceedings of the 2014 ACM SIGSAC Conference on Computer and Communications Security, pp. 251–262 (2014)
4. Chen, R., Fung, B.C.M., Desai, B.C.: Differentially private trajectory data publication. Computer Science (2011)
5. Chen, R., Fung, B.C., Mohammed, N., Desai, B.C., Wang, K.: Privacy-preserving trajectory data publishing by local suppression. Inf. Sci. **231**, 83–97 (2013)
6. Domingo-Ferrer, J.: Microaggregation- and permutation-based anonymization of movement data. Inf. Sci. **208**(21), 55–80 (2012)
7. Dwork, C.: Differential Privacy. Automata, Languages and Programming, pp. 1–12 (2006)
8. Fang, C., Chang, E.C.: Differential privacy with δ-neighbourhood for spatial and dynamic datasets. In: Proceedings of the 9th ACM Symposium on Information, Computer and Communications Security, pp. 159–170 (2014)
9. Gu, K., Yang, L., Liu, Y., Liao, N.: Trajectory data privacy protection based on differential privacy mechanism. In: IOP Conference Series: Materials Science and Engineering, vol. 351, pp. 12–17 (2018)
10. Hao, W., Xu, Z.: CTS-DP: publishing correlated time-series data via differential privacy. Knowl.-Based Syst. **122**, 167–179 (2017)
11. Huo, Z., Meng, X.F.: A trajectory data publication method under differential privacy. Chin. J. Comput. **41**(2), 400–412 (2018)
12. Jiang, K., Shao, D., Bressan, S., Kister, T., Tan, K.L.: Publishing trajectories with differential privacy guarantees. In: Proceedings of the 25th International Conference on Scientific and Statistical Database Management, pp. 12:1–12:12 (2013)

13. Li, J., Bai, Z.H., Yu, R.Y., Cui, Y.M., Wang, X.W.: Mobile location privacy protection algorithm based on PSO optimization. Chin. J. Comput. **41**(5), 1037–1051 (2018)
14. Nergiz, M.E., Atzori, M., Saygin, Y.: Towards trajectory anonymization: a generalization-based approach. In: SIGSPATIAL ACM GIS International Workshop on Security and Privacy in GIS and LBS, vol. 2(1), pp. 52–61 (2008)
15. Shao, D., Jiang, K., Kister, T., Bressan, S., Tan, K.-L.: Publishing trajectory with differential privacy: a priori vs. a posteriori sampling mechanisms. In: Decker, H., Lhotská, L., Link, S., Basl, J., Tjoa, A.M. (eds.) DEXA 2013, Part I. LNCS, vol. 8055, pp. 357–365. Springer, Heidelberg (2013). https://doi.org/10.1007/978-3-642-40285-2_31
16. Tian, F., Zhang, S., Lu, L., Liu, H., Gui, X.: A novel personalized differential privacy mechanism for trajectory data publication. In: 2017 International Conference on Networking and Network Applications (NaNA), pp. 61–68 (2017)
17. Wang, C., Yang, J., Zhang, J.P.: Privacy preserving algorithm based on trajectory location and shape similarity. J. Commun. **36**(2), 144–157 (2015)
18. Wang, H., Xu, Z.Q., Xiong, L.Z., Wang, T.: CLM: differential privacy protection method for trajectory publishing. J. Commun. **38**(6), 85–96 (2017)
19. Xiong, W., Xu, Z., Wang, H.: Privacy level evaluation of differential privacy for time series based on filtering theory. J. Commun. **38**, 172–181 (2017)
20. Yuan, J., Zheng, Y., Xie, X., Sun, G.: Driving with knowledge from the physical world. In: Proceedings of the 17th ACM SIGKDD International Conference on Knowledge Discovery and Data Mining, pp. 316–324 (2011)
21. Zheng, Y., Zhang, L., Xie, X., Ma, W.Y.: Mining interesting locations and travel sequences from GPS trajectories. In: Proceedings of the 18th International Conference on World Wide Web, pp. 791–800 (2009)
22. Zhu, T., Ping, X., Gang, L., Zhou, W.: Correlated differential privacy: hiding information in non-IID data set. IEEE Trans. Inf. Forensics Secur. **10**(2), 229–242 (2014)

Data Privacy Protection in Medical Alliance Chain Based on K-Anonymity

Hui Sun[1], Cheng Huang[1], Xu Cheng[1], and Fulong Chen[1,2(✉)]

[1] School of Computer and Information, Anhui Normal University, Wuhu, China
long005@mail.ahnu.edu.cn
[2] Anhui Provincial Key Lab of Network and Information Security, Wuhu, China

Abstract. At present, there are many threats to medical data security. Because of the different standards of data storage and system, it is very difficult to share medical data and protect data privacy. This paper proposes a data privacy protection method based on K-anonymity for medical alliance chain. The data privacy protection method of Medical Alliance chain in this paper consists of four steps: (1) constructing equivalent classes; (2) medical data slicing; (3) data iteration; (4) medical data reorganization. The scheme of data privacy protection in Medical Alliance chain proposed in this paper has high security, no trusted third party and low energy consumption. It is a privacy protection method suitable for application and medical alliance chain data.

Keywords: K-anonymity · Data slicing · Data iteration · Privacy protection

1 Introduction

1.1 Risks of Medical Data Sharing and Data Privacy Protection Method of Medical Alliance Chain Based on K-Anonymity and QLDS

Medical Internet of Things faces many security threats. In embedded, mobile and network physical systems, a large number of security-critical and privacy-sensitive data are generated, processed and exchanged, which makes them attractive targets for attacks [1]. There are many kinds of security threats in the network, such as physical attack, Trojan horse attack, virus destruction, key decryption, DOS, eavesdropping and traffic analysis [2]. If a computer is infected with the virus and not handled in time, it will affect the operation of other computers in the LAN and the whole LAN, and even cause the whole LAN system of the unit to collapse completely [3]. Blackmail software is a self-propagating malware. Using encryption to save victims'data blackmail has become one of the most dangerous network threats in recent years, causing extensive damage [4]. Medical alliance chain provides a new idea for medical data sharing, and the data in Medical Alliance chain need to be protected.

Foundation Project: National Natural Science Foundation of China (61572036); Open Project of National Key Laboratory of Computer Architecture (CARCH201810).

Liu et al. proposed a k-anonymous location and data privacy protection method (KPPCS) in [5]. In this method, an equivalent class is constructed based on multi-party secure computing. Then a slice-based trajectory privacy protection method (STPP) is proposed. Liu pointed out in the article that compared with the protocol SMC proposed in [6], it does not need trusted third party and trusted friend and it can resist collusion attack at the same time. Compared with the method in document [7], trusted friend is not needed and it can resist collusion attack at the same time. Liu also mentioned that the security of a k-anonymous location and data privacy protection method (KPPCS) is reflected in the process of collusion attack. With the increasing number of N in the equivalent class, the number of participants that an attacker can capture is limited, and the probability of attacker confirming data and application users is very small. In addition, Xiao et al. proposed a QLDS algorithm for query logic separate storage in [8]. The core idea of this algorithm is to store the extracted query logic on the client side of the user, and store the location ancestor of the unclustered location on the back-end server, which effectively guarantees the trajectory privacy of the user. This idea is also used in this paper.

2   Algorithm

2.1   Symbolic Description

The symbolic description of this paper is shown in Table 1.

Table 1. Symbolic description

Symbol	Explain
MTI (Medical-data Tuple Index)	A set of universal unique identifiers (UUIDs) that are not associated with any sensitive data or identity of the user. MTI is always attached to some medical data tuples used to identify medical data reconstruction
MT (Medical-data Tuple)	Minimum tuple (xi, yi, ti, li, di) is the smallest data unit that stores medical data information. Different MTs are attached to different UUIDs
QL (Query Logics)	The mapping relationship associated with the index of medical data tuples can be expressed as P (O, TTI), where O represents some kind of system operation

2.2   Algorithm Description

The data privacy protection method of Medical Alliance chain proposed in this paper is based on K-anonymity and QLDS algorithm. QLDS algorithm is a new practical design scheme of participatory sensor orbit privacy protection proposed by Xiao et al. in [8].

This paper proposes that the data privacy protection method of Medical Alliance chain can be divided into four steps:

(1) Construct equivalence classes. Equivalence classes are a group of n medical monitoring terminals. Each medical monitoring terminal has the function of uploading medical data and data directly to the server. In the equivalence classes, all medical monitoring terminals are independent and distrustful, but they can protect the privacy of medical data.

(2) Medical data slice. Medical monitoring terminal divides medical data into medical data tuples, which are expressed as (xi, yi, ti, li, di), I = 1, 2, 3 ... N. The generated UUIDs are assigned to each medical data tuple. At the same time, the mapping relationship between system operation and index of medical data tuple is preserved, expressed as P (O, TTI) = {Oi:{UUIDj | J = 1, 2, 3 ...}| I = 1, 2, 3 ...}.

For example, patients perform time-based medical data retrieval, the algorithm triggers P (O, TTI) queries to search for the corresponding MTI, and then sends the obtained MTI to the back-end server to further retrieve the corresponding medical data tuples for medical data reconstruction.

Because the time stamp, location and doctor information provide the attacker with key information, such as when the server collects the medical data tuple, it can sort the medical data tuple according to the corresponding time stamp, location and doctor information, which can improve the probability of medical data reconstruction, so we process the medical data element ancestor in the data slicing process accordingly.

Medical data element ancestor set before processing can be represented as SMTi, it shows in formula 1.

$$SMT_i = \begin{bmatrix} name & age & sex & nationality & date \\ T & P & R & BP & W \\ \dots & \dots & \dots & \dots & \dots \\ \dots & \dots & \dots & \dots & \dots \\ \dots & \dots & \dots & hospital & doctor \end{bmatrix} \quad (1)$$

Disturbance processing is done to the part of medical data meta-ancestor which involves sensitive information of patients. After processing, the set of medical data meta-ancestors is expressed as SMTi', I = 1, 2, 3 ... n. Perturbed patient sensitive information may prevent attackers or servers from initiating attacks based on sensitive information processing. But in order for users to reconstruct medical data, it is necessary to store sensitive information without disturbance, which is expressed as UUIDi = {namei, agei, sexi, nationalityi, datei, hospitali, doctorI | I = 1, 2, 3 ... n}.

$$SMT_i' = \begin{bmatrix} name' & age' & sex' & nationality' & date' \\ T & P & R & BP & W \\ \dots & \dots & \dots & \dots & \dots \\ \dots & \dots & \dots & \dots & \dots \\ \dots & \dots & \dots & hospital' & doctor' \end{bmatrix} \quad (2)$$

Data permutation: The input array is reassembled according to the randomly generated permutation IP table, assuming that the permutation IP table is shown in

Table 2. But in order for users to reconstruct medical data, it is necessary to store replacement IP tables with encrypted sensitive information without exchange location.

Table 2. Permutation IP table

24	15	8	5	13
10	7	4	20	1
21	23	16	25	17
22	14	19	3	18
12	11	9	6	2

The input data of the 25th digit is replaced by the first digit and the 15th digit by the second digit. By analogy, the last digit is the original second digit, and the result after replacement is as follows:

$$
SMT_i'' = \begin{bmatrix}
hospital' & \cdots & nationality' & date' & \cdots \\
W & P & \cdots & \cdots & name' \\
\cdots & \cdots & \cdots & doctor' & \cdots \\
\cdots & \cdots & \cdots & sex' & \cdots \\
\cdots & \cdots & BP & T & age'
\end{bmatrix} \tag{3}
$$

Data slicing: The medical data element ancestor set $SMTi''$ is sliced and processed as shown in Formula 3 to generate data element ancestors (xi, yi, ti, li, di), $I = 1, 2, 3 \ldots N$. Convert one-dimensional matrix xi, yi, zi, vi, wi into one-dimensional array as shown in formula 4.

$$
\begin{aligned}
x_i &= [hospital' \quad \cdots \quad nationality' \quad date' \quad \cdots] \\
y_i &= [W \quad P \quad \cdots \quad \cdots \quad name'] \\
z_i &= [\cdots \quad \cdots \quad \cdots \quad doctor' \quad \cdots] \\
v_i &= [\cdots \quad \cdots \quad \cdots \quad sex' \quad \cdots] \\
w_i &- [\cdots \quad \cdots \quad BP \quad T \quad age']
\end{aligned} \tag{4}
$$

(3) Data iteration, as shown in Fig. 1, it ensures that other medical terminals and data centers are unable to identify data contributors. Greedy method is used to determine the order of transmission between medical terminal devices in equivalence classes. Choose the device with the smallest number of data transmission as the first, search each adjacent point from C1 in turn, transmit data to the device with the second smallest number of data, transmit the second smallest number of data to the user with the third smallest number of data together with their own medical data and the transmitted data, and so on, until transmission to the device with the largest number of data, then the last one. Each device has all the medical data that needs to be uploaded, and then the data is uploaded to the medical center.

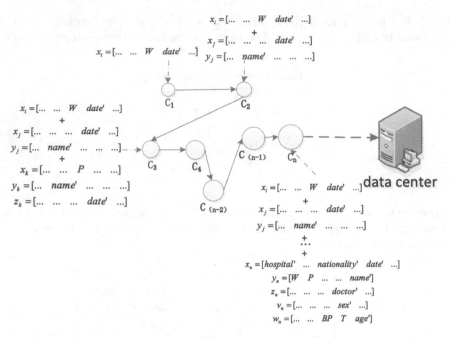

Fig. 1. Data iteration

(4) Medical data reorganization, patients or doctors find the corresponding UUID in the client according to QL, send the UUID to the server, the server finds the corresponding MT according to UUID, and then returns the MT to the client. Patients or doctors reconstruct the medical data in the client.

3 Experiment

3.1 Experimental Results and Analysis

Assuming that the attacker can get all the data at the last node, and the data of this time satisfies the ideal situation, the number of data uploaded by the node n is n pieces, the total number of data transmitted by this time is $\frac{(1+n)n}{2}$ pieces, the attacker obtained $\frac{(1+n)n}{2}$ pieces of data, and knows that the number of data uploaded by each node n is n pieces. When n = 1, the attacker guesses the probability of the correct data slice is $\frac{2}{(1+n)n}$. When n > 1, the attacker guesses that the probability of data slices is $\frac{1}{C_{\frac{(1+n)n}{2}}^{i}}$, the probability that the attacker obtains the correct data slices and ranks them correctly is $\frac{1}{A_i^i}$, and the probability that Attackers guess the correct sequence of data slices is $\frac{1}{C_{\frac{(1+n)n}{n}}^{i}\cdot A_i^i}$. Through calculation, we know that, when the participating medical terminal node reaches 6, the probability of attackers guessing the correct sequence of data slices will be less than 0.05.

3.2 Energy Consumption Analysis

During the experiment, the number of the data transmission of each medical terminal device is shown in Table 3. The medical terminal device can be expressed as Nodei, i = 1, 2, 3, ... N. In the experimental environment, we define n = 10. Data transmission refers to the random transmission of data between 10 different medical terminal devices in Nodei, i = 1, 2, 3, ... 10. Each medical terminal receives data from the previous medical terminal device and transmits it to the next medical terminal device along with its own data until all data transmission from these 10 different medical terminal devices reaches a medical terminal. On the device, in this process, the data that the last medical terminal device receives is called the number of data transmission.

Table 3. Data transmission of medical terminal equipment

Node	1	2	3	4	5	6	7	8	9	10
The number of data transmission (bit)	302	740	297	613	609	893	494	314	651	721

The direction of arrow indicates the direction of data transmission: *Node1* -> *Node2* -> *Node3* -> *Node4* -> *Node5* -> *Node6* -> *Node7* -> *Node8* -> *Node9* -> *Node10*. When all data reaches Node10, the number of data is 5634bit and the number of data transmission is 4913bit.

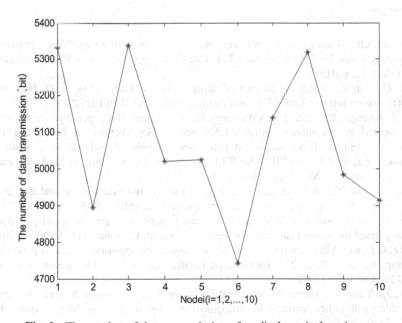

Fig. 2. The number of data transmission of medical terminal equipment

When the total number of data transmission reaches the last node Nodei, the total number of data transmission reaches different last node because of the different transmission order. As shown in Fig. 2, when the last node is Node6, the number of data transmission is the smallest. Therefore, the greedy method can be used to transmit data between medical terminal devices to achieve the minimum number of data transmission.

4   Conclusion

In this paper, a method based on k-anonymity is proposed to protect data privacy in the medical alliance chain. Firstly, an equivalent class composed of n medical monitoring terminals is constructed. Then, medical data is sliced, including specific steps (1) disturbance processing, (2) data replacement, (3) data slicing. The greedy method is used to determine the order of transmission between medical terminal devices in the equivalence class until it is transmitted to the device with the largest number of data. At this time, the last device has all the medical data that need to be uploaded, and then the data is uploaded to the medical center. Therefore, the algorithm can protect data privacy in the medical alliance chain. Experiments show that the proposed algorithm can protect the privacy of data in the medical alliance chain and reduce the cost of medical terminal equipment.

Acknowledgements. This research was supported by National Natural Science Foundation of China (No. 61572036) and National Key Laboratory of Computer Architecture (CARCH201810).

References

1. Sadeghi, A.R., Wachsmann, C., Waidner, M.: Security and privacy challenges in industrial internet of things. In: 2015 52nd ACM/EDAC/IEEE Design Automation Conference (DAC), pp. 1–6. IEEE (2015)
2. Gan, G., Lu, Z., Jiang, J.: Internet of things security analysis. In: 2011 International Conference on Internet Technology and Applications, pp. 1–4. IEEE (2011)
3. Liu, Z., Chengli, Y.: Starting with Wannacry blackmail virus, this paper explores the security defense strategy of computer viruses in LAN. Secrecy Sci. Technol. **06**, 19–22 (2017)
4. Chen, Q., Bridges, R.A.: Automated behavioral analysis of malware: a case study of wannacry ransomware. In: 2017 16th IEEE International Conference on Machine Learning and Applications (ICMLA), pp. 454–460. IEEE (2017)
5. Wang, T., Liu, Y., Jinxin, et al.: Research on k-anonymity-based location and data privacy protection methods in group intelligence perception. J. Commun. **39**(S1), 176–184 (2018)
6. Tian, Y., Li, X., Sangaiah, A.K., et al.: Privacy-preserving scheme in social participatory sensing based on secure multiparty cooperation. Comput. Commun. **119**, 167–178 (2018)
7. Wang, C.J., Ku, W.S.: Anonymous sensory data collection approach for mobile participatory sensing. In: 2012 IEEE 28th International Conference on Data Engineering Workshops, pp. 220–227. IEEE (2012)
8. Xiao, Z., Yang, J.J., Huang, M., et al.: QLDS: a novel design scheme for trajectory privacy protection with utility guarantee in participatory sensing. IEEE Trans. Mob. Comput. **17**(6), 1397–1410 (2017)

IMES: An Automatically Scalable Invisible Membrane Image Encryption for Privacy Protection on IoT Sensors

Songzhan Lv[1], Yining Liu[1], and Jingtao Sun[2(✉)]

[1] School of Computer and Information Security,
Guilin University of Electronic Technology, Guilin, China
yingyu8ji@gmail.com, ynliu@guet.edu.cn
[2] Information System Architecture Research Division,
National Institute of Informatics, Tokyo, Japan
sun@nil.ac.jp

Abstract. With the continuous changes in social needs, Smart City that become a new engine for traditional urban economic transformation, industrial upgrading and urban management. Around the popularity of Smart City, the combination of cloud computing, wireless mobile networks and IoT technology undoubtedly has become a perfect match. However, when the information obtained by the IoT devices are transmitted through the wireless network, people in the city are faced with a lot of personal information leaked without knowing it. This problem, which not only requires the introduction and improvement of relevant laws, but also brings new challenges to the cryptographic technology. This paper proposes an automatically scalable invisible membrane image encryption solution for image privacy issues for the smart city through IoT-based sensors environment. The scheme utilizes the integer vector homomorphic encryption algorithm (VHE) to flexibly generate invisible membrane based on the size of the privacy image to protect private information.

Keywords: Smart City · IoT · Automatic · Image privacy · VHE

1 Introduction

According to the forecast of NISSAY [1], 70% of the world's population will be concentrated in urban areas in the near future, not only energy, housing, transportation, but also the networks and other aspects of human life have to face some of the problems that cannot be ignored, e.g., private protection. However, in order to provide more convenient services to human beings, the concept of the Smart City has become a city's overall development strategy, which will become a new engine for traditional urban economic transformation, industrial upgrading and urban management. In the realization of smart cities, the upgrading of

---

The first author is a master candidate.

© Springer Nature Switzerland AG 2019
J. Vaidya et al. (Eds.): CSS 2019, LNCS 11982, pp. 265–273, 2019.
https://doi.org/10.1007/978-3-030-37337-5_21

sensor technology and the popularity of mobile networks, such as text, symbols and numbers have been rapidly developed, such as intelligent translation, artificial brainless research, but mining rules complexity and application services are still highly dependent on user definition. On the other hands, the unstructured data (such as images and videos) are widely used in object recognition, mobile pursuit, real-time disaster monitoring and virtual implementation of VR, etc. The unstructured data provides more intuitive and more experienced services to users, while user's personal information is leaking frequently. Our research is to solve the problem of personal privacy protection in unstructured data.

Smart City is the mainstream of urban construction at this stage [2–4]. Although people enjoy the convenience of smart cities through the combination of the most advanced technologies, such as cloud computing, wireless mobile networks and IoT sensor technology. When an attacker passes the wireless network to obtain unstructured data by IoT sensor, such as facing personal information in the city, it is leaked and illegally used without knowing it. For solving the personal privacy protection problem, it is not only to be require the introduction and improvement of relevant laws, but also to be needed to bring new challenges to the cryptography technology for researchers. As far as now, traditional image cryptography [5,6] adopts traditional symmetric encryption and chaotic system encryption, but with traditional encryption, encryption is inefficient and insecure [6]. However, the use of chaotic system encryption is efficient and safe, but it cannot flexibly encrypt a part of the image. Therefore, in order to solve such a problem, our proposed a scheme that can generate an invisible membrane according to the size of the privacy location from the image. Invisible membrane image systems can flexibly and efficiently determine whether to allow the user to restore the original image location according to the needs of different users, and can be applied to a wider range of IoT applications without the need for complex environmental deployments and system maintenance.

The contributions of our paper can be summarized as follows:

- Our research provides a container-based mobile deployment IoT platform.
- In view of the lack of security and flexibility of traditional image encryption methods, we propose a new invisible membrane scheme to improve the security and flexibility of image encryption.
- According to different privacy requirements of the user, the cloud control center automatically decides whether to send a decryption key to the user to restore the original image.
- The solution we propose is lightweight and can consume very small amounts of computing resources without affecting IoT data processing.

The rest is organized as follows: Sect. 2 introduces the approach introduces, and our design and discussions in Sect. 3. Performance analyses in Sect. 4. Finally, the conclusion is summarised in Sect. 5.

2   Approach

In this section, we first propose three scenarios, and then introduce to actual requirements. At the end of this section we present our invisible membrane encryption system for privacy protection in IoT society.

2.1   Scenarios

Let's assume an example of using traffic data in a city. In order to prevent illegal situations such as speeding and vehicle theft, it is generally studied to use roadside fixed sensors to collect data, which is usually managed by the national transportation department, however, when chasing illegal vehicles, the general vehicle information and road pedestrians and other information of road need to be protected. Otherwise, it is easy to be tracked by malicious attackers, revealing sensitive personal information such as home address, company address and common driving routes.

These example point out that the user's information needs to be protected during graphics processing to prevent personal information loss, so protects graphics data with new technical will become the biggest problem in Smart City.

2.2   Requirements

Based on the above scenario, we analyzed and summarized the encryption requirements required for the IoT platforms. The requirements are described as follows:

- **Detection Accuracy:** Our system needs to determine the privacy location and size of the image and generate an invisible film based on the privacy location and image size, so we need to improve the accuracy of identifying the coordinate points of the object to help determine the location of the invisible membrane.
- **High Quality and Low Computation:** In the encryption system, we should ensure that the unencrypted part is the same as the original image for image processing. At the same time, due to the limited computing resources of the IoT devices, the encryption algorithm needs to use very low computing resources without affecting the image processing to achieve privacy protection.
- **General-purpose for IoT platforms:** The proposed method needs to meet the needs of different users, while the proposal itself needs a wide range of applicability. The proposal method can not only decide the action of delivering the key according to the requirements of different users, but also restore the image without affecting the information of the image itself.

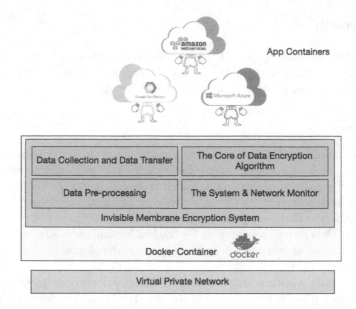

Fig. 1. System architecture

2.3 Approach

Based on the above requirements, we propose the invisible membrane encryption system for image privacy requirements in actual IoT-based sensor environment.

Our invisible membrane encryption system can be divided into four parts (as shown in Fig. 1).

- Data collection and Data transfer part. It is responsible for regularly collecting data from camera sensors which distributed in smart cities, and storing them in edge data center or cloud data center, according to the requirements of IoT applications.
- Data pre-processing part. It is mainly responsible for the preliminary processing of the collected data, and saves the obtained set of coordinate points of the processed object in our relational database.
- The core of data encryption algorithm. It is mainly responsible for matching the set of coordinate points we pre-processed with the encrypted object. After the matching is successful, our core algorithm dynamically generates a transparent film and passes the film to the data for privacy data protection.
- System and Network Monitoring part. It provides services such as detection and notification when there is a dynamic change in the system or network.

2.4 The Processing Steps of Data Encryption Algorithm

In this session, we focus on describing our core encryption and decryption algorithms. Firstly, the cloud generates an invisible membrane of the same size as the privacy part based on the location and size of the privacy part of the image provided by the IoT devices. Secondly, the cloud encrypts an invisible membrane with the secret key K of the cloud and the VHE encryption algorithm [9], and the encrypted invisible membrane is sent to the IoT devices. Finally, the IoT devices position the privacy location and multiply encrypted invisible membrane with the original image pixel in the privacy part to obtain an encrypted image.

On the other hand, about the decryption process, the cloud needs to decide whether to provide the user with a key based on the degree of trust of the users. Once the cloud trusts the user, our cloud platform will provide the secret key to the user. The user should find privacy location coordinates firstly. Then, the user can use the secret key K to decrypt specific encrypted images, ultimately allowing the user to obtain the original images. For system security, the cloud will transform the secret key by completing a invisible membrane encryption and decryption.

3   System Design and Implementation

In this section, we introduce and explain the design of our proposed approaches through the following steps.

3.1   Key Generation

Through application developers access the specific cloud platform and develop appropriate privacy protection rules, then cloud platform input a security parameter a to generate a secret key $K \in \mathbb{Z}^{m \times n}$, where w is a large integer and e is an error term with elements smaller than $\frac{w}{2}$. We further assume that $|S| \ll w$.

3.2   IoT Device Requests Invisible Membrane

The IoT devices which they use the object recognition algorithm, such as Yolo V3 [7] to detect the coordinate position of the object which contains privacy information in that image data. Currently, the Yolo V3 algorithm detects the object is very fast than other recognition algorithms. In our implementation, we adopted this algorithm and combined it with pytorch [8] to improve its recognition accuracy.

3.3   Cloud Generates Invisible Membrane

Once the cloud platform accepts the use-defined required rules and K of cloud platform, the cloud platform generates an invisible membrane depends on the description of the position of the object in the set of coordinate point sets. Assume that the size of the invisible membrane requested by the IoT is 2×2, then cloud platform generates a full one matrix of 2×2 and encrypts the matrix using K.

$$\begin{bmatrix} \frac{w_1+e_1}{K} & \frac{w_2+e_2}{K} \\ \frac{w_3+e_3}{K} & \frac{w_4+e_4}{K} \end{bmatrix} \tag{1}$$

At last, the cloud platform sends encryption matrix to IoT devices.

3.4 Invisible Membrane Encryption

Assuming the original image size is 4×4, the requested privacy location is 2×2 in the lower right corner.

$$
image = \begin{bmatrix} 255 & 255 & 255 & 255 \\ 255 & 255 & 255 & 255 \\ 255 & 255 & 255 & 255 \\ 255 & 255 & 255 & 255 \end{bmatrix} \tag{2}
$$

Note that the encrypting the original image is to multiply the portion of the original image that needs to be encrypted with the invisible membrane point which as shown in (3).

$$
\begin{bmatrix} 255 & 255 & 255 & 255 \\ 255 & 255 & 255 & 255 \\ 255 & 255 & 255 * \frac{w+e_1}{K} & 255 * \frac{w+e_2}{K} \\ 255 & 255 & 255 * \frac{w+e_3}{K} & 255 * \frac{w+e_4}{K} \end{bmatrix} \tag{3}
$$

Finally, IoT devices can send the encrypted image to computation note for image processing.

3.5 Decrypt Image

In contrast to encryption, in decrypt step, cloud platform sends the encrypted image and secret key to trust institution. Once our monitor mechanism detects the proposed system environment is normal, then the trust institution can use K to decrypt image as shown in (4).

$$
\begin{bmatrix} 255 & 255 & 255 & 255 \\ 255 & 255 & 255 & 255 \\ 255 & 255 & \frac{K}{w}\left(255 * \frac{w+e_1}{K}\right) & \frac{K}{w}\left(255 * \frac{w+e_2}{K}\right) \\ 255 & 255 & \frac{K}{w}\left(255 * \frac{w+e_3}{K}\right) & \frac{K}{w}\left(255 * \frac{w+e_4}{K}\right) \end{bmatrix} \tag{4}
$$

Trust institution can get original image.

$$
\begin{bmatrix} 255 & 255 & 255 & 255 \\ 255 & 255 & 255 & 255 \\ 255 & 255 & 255 & 255 \\ 255 & 255 & 255 & 255 \end{bmatrix} \tag{5}
$$

However, other institutions only can obtain encrypted image. Our generates invisible method primarily uses the VHE algorithm [9] to encrypt some of the values in the image matrix, and compares and analyzes the effect of the encrypted part with the most popular chaotic system-based image encryption at the current stage.

4   Performance Analyses

In this session, we evaluate the performance of the proposed algorithm. All experiments were conducted by using Python language on cloud instance with a 2.30 GHz processor, 16G RAM memory and Windows 10. We use image data set[1] with a size of 256 × 256.

We carry out the evaluation of the three scenarios (in 2.1 Scenarios) of our proposal in Fig. 2. Figure 2(a) shows original unencrypted image. Figure 2(b) shows the generated invisible membrane to cover the private location of the original image. Figure 2(c) shows the trusted user who decrypts the original image with a secure key.

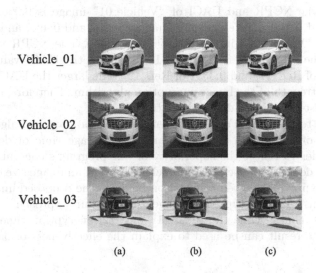

Vehicle_01

Vehicle_02

Vehicle_03

(a)   (b)   (c)

Fig. 2. (a) Image with 256 × 256 pixels; (b) the privacy part encrypt with invisible membrane; (c) decrypt image

We use four values: Peak Signal to Noise Ratio (PSNR)[2], information entropy[3], changing pixel rate (NPCR) and unified averaged changed intensity (UACI)[4] to evaluate the security of the image after encryption. The result as show in Table 1. We believe that the quality of the decrypted image is extremely high according to [10] and PSNR, which is almost the same as the original image

---

[1] OpenCV   data   set.   https://docs.opencv.org/3.0-beta/modules/datasets/doc/datasets.html.

[2] PSNR can evaluate the quality of the decoded image.

[3] Information entropy is the most important measure of randomness in information theory and the maximum entropy of an gray image should be as 8 when all of the pixels are equally distributed, which shows that the information is random.

[4] NPCR and UACI are two most common quantities that used to evaluate the strength of image encryption algorithms with respect to differential attacks.

Table 1. Encrypted image evaluation value.

Image name	PSNR	Information entropy	NPCR	UACI
Vehicle_01	100	7.965	0.996	0.499
Vehicle_02	100	7.998	0.994	0.498
Vehicle_03	100	7.997	0.997	0.500

quality. In our approach, the information entropy of our encrypted "Vehicle_01" image is 7.956, "Vehicle_02" image is 7.998 and "Vehicle_03" image is 7.997, which means the probability of accidental information leakage is very small. We evaluate the NCPR and UACI of "Vehicle_01" image is 0.996 and 0.499; the NCPR and UACI of "Vehicle_02" image is 0.994 and 0.498, and the NCPR and UACI of "Vehicle_03" image is 0.996 and 0.500. The NCPR value in our approach is the same as Refs. [11] and [12], however the UACI value is higher than 0.33424 of Ref. [11] and 0.3351 of Ref. [12]. The larger the UACI value, the stronger the strength of the image encryption algorithm. Therefore, our solution is highly robust for against differential attacks.

According to the results of our implemented of the proposed algorithm, the average time of encryption is 0.007 s, and the average time of decryption is 0.014 s. In order to reflect the superiority of our program's computational efficiency on IoT devices, we use our approach to encrypt an image size of 256×256 pixels, and we provide a speed comparison between the proposed image encryption algorithms. The encryption average time of our approach is 0.352 s by evaluating 100 times, while the Refs. [11] and [12] encryption times are 0.62 s and 3.80 s. The result can be used to explain the effectiveness of our proposed approach.

5   Conclusion

In the next step, our plan to implement. In this paper, we propose an image encryption scheme in order to solve the actual needs of image privacy for IoT-based sensor environments. The scheme encrypts and decrypts objects in the image from the IoT device according to the set of coordinate points of the privacy information of the objects in the image, the cloud computing platform and our proposed invisible membrane. The solution is not only effective but also ensures that the unencrypted portion has the same quality as the original image, and can also quickly deploy the development environment to different IoT platforms via docker [13] several applications, and evaluate our approach in those actual IoT applications with the migration time of invisible membrane through Ethernet.

References

1. NIISAY asset management. Seventy percent of the world population in 2050 will be urban residents (2018)

2. Gaur, A., Scotney, B., Parr, G., et al.: Smart city architecture and its applications based on IoT. Procedia Comput. Sci. **52**, 1089–1094 (2015)
3. Yang, B., Zhang, C., Yong, T., et al.: Vehicle detection and recognition for intelligent traffic surveillance system. Multimed. Tools Appl. **76**, 5817–5832 (2015)
4. Pramkeaw, P., Ngamrungsiri, P., Ketcham, M.: CCTV face detection criminals and tracking system using data analysis algorithm. In: Theeramunkong, T., et al. (eds.) iSAI-NLP 2017. AISC, vol. 807, pp. 105–110. Springer, Cham (2019). https://doi.org/10.1007/978-3-319-94703-7_10
5. Sachdeva, A., Mahajan, P.: A study of encryption algorithms AES, DES and RSA for security. Global J. Comput. Sci. Technol. **13**, 15–22 (2013)
6. Manimurugan, S., John Justin, M.: A survey on various encryption techniques. Int. J. Soft Comput. Eng. **2**, 429–432 (2013)
7. Redmon, J., et al.: You only look once: unified, real-time object detection. In: Proceedings of the IEEE Conference on Computer Vision and Pattern Recognition, pp. 779–788 (2016)
8. Pytorch. https://pytorch.org/
9. Zhou, H., Wornell, G.: Efficient homomorphic encryption on integer vectors and its applications. In: Proceedings of 2014 Information Theory and Applications Workshop (ITA), pp. 22–31 (2014)
10. Huynh-Thu, Q., Ghanbari, M.: Scope of validity of PSNR in image/video quality assessment. Electron. Lett. **44**, 800–801 (2008)
11. Alawida, M., Samsudin, A., Teh, J.S.: A new hybrid digital chaotic system with applications in image encryption. Signal Process. **160**, 44–58 (2019)
12. Xu, L., Li, Z., Li, J., et al.: A novel bit-level image encryption algorithm based on chaotic maps. Opt. Lasers Eng. **78**, 17–25 (2016)
13. Docker. https://www.docker.com/

Privacy-Awareness Fair Contract Signing Protocol Based on Blockchain

Dongfeng Wang[1], Qinghua Li[1], Fengyin Li[1(✉)], Quanxin Zhang[2],
and Banghai Xu[3]

[1] School of Information Science and Engineering,
Qufu Normal University, Rizhao 276800, China
lfyin318@126.com
[2] School of Computer Science and Technology, Beijing Institute of Technology,
Beijing 100081, China
[3] School of Information and Electrical Engineering, Ludong University,
Yantai 264025, China

Abstract. With the rise of network technology in recent years, e-commerce has occupied an important part in trade activities. How to ensure fair transactions between untrustworthy parties is a current research hotspot. This paper combines RSA blind signature and blockchain technology to design a fair contract signing protocol based on blockchain privacy protection. The RSA blind signature generates a contract blind signature, which guarantees the sensitive details of the transaction contract; the blockchain technology provides a decentralized trusted third party for the contract, ensuring fair and equitable transactions. After analysis, the protocol has the characteristics of correctness, unforgeability, blindness, and untraceability.

Keywords: Blockchain · RSA · Blind signature · Contract protocol

1 Introduction

With the development of electronic commerce, people urgently need fair, safe and efficient electronic contract protocol to ensure their own interests in the process of transaction [2]. Unlike traditional paper contracts, electronic contracts are difficult to ensure fair transactions in an untrustworthy network environment and in the case of both parties. At present, most of the contract signing protocols used most are centralized [4], However, there are some shortcomings in this type of protocol.

The rise of blockchain technology has provided people with a decentralized trading environment. Since the blockchain has the characteristics of decentralization, traceability, and non-removability, the application of the blockchain to the fair contract signing agreement can get rid of the constraints of the third party, and the RSA public key encryption system has the advantages of confidentiality and security. When considering the privacy protection problem at the

J. Vaidya et al. (Eds.): CSS 2019, LNCS 11982, pp. 274–278, 2019.
https://doi.org/10.1007/978-3-030-37337-5_22

time of transaction, the blind signature is used in the cryptosystem for good anonymity, and it is applied to the fair contract signing agreement to realize privacy protection.

Here have been many studies on fair contract signing. For example, some protocols use centralized third parties [10], the fairness of the protocol depends on the third party and is vulnerable to attack. At the same time, it requires the third party to be online all the time, which is inefficient. Later, some scholars proposes a de-centralization protocol, which achieves fair de-centralization signing through timestamp service [1]. Then, some scholars designs a contract signing protocol based on blockchain technology and adopts a penalty mechanism for breach of contract to ensure fairness [3]. At the same time, the address of block chain is used as transaction identity to protect privacy. Tian et al. designed a blind signature based on bilinear pairings on block chains [5], introduces blind factor to blind sensitive information, and ensures the privacy of both sides of the transaction, but the computation is heavy. Gao et al. combined verifiable encryption signature and aggregate signature [7], and designs an efficient multi-party contract signing protocol based on block chain.

In this paper, a new blind signature based on RSA is designed by introducing blind factor into the traditional RSA algorithm [8], and a new fair contract signing association is conceived by combining blockchain technology [6] and RSA blind signature [9]. This protocol not only achieves the fair contract signing, but also guarantees the relevant privacy information of the contract, and has high efficiency of execution.

2 A New RSA Blind Signature Scheme

2.1 RSA Blind Signature Scheme

The RSA blind signature scheme requires three parties to participate, namely the digital signature extractor Alice, the blind signer Bob and the random verifier Minter. Alice blinds the message m that needs to be signed, Bob performs blind signature, and the final verification is performed by the random third-party verifier Minter after the signature is completed. Alice can bluff the Bob signed message.

The signature scheme consists of the following six algorithms:

(1) Setup:
   (a) Bob randomly selects two large prime numbers p and q, computing $n = p*q$, $\phi(n) = (p-1)*(q-1)$;
   (b) Bob randomly selects a large integer e, have $(e, \phi(n)) = 1$;
   (c) According to the extended Euclidean algorithm, d is calculated to satisfy $ed = 1 \mod (\phi(n))$;

   Where (e,n) is the key publicly disclosed by Bob, (p,q,d) is privately stored by Bob, and a secure one-way hash $h(\cdot)$ is published.

(2) Sign:
   (a) Alice randomly selects the message m ϵ Z_n^* to be signed, and two different random numbers r_1 ϵ Z_n^*, a ϵ Z_n^* ;
   (b) Alice calculates $m_1 = r_1^{ae}$ h(m) and send m_1 to Bob;
   (c) Alice calculates H = h(m) mod n. Open H for public verification;
(3) BlindSign:
   Bob calculate $t_1 = m_1^d$ mod n after receiving m_1, $\delta_{pves} = t_1$ is a blind signature;
(4) BlindSign:
   Alice receives Bob's blind signature δ_{pves} for bluffing, calculates S = $\left(\frac{\delta_{pves}}{r_1^a}\right)$, and obtains Bob's signature S for message m;
(5) BlindSignVer:
   The random verifier Minter takes the triple as an input and verifies whether the following equation is true.

$$S^e = H$$

If it is true, the signature is successful; otherwise the signature is fails. Where e, S and H are public parameters.

3   Fair Contract Signing Protocol

3.1   Fair Contract Signing Protocol

Figure 1 is a flow chart of the fair contract signing protocol. The specific implementation process of the contract is as follows:

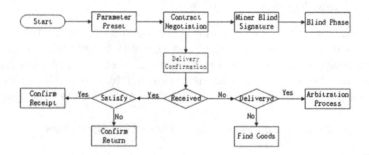

Fig. 1. Contract signing agreement flow chart

Suppose each miner has a pair of blind signature keys. Before the transaction begins, Customer and Seller negotiate the contract and construct the parameters, Customer, as a buyer, confirms the purchase transaction and generates the transaction T_c. Seller confirms the sale transaction and generates transaction T_s, then, trading parties use their own random numbers to blind T_c and T_s respectively and publish the blinded messages m_a and m_b to the Bitcoin network, first seeing the traded miners signing the transaction blindly and broadcasting it to the Bitcoin network. When Customer and Seller see their blind signature, they perform the blinding operation and retain the blind signature respectively. Then Seller starts shipping and issues delivery confirmation, after the miner receives the delivery confirmation, it generates $Open_B$. If Customer receives the goods and is satisfied with them before the pre-deadline, Customer issues a receipt confirmation indicating the receipt of the goods. When the miner sees the receipt of the goods issued by Customer, it generates $Open_{A1}$. When Customer receives the goods but is not satisfied, it generates a return request, and after the miner receives the return request, it generates $Open_{A2}$.

After the transaction is over, if $Open_B$ and $Open_{A1}$ appear in the Bitcoin network within seven days, indicating that the transaction is successful, then the money in both T_c and T_s is returned to Seller, and Customer loses dB; if both $Open_{A1}$ and $Open_{A2}$ appear, it indicates that Customer has not bought Satisfied goods, apply for a return, then deduct some bitcoin in T_c, as a handling fee, all the T_s in dB are returned to Seller; if there is no within three days in the Bitcoin network, it means that Seller has not shipped, the system deducts T_s Part of the bitcoin, as a handling fee; if there is only $Open_B$ in the Bitcoin network within seven days and the customer's trading status is not available, then Seller has shipped, but Customer has not received the goods, Seller needs to find the goods. While deducting some of the bitcoin in T_s. If there is a dispute between the two parties, then both parties can announce their ordinary signature. The miner passed the verification and made a ruling.

3.2 Performance Evaluation

Table 1 compares the fair contract signing protocol with the performance analysis of the other two cryptographic signature schemes. The specific content of the comparison includes operational efficiency, number of verifications, and traffic. The operational efficiency reflects the number of mathematical operations performed by the algorithm of the running protocol; the number of verifications refers to the sum of the number of times that the transaction between the two parties and the verifier needs to be verified in a complete transaction; the traffic represents the sum of the number of times that broadcast or multicast is required. Where m denotes a multiplication operation, d denotes a division operation, e denotes a power operation, MO denotes a modulo operation, and p denotes a bilinear pair.

Table 1. Protocol performance analysis table.

Protocol	Operating efficiency			Number of verifications	Traffic
	14	12	12		
Ref. [7]	$8m + d + 2p$	$5m + p$	p	2	7
Ref. [1]	5m	4m	$(n+4)p + 5m$	6	3
This program	$2m + d + e + 2MO$	$4m + e + MO$	e	1	6

It can be seen from the above table that in terms of operational efficiency, the comparison between the scheme and the scheme in Ref. [7] is relatively simple in terms of calculation amount; in the number of verifications, the scheme only needs to be verified once after the transaction is completed, and does not need to be used for all nodes. To verify, the scheme in Ref. [1] requires the signator to repeat the verification, so the cost of the scheme is less; in terms of traffic, the scheme has fewer communications than the scheme in Ref. [7], this solution has improved in terms of operational efficiency, number of verifications and traffic.

4   Conclusions

This paper combines RSA blind signature and blockchain technology to design a privacy protection contract signing protocol. The protocol introduces blockchain technology, which realizes decentralization, effectively avoids the disadvantages brought by the centralized third party. At the same time, because the blockchain public verification feature can not protect the sensitive information of the contract protocol, it introduces RSA based. Blind signature of the algorithm. After numerous analysis, the contract agreement can meet the requirements of the electronic contract protocol.

Acknowledgement. Shandong educational science planning "special research subject for educational admission examination", no.: ZK1337123A002

References

1. Tian, H.B., He, J.J., Fu, L.Q.: A privacy preserving fair contract signing protocol based on public block chains. J. Cryptologic Res. **4**(2), 187–198 (2017)
2. Ye, C.C., Li, G.Q., Cai, H.M., Gu, Y.G.: Security detection model of blockchain. Ruan Jian Xue Bao/J. Softw. **29**(05), 176–187 (2018)
3. L, L., J, H.J., B, T.H.: Fair contract signing agreement based on blockchain. J. Inf. Secur. **3**(3), 6–12 (2018)
4. M, W.C.: Design of RSA blind signature scheme based on hash algorithm. Inf. Comput. (Theor. Ed.) **4**(5) (2015)
5. X, W.F.: A blind signature scheme based on RSA algorithm. Comput. Knowl. Technol. Acad. Exch. **15**(1Z), 271–272 (2019)
6. X, W.J., Y, G., Y, Z.Z., P, Y.D.: Multi-party privacy protection fair contract signing agreement based on blockchain. J. Inf. Secur. **3**(3), 13–21 (2018)
7. Gao, Y., Jin-Xi, W.: Efficient multi-party fair contract signing protocol based on blockchains. J. Cryptologic Res. **5**(5), 556–567 (2018)
8. Y, H.L.: Research and implementation of RSA encryption algorithms. Ph. D. thesis, Central South University (2016)
9. Wang, Y., Lu, D.J.: An efficient fair electronic exchange protocol based on RSA blind signature. J. Changsha Univ. **2**(5), 40–41 (2015)
10. Zhou, J., Gollmann, D.: An efficient non-repudiation protocol. In: Computer Security Foundations Workshop (2017)

Efficient Privacy Protection Authentication Scheme in Vehicle Ad Hoc Networks

Lv ShanGuo[✉]

Software School, East China Jiaotong University, Nanchang, China
42883824@qq.com

Abstract. In this paper, a group signature-based vehicle information sharing scheme for vehicular ad hoc networks with effective privacy protection is proposed. The design goals are achieved by technologies such as distributed management, HMAC, batch signature verification and cooperative authentication. First, divide the entire network into different domains for local management. Second, HMAC is used instead of time-consuming revocation list checking, and the integrity of messages prior to bulk authentication is ensured to avoid the number of invalid messages in bulk verification. Finally, we also use the cooperative certification method to further improve the efficiency of the program. By adopting the above technology, our proposed solution can meet the verification requirements. Security and performance analysis shows that our proposed solution enables efficient group signature-based authentication while maintaining conditional privacy.

Keywords: Group signature · Ad Hoc networks · Privacy protection authentication

1 Introduction

With the rapid development of wireless communication, ad hoc networks and Internet of things technology, in recent years, vehicular ad hoc networks have been widely concerned by academia, industry and government departments. In order to improve the traffic situation, vehicles need to periodically perceive the relevant information of their own driving process, such as the position, speed and direction of the vehicle, and broadcast these information to the surrounding vehicles by wireless communication, so as to realize the sharing of traffic-related information between them, so that drivers and traffic managers can obtain the vehicles of other vehicles beyond the visual range. Real-time and comprehensive road condition information can effectively improve traffic safety and efficiency, and fundamentally solve the existing road traffic accidents and congestion problems [1]. In the vehicular ad hoc network, between the vehicle and the vehicle, the vehicle and the roadside unit communicate wirelessly. Once the user's hidden information, such as identity, trajectory and references are not well protected [2], the attacker can easily get this information.

In order to achieve efficient anonymous authentication in vehicular ad hoc networks, group signature technology is widely used in vehicular ad hoc networks [3]. Because it allows group members to sign messages in the name of the group, while not

© Springer Nature Switzerland AG 2019
J. Vaidya et al. (Eds.): CSS 2019, LNCS 11982, pp. 279–288, 2019.
https://doi.org/10.1007/978-3-030-37337-5_23

revealing the true identity of the signer. In order to verify a group signature, it takes 11 ms [8], which means that only 91 messages can be authenticated per second. However, when there is 180 vehicles in the communication range of a roadside unit [1], it needs to authenticate 600 safety-related messages per second. Additional authentication and decryption time will be consumed if the value service is considered again [4]. In addition, before group signature verification, vehicles need to check the revocation list to avoid communication with revoked vehicles. According to the literature [1], it takes 9 ms to check an identity in the revocation list. If there are n vehicles that are revoked in the revocation list, each message takes 9n + 11 ms. In this way, the number of messages that can be authenticated per second is 1000/(9n + 11), which is far from the target 600 messages. Therefore, it is necessary to reduce the delay due to the authentication of the revocation list check and the group signature to achieve fast authentication.

In order to solve the problem of revocation list checking, Wasef et al. [5] and Jiang et al. [6] used the hash message digest code HMAC instead of the revocation list, which greatly reduced the inspection time. In the scheme of Wasef et al., the key for calculating the HMAC is global. Once an illegal vehicle is discovered, a global key update process will be performed, which is another form of revocation list and is difficult to implement. Jiang et al. adopted a distributed approach to further improve the efficiency of HMAC inspection. However, both schemes are based on pseudonym authentication schemes and may not be directly applicable to group signature-based schemes. In order to reduce the time of signature verification, Wasef et al. [7] and Zhang et al. [3] adopted the method of batch verification of group signatures, which made a large number of messages can be authenticated in time. However, the problem is that they do not check the integrity of messages before batch authentication. Once there is an invalid message caused by packet loss or malicious injection in the wireless channel, it will lead to additional authentication delay and loss of efficiency. Even if we do not consider the problem of re-authentication, the computational overhead of group signature batch authentication in document [3] is $2T_{pai} + 13nT_{mul}$, while that in document [7] is $3T_{pai} + (6n + 7)T_{mul}$. T_{pai} is the time to perform pairing operation, T_{mul} is the time to perform point multiplication [7]. According to literature [1], it runs on Intel Pentium IV3.0GHZ main frequency computer. T_{pai} is 4.5 ms, T_{mul} is 0.6 ms. Therefore, without considering invalid messages, literature [3] can only authenticate 127 and 274 messages per second, which still fails to meet the requirements of the number of authenticated messages.

The solutions mentioned above focus only on how to achieve fast certification in a single vehicle. However, based on the fact that nearby vehicles require authentication to be almost identical, Zhang et al. [8] and Hao et al. [9] proposed a scheme based on inter-vehicle cooperative certification. By allowing neighboring vehicles to collaborate for certification, their solution allows a vehicle to know the legitimacy of all received messages without having to verify all received messages. Zhang et al.'s scheme uses a Pseudonym-based authentication scheme, while Hao et al.'s scheme is based on group signature. However, although Hao et al.'s scheme can meet the authentication requirement per second, their scheme does not consider revocation list checking. Therefore, the efficiency of their schemes will be reduced in practical application.

In order to achieve efficient and anonymous authentication in vehicular ad hoc networks, Zhu et al. [10] proposed an efficient conditional privacy protection authentication scheme. In this scheme, RSUs are assumed to be credible. However, in practical applications, RSUs may want to obtain user's privacy information. Some existing schemes, such as document [11], consider the security of semi-trusted RSUs in vehicular ad hoc networks.

Under the model of semi-trusted RSUs, by combining distributed management technology, HMAC, batch verification group signature and cooperative authentication, this paper proposes an efficient conditional privacy authentication scheme to realize real-time information sharing during vehicle driving. First, the jurisdictional area is divided into several domains to implement regional management; then, the HMAC is calculated using the key generated by the self-healing group key generation algorithm [12], thereby replacing the time-consuming revocation list checksum. Ensure the integrity of the message before batch verification of the group signature; finally, an example of the Hao et al. cooperative authentication scheme [9] is given to improve its authentication efficiency. Security and performance analysis show that the proposed scheme can achieve higher group signature-based authentication efficiency while achieving conditional concealment.

2 System Model

As shown in Fig. 1, the system model involved in this paper consists of TMC, RSUs fixed to the roadside unit, and OBUs loaded on the moving vehicle:

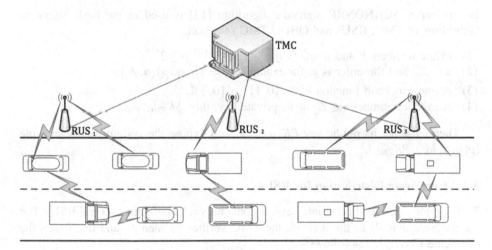

Fig. 1. System model of vehicular ad hoc network.

(1) TMC is a trusted management center for the entire network. When joining the network, RSUs and OBUs need to register at the TMC and obtain a certificate. The TMC also divides its entire jurisdiction into several different domains,

and generates a corresponding group key and group signature material for each domain, and then the TMC sends these security materials to all RSUs in the domain. In general, assume that the TMC has unlimited communication capabilities, computing power, and storage space, and assumes that the attacker is unable to capture the TMC.

(2) RSUs manage vehicles within their communication range. The RSUs connect to the TMC through a wired channel and connect to the OBUs through a wireless channel. They are the bridge between the connecting TMC and the user. In this article, assume that RSUs are semi-trusted [11], for example, they will run as predefined by the system, but they may reveal some secret information to the attacker. The RSUs also have the function of distributing the group key material and the group signing key to the legal OBUs entering the domain.

(3) The OBUs periodically broadcast traffic-related status information including location, speed, and direction of travel to improve the road environment and traffic safety of drivers and pedestrians. We also assume that each vehicle has a Tamper-Proof Device to store safety-related materials.

Without loss of generality, this paper does not consider sharing secrets between vehicles and other users, because almost all security systems cannot prevent this type of active attack.

3   Solution

3.1   System Initialization

In this paper, SCHNONRR signature algorithm [13] is used as the basic signature algorithms of TMC, RSUs and OBUs. TMC selection:

(1) Prime numbers P and g satisfy $q|p-1, q \geq 2^{140}, p \geq 2^{512}$;
(2) $\alpha \in \mathbb{Z}_p$, and the order is g, for example $\alpha^q = 1(\bmod p), \alpha \neq 1$;
(3) A one-way hash function $h(\cdot) : \{0,1\}^* \rightarrow \{0,1\}^l$;
(4) A random number s $\in \mathbb{Z}_q^*$ as its private key, then $SK_{TMC} = s$.

Then calculate its public key $PK_{TMC} = p^s$ and expose the system parameter tuple $(p, q, \alpha, h(\cdot), PK_{TMC})$.

3.2   Certificate Distribution for RSUs

TMC divides the jurisdiction into several domains, each containing several RSUs. For the roadside unit R_x in the domain, the TMC verifies its identity and distributes the certificate $Cert_{TMC,R_x}$ as follows:

(1) TMC selects a random number $Sk_{R_x} \in \mathbb{Z}_q^*$ as the private key of R_x, and calculates the public key $PK_{R_x} = p^{SK_{R_x}}$;
(2) TMC calculates the signature $\sigma_{TA,R_x} = Sig_{SK_{TA}}(PK_{R_x}||D_A)$;
(3) TMC transmits SK_{R_x} and $Cert_{TMC,R_x}$ to R_x through the secure channel, where $Cert_{TA,R_x} = (PK_{R_x}||D_A, \sigma_{TA,R_x})$.

3.3 Certificate Distribution of Vehicles

For the vehicle V_i, after the TMC has verified its identity, the certificate $Cert_{TMC,R_x}$ is distributed as follows:

(1) TMC selects a random number $Sk_{V_i} \in \mathbb{Z}_q^*$ as the private key of V_i, and calculate its corresponding public key $PK_{V_i} = p^{SK_i}$;
(2) TMC calculates the certificate $Cert_{TA,V_i} = Sig_{SK_{TA}}(PK_{V_i})$ of V_i;
(3) TMC securely transmits Sk_{V_i} and $Cert_{TMC,V_i}$ to the vehicle V_i.

3.4 Secure Group Key Distribution and Batch Authentication

For the domain D_A, the TMC generates the group signature key, the public material and the group public key GPK_{D_A}. This paper uses the Wasef scheme [7] to implement the batch verification group signature.

Given the linear pair parameters $(p, \mathbb{G}_1, \mathbb{G}_2, \mathbb{G}_T, e)$, the TMC generates the group public key as follows:

(1) TMC selects a random generator $g_2 \in \mathbb{G}_2$ and calculates $g_1 \in \psi(g_2)$, where g_1 is the generator of $\mathbb{G}_1$, and the isomorphism from $\mathbb{G}_2$ to $\mathbb{G}_1$, such as $g_1 \in \psi(g_2)$;
(2) TMC selects the random numbers $h, u, v \in \mathbb{G}_1$ and $s_1, s_2 \in Z_p$, makes $u^{s_1} = v^{s_2} = h$;
(3) TMC selects the random numbers $\gamma \in \mathbb{Z}_p$ and $\lambda \in \mathbb{Z}_p^*$, makes $\omega = g_2^\gamma$.

Where s_1 and s_2 are the master private keys of the domain D_A that are managed by the TMC. The public system parameters of the domain D_A are $(g_1, g_2, u, v, h, \lambda)$, the group public key is $GPK_{D_A} = \omega$, the TMC sends the system public parameters and the group public key to all RSUs of the domain. Vehicles and roadside units can use these pre-stored information to achieve mutual authentication. When a vehicle V_i joins a new domain D_A, it needs the first RSUs registry in the domain D_A, which prevents illegal vehicles from joining the domain D_A.

Registration: When V_i joins a new domain, a mutual authentication protocol will be executed between V_i and the first roadside unit it encounter It should be noted that if a roadside unit is captured, the TMC will revoke the roadside unit by broadcasting its domain and its identity, so that all vehicles will also know the revocation information.

(1) Each roadside unit periodically broadcasts its certificate, its domain and group public key. For the way unit R_x in the domain D_A, it broadcasts the message message 1: $\left(PK_{R_x}, D_A, Cert_{TMC,R_x}, GPK_{D_A}, Sig_{SK_{R_x}}(GPK_{D_A})\right)$. When V_i receives the message, it first verifies whether D_A is a new domain. If D_A is a new domain, V_i will begin the registration process. V_i first authenticates the legitimacy of R_x by running $Verify(PK_{TMC}, PK_{R_x}||D_A, \sigma_{TMC,R_x})$, if $Cert_{TMC,R_x}$ is Legally, V_i will verify $Sig_{SK_{R_x}}(GPK_{D_A})$ by PK_{R_x}.
(2) After authenticating R_x and D_A is a new domain, V_i will reply to the message message 2: $\left\{PK_{V_i}, Cert_{TMC,V_i}, x_i, Sig_{SK_{V_i}}(x_i)\right\}_{PK_{R_x}}$ to R_x, where x_i is the random number used to calculate the group private key GSK_{D_A,V_i}. It is worth noting the

public key and certificate $Cert_{TA,V_i}$ of V_i is unique throughout the system. Therefore, it is also an identity of V_i. In the proposed scheme, the public key and certificate of V_i are encrypted by PK_{R_x} of R_x, which allows only R_x to obtain the corresponding plaintext, thus protecting the identity privacy of R_x.

(3) After obtaining GSK_{D_A,V_i}, R_x will reply V_i message 3: $\{H(GSK_{D_A V_i}), Sig_{SK_{R_x}}(H(GSK_{D_A V_i}), x_i)\}_{PK_{V_i}}$. When V_i receives the message 3, it first decrypts the message with its private key SK_{V_i} and then verifies the signature.

(4) If the signature is valid, V_i will reply message 4: $\{T, H(V_i||x_i), Sig_{SK_{V_i}}(H(V_i||x_i), T)\}$ to R_x, where T is a timestamp. When R_x receives message 4 at T^*, Algorithm will be executed. Where, $f(TID_i, y)$ is such as $s_{0,0} + s_{1,0} \cdot x + s_{0,1} \cdot y + s_{1,1} \cdot xy + \cdots + s_{t,t} \cdot x^t y^t$ A binary polynomial, where x and y are two variables and $s_{i,j}$ is a constant coefficient. K^B_{m-j-l} and K^F_j are seeds for calculating the group key, l is the length of the backward hash chain, and LC is the life cycle of the group key.

(5) Then, R_x sends a message 5 $\{GSK_{D_A V_i}, LC, l, K^B_{m-j-l}, K^F_j, TID_i, f(TID_i, y), \mathrm{Sig}_1\}_{PK_{V_i}}$ to V_i. After receiving the message 5 sent from R_x, V_i will execute Algorithm to obtain the group key required to calculate the HMAC. We use the formula (1) to calculate the current group key GK_j, where K^F_j and K^B_{m-j+1} are the forward keychain and backward key chain respectively.

$$GK_j = H\left(K^F_j + K^B_{m-j+1}\right) \tag{1}$$

Finally, R_x stores the information shown in Fig. 2, V_i also stores the information shown in Fig. 3.

χ_i	GPR_{D_y,V_i}	$H(V_i \| \| \chi_i)$	PK_{V_i}	T

Fig. 2. Records stored at R_x

χ_i	GPR_{D_y,V_i}	$Sig_{SK_{R_x}}(H(GPR_{D_y,V_i}), \chi_i)$

Fig. 3. Records stored at V_i

Batch Verification: According to DSRC [2], vehicles need periodic broadcast security-related messages every 300 ms. In order to ensure the legitimacy of the message source and the integrity of the message, the receiver of the message should verify the received message. Cancellation list checking is a commonly used method to exclude illegal vehicles before authentication. However, according to document [1], group signatures take about 9 ms to check whether an identity is in the revocation list. Therefore, if a vehicle receives n messages and the number of vehicles revoked is m, it takes 9 ms for the vehicle to verify the identity legitimacy of the sender. Obviously, revocation list checking results in a lot of computational overhead, which seriously reduces the performance of the system.

3.5 Periodic Update of Group Key

When V_i is authenticated by an RSUs in the domain D_A, it periodically receives a message of the group key update broadcast by the RSUs in the domain D_A. The message B_{j+1} of the $(j+1)$th update period is as shown in the formula (2):

$$\begin{cases} B_{j+1} = \{r_{j+1}(x)\} \cup \{p_{j+1}(x)\} \\ r_{j+1}(x) = (x - TID_{r_1})(x - TID_{r_2}) \cdots (x - TID_{r_w}) \\ p_{j+1}(x) = r_{j+1}(x)K_{m-j}^B + f\left(x, K_{j+1}^F\right) \end{cases} \tag{2}$$

Where $TID_{r_1}, TID_{r_2}, \ldots, TID_{r_w}$ is the temporary identity of the vehicle being revoked, It has obtained the group key material $f(TID_i, y), K_{m-j+1}^B$ and K_j^F in the domain D_A before the $(j+1)$th period, and Vehicles that were revoked during the $(j+1)$ period. $r_{j+1}(x)$ is the undoing polynomial of the $(j+1)$th cycle, $p_{j+1}(x)$ is a hidden polynomial of the $(j+1)$th cycle.

It is worth noting that only the vehicle that is legally certified by domain D_A can obtain the group key material, and the RSUs only need to manage the vehicles in the domain. Therefore, the vehicles that are revoked are very few, and each vehicle has only one temporary identity to calculate $f(TID_i, y)$, so $p_{j+1}(x)$ is very small.

After V_i receives the broadcast revocation B_{j+1}, it uses K_j^F to calculate $K_{j+1}^F = H\left(K_j^F\right)$ and $f\left(TID_i, K_{j+1}^F\right)$. Then, V_i calculates $p_{j+1}(TID_i)$, and obtains K_{m-j}^B by formula (3):

$$K_{m-j}^B = \frac{p_{j+1}(TID_i) - f\left(TID_i, K_{j+1}^F\right)}{r_{j+1}(TID_i)} \tag{3}$$

After obtaining K_{m-j}^B, V_i calculates whether $H^l\left(K_{m-j-l}^B\right) = K_{m-j}^B$ is formed. If it is established, V_i will calculate a new group key according to formula (1).

4 Cooperative Certification

In the basic solution, even if only legal vehicles are added to the domain, and there is no invalid signature at the time of batch verification, the scheme can only verify at most 274 messages per second, and still cannot meet the certification speed requirement. Because of this, we must design new solutions to solve this problem. According to the work of Zhang et al. [8] and Hao et al. [9], the efficiency of certification can be improved by using cooperative authentication. By cooperating with neighboring vehicles, their solution can ensure that the vehicle knows the reliability of the received message without having to verify each message signature. Selecting a co-certifier requires the following requirements:

(1) The physical location of a cooperating verifier must precede V_i while the other must be after V_i. This means that the selected cooperating verifiers are preferably paired and can broadcast the authentication results to other users;
(2) Co-verifiers need to be far enough apart from each other;
(3) The number of co-verifiers should be moderate.

Assume that each security-related message contains the sender's location information. When the vehicle V_i receives a message sent from a different message sender at the same time, it first extracts the location information of the message sender, and then executes a selection procedure of the cooperation certifier that satisfies the above requirements to determine who will be selected as the cooperative certifier.

V_i checks the received message every 300 ms and calculates the distance between the sender of the message and itself based on the location information. Then, create a table as shown in Table 3.2, where the message ID is a random sequential index, the direction is whether the sender of the message before or after the recipient, and the distance is the distance between the receiver and the sender.

Assuming that the vehicles are evenly distributed, as shown in Fig. 3.6, the communication range is divided every 60 m according to the basic needs selected by the collaborators and the number of authenticated messages. We define vehicles from the sender (50 ± 5) m, (110 ± 5) m, (170 ± 5) m, (230 ± 5) m and (290 ± 5) m away. As shown in Fig. 3.6, V_i simultaneously receives 10 messages sent from senders 1 through 10, and then calculates its distance from each sender to obtain Table 3.2. Thus V_i should add messages 1, 2, 3 to the bulk verification. Because the cooperation program can reduce the number of messages verified, thus increasing the speed of authentication. Performance analysis indicates that the cooperative certification can meet the demand for the number of messages authenticated per second in the on-board ad hoc network.

5 Safety Analysis

Considering the problem that the roadside unit is captured, in the process of mutual authentication and group key generation, V_i can obtain the service without revealing its identity to the roadside unit. Therefore, even in the presence of some roadside units being captured, the proposed protocol can still protect the identity of the vehicle. Resist the obituary: If a vehicle is investigated, the TMC will begin an audit process and ask some roadside units for information about the vehicle being surveyed. However, RSUs may be captured to protect the vehicle being investigated by the information of the TA-some other vehicles, and this behavior is called obituary. In the delivery we will show that the proposed solution can resist such attacks.

In the designed protocol, each message sent by the vehicle V_i is signed by its private key SK_{V_i}, and the group private key and V_i are bound together. Since R_x does not have SK_{V_i}, it cannot forge the signature of the legal V_i. More importantly, the group private key and the private key are bound together, which adds to the falsification difficulty of R_x. We also store mutual authentication information in Figs. 2 and 3. When the dispute occurs, the TA can ask the vehicle and the roadside unit to present the information.

The non-repudiation of the vehicle's group private key: once R_x has distributed the group private key to V_i, it cannot be denied. In the message messages, the roadside unitization sends a hash value $GSK_{D_AV_i}$, and the signature of the group private key. After V_i receives the message message 5 and obtains $GSK_{D_AV_i}$, it can verify the validity of $GPR_{D_AV_i}$ by hash value. In order to ensure that the group private key is generated by x_i, V_i stores the signature status sent by R_x $Sig_{SK_{R_x}}(H(GSK_{D_AV_i}), x_i, x_i$ At the same time, R_x also stores x_i and $H(V_i\|x_i)$. When an argument occurs, R_x can present this information to the TA. Since the public parameters of the group signature are generated by the TA, it can calculate the group of V_i. The private key. The TA can obtain the identity of V_i according to PK_{V_i}, so that $H(V_i\|x_i)$ can be verified. If $H(V_i\|x_i)$ passes the legality verification, the group private key is $GSK_{D_AV_i}$ is valid, otherwise, $GSK_{D_AV_i}$ is invalid. For V_i, V_i sends x_i to TMC, then TMC can calculate the group private key $GSK_{D_AV_i}$ of V_i. If $GSK_{D_AV_i}$ is correct, the TMC verifies the signature to ensure that it is generated.

Preventing the collusion of the vehicles: A captured roadside unit may collude with a malicious vehicle and send the group private key of the other vehicle to its colluder. The malicious vehicle can then broadcast a message to represent the behavior of the other vehicle. In order to prevent such attacks, in the designed protocol, the signature of the message contains the identity information. At the same time, R_x and V_i also store this information after completing mutual authentication with each other. In the event of an argument, V_i can send its stored information to the TMC. By calculating the group key $GSK_{D_AV_i}$ and verifying the signature $Sig_{SK_{R_x}}(H(GSK_{D_AV_i}), x_i$, TMC can confirm The owner of $GSK_{D_AV_i}$.

6 Conclusion

In this paper, a group signature-based vehicle information sharing scheme for vehicular ad hoc networks with effective privacy protection is proposed. The design goals are achieved by technologies such as distributed management, HMAC, batch signature verification and cooperative authentication. First, divide the entire network into different domains for local management. Second, HMAC is used instead of time-consuming revocation list checking, and the integrity of messages prior to bulk authentication is ensured to avoid the number of invalid messages in bulk verification. Finally, we also use the cooperative certification method to further improve the efficiency of the program. By adopting the above technology, our proposed solution can meet the verification requirements. Security and performance analysis shows that our proposed solution enables efficient group signature-based authentication while maintaining conditional privacy.

Acknowledgment. The work of this paper were supported in part by East China Jiaotong university research fund under Grant No. 14RJ02 and Jiangxi provincial department of science and technology research found under Grant No. 20122BAB201040.

References

1. Author, F.: Article title. Journal **2**(5), 99–110 (2016). Zhang, C., Lu, R., Lin, X., et al: An efficient identity-based batch verification scheme for vehicular sensor networks. In: Proceedings of the 27th IEEE Conference on Computer Communications, INFOCOM 2008, pp. 246–250 (2008)
2. Sun, Y., Lu, R., Lin, X., et al.: An efficient pseudonymous authentication scheme with strong privacy preservation for vehicular communications. IEEE Trans. Veh. Technol. **59**(7), 3589–3603 (2010)
3. Zhang, L., Wu, Q., Solanas, A., et al.: A scalable robust authentication protocol for secure vehicular communications. IEEE Trans. Veh. Technol. **59**(4), 1606–1617 (2010)
4. Mershad, K., Artail, H.: A framework for secure and efficient data acquisition in vehicular Ad Hoc networks. IEEE Trans. Veh. Technol. **62**(2), 535–551 (2013)
5. Wasef, A., Shen, X.: Expedite message authentication protocol for vehicular Ad Hoc networks. IEEE Trans. Mob. Comput. **12**(1), 78–89 (2013)
6. Jiang, S., Zhu, X., Wang, L.: A conditional privacy scheme based on anonymized batch authentication in vehicular ad hoc networks. In: Proceedings of 2013 IEEE International Conference on Wireless Communications and Networking, WCNC 2013, pp. 2375–2380 (2013)
7. Wasef, A., Shen, X.: Efficient group signature scheme supporting batch verification for securing vehicular networks. In: 2010 IEEE International Conference on Communications, ICC 2010, pp. 1–5 (2010)
8. Zhang, C., Sun, X.R., Lu, P.-H.H., et al.: An efficient message authentication scheme for vehicular communications. IEEE Trans. Veh. Technol. **57**(6), 3357–3368 (2008)
9. Hao, Y., Chen, Y., Zhou, C., et al.: A distributed key management framework with cooperative message authentication in VANETs. IEEE J. Sel. Areas Commun. **29**(3), 616–629 (2011)
10. Zhu, X., Jiang, S., Wang, L., et al.: Privacy-preserving authentication based on group signature for VANETs. In: Proceedings of the 2013 IEEE Global Communications Conference, GLOBE-COM 2013, pp. 4609–4614 (2013)
11. Hao, Y., Cheng, Y., Ren, K.: Distributed key management with protection against RSU compromise in group signature based VANETs. In: Proceedings of IEEE GLOBECOM 2008, pp. 1–5 (2008)
12. Dutta, R., Mukhopadhyay, S., Collie, R.M.: Computationally secure self-healing key distribution with revocation in wireless ad hoc networks. Ad Hoc Netw. **8**(6), 597–613 (2010)
13. Schnorr, C.: Efficient signature generation by smart cards. J. Cryptol. **4**(3), 161–174 (1991)

Cooperative Privacy Preservation for Internet of Vehicles with Mobile Edge Computing

Jun Luo[1], Hong Liu[2(✉)], and Qianyang Cheng[3]

[1] The Third Research Institute of the Ministry of Public Security,
Shanghai 200031, China
wiselj@qq.com
[2] East China Normal University and Shanghai Trusted Industrial Control Platform
Co., Ltd., Shanghai 200063, China
liuhongler@ieee.org
[3] School of Computer Science and Software Engineering,
East China Normal University, Shanghai 200063, China
chengqysh@163.com

Abstract. The mobile edge computing is an attractive system paradigm to perform the local data processing and interactions at the edge of networks. The mobile edge computing enabled the internet of vehicles (MEC-IoV) is emerging as a convergence of the internet of things and mobile vehicular networks. The virtual vehicle shadow based privacy preservation scheme is proposed to address the cooperative scenarios, in which predictive location and segmented secret are jointly considered for protocol design. Meanwhile, the MinHash based similarity computing and the selective disclosure mechanism are respectively introduced for location and identity privacy preservation. The proposed scheme launches a new perspective of cooperative privacy preservation in the MEC-IoV with enhanced security requirements; it is suitable for the cooperative edge computing applications.

Keywords: Mobile edge computing · Internet of vehicles · Internet of things · Privacy preservation · Wireless communications

1 Introduction

Mobile edge computing (MEC) is an emerging system paradigm to perform efficient data processing and local interactions at the edge of networks. The distributed computing and communication resources are adaptively allocated according to the demands and capabilities of the interactive entities and are applied to support data collection, information extraction, knowledge generation, and intelligent decision at or near the sources of data [4]. The internet of vehicles (IoV) realizes an inevitable convergence of the internet of things and mobile vehicular networks. The mobile edge computing enabled the internet of

J. Vaidya et al. (Eds.): CSS 2019, LNCS 11982, pp. 289–303, 2019.
https://doi.org/10.1007/978-3-030-37337-5_24

vehicles (MEC-IoV) is noteworthy for involving the seamless connections in heterogeneous contexts to aggregate the distributed vehicles into cooperative interactions and to invoke the vehicles to establish flexible communications. Thus, MEC-IoV becomes the trend for combining the advantages of MEC and IoT for dynamical resource integration.

In the MEC-IoV, the vehicles are associated with the corresponding users and establish interconnections with different entities to achieve the ubiquitous vehicle-to-anything communications, including vehicle-to-infrastructure (V2I), vehicle-to-vehicle (V2V), and vehicle-to-person (V2P). During the wireless communications, sensitive vehicular data refers to locations and identities of the associated vehicle users. Along with the emergence of autonomous vehicles, the MEC-IoV becomes attractive to promote the combination of distributed vehicular resources, which are available to be aggregated. For instance, BMW had presented an ongoing project "vehicular crowd cell", which provides 4G coverage when a vehicle was in use or provided coverage to other nearby users when a vehicle parked. It makes that a vehicle owns dual roles (i.e., the vehicle itself, and a base station) during communications, and the vehicle acts as a moving base station to realize communication capability extension at the network edges (Fig. 1).

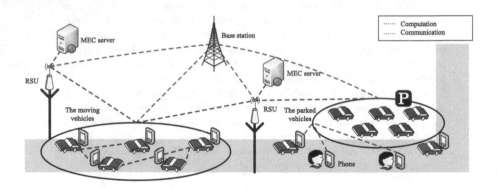

Fig. 1. The network architecture of the MEC-IoV.

For the traditional IoV, there are several privacy preservation schemes referring to anonymity [2], dummy generation [13], obfuscation [9], k-anonymity [3], and mainly address privacy aware issues for avoiding accurate location and identity-related data acquisition. While, current privacy preservation schemes pay less attention to the existence of emerging MEC-IoV applications, without considering the vehicles' dual roles and cooperative interaction requirements. The schemes above are not sufficient to guarantee the anonymity and obfuscation in the MEC-IoV since the cooperative interactions of vehicles and other entities bring more privacy challenges. Particularly, the vehicles' dual roles make privacy issues noteworthy compared with existing studies.

In this work, unique privacy preservation is identified for the moving vehicles and the parked vehicles during cooperative computation and communication scenarios, and the main contributions are as follows:

- Virtual vehicle shadow is defined for privacy preservation, and predictive location and segmented secret are jointly considered. The semigroup property of the Chebyshev polynomial is adopted to establish authentication operator to enhance anonymous data transmission during the vehicular interactions.
- Towards location privacy of the moving vehicles, MinHash based data similarity computing is performed to evaluate the location similarity without revealing any sensitive information with location prediction considerations.
- Towards identity privacy of the parked vehicles, secret sharing and hash-based selective disclosure mechanisms are applied for sensitive data fields protection and access control.

The virtual vehicle shadow is defined for privacy preservation, and predictive location and segmented secret are applied for designing a privacy-preserving scheme. For the moving vehicles, predictive location based privacy-preserving protocol is designed by the Chebyshev chaotic map and MinHash based similarity computing. For the parked vehicles, segmented secret based privacy-preserving protocol is designed by applying hash based selective disclosure mechanism.

The remainder of this work is organized as follows. Section 2 introduces the related works. Section 3 presents a virtual vehicle shadow based privacy preservation scheme, and Sect. 4 introduces the security analysis and performance analysis. Finally, Sect. 5 draws a conclusion.

2   Related Works

Gao et al. [3] designed a mixing zone to address location privacy in vehicular networks, in which pseudonym is applied to protect the location privacy of vehicles. At least k number of vehicles change pseudonyms to obtain k anonymity in collaborative interaction. To address pseudonym change, indMZ is designed to identify a pseudonym scheme for the vehicular networks referring to certification issuance and pseudonym issuance. It indicates that indMZ ensures k anonymity with $k/2$ average cost of extended beacon message, and is independent on the trusted third party.

Kang et al. [8] proposed a privacy-preserved pseudonym scheme for the fog computing enabled IoV and exploited vehicular resources at the network edge for pseudonym management. The proposed scheme satisfies context-aware pseudonym changing, supports dynamic pseudonym distribution; and provides reduced pseudonym management cost. A hierarchical architecture is established to address a context-aware pseudonym changing situation. According to the security analysis, both secure communication and privacy preservation are addressed with lightweight communication overheads.

Wang et al. [14] established an on-board unit (OBU) with three-level security architecture for the IoV and addressed the issues due to current on OBUs fail to protect the in-vehicle network. A security protocol with multiple security levels is designed for wireless network access control, and it is feasible and efficient with enhanced time overhead, secure interactions, and network reliability.

Liu et al. [11] proposed an efficient privacy-preserving dual authentication and key agreement scheme. This scheme prevents unauthorized visitors by developing a dual authentication mode, in which an OBU self-generates an anonymous identity and temporary encryption key during each session. The validity of the vehicle's real identity and anonymous identity could be verified by trust authority, and vehicle behavior attributes are also considered for reputation evaluation. Meanwhile, the correctness of this scheme is performed based on the Burrows-Abadi-Needham (BAN) logic, and it indicates that there is no obvious design flaw for the authentication scheme.

Joy et al. [6] focused on the privacy and security issues for an autonomous, connected vehicle in the IoV, and different vehicular applications are described for the V2V and V2I. The anonymized local privacy mechanism is evaluated based on a real dataset rather than arbitrary distributions, and the virtual identities are assigned to each vehicle for location privacy preservation. The anonymous uploading of urban sensor data is also exchanged during vehicular networking.

Hussain et al. [5] provides a privacy-aware incentives-based witness service in social IoV clouds, and a new service employed the moving vehicles as the witnesses to designated events. An identity-exchange based privacy-preserving service framework and incentive mechanism are respectively designed to promote the wide adoption of social services. The vehicles collaborate with other roadside unit for data collection and transmit the sensing data to the cloud infrastructure based on anonymous communications. The privacy-aware proportionate receipt collection is realized, in which each contributor is credited with incentives according to their contribution. The proposed scheme realizes that privacy is preserved in terms of event reporting and incentives redemption.

Liu et al. [10] addressed blockchain enabled security issue in electric vehicles cloud and edge computing, in which the EVs act as potential resource infrastructures referring to both information and energy interactions. Based on the context-aware vehicular applications, the blockchain inspired data coins, and energy coins are proposed based on distributed consensus. The data contribution frequency and energy contribution amount are jointly applied to achieve the proof-of-work, and security solutions are presented for securing vehicular interactions in both edge and cloud computing.

3 Virtual Vehicle Shadow Based Cooperative Privacy Preservation Scheme

3.1 System Initialization

In system initialization, there are multiple vehicles $\{V_1, V_2, ..., V_n\}$ (i.e., the moving vehicles and the parked vehicles), an RSU, an MEC, and a phone. A vehicle

Table 1. Notations

Notation	Description
PID_R	The pseudo-random identifier of the RSU
PID_E	The pseudo-random identifier of E
r_{V_*}, r_R, r_P	The pseudo-random numbers generated by V_*, RSU, and P
$S_{V_*}, S_{\tilde{V}_*}$	V_*'s secret, and virtual vehicle shadow's secret
$L_{V_*}, L_{\tilde{V}_*}^*$	V_*'s location, and virtual vehicle shadow's location
$L_{V_*}'^*$	V_*'s predictive location
$\mathcal{H}(.), \mathcal{T}(.), \mathcal{F}(.)$	The hash function, Chebyshev polynomial, and a defined function

V_1 owns its secret S_{V_1} and location L_{V_1}, and the RSU owns its pseudo-random identifier PID_R, and other pre-assigned vehicular data for establishing authentication operators. A virtual vehicle shadow $\tilde{V}$ is defined as a vehicle's accompanying copy during a certain time within a certain range. Assume that a virtual vehicle shadow owns its secret $S_{\tilde{V}_1}$, possible locations $\{L_{\tilde{V}_1}^1, L_{\tilde{V}_1}^2, ..., L_{\tilde{V}_1}^i\}$ ($i \in \mathbb{N}^*$). The notations are introduced in Table 1.

During running on the road, V_1 could obtain the locations of the neighboring vehicles $\{V_2, V_3, ..., V_n\}$ ($n \in \mathbb{N}^*$) within a certain range by receiving the broadcasting messages. The location information includes GPS data, velocity, and direction. $\tilde{V}_1$ acts as the virtual vehicle shadow of V_1, and it is determined based on the similarity computing according to the location and identity information. If there is no accompanying vehicle at a certain time and at the nearby place, $\tilde{V}_1$ will be generated according to V_1's historical data.

- *Location prediction*: The virtual vehicle shadow's possible locations $\{L_{\tilde{V}_1}^1, L_{\tilde{V}_1}^2, ..., L_{\tilde{V}_1}^i\}$ ($i \in \mathbb{N}^*$) are obtained for location prediction. $L_{\tilde{V}_1}^*$ is computed according to V_1's location and other neighboring vehicles' locations.
- *Secret segmentation*: The virtual vehicle shadow's secret $S_{\tilde{V}}$ is computed by the interactive vehicles. For instance, V_1 establishes the interactions with the neighboring vehicles $\{V_2, ..., V_n\}$, during which these vehicles respectively generate pseudo-random numbers for broadcasting.

The Chebyshev chaotic map is applied for authentication [12]. A Chebyshev polynomial $\mathcal{T}_l(t)$ is in t of degree l, and $\mathcal{T}_l(t) : [-1, 1] \to [-1, 1]$ is defined:

$$\mathcal{T}_l(t) = \cos(l \cdot \arccos(t))$$

The Chebyshev polynomials satisfy the recurrence.

$$\mathcal{T}_0(t) = 1$$
$$\mathcal{T}_1(t) = t$$
$$\mathcal{T}_l(t) = 2t\mathcal{T}_{l-1}(t) - \mathcal{T}_{l-2}(t); \quad (l \geq 2)$$

Define the degrees $\{l_1, l_2\}$ are positive integer numbers, and the semigroup property is achieved.

$$\mathcal{T}_{l_1}(\mathcal{T}_{l_2}(t)) = \mathcal{T}_{l_2 l_1}(t) = \mathcal{T}_{l_2}(\mathcal{T}_{l_1}(t))$$

The commutativity of Chebyshev polynomials could be extended within $(-\infty, \infty)$, and $\mathcal{T}_{l_1}(t)$ and $\mathcal{T}_{l_2}(t)$ ($t \in (-\infty, \infty)$) also satisfy the semigroup property.

For $l \geq 2$, $t \in (-\infty, \infty)$, it is obtained as follows.

$$\begin{aligned}\mathcal{T}_{l_1}(\mathcal{T}_{l_2}(t)) &= \cos(l_1 \cdot \arccos(\cos(l_2 \cdot \arccos(t)))) \\ &= \cos(l_1 l_2 \cdot \arccos(t)) \\ &= \mathcal{T}_{l_2 l_1}(t) \\ &= \mathcal{T}_{l_2}(\mathcal{T}_{l_1}(t))\end{aligned}$$

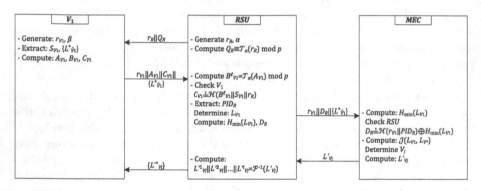

Fig. 2. The predictive location based privacy-preserving protocol for the moving vehicles.

3.2 Predictive Location Based Privacy Preservation for the Moving Vehicles

Figure 2 illustrates the predictive location based privacy-preserving protocol for the moving vehicles. A moving vehicle V_1, an RSU, a MEC server establish interactions. Assume that V_1 runs to a theater for attending a vocal concert, and the RSU and the MEC jointly provide services for V_1.

Challenge and Response Between the RSU and V_1. An RSU firstly generates a pseudo-random number r_R and a positive integer α to launch a new session. Here, α is applied to compute a public key Q_R.

$$Q_R \equiv \mathcal{T}_\alpha(r_R) \pmod{p}$$

The RSU transmits the cascaded message $r_R \| Q_R$ to V_1 as an access challenge. V_1 generates a pseudo-random number r_{V_1} and a positive integer β. Here, β is the maximum degree of a Chebyshev polynomial $T_\beta(.)$. V_1 further extracts its pre-shared secret S_{V_1}, and a set of location data $\{L^1_{\tilde{V}_1}, L^2_{\tilde{V}_1}, ..., L^i_{\tilde{V}_1}\}$ ($i \in \mathbb{N}^*$). $\{L^*_{\tilde{V}_1}\}$ is associated with V_1's virtual vehicle shadow $\tilde{V}_1$ for location confusion.

V_1 computes A_{V_1}, B_{V_1}, C_{V_1} as the authentication operators.

$$A_{V_1} = T_\beta(r_R) \pmod p$$
$$B_{V_1} = T_\beta(Q_R) \pmod p$$
$$C_{V_1} = \mathcal{H}(B_{V_1} \| S_{V_1} \| r_R)$$

V_1 transmits the cascaded message $r_{V_1} \| A_{V_1} \| C_{V_1} \| \{L^*_{\tilde{V}_1}\}$ to the RSU as a response.

The RSU Authenticates the Validity of V_1. The RSU computes $B^\ell_{V_1}$ based on the Chebyshev polynomial $T_\alpha(.)$.

$$B^\ell_{V_1} = T_\alpha(A_{V_1}) \pmod p$$

Theoretically, the semigroup property of Chebyshev polynomials is established.

$$T_\alpha(T_\beta(x)) = T_{\beta\alpha}(x) = T_\beta(T_\alpha(x))$$

It is obtained that $B^\ell_{V_1} = B_{V_1}$ according to the defined semigroup property and $Q_R \equiv T_\alpha(r_R) \pmod p$.

$$
\begin{aligned}
B^\ell_{V_1} &= T_\alpha(A_{V_1}) \pmod p \\
&= T_\alpha(T_\beta(r_R)) \pmod p \\
&= T_\beta(T_\alpha(r_R)) \pmod p \\
&= T_\beta(Q_R) \pmod p \\
&= B_{V_1}
\end{aligned}
$$

After that, the RSU authenticates V_1's validity according to the following operations. If the consistency of the computed value $\mathcal{H}(B^\ell_{V_1} \| S_{V_1} \| r_R)$ equals the received message C_{V_1}, V_1 will be regarded as a legal entity. Otherwise, the protocol will terminate.

The MEC Authenticates the RSU's Validity. The RSU extracts the pseudo-random identifier PID_R, and determines L_{V_1} based on the virtual vehicle shadow's possible locations.

$$L_{V_1} = \{L^1_{\tilde{V}_1}, L^2_{\tilde{V}_1}, ..., L^i_{\tilde{V}_1}\}$$

The MinHash algorithm $H_{min}(.)$ is applied to transferring L_{V_1} into $H_{min}(L_{V_1})$ [1,7]. L_{V_1} refers to an i-dimensional vector, and the main operation is as follows:

- Determine the number i of the hash values, and compute the minimal hash value;
- Linearhash and polynomialhash are jointly applied to determine the odd and even elements of L_{V_1}.

$\{L_{\tilde{V}_1}^1, L_{\tilde{V}_1}^2, ..., L_{\tilde{V}_1}^i\}$ are mapped into multiple integers, and $H_{min}(L_{V_1})$ is accordingly obtained as the minimal elements. The RSU computes D_R based on r_{V_1}, PID_R, and $H_{min}(L_{V_1})$, and further transmits the cascaded message $r_{V_1}\|D_R\|\{L_{\tilde{V}_1}^*\}$ to the MEC for authentication.

$$D_R = \mathcal{H}(r_{V_1}\|PID_R) \oplus H_{min}(L_{V_1})$$

Afterwards, the MEC re-computes $H_{min}(L_{V_1})$ according to the received $\{L_{\tilde{V}_1}^*\}$ based on the pre-shared MinHash algorithm. The MEC checks the RSU's validity by comparing the consistency of the received value D_R and the re-computed value $\mathcal{H}(r_{V_1}\|PID_R) \oplus H_{min}(L_{V_1})$. If it holds, the RSU will be regarded as a legal entity. Otherwise, the protocol will terminate.

The MEC Determines the Similarity of the Vehicles. The MEC performs similarity computing based on the Jaccard similarity coefficient of $H_{min}(L_{V_1})$ and $H_{min}(L_{V_*})$. Here, L_{V_*} is related to the historical location data during a vehicle's former traveling. The Jaccard similarity coefficient $\mathcal{J}(L_{V_1}, L_{V_*})$ is defined as the ratio of the number of elements of intersection and the number of elements of the union.

$$\mathcal{J}(L_{V_1}, L_{V_*}) = \frac{|L_{V_1} \cap L_{V_*}|}{|L_{V_1} \cup L_{V_*}|}$$

If $\mathcal{J}(L_{V_1}, L_{V_*})$ approaches 1, L_{V_1} and L'_{V_*} will be regarded to have higher similarity. The MEC determines the specific vehicle V_j with the most similarity for further predictive location extraction. For multiple vehicles $\{V_1, V_2, ..., V_n\}$, the Jaccard similarity coefficient $\mathcal{J}(L_{V_1}, L_{V_2}, ..., L_{V_n})$ should also be computed.

Assume that $\mathcal{J}(L_{V_1}, L'_{V_j})$ has the most similarity, and the MEC computes L'_{V_j} to involve the predictive location.

$$L'_{V_j} = \mathcal{F}(L'^1_{V_j}\|L'^2_{V_j}\|...\|L'^i_{V_j})$$

Thereafter, the MEC transmits L'_{V_j} to the RSU. The RSU further obtains $L'^1_{V_j}\|L'^2_{V_j}\|...\|L'^i_{V_j}$ according to an inverse operation $\mathcal{F}^{-1}(.)$, and continues to transmit $\{L'^*_{V_j}\}$ to V_1 for location services without revealing any sensitive information.

In this scheme, the RSU and the MEC can only obtain the aggregated locations of the virtual vehicle shadow, the MEC performs similarity computing and location service based on $H_{min}(L_{V_1})$ and $H_{min}(L_{V_*})$, and V_1 could obtain a set of predictive location data $\{L'^1_{V_j}, L'^2_{V_j}, ..., L'^i_{V_j}\}$ for possible location services. The location privacy preservation is achieved by the cooperative interactions of other neighboring vehicles.

3.3 Segmented Secret Based Privacy Preservation for the Parked Vehicles

Figure 3 illustrates the segmented secret based privacy-preserving protocol for the parked vehicles. The communication entities refer to phones, vehicles, and a base station. Assume that the vehicle V_1 arrives the theater, and its user's phone is denoted as P with the same subscript. After the theatre let out, the agglomerated users usually phone someone with strong demands to access mobile communication networks, and the parked vehicles may act as the temporary base station for the neighboring phones.

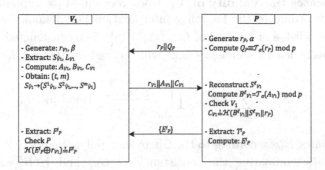

Fig. 3. The segmented secret based privacy-preserving protocol for the parked vehicles.

A vehicle V_1 determines its virtual vehicle shadow's secret $S_{\tilde{V}_1}$, and acts as a temp base station to generate a set of pseudo-random numbers $\{r_P^1, r_P^2, ..., r_P^x\}$ (denoted as $\{r_P^i\}, i = \{1, 2, ..., x\}$). V_1 computes T_P^i and F_P^i.

$$T_P^i = S_P^i \sharp r_P^i$$
$$F_P^i = \mathcal{H}(T_P^i)$$

Here, "$\sharp$" is a numeric symbol for distinguishing $\{V_P^1, V_P^2, ..., V_P^l\}$ and $\{r_P^1, r_P^2, ..., r_P^x\}$. $\{T_P^i\}$ and $\{F_P^i\}$ are checked for the one-to-one correspondence, and $\{F_P^i\}$ is broadcasted to P for further authentication.

Challenge-Response Between P and V_1. During challenge and response, the similar operations are performed: P first generates r_P and α to obtain $Q_P \equiv \mathcal{T}_\alpha(r_P) \pmod{p}$. P transmits $r_P \| Q_P$ to V_1 to launch a new session.

V_1 generates r_{V_1} and β, extracts its virtual vehicle shadow's secret $S_{\tilde{V}_1}$ and location L_{V_1}, and computes A_{V_1}, B_{V_1}, and C_{V_1}.

$$A_{V_1} = \mathcal{T}_\beta(r_R) \pmod{p}$$
$$B_{V_1} = \mathcal{T}_\beta(Q_R) \pmod{p}$$
$$C_{V_1} = \mathcal{H}(B_{V_1} \| L_{V_1} \| r_P)$$

Thereafter, V_1 distributes the secret $S_{\tilde{V}_1}$ into m pieces of secret shares ($S_{\tilde{V}_1}^1$, $S_{\tilde{V}_1}^2, ..., S_{\tilde{V}_1}^m$) with a threshold (t, m). It is required that at least t pieces could deduce $S_{\tilde{V}_1}$. In the case that an entity owns less than t pieces, it will not obtain $S_{\tilde{V}_1}$'s sensitive secret pieces.

V_1 defines a polynomial interpolation $f(x)$ for establishing the secret sharing, and $\{f_1, f_2, ..., f_{t-1}\}$ $(1 \leq t \leq j)$ are the coefficients of $f(x)$. Each share is denoted as $(x_i, f(x_i))$ for $x_i = 1, 2, ..., m$. These coefficients could be randomly chosen for generating n shares based on the following polynomial.

$$f(x) = S_{\tilde{V}_1} + f_1 x + f_2 x^2 + ... + f_{t-1} x^{t-1} \pmod{p}$$

V_1 transmits $r_{V_1} \| A_{V_1} \| C_{V_1}$ to the RSU as a response.

P Authenticates the Validity of V_1. Upon receiving V_1's response, P reconstructs $S_{\tilde{V}_1}$ according to the Lagrange interpolation polynomial. Based on the pre-shared knowledge of t pieces of $(x_i, f(x_i))$, $S_{\tilde{V}_1}^{\ell}$ is reconstructed and equals $S_{\tilde{V}_1}$. If P owns at least t secret pieces, it will successfully deduce $S_{\tilde{V}_1}$.

$$S_{\tilde{V}_1}^{\ell} = \sum_{a=1}^{t} f(x_a) [\prod_{i=1, i \neq a}^{t} \frac{-x_i}{x_a - x_i}] \pmod{p}$$

P recomputes $B_{V_1}^{\ell}$ according to the Chebyshev polynomial $T_{\alpha}(.)$, and checks V_1's validity by comparing the consistency of C_{V_1} and $\mathcal{H}(B_{V_1}^{\ell} \| S_{\tilde{V}_1}^{\ell} \| r_P)$. If it holds, V_1 will be regarded as a legal entity. Otherwise, the protocol will terminate.

V_1 Authenticates P's Validity. P extracts the sensitive data fields for secret data sharing, which is established for selective disclosure between V_1 and P. P first extracts $T_P^i = S_P^i \sharp r_P^i$, and computes E_P^i.

$$E_P^i = T_P^i \oplus r_{V_1}$$

It realizes that the selected data fields $\{T_P^i\}$ are randomized by r_{V_1} to obtain $\{E_P^i\}$, which will be transmitted to P for selected data fields sharing. When V_1 receives $\{E_P^i\}$, it further extracts the locally stored F_P^i to check P's validity. If the consistency of the re-computed value $\mathcal{H}(E_P^i \oplus r_{V_1})$ and F_P^i holds, P will be regarded as a legal entity. Accordingly, V_1 derives the corresponding data fields $\{S_P^i\}$ according to the special numeric symbol "$\sharp$".

Assume that there are five data fields $\{S_P^1, S_P^2, S_P^3, S_P^4, S_P^5\}$ referring to different vehicular data such as user attributes, user preference, vehicle brand, vehicle parameters, and context requirements. P shares certain data fields (e.g., $\{S_P^2, S_P^4, S_P^5\}$) instead of disclosing full data fields. Thus, E_P^2, E_P^4 and E_P^5 are transmitted to V_1 for authentication.

$$E_P^i = T_P^i \oplus r_{V_1}, (i = \{2, 4, 5\})$$

Upon receiving $\{E_P^i\}$ $(i = \{2, 4, 5\})$, V_1 extracts $\{F_P^2, F_P^4, F_P^5\}$, and checks the P's validity by comparing the consistency of $\mathcal{H}(E_P^i \oplus r_{V_1})$ and the locally stored F_P^i. It indicates that V_1 could obtain $\{S_P^2, S_P^4, S_P^5\}$ without revealing any sensitive data such as S_P^1 and S_P^3.

In this scheme, V_1's secret sharing is applied for distributing a secret into multiple pieces for different users. If P owns more than a certain threshold of the secret, it will deduce the full data fields for further authentication. Any identity-related information is not revealed during interactions. If P owns more than t pieces of the secret $S_{\tilde{V}_1}$, it will have the authority for accessing V_1's communication resources. Furthermore, the hash-based selective disclosure mechanism is applied to realize that P could freely select the sensitive data fields without the disclosure of full data fields.

4   Security and Performance Analysis

4.1   Security Analysis

Data Confidentiality and Integrity. Data confidentiality is achieved by the semigroup property and chaotic property of the Chebyshev chaotic map and Chebyshev polynomials. The Chebyshev polynomials $\mathcal{T}_\alpha$ and $\mathcal{T}_\beta$ are defined to describe the relationship of the pair of the public key and private key: $Q_R \equiv \mathcal{T}_\alpha(r_R) \pmod{p}$. It is obtained that $\mathcal{T}_\alpha(\mathcal{T}_\beta(x)) = \mathcal{T}_\beta(\mathcal{T}_\alpha(x))$, in which α and β are random positive integers. The pseudo-random numbers $\{r_P^i\}$ are applied to distort the data fields $\{S_P^i\}$ into the temp data fields $\{T_P^i\}$ by computing $T_P^i = S_P^i \sharp r_P^i$. The messages are exchanged via open wireless communications without any sensitive data disclosure.

Data integrity is achieved by hash functions. For the moving vehicles, an authentication operator C_{V_1} is computed by hashing B_{V_1}, S_{V_1}, and r_R, and C_{V_1} is applied for authenticating the validity of V_1. Another authentication operator D_R is obtained by involving $\mathcal{H}(r_{V_1}\|PID_R)$ and $H_{min}(L_{V_1})$. For the parked vehicles, the hashed value C'_{V_1} is also transmitted to avoid sensitive data disclosure. Meanwhile, $F_P^i = \mathcal{H}(T_P^i)$ is wrapped by a hash function for achieving selective disclosure.

Privacy Preservation. Both location and identity privacy preservation are considered, and the RSU cannot correlate V_1's predictive location and segmented secret with its real identity.

– *Location privacy:* The RSU obtains the possible location $\{L_{\tilde{V}_1}^1, L_{\tilde{V}_1}^2, ..., L_{\tilde{V}_1}^i\}$ of the virtual vehicle shadow for interactions. The location data is aggregated as L_{V_1}, which is applied to obtain $H_{min}(L_{V_1})$ for further computing D_R. The MEC performs similarity computing based on $H_{min}(L_{V_1})$ and other vehicle's $H_{min}(L_{V_*})$ to determine V_j. The Jaccard similarity coefficients are computed for evaluating similarity of the vehicles. L'_{V_j} is established by computing $\mathcal{F}(L_{V_j}'^1\|L_{V_j}'^2\|, ..., \|L_{V_j}'^i)$, and the predictive location $\{L_{V_j}'^1, L_{V_j}'^2, ..., L_{V_j}'^i\}$ is transmitted to V_1 without revealing any sensitive information.

– *Identity privacy:* The secret $S_{\tilde{V}_i}$ is distributed into n pieces of shares ($S^1_{\tilde{V}_i}$, $S^2_{\tilde{V}_i}$,..., $S^n_{\tilde{V}_i}$). Lagrange interpolation polynomial with the pre-shared knowledge of t pairs of $(x_i, f(x_i))$, $S_{\tilde{V}_i}$ could be reconstructed for authentication. Hash based selective disclosure mechanism is also applied for sensitive data protection.

Authentication and Anonymity. The RSU performs authentication on V_1 by verifying whether there is a suitable $B^{\ell}_{V_1}$ to satisfy that C_{V_1} equals $\mathcal{H}(B^{\ell}_{V_1}\|S_{V_1}\|r_R)$. Here, the semigroup property of Chebyshev polynomials is applied for authentication according to $Q_R \equiv T_{\alpha}(r_R) \pmod{p}$. The MEC performs authentication on the RSU by verifying the consistency of the computed value $\mathcal{H}(r_{V_1}\|PID_R)\oplus H_{min}(L_{V_1})$ and the received D_R, during which the pseudo-random identifier is introduced as an authentication operator. Moreover, mutual authentication is established between V_1 and P.

Anonymous data transmission is performed instead of exposing the real identifiers and sensitive secrets in the open and wireless channels. The hashed values are exchanged by involving pseudo-random numbers, which realize dynamic session interactions. Even if an attacker intercepts the exchanged messages, it can only obtain the randomly wrapped data with forward security.

Forward Security. Forward security refers to the session freshness and unlinkability, and pseudo-random numbers r_R, r_{V_1} and r_P are respectively generated by the RSU, V_1, and P. Pseudo-random numbers $\{r^1_P, r^2_P,..., r^x_P\}$ is generated by P for computing $T^i_P = S^i_P\natural r^i_P$. Furthermore, F^i_P is obtained by computing $F^i_P = \mathcal{H}(T^i_P)$, in which r^i_P is applied to enhance session unlinkability. Any attacker will not correlate the currently ongoing session with other former sessions.

4.2 Performance Analysis

Performance analysis is performed in terms of storage requirement, communication overhead, and computation cost. In the MEC-IoV, the vehicles, an RSU, and a phone own a certain hardware resources, which are regarded as resource restricted entities. The MEC acts as a distributed computing unit, which has relatively rich resources during interactions. During protocol implementation, performance simulation is performed based on C programs running on the Intel Core i7, 64-bit, 4*CPUs, 3.40 GHz PC.

Towards storage requirement, V_1 stores the secrets $\{S_{V_1}, S_{\tilde{V}_1}\}$, its location L_{V_1}, and other possible locations $\{L^1_{\tilde{V}_1}, L^1_{\tilde{V}_2},..., L^i_{\tilde{V}_1}\}$. The secrets are assumed as 64-bit length, $L^1_{\tilde{V}_1}$ is assumed as 8-bit length, and the pseudo-random numbers $\{r_R, r_{V_1}, r_P\}$ are assumed as 16-bit length. Such storage could be easily satisfied for current hardware conditions. Additionally, the hash function is based on 128-bit MD5 algorithm, requires 23.0K additional gates, which is suitable for lightweight applications.

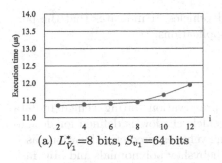
(a) $L_{\tilde{V}_1}^*$=8 bits, S_{v_1}=64 bits

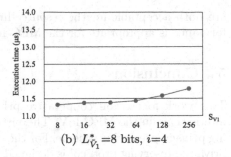
(b) $L_{\tilde{V}_1}^*$=8 bits, i=4

Fig. 4. The execution time of the edge computing mode.

Communication overhead depends on the exchanged message number during the protocol execution. Based on the length assessment, the interactions among V_1, RSU, and MEC complete via 5 steps. For the moving vehicles, communication overhead is estimated as $36 + 2i$ bytes between V_1 and RSU, and is estimated as $18 + 2i$ bytes between the RSU and the MEC. For the parked vehicles, communication overhead is estimated as $30 + 8n$ bytes between V_1 and the RSU.

Computation cost mainly refers to the pseudo-random number generation (PRNG) function, hash function, Chebyshev polynomial, and MinHash based similarity computing, and the maximum amount of computation refers to the hash functions. For the moving vehicles, V_1 mainly performs two times PRNG function, one-time hash operations, and two times Chebyshev polynomial. The RSU mainly performs two times PRNG function, three times hash operations, two times Chebyshev polynomial, and other algebraic operations. For the parked vehicles, V_1 mainly performs two times PRNG function, two times hash operations, and two times Chebyshev polynomial. The RSU mainly performs two times PRNG function, one times hash operations, and two times Chebyshev polynomial.

Figure 4 shows the execution time for the moving vehicle with variables of element number of L_{V_1}, and length of S_{V_1}. The execution time is applied for emulating the computation cost. Considering the unavoidable deviation of protocol simulation, the protocol implementation is performed 1000 thousand times to obtain an average.

1. In Fig. 4(a), let $L_{\tilde{V}_1}^* = 8$ bits, and $S_{v_1} = 64$ bits, the execution time is within 12 µs, and the execution time is almost smooth when $SLen$ is less than $8 * 8$ bits.
2. In Fig. 4(b), let $L_{\tilde{V}_1}^* = 8$ bits, and $i = 4$, the execution time varies from 11.32 µs to 12.44 µs, and the execution time is relatively smooth when S_{V_1} is less than 64 bits.

Thus, the MEC is regarded as resource-rich entities, and the main computation cost is performed due to hash functions and Chebyshev polynomials, which are both acceptable for the resource-limited vehicles. It indicates that the performance is appropriate for the MEC-IoV applications.

5   Conclusions

This work focuses on cooperative privacy preservation during vehicular data interactions in the MEC-IoV. The virtual vehicle shadow is defined for designing privacy-preserving scheme. For the moving vehicles, predictive location based privacy-preserving protocol is designed by Chebyshev polynomials and MinHash based similarity computing. For the parked vehicles, segmented secret based privacy-preserving protocol is designed by applying hash based selective disclosure mechanism. The main security requirements including data confidentiality, data integrity, authentication, and forward security are achieved along with location and identity privacy preservation. The proposed authentication scheme launches a new perspective of cooperative privacy preservation in the MEC-IoV.

Acknowledgment. This work is funded by the National Key R&D Program of China (2017YFB0802300), and National Natural Science Foundation of China (61601129). This work is partially supported by the Shanghai Science and Technology Commission Program (No. 18511105700).

References

1. Ding, J., Ni, C.C., Zhou, M., Gao, J.: Minhash hierarchy for privacy preserving trajectory sensing and query. In: 2017 16th ACM/IEEE International Conference on Information Processing in Sensor Networks (IPSN), pp. 17–28. IEEE (2017)
2. Guo, L., et al.: A secure mechanism for big data collection in large scale Internet of vehicle. IEEE Internet Things J. **4**(2), 601–610 (2017). https://doi.org/10.1109/JIOT.2017.2686451
3. Guo, N., Ma, L., Gao, T.: Independent mix zone for location privacy in vehicular networks. IEEE Access **6**, 16842–16850 (2018). https://doi.org/10.1109/ACCESS.2018.2800907
4. He, Y., Zhao, N., Yin, H.: Integrated networking, caching, and computing for connected vehicles: a deep reinforcement learning approach. IEEE Trans. Veh. Technol. **67**(1), 44–55 (2018). https://doi.org/10.1109/TVT.2017.2760281
5. Hussain, R., et al.: Secure and privacy-aware incentives-based witness service in social Internet of vehicles clouds. IEEE Internet Things J. **5**(4), 2441–2448 (2018). https://doi.org/10.1109/JIOT.2018.2847249
6. Joy, J., Gerla, M.: Internet of vehicles and autonomous connected car-privacy and security issues. In: 2017 26th International Conference on Computer Communication and Networks (ICCCN), pp. 1–9. IEEE (2017). https://doi.org/10.1109/ICCCN.2017.8038391
7. Kalnis, P., Mamoulis, N., Bakiras, S.: On discovering moving clusters in spatio-temporal data. In: Bauzer Medeiros, C., Egenhofer, M.J., Bertino, E. (eds.) SSTD 2005. LNCS, vol. 3633, pp. 364–381. Springer, Heidelberg (2005). https://doi.org/10.1007/11535331_21

8. Kang, J., Yu, R., Huang, X., Zhang, Y.: Privacy-preserved pseudonym scheme for fog computing supported Internet of vehicles. IEEE Trans. Intell. Transp. Syst. **19**(8), 2627–2637 (2017). https://doi.org/10.1109/TITS.2017.2764095
9. Lim, J., Yu, H., Kim, K., Kim, M., Lee, S.B.: Preserving location privacy of connected vehicles with highly accurate location updates. IEEE Commun. Lett. **21**(3), 540–543 (2017). https://doi.org/10.1109/LCOMM.2016.2637902
10. Liu, H., Zhang, Y., Yang, T.: Blockchain-enabled security in electric vehicles cloud and edge computing. IEEE Netw. **32**(3), 78–83 (2018). https://doi.org/10.1109/MNET.2018.1700344
11. Liu, Y., Wang, Y., Chang, G.: Efficient privacy-preserving dual authentication and key agreement scheme for secure V2V communications in an IoV paradigm. IEEE Trans. Intell. Transp. Syst. **18**(10), 2740–2749 (2017). https://doi.org/10.1109/TITS.2017.2657649
12. Mason, J.C., Handscomb, D.C.: Chebyshev Polynomials. Chapman and Hall/CRC (2002)
13. Niu, B., Zhang, Z., Li, X., Li, H.: Privacy-area aware dummy generation algorithms for location-based services. In: 2014 IEEE International Conference on Communications (ICC), pp. 957–962. IEEE (2014). https://doi.org/10.1109/ICC.2014.6883443
14. Wang, L., Liu, X.: NOTSA: novel OBU with three-level security architecture for Internet of vehicles. IEEE Internet Things J. **5**(5), 3548–3558 (2018). https://doi.org/10.1109/JIOT.2018.2800281

Machine Learning and Security

DeT: Defending Against Adversarial Examples via Decreasing Transferability

Changjiang Li[1], Haiqin Weng[1], Shouling Ji[1(✉)], Jianfeng Dong[2], and Qinming He[1]

[1] Zhejiang University, Hangzhou, China
{cj_li,hq_weng,sji,hqm}@zju.edu.com
[2] Zhejiang Gongshang University, Hangzhou, China
danieljf24@gmail.com

Abstract. Deep neural networks (DNNs) have made great progress in recent years. Unfortunately, DNNs are found to be vulnerable to adversarial examples that are injected with elaborately crafted perturbations. In this paper, we propose a defense method named DeT, which can (1) defend against adversarial examples generated by common attacks, and (2) correctly label adversarial examples with both small and large perturbations. DeT is a transferability-based defense method, which to the best of our knowledge is the first such attempt. Our experimental results demonstrate that DeT can work well under both black and gray box attacks. We hope that DeT will be a benchmark in the research community for measuring DNN attacks.

Keywords: Deep learning · Adversarial examples · Transferability

1 Introduction

Deep neural networks (DNNs) have been widely used in many challenging tasks, showing impressive performance. For some tasks, DNNs have already exceeded human beings, e.g., image recognition, text classification, and speech recognition [4,6,13,14,21,23,25]. Not surprisingly, however, researchers have found that DNNs are vulnerable to some specially perturbed examples called adversarial examples [3,5]. Such adversarial examples are so harmful since they are injected with elaborately crafted perturbations that are imperceptible to humans, even the model interpretation methods, while can fool DNNs [27].

To defend against adversarial examples, researchers have proposed various defense methods. Goodfellow et al. proposed adversarial training [5], which trains the model on the augmented dataset containing adversarial examples. Papernot et al. proposed the defensive distillation to improve the robustness of the model [20]. They first train one DNN model to predict soft labels for training examples, and then train another model on the same training examples with the predicted soft labels. Meng et al. proposed a novel method called Magnet which combines with detectors and reformers [16]. Detectors are designed to detect adversarial

© Springer Nature Switzerland AG 2019
J. Vaidya et al. (Eds.): CSS 2019, LNCS 11982, pp. 307–322, 2019.
https://doi.org/10.1007/978-3-030-37337-5_25

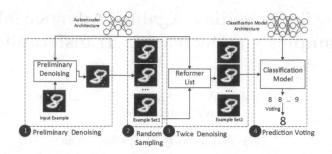

Fig. 1. Working flow of our proposed DeT.

examples and reformers are designed to reconstruct input examples. Cao et al. proposed a region-based classification which selects examples in a hypercube centered on the input example [1] and sends them to the classifier. The most frequent label is deemed as the final predicted label.

The above methods however have their own limitations. Adversarial training can only defend against specific adversarial examples similar to those in the training set. Defensive distillation cannot significantly improve the robustness of the classifier, and it is easy to be attacked [3]. Region-based methods work poorly to defend against adversarial examples with large perturbations. Magnet has been broken by Carlini&Warner leveraging the transferability of adversarial examples and requires extensive human labors [2]. In summary, the existing defenses have the following limitations: (1) it can only defend against specific adversarial examples [5] and adversarial examples with slight perturbations [1]; and (2) it needs extensive human labors [16]. Therefore, there is a long-term arms race between the attackers and the defenders [15].

To address the above limitations, we propose a robust defense method called DeT. It uses a list of reformers[1] to reduce the transferability of adversarial examples and thus mitigates the threat posed by the adversary. We propose a cross training algorithm to generate several complementary reformers, among which the transferability of adversarial examples is low. The defense ability of DeT is mainly based on the low transferability of adversarial examples among the reformers. DeT can (1) defend against adversarial examples generated by common attacks, and (2) still give the correct output for adversarial examples with large perturbations.

Figure 1 illustrates the working flow of DeT. Given an input example, DeT first adds Gaussian noises on the input example and then sends the noised example to a specific reformer for preliminary denoising. After preliminary denoising, we can get a denoised example close to the original input. Then, we perform a non-differentiable random sampling operation on the denoised example. Under the gray box circumstance, this makes the attack method unable to perform the gradient-based optimization. By the sampling operation, we obtain an example set

---

[1] The details of reformers will be explained in Sect. 3.

where each example is very close to the original input. We use several reformers to reconstruct all the examples from the example set, and send the reconstruction results to the classifier for labeling. We select the most frequently appeared label in the predicted label collection as the output label.

The contributions of this paper are summarized as follows.

- We propose an algorithm that can significantly decrease the transferability of adversarial examples among different reformers. This algorithm can be used to defend against the gray box attack. To our knowledge, it is the first attempt to defend against adversarial examples through reducing the transferability of adversarial examples.
- We introduce a robust defense method DeT which can significantly increase the accuracy of the classifier under common attacks.
- DeT can give the correct output even if adversarial examples are with large adversarial perturbations.

2 Background

In this section, we first introduce the threat model considered in this paper, followed by reviewing the related work.

2.1 Threat Model

The attack situation can be divided into the following two situations based on the adversary's understanding of our defense methods.

Black Box Attack. The adversary only knows the structure and parameters of the classifier while does not know anything about the defense method.

Gray Box Attack. The adversary not only knows the structure and parameters of the classifier but also knows the defense method. In this paper, we assume a more powerful adversary who can get the structure and parameters of one reformer used in the Reformer List.

Below we briefly review the related work from four fields: deep neural networks, adversarial examples, common attacks, and defenses.

2.2 Deep Neural Networks

Deep neural networks (DNNs) have made great progress in recent years, especially the convolutional neural network (CNN) [12]. DNN is widely used in many fields, such as image recognition [10,23], speech recognition [6,8], medical treatments [26] and information security [9,25].

Notation. For simplicity, let $X = \{x_i | \ i = 1, 2, ...\}$ denote the set of input examples, where x_i is an example. Let $X' = \{x'_i | \ i = 1, 2, ...\}$ denote the set of adversarial examples corresponding to X. Given X, let $C(x_i)$ denote the estimated label of x_i.

A DNN is a function model, denoted by $y = F(x) = f_L(f_{L-1}(...(f_1(x))))$, where y represents the output vector and $y \in \mathbb{R}^m$. f_i represents layer i in DNN, and f_L is often a *softmax* layer which maps from logits (the result vector before the softmax layer) to the output vector. The output vector is in the range $[0, 1]$ that adds up to 1. The value of $F(x_i)_j$ is regarded as the probability of the input x_i belonging to class j. The classifier will consider the label $C(x_i) = argmax_j F(x_i)_j$ as the predicted label.

2.3   Adversarial Examples

The concept of adversarial examples was first proposed by Szegedy et al. [24]. Those examples with elaborately crafted perturbations are called adversarial examples.

To measure the perturbations, researchers usually adopt three distance metrics: L^0, L^2, and L^∞. If the distances are small enough, we can guarantee that the adversarial perturbations of adversarial examples are undetectable to humans.

Transferability is of key importance to adversarial examples. Transferability means that adversarial examples generated for one model can also lead to the misclassification of another, even if these two models have different structures and are trained on different datasets [19]. DeT significantly decreases the transferability of adversarial examples among reformers.

2.4   Common Attacks

Fast Gradient Sign Method (FGSM) utilizes the gradient information to generate adversarial examples [5]. Specially, the adversarial examples generated by FGSM can be formulated as $x' = x + \epsilon * sign(\nabla_x L(F(x), y))$, where $L(.,.)$ denotes the loss between the model output of x and the ground truth label y and $sign$ is a function that extracts the sign of its inputs. The generated adversarial examples maximize the loss function. The parameter ϵ controls the attack strength. An increase of ϵ can improve the success rate of the attack, though it might result in human-perceptible noises.

Basic Iterative Method (BIM) is an extension of FGSM [11]. Different from FGSM that takes one step to change the original examples, BIM takes multiple small steps with step-width α. Compared with FGSM, we can see that BIM is designed as the multiple iterations version of FGSM.

Deepfool iteratively searches the minimal L^2 adversarial perturbations for a given example [17]. In the iterative process, it adds small perturbations to the given example at a time until the example crosses the decision boundary.

Carlini&Wagner Attacks (C&W) include three attacks that can almost reach an incredible success rate of 100% with human imperceptible perturbations [3]. The attacks included in C&W can be classified as the targeted and non-targeted attacks. The targeted attack makes the output to meet the target requirements (e.g., misclassify the input example to the specified target class) while the non-targeted attack only requires the target model to misclassify the input examples. Due to the space limitation, we refer interesting authors to [3] for more details.

In this paper, we focus on non-targeted attacks since they are more easy to be achieved for the adversary. As L^2-based C&W attack is the strongest attack method, we use it to evaluate our proposed defense method.

2.5 Common Defenses

Adversarial Training aims to train a more robust classification model by adding extra adversarial examples with ground truth label to the training dataset [24]. This method requires a great deal of computational cost to generate adversarial examples as well as retraining the model. The effectiveness of adversarial training depends on whether the attack methods being available.

Region-based Classification randomly selects a number of examples in the hypercube centered on the original input example [1]. These selected examples are then fed to the model. The model gives all labels of these selected examples, and it considers the most frequent label as the final output. The basic idea of this method is to assume that *the adversarial example is close to the decision boundary.*

Magnet is a framework for defending against adversarial examples [16]. Upon receiving an example, Magnet determines whether this example is adversarial or not. Magnet then refuses to classify the example if the example is detected as adversarial, otherwise Magnet reconstructs the input example to reduce its potential threat and sends the reconstructed example to the classifier.

Adversarial training can only defend against known attacks, and therefore it is not within our scope of comparison. In our experimental evaluation, we compare our method with Region-based method and Magnet.

3 Our Defense Method

In this paper, we propose a robust defense method called DeT to defend against adversarial examples. Figure 1 shows the overall architecture of DeT. DeT has four processes: *preliminary denoising, random sampling, twice denoising* and *prediction voting.*

Below, we introduce the four processes of DeT in detail.

3.1 Preliminary Denoising

We first briefly introduce the details of the reformer used in the process of preliminary denoising.

Reformer. The reformer is a function that reconstructs the input example throughout denoising it. The reconstructed example is very close to the original example only with several details lost (these details are regarded as noise by the reformer). Usually, the reformer is built upon the autoencoder.

Given an input example x_t, DeT first adds Gaussian noises to the example for obtaining a noised example x'_t. This process is helpful for the reformer to reconstruct examples, since it amplifies noises to the same level as the noises used to train our reformer. Then, we use the reformer to preliminarily denoise x'_t for obtaining a relatively clean example x''_t. This operation can eliminate potential threats.

3.2 Random Sampling

After preliminary denoising, we obtain a relatively clean example x''_t. However, we cannot guarantee that x''_t is not an adversarial example. There still exists the possibility that x''_t is near the decision boundary. Therefore, inspired by the Region-based method, we randomly sample a set of examples in a hypercube centered at x''_t and can get an example set $X_t = \{x''_i | i = 1, 2, ...\}$. The generation of x''_i can be formulated as follows:

$$x''_i = Clip(x''_t + \epsilon * Noise), \tag{1}$$

where $Noise$ denotes the Gaussian noise, and ϵ is a parameter that controls the side length of the hypercube.

3.3 Twice Denoising

To further improve the effectiveness of DeT, we again use several other reformers to form a Reformer List to further denoising. A single reformer can be easily attacked by the adaptive attack. DeT uses several reformers that can prevent the adversarial examples that fool one reformer from fooling the other reformer, since the transferability of adversarial examples among these reformers is relatively low. We believe that the diversity of the reformer architectures in the Reformer List will help reduce the transferability of the adversarial examples and thus enhance the defense capabilities of DeT. Therefore, we employ three autoencoders with different architectures as our reformers. The architectures of the three autoencoders used in this paper are based on the open source implementations[2]. For the ease of reference, we denote the $Reformer\ i$ as R_i in the paper. We also propose an algorithm called cross training to further reduce the transferability of adversarial examples among reformers, as shown in Algorithm 1.

Cross Training Algorithm. The input of the cross training algorithm includes the training epoch e, the reformer set R with n already trained reformers, the batch size s, the training dataset X and the noise length l. The output is a reformer set R' corresponding to R. Note that all the reformers in the input reformer set are already trained and can reconstruct examples well.

In the following, we show several examples, based on two re-trained reformers R'_1 and R'_2

---

[2] https://github.com/Trevillie/MagNet

Algorithm 1: Cross Training

Input: e: Training epoch.
s: The size of a batch of data.
X: Training dataset.
R: $[R_1, R_2, ..., R_n]$
l: The noise strength added to the clean example.
Output: R'=$[R'_1, R'_2, ..., R'_n]$

1 $sub\_list = Combinations(0, n-1, 2);$
2 **while** *epoch less than e* **do**
3      $train_x, train_y = GenetrateData(X);$
4      $temp_x = Clip(train_x + l * random(s));$
5   **for** *p in sub_list* **do**
6          $p0 = P[0], p1 = p[1];$
7          $X_1 = R[p0](temp_x);$
8          $X_{1\_2} = R[p1](X_1);$
9          $Loss1 = EuclideanDistance(X_{1\_2}, train_x);$
10         $Train1 = Optimizer.min(Loss1, R[p1]);$
11         $Run(Train1);$
12         $X_2 = R[p1](temp_x);$
13         $X_{2\_1} = R[p0](X_2);$
14         $Loss2 = EuclideanDistance(X_{2\_1}, train_x);$
15         $Train2 = Optimizer.min(Loss2, R[p0]);$
16         $Run(Train2);$
17   **end**
18     $epoch+ = 1$
19 **end**
Result: $R'=[R'_1, R'_2, ..., R'_n]$

Figure 2 illustrates reconstructed examples on MNIST. From Fig. 2, we can see that R'_1 makes the outline of the input example thicker while R'_2 makes the outline of the input example thinner, which are equivalent to expansion and corrosion operations in image processing, respectively. Intuitively, R'_1 and R'_2 deal with the image in two opposite ways, and thus the adversarial perturbations for one reformer can be removed by the other.

Figure 3 also shows two adversarial examples reconstructed by our two other reformers trained on CIFAR. As we can see from Figs. 2 and 3, the cross training algorithm can re-train reformers in two different directions.

We do not explicitly specify the change directions in the cross training. Interestingly, it is the cross training algorithm that automatically searches for two different directions of the change.

We select several reformers from R' to form the Reformer List. Assume there are k re-trained reformers in the Reformer List, R'_1, R'_2,..., and R'_k. We use R'_i ($i = 1, 2, ..., k$) to reconstruct all the examples in X_t and get a reconstructed example set denoted by X_{ti}. Up to now, we get k reconstructed example sets, X_{t1}, X_{t2}, ..., and X_{tk}.

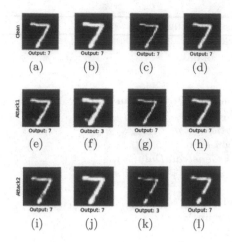

Fig. 2. Examples reconstructed by R'_1 and R'_2. (a)–(d) indicate that the input example is a clean example, (e)–(h) indicate that the input example is an adversarial example for R'_1, and (i)–(l) indicate that the input example is an adversarial example for R'_2. (a), (e), where (i) presents the input example itself; (b), (f), and (j) present the input examples processed by the R'_1; (c), (g), and (k) present the input examples processed by the R'_2; (d), (h), and (l) present the examples processed by the R_1. The number below each picture presents the classification result.

Fig. 3. The first image is a clean image, and the latter two are the images reconstructed by the two reformers re-trained on CIFAR.

3.4 Prediction Voting

For a reconstructed set X_{ti} ($i = 1, 2, ..., k$), we feed all the examples in it to the classifier. The most frequent label is selected as the predicted y_i label for this set. After this, we can get a label set $Y = [y_1, y_2, ..., y_k]$. Finally, the most frequent label in Y is deemed as the final output. If several labels in Y have the same highest frequency, we randomly select one from them as the final output.

4   Evaluation

In this section, we first describe the experimental setup. After that, we evaluate the effectiveness of cross training, test DeT against black and gray box attacks, and compare DeT with the state-of-the-arts.

4.1 Setup

Datasets: We employ two commonly used datasets: MNIST and CIFAR. MNIST, includes 55,000 training examples, 5,000 validation examples, and 10,000 testing examples. CIFAR, includes 45,000 training examples, 5,000 validation examples, and 10,000 testing examples.

Implementation:

- **Classifier:** On MNIST, we train a classification model (a seven-layer CNN [3]) with the accuracy of 99.43%. On CIFAR, we train a classification model (a Residual Neural Network [7]) with the accuracy of 92.43%.
- **Reformer:** For each of the datasets, we train three reformers using three different structures. Note that we train all the reformers on the noise-added examples and the reconstruction error (i.e., the L^2 distance between the reconstructed example and the clean example) is used to optimize the reformer.
- **Cross Training:** We re-train the reformers according to the cross training algorithm. After the re-training process, we get nine reformers for each dataset. Then, we select a few reformers to form the Reformer List. Our selection strategy are according to: (1) the selected reformer does not have much influence on the accuracy of the classifier after the input reconstruction; and (2) the transferability of adversarial examples among the reformers should be as low as possible.

Metrics: To evaluate DeT and compare it with other defense methods, we adopt the following evaluation metric named *Accuracy*.

$$Accuracy = \frac{Number\ of\ correctly\ classified\ examples}{Total\ number\ of\ input\ examples},$$

Accuracy measures the proportion of correctly classified examples in the input examples.

All experiments in this paper are run on a server with 2 Intel Xeon E5-2640 V4 GPUs, 64 GB memory, 4 TB HDD and 1 GeForce GTX-1080TI GPU.

4.2 Effectiveness of Cross Training

Figure 4 shows the classification accuracy comparison of the classifier equipped with the re-trained and the original reformers under L^2-based C&W attack. As can be seen from Fig. 4(a), the adversarial examples fool the classifier with R_1 perfectly. While feeding these examples to the classifier with R_2, the classification accuracy decreases from 99% to 0% as the *Confidence* increases from 0 to 40. It can be seen from Fig. 4(a) that the transferability of adversarial examples becomes stronger as the *Confidence* increases. Even when *Confidence* is greater than 30, adversarial examples can also attack R_2 perfectly. Figure 4(b) shows the classification accuracy of the classifier equipped with re-trained reformers. From this figure, we can see that when *Confidence* is 40, the classifier equipped with R'_2 still achieves the classification accuracy of 89%. The above results suggest that our algorithm can significantly decrease the transferability of adversarial examples among reformers.

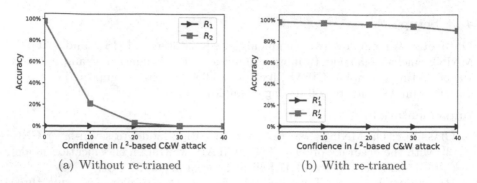

(a) Without re-trianed

(b) With re-trianed

Fig. 4. The classification accuracy on MNIST under attack, where the adversarial example in (a) is generated for $R1$, and the adversarial example in (b) is generated for $R1'$.

4.3　Evaluation Against Black Box Attacks

Table 1. Classification accuracy.

Dataset	Accuracy (no defense)	Accuracy (with DeT)
MNIST	99.43%	98.6%
CIFAR	92.43%	86.7%

Performance of DeT. Table 1 shows the decrease of the classification accuracy, which is within our tolerance range. Then, we adopt four common attacks, i.e., Deepfool, BIM, FGSM, and C&W, to evaluate DeT. Among them, Deepfool, BIM and FGSM are implemented based on the Cleverhans library [18], and C&W is implemented based on the open source code [3].

On MNIST, the classification performance with and without DeT against common attacks are shown in Table 2. It is obvious that the classifier protected by DeT outperforms that without any protection. Especially, the classification accuracy of the classifier without defense is 0.0% while it can still obtain a 96%+ classification accuracy with DeT's protection.

On the CIFAR dataset, the classification accuracy with and without DeT against common attacks are shown in Table 2. We can observe that the accuracy of the classifier with DeT has been significantly improved compared to that without any protection.

4.4　Evaluation Against the Gray Box Attack

Following Meng et al. [16], in this section, we evaluate DeT against gray box attacks under L^2-based C&W attack.

Table 2. The classification accuracy of the classifier without defense v.s. with DeT.

Attack	No defense	with DeT
MNIST		
FGSM L^∞ $\epsilon = 0.1$	90.0%	97.95%
BIM L^∞ $\epsilon = 0.05$	93.05%	98.45%
BIM L^∞ $\epsilon = 0.1$	64.85%	97.85%
DeepFool L^∞	0.85%	97.8%
C&W L^2 $Confidence = 0$	0.0%	98.44%
C&W L^2 $Confidence = 20$	0.0%	96.79%
CIFAR		
FGSM L^∞ $\epsilon = 0.01$	29.2%	78.8%
BIM L^∞ $\epsilon = 0.005$	12.95%	82.1%
BIM L^∞ $\epsilon = 0.01$	5.15%	78.2%
DeepFool L^∞	4.55%	86.1%
C&W L^2 $Confidence = 0$	0.0%	86.4%
C&W L^2 $Confidence = 10$	0.0%	85.6%

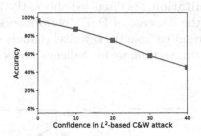

Fig. 5. The accuracy of DeT under the gray-box attack.

Figure 5 shows the gray box attack results, from which we can see that DeT can efficiently defend against gray box attack. Even when the adversarial examples are generated with $Confidence = 40$, the classifier with DeT still achieves 43.7% accuracy. The decrease of transferability in this experiment is not as significant as that in Fig. 4. We speculate that it may because we first send the adversarial example to the preliminary denoising. How to improve this is an interesting future work of DeT.

4.5 Comparison with the State-of-the-Art Defense

Since L^2-based C&W attack is one of the strongest attacks at present, we compare with other defenses under this attack. We conduct comparative experiments on the MNIST and the CIFAR datasets. Figure 6 illustrates the comparison between DeT and the state-of-the-art defenses.

Magnet. We find that the defense capability of Magnet depends heavily on the detectors. Magnet can detect an adversarial example with slightly large adversarial perturbations. It will not send the example to the classifier, and therefore, will not produce the correct classification. Magnet's classification accuracy is shown in the black lines of Fig. 6. It can be found that with the increase of $Confidence$, the classification accuracy of Magnet is significantly reduced. Notably, according to Fig. 6(a), on the MNIST dataset, when $Confidence = 40$, the classification accuracy of Magnet reduced to near 0% while DeT can still achieve the accuracy of around 84%. According to Fig. 6(b), on the CIFAR dataset, Magnet can only reach the accuracy of 44% when the $Confidence = 50$, and achieve the accuracy of about 13% when $Confidence = 100$. On the other hand, DeT can reach the accuracy of 80% when $Confidence = 50$, and we can still achieve the accuracy of about 65% when $Confidence = 100$. These results show that our classification accuracy has improved significantly compared to Magnet.

Region-Based Classification. For Region-based classification defense methods [1], the basic assumption is that *the adversarial examples exist near the decision boundary*. Our experimental results show that this assumption is not necessarily true.

Exploring DeT's Limitation. As discussed above, the increase of adversarial perturbations leads to the decrease of DeT's performance. We conjecture that such decrease might be resulted from the key pixel changes caused by large adversarial perturbations. In this section, we use Saliency Maps [22] to experimentally verify our conjecture.

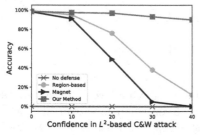 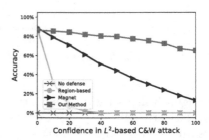

(a) The accuracy on MNIST datatset   (b) The accuracy on CIFAR datatset

Fig. 6. Classification accuracy comparison of DeT and other defenses against the L^2-based C&W attack.

Figure 7(b) shows our experimental results, where the ground truth label is "Airplane". We can see that (1) key pixels of the clean example are the outline of the airplane, and (2) key pixels of the adversarial example with $Confidence = 10$ are very close to the former. Therefore, our proposed method, DeT, removes the adversarial perturbations through the reformer. However, for the adversarial example with $Confidence = 100$, we can see from the third image in Fig. 7(b)

| Clean | Confidence:10 | Confidence:100 | Clean | Confidence:10 | Confidence:100 |

(a) Original Image and Adversarial Images   (b) Saliency Maps of the Imgae

Fig. 7. (a) One clean example and two adversarial examples with different perturbations generated by the L^2-based C&W attack. (b) Saliency Maps corresponding to the images in (a).

that the outline of the aircraft is completely invisible. We have sufficient reasons to believe that many key pixels have already been changed, and it is difficult to classify it correctly.

Table 3. The proportion of the adversarial examples with human imperceivable perturbations and the estimated best accuracy under each *Confidence*. The classification accuracy of DeT on clean examples is 86.7%.

Confidence	Proportion	Best accuracy
0.0	99.7%	86.4%
10.0	99.2%	86.0%
20.0	98.7%	85.5%
30.0	97.4%	84.4%
40.0	95.5%	82.8%
50.0	93.7%	81.2%
60.0	91.2%	79.0%
70.0	89.1%	77.2%
80.0	85.3%	73.9%
90.0	80.4%	69.7%
100.0	78.4%	67.9%

Then we do another statistical experiment to count the adversarial examples with human imperceivable perturbations under different *Confidence*. We first randomly sample 1000 examples from the CIFAR dataset. Then, we invite an expert in adversarial machine learning to label how many examples with human imperceivable perturbations under each *Confidence*. Table 3 lists the proportion of the adversarial examples with human imperceivable perturbations under each *Confidence*.

We conclude the DeT can correctly classify most of the adversarial examples. The decrease in accuracy is may due to the fact that those adversarial perturbations are perceptible to the humans while not meeting the definition of adversarial examples.

5   Conclusion

In this paper, we propose DeT, which obtains high accuracy in both scenarios of classifying adversarial examples with small and large perturbations. We also propose an algorithm that can significantly reduce the transferability of adversarial examples among different reformers. In the future work, we will consider to improve the robustness of the model by further reducing the transferability of adversarial examples.

Our method also has some limitations. The first is the efficiency problem, which can be solved by adding hardware at this moment. In addition, our reformer is trained under Gaussian noises. For some of the adversarial noises that differ greatly from Gaussian noises, they cannot be denoised by the reformer, which also needs to be resolved in the future.

In general, our method significantly improves the robustness of a classifier, and we hope that DeT will be used as a benchmark in the research community for measuring neural network attacks.

Acknowledgements. This work was partly supported by NSFC under No. 61772466 and U1836202, the Zhejiang Provincial Natural Science Foundation for Distinguished Young Scholars under No. LR19F020003, and the Provincial Key Research and Development Program of Zhejiang, China under No. 2017C01055.

References

1. Cao, X., Gong, N.Z.: Mitigating evasion attacks to deep neural networks via region-based classification. In: Proceedings of the 33rd Annual Computer Security Applications Conference, pp. 278–287. ACM (2017)
2. Carlini, N., Wagner, D.: MagNet and efficient defenses against adversarial attacks are not robust to adversarial examples. arXiv preprint arXiv:1711.08478 (2017)
3. Carlini, N., Wagner, D.: Towards evaluating the robustness of neural networks. In: 2017 IEEE Symposium on Security and Privacy (SP), pp. 39–57. IEEE (2017)
4. Du, T., Ji, S., Li, J., Gu, Q., Wang, T., Beyah, R.: SirenAttack: generating adversarial audio for end-to-end acoustic systems. arXiv preprint arXiv:1901.07846 (2019)
5. Goodfellow, I.J., Shlens, J., Szegedy, C.: Explaining and harnessing adversarial examples. Computer Science (2014)
6. Graves, A., Mohamed, A.R., Hinton, G.: Speech recognition with deep recurrent neural networks. In: 2013 IEEE International Conference on Acoustics, Speech and Signal Processing (ICASSP), pp. 6645–6649. IEEE (2013)

7. He, K., Zhang, X., Ren, S., Sun, J.: Identity mappings in deep residual networks. In: Leibe, B., Matas, J., Sebe, N., Welling, M. (eds.) ECCV 2016. LNCS, vol. 9908, pp. 630–645. Springer, Cham (2016). https://doi.org/10.1007/978-3-319-46493-0_38

8. Hinton, G., et al.: Deep neural networks for acoustic modeling in speech recognition: the shared views of four research groups. IEEE Signal Process. Mag. **29**(6), 82–97 (2012)

9. Javaid, A., Niyaz, Q., Sun, W., Alam, M.: A deep learning approach for network intrusion detection system. In: Proceedings of the 9th EAI International Conference on Bio-inspired Information and Communications Technologies (formerly BIONETICS), pp. 21–26. ICST (Institute for Computer Sciences, Social-Informatics and Telecommunications Engineering) (2016)

10. Krizhevsky, A., Sutskever, I., Hinton, G.E.: ImageNet classification with deep convolutional neural networks. In: Advances in Neural Information Processing Systems, pp. 1097–1105 (2012)

11. Kurakin, A., Goodfellow, I., Bengio, S.: Adversarial examples in the physical world. arXiv preprint arXiv:1607.02533 (2016)

12. LeCun, Y., Bottou, L., Bengio, Y., Haffner, P.: Gradient-based learning applied to document recognition. Proc. IEEE **86**(11), 2278–2324 (1998)

13. Li, J., Ji, S., Du, T., Li, B., Wang, T.: TextBugger: generating adversarial text against real-world applications. In: NDSS (2019)

14. Li, X., et al.: Adversarial examples versus cloud-based detectors: a black-box empirical study. arXiv preprint arXiv:1901.01223 (2019)

15. Ling, X., et al.: DEEPSEC: a uniform platform for security analysis of deep learning model. In: IEEE S&P (2019)

16. Meng, D., Chen, H.: MagNet: a two-pronged defense against adversarial examples. In: Proceedings of the 2017 ACM SIGSAC Conference on Computer and Communications Security, pp. 135–147. ACM (2017)

17. Moosavi-Dezfooli, S.M., Fawzi, A., Frossard, P.: DeepFool: a simple and accurate method to fool deep neural networks. In: Proceedings of the IEEE Conference on Computer Vision and Pattern Recognition, pp. 2574–2582 (2016)

18. Papernot, N., et al.: Cleverhans v2. 0.0: an adversarial machine learning library. arXiv preprint arXiv:1610.00768 (2016)

19. Papernot, N., McDaniel, P., Goodfellow, I.: Transferability in machine learning: from phenomena to black-box attacks using adversarial samples. arXiv preprint arXiv:1605.07277 (2016)

20. Papernot, N., McDaniel, P., Wu, X., Jha, S., Swami, A.: Distillation as a defense to adversarial perturbations against deep neural networks. In: 2016 IEEE Symposium on Security and Privacy (SP), pp. 582–597. IEEE (2016)

21. Shi, C., et al.: Adversarial captchas. arXiv preprint arXiv:1901.01107 (2019)

22. Simonyan, K., Vedaldi, A., Zisserman, A.: Deep inside convolutional networks: visualising image classification models and saliency maps. arXiv preprint arXiv:1312.6034 (2013)

23. Simonyan, K., Zisserman, A.: Very deep convolutional networks for large-scale image recognition. arXiv preprint arXiv:1409.1556 (2014)

24. Szegedy, C., et al.: Intriguing properties of neural networks. arXiv preprint arXiv:1312.6199 (2013)

25. Xu, L., Zhang, D., Jayasena, N., Cavazos, J.: HADM: hybrid analysis for detection of malware. In: Bi, Y., Kapoor, S., Bhatia, R. (eds.) IntelliSys 2016. LNNS, vol. 16, pp. 702–724. Springer, Cham (2018). https://doi.org/10.1007/978-3-319-56991-8_51

26. Xu, Y., et al.: Deep learning of feature representation with multiple instance learning for medical image analysis. In: 2014 IEEE International Conference on Acoustics, Speech and Signal Processing (ICASSP), pp. 1626–1630. IEEE (2014)
27. Zhang, X., Wang, N., Shen, H., Ji, S., Luo, X., Wang, T.: Interpretable deep learning under fire. In: USENIX Security (2020)

ADS-B Data Attack Detection Based on Generative Adversarial Networks

Tengyao Li[1]([✉])(iD), Buhong Wang[1], Fute Shang[1], Jiwei Tian[1],
and Kunrui Cao[1,2]

[1] Information and Navigation College, Air Force Engineering University,
Fenghao East Road 1st, Xi'an, Shaanxi, China
totopcoder@gmail.com
[2] School of Information and Communications,
National University of Defense Technology, Xi'an, Shaanxi, China

Abstract. With the requirements on accuracy, coverage and reliability,
the air traffic surveillance is being developed into the next generation. In
2020, ADS-B data is becoming the foundation to establish air traffic situation awareness capabilities. However, ADS-B is designed without sufficient security guarantees, which results in diverse attack threats. Hence,
it is in demand of effective attack detections to keep attack data away
from decision flows. To improve the accuracy and robustness, attack
detection based on generative adversarial network for ADS-B data is
proposed. The LSTM networks are the core components to set up the
generator and discriminator to make the most of temporal spatial correlations. Utilizing the reconstruction error and discriminative loss, the
comprehensive detection metric is obtained to identify attack behaviors.
To enhance the robustness, the analysis threshold for detection decision
is determined in terms of normal data intrinsic features. By experimental analysis on real ADS-B data, the accuracy and robustness of the
proposed method is validated.

Keywords: Automatic Dependent Surveillance - Broadcast ·
Generative Adversarial Networks · Attack detection · Air traffic
surveillance · Cyber security

1 Introduction

With the fast increase of airspace density, more requirements on accuracy, reliability, safety and security are emerging in ATM (Air Traffic Management) systems [1]. As a result, the systems are developed into the next generation with
high performances, which pushes them into cyber physical systems with more
vulnerabilities [2]. Recently, cyber security for the ATM systems is becoming
the essential focus to support flight safety. With the information as the core
component in the next generation ATM systems, its security, especially the data
security, is vital to ensure and improve system performances [3]. For the ATM

© Springer Nature Switzerland AG 2019
J. Vaidya et al. (Eds.): CSS 2019, LNCS 11982, pp. 323–336, 2019.
https://doi.org/10.1007/978-3-030-37337-5_26

systems, the surveillance data is one of the primary data source to support various system functions [4], of which security is the foundation to enhance the security for the whole system.

Due to the shortage of accuracy, coverage and economy cost, the traditional surveillance methods such as PSR (Primary Surveillance Radar), SSR (Secondary Surveillance Radar), MLAT/WAM (MultiLATeration/ Wide Area Multilateration) and so on are in demand of improvements or replacements. Relying on high accuracy, wide coverage and low economy cost, ADS-B (Automatic Dependent Surveillance - Broadcast) is put forward to deal with the challenges during developments and deployed in the majority of countries in the world. At present, ADS-B has been listed as the core technology with the highest priority by ICAO (International Civil Aviation Organization) [5], which is supported by quantities of research projects such as NextGen (the NEXT GENeration air transportation project), SESAR (the Single European Sky Advanced Research) and CNGATM (the China Next Generation Air Traffic Management). Thus, ADS-B data is the foundation to establish essential situation awareness capabilities and support decision making, of which security is related tightly with the safety of the whole system [6].

Unfortunately, the attack behaviors for ADS-B data has been emerged with diverse patterns, which has been verified on attack feasibilities and impacts by real experiments [7]. When data is transmitted by datalink, the data is plain without any encryption, which enables attackers to collect ADS-B data conveniently. The integrity, authentication and availability are possible to be destroyed so that the ADS-B data is threatened to be manipulated with attack intents. To eliminate the attack impacts, it is necessary to set up attack detection strategy to detect attack behaviors in time [8], which enables it to remove the attack data before decision procedures and remain more time for effective responses. Though there are many detection strategies for ADS-B data up to now, the strategies are constricted with more prior knowledge, low accuracy and high time delay. To make up with the weakness, we proposed the attack detection model based on GAN (Generative Adversarial Network), which is dependent on the reconstruction deviations and discriminator loss to distinguish the attack behaviors.

The whole paper is organized as following: Sect. 2 introduces the workflow of ADS-B and current researches on novelty detection with GAN, Sect. 3 explains the detailed model of our methods, including normal data pattern, GAN reconstruction model and attack behavior discriminator, Sect. 4 shows the main results on the performance of the proposed model, Sect. 5 offers the further discussion about the challenges for GAN on the ADS-B attack detection field, Sect. 6 summaries the pros and cons of the proposed method.

2 Related Work

2.1 ADS-B

ADS-B is the primary surveillance method in the next generation ATM system, which will be used simultaneously with SSR to improve the surveillance performance. In 2020, ADS-B will be mandated to be deployed in the majority of countries [9]. The ADS-B data is more abundant with multiple attributes, including latitude, longitude, altitude, heading and velocity, etc., which are applied to improve the surveillance accuracy. The location information of ADS-B data is updated per second to support TBO (Trajectory Based Operation) on efficient predictions [10].

As illustrated in Fig. 1, current flights obtain ADS-B data from GNSS (Global Navigation Satellite System) and airborne navigation systems by ADS-B receivers [11]. According to the ADS-B data format, the corresponding data is encapsulated into message packages for transmission. Via 1090ES (1090 MHz Extend Squitter) or UAT (Universal Access Transceiver) data link, ADS-B data is transmitted to the neighbor flights and the corresponding ground stations. The neighbor flights receive the ADS-B data and construct the local situation awareness capabilities to enhance its safety and security. The ground stations receive the ADS-B data and push it into complicated processing procedures for air traffic control. On the one hand, the ADS-B data is rebroadcast with the traffic broadcast service to meet the compatibility and data share. On the other hand, the ADS-B data is sent to the ATC (Air Traffic Control) center to support decision making.

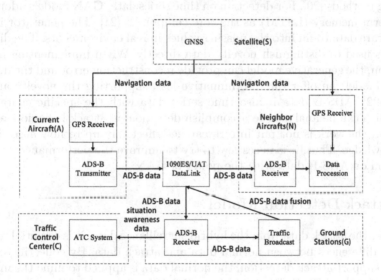

Fig. 1. The workflow for ADS-B data [11]

For the whole cycle of ADS-B data, there are vulnerabilities during generation, transmission, exchange and share [12]. The data is prone to being attacked by manipulation, replay and injection, etc. When the data is manipulated in terms of attack behaviors, it is inevitable to capture features of attack behaviors, which is feasible to mine attack data to detect novelties caused by attackers.

2.2 Novelty Detection with GAN

Generative adversarial network (GAN) theory is proposed by Goodfellow [13], which is integrated with minmax game theory and deep learning [14]. GAN is comprised of generator and discriminator, which is trained jointly to optimize with each other. The generator is trying to generate data which can be classified as normal sample by discriminator with high probability. The discriminator is trying to distinguish novelty data if the input is generated with noise or malicious data. With the adversarial training, performances of the generator and discriminator reach to the balance states, establishing the GAN model. By validation with various problems, GAN is proved to be superior with traditional methods on accuracy and efficiency [15]. These years, various GANs are emerging, which is proved to be similar with performances on common problems [16].

For novelty detection, GAN is the representative methods on deep learning [17], which is selected to improve detection accuracy. Auto encoder [18] is used to detect novelty data based on reconstruction error, which is hindered with threshold setting. Deep one class classification [19] is used to detect novelty data based on support vector data description, which is in need of positive and negative data. But for GAN model, it can be established without prior knowledge and pre-configured thresholds, which is adaptive to unsupervised and supervised learning methods [20]. For detection on time series data, GAN models adopt long short term memory (LSTM) as the core component [21]. The generator is used to generate data to fill into the missing values in real environments. The discriminator is used to distinguish novelty data directly. When implementing novelty detection, the generative model can provide reconstruction error and the discriminative model can offer the discriminative loss, supporting the novelty analysis better [22]. ADS-B data is also time series data with the specific characteristics, which can be analyzed to accomplish detection on attack behaviors as well. However, the work is not put into researches effectively up to now according to our knowledge. Thus, it is necessary to try to improve the performance of attack detection on ADS-B data with the power of GAN.

3   Attack Detection Model

To detect the attack data from the hybrid surveillance data, it is essential to identify the differences between normal data and attack data. By collecting enough data to support attack detection, the normal data is applied to mine the intrinsic features for the ADS-B data sequences. Relying on the extractive features, it is feasible to detect attack data from complicated behaviors. However, the feature of data is difficult to choose manually, which is hidden in the latent spaces. In machine learning, the generative model is practical to depict the internal features to set up the detection models.

As illustrated in Fig. 2, the generative model is dependent on reconstruction error to detect attack data. By training on the normal data sequences, the generative model is established to construct models to match with the original data, which can be used to generate the data with high similarity for normal data.

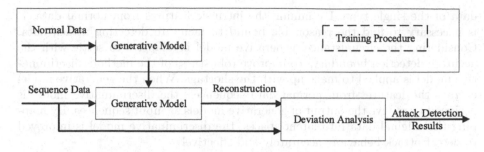

Fig. 2. Attack detection based on generative model

Once the generative models are set up, the sequential data is input to generate the output data with the trained models. The output sequence data is regarded as the reconstructions, which reemerges the normal data. Subsequently, the deviation analysis is taken to highlight the differences between reconstructions and normal data, obtaining the comprehensive detection probability. However, the method is absent of robustness due to the dependency on thresholds to acquire detection results. If the parameter tuning is proper and optimized, the differences between reconstruction and normal data is magnified sufficiently, which still calls for suitable thresholds to improve accuracy and eliminate false alarm ratio.

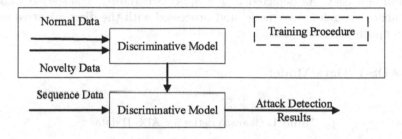

Fig. 3. Attack detection based on discriminative model

To relieve the threshold construction, the discriminative model for machine learning is also an alternative choice to detect attack behaviors fast. As illustrated in Fig. 3, the discriminative model is in demand of labeled data to be trained with supervised learning. Once the model is obtained, it is convenient and efficient to detect attack data, which is a kind of direct and practical method. For the model, one of the key difficulty is the need of attack data to accomplish training procedures.

Unfortunately, there is no credible attack data from actual industrial environments. For ADS-B data, the data collected from airspaces is regarded as the normal sequences generally. Thus, the model is only possible to be trained by data of the single type. By mining the intrinsic features from normal data, it is necessary to find the reasonable bound to facilitate detecting attack data. Considering the circumstance, generative model is adaptive to settle with the accurate detection boundary. To improve robustness of the method, discriminative model is applied to make up with the shortage. When the generative model extract the features from normal data sequences, the discriminative model is designed to receive the output of generative models as input sequences. By mapping the original data into latent spaces, the discriminative model is improved to detect attack behaviors accurately and effectively.

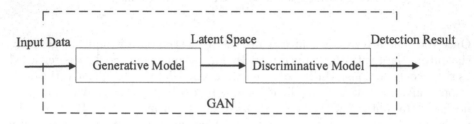

Fig. 4. GAN model

Utilizing the power of generative adversarial network, the ADS-B data sequence is analyzed with dynamic game theory to improve detection accuracy and efficiency. As depicted in Fig. 4, ADS-B data is transferred into the latent space via generative model and processed with the discriminative model to accomplish detection tasks.

3.1 ADS-B Data Model

Table 1. Characteristics for ADS-B data

No.	Characteristic	Description
1	Temporal correlations	ADS-B data is typical time series data, which is related tightly for the data points of the neighbor time
2	Spatial correlations	The ADS-B data collected from the neighbor flights is relative for the sequential time
3	Multiple dimensions	ADS-B data consists of multiple attribute data
4	High generation frequency	ADS-B data is sent with two pieces per second for location, velocity message and one piece per five seconds for identity message
5	Noise influences	ADS-B data is impacted with data and channel noise

ADS-B data is comprised of multiple attributes to provide more accurate and abundant information on surveillance. By analyzing the data characteristics, it is typical temporal spatial stream data. The current data is relative strongly with the last data points and the ADS-B data of neighbor flights. Based on the phenomenon, ADS-B data is regarded as multivariate time series data, which is the vital factor when designing attack detection methods. In addition, the ADS-B data is generated and transmitted fast with two messages per second. When the message is transmitted and received, it is impacted with noise and unreliability of communication channel, which causes the absence and fluctuation of ADS-B data (Table 1).

For the ADS-B data sequence, it is denoted as the following equation:

$$\begin{cases} X_j = \{x_{ji}|i = t_0, t_1, \cdots, t_n\} \\ x_{ji} = \{x_{ji}^k|k \in Q\} \end{cases} \tag{1}$$

where X_j is the ADS-B data sequences of jth flights, x_{ji} is the ADS-B data point on time i, x_{ji}^k is the corresponding attribute value of flight j for the specific time i, Q is the attribute set for ADS-B data.

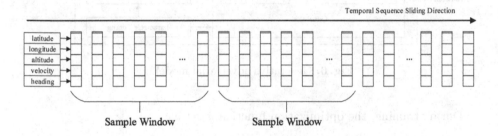

Fig. 5. Temporal sequence separation

As depicted in Fig. 5, ADS-B sequences are sliced into snippets. Setting the sample window is T_s, the ADS-B data is separated into several parts with equal length. Five essential attribute values, including latitude, longitude, altitude, velocity and heading, are selected as the basic information, which manifest the position, velocity and direction of flights. Considering all the data is collected from the actual industrial environments, the missing data is filled with linear interpolation to ensure updating the status message once per second.

3.2 GAN Model

When designing the GAN model, the original framework proposed is chosen as the foundation. Considering the temporal spatial characteristics, LSTM is opted for enhancing the temporal correlation learning. As illustrated in Fig. 6, the generative model consists of LSTM encoder and decoder, which transfers the ADS-B data into latent space and regenerate the data with the potential features of normal data. The discriminative model is comprised of LSTM networks to detect the attack behaviors. When training the model, normal data is applied to generate positive samples and random noise is applied to generate negative samples. The reconstruction output of generator, detection labels and discriminator loss of discriminator is push to the model output, which construct the foundation of attack behavior analysis module. The essential factor for the model training is effective data volume and parameter tuning. On the one hand, ADS-B data is collected from actual industrial environments where large scale data from thousands of flights can be obtained. On the other hand, the parameter can be optimized with plenty of iterations.

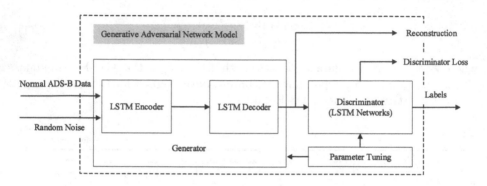

Fig. 6. Generative adversarial model

During training, the optimization function is set as:

$$\min_{G} \max_{D} V(D,G) = \mathcal{E}_{x \sim p_{data}(X)}[log D(x)] + \mathcal{E}_{z \sim p_z(Z)}[log(1 - D(G(z)))] \quad (2)$$

where G, D are the map functions for generator and discriminator respectively, x is the normal ADS-B data sequences, z is the random noise sequences. Relying on the min-max game, the generator tends to generate data that is difficult to identify from normal data, the discriminator tends to detect all the generated data with the high probability. When reaching the balance conditions or maximum iteration limitations, the GAN model is obtained, which is the core component to detect attack behaviors.

3.3   Attack Behavior Analysis

When the GAN model is obtained, it is feasible to analyze the ADS-B sequential data to detect attack behaviors. The discriminative model in GAN is convenient to apply into attack detections. But in order to improve the accuracy and robustness, the attack behavior analysis module is designed based on both the generative and discriminative parts.

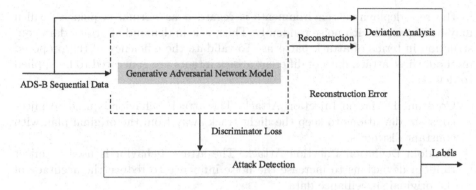

Fig. 7. Attack behavior analysis

As depicted in Fig. 7, two metrics are selected to put into attack detection. One is the reconstruction error, the error is calculated within deviation analysis module, in which the data is analyzed with mean square error. The other is the discriminator loss that is obtained with cross entropy calculations. To integrate with the two metrics effectively, the comprehensive detection metric Φ is:

$$\Phi = \frac{\delta_r}{ln(e - l_d)}, \quad \delta_r, l_d \in [0, 1] \tag{3}$$

where δ_r is the reconstruction error, l_d is the discriminative loss, both the two metric is constricted within $[0, 1]$.

According to the training procedure, the expected value of Φ is determined based on the detection labels of GAN model, which is chosen as the reasonable threshold to accomplish detection. Assuming the Φ_h is the detection threshold, some small slack variables are attached to enhance the robustness:

$$\tilde{\Phi}_h = \Phi_h + \epsilon, \epsilon > 0 \tag{4}$$

where ϵ is the slack variable. Thus, the final decision for attack detection is:

$$\Gamma = \begin{cases} 1, & \Phi > \tilde{\Phi}_h \\ 0, & \Phi \le \tilde{\Phi}_h \end{cases} \tag{5}$$

If the comprehensive detection metric Φ is beyond the threshold $\tilde{\Phi}_h$, then the attack behaviors are detected with high probability. Otherwise, the ADS-B data is normal without novelties caused by attackers.

4   Experiment Analysis

In actual industrial environments, the data manipulation attack is common and easy to be implemented. However, with constriction of laws, attack data is difficult to collect directly. Generally, the data that is collected from ADS-B receivers in the real deployment environments is regarded as normal sequences, which may be impacted with noise randomly. Thus, it is in demand of attack data construction in terms of attack patterns. To validate the efficiency of the proposed method, three attack data of different attack intents are generated to be applied to detect:

– Constant Deviation Injection Attack. The attack behavior is used to inject constant deviations to keep the flight track away from the original plan with constant distances.
– Random Deviation Injection Attack. The attack behavior is used to inject random deviations to increase the noise influence to reduce the accuracy of the original surveillance data.
– Increased Deviation Injection Attack. The attack behavior is used to inject deviations gradually with time elapsing, of which values are increasing slowly to enhance stealth of attack behaviors.

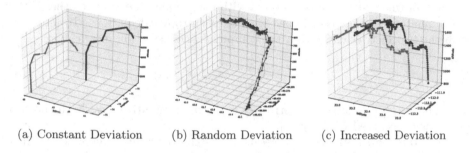

(a) Constant Deviation   (b) Random Deviation   (c) Increased Deviation

Fig. 8. Data manipulation attack (Color figure online)

As illustrated in the Fig. 8, the tracks of attack examples are given. The above three constructed attack data is mixed with normal ADS-B data, setting up the basic data for attack detection. In comparison with the original track

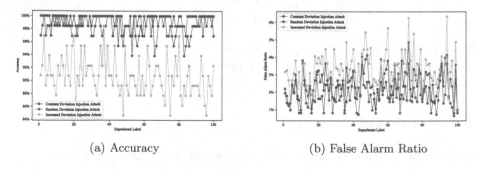

(a) Accuracy   (b) False Alarm Ratio

Fig. 9. Attack detection performance (Color figure online)

(marked with red), the attack influences (marked with blue) are depicted and the flight safety is possible to be eliminated under these attack behaviors.

As depicted in Fig. 9, two metrics are adopted to evaluate and analyze: Accuracy and False Alarm Ratio. The accuracy analysis is used to confirm the accuracy of detection on attack behaviors, which is essential to hinder with attack data to enter decision flow. The false alarm ratio is used to enhance the robustness of detection methods, which is vital to ensure normal data is reported accurately. In the experiments, the ADS-B data of 1297 flights are utilized, of which 5% is chosen as attack targets randomly. By implementing the proposed method, the accuracy and false alarm ratio is analyzed to confirm the performance as Eq. 6.

$$\begin{cases} c_{acc} = r_{aa}/d_a \\ c_{far} = r_{an}/d_n \end{cases} \tag{6}$$

where c_{acc} and c_{far} are accuracy and false alarm ratio respectively, r_{aa} is attack data with the attack label, r_{an} is normal data with the attack label, d_a, d_n are attack data and normal data for the sample data respectively.

In the experiments, each attack pattern is detected for 100 times. On average accuracy, constant deviation injection attack detection accuracy is 98.2%, random deviation injection attack detection accuracy is 99.3%, increased deviation injection attack detection accuracy is 90.6%. The constant and random deviation attack is detected with high probability while the detection on increased deviation attack is in need to enhance. On average false alarm ratio, three attack patterns are about 2.5%, 1.8%, 3.3% respectively, which depicts the intrinsic features are learned effectively.

According to the results, the accuracy and robustness of the proposed method are proved by the higher accuracy and low false alarm ratio. For constant and random deviation injection attack patterns, it is easy to detect the attack behaviors accurately. For the increased deviation injection attack pattern, the performance of the method is eliminated due to the slow deviation increase. When the features that attack data is deviated from normal data is captured with high probability by the model, it is practical to detect attack behaviors based on the method.

5   Discussion

ADS-B data is typical temporal spatial sequential data, which is in demand of sequential online analysis capability on attack detection. Considering the air traffic surveillance is critical infrastructure, the security of ADS-B data is essential to ensure the flight safety [23]. To improve the data security, effective attack detection strategy is necessary to detect attack behaviors fast, identify attack data accurately, process attack data properly and repair attack data reasonably. At present, the attack detection on ADS-B data is focused due to the mandated deployment deadline (2020 year) coming. Generally, the attack detection on ADS-B data mainly takes advantage of the motion laws [24] and third reference data [25]. On the one hand, the ADS-B data is validated with motion laws. Considering the complicated flying tracks, the adopted motion laws to detect is hybrid with multiple ways such as uniform linear motion, uniform accelerated motion, circular motion and so on. On the other hand, the third reference data, such as SSR, PSR, WAM and so on, is utilized to accomplish data fusion. After data associations, cross validations are implemented for ADS-B data sequences with different surveillance data. However, the performance of attack detection is limited on accuracy, time delay and false alarm ratio.

In terms of ADS-B data attack detection, the primary challenges are listed as the following:

1. **Large Data Processing Capability.** The data collected from actual industrial environment is increasing fast. For one hour, the amount of flights reach to 10^3–10^4 level. Meanwhile, for one day, the size of data can reach to 10^2–10^3 GB [26].
2. **Low Analyzing Time Delay.** Considering the high velocity of flight motion, the processing and analysis time ought to be limited within short time, supporting fast decision making and ensuring flying safety.
3. **Low False Alarm Ratio.** Obviously the ADS-B data is influenced with noise brought by communication unreliability and device performance. Hence, the data is fluctuated naturally to cause high probability of false alarm, which is in demand of processing properly.
4. **High Detection Accuracy.** Due to the critical safety and security of air traffic surveillance, high accuracy is significant to be guaranteed with high priority. To avoid the malicious data into decision flow, it is necessary to detect the attack data accurately and make responses in time.
5. **Dynamic and Robustness.** The detection model should not be static while it should be dynamic to enhance its robustness, adapting to the uncertainty and variety of attack behaviors.

The proposed detection method (For simplicity, it is entitled **DAD-GAN**) is based on big data to mine intrinsic features of normal ADS-B data, which is the foundation to distinguish attack data from hybrid stream data sets. When the model is trained offline with strong computation capability, it is practical to apply online to detect with low time delay. With the offline-online scheme, DAD-GAN method is adaptive to the stream data detection challenges. Due to the joint training and integrated usage of generative and discriminator, the method is improved on accuracy and false alarm ratio. Meanwhile, the threshold is analyzed based on large data, enhancing the robustness on detecting attack behaviors.

Nevertheless, DAD-GAN is in face of some pivotal challenges on attack detection. (1) The internal network structure is hard to determine. The amount of LSTM units and the concrete parameters are in demand of quite a few iterations to be obtained and optimized. (2) It is affected with ADS-B data quality and scale, which is relative with detection performance tightly. (3) The offline-online scheme is not flexible in comparison with online detection methods. The pre-trained model may vary with the concept shift for ADS-B data status, which eliminates the efficiency on attack behavior analysis. All the above deficiencies exist in the majority of deep novelty detection methods, which is in demand of improvements in the future.

6 Conclusion

The DAD-GAN is proposed to focus on the attack detection on ADS-B data, improving the accuracy and robustness. Taking advantage of reconstruction error and discriminative loss based on GAN, the differences between normal ADS-B data sequences and attack data sequences are magnified and identified effectively. By setting up the threshold with large scale data, the empirical factors are eliminated to support robust detection performances. However, the internal structure of DAD-GAN is difficult to determine, which is in demand of quite a few iterations to obtain optimized parameters. Meanwhile, the online sequential attack detection performance should be strengthened for DAD-GAN, which is the next work to improve its performances.

References

1. Strohmeier, M., Schafer, M., Pinheiro, R., Lenders, V., Martinovic, I.: On perception and reality in wireless air traffic communication security. IEEE Trans. Intell. Transp. Syst. **18**(6), 1338–1357 (2017). https://doi.org/10.1109/tits.2016.2612584
2. Sampigethaya, K., Poovendran, R.: Aviation cyber-physical systems: foundations for future aircraft and air transport. Proc. IEEE **101**(8), 1834–1855 (2013). https://doi.org/10.1109/JPROC.2012.2235131
3. Buczak, A.L., Guven, E.: A survey of data mining and machine learning methods for cyber security intrusion detection. IEEE Commun. Surv. Tutor. **18**(2), 1153–1176 (2016). https://doi.org/10.1109/COMST.2015.2494502
4. International Civil Aviation: Aeronautical surveillance manual. Report (2010)
5. RTCA (Firm). SC-186: Minimum Operational Performance Standards (MOPS) for 1090 MHz Extended Squitter Automatic Dependent Surveillance - Broadcast (ADS-B) and Traffic Information Services - Broadcast (TIS-B). Document (RTCA (Firm))), RTCA, Incorporated (2011). https://books.google.com/books?id=H69enQEACAAJ
6. Strohmeier, M., Lenders, V., Martinovic, I.: On the security of the automatic dependent surveillance-broadcast protocol. IEEE Commun. Surv. Tutor. **17**(2), 1066–1087 (2015). https://doi.org/10.1109/comst.2014.2365951
7. Costin, A., Francillon, A.: Ghost in the air (traffic): on insecurity of ADS-B protocol and practical attacks on ADS-B devices. Black Hat USA (2012)
8. Riahi Manesh, M., Kaabouch, N.: Analysis of vulnerabilities, attacks, countermeasures and overall risk of the automatic dependent surveillance-broadcast (ADS-B) system. Int. J. Crit. Infrastruct. Prot. **19**(Suppl. C), 16–31 (2017). https://doi.org/10.1016/j.ijcip.2017.10.002
9. Ali, B.S.: System specifications for developing an automatic dependent surveillance-broadcast (ADS-B) monitoring system. Int. J. Crit. Infrastruct. Prot. **15**, 40–46 (2016). https://doi.org/10.1016/j.ijcip.2016.06.004

10. Zhang, J.F., Liu, J., Hu, R., Zhu, H.B.: Online four dimensional trajectory prediction method based on aircraft intent updating. Aerosp. Sci. Technol. **77**, 774–787 (2018). https://doi.org/10.1016/j.ast.2018.03.037

11. Li, T.Y., Wang, B.H.: Sequential collaborative detection strategy on ADS-B data attack. Int. J. Crit. Infrastruct. Prot. **24**, 78–99 (2019). https://doi.org/10.1016/j.ijcip.2018.11.003

12. Zhang, T., Wu, R., Lai, R., Zhang, Z.: Probability hypothesis density filter for radar systematic bias estimation aided by ADS-B. Sig. Proces. **120**(Suppl. C), 280–287 (2016). https://doi.org/10.1016/j.sigpro.2015.09.012

13. Goodfellow, I.J., et al.: Generative adversarial nets. In: International Conference on Neural Information Processing Systems (2014)

14. Chalapathy, R., Chawla, S.: Deep learning for anomaly detection: a survey (2019). arXiv preprint arXiv:03407

15. Creswell, A., White, T., Dumoulin, V., Arulkumaran, K., Sengupta, B., Bharath, A.A.: Generative adversarial networks: an overview. IEEE Sig. Process. Mag. **35**(1), 53–65 (2018). https://doi.org/10.1109/MSP.2017.2765202

16. Lucic, M., Kurach, K., Michalski, M., Gelly, S., Bousquet, O.: Are GANs created equal? A large-scale study (2017)

17. Han, J., Zhang, Z., Cummins, N., Schuller, B.: Adversarial training in affective computing and sentiment analysis: recent advances and perspectives [review article]. IEEE Comput. Intell. Mag. **14**(2), 68–81 (2019). https://doi.org/10.1109/MCI.2019.2901088

18. Tian, K., Zhou, S., Fan, J., Guan, J.: Learning competitive and discriminative reconstructions for anomaly detection. arXiv preprint arXiv:07058

19. Ruff, L., et al.: Deep one-class classification. In: International Conference on Machine Learning, pp. 4390–4399

20. Kahng, M., Thorat, N., Chau, D.H., Viégas, F.B., Wattenberg, M.: GAN lab: understanding complex deep generative models using interactive visual experimentation. IEEE Trans. Vis. Comput. Graph. **25**(1), 310–320 (2019). https://doi.org/10.1109/TVCG.2018.2864500

21. Esteban, C., Hyland, S.L., Rätsch, G.: Real-valued (medical) time series generation with recurrent conditional GANs (2017)

22. Li, D., Chen, D., Shi, L., Jin, B., Goh, J., Ng, S.K.: MAD-GAN: multivariate anomaly detection for time series data with generative adversarial networks (2019)

23. Mahmoud, M.S.B., Pirovano, A., Larrieu, N.: Aeronautical communication transition from analog to digital data: a network security survey. Comput. Sci. Rev. **11–12**, 1–29 (2014)

24. Strohmeier, M., Lenders, V., Martinovic, I.: A localization approach for crowdsourced air traffic communication networks. IEEE Trans. Aerosp. Electron. Syst. **PP**(99), 1 (2016)

25. Jeon, D., Eun, Y., Kim, H.: Estimation fusion with radar and ADS-B for air traffic surveillance. Int. J. Control Autom. Syst. **13**(2), 336–345 (2015). https://doi.org/10.1007/s12555-014-0060-1

26. Schafer, M., Strohmeier, M., Smith, M., Fuchs, M., Lenders, V., Martinovic, I.: IEEE: OpenSky report 2018: assessing the integrity of crowdsourced mode S and ADS-B data. In: IEEE-AIAA Digital Avionics Systems Conference, pp. 1388–1396. IEEE, New York (2018)

Stealthy and Sparse False Data Injection Attacks Based on Machine Learning

Jiwei Tian[1](✉) ⓘ, Buhong Wang[1], Tengyao Li[1], Fute Shang[1],
Kunrui Cao[2], and Jing Li[3]

[1] Information and Navigation College,
Air Force Engineering University, Xi'an, China
tianjiwei2016@163.com
[2] National University of Defense Technology, Xi'an, China
ckredu@sina.com
[3] Henan University of Technology, Zhengzhou, China
503245609@qq.com

Abstract. Power grid cyber-physical systems face a variety of cyber-attacks. Machine learning based stealthy false data injection attacks are explored in this paper. To avoid the detection of the Bad Data Detector, two issues are considered in the machine learning based attack strategy. One is how to use machine learning to generate suitable attack vectors based on eavesdropping measurements. The other is how to improve the robustness of the attack strategy if there are corrupted measurements or outliers. Considering these two problems, a robust linear regression based false data injection attack strategy is proposed. Moreover, a more sparse attack strategy is also explored to further reduce the cost of attackers. Simulations conducted on the IEEE 14-bus system verify the effectiveness of the attack strategies.

Keywords: Machine learning · Linear regression · Cyber security · False data injection

1 Introduction

The autonomous decentralized system model is not only widely used in the computer [1] and transportation [2] fields, but also gradually adopted in the power system [3]. With the development of information and communication technology, the power system cyber-physical system (PGCPS) is accelerating the transition to the Smart Grid, which is more vulnerable to various cyber-attacks. As a typical infrastructure, cyber-attacks against the power grid can have catastrophic effects, such as the 2015 Ukraine Blackout event.

In various cyber-attacks, false data injection (FDI) attacks proposed in [4] pose a huge threat to the security of the power system. The reason is twofold. One is that well-designed FDI attacks [5, 6] are stealthy, the other is that these attacks can manipulate electricity for profit [7, 8] or even result in cascading failures [9]. In order to improve the security of the power system, a large number of researches on FDI attacks have been conducted. These researches can be divided into three categories: attack strategies,

© Springer Nature Switzerland AG 2019
J. Vaidya et al. (Eds.): CSS 2019, LNCS 11982, pp. 337–347, 2019.
https://doi.org/10.1007/978-3-030-37337-5_27

detection methods, and defense technologies. Machine learning and deep learning (ML/DL) have made great progress in the past few years and have also been used in the research on FDI attacks, discussed below.

Two machine learning based techniques (Distributed SVM and Anomaly Detection) for stealthy attack detection were proposed in [10]. Popular batch and online learning algorithms were used to detect cyber-attacks [11]. An online attack detection algorithm using a model-free reinforcement learning (RL) framework was explored in [12]. Besides, many deep learning methods [13–15] were proposed to detect cyber-attacks in the power system, including convolutional neural network (CNN), recurrent neural networks (RNN). A novel approach based on deep neural network (DNN) [16] was proposed to help identify and classify various cyber-attacks.

As a widely used technology, machine learning can be used not only to detect various faults and attacks but also to carry out cyber-attacks. However, in the literature, there is very little research on FDI attacks based on machine learning. A novel attack strategy using linear regression (LR) was proposed in [17]. The LR based FDI attacks can circumvent the detection of the Bad Data Detector (BDD). Besides, attackers do not need knowledge about the topological and electrical parameters of the power system to generate attack vectors. This makes LR based FDI attacks more practical because the above parameters belong to the confidential information of the system and are usually strongly protected. As far as we know, it is the first paper trying to design FDI attacks based on machine learning.

Although the FDI attack based on LR is more practical, the assumption is not realistic because attackers should eavesdrop all the sensor measurements correctly. As we all know, although the interception from the meters is applicable during the transmission of meter data [18], missing and grossly corrupted observations are also ubiquitous due to sensor failures or communication errors [19].

Normal LR estimator is very sensitive to unusual values or outliers. Even one outlier can have a large effect on the parameter estimates [20]. In this case, the LR based FDI attacks may be detected by the BDD. To improve the hiddenness of the LR based FDI attacks, we proposed an attack strategy based on robust linear regression (RLR). Besides, to further reduce the cost of attackers, a more sparse attack strategy is also presented.

The remainder of this paper is organized as follows. The state estimation and LR based FDI attacks are introduced in Sect. 2. In Sect. 3, an RLR-based FDI attack strategy is proposed to overcome the issue of outliers. Extensive experimental results based on IEEE 14-bus system are presented in Sect. 4. Conclusions are given in Sect. 5.

2 State Estimation and LR Based FDI Attacks

2.1 State Estimation

Sensor measurements are collected through SCADA (Supervisory Control And Data Acquisition) for further processing. In DC state estimation, the linearized model is as follows:

$$z = Hx + e \tag{1}$$

where z and x represent measurement vector and state vector respectively, H is the system matrix, and e denotes random noises in measurements. In general, weighted least square (WLS) method is applied to obtain the system state vector:

$$\hat{x} = (H^T W H)^{-1} H^T W z \tag{2}$$

where W denotes diagonal covariance matrix. Once the estimated state is derived, the Bad Data Detector (BDD) is applied to detect bad measurement data based on chi-square (χ^2) test. The residue is calculated as follows:

$$\hat{z} = H\hat{x} \tag{3}$$

$$r = z - \hat{z} \tag{4}$$

where $\hat{z}$ denotes estimated measurements. If z and $\hat{z}$ match each other, i.e., $\|r\| \leq \tau$, z is regarded as the normal measurement. Otherwise, bad data is detected.

2.2 LR Based FDI Attacks

In [17], FDI attacks based on LR are proposed. Using the eavesdropped data, attackers can explore the intrinsic linear correlations between the sensor measurements based on LR.

$$h_\theta(z_j) = \theta_{0(j,i)} + \theta_{1(j,i)} z_j \quad i = 1, 2, 3, \cdots, m \tag{5}$$

where z_j is the jth measurement, z_i is the ith measurement, $\theta_{0(j,i)}$ and $\theta_{1(j,i)}$ are learned best-fit coefficients by minimizing the cost as follows:

$$J = \frac{1}{2n} \sum_{l=1}^{n} (h(z_l) - z_l)^2 \tag{6}$$

Then attackers can choose arbitrary sensor to attack and the whole attack vector will be generated based on derived linear correlations:

$$z_{ia} = \theta_{0(j,i)} + \theta_{1(j,i)} z_{ja} \quad i = 1, 2, 3, \cdots, m \tag{7}$$

3 FDI Attacks Based on RLR

Although the LR based FDI attacks in [17] can circumvent the detection of BDD, the assumption is not realistic because attackers need to obtain all true measurements in the complex and changing environment. As we all know, during the transmission of meter data, missing and grossly corrupted observations are ubiquitous due to sensor failures

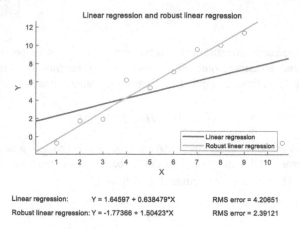

Linear regression: Y = 1.64597 + 0.638479*X   RMS error = 4.20651
Robust linear regression: Y = -1.77366 + 1.50423*X   RMS error = 2.39121

Fig. 1. Comparison of LR and RLR

or communication errors. These outliers will seriously affect the estimation parameter of LR as shown in Fig. 1.

In this case, based on the seriously affected fit coefficients, the LR based FDI attacks may be detected by the BDD. Then the attack is valid. To overcome this issue, a robust version of LR based FDI attack strategy is proposed. The main idea of the method in robust estimation is to modify the objective function in classical least squares regression which is very sensitive to outliers.

The principle of robust regression is to mitigate the influence of outliers on regression coefficients and choose a function with slower growth. M-estimation (Maximum Likelihood Estimation) is often used as a method for robust regression parameter estimation. The purpose is to ensure the correctness of the regression parameters as much as possible under the premise that the samples may have outliers. The principle is shown as follows:

$$\hat{\beta}_M = \arg \min_{\beta} \sum_{i=1}^{n} \rho(y_i - x_i^T \beta) = \arg \min_{\beta} \sum_{i=1}^{n} \rho(r_i(\beta)) \tag{8}$$

where ρ represents the objective function, r_i is the residual item, $r_i = y_i - x_i^T \beta$.

As shown in Fig. 1, the M-estimation based RLR has a better performance than LR. The proposed robust attack strategy is summarized in Algorithm 1.

In general, attack vectors usually comprise a large number of small entry values, which are always tolerated if their average energy is within the variance of the measurement noise. On the contrary, the large elements of the attack vector are the focus of our attention. Therefore, a shrinkage operator is defined as follows:

$$S_\tau(x) = \begin{cases} x, & |x| \geq \tau \\ 0, & |x| < \tau \end{cases} \tag{9}$$

Algorithm 1: Robust linear regression based FDI attacks

Input: Z =data matrix (with outliers);

1. **Calculate fit coefficients** θ by keeping arbitrarily chosen measurement as input and all other measurements as output one by one based on **Robust linear regression**

2. **Set the attack magnitude** for the chosen measurement

3. **Calculate the whole attack vector** a based on calculated fit coefficients

Output: corrupted measurement data $z_a = z + a$

where τ is a threshold that should be adjusted considering the stealth and sparsity of the designed attack vector. The sparse RLR based strategy is presented in Algorithm 2.

Algorithm 2: Sparse RLR based FDI attacks

Input: Z =data matrix (with outliers);

1. **Calculate fit coefficients** θ by keeping arbitrarily chosen measurement as input and all other measurements as output one by one based on **Robust linear regression**

2. **Set the attack magnitude** for the chosen measurement

3. **Calculate the whole attack vector** a based on calculated fit coefficients

4. **Calculate the sparse attack vector** a based on

$$S_\tau(x) = \begin{cases} x, & |x| \geq \tau \\ 0, & |x| < \tau \end{cases}$$

Output: corrupted measurement data $z_a = z + a$

4 Results and Discussion

4.1 Test System

To evaluate the performance of the proposed strategy, simulations are conducted on IEEE 14-bus system, as shown in Fig. 2.

Every load bus in IEEE 14-bus system is linked with corresponding load zone of NYISO [21] as shown in Table 1. Based on NYISO data from Jan 1, 2018 to Jan 31, 2018, all the measurements are derived. The procedure to generate measurements is given in [22]. Gaussian noise cases are considered, i.e., the signal-to-noise ratio (SNR) is set as 5 dB. Besides, we add 0.01% outliers to the measurement matrix.

342   J. Tian et al.

Table 1. Corresponding relations between load buses of the test system and load regions of NYISO.

Load zone	A	B	C	D	E	F	G	H	I	J	K
Load bus	2	3	4	5	6	9	10	11	12	13	14

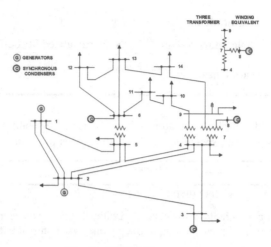

Fig. 2. IEEE 14-bus system

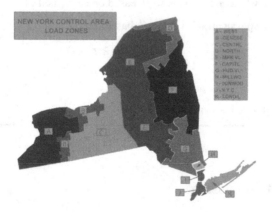

Fig. 3. NYISO map of 11 load regions in New York State, USA

4.2 Simulations Analysis

In the simulations, measurement z_5 is set as the input, fit coefficients θ are calculated by keeping z_5 as input and all other measurements as output one by one. The derived coefficients based on RLR are shown in Table 2. For comparison, LR based on coefficients using normal measurements and measurements with outliers are also listed.

Table 2. Corresponding relations between load buses of the test system and load regions of NYISO.

	LR (with outliers)		LR (no outliers)		RLR (with outliers)	
	θ_0	θ_1	θ_0	θ_1	θ_0	θ_1
$\theta_{(5,1)}$	55.43	−21.32	63.60	−20.44	60.63	−20.86
$\theta_{(5,2)}$	29.27	1.42	28.28	1.31	28.50	1.34
$\theta_{(5,3)}$	−35.21	7.92	−45.28	6.43	−43.96	6.62
$\theta_{(5,4)}$	−12.93	4.82	−16.68	4.09	−16.01	4.18
$\theta_{(5,5)}$	0.00	1.00	0.00	1.00	0.00	1.00
$\theta_{(5,6)}$	−4.95	0.79	−3.19	1.05	−3.07	1.07
$\theta_{(5,7)}$	0.00	0.00	0.00	0.00	0.00	0.00
$\theta_{(5,8)}$	0.00	0.00	0.00	0.00	0.00	0.00
$\theta_{(5,9)}$	−14.70	2.00	−8.87	2.71	−8.54	2.76
$\theta_{(5,10)}$	−3.00	0.79	−3.00	0.79	−2.95	0.80
$\theta_{(5,11)}$	0.57	0.40	−0.20	0.43	−0.17	0.44
$\theta_{(5,12)}$	−10.32	−0.36	−1.89	0.55	−1.83	0.56
$\theta_{(5,13)}$	−8.75	0.53	−5.51	1.05	−5.32	1.08
$\theta_{(5,14)}$	5.41	2.66	−3.80	1.46	−3.70	1.47
$\theta_{(5,15)}$	45.97	−13.60	40.23	−14.15	38.12	−14.45
$\theta_{(5,16)}$	29.94	−5.49	23.18	−6.31	22.29	−6.44
$\theta_{(5,17)}$	36.19	−4.60	31.29	−5.09	30.39	−5.22
$\theta_{(5,18)}$	37.19	−1.90	21.23	−4.46	20.64	−4.54
$\theta_{(5,19)}$	14.87	−3.07	16.08	−3.27	15.70	−3.33
$\theta_{(5,20)}$	−14.16	1.32	−14.16	1.32	−13.73	1.38
$\theta_{(5,21)}$	−22.77	5.12	−22.77	5.12	−21.90	5.25
$\theta_{(5,22)}$	8.23	−2.65	8.23	−2.65	7.98	−2.68
$\theta_{(5,23)}$	4.74	−1.55	4.74	−1.55	4.63	−1.57
$\theta_{(5,24)}$	13.39	3.87	13.39	−3.87	12.98	−3.92
$\theta_{(5,25)}$	1.59	−0.68	1.59	−0.68	1.53	−0.68
$\theta_{(5,26)}$	2.59	−0.66	2.59	−0.66	2.50	−0.67
$\theta_{(5,27)}$	5.91	−1.49	5.91	−1.49	5.73	−1.52
$\theta_{(5,28)}$	0.00	0.00	0.00	0.00	0.00	0.00
$\theta_{(5,29)}$	8.38	−2.63	8.38	−2.63	8.15	−2.66
$\theta_{(5,30)}$	28.99	2.89	1.59	−0.55	1.57	−0.55
$\theta_{(5,31)}$	0.84	−1.18	2.69	−0.91	2.63	−0.92
$\theta_{(5,32)}$	−1.32	0.25	−1.32	0.25	−1.29	0.25
$\theta_{(5,33)}$	0.59	−0.12	0.59	−0.12	0.57	−0.12
$\theta_{(5,34)}$	4.63	0.01	1.11	−0.55	1.10	−0.55

From Table 2, we can see that with outliers, fit coefficients based on RLR and LR are significantly different. However, fit coefficients based on RLR are very similar with fit coefficients with normal measurement (no outliers). It means that with outliers RLR can explore the linear correlations correctly but LR cannot.

Based on derived fit coefficients, attack vectors are generated. As the IEEE 14 bus system has 34 sensors and 13 states, the degree of freedom is 21. Considering the chi-square test of the 95% confidence interval, the threshold of the BDD is 32.67. For comparison, three cases are considered and in each case, the original attack input for measurement z_5 is the same. The three cases are shown from Figs. 4, 5 and 6. In the case (LR with outliers) Fig. 4, there is a clear difference between attacked and estimated measurements, resulting in the residual 140.27, which is large than the threshold 32.67. It means that the LR based FDI attacks will be detected by the BDD. However, in the case (RLR with outliers) Fig. 5, the estimated measurements follow the attacked measurements closely, leading to the residual 7.95, which is small than the threshold 32.67. This means that even with outliers our proposed RLR based FDI attacks can remain stealthy. In the case (LR without outliers) Fig. 6, measurements without outliers are considered as in [17]. The residual is 7.88, which is close to the residual 7.95 in the RLR based case. These residuals are mainly due to the Gaussian noises introduced in the measurements and nearly equal residuals mean that RLR based FDI attacks can overcome the adverse effects of outliers.

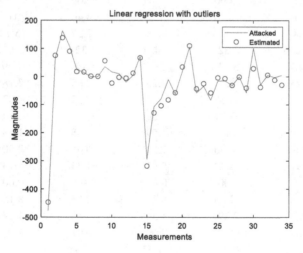

Fig. 4. Attacked and estimated measurements based on LR with outliers

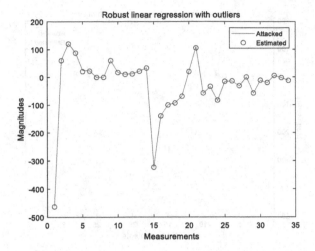

Fig. 5. Attacked and estimated measurements based on RLR with outliers

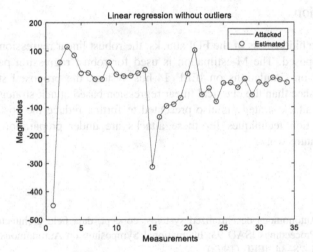

Fig. 6. Attacked and estimated measurements based on LR without outliers

Finally, we also evaluate the performance of the sparse RLR based strategy. Take the case (RLR with outliers, Fig. 5) for example, attackers need control 33 sensors to carry out the FDI attack. If the sparse RLR based strategy adopted, we can reduce the number of controlled sensors to 22 (the threshold τ is set as 20). The new attack vector is shown in Fig. 7. The new residual is 24.7, which is also small than the threshold 32.67. For attackers, it is a suitable strategy to further reduce the attack cost because controlling more sensors means more cost and energy.

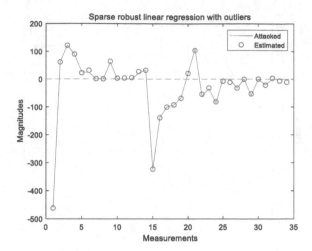

Fig. 7. Attacked and estimated measurements based on Sparse RLR with outliers

5 Conclusion

To improve the hiddenness of the FDI attacks, the robust linear regression based attack strategy is proposed. The M-estimation is used for robust regression parameter estimation. Based on simulations on IEEE 14-bus system, the proposed strategy has a better performance than the classical linear regression based attack strategy. Moreover, a more sparse attack strategy is also presented to further reduce the cost of attackers. Effective detection techniques for these attacks are under preparation and will be presented in future work.

References

1. Mori, K.: Autonomous decentralized systems: concept, data field architecture and future trends. In: Proceedings ISAD 93: International Symposium on Autonomous Decentralized Systems, pp. 28–34. IEEE (1993)
2. Vallee, M., Merdan, M., Lepuschitz, W., Koppensteiner, G.: Decentralized reconfiguration of a flexible transportation system. IEEE Trans. Industr. Inf. **7**(3), 505–516 (2011)
3. Xu, Q., et al.: A decentralized dynamic power sharing strategy for hybrid energy storage system in autonomous DC microgrid. IEEE Trans. Industr. Electron. **64**(7), 5930–5941 (2017)
4. Liu, Y., Ning, P., Reiter, M.K.: False data injection attacks against state estimation in electric power grids. ACM Trans. Inf. Syst. Secur. (TISSEC) **14**(1), 13 (2011)
5. Tian, J., Wang, B., Li, X.: Data-driven and low-sparsity false data injection attacks in smart grid. Secur. Commun. Netw. **2018**, 11 (2018). Art. no. 8045909
6. JiWei, T., BuHong, W., FuTe, S., Shuaiqi, L.: Stealthy false data injection attacks using matrix recovery and independent component analysis in smart grid. In: IOP Conference Series: Materials Science and Engineering, vol. 199, no. 1, p. 012034. IOP Publishing (2017)

7. Xie, L., Mo, Y., Sinopoli, B.: False data injection attacks in electricity markets. In: First IEEE International Conference on Smart Grid Communications, pp. 226–231 (2010)
8. Tajer, A.: False data injection attacks in electricity markets by limited adversaries: stochastic robustness. IEEE Trans. Smart Grid **10**, 128–138 (2017)
9. Che, L., Liu, X., Ding, T., Li, Z.: Revealing impacts of cyber attacks on power grids vulnerability to cascading failures. IEEE Trans. Circuits Syst. II Express Briefs **66**, 1058–1062 (2018)
10. Esmalifalak, M., Liu, L., Nguyen, N., Zheng, R., Han, Z.: Detecting stealthy false data injection using machine learning in smart grid. IEEE Syst. J. **11**(3), 1644–1652 (2017)
11. Ozay, M., Esnaola, I., Vural, F.T.Y., Kulkarni, S.R., Poor, H.V.: Machine learning methods for attack detection in the smart grid. IEEE Trans. Neural Netw. Learn. Syst. **27**(8), 1773–1786 (2016)
12. Kurt, M.N., Ogundijo, O., Li, C., Wang, X.: Online Cyber-Attack Detection in Smart Grid: A Reinforcement Learning Approach, arXiv preprint arXiv:1809.05258 (2018)
13. Niu, X., Sun, J.: Dynamic Detection of False Data Injection Attack in Smart Grid using Deep Learning, arXiv preprint arXiv:1808.01094 (2018)
14. Ayad, A., Farag, H.E.Z., Youssef, A., El-Saadany, E.F.: Detection of false data injection attacks in smart grids using recurrent neural networks. In: IEEE Power & Energy Society Innovative Smart Grid Technologies Conference, pp. 1–5 (2018)
15. Ashrafuzzaman, M., et al.: Detecting stealthy false data injection attacks in power grids using deep learning. In: 2018 14th International Wireless Communications & Mobile Computing Conference (IWCMC), pp. 219–225. IEEE (2018)
16. Zhou, L., Ouyang, X., Ying, H., Han, L., Cheng, Y., Zhang, T.: Cyber-attack classification in smart grid via deep neural network. In: Proceedings of the 2nd International Conference on Computer Science and Application Engineering, p. 90. ACM (2018)
17. Nawaz, R., Shahid, M.A., Qureshi, I.M., Mehmood, M.H.: Machine learning based false data injection in smart grid. In: 2018 1st International Conference on Power, Energy and Smart Grid (ICPESG), pp. 1–6. IEEE (2018)
18. Li, H., Lai, L., Zhang, W.: Communication requirement for reliable and secure state estimation and control in smart grid. IEEE Trans. Smart Grid **2**(3), 476–486 (2011)
19. Anwar, A., Mahmood, A.N., Pickering, M.: Modeling and performance evaluation of stealthy false data injection attacks on smart grid in the presence of corrupted measurements. J. Comput. Syst. Sci. **83**(1), 58–72 (2017)
20. Yu, C., Yao, W.: Robust linear regression: a review and comparison. Commun. Stat. Simul. Comput. **46**(8), 6261–6282 (2017)
21. Load Data: Market and Operational Data (NYISO). http://www.nyiso.com/public/marketsoperations/index.jsp
22. Chaojun, G., Jirutitijaroen, P., Motani, M.: Detecting false data injection attacks in ac state estimation. IEEE Trans. Smart Grid **6**(5), 2476–2483 (2015)

Automated Detection System for Adversarial Examples with High-Frequency Noises Sieve

Dang Duy Thang$^{(\boxtimes)}$ and Toshihiro Matsui

The Institute of Information Security, Yokohama, Japan
{dgs174101,matsui}@iisec.ac.jp
http://lab.iisec.ac.jp/matsui_lab/

Abstract. Deep neural networks are being applied in many tasks with encouraging results, and have often reached human-level performance. However, deep neural networks are vulnerable to well-designed input samples called adversarial examples. In particular, neural networks tend to misclassify adversarial examples that are imperceptible to humans. This paper introduces a new detection system that automatically detects adversarial examples on deep neural networks. Our proposed system can mostly distinguish adversarial samples and benign images in an end-to-end manner without human intervention. We exploit the important role of the frequency domain in adversarial samples, and propose a method that detects malicious samples in observations. When evaluated on two standard benchmark datasets (MNIST and ImageNet), our method achieved an out-detection rate of 99.7–100% in many settings.

Keywords: Deep Neural Networks · Adversarial examples · Detection systems

1 Introduction

Deep Neural Networks (DNNs) were developed as a machine learning approach to many complex tasks. Traditional machine learning methods are successful when the final value is a simple function of the input data. Conversely, DNNs can capture the composite relations between millions of pixels and textual descriptions, brand-related news, future stock prices, and other contextual information. DNNs attain state-of-the-art performance in practical tasks of many domains, such as natural language processing, image processing, and speech recognition [9]. Current state-of-the-art DNNs are usually designed to be robust to noisy data; that is, the estimated label of a DNN output is insensitive to small noises in the data. Noise robustness is a fundamental characteristic of DNN applications in real, uncontrolled, and possibly hostile environments. However, recent research has shown that DNNs are vulnerable to specially-crafted adversarial perturbations (also known as adversarial examples) [3,5], well-designed fluctuating inputs

© Springer Nature Switzerland AG 2019
J. Vaidya et al. (Eds.): CSS 2019, LNCS 11982, pp. 348–362, 2019.
https://doi.org/10.1007/978-3-030-37337-5_28

that are added to clean inputs. Developers of machine learning models assume a legitimate environment in both training and testing. Intuitively, the inputs X are assumed to come from the same distribution during both training and test times. That is, if the test inputs X are new and previously unseen during the training process, they at least have the same properties as the inputs used for training. These assumptions ensure a powerful machine learning model, but any attacker can alter the distribution during either the training time [20] or the testing time [1]. Typical training attacks [6] try to inject adversarial training data into the original training set. If successful, these data will wrongly train the deep learning model. However, most of the existing adversarial methods attack the testing phase [2,12], which is more reliable than attacking the training phase. Especially, training-phase attacks are more difficult to implement and should not be launched without first exploiting the machine learning system. For example, an attacker might slightly modify an image [20], causing it to be recognized incorrectly, or adjust the code of an executable file to enable its escape by a malware detector [4]. Many researchers have developed defense mechanisms against adversarial examples. For example, Papernot et al. [15] deployed a distillation algorithm against adversarial perturbations. However, as pointed out by Carnili et al. [2], this method cannot improve the robustness of a DNN system. Several other adversarial defense approaches have also been published [2,12]. Carlini et al. [2] proposed new attacks based on three previously used distance metrics: L_0, L_2 and L_∞, and evaluated the defenses of DNNs under the proposed attack methods. Madry et al. [12] applied a natural saddle-point method that guards against adversarial examples in a principled manner. They found that the network architecture affects the adversarial robustness of a DNN, so the robust decision boundary of the saddle-point problem can be more complicated than a decision boundary that simply categorizes the legitimate data. Preprocessing-based defense strategies against adversarial examples, which are the focus of our current work, will be reviewed and discussed in Sect. 2.

Our Contributions. This paper introduces new techniques for overcoming adversarial examples. Our proposed system can automatically detect and classify both adversarial and legitimate samples. Assuming that most of the adversarial perturbations are created in the high frequencies of the image, we seek to reduce the high-frequency adversarial noises while retaining the benign high-frequency features. To prove our hypothesis, we first installed a low-pass filter layer between the adversarial example and target classifier. The probability of detecting the target class by the classifier dropped significantly (to nearly zero), but the recognition results of the primary class were retained. In Sect. 3, we demonstrate the correctness of these implementations in a theoretical proof. Based on the previous observation, we propose a new end-to-end system that automatically detects adversarial examples by a sieve layer inserted between the input and DNN, which traps suspicious noises. In parallel with this process, the un-sieved input is fed to the classifier and the highest-confidence class is marked as an anchor. The probabilities of the anchor and sieved input from the classifier are then compared, and the final decision on the input (adversarial or benign) is determined by a specified fixed threshold. Our main idea is depicted in Fig. 1.

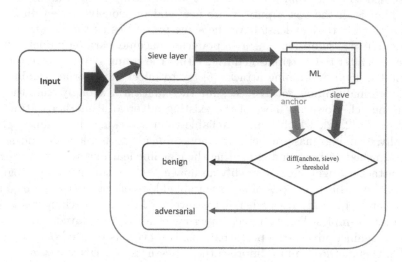

Fig. 1. Processes of our automated detection system: an input is duplicated and the actual and duplicated inputs are directed into two parallel processing flows. In one processing direction (green arrow), the high-frequency adversarial noises are captured by the sieve layer; in the other direction (yellow arrow), all data are forwarded to the target model. The probability of the highest-confidence class is designated as the anchor for tracking in the green direction (called the sieve in our system). By comparing the difference between the anchor and sieve based on a fixed threshold, our system identifies the input as benign or adversarial. (Color figure online)

The main contributions of this paper are as follows:

- We investigated and analyzed various attack approaches for crafting adversarial examples. By summarizing the different attack strategies, we provide an intuitive overview of these attack methods.
- We investigated the modern defense approaches and their variants in adversarial settings. We assumed that most of the adversarial perturbations are created at high frequencies. After implementing many experiments based on our theoretical framework, we confidently affirm our hypothesis.
- After thoroughly analyzing our experimental and theoretical observations, we created a new automated detection method for adversarial examples. Our approach differs from previous researches, in which the experimental steps are typically based only on the original hypothesis. Our approach was successfully applied to two types of common datasets: a small-scale dataset (Modified National Institute of Standards and Technology [MNIST]) and a large-scale dataset (ImageNet). Our defense method accurately classified the adversarial examples and legitimate samples. Moreover, in some cases, it recovered the high accuracy rates of the DNN classification.

Outlines of the Paper. The remainder of this paper is organized as follows. Section 2 introduces related works, the background of adversarial examples, and current adversarial attack/defense approaches. Section 3 describes our proposed method, and Sect. 4 presents our experiments and evaluation results on both benchmark datasets (MNIST and ImageNet). Section 5 summaries our work.

2 Related Works and Background

2.1 Related Works

Removing the adversarial noises and regaining the recognition integrity of classifiers have been attempted in several works. Liao et al. [11] developed High-level representation Guided Denoiser (HGD) as a defense for image classification systems. They argued that many defense models cannot remove all adversarial perturbations, and that the non-removed adversarial noises are greatly amplified in the top layers of the target model. Consequently, the model will output a wrong prediction. To overcome this problem, they trained a denoiser by an HGD loss function. However, their proposed system was implemented only on ImageNet, which contains color images, and was not trialed on grayscale datasets such as MNIST. Although this omission is not highly important, the performance of a method based on high-level representation in a very deep neural network may degrade on grayscale images, whereas a simple neural network performs accurately on MNIST data. The strategy of Xu et al. [21], which they called "feature squeezing", reduces the number of degrees of freedom available to an adversary by squeezing out the unnecessary input features. The squeezing is performed by two denoisers performing different denoising methods: (1) squeezing the color bit depth, and (2) spatial smoothing. The prediction results are then compared with those of the target model, and the input is inferred as adversarial or legitimate. Although Xu et al. [21] evaluated their proposed method on various adversarial attacks, how they specified their thresholds on different benchmark datasets is unclear. Deciding appropriate thresholds for their system will overburden operators, and the method cannot easily adapt to new and unknown datasets.

2.2 Background

Deep Neural Networks. In this subsection, we review neural networks in detail and introduce the required notation and definitions. Neural networks consist of elementary computing units named neurons organized in interconnected layers. Each neuron applies an activation function to its input, and produces an output. Starting with the input to the machine learning model, the output produced by each layer of the network provides the input to the next layer. Networks with a single intermediate hidden layer are called shallow neural networks, whereas those with multiple hidden layers are DNNs. The multiple hidden layers hierarchically extract representations from the model input, eventually producing a representation for solving the machine learning task and outputting a prediction. A neural network model F can be formalized as multidimensional and parametrized functions f_i, each corresponding to one layer of the network architecture and one representation of the input. Specifically, each vector θ_i parametrizes layer i of the network F and includes weights for the links connecting layer i to layer i_1. The set of model parameters $\theta = \{\theta_i\}$ is learned during training. For instance, in supervised learning, the parameter values are learned by computing the prediction errors $f(x) - y$ on a collection of known input–output pairs (x, y).

Adversarial Attacks. The adversarial examples and their counterparts are considered to be indistinguishable by humans. Because human perception is difficult to model, it is often approximated by three distance metrics based on the L_p norm:

$$||x||_p = \left(\sum_{i=1}^{n} |x_i|^p \right)^{\frac{1}{p}}. \tag{1}$$

The L_0, L_2, L_∞ metrics are usually used for expressing different aspects of visual significance. L_0 counts the number of pixels with different values at the corresponding positions in two images. This measure describes the number of pixels that differ between two images. L_2 measures the Euclidean distance between two images, and L_∞ helps to measure the maximum difference among all pixels at the corresponding positions in two images. The best distance metric depends on the proposed algorithms.

Szegedy et al. [19] created targeted adversarial examples by a method called Limited-memory Broyden-Fletcher-Goldfarb-Shanno (L-BFGS), which minimizes the weighted sum of the perturbation size ε and loss function $L(x^*, y_{target})$ while constraining the elements of x^* to normal pixel values.

According to Goodfellow et al. [3], adversarial examples can be caused by the cumulative effects of high-dimensional model weights. They proposed a simple attack method called the Fast Gradient Sign Method (FGSM):

$$x^* = x + \varepsilon \cdot sign(\nabla_x L(x, y)), \tag{2}$$

Where ε denotes the perturbation size for crafting an adversarial example x^* from an original input x. Given a clean image x, this method attempts to create a similar image x^* in the L_∞ neighborhood of x that fools the target classifier. This process maximizes the loss function $L(x, y)$, which defines the cost of classifying image x as the target label y. The FGSM solves this problem by performing one-step gradient updates from x in the input space with a small perturbation ε. Increasing ε increases the magnitude and speed of the attack-success rate, but widens the difference between the adversarial sample and the original input. FGSM computes the gradients only once, so is much more efficient than L-BFGS. Despite its simplicity, FGSM is a fast and powerful generator of adversarial examples. FGSM maximizes the loss function $L(x, y)$ by gradient descent (GD), a standard method for solving unconstrained optimization problems. Meanwhile, constrained problems can be solved by projected gradient descent (PGD). Madry et al. [12] applied PGD in a new adversarial attack method defined as:

$$x^* = x + \delta \cdot (\triangledown L\,(x, y))\ \text{respect to project}_{(x,\epsilon)}(x^*) \tag{3}$$

where $\text{project}_{(x,\epsilon)}(x^*)$ defines a projection operator with parameter x^* on the circle area around x with radius ϵ, δ is a clip value that is searched in a box (x, ϵ). In this paper, we employ both FGSM and PGD in the attack phase. The adversarial attacks are created by a method called the attacking model. When the attacking model is the target model itself or contains the target model, the resulting attacks are white-box. In the present work, our method also operates in a white-box manner.

Adversarial Defenses. Adversarial training of machine learning systems has been extensively researched [7,8]. This strategy trains the models on adversarial examples to improve their attack robustness. Some researchers have combined data augmentation with adversarial perturbed data for training [7,8,19]. However, this training is more time consuming than traditional training on clean images alone, because it adds an extra training dataset to the training set, which clearly extends the training time. In other defense strategies based on pre-processing, the perturbation noise is removed before feeding the data into a machine learning model. Meng et al. [13] proposed a two-phase defense model that first detects the adversarial input, and then reforms the original input based on the difference between the manifolds of the original and adversarial examples. Another adversarial defense direction is based on the gradient masking method [7]. By virtue of the gradient masking, this defense strategy typically ensures high smoothness in specific directions and neighborhoods of the training data, inhibiting attackers from finding the gradients of the good candidate directions. Accordingly, they cannot perturb the input in a damaging way. Papernot et al. [15] adapted distillation to adversarial defense, and trained the target model on soft labels output by another machine learning model. Nguyen and Sinha [14] developed a gradient masking method to defend against C&W attacks [2], in which the noise is appended to the network logit layer. Gu et al. [5] proposed the deep contrastive network, which imposes a layer-wise contrastive penalty to achieve output invariance under input perturbations. However, methods based on gradient masking can be replaced by a substitute model (a copy that imitates the defended model), which attackers can train by observing the labels assigned by the defended model to inputs that are chosen carefully by the adversary.

3 Proposed End-to-End System

3.1 Attack Phase

Our targeted attack settings are white-box, meaning that attackers can fully access the model type, model architecture, and all trainable parameters.

The adversary aims to change the classifier's prediction to some specific target class. Using the available information, the attackers identify the vulnerable portion of the feature space, or seek the victim decision boundaries. The clean input of the victim model is then altered by adversarial example methods. Adversarial samples that will be misclassified by machine learning models are generated by an adversary with knowledge of the model's classifier f and its trainable parameters. In this work, adversarial examples are created by the FGSM [3] and PGD methods [12]. We first define a classifier function $f : \mathbb{R}^n \to [1...k]$ that maps the image pixel-value vectors to a particular label. We then assume a loss function $L : \mathbb{R}^n \times [1...k] \to \mathbb{R}$ for function f. Given an input image $x \in \mathbb{R}^n$ and target label $y \in [1...k]$, our system attempts to optimize $\delta + L(x + \delta, y)$ subject to $x + \delta \in [0,1]^n$, where δ is a perturbation noise added to the original image x. Note that this function solves $f(x)$ in the case of convex losses, but can only approximately solve neural network problems, which involve non-convex losses. In this case, the gradient is computed not from the Softmax output, but from the output of the second-to-last layer logits. Our PGD-based attack phase is described by Algorithm 1. In FGSM, Algorithm 1 is executed without constraining $||\delta_x||_\infty$. In the attack phase, the learning rate for crafting adversarial examples was set to 0.01 and the process was iterated 500 times. The targeted output images were created from clean input images.

Algorithm 1: Algorithm for Crafting Adversarial Examples

---

    input   : $x, y_{true}, y^*, f, \epsilon, \alpha$
    output   : x^*
    parameter : learning rate $= 0.01$, epochs $= 500$

1 $x \leftarrow x^*$ // initial adversarial sample
2 $\delta_x \leftarrow 0$ // initial perturbation factor
3 **while** $||\delta_x||_\infty < \epsilon$ *and* $f(x^*) \neq y^*$ **do**
4      $x^* \leftarrow x + \alpha \cdot sign(\triangledown L(y^*|x^*))$
5   maximize $L(y^*|x^*)$ with respect to $||\delta_x||_\infty$
6      $x^* \leftarrow clip(x^*, x - \alpha, x + \alpha)$
7      $\delta_x \leftarrow (x^* - x)$
8 **end**
9 **return** x^*

3.2   Detection Phase

To create a new benchmark dataset for our detection system, we combined benign images with the adversarial images created in the attack phase. Assuming that the adversarial noises are high- frequency features on the images, we targeted the high-frequency domains on the images while retaining all features in the low-frequency areas. Various common algorithms are available for reducing image noises before further processing such as classification. In this work, we investigate the two most well-known filters in image denoising studies: linear and non-linear filters. For example, consider a new array with the same dimensions as the specified image. Fill each location of this new array with the weighted sum of the pixel values from the locations surrounding the corresponding location in the image, using a constant weight set. The result of this procedure is shift-invariant meaning that the output value depends on the pattern (not the positions) of the image neighborhood. It is also linear, meaning that summing the two images yields the same output as summing the separate outputs of both images. This procedure, known as linear filtering, smooths the noises in the images. One famous linear filter is the Gaussian filter, defined as

$$G_\sigma(i,j) = \frac{1}{2\pi\sigma^2} e^{-\frac{i^2+j^2}{2\sigma^2}}. \tag{4}$$

Here, i, j denotes the coordinate signal of the input and σ is the standard deviation of the Gaussian distribution. Alternatively, noise removal can be considered as filtering by a statistical estimator. In particular, the goal is to estimate the actual image value of a pixel in a noisy measurement scenario. The class of noise-removal filters is difficult to analyze, but is extremely useful. Smoothing an image by a symmetric Gaussian kernel replaces a pixel value with some weighted average of its neighbors. If an image has been corrupted by stationary additive zero-mean Gaussian noise, then this weighted average can reasonably estimate the original value of the pixel. The expected noise response is zero. Weighting the spatial frequencies provides a better estimate than simply averaging the pixel values. However, when the image noise is not stationary additive Gaussian noise, the situation becomes more complicated. In particular, consider that a region of the image has a constant dark value with a single bright pixel composed of noise. After smoothing with a Gaussian, a smooth, Gaussian-like bright bump will be centered on the noise pixel. In this way, the weighted average can be arbitrarily and severely affected by very large noise values. The bump can be rendered arbitrarily bright by introducing an arbitrarily bright pixel, possibly by transient error in reading a memory element. When this undesirable property does not develop, the estimator outputs robust estimates. The most well-known robust estimator computes the median of a set of values from its neighborhood. A median filter assigns a neighborhood shape (which can significantly affect the behavior of the filter). As in convolution, this neighborhood shape is passed over the image, but the median filter replaces the current value of the element by median of the neighborhood values. For the neighborhood surrounding (i, j), the filter is described by:

$$x_{ij} = median(X_{uv}|X_{uv} \in \mathbb{N}_{ij}), \tag{5}$$

where X_{uv} denotes the neighborhood points of x_{ij}. Any adversarial noises can be attenuated by smoothing the pixels in the image. When adversarial noises are absent, smoothing the pixels does not severely affect the input-image quality, so the target classifier still recognizes the correct label. We name this process the sieve process (indicated by the green arrow in Fig. 1).

Our proposed detection system runs the sieve and anchor processes in parallel. The sieve process arrests the high frequencies in the input processing while the anchor process transfers the input directly to the machine learning model. The probability of the highest-confidence class from the machine learning model is assigned as the anchor. The sieve process then tracks the oscillations of classes similar to the anchor class. If the probabilities p of the anchor and sieve differ by more or less than the fixed threshold Θ, our system confidently determines the input as adversarial or benign, respectively. Our system proceeds by Algorithm 2, where κ denotes the kernel size, f is a machine learning function that computes the probabilities of the predicted class, and s is the sieve function. The sieve function based on the Gaussian filter is called the Detection System based on Gaussian (DSG); the other sieve function is Detection System based on Median (DSM).

Algorithm 2: Automated Detection System of Adversarial Examples with a High-Frequency Sieve

---

    input   : X, Θ, s, f
    output   : $0, 1$
    // 0: benign; 1: adversarial
    parameter : $\kappa = [(3 \times 3); (5 \times 5)]$

1 **for** k_{size} *in* κ **do**
2 | **for** x *in* X **do**
3 | | $anchor_x \leftarrow x$
4 | | $sieve_x \leftarrow x$
5 | | $sieve_x \leftarrow s(sieve_x, k_{size})$
6 | | $p(anchor_y) \leftarrow f(anchor_x)$
7 | | $p(sieve_y) \leftarrow f(sieve_x | anchor_y)$
8 | **end**
9 **end**
10 **if** $diff(p(anchor_y), min(p(sieve_y))) > \Theta$ **then**
11 | **return** 1
12 **else**
13 | **return** 0
14 **end**

---

4 Implementation and Results

4.1 Datasets

The classification task was evaluated on two common benchmark datasets, namely, MNIST and ImageNet.

Setup of MNIST. The MNIST dataset [10] includes 70,000 gray images of hand-written digits ranging from 0 to 9. It is separated into 60,000 training images and 10,000 testing images. A single MNIST image is composed of 28×28 pixels, each encoded by an 8-bit grayscale. We randomly extracted 200 images of the digit "0" from the 10,000 testing images. From each of these 200 images, we created nine adversarial images targeting the remaining digits (1–9). Finally we created a new benchmark dataset of 2,000 images (200 benign images and 1,800 adversarial images).

Setup of ImageNet. The ImageNet dataset [16] is a very large database designed for visual object recognition research. The original ImageNet includes more than 14 million images in 20,000 categories. Typical categories such as "computer mouse" and "vending machine" comprise several hundred images. As the machine learning model, we adopted Google Inception V3 [18] trained on 1,000 common categories in ImageNet. We randomly selected 1,000 testing images (excluding "ostrich" images). This selection of targeted class does not compromise the generality of our system. Applying the FGSM and PGD methods, we crafted 2,000 adversarial "ostrich" images. Both image sets were combined into a new benchmark repository of 3,000 images for our experiment.

4.2 Implementation

Although adversarial examples have recently attracted much interest from researchers, a public benchmark dataset for evaluating the robustness of defense systems remains lacking. In the attack phase of our system, we thus created a new benchmark dataset for evaluating the detection capabilities of our detection system.

The 200 random images of digit "0" extracted from the MNIST dataset were converted to adversarial images of digits 1–9 by the FGSM method. The FGSM was run through 1,000 iterations (epochs). The adversarial images were combined with original images into the new benchmark dataset for evaluating our detection system. The proposed detection system knows the true labels of the input. When presented with the unknown input, our system automatically processes the input and returns a decision (adversarial or benign).

Applying FGSM and PGD, we created adversarial "ostrich" images from 1,000 random ImageNet testing images. The original images were selected from categories other than "ostrich". The FGSM and PGD were each run through 500 iterations (epochs). Figure 2 shows five samples among the 1,000 randomly picked images used for crafting the adversarial examples. The first row displays the original (benign) images of a dish, hammerhead, mosque, oscilloscope and parachute. Below the images, the probabilities present the highest probability of each image class (indicated in parentheses).

In the sieve process, the kernel sizes of the Gaussian and median filters were set to (3×3) and (5×5), respectively. Observing the probability changes of the anchor before and after sieving, the input data were assessed as benign or adversarial based on the given threshold.

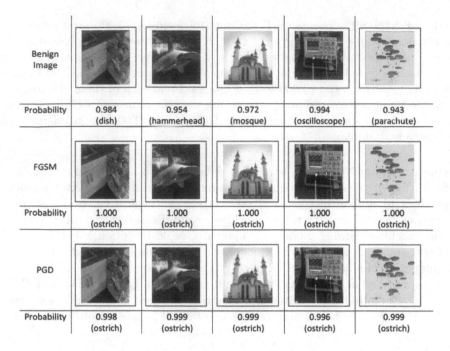

Benign Image					
Probability	0.984 (dish)	0.954 (hammerhead)	0.972 (mosque)	0.994 (oscilloscope)	0.943 (parachute)
FGSM					
Probability	1.000 (ostrich)	1.000 (ostrich)	1.000 (ostrich)	1.000 (ostrich)	1.000 (ostrich)
PGD					
Probability	0.998 (ostrich)	0.999 (ostrich)	0.999 (ostrich)	0.996 (ostrich)	0.999 (ostrich)

Fig. 2. Attack phase samples.

4.3   Results

Our results were compared with those of Xu et al. [21]. Our system is more convenient that Xu's system, owing to its high detection accuracy and easy setup. Specifically, our system adopts a fixed threshold whereas Xu et al.'s system must adapt the threshold value to individual cases. The performance of our system was evaluated by the F1-score. When based on the Gaussian and median filtering, our detection system is called DSG and DSM, respectively.

We observed and analyzed a typical oscilloscope image. From a benign oscilloscope image with a detection probability of 99.4%, we created two adversarial images with the targeted label is ostrich, one by FGSM method, the other by PGD method (Fig. 2). Afterward, the adversarial ostrich noises were sieved by the DSG and DSM functions, and the oscilloscope features were regained. As shown in Fig. 3, the probabilities of the targeted ostrich and legitimate oscilloscope dramatically differed when processed by the DSG and DSM functions. When an input is Original Oscilloscope, classification probability is 99.4% for oscilloscope label and the probabilities for true label are still remained round 99% after using DSG or DSM algorithms. Conversely, with an adversarial image with targeted class ostrich, DSG and DSM not only remove adversarial noises but only regain the probabilities of true label nearly equal to when using original input. This observation confirms our assumption that adversarial noises are high-frequency noises, and that adversarial samples are powerfully detected by adopting the low-pass filter in our model.

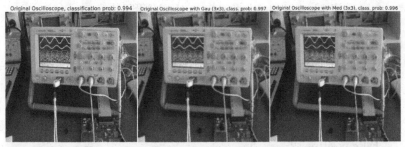

(a) Orginal Oscilloscope (b) Orginal Image with (c) Orginal Image with
Image   DSG (3x3)   DSM (3x3)

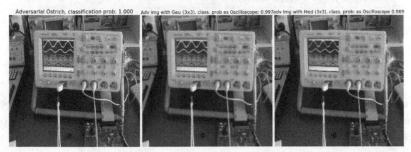

(d) Adversarial Image (e) Adversarial Image (f) Adversarial Image
(Ostrich)   with DSG (3x3)   with DSM (3x3)

Fig. 3. Original image (true class: Oscilloscope) and Adversarial image suffer to DSG and DSM with kernel size is (3×3). (3a) for original input, classification probability for oscilloscope label is 99.4%, (3b) for original input with DSG, classification probability for oscilloscope label is 99.7%, (3c) for original input with DSM, classification probability for oscilloscope label is 99.6%, (3d) for adversarial input, classification probability for ostrich label is 100%, (3e) for adversarial input with DSG, classification probability for oscilloscope label is 99.7%, (3f) for DSM input with classification probability for oscilloscope label is 98.9%

The detection results on the MNIST dataset are reported in Table 1. The dashes in this table signify a lack of information from earlier research. Although the same number of images was compared in ours and Xu et al.'s methods, we created a more challenging test set than Xu et al. [21]. Whereas Xu et al. created a balanced dataset of 1,000 legitimate images and 1,000 adversarial examples, we created 1,800 adversarial images from 200 legitimate inputs, thus imposing an imbalanced [17] dataset in our experimental test. Nevertheless, our detection rates are highly competitive with those of Xu et al. and slightly surpass the earlier detection rates. Moreover, our system applies a fixed threshold for all settings, whereas in Xu et al.'s work, the threshold must be adjusted in different settings.

On the ImageNet dataset, our detection rates exceeded those of Xu et al. As highlighted in Table 2, we analyzed more files in this implementation than

Table 1. Detection rates on the MNIST dataset

	Our method		Xu et al. [21]		
	DSG	DSM	Bit-depth	Smoothing	Best-joint
No. Files	2,000	2,000	2,000	2,000	2,000
Threshold	0.1	0.1	0.0005	0.0029	0.0029
True positive	1799	1796	–	–	–
True negative	198	195	–	–	–
False positive	2	5	–	–	–
False negative	1	4	–	–	–
Accuracy	0.999	0.996	–	–	–
Precision	0.999	0.997	–	–	–
Recall	**0.999**	0.998	0.903	0.868	0.982
F1 score	0.999	0.998	–	–	–

Xu et al., while maintaining the imbalance in our benchmark dataset. Our detection rate was 99.7% amd 100% with DSG and DSM, respectively, greatly outperforming Xu et al.'s system.

Table 2. Detection rates on the ImageNet dataset

	Our method		Xu et al. [21]		
	DSG	DSM	Bit-depth	Smoothing	Best-joint
No. files	3,000	3,000	1,800	1,800	1,800
Threshold	0.92	0.92	1.4417	1.1472	1.2128
True positive	1994	2000	–	–	–
True negative	995	875	–	–	–
False positive	45	125	–	–	–
False negative	6	0	–	–	–
Accuracy	0.983	0.958	–	–	–
Precision	0.978	0.941	–	–	–
Recall	0.997	**1.000**	0.751	0.816	0.859
F1 score	0.987	0.999	–	–	–

5   Conclusion

We investigated the high-frequency noises in adversarial image examples. Based on the high-frequency noise assumption and a theoretical framework, we demonstrated the effectiveness of a low-pass filter in removing these noises. This observation guided the development of our automated detection system for adversarial examples. On the MNIST and ImageNet datasets, our system achieved maximum accuracy rates of 99.9% and 100%, respectively. For evaluating our system, we constructed new benchmark datasets posing more challenges than previously constructed datasets [11,21]. Whereas the earlier studies evaluated their systems on images from the training set, our evaluation employed the testing images. Although we also challenged our model on imbalanced datasets, our detection system delivered state-of-the-art performance. As another important contribution to the existing corpus, our system not only defeated adversarial noises, but also regained the legitimate class from adversarial examples.

Acknowledgement. We would like to thank Professor Akira Otsuka for his helpful and valuable comments. This work is supported by Iwasaki Tomomi Scholarship.

References

1. Biggio, B., et al.: Evasion attacks against machine learning at test time. In: Blockeel, H., Kersting, K., Nijssen, S., Železný, F. (eds.) ECML PKDD 2013. LNCS (LNAI), vol. 8190, pp. 387–402. Springer, Heidelberg (2013). https://doi.org/10.1007/978-3-642-40994-3_25
2. Carlini, N., Wagner, D.: Towards evaluating the robustness of neural networks. In: 2017 IEEE Symposium on Security and Privacy (SP), pp. 39–57. IEEE (2017)
3. Goodfellow, I., Shlens, J., Szegedy, C.: Explaining and harnessing adversarial examples. In: International Conference on Learning Representations ICLR (2015). http://arxiv.org/abs/1412.6572
4. Grosse, K., Papernot, N., Manoharan, P., Backes, M., McDaniel, P.: Adversarial examples for malware detection. In: Foley, S.N., Gollmann, D., Snekkenes, E. (eds.) ESORICS 2017. LNCS, vol. 10493, pp. 62–79. Springer, Cham (2017). https://doi.org/10.1007/978-3-319-66399-9_4
5. Gu, S., Rigazio, L.: Towards deep neural network architectures robust to adversarial examples. CoRR. arXiv:1412.5068 (2014)
6. Huang, L., Joseph, A.D., Nelson, B., Rubinstein, B.I., Tygar, J.: Adversarial machine learning. In: Proceedings of the 4th ACM Workshop on Security and Artificial Intelligence, pp. 43–58. ACM (2011)
7. Kurakin, A., Boneh, D., Tramr, F., Goodfellow, I., Papernot, N., McDaniel, P.: Ensemble adversarial training: attacks and defenses. In: International Conference on Learning Representations ICLR (2018)
8. Kurakin, A., Goodfellow, I., Bengio, S.: Adversarial machine learning at scale. In: International Conference on Learning Representations ICLR (2017)
9. LeCun, Y., Bengio, Y., Hinton, G.: Deep learning. Nature **521**(7553), 436 (2015)
10. LeCun, Y., Cortes, C., Burges, C.: MNIST handwritten digit database. AT&T Labs. http://yann.lecun.com/exdb/mnist2 (2010)
11. Liao, F., Liang, M., Dong, Y., Pang, T., Hu, X., Zhu, J.: Defense against adversarial attacks using high-level representation guided denoiser. In: Proceedings of the IEEE Conference on Computer Vision and Pattern Recognition, pp. 1778–1787 (2018)
12. Madry, A., Makelov, A., Schmidt, L., Tsipras, D., Vladu, A.: Towards deep learning models resistant to adversarial attacks. In: 6th International Conference on Learning Representations, ICLR 2018, Vancouver, BC, Canada, April 30–May 3, 2018, Conference Track Proceedings (2018)

13. Meng, D., Chen, H.: Magnet: a two-pronged defense against adversarial examples. In: Proceedings of the 2017 ACM SIGSAC Conference on Computer and Communications Security, pp. 135–147. ACM (2017)
14. Nguyen, L., Wang, S., Sinha, A.: A learning and masking approach to secure learning. In: Bushnell, L., Poovendran, R., Başar, T. (eds.) GameSec 2018. LNCS, vol. 11199, pp. 453–464. Springer, Cham (2018). https://doi.org/10.1007/978-3-030-01554-1_26
15. Papernot, N., McDaniel, P., Wu, X., Jha, S., Swami, A.: Distillation as a defense to adversarial perturbations against deep neural networks. In: 2016 IEEE Symposium on Security and Privacy (SP), pp. 582–597. IEEE (2016)
16. Russakovsky, O., et al.: Imagenet large scale visual recognition challenge. Int. J. Comput. Vis. **115**(3), 211–252 (2015)
17. Sun, Y., Wong, A.K., Kamel, M.S.: Classification of imbalanced data: a review. Int. J. Pattern Recogn. Artif. Intell. **23**(04), 687–719 (2009)
18. Szegedy, C., Vanhoucke, V., Ioffe, S., Shlens, J., Wojna, Z.: Rethinking the inception architecture for computer vision. In: Proceedings of the IEEE Conference on Computer Vision and Pattern Recognition, pp. 2818–2826 (2016)
19. Szegedy, C., et al.: Intriguing properties of neural networks. In: International Conference on Learning Representations ICLR (2014)
20. Xiao, C., Li, B., Zhu, J.Y., He, W., Liu, M., Song, D.: Generating adversarial examples with adversarial networks. In: Proceedings of the Twenty-Seventh International Joint Conference on Artificial Intelligence, IJCAI-2018, pp. 3905–3911 (July 2018)
21. Xu, W., Evans, D., Qi, Y.: Feature squeezing: detecting adversarial examples in deep neural networks. In: 25th Annual Network and Distributed System Security Symposium, NDSS 2018, San Diego, California, USA, February 18–21 (2018)

An Improvement of the Degradation of Speaker Recognition in Continuous Cold Speech for Home Assistant

Haojun Ai[1,2], Yifeng Wang[1], Yuhong Yang[3(✉)], and Quanxin Zhang[4]

[1] School of Cyber Science and Engineering, Wuhan University, Hubei, China
{aihj,whuyifeng}@whu.edu.cn
[2] Key Laboratory of Aerospace Information Security and Trusted Computing,
Ministry of Education, Wuhan, China
[3] National Engineering Research Center for Multimedia Software,
School of Computer Science, Wuhan University, Hubei, China
ahka_yang@yeah.net
[4] School of Computer Science and Technology, Beijing Institute of Technology,
Beijing, People's Republic of China
zhangqx@bit.edu.cn

Abstract. Home assistant with speech user interfaces is quite welcomed due to its convenience in recent years. With speaker recognition (SR) technology in this application, personalized services (e.g., playing music, making to-do lists) for different family members become reality. However, the SR accuracy may decline sharply when a family has a cold due to the restriction of hardware and response time. In this paper, we propose a dual model updating strategy based on cold detection to maintain all speaker voice models. In this method, time domain and frequency domain features would be combined to detect continuous cold speech. And then, corresponding models would be selected to determine the identity according to the results of the detection. In order to continuously track SR performance based on data of mobile phone usage, a new mobile phone-based speech dataset (PBSD) which contains voice, phone model, and user's state of physical wellness has been constructed. Besides, the relationship between SR accuracy and users' state of physical wellness also has been analyzed based on a GMM-UBM framework. Finally, to evaluate performance of the proposed method, experiments focused on SR accuracy of 10 speakers from both cold-suffering and healthy states have been conducted. The results demonstrated that the SR accuracy can be improved effectively by the cold detection-based model updating strategy, especially in a cold-suffering circumstance.

Keywords: Speaker recognition · Database · Cold · MFCC · GMM

1 Introduction

As a representative application of the biometrics field, speaker recognition (SR) [1, 2] has become increasingly ubiquitous as home assistants become more and more popular. Amazon Alexa is a virtual voice assistant which is capable of recognizing speakers to

© Springer Nature Switzerland AG 2019
J. Vaidya et al. (Eds.): CSS 2019, LNCS 11982, pp. 363–373, 2019.
https://doi.org/10.1007/978-3-030-37337-5_29

assist them in placing orders on the Amazon. Similarly, the TmallGenie (Alibaba AI Labs) also has a built-in SR function which supports voice registration for up to six individuals.

In spite of the wide deployment of SR in home assistants, there are still some challenges of SR in a real application. First of all, SR assistants would be affected by intra-speaker variabilities (such as voice aging, emotion, changes related on sickness, etc.) and extra-speaker variabilities (such as noise, echo, etc.). The natural variabilities of intra-speaker are inevitable and generally time-varying. When there is a mismatch between training conditions of speaker models, the verification system would be less accurate. which would cause a serious challenge to speaker recognition. For example, the performance of speaker models with neutral speech would be degraded when it is tested on emotional utterances [3]. Besides, there are many studies have proved that voice is long-term aging. While, Yuri et al. [4] analyzed NIST 2005 and 2006 dataset [5] to find that recognition accuracy has declined in the short term (about one month). Nevertheless, there are various factors except aging in their experiment, which makes the conclusion that short-term voice aging is not much convincing. For a family assistant, TmallGenie's SR accuracy drops to 80.8% in three months after registering the initial speaker models. Alexa is "smarter", for it can automatically learn users' voice and update the speaker model without fixed phrases uttered by them.

Moreover, the changes related to sickness is another key factor which would affect speaker recognition performance. Taking a cold as an example, the nose and throat play an important role in speech production [6] and may be significantly affected by the symptoms of a cold. Some of the related studies [7–11] also have considered the impact of the common cold on automatic speech recognition. Hansen et al. have successfully characterized vocal fold pathology by extracting novel features such as the non-linear Teager Energy Operator (TEO) [7–10]. Tull et al. [11] have studied how a cold affect certain speech features to acquire a clear low-order Mel-frequency cepstral coefficients (MFCC) pattern.

In conclusion, there are three challenges to using a cold continues speech for SR. The first one is voice pathological features are temporary, which would disappear after a few days. The second is, the change of voice caused by a cold may differ vastly from person to person and the pattern may not be fixed. The final one is, the previous challenges make it difficult to distinguish whether speech variability originates from separate users or from differences in a single user's voice features. Due to such fluctuations in voice pathology, ensuring high SR accuracy in the home assistant scenario is a very challenging endeavor.

In order to deal with these problems in speaker recognition, the goal of this work is to continuously track SR performance based on mobile phone usage data. The primary contributions can be summarized as follows.

1. A new mobile phone-based speech dataset, named PBSD, has been proposed. Based on this dataset, SR performance variations in the short-term has been analyzed, and it can be conclude that there is no voice aging within a period of about 30 days. We center our investigation on the effects of the common cold on SR performance.

2. A dual model updating strategy has been designed based on the cold detection. A Gaussian Mixture Model (GMM) based speaker verification technique has been used in this process. This method is independent of the content in speech, and SR accuracy can be guaranteed even when the user is suffering a cold which affects his or her voice.
3. Time-domain and frequency-domain features have been combined to form a new set of feature vectors for more accurate cold speech detection.

2 Database (PBSD) Construction

Obtaining usable data can be difficult in studies on SR. There is currently no publicly available long-term longitudinal speaker database [12] that meets our requirements, because the interval between each session is too long, it is difficult to ignore the effects of aging. The number of short-term speaker databases are limited, for example, Beigi et al. [13] only recorded three sessions in five consecutive months. Databases based on readily available, daily devices (e.g., mobile phones) are more suitable for our research but rare to find.

To this end, we created a new database, the "phone-based speech database" (PBSD[1]), for the purposes of this study. It contains 25 speakers (13 male and 12 female, mean age 25 years). We also designed several guidelines and requirements for recording.

The prompt text is 0–9 numbers and sentences in Chinese. The time of one session varies from person to person. The length of reading materials is approximately 2.5–4 min. All sessions were recorded in lossless pcm-encoded WAV format via the Luyinbao app (form Iflytek CO., LTD.) with sampling rate of 16 kHz. Speakers were required to use the same phone throughout the entire recording time. Each session was recorded in a relatively quiet environment be it indoor or outdoor (i.e., their daily environment like Fig. 1) with background noise below 45 dB. Each session was given three tags: date, phone model, and physiological state (cold or health).

Fig. 1. Recording way and scene.

We removed any audible unwanted noises to limit variable factors (apart from aging) for the sake of consistency, since the recording conditions were varied. We examined the recorded spectral content and any with significant frequency artefacts (e.g., microphone interference, popping) were discarded. So far, each speaker produced 14–40 effective sessions spanning a range of 30–60 days. There were 14 sessions in total with common time nodes, so the current database contains $25 \times 14 = 350$ sessions, totally 14 h of speech data. Note that the PBSD continues to expand as new sessions are added every day.

3 Speaker Recognition Test

3.1 Feature Extraction and Model Training

Mel-Frequency Ceptral Coefficients, MFCC is an acoustic feature derived from the research results of human auditory mechanism. In this paper, we adopt MFCC (with DCT) as an acoustic features that use a 20 ms window size and a 10 ms frame shift to generate a 13-dimensional MFCC features.

Furthermore, a well-known technology GMM is used for classification by using the Expectation-Maximization algorithm, in which various model parameters (mean, variance and mixing coefficients) are adjusted to converge to a model giving a maximum log likelihood value. We used 16 single Gaussian distributions to train a 16-order GMM model for each speaker in the GMM-UBM (Universal Background Model) baseline system [14]. The GMM model formula is defined as follows.

$$\Pr(x) = \sum_{k=1}^{K} \pi_k N(x; u_k; \sum_k)$$

(1)

Where, the GMM model is given by the weighted sum of K single Gaussians, and k is the weighting factor. Any one of the Gaussian distributions $N(x; u_k; \sum_k)$ is called a component of this model.

3.2 Voice Aging

Experiments must follow a guideline: control variables. Eight speakers (healthy speakers, labeled "hS1" ~ "hS8") who did not catch a cold in one month were selected from the PBSD data set to conduct the short-term aging studies in the home scene. Each produced 10 valid session samples in one month; again, the length of each sessions is between about 2.2 and 4 min.

We designed experiments based on the GMM-UBM framework to calculate the overall SR accuracy curve of eight speakers over time. After VAD operation, we took 99 frames of effective speech data about 1 s long for testing with more than 100 test samples per person per day.

The results based on the GMM-UBM framework are shown in Fig. 2. Almost everyone has a recognition accuracy of more than 90% every day, and there is no obvious downward trend with the passage of time. However, in the experiment we

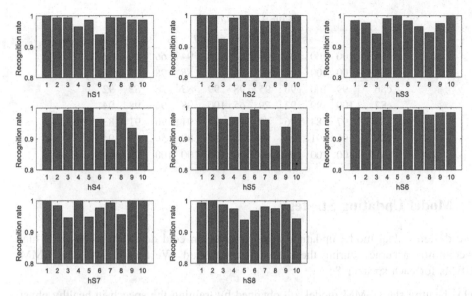

Fig. 2. The recognition rate of eight healthy speakers ("hS1" ~ "hS8") in a month.

selected a small number of speakers, so we can only concluded that in the home assistant, the voice of the in-set speakers did not significantly age in the short term.

3.3   Cold-Suffering Voice

In the section, we selected ten speakers (cold speakers, labeled "cS1" ~ "cS10") who caught a cold during the recording time, using each 10 sessions for experiments. We observed changes in their SR accuracy over time. The recording time was about 30 days and covered the whole process of physiological changes from healthy to cold-suffering, even to healthy again. We concluded that there was no voice aging in the short term (about one month) from Sect. 3.2, that is, in the experiment of this section, the unique variable can be basically determined to be cold or not.

Table 1 shows that the recognition accuracy of each speakers during the cold-suffering period, and indicates various degrees of decline related to the severity of the cold. Although the SR accuracy of some speakers remain stable during a cold, indeed, suffering a cold still poses a certain challenge to the SR task.

Table 1. SR accuracy (%) of 10 cold speakers ("cS1" ~ "cS10"). All results in the table is based on the GMM-UBM model trained by 10 s healthy speech data. The bold values are the recognition results of the cold speech, and the italic values indicate that the SR rate is significantly reduced.

Times	1	2	3	4	5	6	7	8	9	10
cS1	97	98	97	93	*47*	*25*	*49*	*26*	79	99
cS2	99	97	98	**96**	*81*	99	**100**	94	98	98
cS3	100	100	*68*	*49*	*85*	93	100	96	82	93

(continued)

Table 1. (*continued*)

Times	1	2	3	4	5	6	7	8	9	10
cS4	100	100	100	100	100	100	94	*66*	*40*	*83*
cS5	100	100	94	100	100	*71*	*88*	98	100	95
cS6	99	100	96	95	98	99	*83*	78	82	**92**
cS7	100	99	93	*79*	*65*	100	98	94	98	94
cS8	97	84	96	*89*	*76*	*78*	91	90	91	83
cS9	96	91	94	**93**	*88*	*85*	88	*50*	*73*	94
cS10	100	100	100	100	100	100	100	100	**100**	**100**

4 Model Updating Strategy

We design a dual model updating strategy based on cold detection to ensure a high recognition accuracy during the cold-suffering period. We trained two state GMM-UBMs for each speaker S_i:

(1) healthy state GMM model λ_{iH} obtained by training the speech in healthy physiological state;
(2) Correspondingly, λ_{iC} is the GMM model in the cold state.

Based on the GMM-UBM model, we train a dual model λ_{iH} (Healthy) and λ_{iC} (Cold) for each speaker S_i, the training process and the whole framework are shown in Fig. 3.

In the recognition phase, when someone speaks a speech to be recognized, the first step of my framework is to perform automatic speech pathology. According to the results of the cold/health binary classification, the GMM model with different states is selected to calculate the confidence score, and the discriminant result is given.

4.1 Cold/Healthy Voices Discrimination

The detection of voice disorder with a sustained vowel is relatively easy to detection with continuous speech [15]. However, for home assistant, people do use continuous speech instead of sustained voice, in reality, it will be more natural to detect pathology from continuous sentences. Which we did a simple neural network and GMM binary classification experiments, and founded that voice features such as pitch, jitter, shimmer and harmonic-to-noise ratio values [16, 17] do not perform well in the pathology of continuous speech. Many of features (such as shimmer, pitch) fluctuate and lose stability when using the continuous speech. However, the jitter parameters are basically maintained at a stable value, as shown in Fig. 4, so it is effective in using continuous speech to detect cold voice. Besides, short-term MFCC [18–21] is a good parameterization method compared to LPC (Linear Prediction Coefficient).

Feature Fusion. The jitter parameters and MFCC are directly fused at the feature level to form a set of 41-dimensional feature vectors, the jitter parameters are four-dimensional, which is *jitta, jitt, rap*, and *ppq5*, see [16] for details.

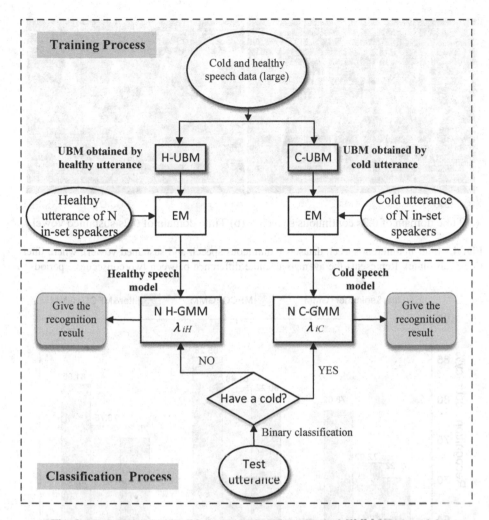

Fig. 3. Training and recognition process based on the dual GMM-UBM model.

Since the standard MFCC only characterizes the static properties of the speech data, the MFCC parameters used herein are the standard 37-dimensional, consisting of 1-dimensional logE frame energy, 12-dimensional MFCC coefficients, 12-dimensional first-order differential coefficients, and 12-dimensional second-order differential coefficients.

Detecting Cold Voice. Finally we did cold voice detection by using the 41-dimensional parameters and GMM [17], where we adopted 128 single Gaussian distributions to train a 128-order GMM model for binary-class classification. Though the classification accuracy is also not satisfactory, with only 80 ± 2% accuracy. However, as shown in Fig. 5, under the same experimental conditions, the fusion features proposed in the paper performed best in the detection of cold speech experiments.

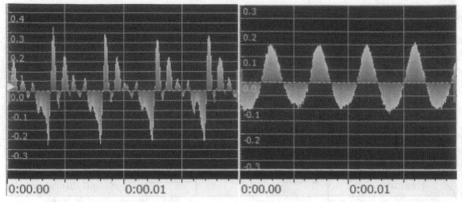

(a)Time domain of 0.2s continuous speech.   (b) Time domain of 0.2s sustained vowel.

Fig. 4. Jitter in different speech datasets (continuous speech and sustained vowel), where jitter (local, absolute): Represents the average absolute difference between two consecutive periods.

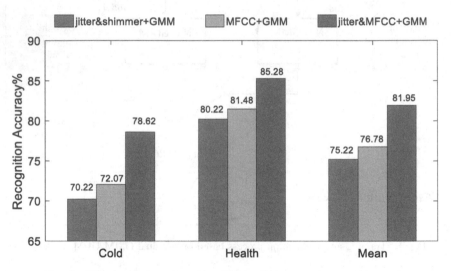

Fig. 5. Experimental results using different features to detect cold speech.

4.2   Cold–Based Speaker Recognition Phrase

In the training process, the cold-based framework uses MFCC features and GMM model that are consistent with Sect. 3.1 for supervised model training. As shown in Fig. 3, we collected the cold and healthy speech of each speaker separately, to train the cold GMM λ_{iC} and the healthy GMM λ_{iH} for each speaker S_i.

Next we would select different cold/healthy GMMs for recognition based on the result of detecting the cold speech, and give the final result. Besides, our framework also updates the speaker model more intelligently, as time passes, constantly using the cold or healthy speech to update the corresponding speaker models in real time.

4.3   Experimental Results

As shown in Fig. 6, all speakers have a significant improvement in the SR accuracy during the cold-suffering period or still maintain a high accuracy (cS10), which shows that to some extent our algorithm can improve the problem of low accuracy during the cold period. However, our algorithm has slightly reduced the recognition accuracy during the healthy periods, but still within an acceptable range.

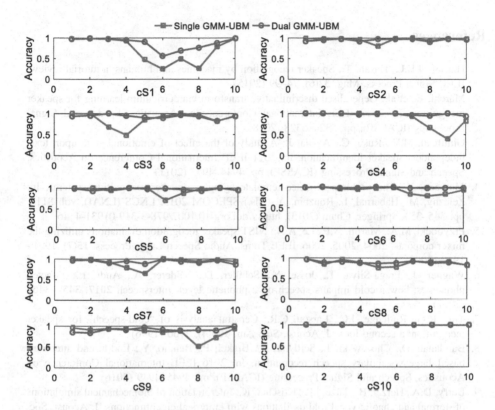

Fig. 6. 10 speakers based on single or dual model recognition accuracy

5   Conclusion

In this paper, we introduced an available dataset PBSD for assessing SR accuracy in daily users. PBSD consists of data collected from 25 individuals and spans 40 days, where each session is recorded in lossless pcm-encoded WAV format. Based on PBSD, 10 cold speakers were selected to study the problem of cold speech degradation. Moreover, a dual model updating strategy based on cold detection has been proposed to maintain the speech model. Using samples of training speech with a length of 10 s and the test voice with a length of 1 s to analyze the recognition performance based on GMM-UBM frameworks, the results of experiments demonstrated that the proposed dual model updating strategy is outperformed than the single model. When using a single model, the recognition accuracy decreases with the occurrence of a cold. However, with the dual model updating strategy, high SR accuracy can be ensured as the users recovering from cold-suffering to healthy.

Acknowledgment. This work is partially supported by The National Key Research and Development Program of China (2016YFB0502201) and the National Natural Science Foundation of China (General Program), Grant No. 61971316.

References

1. Hansen, J.H.L., Hasan, T.: Speaker recognition by machines and humans: a tutorial review. IEEE Signal Process. Mag. **32**(6), 74–99 (2015)
2. Marchi, E., et al.: Generalised discriminative transform via curriculum learning for speaker recognition. In: 2018 IEEE International Conference on Acoustics, Speech and Signal Processing (ICASSP), pp. 5324–5328 (2018)
3. Ghiurcau, M.V., Rusu, C., Astola, J.: A study of the effect of emotional state upon text-independent speaker identification. In: 2011 IEEE International Conference on Acoustics, Speech and Signal Processing (ICASSP), pp. 4944–4947 (2011)
4. Matveev, Y.: The problem of voice template aging in speaker recognition systems. In: Železný, M., Habernal, I., Ronzhin, A. (eds.) SPECOM 2013. LNCS (LNAI), vol. 8113, pp. 345–353. Springer, Cham (2013). https://doi.org/10.1007/978-3-319-01931-4_46
5. Przybocki, M.A., Martin, A.F., Le, A.N.: NIST speaker recognition evaluations utilizing the mixer corpora—2004, 2005, 2006. IEEE Trans. Audio Speech Lang. Process. **15**(7), 1951–1959 (2007)
6. Wagner, J., Fraga-Silva, T., Josse, Y., Schiller, D., Seiderer, A., Andr, E.: Infected phonemes: how a cold impairs speech on a phonetic level. Interspeech **2017**, 3457–3461 (2017)
7. Tull, R.G., Rutledge, J.C., Larson, C.R.: Cepstral analysis of "cold-speech" for speaker recognition: a second look. J. Acoust. Soc. Am. **100**(4), 2760 (1996)
8. Bahdanau, D., Chorowski, J., Serdyuk, D., Brakel, P., Bengio, Y.: End-to-end attention-based large vocabulary speech recognition. In: 2016 IEEE International Conference on Acoustics, Speech and Signal Processing (ICASSP), pp. 4945–4949 (2016)
9. Berry, D.A., Herzel, H., Titze, I.R., Krischer, K.: Interpretation of biomechanical simulations of normal and chaotic vocal fold oscillations with empirical eigenfunctions. J. Acoust. Soc. Am. **95**(6), 3595–3604 (1994)
10. Henrquez, P., Alonso, J.B., Ferrer, M.A., Travieso, C.M., Godino-Llorente, J.I., Daz-de-Mara, F.: Characterization of healthy and pathological voice through measures based on nonlinear dynamics. IEEE Trans. Audio Speech Lang. Process. **17**(6), 1186–1195 (2009)
11. Hansen, J.H.L., Gavidia-Ceballos, L., Kaiser, J.F.: A nonlinear operator-based speech feature analysis method with application to vocal fold pathology assessment. IEEE Trans. Biomed. Eng. **45**(3), 300–313 (1998)
12. Cole, R.A., Noel, M., Noel, V.: The CSLU speaker recognition corpus. In: ICSLP (1998)
13. Beigi, H.: Effects of time lapse on speaker recognition results. In: 2009 16th International Conference on Digital Signal Processing, pp. 1260–1265 (2009)
14. Reynolds, D.A., Rose, R.C.: Robust text-independent speaker identification using gaussian mixture speaker models. IEEE Trans. Speech Audio Process. **3**(1), 72–83 (1995)

15. Ali, Z., Alsulaiman, M., Muhammad, G., Elamvazuthi, I., Mesallam, T.A.: Vocal fold disorder detection based on continuous speech by using MFCC and GMM. In: 2013 7th IEEE GCC Conference and Exhibition (GCC), pp. 292–297 (2013)
16. Teixeira, J.P., Oliveira, C., Lopes, C.: Vocal acoustic analysis – jitter, shimmer and HNR parameters. Procedia Technol. **9**, 1112–1122 (2013)
17. Sabir, B., Rouda, F., Khazri, Y., Touri, B., Moussetad, M.: Improved algorithm for pathological and normal voices identification. Int. J. Electr. Comput. Eng. **7**(1), 238–243 (2017)
18. Godino-Llorente, J., Gomez-Vilda, P.: Automatic detection of voice impairments by means of short-term cepstral parameters and neural network based detectors. IEEE Trans. Biomed. Eng. **51**(2), 380–384 (2004)
19. Gelzinis, A., Verikas, A., Bacauskiene, M.: Automated speech analysis applied to laryngeal disease categorization. Comput. Methods Programs Biomed. **91**(1), 36–47 (2008)
20. Dibazar, A.A, Berger, T.W., Narayanan, S.S.: Pathological Voice Assessment. International Conference of the IEEE Engineering in Medicine & Biology Society (2006)
21. Costa, S.C., Neto, B.G.A., and Fechine, J.M.: Pathological voice discrimination using cepstral analysis, vector quantization and hidden markov models. In 2008 8th IEEE International Conference on BioInformatics and BioEngineering, pp. 1–5 (2008)

Evading PDF Malware Classifiers
with Generative Adversarial Network

Yaxiao Wang[1]([⊠]) [ID], Yuanzhang Li[1], Quanxin Zhang[1], Jingjing Hu[1],
and Xiaohui Kuang[2]

[1] School of Computer Science and Technology,
Beijing Institute of Technology, Beijing 100081, China
1989941673@qq.com, {popular,zhangqx,
hujingjing}@bit.edu.cn
[2] National Key Laboratory of Science and Technology on Information System
Security, Beijing 100081, China
xiaohui_kuang@163.com

Abstract. Generative adversarial networks (GANs) have become one of the
most popular research topics in deep learning. It is widely used in the term of
image, and through the constant competition between generator and discriminator, it can generate so remarkably realistic images that human can't distinguish. However, Although GAN has achieved great success in generating
images, it is still in its infancy in generating adversarial malware examples. In
this paper, we propose an PDF malware evasion method that is using GAN to
generate adversarial PDF malware examples and evaluate it against four local
machine learning based PDF malware classifiers. The evaluation is conducted
on the same dataset which contains 100 malicious PDF files. The experimental
results reveal that the proposed evasion attacks are effective, with attacks against
three classifiers all attaining 100% evasion rate and attack against the last
classifier also attaining 95% evasion rate on the evaluation dataset.

Keywords: Malware evasion · Generative adversarial network · PDF
malware · Machine learning · Adversarial examples

1 Introduction

PDF documents are widely used in study or work for their efficiency, stability, and
interactivity. However, in recent years, with the development of non-executable file
attack technology, the security of PDF documents has been greatly threatened. Many
attackers are committed to exploiting the vulnerabilities of PDF readers to trigger the
download or direct execution of executable payloads.

The security of PDF documents is mainly reflected in three aspects. Firstly, PDF file
format is a very flexible infectious vector [1], which can be embedded with various types
of attacks, such as JavaScript code, ActionScript code, malicious executable files and
malicious PDF files. Secondly, the complexity of PDF file format allows attackers to use
various solutions to hide code injection or other attack strategies, making detection of
malicious code more difficult. Finally, attackers can exploit specific vulnerabilities in

© Springer Nature Switzerland AG 2019
J. Vaidya et al. (Eds.): CSS 2019, LNCS 11982, pp. 374–387, 2019.
https://doi.org/10.1007/978-3-030-37337-5_30

PDF readers by triggering them in PDF documents. While vulnerabilities in third-party applications are often publicly exposed, they are not fixed in a timely manner. As a result, attacks last longer due to the lack of proper security updates.

Machine learning has been widely used in various application domains such as image classification [2] and natural language processing [3]. Many machine learning based systems have been reported to achieve excellent performance [4, 5]. Also, machine learning methods are adopted in many security tasks, such as PDF malware detection [6–9]. However, researchers begin to question the reliability of learning algorithms against adversarial attacks carefully-crafted against them [10–12]. Such attacks became widespread when researchers demonstrated that it was possible to evade deep learning algorithms for computer vision with adversarial examples, i.e., minimally-perturbed images that mislead classification [13, 14]. Adversarial attacks can be applied not only to images, but also to the generation of adversarial malware examples and infection vectors, as first shown in [11], and subsequently studied in [15–18]. By making some fine-grained changes to correctly detected malicious samples, attackers can effectively evade machine-learning detection without making invasive changes.

In this work, we study the problem of PDF malware evasion with generative adversarial network. And we investigate an evasion scenario in which only the feature set employed by the target classifier is exposed to the adversary and the adversary doesn't have access to the training dataset, classification algorithm and its parameters adopted by the classifier. Moreover, the target classifier only reveals its final classification decision (e.g., benign or malicious) about a given PDF instance. Our contributions are summarized as follows:

(1) We propose a novel PDF malware evasion method based on generative adversarial network.
(2) We craft real PDF malware instances instead of only performing attacks in feature space.
(3) We conduct experimental evaluation against four local PDF malware classifiers. The empirical results demonstrate the efficiency of our proposed method, with three attacks attaining 100% evasion rate and one attaining 95% evasion rate.

The remaining of this paper is organized as follows: Sect. 2 reviews the background of PDF structure and MalGAN before proposing our evasion method. Next, we introduce our approach in detail in Sect. 3 and report the experimental evaluation in Sect. 4. We survey related works in Sect. 5 and finally conclude our work in Sect. 6.

2 Background

2.1 PDF Structure

The PDF file structure is shown in Fig. 1, which contains the following four parts:

(1) Header: A line of text containing information about PDF file version, introduced by the marker %.
(2) Body: A sequence of objects that define the operation performed by the file. Such objects can contain compressed or uncompressed embedded data, such as text,

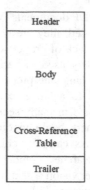

Fig. 1. PDF structure

images, script code and so on. Each object has a unique reference number, usually introduced by the sequence *number 0 obj*, where *number* is the correct object number. PDF objects can also be referenced by other objects using the sequence *number 0 R*, where *number* identifies the referenced target object. Each object ends with *endobj*. The *keywords* (also known as *name objects*) are used to describe the functionality of each object, usually introduced by the marker/.

(3) Cross-Reference (X-Ref) Table: A list of offsets that indicate the position of each object in the file. Such a list gives readers precise indication on where to start parsing each object. It is introduced by the marker *xref*, followed by a sequence of numbers, the last of which indicates the total number of objects in the file. Each row in the table corresponds to a specific object, but only rows ending in *n* are relevant to the specific object stored in the file. It is worth noting that the reader only parses objects referenced by the X-Ref Table. Therefore, it is possible to find objects stored in files but lacking references in the table.

(4) Trailer: A special object that describes some basic elements in a file, such as the first object in the object graph. In addition, it contains references to file metadata, which are typically stored in one single object. A trailer object is usually introduced by the keyword *trailer*.

2.2 MalGAN

GAN proposed by Goodfellow et al. [19] is a generative model, which consists of two models, namely generator G and discriminator D. Generator G is mainly used to learn the distribution of real data, while discriminator D is mainly used to determine the probability of data coming from real data. Generator G and Discriminator D are trained alternately, finally reaching a Nash equilibrium state. In this state, generator G can learn the distribution of real data, while discriminator D has a result of 1/2 everywhere, i.e., it cannot tell whether the input data comes from generator or real data.

Hu et al. [20] proposed a GAN based algorithm named MalGAN to generate adversarial malware examples, which are able to bypass black-box machine learning based detection models. The architecture of MalGAN is shown in Fig. 2.

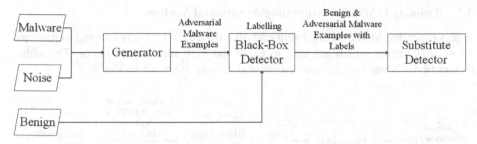

Fig. 2. The architecture of MalGAN

MalGAN only contains a generator and a substitute detector, which are both feed-forward neural networks. The black-box detector which adopts machine learning based algorithm is the target system and used as an external system here. The authors assume that the only thing they know about the black-box detector is the feature set it employed. They don't have access to the classification algorithm and parameters of the black-box model, but they can get the detection results of their programs from it. The substitute detector is trained to fit the black-box malware detection algorithm, while the generative network is used to transform malware samples into their adversarial version.

3 Scheme

The overall framework of evading PDF malware classifiers we proposed is shown in Fig. 3. We first extract features of PDF files and represent them as feature vectors. Next, we use these vectors to train a GAN and use the GAN to generate adversarial vectors which are able to evade the PDF malware classifier. Finally, we craft real adversarial PDF malware examples according to adversarial vectors.

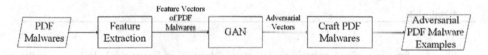

Fig. 3. The overall framework of evading PDF malware classifiers

3.1 Feature Extraction

We use MIMICUS implemented by Šrndić et al. [21] to extract the features of the PDF file and represent these features as n-dimensional feature vector $X = \{x_1, x_2...x_n\}$, where x_i represents the value of feature i and n is the total number of features.

By running a set of regular expressions on the original bytes of the PDF file to extract features, a total of 135 integer, floating point and boolean features that were exposed by Smutz et al. [22] can be extracted. These features reflect various properties of PDF files, such as the size and version of the file, PDF metadata items such as author names, the number of characters for creation and modification dates, and structural properties such as the number of Acrobat tables and their relative positions in the file.

3.2   Training GANs for Generating Adversarial Vectors

In this paper, the MalGAN algorithm proposed by Hu et al. [20] is adopted to generate adversarial vectors which are able to evade the PDF malware classifier. The architecture of GAN used to generate adversarial vectors is shown in Fig. 4.

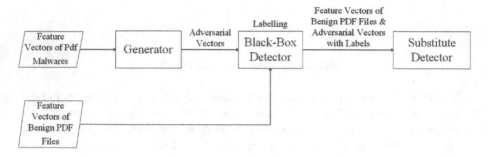

Fig. 4. The architecture of GAN used to generate adversarial vectors

---

Algorithm 1 The Training Process of GAN

1: **while** not converging **do**
2:      Sample a minibatch of malicious PDF samples M={ $m^{(1)},\ldots,m^{(n)}$}
3:      Generate adversarial examplesM' from the generator for M
4:      Sample a minibatch of benign PDF samples B={ $x^{(1)},\ldots,x^{(n)}$}
5:      Label M' and B using the black-box detector
6:      Update the substitute detector by descending it's gradient:
            $\nabla_{\theta_d} \frac{1}{n} \sum_{i=1}^{n} [-\log D(m^{(i)}) - \log(1-D(x^{(i)}))], m \in BB_{Malware}, x \in BB_{Benign}$
7:      Update the substitute detector by descending it's gradient:
            $\nabla_{\theta_g} \frac{1}{n} \log D(G(m^{(i)})), m \in S_{Malware}$
8: **end while**

The loss function of the substitute detector is defined in Formula 1. BB_{Benign} is the set of PDF samples that are recognized as benign by the black-box detector, and $BB_{Malware}$ is the set of samples that are recognized as malicious by the black-box detector.

$$L_D = -E_{x \in BB_{Benign}} \log(1 - D_{\theta_d}(x)) - E_{m \in BB_{Malware}} \log D_{\theta_d}(m) \tag{1}$$

The loss function of the generator is defined in Formula 2. $S_{Malware}$ is the actual malicious PDF dataset, not the malicious set labelled by the black-box detector.

$$L_G = E_{m \in S_{Malware}} \log D_{\theta_d}(G_{\theta_g}(m)) \tag{2}$$

In this paper, GAN is trained by means of alternate training, i.e., fixing the generator and training substitute detector first and then fixing the substitute detector and training generator. The training process of GAN in this paper is shown in Algorithm 1.

3.3 Crafting Adversarial PDF Malware Examples

MIMICUS is used as a tool in this paper to craft adversarial PDF malware examples according to the adversarial vectors. The crafting method is to modify the original PDF malware so that its feature vector is closer to the adversarial vector.

The modification method is to inject a set of whitespace-separated string patterns into the gap between the X-Ref Table and the trailer of the target PDF file. Figure 5 shows the layout before and after the PDF file is modified.

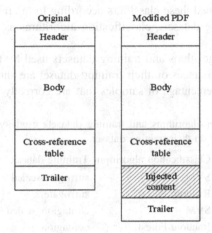

Fig. 5. Layout before and after PDF file is modified

Two unavoidable problems arise during the process of modifying PDF malware. The first problem is that the extracted features of the PDF malware are heavily interdependent, i.e., the change of one feature may affect the value of other features. Another problem is that the value of some components in the adversarial vector generated by GAN may be out of the boundary value of PDF file features. Due to the two problems, there are some subtle differences between the features of the crafted PDF malware and the adversarial vector.

4 Experiment

4.1 Datasets

Three datasets are used in our experiments: two datasets, Contagio and Surrogate, collected from MIMICUS, are used for training of PDF malware classifiers and GAN models, while the Attack dataset are used as evaluation dataset to evaluate our evasion method.

(1) Contagio dataset: This dataset contains 5000 benign PDF samples and 4999 PDF malwares (in the form of feature vectors).
(2) Surrogate dataset: This dataset contains 5000 benign PDF samples and 5000 PDF malwares (in the form of feature vectors). 5000 benign PDF samples and 5000 PDF malwares are used when training PDF malware classifiers while 5000 benign PDF samples and 4999 PDF malwares are used when training GAN in our experiments.
(3) Attack dataset: This dataset contains 100 PDF malwares, mainly used to evaluate our evasion method and craft adversarial PDF malware examples.

4.2 Classifiers

In our experiments, we mainly attacked four PDF malware classifiers involved in MIMICUS. We first trained these classifiers according to the information provided by MIMICUS about training datasets, classification algorithms as well as its parameters and so on.

The classification algorithms and training datasets used by the four PDF malware classifiers and the performances on their training dataset are shown in Table 1, where *Accuracy* refers to the percentage of samples that are correctly classified.

Table 1. The classification algorithms and training datasets used by the four PDF malware classifiers and the accuracy on their training dataset.

PDF malware classifier	Classification algorithm	Training dataset	Accuracy
F	SVM	surrogate-scaled	0.9995
FC	Random Forest	surrogate	1.0
FT	SVM	contagion_scaled	0.998999899989999
FTC	Random Forest	contagion	1.0

4.3 GAN Models

We trained a GAN model for each PDF classifier. In our experiment, we performed an incomplete black-box attack and assumed that we only known about the feature set employed by the target classifier. Therefore, we used the dataset which were different from the training dataset of the target classifier to train GAN. The training datasets of the four GAN models are shown in Table 2.

The four GAN models used the same architecture and parameters of network. In our experiment, we fed binary feature vectors to generator, so it was necessary to convert the feature vector of a PDF malware into its binary version before training GAN. We set the feature whose value is less than or equal to 0 as 0, and the feature whose value is greater than 0 as 1.

In our experiment, both generator and substitute detector contained an input layer, two hidden layers and an output layer. The network size of generator was 135-250-300-135, and the network size of substitute detector was 135-250-300-1. The learning rates of generator and substitute detector were both 0.001, and Adam was chosen as the optimizer.

Table 2. The training datasets of the four GAN models.

GAN	Black-box detector	Training dataset of black-box detector	Training dataset of GAN
A	F	surrogate_scaled	contagio
B	FC	surrogate	contagio
C	FT	contagio_scaled	surrogate
D	FTC	contagio	surrogate

We set the largest training epoch as 500 and saved the model when vectors generated by generator attained highest evasion rate. Due to the two unavoidable problems mentioned in Sect. 3.3, it is not possible to craft PDF malwares whose feature vectors are the same as the adversarial vectors. Therefore, there may be a case where adversarial vectors attain a high evasion rate, but the crafted PDF malwares attain a low evasion rate. In order to save the model whose generated PDF malwares have the highest evasion rate, we also saved a model every 50 epochs. When the maximum training times was reached, a total of 11 models were saved. The 11 models were then evaluated on Attack dataset to compare their performance, i.e., the evasion rate of the crafted PDF malwares. The model with the best performance was chosen as the optimal model of this training.

4.4 Results

We evaluated the four GAN models on the same evaluation dataset. We first used the four classifiers to detect the original 100 PDF malwares in Attack dataset. The evasion rates of these malwares against different classifiers are shown in Table 3 and provide a baseline with which we compare the evasion rates of crafted PDF malwares.

We used four GAN models to generate adversarial vectors and then crafted PDF malwares according to them. Then we evaluated the 100 generated PDF malwares on the four PDF classifiers. The evasion rates of generated vectors and crafted PDF malwares are shown in Table 4.

As can be seen from Table 4, all the vectors generated by four GAN models could evade the PDF malware classifier, but not all of the PDF malwares crafted according to these vectors were able to evade the classifier. For example, Only 95% of the PDF malwares generated from model D could evade PDF malware classifier. The main reason for this is our limited ability to process features. Due to the two reasons mentioned before, the features of crafted PDF malwares and the generated vectors are

Table 3. Evasion rates of original PDF malwares

PDF classifier	Evasion rate
F	47%
FC	8%
FT	1%
FTC	0%

Y. Wang et al.

Table 4. Evasion rates of generated vectors and crafted PDF malwares

GAN	PDF malware classifier	Evasion rate of crafted malwares	Evasion rate of generated vectors	Epoch
A	F	100%	100%	1
B	FC	100%	100%	450
C	FT	100%	100%	1
D	FTC	95%	100%	300

hardly the same, as can be seen from Fig. 6. The BEFORE column shows the value of features extracted from a PDF malware F_B. The AFTER column shows the vector generated by GAN and this vector was used to modify file F_B and crafted the PDF malware F_A. However, the file F'_A was crafted instead, with slightly different feature values shown in FILE column.

In term of training time, the crafted PDF malwares could attain 100% evasion rate when model A and C were trained for only one epoch, i.e., the network was almost not trained, while it took a long time for model B and D to reach such level. After several times of training, we found that model A and C can attain this evasion rate in one epoch in every training. Since both model A and C attacked the black-box detector whose classification algorithm is Support Vector Machine (SVM), and the structure of SVM is similar to that of neural network, the substitute detector can well fit them, so the PDF malwares generated from model A and C could attain 100% evasion rate. However, both model B and D attacked the black-box detector whose classification algorithm is Random Forest (RF). The structure of RF is very different from neural network, so it is difficult to fit it.

	BEFORE	AFTER	FILE
author_dot	0	24	22
author_lc	12	-16	0
author_len	15	13	70
author_mismatch	1	4	2
author_num	0	22	20
author_oth	1	29	48
author_uc	2	2	2
box_nonother_types	0	-1	0
box_other_only	TRUE	FALSE	TRUE
company_mismatch	0	24	0
count_acroform	1	-34	1
count_acroform_obs	0	-12	0
count_action	0	8	7
count_action_obs	0	27	0
count_box_a4	0	-24	0
count_box_legal	0	-35	0
count_box_letter	0	-25	0
count_box_other	2	32	29
count_box_overlap	0	-10	0
count_endobj	19	1	19
count_endstream	9	7	9
count_eof	1	11	10
count_font	2	-9	2

Fig. 6. Differences between features of crafted PDF malwares and generated vectors

The specific scores of the 100 original PDF malwares and crafted PDF malwares revealed by the four classifiers are respectively shown in Figs. 7, 8, 9 and 10. For the classifiers with random forest classification algorithm, the scores of the crafted PDF malwares decrease obviously compared with original PDF malwares. For the classifiers with support vector machine classification algorithm, the scores of crafted PDF malwares are almost the same and most of them drop significantly and only a few of them increase. The possible reasons are left for further study.

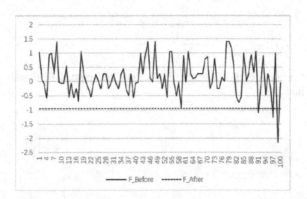

Fig. 7. Scores of original PDF malwares (F_Before) and crafted PDF malwares (F_After) revealed by classifier F

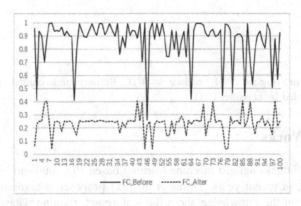

Fig. 8. Scores of original PDF malwares (FC_Before) and crafted PDF malwares (FC_After) revealed by classifier FC

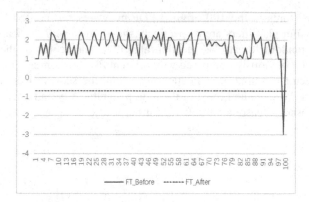

Fig. 9. Scores of original PDF malwares (FT_Before) and crafted PDF malwares (FT_After) revealed by classifier FT

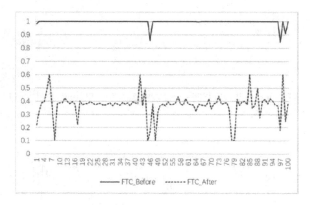

Fig. 10. Scores of original PDF malwares (FTC_Before) and crafted PDF malwares (FTC_After) revealed by classifier FTC

5   Related Works

Various evasion attacks against machine learning based PDF malware classifiers have been carried out in recent years. Šrndić et al. [21] proposed a taxonomy of evasion scenarios based on the knowledge about the feature set, training dataset and classification algorithms together with their parameters of the targeted system.

Without knowing about the learning algorithm employed by the system, Maiorca et al. [23] performed reverse mimicry attack by injecting a small malicious payload into benign files with the hope that the files could still be classified as benign.

If the attacker knows at least the feature set used by the target classifier, they can carry out mimicry attack, by injecting the information of the benign sample into the malicious sample, so that the malicious sample is classified as benign sample by the classifier. For example, Smutz et al. [22] injected information of the most discriminating features of PDFRate into malicious samples, and the results showed that the accuracy of PDFRate could be reduced by more than 20% by changing only six features. Corona et al. [24] adopted different injection strategies to try to evade LuxOR. They added all features of many benign samples to the malicious samples, and the results showed that most modified malicious samples could still be detected due to the dynamic characteristics of the features adopted by LuxOR.

Biggio et al. [11, 12] were the first to perform attacks against linear and non-linear models in the case of knowing about the learning algorithm employed by the system. They attacked Slayer [25] by using gradient descent based methods on three types of classifiers, including neural networks, linear and RBF support vector machines. The results showed that it was easy to evade any classifier by injecting very few keywords if also the targeted classifier was known to the attacker. If the classifier was not known, the efficacy of such an attack was reduced because the attacker had to train a substitute classifier to perform attack. However, by increasing the number of changes to the file, it could completely evade all classifiers. Most classifiers were evaded after 30 to 40 changes, which meant injecting 30 to 40 keywords.

Šrndić et al. [21] extended the concept proposed by Biggio et al., by performing a practical evasion of PDFRate, i.e., crafting real samples that reflected the changes made to the feature vector. Based on the information about PDFRate they obtained, they locally cloned the classifier and then created the actual evasive samples by injecting the selected features for evasion after the file EOF. Xu et al. [26] attacked PDFRate and Hidost by injecting target features directly into PDF file objects. Instead of using gradient descent algorithm, they used genetic algorithm. Their method is the only one to remove features from malicious files, and it has been shown to be very effective in evading both systems.

6 Conclusion

In this paper, we propose a novel PDF malware evasion approach based on GAN to evade machine learning based PDF malware classifiers. We evaluate our approach against four local PDF malware classifiers and the evaluation is conducted on the same evaluation dataset. In our experiment, MIMICUS is used as a tool for extracting features and crafting real PDF malwares. The experimental results reveal that attacks against three local classifiers are all able to attain 100% evasion rate and attack against the last classifier can also attain 95% evasion rate.

Through this experiment, it is found that applying GAN on the generation of adversarial PDF malware examples could achieve some good results, but there are still some problems that need to be further studied in the future. Since the features of PDF files are heavily interdependent and the values generated by GAN may be out of the boundary value of PDF file features, so it is not possible to craft PDF malwares whose features are the same as the vector generated by GAN. The PDF malware crafted according to the vector does not necessarily evade the PDF malware classifier even though the vector can evade it.

Acknowledgment. This work is supported by National Natural Science Foundation of China (No. 61876019 & U1636213).

References

1. Symantec: Internet Security Threat Report, vol. 23 (2018)
2. Taigman, Y., Yang, M., Ranzato, M.A., Wolf, L.: DeepFace: closing the gap to human-level performance in face verification. In: CVPR (2014)
3. Vinyals, O., Kaiser, Ł., Koo, T., Petrov, S., Sutskever, I., Hinton, G.: Grammar as a foreign language. In: NIPS (2015)
4. He, K., Zhang, X., Ren, S., Sun, J.: Delving deep into rectifiers: surpassing human-level performance on ImageNet classification. In: ICCV (2015)
5. Silver, D., et al.: Mastering the game of Go with deep neural networks and tree search. Nature **529**, 484 (2016)
6. Maiorca, D., Ariu, D., Corona, I., Giacinto, G.: An evasion resilient approach to the detection of malicious PDF files. In: Camp, O., Weippl, E., Bidan, C., Aïmeur, E. (eds.) ICISSP 2015. CCIS, vol. 576, pp. 68–85. Springer, Cham (2015). https://doi.org/10.1007/978-3-319-27668-7_5
7. Maiorca, D., Ariu, D., Corona, I., et al.: A structural and content-based approach for a precise and robust detection of malicious PDF files. In: 1st International Conference on Information Systems Security and Privacy (ICISSP 2015). IEEE (2015)
8. Smutz, C., Stavrou, A.: When a tree falls: using diversity in ensemble classifiers to identify evasion in malware detectors. In: 23rd Annual Network and Distributed System Security Symposium, NDSS 2016, San Diego, California, USA, 21–24 February 2016
9. Šrndić, N., Laskov, P.: Hidost: a static machine-learning-based detector of malicious files. EURASIP J. Inf. Secur. **2016**(1), 22 (2016)
10. Biggio, B., Roli, F.: Wild patterns: ten years after the rise of adversarial machine learning. Pattern Recognit. (2017)
11. Biggio, B., et al.: Evasion attacks against machine learning at test time. In: Blockeel, H., Kersting, K., Nijssen, S., Železný, F. (eds.) ECML PKDD 2013. LNCS (LNAI), vol. 8190, pp. 387–402. Springer, Heidelberg (2013). https://doi.org/10.1007/978-3-642-40994-3_25
12. Biggio, B., et al.: Security evaluation of support vector machines in adversarial environments. In: Ma, Y., Guo, G. (eds.) Support Vector Machines Applications, pp. 105–153. Springer, Cham (2014). https://doi.org/10.1007/978-3-319-02300-7_4
13. Goodfellow, I.J., Shlens, J., Szegedy, C.: Explaining and harnessing adversarial examples. Comput. Sci. (2014)
14. Szegedy, C., Zaremba, W., Sutskever, I., et al.: Intriguing properties of neural networks. Comput. Sci. (2013)
15. Demontis, A., Melis, M., Biggio, B., et al.: Yes, machine learning can be more secure! A case study on android malware detection. IEEE Trans. Dependable Secur. Comput., 1 (2017)
16. Grosse, K., Papernot, N., Manoharan, P., Backes, M., McDaniel, P.: Adversarial Examples for Malware Detection. In: Foley, Simon N., Gollmann, D., Snekkenes, E. (eds.) ESORICS 2017. LNCS, vol. 10493, pp. 62–79. Springer, Cham (2017). https://doi.org/10.1007/978-3-319-66399-9_4
17. Kolosnjaji, B., Demontis, A., Biggio, B., et al.: Adversarial malware binaries: evading deep learning for malware detection in executables (2018)
18. Wang, Q., et al.: In KDD 2017 - Proceedings of the 23rd ACM SIGKDD International Conference on Knowledge Discovery and Data Mining, vol. Part F129685, pp. 1145–1153. Association for Computing Machinery (2017)
19. Goodfellow, I.J., Pouget-Abadie, J., Mirza, M., et al.: Generative adversarial nets. In: International Conference on Neural Information Processing Systems (2014)

20. Hu, W., Tan, Y.: Generating adversarial malware examples for black-box attacks based on GAN (2017)
21. Šrndić, N., Laskov, P.: Practical evasion of a learning-based classifier: a case study. In: IEEE S&P (2014)
22. Smutz, C., Stavrou, A.: Malicious PDF detection using metadata and structural features. In: ACM Press the 28th Annual Computer Security Applications Conference, Orlando, Florida, 03 December 2012–07 December 2012
23. Maiorca, D., Corona, I., Giacinto, G.: Looking at the bag is not enough to find the bomb: an evasion of structural methods for malicious PDF files detection. In: ACM SIGSAC Symposium on Information. ACM (2013)
24. Corona, I., Maiorca, D., Ariu, D., et al.: Lux0R: detection of malicious PDF-embedded JavaScript code through discriminant analysis of API references. In: Workshop on Artificial Intelligent & Security Workshop. ACM (2014)
25. Maiorca, D., Giacinto, G., Corona, I.: A Pattern Recognition System for Malicious PDF Files Detection. In: Perner, P. (ed.) MLDM 2012. LNCS (LNAI), vol. 7376, pp. 510–524. Springer, Heidelberg (2012). https://doi.org/10.1007/978-3-642-31537-4_40
26. Xu, W., Qi, Y., Evans, D.: Automatically evading classifiers: a case study on PDF malware classifiers. In: NDSS. The Internet Society (2016)

Cyberspace Safety

Non-linguistic Features for Cyberbullying Detection on a Social Media Platform Using Machine Learning

YuYi Liu[1], Pavol Zavarsky[2(✉)], and Yasir Malik[2]

[1] Edmonton Public Schools, Edmonton, Canada
mandy.liu@epsb.ca
[2] Concordia University of Edmonton, Edmonton, Canada
pavol.zavarsky@concordia.ab.ca

Abstract. Cyberbullying on social media platforms has been a severe problem with serious negative consequences. Therefore, a number of researches on automatic detection of cyberbullying using machine learning techniques have been conducted in recent years. While cyberbullying detection has traditionally utilized linguistic features, the cyberbullying on social media does not have only linguistic features. In this paper, a holistic multi-dimensional feature set is developed which takes into account individual-based, social network-based, episode-based and linguistic content-based cyberbullying features. To test performance of the proposed multi-dimensional feature set, we designed and built cyberbullying detection models on the KNIME machine learning platform. Six different machine learning algorithms - Naïve Bayes, Decision Tree, Random Forest, Tree Ensemble, Logistic Regression, and Support Vector Machines - were used in our cyberbullying detection models. Our experimental results demonstrate that applying the proposed multi-dimensional feature set (i.e. the set not limited to the linguistic features) results in an improved cyberbullying detection for all tested machine learning algorithms.

Keywords: Cyberbullying detection · Cyberbullying features · Machine learning · Cyber safety

1 Introduction

Over the past few years, researchers and national organizations have been conducting studies to protect children and youths from cybercrimes. Progresses have been made in developing models to detect cyberbullying using machine learning techniques. It has been recognized that feature extraction of cyberbullying acts is the core component for an effective detection of cyberbullying. The major limitation of the existing models is that the feature extraction focuses primarily on linguistic analysis of bullying comments. However, considering cyberbullying as a behavior, the features of the behavior are not limited to linguistic features. For the reason, a holistic multi-dimensional feature set is developed in this paper based on our study and analysis of cyberbullying activities on a social media platform. The proposed multi-dimensional feature set can be used for an automatic detection of bullying incidents using machine learning and

J. Vaidya et al. (Eds.): CSS 2019, LNCS 11982, pp. 391–406, 2019.
https://doi.org/10.1007/978-3-030-37337-5_31

natural language processing techniques. The proposed multi-dimensional feature set takes into account individual-based, social network-based, episode-based and linguistic content-based features to detect cyberbullying on social media. Our experimental results confirm improvement in cyberbullying detection by using the proposed multi-dimensional feature set.

The remainder of this paper is organized as follows. Section 2 reviews the previous work on cyberbullying detection. In Sect. 3, the multi-dimensional feature set engineering for cyberbullying detection is proposed and justified. Section 4 discusses the design and construction of the cyberbullying detection model. The results of cyberbullying detection for three- and four-dimensional data sets processed by six machine learning algorithms - Naïve Bayes, Decision Tree, Random Forest, Tree Ensemble, Logistic Regression, and Support Vector Machines - are presented in Sect. 5. The performance of machine learning algorithms in detection of cyberbullying for the three- and four-dimensional sets are evaluated by the Precision, Recall, F1-measure, Accuracy, and Area Under Curve (AUC) metrices. We conclude the paper with final remarks and directions for future research in Sect. 6.

2   Related Work

Cyberbullying phenomenon, forms and impacts have been studied extensively in the realm of sociology and psychology. The theoretical interactional-normative framework for recognizing hostile content has been proposed in [2]. Different types of cyberbullying have been discussed in [3, 4]. Price and Dalgleish [1], Cowie [5] and Smith et al. [6] demonstrated the severe consequences and impact on youngsters induced by cyberbullying. 'Snowball effect' described in [7] illustrates that one single post can cause continuous harm to the victim if the post is reposted or liked by others.

Research on detecting and preventing cyberbullying has also made important advances in the recent years. As cyberbullying detection requires to distinct bullying from non-bullying posts, the dominant approaches are based on supervised algorithms with binary classifiers in the machine learning domain. The general solution is that the positive class represents post units containing cyberbullying, while the negative class includes posts containing non-bullying text. It is important in apply natural language processing approaches in cyberbullying detection research as the study object is mainly text generated by individuals.

Among the studies on cyberbullying detection, the chi-square information gain and odd ratio mutual information algorithms to detect and document evidence of email-based cybercrimes are explored in [8]. N-grams, Linguistic Inquiry and Word Count (LIWC) [10], Term Frequency/Inverse Document Frequency (TF/IDF), Part-of-Speech (POS) information [12], and Bag-of-Words (BoW) [11] have been applied in the detection of cyberbullying. More recent studies have demonstrated the value of considering other features, such as geoposition, time of publication [9] and network-based features. Moreover, cyberbullying detection in other languages than English has been explored by researchers in [14] for Arabic and in [16] for Dutch. Convolutional Neural Network (CNN), Long Short-Term Memory (LSTM) deep learning approaches have been used in cyberbullying detection models in [15].

Although the natural language processing techniques contributed to the development of cyberbullying detection, authors of [9, 13] found that language analysis of comments or postings is not enough to effectively detect cyberbullying. False positives are inevitable when only text features are fed to machine learning classifiers. The findings in [17] confirmed that a number of swear words were found in non-cyberbullying media conversation sessions. Authors of [7, 18, 19] proposed that cyberbullying feature study should be broadened to include both psychologic and behavioral analysis areas.

The key challenge in cyberbullying detection research is the feature set extraction which is essential for development of cyberbullying detection models. However, most of the cyberbullying detection methods are limited to studying linguistic characteristics of comments in cyberbullying activities. The holistic feature set for an effective detection of cyberbullying has not been developed. To address the gap, we present in this paper a multi-dimensional feature set engineering as an approach to improve the effectiveness of cyberbullying detection.

3   Multi-dimensional Feature Set for Cyberbullying Detection

Cyberbullying feature set development is the primary task and core component for the success of detection of cyberbullying on social media platforms by machine learning. The main idea underlying the feature set engineering proposed in this section is that a cyberbullying act on social media platforms can be detected by combining the natural language processing and machine learning techniques. Based on the definitional characteristics of cyberbullying, we propose the cyberbullying feature set with a structure of five dimensions and four layers as shown in Fig. 1.

The five-dimensional feature set shown in Fig. 1 has individual-based dimension, social network-based dimension, content-based dimension, episode-based dimension, and the "others" dimension. The details of the proposed five-dimensional feature set structure are provided in the following paragraphs.

3.1   Feature Set Layer Structure

The proposed cyberbullying feature set for machine learning based detection of cyberbullying has a layered structure. The first layer is formed by four main traits: (1) Participants trait, (2) Behaviour trait, (3) Technology trait, and (4) Sociology trait.

- *Participant's trait* reflects the power imbalance of the bully, victims and bystanders involved in one cyberbullying episode. In the trait, the post owner's age, gender, activeness, popularity, anonymity, and different roles in cyberbullying incident are considered.
- *Behavior trait* derives from the aggressiveness and repetition of cyberbullying. Attributes under this trait are the language linguistic characteristics, intention to spread the rumours, influence scope, episode duration, and inter-arrival time of negative comments.

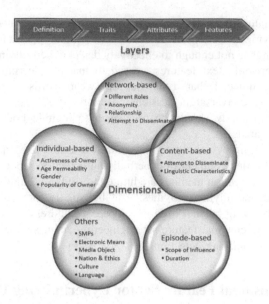

Fig. 1. Five-dimensional cyberbullying detection feature set structure

- *Technology trait* represents different online social media platforms' functions and regulations, diverse electronic means, the posting media types besides the text comments, such as pictures or video clips.
- *Sociology trait* considers national, ethnic and cultural differences. Besides cyberbullying posts in English, cyberbullying in other languages can be explored.

3.2 Feature Set Dimension Structure

Several datasets have become publicly available for cyberbullying research in the recent years. In our research, we adopted the labelled cyberbullying datasets on social media platform Instagram generously shared by the CU CyberSafety Research Center of the University of Colorado Boulder [20]. Using the dataset, we explored the Participant's and Behaviour Traits (see Fig. 2) that cover twelve Attributes with twenty-six Features to describe cyberbullying on the social media platforms. The twenty-six features were categorized into four dimensions: (1) individual-based, (2) social network-based, (3) content-based, and (4) episode-based dimension.

(1) *Individual-Based Dimension*

In this dimension, see Figs. 1 and 2, we identified four Attributes with nine Features to differentiate cyberbullying postings by the participants.

(a) *Activeness of Owner*
We consider the online age as time since the user account was created in a given social media platform. The frequency of postings an account produced in the latest half-year can be used to estimate the activeness of the account user.

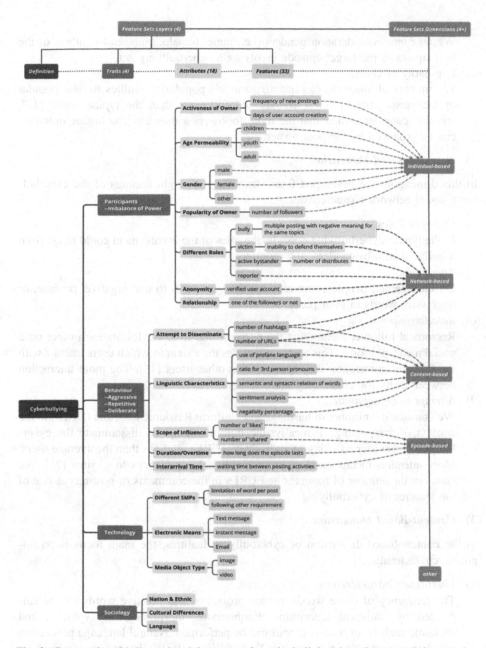

Fig. 2. Proposed multi-dimensional feature set for cyberbullying detection on social networks

(b) *Age Permeability*

   We classify the participants of a cyberbullying episode into three categories based on the age range. Age under 14 are children, between 15 and 29 are youth, and 30 and over are classified into an adult group.

(c) *Gender*

We take into consideration genders (i.e., male, female, transgender, other) of the participants in the target episode involving a cyberbullying act.

(d) Popularity of Owner

The number of followers can quantify a user's popularity. Bullies are less popular in the perspective of fewer friends and followers than the typical users [13]. Another consideration is that the more followers a user has, the higher influence can be produced by the post owner.

(2) *Network-Based Dimension*

In this dimension, we developed four Attributes with eight features of the cyberbullying social network characteristics.

(a) *Different Roles*

In the typical cyberbullying episode, the roles of the involvement could range from a bully, victim, bystanders, and reporters.

(b) *Anonymity*

On the Internet, people commonly use fake accounts to use negative, profane, or aggressive words in their posts.

(c) *Relationship*

Reciprocal follower means that the user and the follower follow each other on a social media platform. This metric quantifies the extent to which users interact with the follower connection they receive from other users [18]. The more interaction between them, the closer they are.

(d) *Attempt to Disseminate*

We consider the number of hashtags and Uniform Resource Locators (URLs) in the context of the posting. Typically, the bullies attempt to disseminate the cyberbullying behaviour by using more hashtags, URLs, and @s than the average users. More attention means more negative emotional experiences to victims [21]. We consider the number of hashtags and URLs in the comments or postings as one of the features of cyberbullying.

(3) *Content-Based Dimension*

In the content-based dimension of cyberbullying features, the main focus is on linguistic characteristics.

(a) *Linguistic Characteristics*

The frequency of curse words, person pronouns, and positive words can be calculated by statistical algorithms. Furthermore, morphological, syntactic, and semantic analysis of dataset corpus can be performed. Natural language processing and data mining techniques, such as Bag-of-Words (BoW), latent semantic analysis (LSA), continuous Bag-of-Words (CBoW), skip-gram are practical word embedding methods that can be applied to represent words in vectors.

- Use of profane language
  We examine the number and frequency of abusive words in the postings and comments. For this purpose, word lists from noswearing.com [22] and the hatebase database [23] can be employed to score the extent of swear and hateful words on [0,100] scale. Besides profane words, other topics, such as religion, death, body, and sexual hints commonly have highly-frequent occurrence in cyberbullying postings.
- Use of the third person pronoun
  The occurrence of the third-person pronouns (i.e., he, she, and they) is higher than the use of the first person singular pronoun (i.e., I) in cyberbullying involving comments [17]. Therefore, we consider the use of third-person pronouns as a feature of cyberbullying.
- Semantic and syntactic relation of words
  Word embedding, a class of techniques which allows words with similar meaning to have a similar representation as real-valued vectors, can find both semantic and syntactic relation of words. We applied TF/IDF (term frequency, inverse document frequency) scheme to calculate weight of the importance of words.
- Sentiment analysis
  We consider metrics across the user's posting and other users' comments, such as the number of uppercase text which could indicate an intense emotion. SentiStrength is a tool to estimate the strength of sentiment in short texts from extremely positive (+5) to extremely negative (−5).
- Negativity percentage
  An interesting and unexpected founding in [17] is that most cyberbullying have the percentage of negativity in the comments between 50%–60%, rather than the higher percentage such as more than 60%–70%. We consider this pattern as one of the features to detect cyberbullying incidents.

(4) *Episode-Based Dimension*

In this dimension, we identified three attributes to describe the cyberbullying phenomenon based on the episode criteria. Since the cyberbullying happens under a context, we set the threshold of fifteen comments for each episode.

(a) *Scope of Influence*

- Number of 'likes'
  The average number of likes per posting for non-cyberbullying is four times the average number for cyberbullying episodes [17], which means the cyberbullying conversations have a lower number of likes than the regular posts.
- Number of 'shared'
  Count of 'shared' episodes on social media can give an aggregated numerical view of the spread of those shares and imply the impact of the cyberbullying episodes across social networks.

(b) *Duration/Overtime*
  Although each social media platform has its average content lifespan, most social content peaks their impressions within a few hours after the posts publishing. 75%

of total comments in one post episode is received at 2.5-h mark on Facebook and 6-h on Instagram. Since the cyberbullying is a hostile act and derogatory message that bully tries to impose to victim repeatedly, the period of such posts and their comments can be longer than the average online conversations.

(c) *Interarrival Time*

Bullies and aggressors tend to be more impatient compared to the spam and normal users. According to results in [17], 40% of the cyberbullying comments were generated in less than one hour after the previous comments in one cyberbullying session.

4 Cyberbullying Detection Using the Proposed Multi-dimensional Feature Set

4.1 Machine Learning Models for Cyberbullying Detection

For cyberbullying detection experiments, we constructed six machine learning models for six algorithms. We employed the Konstanz Information Miner (KNIME) [24] to establish the experimental environment to build and test the machine learning models. The models are Naïve Bayes model, Decision Tree model, Random Forest model, Tree Ensemble model, Logistic Regression model, and Support Vector Machines model. The Random Forest model of the cyberbullying detection is shown in Fig. 3. Other five cyberbullying detection models have a similar work flow as the Random Forest model. In the cyberbullying detection model, Document Creation and Preprocessing are two meta nodes for processing text type data in the work flow. The process of creation of the two meta nodes is shown in Figs. 4 and 5.

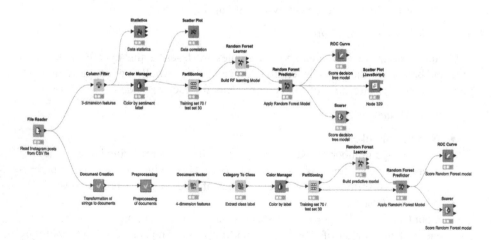

Fig. 3. Cyberbullying detection machine learning model with the Random Forest classifier

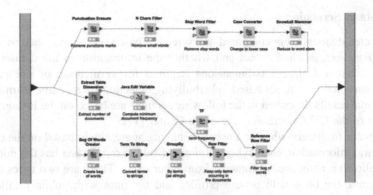

Fig. 4. The process of the Preprocessing meta node

Fig. 5. The process of meta node document creation

4.2 Dataset Collection

We used nine datasets from different social media, such as Twitter, Facebook, and Formspring, available at the ChatCoder, Kaggle Dataset, University of Wisconsin-Madison, and CU CyberSafety Research Center of the University of Colorado Boulder sharing resources. The datasets used in our experiments are listed in Table 1.

Table 1. Dataset collection

Dataset	Social media platform	Format	Size	Label
Bayzick Bullying Data	Myspace	XML	17.8 MB	Yes
University of Wisconsin-Madison	Tweet (7321 tweets)	csv	53.5 MB	Yes
CU CyberSafety Research Center	Ask.fm	txt	2.94 GB	Yes
			4.56 GB	
	Instagram	csv, jpg, txt	186.9 MB	Yes
	Vine	csv, json, txt, mp4	18.06 GB	Yes
Unknown	Facebook	mat	209.8 MB	unknown
Kelly Raynolds	Formspring.me	XML, csv	15.5 MB	Yes
General Data	unspecified	XML, csv	12.7 MB	No
Text mining and cybercrime data	unspecified	txt, HTML	77.4 MB	No

4.3   Dataset Screening

The collected datasets were compared and screened based on criteria, such as whether the data had been labelled or not and whether the information in the dataset corpus included different feature set dimensions required for verification of our proposed multi-dimensional feature set based cyberbullying detection by machine learning. The experimental results described in the following sections are based on the Instagram API collection of the CU CyberSafety Research Center [17].

To be able to discern whether a user is behaving aggressively based on the contexts and scenario information, each cyberbullying episode in our dataset has the initial post and its following associated comments from other users. There are two types of users on Instagram, the ones with private profiles and the ones with public profiles. Our sample dataset comprised the information from public profiles. According to [19], there are approximately sixteen related comments following the original post in one conversation by the users other than friends on Instagram. In our study, the threshold for the lowest number of comments in each episode was set to 15. The basic requirement for episodes being chosen is that either in the posting or in related comments, the profane language or swear words [22] were found at least once in the context. The datasets then were labelled manually by five people. For an episode to be labelled as containing cyberbullying, at least 3 out of the five people had to label it as cyberbullying according to the same standards for the judgment. In the resulting sample dataset, 478 sessions are labelled as cyberbullying and 444 sessions are labelled as non-cyberbullying. The dataset is in csv format, with 922 rows and 215 columns. Each row represents one episode with 215 criteria to describe one-episode instance. In total, 59459 comments from 922 conversation episodes with different topics comprise the dataset used in our experiments.

4.4   Dataset Preparation

The procedure we used to prepare the dataset for further processing by the machine learning algorithms has the following three components.

- Criteria reduction
  Four statistical techniques, Missing Value, Low Standard Deviation, High Correlation, and Low Skewness are applied to eliminate unneeded data columns.
- Record cleaning
  Outliers, noisy and empty or sparsely populated records are removed.
- Transformation
  In this step, we transform raw data to the format that can be processed by the machine learning tool, e.g. by changing the 'likes' criteria format from 'string' to 'number (integer)'. Each episode in the prepared dataset includes the criteria 'episode_id', 'class', 'comments', 'likes', 'owner_id', 'shared_media', 'followed_by' and 'follows'.

The three-dimensional feature set for our cyberbullying detection experiments shown in Table 2 includes two features from the episode-based dimension, one feature from the individual-based dimension, and one feature from network-based dimension. The

Table 2. Three-dimensional and four-dimensional feature sets

a) 3-dimensional feature set

Feature	Dimension	Criteria	Type
Number of 'likes'	Episode-based	'likes'	number
Number of 'shared'	Episode-based	shared_media	number
Number of followers	Individual-based	followed_by	number
One of followers	Network-based	follows	number

b) 4-dimensional feature set

Feature	Dimension	Criteria	Type
Number of 'likes'	Episode-based	'likes'	number
Number of 'shared'	Episode-based	shared_media	number
Number of followers	Individual-based	followed_by	number
One of followers	Network-based	follows	number
Sentiment analysis	Content-based	comments	string

feature Sentiment analysis from the content-based dimension is added into the feature set to form the four-dimensional feature set. The features are explained in Sect. 3.

Before the three- and four-dimensional feature set data is fed into the machine learning models, certain preprocessing steps are required to process the textual data. We applied natural language processing, text mining, and information retrieval techniques to enable the cyberbullying detection model to read, process, mine and visualize textual data in KNIME. The preprocessing includes (a) cleaning of the columns without any comments; (b) integration of all the initial comments and following posts into one column for each episode; (c) removing punctuation marks; (d) filtering of small words and stop words [33]; and (e) conversion of the terms to the lower case formatting. Then the word stem is extracted using 'snowball stemming' technique to make sure the words referring to the same lexical concept reflect the same information in our cyberbullying detection models.

Word embedding requires the conversion of text to word vectors for the latent language sentiment analysis. We extract the terms, create the Bag-of-Words (BoW) data table which can be used as the input to generate document vector. After the BoW table has been created, we filter out all terms that occur in less than nine documents. We set the minimum number of documents to 9 since we assume that a term has to occur in at least 1% of all documents (9 out of 922) to represent useful information for classification. Based on these extracted words, the document vectors are numerical representations of the text and can be used for classification by a binary classifier.

4.5 Classification

For cyberbullying detection, we performed binary classification experiments using KNIME [24] with six different classifiers: Naïve Bayes, Decision Tree, Random Forests, Tree Ensemble, Logistic Regression and Support Vector Machines (SVM). The 3-dimensional and 4-dimensional feature set data corpora were independently used by all six machine learning algorithms. In supervised learning, a machine learning algorithm takes a set of training instances of which the label is known, and seeks to build a pattern that generates a desired prediction for the unseen instances. In our cyberbullying detection models, the portion of the training set and test set was set to 70 to 30, which means that of all the 922 instances (conversation episodes) in the dataset, 645 episodes were in the training set and 277 episodes in the test set.

5   Experimental Results

In this section, performance of the six machine learning algorithms is compared for the 3-dimensional and 4-dimensional feature sets. The Instagram posting dataset with 59459 comments in 922 conversation episodes used in the experiments is described in Sect. 4. Precision, Recall, F1-measure, and Accuracy performance metrics are calculated on the cyberbullying positive class. We also report Area Under Curve (AUC) scores, a performance metric that is considered to be more robust to data imbalance than Precision, Recall and F1-measure [25]. The results are shown in Table 3.

The metrics used to evaluate the performance of machine learning algorithms in cyberbullying detection using the feature sets of different dimensions are as follows.

(1) *Confusion Matrix:* The confusion matrix is a summary of prediction results of an algorithm or classifiers and provides an assessment of the selected algorithm by the values of true positive (TP), false positive (FP), false negative (FN), and true negative (TN).

(2) *Precision:* Precision is the value of instances that are genuine of a class divided by the total instances classified as that class (also called Positive Predictive Value).

$$Precision = \frac{TP}{TP + FP}$$

(3) *Recall:* Recall is the proportion value of instances classified as a given class divided by the actual total in that class (equivalent to TP rate, also called Sensitivity). Recall means what proportion of actual positives has been identified correctly.

$$Recall = TP\ Rate = \frac{TP}{TP + FN}$$

(4) *F-Measure:* F-Measure is a weighted harmonic mean of Precision and Recall.

$$F - measure = \frac{\left(\beta^2 + 1\right) \times Precision \times Recall}{\beta^2\ Precision + Recall}$$

The weight $\beta \in [0, \infty]$. $\beta = 1$ is for equal weight on Precision and Recall. This situation is referred as F1-measure. We used the F1-measure in our experiments.

(5) *Accuracy:*

$$Accuracy = \frac{TP + TN}{TP + FP + FN + TN}$$

(6) *Area Under Curve (AUC):* AUC represents the probability that a classifier will rank a randomly chosen positive instance higher than a randomly chosen negative one [25]. The curve is the Receiver Operating Characteristic (ROC) curve that is a function of TPR against FPR at various threshold settings. The TPR is defined as TP/((TP + FN)) and FPR is defined as FP/((FP + TN)). The AUC is scale-invariant and can measure how well predictions are ranked.

Table 3. Assessment of performance of cyberbullying detection by machine learning for the three-dimensional and four-dimensional feature sets

Algorithm	Three-dimensional feature set					Four-dimensional feature set				
	Precision	RecaU	Fl-measure	Accuracy	AUC	Precision	RecaU	Fl-measure	Accuracy	AUC
Naïve Bayes	80.36	29.03	42.65	56.32	59.97	68.25	**89.58**	77.48	72.92	73.46
Decision Tree	71.21	60.65	65.51	64.26	66.08	75.33	78.47	76.87	75.45	77.50
Tree Ensemble	73.13	63.23	67.82	66.43	71.18	78.21	84.72	81.33	79.78	85.87
Random Forest	74.63	64.52	69.20	67.87	71.54	78.15	81.94	80	78.7	84.99
Logistic Regression	59.43	43.75	50.40	55.23	56.85	**86.15**	77.78	**81.75**	**81.95**	**90.39**
Support Vector Machines	74.55	26.45	39.05	53.79	58.89	82.96	77.78	80.29	80.14	87.36

The results in Table 3 are shown in their graphical forms in Figs. 6 and 7. The results demonstrate better performance of the cyberbullying detection models with the four-dimensional feature set than with the three-dimensional for all algorithms except the Precision metric results of the Naïve Bayes probabilistic classifier.

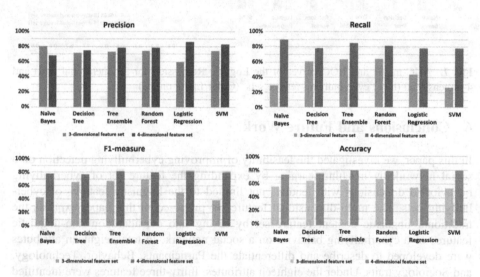

Fig. 6. Precision, Recall, Fl-measure and Accuracy metric of cyberbullying detection performance using 3-dimensionional and 4-dimensional feature sets

Figure 7 shows the AUC metric of cyberbullying detection performance of the selected six machine learning algorithms. Similar to the Recall and Accuracy results, the four-dimensional feature set outperforms the three-dimensional feature set in all machine learning algorithms for the cyberbullying detection. The ROC curves for the Logistic Regression model are also shown in Fig. 7.

Although the Naïve Bayes has the highest Recall score, the Precision value makes its overall performance lower compared to the other machine learning classifiers. The Tree Ensemble and Random Forest have a very similar performance as they both belong to the ensemble classification algorithm category. In our experiments, both the Tree Ensemble and Random Forest outperformed the Decision Tree in the cyberbullying detection. Support Vector Machines performed better than Tree Ensemble and Random Forest algorithms, with the respective AUC scores of 87.36%, 85.87% and 84.99% respectively. The Logistic Regression provided the best results regarding Precision, F1-Measure, Accuracy and AUC. The Area Under Curve for the Logistic Regression in Fig. 7 illustrates the improvement of in the cyberbullying detection task with the AUC score being increased from 56.85% to 90.39%.

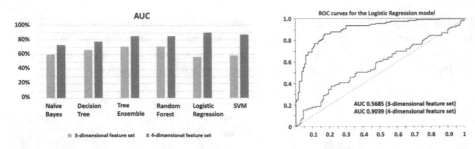

Fig. 7. AUC metric and ROC curves of the Logistic Regression for 3-dimensional (red) and 4-dimensional (blue) cyberbullying feature sets. (Color figure online)

6   Conclusions and Future Work

In this paper, we investigated the feasibility of improving cyberbullying detection on a social network by machine learning by expanding the feature set of cyberbullying behavior to dimensions with features not limited to the linguistic features of cyberbullying acts. The multi-dimensional feature set proposed in this paper expands the traditional linguistic content feature set by taking into consideration non-linguistic features of a cyberbullying behavior on a social network. In total, eighteen attributes were developed to describe and differentiate the Participants, Behavior, Technology, and Sociology traits. Under the eighteen attributes, thirty-three features were identified to facilitate a more accurate detection of cyberbullying incidents and to distinguish cyberbullying from another behavior, such as cyber harassment and cyber stalking. We applied the multi-dimensional feature set in the cyberbullying detection data pipeline built on KNIME machine learning platform. In our experiments, we tested 922 episodes with 59459 comments from Instagram. The experimental results demonstrate that cyberbullying incidents on social media platforms can be more effectively detected by using cyberbullying feature sets that are not limited to the linguistic content dimension. The improved detection of cyberbullying was achieved for all six machine learning algorithms used in our experiments - Naïve Bayes, Decision Tree, Random Forest, Tree Ensemble, Logistic Regression, Support Vector Machines - by using 5-set evaluation metrics. Our experimental results and evaluation show that Logistic Regression and Support Vector Machines outperform the Naïve Bayes, Decision Tree, and Ensembles classification on the cyberbullying detection task.

Regarding the future research, an interesting direction for future work would be the use of advanced Deep Learning techniques, such as Convolutional Neural Network (CNN) and Recurrent Neural Network (RNN) algorithms, in constructing cyberbullying detection models, given that a large amount of cyberbullying related dataset is available. State-of-the-art natural language processing techniques, such as Continuous Bag-of-Words, skip-gram, N-gram, dictionary tagger, Node2vec could be integrated into the Deep Learning model for a better performance in cyberbullying detection.

References

1. Price, M., Dalgleish, J.: Cyberbullying: experiences, impacts and coping strategies as described by Australian young people. Youth Stud. Aust. **29**, 51 (2010)
2. O'Sullivan, P.B.: Reconceptualizing 'flaming' and other problematic messages. New Media Soc. **5**(1), 69–94 (2003)
3. Vandebosch, H., van Cleemput, K.: Cyberbullying among youngsters: profiles of bullies and victims. New Media Soc. **11**(8), 1349–1371 (2009)
4. Willard, N.E.: Cyberbullying and Cyberthreats: Responding to the Challenge of Online Social Aggression, Threats, and Distress. Research Publishers LLC, Champaign (2007)
5. Cowie, H.: Cyberbullying and its impact on young people's emotional health and well-being. Psychiatrist **37**(5), 167–170 (2013)
6. Smith, P.K., et al.: Cyberbullying: its nature and impact in secondary school pupils. J. Child Psychol. Psychiatry Allied Discip. **49**(4), 376–385 (2008)
7. Slonje, R., Smith, P.K., Frisén, A.: The nature of cyberbullying, and strategies for prevention. Comput. Hum. Behav. **29**(1), 26–32 (2013)
8. Ghasem, Z., Frommholz, I., Maple, C.: Machine learning solutions for controlling cyberbullying and cyberstalking. J. Inf. Secur. Res. **6**(2), 55–64 (2015)
9. Galán-García, P., et al.: Supervised machine learning for detection of troll profiles in twitter social network: application to real case of cyberbullying. Log. J. IGPL **24**(1), 42–53 (2015)
10. Kasture, A.S., Nand, P., Tegginmath, S.: A predictive model to detect online cyberbullying (2015)
11. Zhao, R., Zhou, A., Mao, K.: Automatic detection of cyberbullying on social networks based on bullying features. In: 17th International Conference on Computer Networks - ICDCN 2016 (2016)
12. Engman, L., Janlert, L.E., Bjorklund, H.: Automatic detection of cyberbullying on social media. In: Proceedings of 16th International Multidisciplinary Scientific Conference SGEM 2016, pp. 505–512 (2016)
13. Chatzakou, D., et al.: Mean birds: detecting aggression and bullying on Twitter (2017)
14. Haidar, B., Chamoun, M., Serhrouchni, A.: A multilingual system for cyberbullying detection: Arabic content detection using machine learning. ASTES J. **2**(6), 275–284 (2017)
15. Agrawal, S., Awekar, A.: Deep learning for detecting cyberbullying across multiple social media platforms. In: Pasi, G., Piwowarski, B., Azzopardi, L., Hanbury, A. (eds.) ECIR 2018. LNCS, vol. 10772, pp. 141–153. Springer, Cham (2018). https://doi.org/10.1007/978-3-319-76941-7_11

16. Van Hee, C., et al.: Automatic detection of cyberbullying in social media text. Plos One 1–21 (2018)
17. Hosseinmardi, H., Mattson, S.A., Ibn Rafiq, R., Han, R., Lv, Q., Mishra, S.: Analyzing labeled cyberbullying incidents on the instagram social network. Social Informatics. LNCS, vol. 9471, pp. 49–66. Springer, Cham (2015). https://doi.org/10.1007/978-3-319-27433-1_4
18. Hosseinmardi, H., et al.: Towards understanding cyberbullying behavior in a semi-anonymous social network. In: Proceedings of 2014 International Conference on Advances in Social Networks Analysis and Mining, ASONAM 2014, pp. 244–252 (2014)
19. Hosseinmardi, H., et al.: A comparison of common users across Instagram and Ask.fm to better understand cyberbullying. In: Proceedings of 4th IEEE International Conference on Big Data and Cloud Computing, pp. 355–362 (2014)
20. Hosseinmardi, H.: Dataset - CU Cyber Safety Research Center, Univ. Colorado at Boulder. https://sites.google.com/site/cucybersafety/home/cyberbullying-detection-project/dataset
21. Pieschl, S., et al.: Relevant dimensions of cyberbullying - results from two experimental studies. J. Appl. Dev. Psychol. **34**(5), 241–252 (2013)
22. NoSwearing.com: Swear word list, dictionary, filter, and API. https://www.noswearing.com
23. Hatebase. https://www.hatebase.org/
24. Berthold, M.R., et al.: KNIME-the Konstanz information miner: ver. 2.0 and beyond. ACM SIGKDD Explor. Newsl. **11**(1), 26–31 (2009)
25. Fawcett, T.: An introduction to ROC analysis. Pattern Rec. Lett. **27**(8), 861–874 (2006)
26. Textfixer.com English stop words list. https://www.textfixer.com/tutorials/common-english-words.txt

Another Look at a Proposed Cubic Chaotic Mapping

Qi Wu[✉]

Jiangxi University of Finance and Economics, Nanchang 330032, Jiangxi, China
wuqiocjzd@126.com

Abstract. In this paper, we take another look at a cubic chaotic mapping proposed before, in which a case was left unconcerned. For this case, we could form a cubic mapping easily almost as same as we did before. Analysis illustrates that the mapping formed demonstrates perfect chaotic properties for anti-control of chaos. At last, a simple pseudorandom bit generator is designed and excellent results are achieved for all statistical tests.

Keywords: Chaotic mapping · Anti-control of chaos · Pseudorandom bit generator

1 Introduction

Among chaotic systems, 1-dimensional discrete chaotic mappings (abbreviated as **1DDCM** hereafter) are of the easiest form and highest efficiency [1]. However, in terms of our experiments [2–9], classic 1DDCM, such as piecewise linear mapping (skew tent mapping in most cases), Logistic mapping, and Chebyshev mapping, are defective: The chaotic area of Logistic mapping is highly narrow and incontinuous, which makes it difficult to select strong parameters; Although skew tent mapping owns broad chaotic area, when applied to devising pseudorandom bit generators (abbreviated as **PRBG** sometimes hereafter), its strong cipher space is confined in a small adjacent area of 0.5; Chebyshev mapping invokes cosine and arccosine functions once respectively during each iteration, which makes it inefficient, as cosine and arccosine functions are usually implemented by means of Taylor Expansion.

Nowadays, research on 1DDCM focuses on analysis, comparison and application of existing mappings [10–13], whereas novel ones are seldom proposed. Though 1DDCM owns too few parameters, which makes it apt to reveal its phase trajectory, and had better not be put into use directly [14], we persist that design and analysis of novel 1DDCM are significant. For one thing, owing to its simple computation and lucid chaotic properties, 1DDCM is the best tutorial for beginners of chaos. For another, thanks to its high efficiency, 1DDCM provides a sound base for high-dimensional mappings, for instance, coupling several 1-dimensional ones.

In the literature, many efforts have been made via making a 1DDCM piecewise [15–17]. Although this way could bring more parameters easily and enlarge the cipher space naturally, it dramatically decreases the efficiency. In terms of our experiments, skew tent mapping is much slower than Logistic mapping, due to its need for branch

© Springer Nature Switzerland AG 2019
J. Vaidya et al. (Eds.): CSS 2019, LNCS 11982, pp. 407–412, 2019.
https://doi.org/10.1007/978-3-030-37337-5_32

structure when implemented. In our opinion, another way for bringing more parameters is much more efficient, namely, degree raising.

In Ref. [18], a cubic chaotic mapping is constructed by us by means of raising the degree of Logistic mapping while keeping it a unimodal surjection. However, a case in Ref. [18] is left unconcerned, to which will be paid attention in this paper.

The paper is organized as follows. Section 2 takes another look at a proposed cubic chaotic mapping. Section 3 constructs a simple PRBG and tests it. Section 4 concludes.

2 A Cubic Chaotic Mapping Revisited

A Logistic mapping $g(x) = ux(1 - x)$ is a surjection iff $u = 4$, whereas non-surjection degrades dramatically during iterations. As a quadratic mapping is axisymmetric, given two points $(0, 0)$ and $(1, 0)$, no adjustment could be made. Thus, in Ref. [18] we raise its degree and obtain good results.

Given $(0, 0)$ and $(1, 0)$, owing to imaginary roots of equations with real coefficients always appear in pairs, the cubic equation must have a 3rd real root, say c. Let the cubic mapping be $f(x) = dx(1 - x)(x - c)$. To make the cubic mapping unimodal in interval $(0, 1)$, we have $c \geq 1$ or $c \leq 0$. In Ref. [18], only $c \geq 1$ is taken into account. In this paper, we focus on $c \leq 0$.

Let's set the peak value 1 in interval $(0, 1)$, then we have

$$d = \frac{27}{(c + 1 + \sqrt{c^2 - c + 1})(2 - c - \sqrt{c^2 - c + 1})(1 - 2c + \sqrt{c^2 - c + 1})}. \tag{1}$$

That's to say, we could fetch a nonpositive c at will, then compute d via Eq. (1), then a concrete mapping is formed. To distinguish it from the mapping in Ref. [18], we name it *Cubic Chaotic Mapping 2*, sometimes abbreviated as **CCM2**.

Next, we give the bifurcation graph of CCM2.

Let $x_0 = 0.1$, c go from -1000 to 0 with step $= 0.01$, for the 100001 parameters, we iterate CCM2 500 times. After filtering the first 200 times, we depict the value of x for the last 300 times, as shown in Fig. 1.

Apparently, as same as CCM in Ref. [18], the bifurcation graph of CCM2 covers the entire space, which is superb.

Then, we depict the Lyapunov exponent graph of CCM2.

Let $x_0 = 0.1$, c go from -1000 to 0 with step $= 0.01$, for the 100001 parameters, we iterate the system 2000 times and compute the Lyapunov exponent from the last 1000 times, as shown in Fig. 2.

Obviously, when c traverses $[-1000, 0]$, CCM2 always resides in chaotic area, which is excellent.

The running time of CCM2 is approximately the same as CCM, which will be omitted in this paper.

Therefore, CCM2 owns broad and continuous chaotic area and comparatively ideal running time.

In Ref. [18], CCM is applied to a hash function. Here, we apply CCM2 to a different field, namely, PRBG.

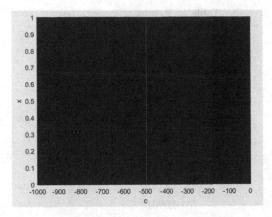

Fig. 1. Bifurcation graph of CCM2

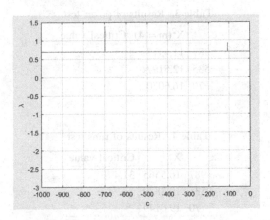

Fig. 2. Lyapunov exponent graph of CCM2

3 A Simple Pseudorandom Bit Generator

Here, we design a simple PRBG. Given x_0, c, after each iteration, emit a bit s_i via comparing x_i and 0.5:

$$s_i = \begin{cases} 0, & x_i < 0.5 \\ 1, & x_i \geq 0.5 \end{cases}. \tag{2}$$

When c goes from -1000 to 0 with step = 0.01, for the 100001 parameters, 60841 ones pass all 5 tests for pseudorandomness. Compared to our previous work [2–9], we could expect that CCM2 overwhelms skew tent mapping while designing PRBG based on coupled chaotic systems.

Next, we give some results of the tests without explanation (level of significance 0.05, length of sequence 50000, c = $-987, -535, -70$ respectively). Readers could refer to Refs. [2–9] for basic knowledge of pseudorandom tests (Tables 1, 2, 3, 4, 5 and 6).

Table 1. Results of monobit test

c	X^2	Critical value
−987	0.2509	3.84
−535	0.8820	
−70	0.0180	

Table 2. Results of serial test

c	X^2	Critical value
−987	1.2366	5.99
−535	3.1434	
−70	0.0901	

Table 3. Results of poker test

c	$X^2(m = 4)$	Critical value
−987	11.4317	25
−535	12.5197	
−70	16.6080	

Table 4. Results of runs test

c	X^2	Critical value
−987	16.5565	31.4
−535	19.3820	
−70	19.0149	

Table 5. Results of auto-correlation test

c	$|X|(d = 10000)$	Critical value
−987	0.93	1.96
−535	0.96	
−70	1.05	

Table 6. Results of linear complexity

c	Linear complexity	N/2
−987	500	500
−535	500	
−70	501	

Due to the time-consuming BM algorithm, we reduce the length to 1000 for testing the linear complexity.

4 Conclusion

In this paper, we take another look at a proposed cubic chaotic mapping, in which a case is left unconcerned. For that case, a similar cubic chaotic mapping could be formed, which possesses excellent chaotic property for anti-control of chaos. Then, based on the mapping, a simple PRBG is devised. Pseudorandom tests illustrate that the proposed PRBG could generate good sequences for most cases of parameters, which is superb. In the future, we tend to apply the mapping to some other fields, such as designing coupled chaotic systems.

Acknowledgments. This research is financially supported by the National Natural Science Foundation of China under Grant No. 61862028 & No.61762041, Natural Science Foundation of Jiangxi Province under Grant No. 20181BAB202016, the Science and Technology Project of Provincial Education Department of Jiangxi (GJJ160430), the Science and Technology Project of Provincial Education Department of Jiangxi for Youth (GJJ180288). Thanks for my supervisors Changxuan Wan & Zuowen Tan.

References

1. Hao, B.: Starting with Parabolas: An Introduction to Chaotic Dynamics. Shanghai Science and Technology Education Press, Shanghai (1993)
2. Tan, Z., Wu, Q.: Study of linearly cross-coupled chaotic systems for a random bit generator. In: 2008 International Conference on Computational Intelligence and Security, Suzhou. IEEE (2008)
3. Tan, Z., Wu, Q.: Study of exponentially cross-coupled chaotic systems for a random bit generator. In: 2008 International Symposium on Intelligent Information Technology Application, Shanghai, pp. 224–227. IEEE (2008)
4. Wu, Q., Tan, Z., Wan, C.: A harmonically coupled chaotic system for a pseudo-random bit generator. J. Chin. Comput. Syst. **32**(4), 639–643 (2011)
5. Wu, Q.: Independent variable exclusively coupled chaotic pseudorandom bit generator. Comput. Eng. Sci. **38**(11), 2197–2201 (2016)
6. Wu, Q.: An independent variable exclusively coupled chaotic system for a pseudorandom bit generator. In: 2016 International Conference on Industrial Informatics – Computing Technology, Intelligent Technology, Industrial Information Integration, Wuhan, pp. 341–344. IEEE (2016)
7. Wu, Q.: A dependent variable harmonically coupled chaotic system for a pseudorandom bit generator. In: 2018 International Conference on Smart Materials, Intelligent Manufacturing and Automation, Hangzhou. IEEE (2018)
8. Wu, Q.: A dependent variable exclusively coupled chaotic system for a pseudorandom bit generator. In: 2018 International Conference on Network and Information Systems for Computers, Wuhan. IEEE (2018)

9. Wu, Q.: A pseudorandom bit generator based on a dependent variable exclusively coupled chaotic system. In: 2018 International Conference on Intelligent Information Processing, Guilin, pp. 11–16. IEEE (2018)
10. Zhao, X.: Research on optimization performance comparison of different one-dimensional chaotic maps. Appl. Res. Comput. 29(3), 913–915 (2012)
11. Liu, L., Song, H.: Parameter estimation of one-dimensional discrete chaotic system based on chaotic synchronization. Electron. Des. Eng. 22(13), 123–125 (2014)
12. Li, C., Li, Y., Zhao, L., et al.: Research on statistical characteristics of chaotic pseudorandom sequence for one-dimensional logistic map. Appl. Res. Comput. 31(5), 1403–1406 (2014)
13. Chen, W.: The iterations of a class of level top unimodal mappings. J. Sichuan Norm. Univ. (Nat. Sci.) 38(3), 391–397 (2015)
14. Li, S., Mou, X., Cai, Y.: Pseudo-random bit generator based on couple chaotic systems and its applications in stream-cipher cryptography. In: 2nd International Conference on Cryptology in India, Chennai, pp. 316–329. IEEE (2001)
15. Guo, Z., Liu, D.: Image encryption and compression algorithm based on 2D phased linear chaotic map coupling Chinese remainder theorem. Comput. Appl. Softw. 32(5), 288–291, 329 (2015)
16. Cai, D., Ji, X., Shi, H., et al.: Method for improving piecewise logistic chaotic map and its performance analysis. J. Nanjing Univ. (Nat. Sci.) 52(5), 809–815 (2016)
17. Xu, H., Li, Q., Ning, M., et al: Analysis of the chaotic boundary in a class of piecewise nonlinear mapping. J. Hainan Norm. Univ. (Nat. Sci.) 29(4), 363–368, 383 (2016)
18. Wu, Q.: A chaos-based hash function. In: 2015 International Conference on Cyber-Enabled Distributed Computing and Knowledge Discovery, Xi'an. IEEE (2015)

Research on Drug Regulation Mode in the Age of the Internet of Things

Yan Zhao[1(⊠)], HuWei Liu[1], and Ning Cao[2]

[1] School of Information, Beijing Wuzi University, Beijing, China
zhaoyanxn@163.com, liuhuwei@outlook.com
[2] School of Internet of Things, Wuxi Commercial Vocational and Technical
College, Wuxi, China
ning.cao2008@hotmail.com

Abstract. The Internet of things is the third information technology revolution after the computer and the Internet. The center of this technological revolution is the [1] of the Internet of things. The Internet of things is not a communication network, but a collection of sensing technology, communication technology and computing technology. The State Council emphasizes that in the field of people's livelihood, the model application and demonstration project of the Internet of things should be implemented around the innovation of management model and service model. The drug regulatory code is the information label of each drug given by the State Administration of drugs to supervise the implementation of electronic drugs. It is used to indicate the information mark of store automatic sale management system or to mark the classification and coding of goods. To find the feasibility of the interconnection between the two has a broad prospects for development. In the 2008 government work report, Premier Wen Jiabao pointed out that the strict market access system and product quality traceable system and recall system were implemented. At present, the State Food and drug administration has carried out the electronic supervision of pharmaceuticals, which is a work that embodies the technology characteristics of the Internet of things and has the concept of forward-looking supervision. Using modern information technology, network technology, coding technology and the built third party technology platform, we set up a monitoring and traceable system for drug. At the same time, the problem of drug safety has also become a major concern. At present, there is not an effective drug safety supervision mode to supervise drugs.

Keywords: Internet of Things · Drug regulatory code · Pattern innovation

1 An Overview of the Internet of Things

The concept of the Internet of things has attracted more and more attention since it was put forward in 1999. The Internet of things is designed to connect all items to the Internet through a variety of information sensing devices to realize intelligent identification and management.

J. Vaidya et al. (Eds.): CSS 2019, LNCS 11982, pp. 413–424, 2019.
https://doi.org/10.1007/978-3-030-37337-5_33

1.1 The Concept of the Internet of Things

At present, a more authoritative definition of "Internet of things" is put forward by the European Commission on information society and the media in 2008 (the 2020 Internet of things: the way ahead). The "Internet of things" is defined as "has some identity and virtual individual features, related operations can be carried out in a smart space by using the intelligent interface, and can be with the social, environmental, user context and connected and effective communication network of objects, think of things with" integration "that is the future of the Internet, one of the objects which are communicated with each other and play a positive angle. In 2010, the government work report in our definition of things: IOT refers to the information sensing device (RFID radio frequency identification (RFID), infrared sensors, GPS, laser scanners, etc.) in accordance with the contract agreement, any items and the Internet together to exchange information and communication, in order to achieve a network intelligent identification, positioning, tracking, monitoring and management. It is an extended and extended network based on the Internet.

1.2 Features of the Internet of Things

(1) Connectivity. Connectivity at any time, connectivity of any place, connectivity of any object.
(2) Intelligence. The material world in which people are located can be digitized and networked to a great extent, making objects in the world not only connected in a sensory manner but also in an intelligent way, and network services can also be intelligent.
(3) Embeddedness. First, all kinds of objects are embedded in people's living environment. Two, Internet services provided by Internet of things will be seamlessly embedded in people's daily work and life.

1.3 The Application of the Internet of Things in Domestic Related Fields

At present, the Internet of things has been in our country in the field of health hospital intelligent management (patient information management, mobile nursing, medication management), remote monitoring, drugs and equipment management in Colleges and universities in the field of [2], teaching technology (teaching methods and teaching methods), student management (student attendance management and student safety management), the logistic service (campus card, campus material distribution and storage use) applied [3] etc. In particular, the Internet of things has made notable progress in environmental protection and health. The main manifestations are: clear the general idea, actively and steadily push forward, strengthen the support strength, and strengthen the system design. These practices can be used for reference for the construction of the Internet of drugs.

2 A Summary of China's Drug Regulatory Code

2.1 The Definition of China's Drug Regulatory Code Network

According to the definition of things, we give the definition of Chinese drug regulatory code of things, is refers to through the information sensing device to connect all China drug regulatory code and Internet services, information exchange and communication, to a network to realize intelligent identification, positioning, tracking, monitoring, management and service.

2.2 The Basic Form of Drug Electronic Regulatory Code

(1) The Composition of the Code

One - dimensional bar code, 20 bits. The first number is 8, representing the drug. The next 6 bits represent the class code; the next 9 represents a single sequence number; the next 4 is a cipher (Table 1).

Table 1. Regulatory code printing parameters specification

Regulatory code printing parameters specification	
Bar code type	Code 128C
Bar code density	$\geq$ 7mils
Height of bar code	$\geq$ 8 mm
data type	number
Data length	20

(2) Regulatory Code Printing Parameters Specification

When printing the regulatory code, the minimum bar code density is 7mils and the bar code width is about 28 mm according to the requirements. In order to improve the success rate and scan speed of the first scan code, it is recommended to use 10mils above density (the smallest module width is 10mils, and the bar code width is about 42 mm).

2.3 The Theory of the Internet of Drug Supervision and Code in China

The Internet of things is a new network produced by the combination of technology such as object recognition and perception and Internet. It mainly solves the connection between objects, people, objects [4] and people to people. The basic characteristics, basic functions and basic structure of China's drug regulatory code are the same as the Internet of things, but China's drug regulatory code has its own characteristics. The basic characteristics of things, mainly refers to the network, networking, Internet, automation, intelligent sensing [5]; basic functions, mainly through networking related technology can achieve a comprehensive perception, reliable transmission between items and intelligent processing, its essence is the acquisition of equipment items will be the greatest degree of information data the use of modern sensor and data embedded in the prior articles or facilities, then use item identification technology and communication technology of the data items of information connected to the Internet, and then get the information to the server collation, processing, analysis and processing, and finally the goods management and the corresponding control using [6] analysis and processing the results of.

3   The Significance of the Internet of Things Technology in the Electronic Supervision of Drugs

At present, although there are standard networking technology, safety protection, electromagnetic interference and other key technology development is not mature, application of the relatively high cost of things, most of the medicine enterprise scale lag strength is not strong, modernization, environment using the Internet for electronic monitoring is not mature and other obstacles, but things in the electronic supervision the effect of drugs has is of great significance to allow all doubt, that is mainly reflected in the following aspects.

3.1   Realize Real-Time Monitoring and Guarantee the Quality and Safety of Drug Circulation

Drugs especially vaccines and other biological products easily affected by environmental factors such as temperature, so as to ensure the quality of drugs, the drug must ensure that the environment temperature is always within the range or once the temperature anomaly can be found in a timely manner, which requires the environmental temperature on the drug of real-time monitoring. At present, the production of drugs from the production, circulation to the last use involves many links. It is easy to produce the problem of "chain breaking". In addition, the temperature of the external environment varies greatly at different time and place. Once the problem arises, it will easily affect the quality of the drug. At present, the main is to check the temperature through the derived temperature recorder data on real-time monitoring of the whole process of drug circulation temperature not to control after behavior; moreover, existing problems in chain breaking out of storage link, can not achieve the whole record at ambient temperature on the drug. On the one hand, we can't find the impact of environmental abnormality on the quality of drugs in time, and take remedial measures in time. On the other hand, once there is a problem, it is difficult to identify the cause of the accident due to the failure to record the whole environmental temperature.

3.2   Realizing the Effective Tracking of the Whole Process of Drug Circulation

In the current electronic supervision of pharmaceuticals, when the drug is out and in storage, we need to scan the electronic supervision code one by one with the scanning code gun. After the information is completed, click the upload button to upload the information to the China Pharmaceutical electronic supervision network [7]. Due to the information after scanning, enterprises need to manually click "Upload" button to upload. There are some problems that enterprises upload information, nuclear notes and write off, which results in the fact that regulatory authorities can not grasp the real drug circulation information in time. In addition, the flow of drugs from medical institutions or drugstores to consumers is still a regulatory gap. Because the information of the drug electronic supervision network can not fully reflect the actual direction of the drug, once the adverse drug reaction and other problems need to be recalled immediately, it is impossible to recall all the problem drugs at the first time. Moreover, the drugs that have been sold to consumers are very difficult to recall because of the lack of corresponding records, which makes the electronic supervision of pharmaceuticals lose the meaning of dynamic supervision and timely tracing.

Aiming at the defects of the current regulation, things can achieve real-time automatic upload and drug related information, without manual intervention, not only to ensure the timeliness of information, but also can effectively avoid the illegal operation of the logistics and information flow issues such as inconsistent artificial scan code, upload data. In addition, in the final part of drug sales, because the second generation ID card and medical card contains RFID tags, drug sales need to consumer identity information identification and drug sales information association, in order to complete sales, the true record of the whole process of drug circulation, so as to realize the full traceability.

3.3 Enriching the Content of Drug Supervision and Improving the Ability of Drug Regulation

Through the understanding of China's pharmaceutical electronic supervision network, we can see that the current drug electronic supervision is mainly for drug flow, focusing on the construction of drug circulation tracking platform to track the flow of drugs. In addition, a simple information query platform for drugs is also established, which can query the authenticity of drugs and the information of first tier sellers through the query system of China's drug and electronic supervision network, but the information content is too simple to meet the needs of regulators and consumers.

Drug supervision is the supervision of all kinds of drug related information. The focus of drug electronic supervision under the environment of Internet of things is to collect all kinds of drug information and upload it to the central database after digitalization. According to the regulatory requirements, data information can be processed by intelligent processing technology and uploaded to the corresponding regulatory platform. The powerful information collection and processing capabilities of the Internet of things can build huge data information system, provide information basis for the continuous enrichment of regulatory content, and ensure regulatory capacity to always meet regulatory needs. For example, can increase the drug price information in the monitoring platform, to strengthen the drug price regulation; you can also write information using detailed and popular medicines in the electronic label of the drug product, as a supplement of drug instructions, to maximize the protection of the drug safety of patients.

3.4 Greatly Simplifying the Work of Pharmaceutical Enterprises and Improving the Efficiency of Drug Electronic Supervision

In electronic supervision, the main work of enterprises is the coding of regulatory codes. The traditional electronic bar code is used as the electronic supervision code of drugs, and the scanning gun is used to scan the regulatory code one by one, so that the information can be read. Therefore, in order to overcome the low efficiency caused by a large number of scanning tasks, we need to classify the regulatory codes according to the packaging specifications, and establish correlation relations for different levels of regulatory codes. But in the process of implementation, it is found that it is easy to cause association errors, such as changing difficulties, scanning quickly, missing bar code, bar code easy to damage, slow scanning speed and other issues, which increases the workload of enterprises and reduces the circulation efficiency of drugs [8]. The Internet of things technology can effectively solve the above problems. It uses the RFID technology, the first to read multiple tags in a package isolated case, without one by one scan of the label, greatly reduce the correlation level; secondly, as long as the RFID tags in the reader identification range, label information can be read automatically, there is no leakage to read RFID tags in the bad problem; normally, it is not easy to damage, rarely damaged barcode need to replace the trouble. Therefore, the electronic supervision based on the Internet of things can effectively reduce the workload of the enterprises and improve the efficiency of drug electronic supervision.

4 New Model of Drug Regulation in the Era of Internet of Things

4.1 Electronic Supervision in the Field of Drug Circulation

In the 2008 government work report, Premier Wen Jiabao pointed out that the strict market access system and product quality traceability system and the recall system [9] were implemented. At present, the State Food and drug administration has carried out the electronic supervision of pharmaceuticals, which is a work that embodies the technology characteristics of the Internet of things and has the concept of forward-looking supervision [10]. Using modern information technology, network technology, coding technology and the built third party technology platform, we set up a monitoring and traceability system for drug catalogues. The outer packing in drug minimum sales units, according to a code of principles for drug endowed, at the same time through the pharmaceutical enterprises, real-time upload the production and management of data, to achieve timely access to network traffic and flow control of drugs, inventory information, and through early warning and treatment of drug safety information, to meet the needs of drug supervision work. Electronic monitoring of drug circulation, one can effectively combat counterfeit drugs, to ensure the safety and effectiveness of public administration. The closed loop operation of the electronic regulatory network of drugs makes it difficult for illegal drugs to enter the regular sales channels of the state. Two is the effective implementation of the problem of drug tracing and recall. Because of the traffic flow, and inventory of drugs network capable of performing real-time control, so the injury occurred, the network can in the shortest possible time, with the fastest speed of drug traceability, play a major role for the control of drug harm quickly recall and injury events.

4.2 Drug Electronic Supervision Under the Technology of Internet of Things

The above electronic supervision is only used in the field of drug circulation. With the continuous improvement and wide application of Internet of things technology, we should closely combine the links of drug research, production, circulation and use with electronic supervision to form a comprehensive drug electronic supervision mode.

From the supervision of information collection, analysis, focus, to the redistribution of regulatory resources, to release and carry out the task of supervision, or even a technical review, the administrative examination and approval, mobile law enforcement and judicial transfer, statistical analysis and so on the restructuring of the business aspects of the work, leading towards supervision to intelligent mode. Then, as regulators, not only can grasp the various drug flow, flow, inventory, adverse reactions and other information, area and time statistics of national medicine and the analysis also carried out, under the social public emergencies emergency transfer and drug dispensing, etc. These work information will lay an important foundation for assisting medical reform at the present stage of our country, investigating the situation of national drug use and carrying out the research on medical and health work.

5 Construction of China's Drug Safety Supply Chain Supervision Model

5.1 Non Supply Chain Drug Safety Supervision Model and Existing Problems

Supervision of local governments in China (hereinafter referred to as non current supply chain supervision model) is separate supervision mode (see Fig. 1), the local drug regulatory departments to form separate supervision of sampling, pharmaceutical production enterprises, pharmaceutical wholesale enterprises, pharmaceutical sales units, according to pharmaceutical production and quality management certification (GSP and GMP), detection of adverse drug reactions and for practitioners to ensure drug safety management. In such a regulatory mode, if we can strictly guard against drug sales, we can ensure drug safety, but the drug regulatory authorities are facing a lot of coordination work, especially with the local government departments. For example, in criminal acts against selling counterfeit drugs, need the joint action of industry and commerce, public security, quality supervision and other departments; in the fight against illegal drug advertisements in the process, more just the illegal advertising to inform the Department of industry and commerce, and no law enforcement powers in the corresponding; related legal issues involving imported drug safety, drug administration and customs import and export inspection and quarantine and commerce departments must coordinate the relationship; in the process of supervision of hospital pharmacy, if there is no local health departments support, supervision work is difficult. Therefore, the government supervision departments because of manpower, time and funds are limited, it is difficult to achieve a comprehensive examination, or detection means it is difficult to use cheap, fast and effective monitoring of drug safety, drug market will continue to appear counterfeit medicines and drugs, a fish escaped through the Seine, it is difficult to eliminate substandard drugs. In addition, in addition to some deep-seated problems, there are still many problems in the process of coordination with relevant departments in the lack of unified standard for drug regulation in various provinces and cities.

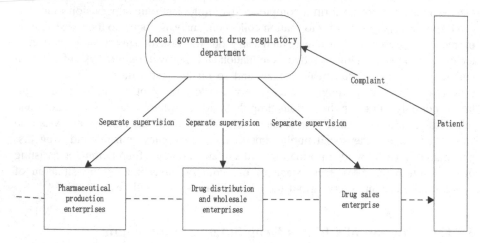

Fig. 1. Drug safety supervision mode

5.2   Construction of Regulatory Model of Drug Safety Supply Chain in China

Europe and the United States has been in the world pharmaceutical research and development, production and consumption of the frontier, the drugs safety supervision very seriously, as early as the end of twentieth Century on the basic realization of the supervision of the whole supply chain of drugs, such as the United Kingdom from the point to the line of drug supply chain supervision system, the drug supply chain information management and drug pedigree information "the EU version of" EU good circulation management standards "(GDP) in the regulation of the entire supply chain based on drug safety, etc. Based on the experience of drug supply chain supervision in Europe and America, this paper puts forward a model for the construction of China's drug safety supply chain supervision. Drug safety supply chain supervision refers to the integration of drug manufacturers, distributors and retailers in a supply chain that ensures drug safety through the means of electronic information and mechanism design, so as to achieve effective management of drug safety.

The basic framework of China's drug regulatory supply chain as shown in Fig. 2, its mode of operation is: the local government supervision of GMP pharmaceutical production enterprises, pharmaceutical production out, through the electronic code stored Fu pharmaceutical production and circulation of information, to the circulation, distributors, wholesalers to information related to the process of drug distribution occurred to add, to sales, hospitals and drug retailers through the doctor and pharmacist to ensure the safety of drugs. At the same time in the reverse circulation of pharmaceuticals, establish a new mechanism to cut off the drug safety risk transfer chain based design, in order to promote the pharmaceutical enterprises on the supply chain cooperation, the formation of the industrial chain between the upstream and downstream enterprises of product quality supervision and other drug safety responsibility system based on traceability system. Drug manufacturers uploaded the drug data to the national unified regulatory platform. The enterprises, hospitals and patients at the downstream of the supply chain can always verify the drug safety at any time. The drug regulatory authorities supervise drug wholesalers, distributors, hospitals and drug retailers, and monitor the safety of drug use for patients and the public.

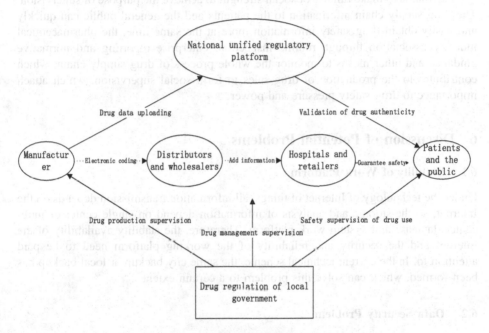

Fig. 2. Drug safety supply chain supervision mode

5.3   Characteristics of the Mode of Drug Safety Supply Chain Supervision

First, the effective integration of regulatory resources can be realized. The drug supply chain supervision mode to distributors and retailers in the integration of a supply chain to ensure drug safety, drug safety inspection through the design of drug supply chain between the upstream and downstream and the reporting system, reduce the risk of drug circulation, while the integration of state and local regulatory power, realize data sharing, the formation of a national drug supervision network.

The two is to save cost effectively and realize real-time online monitoring. Information is the basic feature of supply chain management, and the drug supply chain is no exception. The supervision mode of drug supply chain can make use of various electronic information means to monitor the production, circulation, storage, distribution and sale of drugs online and online, which not only saves human resources, but also effectively monitors enterprises, and saves a lot of manpower supervision costs.

Three is the supervision means which can realize the combination of key and comprehensive. After the implementation of the drug safety supply chain network, the regulatory agency does not need to regulate every link of the drug production and circulation. Those in the drug regulatory mechanism in the key parts (such as sales) is the focus of Drug Supervision checks; and those that can through the system design of internal supply chain in addition to some of the drug supply chain and drug safety, you can put more resources to conduct comprehensive supervision.

The four is to make full use of social strength to achieve the purpose of supervision. The drug supply chain information to the patients and the general public can quickly and easily obtain drug safety information more at the same time, the pharmaceutical industry association through routine inspection, enterprise reporting and normative guidance and other means to monitor the whole process of drug supply chain, which contributes to the production of drug sales to form social supervision, which attach importance to drug safety pressure and power.

6 Discussion of Potential Problems

6.1 Stability of Work Platform

Under the technology of Internet of things, all information transmission depends on the Internet, so the storage and analysis of information depend on single center or multi center database and system work platform. Therefore, the stability availability of the Internet and the security and reliability of the working platform need to be paid attention to. In the current technical scheme, the same city backup or local backup has been formed, which can solve this problem to a certain extent.

6.2 Data Security Problem

A large number of information data are stored in one or more central databases at the same time, and the security of data needs to be paid enough attention to. A large number of data centralized management, once the occurrence of data leakage, the pharmaceutical industry of China's national conditions, drug use and commercial secrets of the important information safety posed a great threat. Therefore, it is necessary to increase the security management of data information by law, regulations and technical means [11].

In short, in the face of the arrival of the era of things, the drug regulatory departments should be in the premise of a clear regulatory direction and task, make full use of the modern government management ideas and information technology, to speed up the reform push to improve the means of supervision and the formation of new regulatory structure have the characteristics of the times and the actual effect of the.

7 Conclusion

The prospects for the development of the drug regulatory code network: since 2006, the drug monitoring code has been for 11 years and has now covered all the basic drug catalogues. Because the system is conducive to improving the level of enterprises, helping the government to strengthen supervision, and helping consumers identify counterfeit drugs and quality queries, which is more and more accepted and welcomed by all parties.

In recent years, consumers pay more and more attention to commodity safety. The media constantly exposures the safety of food, cars and accessories, household appliances, children's toys, clothing and so on. The famous enterprises attach importance to the quality of products. Strengthen product quality supervision level has a good social environment, once the implementation of electronic supervision function, it can further improve product quality, reduce security risks, protect the interests of the consumers, it can better protect the well-known brands, is conducive to the brand bigger and stronger, to improve the overall quality of the image Chinese products. Once the on-line electronic supervision system more and more enterprises, will further promote the development of the national economy, improve the Chinese networking level, strengthen the organic integration of the Internet and the Internet of things.

Acknowledgement. This work was supported in part by the Beijing Great Wall Scholars' Program under Grant CIT and TCD20170317, in part by the Beijing Tongzhou Canal Plan "Leading Talent Plan", in part by the Beijing Collaborative Innovation Center and in part by the Management Science and Engineering High-precision Project.

References

1. Tang, L.: The emergence and development of the strategic emerging industry - the Internet of things. J. Chifeng Univ. (Natural Science Edition) **3**, 30–32 (2011)
2. Xi, J.: Our country from the power network construction has become a powerful network of EB/OL. 20140227
3. Sang, Y.: Security situation and Strategy Research of J big data. Comput. Sci. **42**(11), 372–383 (2015)
4. The central government portal. The State Council on promoting things orderly and healthy development of the guidance of EB/OL. 20160806
5. Yao, W.: On the concept of the Internet of things and its basic connotations. Chin. World Inf. **2010**(5), 22–23 (2010)
6. Gu, L.J.: strengthened The current situation and development strategy of the Internet of Things in China. Enterp. Econ. **2013**(4), 114–117 (2013)
7. Jing, W.: Research on electronic regulatory Countermeasures of drug safety in China. Heilongjiang University of Chinese Medicine, p. 35 (2011)

8. Jiang, J., Li, X.: Common problems and treatment of drug electronic supervision in the process of coding. Chin. Pharm. Equip. **2**, 50–52 (2010)
9. Wen, J.: Government Work Report. People's Publishing House, Beijing (2008)
10. State food and Drug Administration (State Food and Drug Administration). Notifications of relevant issues on the implementation of drug electronic supervision and administration state food and Drug Administration [No. 2008] 165 (2008)
11. Zhang, J.: The government wants to strengthen the supervision of online drug sales. Chin. Pharm. Ind. **16**(2), 2–3 (2007)

Privacy-Aware Service Migration for Edge Computing in Urban Cities

Xihua Liu[1], Lianyong Qi[2], Xiaolong Xu[1(✉)], Xuyun Zhang[3],
and Shaohua Wan[4]

[1] School of Computer and Software, Nanjing University of Information
Science and Technology, Nanjing, China
liuxihua710@gmail.com, njuxlxu@gmail.com
[2] School of Information Science and Engineering,
Qufu Normal University, Shandong, China
lianyongqi@gmail.com
[3] Department of Electrical and Computer Engineering,
University of Auckland, Auckland, New Zealand
xuyun.zhang@auckland.ac.nz
[4] School of Information and Safety Engineering,
Zhongnan University of Economics and Law, Wuhan, China
shaohua.wan@ieee.org

Abstract. Currently, to satisfy the increasing demands for the computing and network resources at the edge of networks, edge computing has emerged as an efficient paradigm for real-time resource provisioning. Due to the unbalanced resource requests of mobile devices in the urban cities, the edge computing nodes (ECN) easily suffers from the underload or overload resource usage. Thus, it is of great importance to devise rational and effective service migration strategies to guarantee the overall performance of edge computing in the urban city. However, during the service migration between ECNs, the privacy information in the services is detected by the network, which may lead to the privacy leakage. To avoid privacy leakage and provide favorable computation performance including load balance as well as transmission time, it is necessary to seek appropriate service migration routes. In this paper, an optimization problem is formulated to minimize the transmission time and the load balance while protecting the privacy data during the service migration. Then, a privacy-aware service migration method, named PSM, is proposed in this paper. Finally, numerous experiments and evaluations are conducted to confirm the effectiveness and efficiency of our designed method.

Keywords: Edge computing · Service migration · Privacy leakage ·
Transmission time · Load balance

Supported by National Natural Science Foundation of China under grant no. 61702277
and no. 61872219.

J. Vaidya et al. (Eds.): CSS 2019, LNCS 11982, pp. 425–436, 2019.
https://doi.org/10.1007/978-3-030-37337-5_34

1   Introduction

Edge computing addresses the problem of limitations on the mobile devices including computing power, battery capacity, etc., which is introduced to process data at the edge of networks [1]. Besides, edge computing is a robust paradigm since the edge nodes (ENs) in edge computing are distributed and they are less impacted by the failures of one centralized point [2]. However, the resource requests of mobile devices in the urban cities are unbalanced. When the EN is filled with dense service requirements, the services in the EN need to be in queue to wait available resources in the EN. In order to mitigate the queuing time, the services are migrated to the other ENs for processing, which minimizes the waiting time so that improves the performance of the networks [3].

However, the process of service migration across ENs is imposed with the privacy and security issues [4]. Although the service migration improves the capability of networks, it leads to the easy leakage of privacy information at the same time. On condition that the contents of migrated services are related to the account information, current location, etc., the network could obtain the information in the services, which may result in the violation of personal privacy. The schemers, who invade the network, could sell the personal information or committing crimes. Clearly, as the service migration carries different privacy information, it is necessary to cope with the problem of privacy leakage during the service migration in edge computing [5,6].

On the other hand, the overall performance of entire service migration, including the transmission time and the load balance, needs to be taken into consideration. When the services need to be migrated, the time consumption is a significant object [7]. On condition that the transmission time is saved, the experience of customers will be highly improved. Furthermore, although the customers are sensitive to the transmission time for executing the services, the load balance also affects the data-processing capability, availability and flexibility of the networks. When all of the services are migrated to the same EN, the tasks need to wait the tasks in front of it, which leads to the waste of time and computing resources. In order to cope with this problem, the load balance of ENs is also a significant object waiting to be improved [8].

With the above observations, it is important to design an appropriate method for the service migration to avoid the privacy leakage while improving the load balance and transmission time. A privacy-aware service migration method, named PSM, is designed for the service migration to avoid the privacy leakage while improving the load balance and transmission time.

In this paper, the main contributions are as follows:

- Analyze the privacy entropy and the overall performance including the transmission time and the load balance during the service migration in edge computing. In addition, this problem is defined as a multi objective optimization problem.
- A privacy-aware service migration method is proposed to make jointly optimization of the load balance, privacy entropy and transmission time and for all the ENs in edge computing.

- Comprehensive experiments and evaluations are conducted to demonstrate the efficiency and effectiveness of our proposed method.

The reminder of this paper is organized as follows. In Sect. 2, the related work is summarized. In Sect. 3, the mathematical modeling and the formulation are introduced. In Sect. 4, a privacy-aware service migration method for edge computing is proposed. In Sect. 5, comprehensive experiments and comparison analysis are presented. Finally, conclusions and future work are shown in Sect. 6.

2 Related Work

Due to the development of the mobile applications, traditional cloud computing no longer satisfied people's need for real-time computing requirements. Fortunately, edge computing emerges as an alternative paradigm. The services can be migrated from the mobile devices to the edge nodes (ENs) for processing in edge computing [9,10].

If all the services are migrated between ENs without managements, the load balance and the transmission time will be affected. The load balance makes contribution to the data-processing capability, and the transmission time leads to the waste of time [11,12].

In [13], Tiago et al. introduced a method to minimize service delay in a scenario where there are two cloudlet servers. This method focuses mainly on the computation and communication by controlling processing delay in the form of virtual machine migration, and improved the transmission delay by power control. In [14], in order to deal with the data streams nearby the mobile edge, Sun et al. introduced edgeIoT which is a new approach to the mobile edge computing in the IoT architecture. In addition, they introduced a hierarchical fog computing architecture to offer flexible IoT services in fog nodes while protecting user privacy. In [15], the service migration problem was denoted as a Markov Decision Process (MDP) by Wang et al. In order to provide optimal service migration policies, they introduced a mathematical framework. In addition, a numerical technique and a novel algorithm is introduced for the optimal solution computation.

In addition, in order to avoid privacy leakage during the service migration, these services need to be handled extra.

In [16], Shen et al. focused on the optimization of the task acceptance rate during the process of protecting participants' privacy by using edge nodes, and a privacy-preserving task allocation framework (P2TA) is introduces for edge computing enhanced MCS. In [17], Lu et al. introduced a lightweight privacy-preserving data aggregation scheme, which is named as Lightweight Privacy-preserving Data Aggregation, in fog computing-enhanced IoT framework. In [18], Gai et al. investigated on the conflict problem between the privacy protection and efficiency, and they introduced a novel approach to provide higher-level security transmission by the technology of the multi-channel communications.

Based on the above investigation, few researches and studies have taken the joint optimization for the load balance, the transmission time and the privacy entropy during the migration between ENs in edge computing.

3   System Model and Problem Formulation

3.1   Resource Model

We assume that there are n ENs, m VMs in each EN and k computing tasks in edge computing, denoted as $SE = \{se_1, se_2, \ldots, se_n\}$, $SV = \{sv_1, sv_2, \ldots, sv_m\}$ and $SC = \{sc_1, sc_2, \ldots, sc_k\}$, respectively. Consider a scenario, the computing tasks are transmitted in the form of VMs between ENs for process. In addition, for the sake of the security of privacy, when the computing task need to be offloaded, the computing task is divided into C types.

3.2   Load Balance Analysis of ENs

VMs are rented for resource allocation in the ENs, and the computing tasks are hosted by VMs. In addition, the capacity of servers in this paper are weighed by the number of VMs.

The resource usage is an important value to evaluate the performance of ENs. O_n is utilitied to judge whether the se_n is occupied, which is determined by

$$O_n = \begin{cases} 1, \text{if } se_n \text{ is occupied}, \\ 0, \text{otherwise}. \end{cases} \tag{1}$$

$JS^n{}_k$ is utilitied to judge whether the sc_k is deployed on se_n, which is defined by

$$JS_k^n = \begin{cases} 1, \text{if } sc_k \text{ is placed on } se_n, \\ 0, \text{otherwise}. \end{cases} \tag{2}$$

The number of occupied servers determined the average resource usage of the EN. The number of occupied servers is determined by

$$NO = \sum_{n=1}^{N} JS_k^n. \tag{3}$$

The resource utilization can measure the usage of VM instances. The resource utilization of sen is calculated by

$$RU_n = \frac{1}{\gamma_n} \sum_{k=1}^{K} CD_k \cdot O_n, \tag{4}$$

where γ_n represents the capacity of n-th EN and CD_k represents the number of consumed VMs for sc_k.

Finally, the average resource usage of the EN is calculated by

$$AR = \frac{1}{NO} \sum_{n=1}^{N} RU_n.$$ (5)

Then, the load balance is considered in edge computing. Based on the variance of resource utilization, the load balance variance of se_n is calculated by

$$BV = (AR - RU_n)^2.$$ (6)

For all the ENs, the average load balance variance is calculated by

$$AB = \frac{1}{NO} \sum_{n=1}^{N} BV \cdot JS_k^n.$$ (7)

3.3   Transmission Time Analysis

If the first EN is full of tasks, the VMs need to be migrated from hosted EN to other ENs. However, the migration consumes a lot of time. The number of the computing tasks, which needs to be offloaded, is C.

At first, transferring the computing tasks follows the Poisson distribution. The probability of transmitting c-th type computing task is denoted as $P_{c,k}^n$, and $P_{c,k}^n$ is calculated by

$$P_{c,k}^n = \frac{\lambda^{s_{c,k}^n}}{S_{c,k}^n!} e^{-\lambda}, c = 1, 2, ...C.$$ (8)

Secondly, the time of k-th type of data transmission in SE is calculated by

$$t_{c,k}^n = \frac{1}{V} S_{c,k}^n.$$ (9)

Based on the above two formulas, the average time of data transmission T is calculated by

$$T = \frac{1}{K} \sum_{k=1}^{K} \sum_{c=1}^{C} P_{c,k}^n t_{c,k}^n.$$ (10)

3.4   Privacy Entropy Analysis

During the transmission of the computing tasks, the security of the computing tasks must need to be taken into consideration. In this paper, the privacy entropy is selected to measure the uncertainty of the computing tasks. If the privacy entropy is great, it is more likely that the probability of the privacy information leakage is small. In addition, the relationship between $SC_{c,k}^n$ and $P_{c,k}^n$ is expressed by

$$\begin{pmatrix} SC_{c,k}^n \\ P_{c,k}^n \end{pmatrix} = \begin{pmatrix} SC_{1,k}^n & SC_{2,k}^n & \cdots & SC_{c,k}^n \\ P_{1,k}^n & P_{2,k}^n & \cdots & P_{c,k}^n \end{pmatrix}.$$ (11)

The privacy entropy in se_n is calculate by

$$H(sc_n) = -\sum_{c=1}^{C} P_{c,k}^n \log_2 P_{c,k}^n. \tag{12}$$

The privacy entropy for all the offloaded computing tasks is calculated by

$$H(SC) = -\frac{1}{K}\sum_{k=1}^{K}\sum_{c=1}^{C} P_{c,k}^n \log_2 P_{c,k}^n. \tag{13}$$

3.5 Problem Definition

In this paper, our goal is to minimize the load balance presented in (7), the data transmission presented in (10) and maximize the privacy entropy presented in (13). The formalized problem is formulated by

$$\min T. \tag{14}$$

$$\max H(SC),\ AB. \tag{15}$$

$$s.t. \sum_{c=1}^{C} P_{c,k}^n = 1. \tag{16}$$

4 A Privacy-Aware Service Migration Method for Edge Computing in Urban Cities

In this paper, our target is to work out a multi-objective optimization problem between the load balance, the transmission time and the privacy entropy at the same time. Due to good robustness and parallel processing mechanism of strength pareto evolutionary algorithm (SPEA2), SPEA2 is utilized to obtain the global optimal strategy. Finally, SAW and MCDM are leveraged to obtain the optimal solutions.

4.1 Encoding

First, both the services and ENs need to be encoded. In traditional genetic algorithm (GA), gene represents the offloading strategy of each computing task. All of the genes make up the chromosome which represents the optimal solution of this problem. In this paper, the chromosome is encoded in integer.

4.2 Fitness Functions and Constraints

The fitness functions, which include three categories: the load balance (7), the transmission time (10) and the privacy entropy (13), aim to evaluate the pros and cons of each individual. As is shown in (14) and (15), this method is leveraged to minimize the load balance and the data transmission and maximize the privacy entropy. Besides, the constraint is shown in (16), and the constraint means that the sum of the probability of transferring c-th type data equals 1.

4.3 Initialization

In this operation, some paraments need to be set up at first, including the size of population SP, the probability of mutation PM, the probability of crossover PC, the number of iterations NI and the size of archive SA. The migration strategy is denoted as $C_s(c_{s,1}, c_{s,2}, ..., c_{s,j})$, where C_α represents the s-th chromosome and $c_{s,j}$ represents the j-th gene of the s-th chromosome in the population.

4.4 Selection

In this operation, the individuals, which have better fitness, are selected from the current evolutionary group. Then, these individuals are put into the mating poor. Furthermore, in the following crossover and mutation operations, the individuals are just selected from the mating pool to bring out a better population.

4.5 Crossover and Mutation

In the crossover operation, in order to generate two new chromosomes, two parental chromosomes are combined. First, one crossover point is selected randomly. Then, the chromosomes below the crossover point are changed.

On condition that the offspring chromosome performs no longer better than their parental chromosome but is not the global optimal solution, the premature convergence will take place. The mutation operation is utilitied to ensure the individual diversity. In addition, the probability of each gene which will mutate is equal.

4.6 Schedule Selection Using SAW and MCDM

In this paper, both the load balance and the transmission time are negative criteria, and the privacy entropy is positive criteria. The effectiveness of the positive criteria will increase while its value increases, and the effectiveness of the negative criteria is opposite. The migration composition set is denoted as CO, and each migration composition in CO contributes to the value of the load balance, the energy consumption and the privacy entropy. The load balance value is denoted as $LB = (LB^i, 1 \leq i \leq P)$ the transmission time value is denoted as $TT = (TT^i, 1 \leq i \leq P)$, and the privacy entropy value is $PE = (PE^i, 1 \leq i \leq P)$, respectively. According to the specifications above, the utility value generated is calculated by

$$U_i = \frac{LB^{\max} - LB^i}{LB^{\max} - LB^{\min}} \cdot w_{lb} + \frac{TT^{\max} - TT^i}{TT^{\max} - TT^{\min}} \cdot w_{tt} + \frac{PE^i - PE^{\max}}{PE^{\max} - PE^{\min}} \cdot w_{pe}, \quad (17)$$

where w_{lb}, w_{tt} and w_{pe} represent the weight of the load balance, the transmission time and the privacy entropy, respectively.

Based on the above formula, the utility value is calculated. Then, MCDM is leveraged to select the optimal strategy from the migration compositions. The migration composition with the maximum utility value is the final strategy.

4.7   Method Review

This paper aims to optimize the load balance, transmission time and privacy entropy at the same time. SPEA2 is leveraged to solve this problem because its good performance in multi-optimization problems. First, the computing tasks need to be encoded. Then, the fitness functions and constraints need to be set up. Besides, the crossover and mutation operations are leveraged to avoid premature convergence and bring out new individuals. At last, the optimal strategy is picked out after using SAW and MCDM methods.

Algorithm 1. Service migration method in edge computing

Require: S, J
Ensure: SS
 1: **for** $s = 1$ to S **do**
 2:      $j = 1$
 3:      **while** $j \leq J$ **do**
 4:          Crossover and mutation operations
 5:          **for** the individuals in the population **do**
 6:              Calculate the load balance by formula (1-7)
 7:              Calculate the transmission time by formula (8-10)
 8:              Calculate the privacy entropy by formula (11-13)
 9:          **end for**
10:          Selection operation to ensure the child generation
11:              $j = j + 1$
12:      **end while**
13:      Evaluate utility function by (23-24)
14:      Pick out the optimal schedule strategy SS by formula 14
15: **end for**
16: **return** SS

---

5   Experiment Evaluation

5.1   Experimental Context

In Table 1, there are four basic parameters and some range of the values which are used in our experiment. For the effectiveness of our experiment, five different numbers of services are set to bring out five different scale datasets, and the numbers of the computing tasks are 5, 10, 15, 20 and 25, respectively.

5.2   Performance Evaluation

In this section, we analyze the load balance, transmission time and privacy entropy to evaluate our proposed method.

Table 1. Parameter settings.

Parameter description	Value
The number of services	5, 10, 15, 20, 25
The number of VMs on each EN	7
The transmission rate between ENs	120 Mb/s
The migrated service (Mb)	[1, 50]

Analysis of the Balance Between Three Objects. There are three objects, which need to be improved, in this paper. Five different numbers of services are analyzed in this part. Figure 1 shows the balance between the load balance variance, transmission time and privacy entropy. It is concluded that the privacy entropy will increase with the increase of the transmission time. The high value of privacy entropy means more parts of the services need to be migrated, which makes contributions to the safety of the service migration. The load balance changes just a little.

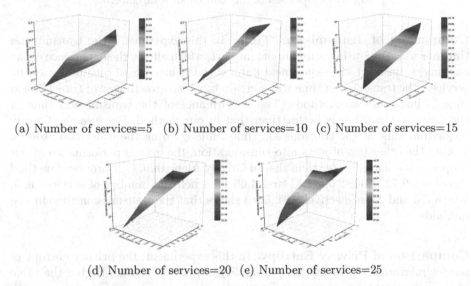

(a) Number of services=5   (b) Number of services=10   (c) Number of services=15

(d) Number of services=20   (e) Number of services=25

Fig. 1. The balance between the load balance variance, transmission time and privacy entropy with different numbers of services.

Comparison of Load Balance. In this experiment, the load balance variance of ENs in edge computing affects the throughput, data-processing capabilitu, and flexibility and availability of the network. Compared with the Greedy Algorithm, with the increase of the number of the services, the difference between the two methods becomes obvious. The value of the load balance variance in our proposed method is larger than that in Greedy Algorithm, which means our proposed method protects the privacy data more safely. The load balance variance of our proposed method is 37.5, 38.8, 40.2, 43.73 and 48.29 when the number of services is 5, 10, 15, 20 and 25, respectively. Figure 2 shows the load balance variance in two methods.

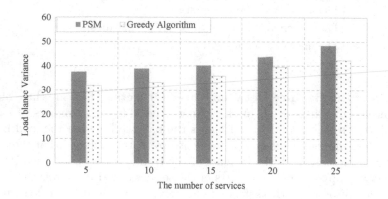

Fig. 2. Comparison of the load balance variance.

Comparison of Transmission Time. In this experiment, the transmission time of service migration is an important part, which affects the experience of the customers. Based on the experiment data, with the increase of the number of the services, the transmission time will increase too. The growth rate of transmission time is linear in two methods. The performance of the transmission time in the Greedy Algorithm is better than that in our method. Because the Greedy Algorithm aims at the transmission time while ignoring the other two objects. Taking the other two objects into consideration, the overall performance of our proposed method is better than that of Greedy Algorithm. Our proposed method consumes 0.72, 1.64, 2.56, 3.45 and 4.65 (s) when the number of services is 5, 10, 15, 20 and 25, respectively. Figure 3 shows that the transmission time in two methods.

Comparison of Privacy Entropy. In this experiment, the privacy entropy of service migration represents the probability of privacy leakage. Higher the value of the privacy entropy is, more safety the service migration is Fig. 4 shows with the increase of the number of the services, the privacy entropy will increase too. The privacy entropy of our proposed method is 14.66, 30.23, 44.37, 60.33 and 74.41 when the number of services is 5, 10, 15, 20 and 25, respectively. Figure 4 shows that the privacy entropy in two methods.

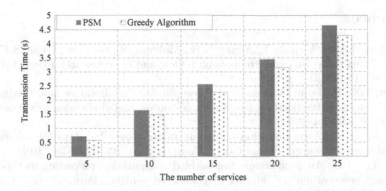

Fig. 3. Comparison of the transmission time.

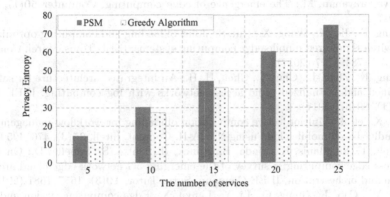

Fig. 4. Comparison of the privacy entropy.

6   Conclusion and Future Work

Nowadays, the edge computing has emerged as an important paradigm, which makes contributions to our life gradually. In order to optimize the load balance, transmission time and privacy entropy during the service migration between ENs, a multi-objective service migration method with privacy preservation is proposed in this paper. First, the service migration method is analyzed. Then, SPEA2 is leveraged to make optimization of the load balance, transmission time and privacy entropy at the same time. Experimental evaluations are conducted to evaluate the effectiveness and efficiency of our method.

For the future work, we plan to extend our proposed method to a scenario in the real-world and make investigation for other specific applications.

References

1. Hashem, I.A.T., Yaqoob, I., Anuar, N.B., Mokhtar, S., Gani, A., Khan, S.U.: The rise of "big data" on cloud computing: review and open research issues. Inf. Syst. **47**, 98–115 (2015)
2. Tran, T.X., Hajisami, A., Pandey, P., Pompili, D.: Collaborative mobile edge computing in 5G networks: new paradigms, scenarios, and challenges. arXiv preprint. arXiv:1612.03184 (2016)
3. Xu, X., et al.: A computation offloading method over big data for IoT-enabled cloud-edge computing. Future Gener. Comput. Syst. **95**, 522–533 (2019)
4. Xu, X., et al.: An edge computing-enabled computation offloading method with privacy preservation for internet of connected vehicles. Future Gener. Comput. Syst. **96**, 89–100 (2019)
5. Mach, P., Becvar, Z.: Mobile edge computing: a survey on architecture and computation offloading. IEEE Commun. Surv. Tutor. **19**(3), 1628–1656 (2017)
6. Satyanarayanan, M.: The emergence of edge computing. Computer **50**(1), 30–39 (2017)
7. Wang, F., Jie, X., Wang, X., Cui, S.: Joint offloading and computing optimization in wireless powered mobile-edge computing systems. IEEE Trans. Wirel. Commun. **17**(3), 1784–1797 (2017)
8. Liang, K., Zhao, L., Chu, X., Chen, H.-H.: An integrated architecture for software defined and virtualized radio access networks with fog computing. IEEE Netw. **31**(1), 80–87 (2017)
9. Xu, X., et al.: Multiobjective computation offloading for workflow management in cloudlet-based mobile cloud using NSGA-II. Comput. Intell. **35**(3), 476–495 (2019)
10. Taleb, T., Samdanis, K., Mada, B., Flinck, H., Dutta, S., Sabella, D.: On multi-access edge computing: a survey of the emerging 5G network edge cloud architecture and orchestration. IEEE Commun. Surv. Tutor. **19**(3), 1657–1681 (2017)
11. Shi, W., Cao, J., Zhang, Q., Li, Y., Lanyu, X.: Edge computing: vision and challenges. IEEE Internet Things J. **3**(5), 637–646 (2016)
12. Shi, W., Dustdar, S.: The promise of edge computing. Computer **49**(5), 78–81 (2016)
13. Rodrigues, T.G., Suto, K., Nishiyama, H., Kato, N.: Hybrid method for minimizing service delay in edge cloud computing through VM migration and transmission power control. IEEE Trans. Comput. **66**(5), 810–819 (2016)
14. Sun, X., Ansari, N.: EdgeIoT: mobile edge computing for the Internet of Things. IEEE Commun. Mag. **54**(12), 22–29 (2016)
15. Wang, S., Urgaonkar, R., Zafer, M., He, T., Chan, K., Leung, K.K.: Dynamic service migration in mobile edge-clouds. In: 2015 IFIP Networking Conference (IFIP Networking), pp. 1–9. IEEE (2015)
16. Hu, Y., Shen, H., Bai, G., Wang, T.: Privacy-preserving task allocation for edge computing enhanced mobile crowdsensing. In: Vaidya, J., Li, J. (eds.) ICA3PP 2018. LNCS, vol. 11337, pp. 431–446. Springer, Cham (2018). https://doi.org/10.1007/978-3-030-05063-4_33
17. Lu, R., Heung, K., Lashkari, A.H., Ghorbani, A.A.: A lightweight privacy-preserving data aggregation scheme for fog computing-enhanced IoT. IEEE Access **5**, 3302–3312 (2017)
18. Gai, K., Qiu, M., Xiong, Z., Liu, M.: Privacy-preserving multi-channel communication in edge-of-things. Future Gener. Comput. Syst. **85**, 190–200 (2018)

A Certificateless Aggregate Signature Scheme Based on Blockchain for EMR

Hong Shu[1,2,3] (ID), Fulong Chen[1,2(✉)] (ID), Dong Xie[1,2], Ping Qi[3] (ID), and Yongqing Huang[3,4]

[1] Anhui Normal University, Wuhu 241002, Anhui, China
shuhongt1@126.com, long005@mail.ahnu.edu.cn,
xiedong@ahnu.edu.cn
[2] Anhui Provincial Key Lab of Network and Information Security,
Wuhu 241002, Anhui, China
[3] Tongling University, Tongling 244061, Anhui, China
qiping929@gmail.com, hyq@tlu.edu.cn
[4] Institute of Information Technology & Engineering Management,
Tongling University, Tongling 244061, China

Abstract. In this paper, a certificateless aggregate signature scheme for blockchain- based electronic medical record (EMR) is proposed, which has the characteristics of decentralization, security, credibility and tamper-proof. Performance analysis shows that the proposed scheme has constant communication cost and low computational cost. This scheme can be utilized to tackle difficult problems in regard to identity authentication in EMR. It can also preserve the integrity of EMR data.

Keywords: EMR · Certificateless aggregate signature · Blockchain · Trapdoor hash function · Privacy preservation

1 Introduction

With the development of big data and Internet of Things technology, smart healthcare has attracted more and more interests from the researchers. The electronic medical record system (EMR) [1] is responsible for collecting information during examination and treatment, such as texts, symbols, charts, graphs, images, etc. Such information will later be used to assist decision making by doctors and nurses. EMR should be protected against forgery, tampering and repudiation [2]. The patient's EMRs can be regarded as a series of static medical record documents. Digital signature on each individual medical record will preserve information integrity in identity authentication, authorization management and responsibility allocation. Therefore, it has become an intriguing topic on how to effectively save computational and storage overhead of digital signatures for batch medical records. At the same time, the needs for secure storage and sharing for EMRs are also satisfied.

Aggregate signature can combine a short digital signature from multiple digital signatures. Thereafter, by verifying the correctness of the short aggregate signature, the verification of each individual signature can be fulfilled. Therefore, the aggregate

© Springer Nature Switzerland AG 2019
J. Vaidya et al. (Eds.): CSS 2019, LNCS 11982, pp. 437–443, 2019.
https://doi.org/10.1007/978-3-030-37337-5_35

signature scheme with low computation, low power consumption, low storage and high reliability becomes an important security guarantee for EMR. Based on blockchain, secure sharing of medical data can be achieved [3]. Each medical record requires the digital signature of a responsible health care provider in order to guarantee the transparency of blockchain [4]. Recently, some scholars have applied aggregate signature schemes to blockchain. Zhao [5] constructed an aggregate signature scheme based on Gamma signature [6], and applied the same to Bitcoin. By doing so, the storage capacity for signature reduced by 49.8%, while the verification efficiency improved by 72%. Combining verifiable encryption signature and aggregate signature, Gao [7] developed a multi-party contract signing protocol based on blockchain. This protocol ensures efficiency and fairness during E-commerce transaction. However, the capacity limitation of the block has been a major bottleneck against performance improvement of the blockchain. Aggregated signatures have natural compression properties. Therefore, in the blockchain-based EMR, the batch individual signatures can be aggregated into a short signature. This makes it possible to increase the information storage of each block without increasing the block capacity, meanwhile effectively preventing spam attacks [5].

The contributions of this paper are as follows:

- We present a two-layer blockchain-based EMR system model, which is used to execute the secure storage and sharing of EMR.
- The proposed aggregate signature scheme is based on multi-trapdoor hash function. Batch trapdoor collision computation of multi-trapdoor hash function can improve the efficiency of aggregate signature.
- Performance analysis shows that the communication cost and computation cost of our scheme are superior to that of other blockchain-based aggregate signature schemes.

The rest of this paper is organized as follows. Section 2 presents the necessary preliminaries and system model. The proposed scheme is described in Sect. 3. Then we give the performance evaluation in Sect. 4. Finally, the conclusion is offered in Sect. 5.

2 Preliminaries

2.1 Trapdoor Hash Function

The trapdoor hash function [8] consists of the following four algorithms:

ParGen: Inputs security parameter k, outputs system parameter *params*;

KeyGen: Inputs *params*, outputs trapdoor/hash key <*HK, TK*>;

HashGen: Inputs *params*, the message m and the auxiliary parameter u, outputs the trapdoor value $TH_{HK}(m, u)$;

TrapColGen: Inputs *params*, <*HK, TK*>, m, u and new message $m'(\neq m)$, outputs u' and HK' such that $TH_{HK}(m, u) = TH_{HK'}(m', u')$;

According to the number of trapdoor information (TK), trapdoor hash functions includes the following categories: single trapdoor hash functions [8], double trapdoor hash functions [9], and multiple trapdoor hash functions [10]. In this paper, a certificateless aggregate signature scheme based on multi-trapdoor hash function is constructed and applied to blockchain based EMR data storage model.

2.2 System Model

In this paper, a two-layer system model of on-blockchain/off-blockchain is used to execute the secure storage and sharing of EMR. As shown in Fig. 1, the off-blockchain layer completes the collection, aggregation and storage of EMRs. When a patient comes to the hospital for treatment, each respondent medical care provider signs the EMRs, calculates their abstracts and encrypts them. Then all the information is sent to the central hospital, where the original encrypted medical data is stored in the medical cloud. After verifying each individual signature, the central hospital aggregates all the medical abstracts of the patient in this treatment. In the end, an aggregate signature is generated. On the other hand, the on-blockchain layer is responsible for EMR sharing. Each transaction in the medical chain consists of the abstract of the patient's medical records, aggregate signatures, access control, and location index of the original medical data in the medical cloud. Patients are the owners of medical data that grant an entity (doctor, institution, researcher, etc.) access to relevant medical records. When an entity gains access, he can look up on the medical chain and obtain an index of medical data in the medical cloud. Then he can access the original medical record.

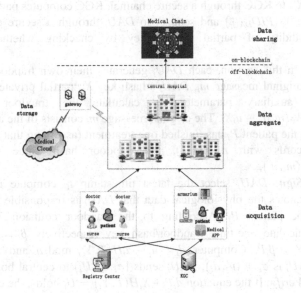

Fig. 1. System model

3 Certificateless Aggregate Signature Scheme Based on Multi-trapdoor Hash Function

This section presents the certificateless aggregate signature scheme based on multi-trapdoor hash function.

Setup: Suppose the system parameter k, Key Generation Center (KGC) chooses tow large prime numbers p, q and an elliptic curve $E(F_k)$ over finite field F_k. Let G be a cyclic subgroup of $E(F_k)$ and P a generator of G with prime order q. Given 5 secure hash functions: W_1, W_2, W_3, W_4: $\{0,1\}^* \to Z_q^*$, $H{:}G \to Z_q^*$. Select randomly $\lambda \in Z_q^*$ as the master key, then the public key is $K_{pub} = \lambda P$. Finally, output the system parameter $params = (G, P, q, W_1, W_2, W_3, W_4, H)$.

Pseudogym-Gen: In this paper, pseudonym system [11] is used to provide conditional privacy protection [12] for doctors, nurses, patients, medical equipment, etc. We define doctors, nurses, medical equipment and medical APP as data acquisition units (DAU). The registry center generates pseudonyms for DAU_i and patient P_j as following:

- Registry center accepts DAU_i's real identity RID_{DAU_i} and calculates its pseudonym $PID_{DAU_i} = W_1(RID_{DAU_i})$. Then send the pseudonym to KGC through a secure channel.
- Registry center accepts P_j's real identity RID_{P_j} and calculates its pseudonym $PID_{P_j} = W_1(RID_{P_j})$. Then send the pseudonym to KGC through a secure channel.

Key-Gen: DAU_i select randomly a secret value α_i, compute $X_i = \alpha_i P$ as public key. Then send (α_i, X_i) to KGC through a secure channel. KGC computes partial private key of DAU_i $\theta_i = \lambda_i W_2(PID_{DAU_i})$ and send θ_i to DAU_i through a secure channel. DAU_i verifies the validity of partial private key by checking whether $\theta_i P = K_{pub} W_2(PID_{DAU_i})$.

Hash-Gen: In this section, each DAU_i generates their own trapdoor hash value. Input $params$, original message m_i, DAU_i's hash key X_i, partial private key θ_i, select randomly an auxiliary parameter u_i, calculate the trapdoor hash value $TH_{X_i}(m_i, u_i) = W_3(m_i)P - u_i X_i$. The original message m_i consists of the attribute values of DAU_i. When the patient P_j has finished one treatment (assuming that the patient has n medical records with n DAU_i), the trapdoor hash value is aggregated $T = \sum_{i=1}^{n} TH_{X_i}(m_i, u_i)$.

Individual-Sign: DAU_i select the latest timestamp t_i, compute $u_i' = W_4(t_i, \theta_i)$, $U_i = u_i' P$. m_i' denotes the physiological data that DAU_i is responsible for during the treatment of the patient P_j. According to the trapdoor collision $TH_{X_i}(m_i, u_i) = TH_{Y_i}(m_i', u_i')$, calculate one-time trapdoor/hash key respectively $\beta_i = u_i'^{-1}(W_3(m_i') - W_3(m_i) + u_i)$, $Y_i = \beta_i P$. Computer $d_i = u_i' - \alpha_i H(T, Y_i)$ mod q and the individual signature of DAU_i is $\sigma_i = (u_i', d_i)$. DAU_i sends (σ_i, Y_i, U_i) to central hospital.

Individual-Verify: If the equation $d_i P + X_i H(T, Y_i) = U_i$ holds, the central hospital accepts P_j's individual signature and outputs 1, otherwise, outputs 0. Since $d_i = u_i' - \alpha_i H(T, Y_i)$ mod q, we can obtain $d_i P + X_i H(T, Y_i) = u_i' P - \alpha_i H(T, Y_i)P + X_i H(T, Y_i) = U_i$.

Aggregate-Sign: For each accepted individual signature, the central hospital calculates $D = \sum_{i=1}^{n} d_i$, $\omega = \sum_{i=1}^{n} u_i'$. Then the aggregate signature is $\sigma = (\omega, D)$. The central hospital constructs a transaction with the patient P_j's medical record abstract, aggregate signature, access control authority and the location of the original medical data in the cloud storage. Then it issues a transaction request to the medical chain.

Aggregate-Verify: Receiving the message, the miner verifies the aggregate signature by a consensus mechanism. If the equation $DP + \sum_{i=1}^{n} X_i H(T, Y_i) = \omega$ holds, then broadcast the information to other nodes in the network. Other nodes begin to perform consensus verification on the transaction and broadcast it on the network. After the verification is successful, the transaction will be added to the block. After a period of time, blocks validated by most nodes are added to the medical chain.

4   Efficiency Analysis

The method of performance evaluation proposed in [12] is adopted in this paper. Table 1 lists the execution time of the encryption operations below.

Table 1. Different encryption operation execution time.

Encryption operation	Description	Time (ms)
T_B	The bilinear pair operation	4.2110
T_{MB}	The scalar multiplication in the bilinear pair	1.7090
T_{AB}	The bilinear pair-to-midpoint addition	0.0071
T_{HB}	The hash-to-point operation in bilinear pair	4.4060
T_{ME}	The scalar multiplication in elliptic curve	0.4420
T_{AE}	The point addition operation in elliptic curve	0.0018
T_H	The general hash operation	0.0001

We compare the performance of the proposed blockchain-based certificateless aggregate signature algorithm with two most recent blockchain-based aggregate signature algorithm. These schemes are measured by communication cost and computation cost, which are considered in terms of the length of the aggregate signature and the running time of the aggregation verification algorithm respectively.

As shown in Table 2 and Fig. 2, we can see that the proposed scheme outperforms the scheme [7] in time efficiency of individual signature and aggregate verification. The time efficiency of the scheme proposed in this paper is lower than that of the scheme [5], while the aggregate verification is slightly better than that of the scheme [5]. From Fig. 3, in terms of storage efficiency, we can see the aggregate signature lengths of scheme [5] and [7] are related to the number of signatures n, that is, the communication overhead increases linearly with n. The signature length of the proposed scheme is a constant, which will greatly reduce the storage space of transactions, so that a block can store more transactions.

Table 2. The performance comparison of related schemes.

Scheme	Individual signature	Aggregate verify	Aggregate signature length	Correlation between signature length and n
Gao [7]	$5T_{MB} + 2T_{HTP}$ $\approx 17.357ms$	$(n+4)T_B + (2n+1)T_{HTP}$ $\approx 13.023n + 21.25ms$	$128*(2n+1)$ bytes	Yes
Zhao [5]	$T_{ME} + 2T_H$ $\approx 0.4422ms$	$(2n+1)T_{ME} + 2nT_H$ $\approx 0.8842n + 0.442ms$	$80n + 20$ bytes	Yes
Our proposed scheme	$2T_{ME} + 4T_H$ $\approx 0.8844ms$	$(n+1)T_{ME} + nT_H$ $\approx 0.4421n + 0.442ms$	40 bytes	No

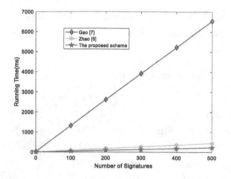

Fig. 2. Execution time

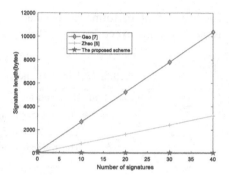

Fig. 3. Aggregate signature length

5 Conclusion

A certificateless aggregate signature scheme based on trapdoor hash function is proposed in this paper. Performance analysis shows that the proposed scheme has constant communication cost and low computational cost. Applying this scheme to blockchain-based EMR storage and sharing model can effectively increase the number of transactions stored in each block, and therefore alleviate the capacity limitation of blockchain to a certain extent.

Acknowledgments. This research is supported by the National Natural Science Foundation of China (nos. 61572036, 61672039 and 61801004); the Natural Science Foundation of Anhui Province (no. 1808085QF211); the Natural Science Foundation of Universities of Anhui Province (nos. KJ2019A0702, KJ2019A0704).

References

1. Zuckerman, A.E.: Restructuring the electronic medical record to incorporate full digital signature capability. Proc. Amia. Symp. **8**(1), 791–795 (2000)
2. Yu, Y.C.: Dual function seal: visualized digital signature for electronic medical record systems. J. Med. Syst. **36**(5), 3115–3121 (2012)
3. Azaria, A., Ekblaw, A., Vieira, T., Lippman, A.: MedRec: using blockchain for medical data access and permission management. In: OBD 2016, pp. 25–30. IEEE Press, Vienna (2016)
4. Dai, H., Zheng, Z., Zhang, Y.: Blockchain for Internet of Things: A Survey (2019). https://doi.org/10.1109/JIOT.2019.2920987
5. Zhao, Y.: Aggregation of Gamma-Signatures and Applications to Bitcoin (2018). https://eprint.iacr.org/eprint-bin/search.pl
6. Yao, A.C.-C., Zhao, Y.: Online/offline signatures for low-power devices. IEEE Trans. Inf. Forensic Secur. **8**(2), 283–294 (2012)
7. Gao, Y., Wu, J.X.: Efficient multi-party fair contract signing protocol based on blockchains (in Chinese). J. Cryptologic. Res. **5**(5), 556–567 (2018)
8. Krawczyk, H., Rabin, T.: Chameleon signatures. In: NDSS 2000, pp. 143–154. San Diego, California (2000)
9. Chandrasekhar, S., Ibrahim, A., Singhal, M.: A novel access control protocol using proxy signatures for cloud-based health information exchange. Comput. Secur. **67**, 73–88 (2017)
10. Chandrasekhar, S., Singhal, M.: Multi-trapdoor hash functions and their applications in network security. In: IEEE CNS 2014. pp. 463–471. IEEE Press, San Francisco (2014). https://doi.org/10.1109/cns.2014.6997516
11. Health informatics - Pseudonymization, ISO 25237 (2017). http://www.doc88.com/p-7824948670236.html
12. He, D., Zeadally, S., Xu, B., Huang, X.: An efficient identity-based conditional privacy-preserving authentication scheme for vehicular ad hoc networks. IEEE Trans. Inf. Forensic Secur. **10**(12), 2681–2691 (2015). https://doi.org/10.1109/TIFS.2015.2473820

The Fuzzy Integral Evaluation Method Based on Feature Weighting for the Level of Complex Social Development

Meifang Du[1]([⊠]) and Haojia Zhu[2]

[1] School of Computer Science and Technology,
Shandong Technology and Business University, Yantai, China
8049870@qq.com
[2] School of Information Science and Engineering,
Qufu Normal University, Rizhao, China

Abstract. This paper puts the thought of the dichotomy of grid used in clustering center extraction algorithm based on grid. The structure optimization of fuzzy clustering neural network model is realized. This paper takes the classification of social development level as an example to verify that this structure has the advantages of overcoming the slow convergence speed and solving the problem of clustering dead point. The paper analyses various factors affecting the comprehensive development level of society, and quotes the concepts of fuzzy measure and fuzzy integral, puts forward the evaluation method of fuzzy integral for the comprehensive development level of society, and establishes the corresponding evaluation model of multi-index and multi-level fuzzy integral for the comprehensive development level of society.

Keywords: Social comprehensive development level · Fuzzy measure · Fuzzy integral · Comprehensive evaluation

1 Introduction

The comprehensive development of society can be said to be the development strategy of most countries today. The comprehensive development of society is influenced by many factors. It is an important method to study a country's development strategy to objectively measure the whole social development situation in an all-round and multi-angle way. Establishing an appropriate and practical evaluation system can help us objectively analyze the current situation of social development, and take certain measures to make every link develop in a balanced way, so as to promote the comprehensive development of society. In recent years, many scholars in various countries have done a lot of research, established some good social evaluation index system, and put forward many mathematical models to evaluate the level of social development. However, since the evaluation of the level of social comprehensive development is a typical multi-level fuzzy comprehensive evaluation problem, the previous evaluation

J. Vaidya et al. (Eds.): CSS 2019, LNCS 11982, pp. 444–454, 2019.
https://doi.org/10.1007/978-3-030-37337-5_36

model needs a lot of fuzzy operations in the evaluation. Based on this, this paper will make some discussions on the establishment of a reasonable evaluation model for the level of comprehensive social development. Fuzzy integral evaluation method is applied to the evaluation system of social comprehensive development level in order to reduce the amount of calculation.

The main work of this paper is to design a structural optimization fuzzy clustering neural network model and apply it to the specific social development level of classification examples. In addition, the feature weighting based fuzzy mean clustering algorithm is used to deal with the problem of non-uniform contribution of each dimension to the classification of real vector fuzzy clustering.

2 Fuzzy Integral

The concept of fuzzy integral is a new kind of integral similar to Lebesgue integral, which was introduced by Japanese scholar Sugeno in his doctoral dissertation in 1974 by using the concept of fuzzy measure. We also call it Sugeno fuzzy integral. Fuzzy integral is introduced on the basis of fuzzy measure. Therefore, the concept of fuzzy measure must be introduced first.

2.1 Fuzzy Measure

We know that classical measure is an additive measure. It is an abstract representation of the length, area, volume and mass of things. But in objective reality, the measurement of things does not satisfy additivity. Therefore, it is necessary to establish a systematic theory of non-additive measure for revealing the essence of objective things in nature more comprehensively and deeply. Fuzzy measure is to study whether an element whose position is not determined beforehand belongs to a subset M of X. So far, scholars at home and abroad have given many different definitions of fuzzy measures, thus establishing different fuzzy integrals. Here, we only introduce the λ-fuzzy measure $g\lambda$ which we need to use in this paper. It is defined as: if the set function $g\lambda$ defined on the Borel field N of A satisfies:

(1) $g\lambda(\varphi) = 0$, $g\lambda(A) = 1$;
(2) M, N $\in$ N, if M $\cap$ N = φ have
$g\lambda(M \cap N) = g\lambda(M) + g\lambda(N) + \lambda g\lambda(M) \cdot g\lambda(N)$, $-1 < \lambda < +\infty$;
(3) Continuity of $g\lambda$ satisfying fuzziness measure
$g\lambda$ is called a λ-fuzzy measure.

2.2   Fuzzy Integral of Fuzzy Measure

Let the function h: $X \rightarrow [0,1]$, then the fuzzy integral of h on $A \subset X$ about the fuzzy measure g is defined as:

$$\int_A h(x) \circ g(\bullet) = \bigvee_{\alpha \in [0,1]} (\alpha \wedge g(A \cap H_\alpha)), \text{ where } H\alpha = \{x|h(x) \geq \alpha\} \tag{1}$$

In particular, when the integral region A = X,

$$\int_A h(x) \circ g(\bullet) = \bigvee_{\alpha \in [0,1]} (\alpha \wedge g(H_\alpha)) = \int h(x) \circ g(\bullet) \tag{2}$$

2.3   Fuzzy Distribution Function

The function H on R, if satisfied

(1) $0 \leq H(x) \leq 1, \forall x \in R$;
(2) if $x \leq y$, have $H(x) \leq H(y)$;
(3) $\lim_{x \to a^+} H(x) = H(a)$;
(4) $\lim_{x \to -\infty} H(x) = 0, \lim_{x \to +\infty} H(x) = 1$.

H is called a fuzzy distribution function.

Let H be a fuzzy distribution function on R. For any left open and right closed interval (a, b], let

$$g_\lambda = ((a,b]) = \frac{H(b) - H(a)}{1 + \lambda H(a)}, -1 < \lambda + \infty \tag{3}$$

Then $g\lambda$ is a λ-fuzzy measure.

2.4   Constructing the Value of g_λ

The value of g_λ can be constructed from H without contradiction for all elements of B, which is useful for evaluating with fuzzy integral.

Let $X = \{x_1, x_2, \ldots, x_n\}$, order

h: $X \rightarrow [0,1]$ and $h(x_1) \geq h(x_2) \geq \ldots \geq h(x_n)$, Then the definition of fuzzy integral is as follows.

$$\int_A h(x_i) \circ g_\lambda(\bullet) = \bigvee_{\alpha \in [0,1]} (\alpha \wedge g_\lambda(H_\alpha)) = \overset{i=1}{\underset{n}{\vee}} (h(x_i) \wedge g_\lambda(X_i)) \tag{4}$$

Where $Xi = \{x1, x2, \ldots, xi\}$.

Let the fuzzy distribution function be $H(xi)$, $i = 1, 2, \ldots, n$, and $H(x1) \leq H(x2) \leq \ldots \leq H(xn) = 1$, order

$g1 = g\lambda(\{x1\}) = g\lambda((-\infty, x1]) = H(x1)$, By formula (3), order

$$g_2 = g_\lambda((x_1, x_2]) = \frac{H(x_2) - H(x_1)}{1 + \lambda H(x_1)}$$

Have $g_\lambda(X_2) = g_\lambda((-\infty, x_1] \cup (x_1, x_2]) = \frac{1}{\lambda}[(1 + \lambda g_1)(1 + \lambda g_2) - 1]$

$$= \frac{1}{\lambda}\left[(1 + \lambda H(x_1))(1 + \lambda \frac{H(x_2) - H(x_1)}{1 + \lambda H(x_1)}) - 1\right] = H(x_2),$$

Easy to get by induction $g_\lambda(X_i) = H(x_i)$ $i = 1, 2, \ldots, n$

At this time, $\int h(x_i) \circ g_\lambda(\bullet) = \overset{i=1}{\underset{n}{\vee}} (h(x_i) \wedge H(x_i))$ can be used as the evaluation value of the whole system μ, which is

$$\mu = \overset{i=1}{\underset{n}{\vee}} (h(x_i) \wedge H(x_i)) \tag{5}$$

Among them, x_i represents the evaluation factors of the evaluated things, $h(x_i)$ represents the satisfaction with factor i, and $g_\lambda(x_i)$ represents the weight distribution of the evaluation factors in the evaluated things.

2.5   Algorithm Process

The classification number and clustering center of the sample can be predicted by applying the algorithm of clustering center extraction based on binary grid to the sample data. Then according to the above established fuzzy clustering neural network model ideas and algorithms, we give a specific program flow chart, as shown in Fig. 1 (MATLAB has developed the corresponding program to be used in the specific clustering example.

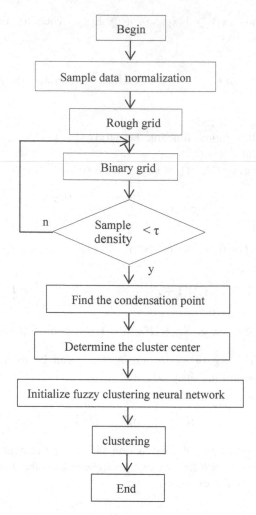

Fig. 1. Program flow chart

3 Fuzzy Integral Evaluation Method

3.1 Determine the Evaluation Index

We know that the reasons for the impact on the overall level of social development come from many aspects: the level of national economic development, social structure, population quality, quality of life and so on are all factors affecting social development. The Chinese Academy of Social Sciences has made a survey of the comprehensive social development of various countries in the world and has established the following social evaluation index system. On the one hand, the index system strives to fully reflect the coordinated development of economy and society, on the other hand, it strives to highlight the human-centered development concept and measurement standards. This indicator system includes four groups of 16 indicators: quality of life (1–4 items in Table 1), population quality (5–9 items in Table 1), social structure (10–15 items in Table 1), and economic development level (16 items in Table 1).

Table 1. Social development indicators

Number	Index	Scoring standard	China score
1	Average number of doctors by population	6	6
2	Inflation rate	6	5
3	Average daily calorie intake per person	6	5
4	Per capita energy consumption	6	5
5	Natural population growth rate	6	6
6	Average life expectancy	7	6
7	Infant mortality rate	6	4
8	The proportion of middle school students aged 12–17	6	4
9	The proportion of college students aged 20–24	6	1
10	The proportion of agricultural value in GNP	6	4
11	Non-agricultural Employed Population's Proportion to Employed Population	6	4
12	The proportion of education expenditure in gross national product	6	3
13	The proportion of tertiary industry in GNP	6	3
14	The proportion of total exports in GNP	6	3
15	The proportion of urban to total population	7	2
16	Per capita GNP	8	2
	Total	**100**	**65**

According to Table 1, we have the following structure:

When evaluating the comprehensive level of social development, the first level of evaluation factors are: x_1 = "quality of life", x_2 = "quality of population", x_3 = "social structure", and x_4 = "level of national economic development".

For each of the above evaluation factors, there are their own sub-evaluation factors, that is, the second level of evaluation factors, respectively, as follows:

For the quality of life, the evaluation factors are as follows: x_{11} = "the average number of doctors per population", x_{12} = "the inflation rate", x_{13} = "the average daily calorie intake per person", and x_{14} = "the energy consumption per person".

For the quality of population, the evaluation factors are: x_{21} = "the natural growth rate of population", x_{22} = "the average life expectancy", x_{23} = "the infant mortality rate", x_{24} = "the proportion of middle school students in the population aged 12–17 years", and x_{25} = "the proportion of college students in the population aged 20–24 years".

For social structure, the evaluation factors are: x_{31} = "the proportion of agricultural output value in GNP", x_{32} = "the proportion of non-agricultural employment population in the employment population", x_{33} = "the proportion of educational expenditure in GNP", x_{34} = "the proportion of tertiary industry in GNP", x_{35} = "the proportion of total export value in GNP", x_{36} = "The proportion of urban population to the total population".

For the level of national economic development, the evaluation factors are: x_{41} = "per capita GNP".

3.2 Determine the Satisfaction of Each Factor and the Weight Distribution of Each Factor Among the Evaluated Objects

According to the table obtained from the survey conducted by the Chinese Academy of Social Sciences on the comprehensive socio-economic development of various countries in the world, we can draw the following data:

$h(x_1)$ = 0.87, $h(x_2)$ = 0.68, $h(x_3)$ = 0.51, $h(x_4)$ = 0.25,
$g\lambda(x_1)$ = 0.24, $g\lambda(x_2)$ = 0.31, $g\lambda(x_3)$ = 0.37, $g\lambda(x_4)$ = 0.08;
$h(x_{11})$ = 1, $h(x_{12})$ = 0.83, $h(x_{13})$ = 0.83, $h(x_{14})$ = 0.83,
$g\lambda(x_{11})$ = 0.25, $g\lambda(x_{12})$ = 0.25, $g\lambda(x_{13})$ = 0.25, $g\lambda(x_{14})$ = 0.25;
$h(x_{21})$ = 1, $h(x_{22})$ = 0.86, $h(x_{23})$ = 0.67, $h(x_{24})$ = 0.67, $h(x_{25})$ = 0.17,
$g\lambda(x_{21})$ = 0.24, $g\lambda(x_{22})$ = 0.19, $g\lambda(x_{23})$ = 0.19, $g\lambda(x_{24})$ = 0.19, $g\lambda(x_{25})$ = 0.19;
$h(x_{31})$ = 0.67, $h(x_{32})$ = 0.67, $h(x_{33})$ = 0.50, $h(x_{34})$ = 0.50, $h(x_{35})$ = 0.50,
$h(x_{36})$ = 0.29;
$g\lambda(x_{31})$ = 0.16, $g\lambda(x_{32})$ = 0.16, $g\lambda(x_{33})$ = 0.16, $g\lambda(x_{34})$ = 0.16, $g\lambda(x_{35})$ = 0.16,
$g\lambda(x_{36})$ = 0.20;
$h(x_{41})$ = 0.25;
$g\lambda(x_{41})$ = 1;

Then the values of $H(x_i)$ are calculated separately.

$H(x_1)$ = 0.24, $H(x_2)$ = 0.55, $H(x_3)$ = 0.92, $H(x_4)$ = 1;
$H(x_{11})$ = 0.25, $H(x_{12})$ = 0.50, $H(x_{13})$ = 0.75, $H(x_{14})$ = 1;
$H(x_{21})$ = 0.24, $H(x_{22})$ = 0.43, $H(x_{23})$ = 0.62, $H(x_{24})$ = 0.81, $H(x_{25})$ = 1;
$H(x_{31})$ = 0.16, $H(x_{32})$ = 0.32, $H(x_{33})$ = 0.48, $H(x_{34})$ = 0.64, $H(x_{35})$ = 0.80,
$H(x_{36})$ = 1;
$H(x_{41})$ = 1;

3.3 Ascertain the Evaluation Value of the Complex Development Level of the Society

From the formula $\mu = \overset{n}{\underset{i=1}{\vee}} (h(x_i) \wedge H(x_i))$, we can first find out the evaluation value of each factor in the second layer:

$$\mu_1 = \overset{4}{\underset{i=1}{\vee}} (h(x_{1i}) \wedge H(x_{1i}))$$
$$= (1 \wedge 0.25) \vee (0.83 \wedge 0.50) \vee (0.83 \wedge 0.75) \vee (0.83 \wedge 1)$$
$$= 0.83$$

$$\mu_2 = \bigvee_{i=1}^{5} (h(x_{2i}) \wedge H(x_{2i}))$$

$$= (1 \wedge 0.24) \vee (0.86 \wedge 0.43) \vee (0.67 \wedge 0.62) \vee (0.67 \wedge 0.81) \vee (0.17 \wedge 1)$$

$$= 0.67$$

$$\mu_3 = \bigvee_{i=1}^{6} (h(x_{3i}) \wedge H(x_{3i}))$$

$$= (0.67 \wedge 0.16) \vee (0.67 \wedge 0.32) \vee (0.50 \wedge 0.48) \vee (0.50 \wedge 0.64) \vee (0.50 \wedge 0.80) \vee (0.29 \wedge 1)$$

$$= 0.50$$

$$\mu_4 = \bigvee_{i=1}^{1} (h(x_{4i}) \wedge H(x_{4i}))$$

$$= (0.25 \wedge 1) = 0.25$$

From this, we can see that the evaluation values of the first level factors calculated by the fuzzy integral are μ_1, μ_2, μ_3, μ_4, which basically coincide with the satisfaction $h(x_1)$, $h(x_2)$, (x_3), $h(x_4)$ of the factors at all levels obtained from the questionnaire.

Next, we take the evaluation values μ_1, μ_2, μ_3, and μ_4 of the factors of the first layer obtained above as the satisfaction degree $h(x_1)$, $h(x_2)$, $h(x_3)$, $h(x_4)$, for each factor of the first layer. that is,

$h(x_1) = \mu_1$, $h(x_2) = \mu_2$, $h(x_3) = \mu_3$, $h(x_4) = \mu_4$, Finally, we ask again

$$\mu = \bigvee_{4}^{i=1} (h(x_i) \wedge H(x_i))$$

$$= (0.83 \wedge 0.24) \vee (0.67 \wedge 0.55) \vee (0.50 \wedge 0.92) \vee (0.25 \wedge 0.08) = 0.55$$

According to the obtained μ value, we can know that China's social development is at the middle and lower level in the world.

3.4   The Experiment

We take the statistical data of Shandong province in 1999 from the National Bureau of Statistics as the research section. The index system of these data is broad and complex. To make a comprehensive evaluation on the level of regional economic development, a series of main indicators should be selected from various indicators reflecting regional economic development. These indicators should reflect the strategy of coordinated development of regional economy and fairness. This paper chooses 6 indicators to evaluate the level of regional economic development. (per capita amount of grain, per capita GDP, per capita local fiscal revenue, per 10,000 students in school, per 10,000 beds in hospitals, agricultural, forestry, animal husbandry and fishery labor force)

First, we normalized all the experimental data. After normalization, we input the network partitioning parameter 0.1 to conduct rough mesh division of the sample space. The density threshold is input, and then the coarse meshes are divided by binary meshes.

Then we extract the aggregation points from the cluster samples according to the definition of aggregation points introduced earlier. The number of condensate points extracted is 4. That is to say, the number of clustering prototypes in the sample space we want to cluster is 4.

Then, the clustering center of the sample was determined step by step from the aggregation point of the maximum density, and the clustering center was obtained as follows:

$$
\begin{array}{cccccc}
0.455 & 0.559 & 0.478 & 0.096 & 0.269 & 0.242 \\
0.507 & 0.277 & 0.329 & 0.362 & 0.231 & 0.458 \\
0.523 & 0.142 & 0.163 & 0.506 & 0.065 & 0.735 \\
0.541 & 0.068 & 0.101 & 0.776 & 0.084 & 0.46
\end{array}
$$

Next, we can use the number of clustering centers and prototypes obtained above to optimize the fuzzy clustering neural network. In this way, the structure optimization of clustering neural network is realized. The specific optimization process is not given in detail here. The clustering results are shown in Table 2.

We can see from the results: The first type is economically developed areas. The second type is more economically developed areas. The third type is economically less developed areas. The fourth type is economically underdeveloped areas. This is the basic portrayal of Shandong reality.

Table 2. The result of structure optimization clustering neural network clustering

Type	Counties and cities
The first type	Changqing, Laixi, Yiyuan, Kenli, Changdao, Pingyin, Longkou, Laizhou, Penglai, Zhaoyuan, Qixia, Qingzhou, Zhucheng, Shouguang, Yanzhou, Feicheng, Wendeng, Rongcheng, Zhangqiu, Rushan, Wulian, Jiaozhou, Jimo, Binzhou, Jiaonan(25)
The second type	Linqu, Changle, Anqiu, Weishan, Yutai, Jinxiang, Jiaxiang, Wenshang, Sishui, Liangshan, QuFU, Zoucheng, Ningyang, Dongping, Mengyin, Qingyun, Liaocheng, Yanggu, Chiping, Dingtao, Chengwu, Juye, Juancheng (23)
The third type	Huantai, Gaoqing, Lijin, Guangrao, Haiyang, Shanghe, Gaomi, Changyi, Jiyang, Ling, Ningjin, Linyi, Qihe, Pingyuan, Xiajin, Wucheng, Leling, Yucheng, Huimin, Yangxin, Wudi, Zhanhua, Boxing, Zouping, Donge, Gaotang (26)
The fourth type	Tengzhou, Laiyang, Xintai, Juxian, Yinan, Yancheng, Yishui, Cangshan, Feixian, Pingyi, Junan, Linshu, Pingdu, Linqing, Shenxian, Guanxian, Heze, Caoxian, Shanxian, Yuncheng, Dongming (21)

This experiment reflects the level of economic development and comprehensive economic strength of Shandong province. The clustering results are in good agreement with the actual situation of the whole province. This shows that it is feasible to use this method to evaluate the level of regional economic development.

4   Conclusions

In this paper, the fuzzy integral is applied to the evaluation system of social development, and a fuzzy integral evaluation model of social development level is established. The evaluation results are consistent with the actual results, and the calculation is much less than the previous evaluation model, which provides a new idea for the comprehensive evaluation of social development.

A fuzzy clustering neural network structure optimization method based on bipartite mesh extraction of aggregation points is proposed in this paper. This method can make the algorithm quickly and globally converge to the optimal solution. However, in the optimization of fuzzy clustering neural network structure, there is still a lot of work to be studied. For example, when a fuzzy pattern clustering problem is proposed, to design a structure-optimized fuzzy clustering neural network model, we must first make clear the so-called complexity and fuzziness of the given pattern from the clustering characteristics. Therefore, the complexity of fuzzy clustering pattern is also a major problem to be solved.

Acknowledgement. This work is supported by Shandong Natural Science Foundation (ZR2013FL020), and Shandong Technology and Business University internal scientific research projects (04010621).

References

1. Tahmoresnezhad, J., Hashemi, S.: Turk. J. Electr. Eng. Comput. Sci. **25**(1), 292–307 (2017). https://doi.org/10.3906/elk-1503-245
2. Amorim, R.: J. Classif. **33**(2), 210–242 (2016). https://doi.org/10.1007/s00357-016-9208-4
3. Baghmisheh, M., Ezzati, R.: Error estimation and numerical solution of nonlinear fuzzy Fredholm integral equations of the second kind using triangular functions. J. Intell. Fuzzy Syst. **30**, 639–649 (2016)
4. Sadatrasoul, S.M., Ezzati, R.: Numerical solution of two-dimensional nonlinear Hammerstein fuzzy integral equations based on optimal fuzzy quadrature formula. J. Comput. Appl. Math. **292**, 430–446 (2016)
5. Chu, J.F., Liu, X.W., Wang, Y.M., Chin, K.S.: A group decision making model considering both the additive consistency and group consensus of intuitionistic fuzzy preference relations. Comput. Ind. Eng. **101**, 227–242 (2016)
6. Chen, S.M., Kao, P.Y.: TAIEX forecasting based on fuzzy time series, particle swarm optimization techniques and support vector machines. Inf. Sci. **247**(Suppl. C), 62–71 (2013)
7. Das, S., Kar, S., Pal, T.: Robust decision making using intuitionistic fuzzy numbers. Granul. Comput. **2**(1), 41–54 (2016)
8. Babolian, E., Sadeghi Goghary, H., Abbasbandy, S.: Numerical solution of linear Fredholm fuzzy integral equations of the second kind by Adomian method. Appl. Math. Comput. **161**, 733–744 (2005)

9. Bede, B., Gal, S.G.: Quadrature rules for integrals of fuzzy-number-valued functions. Fuzzy Sets Syst. **145**, 359–380 (2004)
10. Cai, M.J., Li, Q.G., Lang, G.M.: Shadowed sets of dynamic fuzzy sets. Granul. Comput. **2** (2), 85–94 (2017)
11. Chatterjee, K., Kar, S.: Unified granular-number based AHP-VIKOR multi-criteria decision framework. Granul. Comput. **2**(3), 199–221 (2017)
12. Chen, N., Xu, Z.S., Xia, M.M.: Interval-valued hesitant preference relations and their applications to group decision making. Knowl. Based Syst. **37**(2), 528–540 (2013)

Big Data and Security

Big Data Based E-commerce Search Advertising Recommendation

Ming Tao(✉) , Peican Huang , Xueqiang Li , and Kai Ding

School of Computer Science and Technology, Dongguan University of Technology,
Dongguan 523808, People's Republic of China
ming.tao@mail.scut.edu.cn, {huangpc,lixq,dingkai}@dgut.edu.cn

Abstract. Search engine marketing promoted by search engine companies, e,g., Google and Baidu, and the acknowledgment of brand promotion supported by the search engine have breaking through the limitation of traditional marketing model. However, with the ever-increasing
complexity of internet ecosystem, how to improve the recommendation
efficiency of e-commerce search advertisements has been conducting a
joint academic/industry challenge. To address this issue, through analyzing the popular treatment schemes of search advertising, a recommendation scheme for e-commerce search advertisements using Spark based
big data framework is proposed in this paper, which presents a solid solution to achieve high relevant recommendation for network users' searching behaviors and information needs while implementing the tripartite
benefit of network users, advertising platforms and advertisers. The conducted experiments have been shown to demonstrate the performance.

Keywords: Search engine marketing · Recommendation · Spark · Big
Data

1 Introduction

In the information age with the explosive expanding of data volume, search
engine as a significant technology in artificial intelligence field has been taken as a
powerful means of satisfying the users' accurate information needs [1]. Currently,
such technology has been widely applied in many fields, especially, highlights the
commercial value in the field of e-commerce search advertising, and has been
conducting a joint academic/industry investigation for years [2,3].

In the e-commerce, with the help of search engine, users can generally locate
the target products more quickly. In addition, using and analyzing the information, e.g., the search keywords and the historical log data, the e-commerce
platform also can recommend the product advertisements connecting better with
users expectations. Meanwhile, the placement of search advertisements also concerns to the benefits of advertising platforms and advertisers. Specifically, the
advertisers expect to enhance the influence of brand promotion and the sale

© Springer Nature Switzerland AG 2019
J. Vaidya et al. (Eds.): CSS 2019, LNCS 11982, pp. 457–466, 2019.
https://doi.org/10.1007/978-3-030-37337-5_37

profits, and the advertising platforms expect to gain more profits by recommending more accurate advertisements to network users. If the search advertising platforms could produce more accurate recommendations connecting better with network users' expectations, the tripartite benefit of network users, advertising platforms and advertisers would be achieved. To address the issue of the web search engines in supporting the heterogeneity of the network users in their search behaviors, Rahman et al. [4] attempted to augment web search engines with personalized recommendations of search results. By categorizing all the advertisements in terms of the commercial categories and extracting the keywords from each advertisements, Hwang et al. [5] developed a framework for personalized Internet advertising recommendation service based on keyword similarity. To address the difficult for advertisers of targeting and acquiring new customers with potential interest in the product, Siriaraya et al. [6] developed a recommendation system based on the users' latent interests using categorized web browsing history. By considering the context, modeling, and scale in the advertising recommendation, Gimenes et al. [7] proposed a method named Online-Recommendation Fraud ExcLuder (ORFEL) to detect defamation and/or illegitimate promotion of online products by using vertex-centric asynchronous parallel processing of bipartite (users-products) graphs. By integrating the contextual information from multiple diverse sources which could be used to enrich the decision making process of recommending advertisements to tailor better advertisements for users, Youssef et al. [8] created a targeted advertising system that started off by gathering a rich set of context information, and then provided viewers with recommended advertisements based on their current detected contextual information.

However, with the ever-increasing complexity of internet ecosystem, how to improve the recommendation efficiency of e-commerce search advertising still remains as a challenge issue. To address this issue, a recommendation scheme for e-commerce search advertisements using Spark based big data framework is proposed in this paper to achieve high relevant recommendation for network users' searching behaviors and information needs while implementing the tripartite benefit of network users, advertising platforms and advertisers. In this context, through analyzing the popular treatment schemes of search advertising, the web crawler technology is employed to capture the advertising data which is used to generate the user search log data, and then, the basic process of search advertising recommendation is implemented with the Spark based big data framework. Finally, the elaborately designed experiments are conducted to demonstrate the efficiency of the proposed recommendation scheme.

The rest of this paper is organized as follows. In Sect. 2, a popular architecture of search advertising system is introduced. In Sect. 3, the data preparation including the advertising data collection using web crawler technology and the process of generating the user search log data is discussed. In Sect. 4, the basic process of search advertising recommendation implemented with the Spark based big data framework is discussed. In Sect. 5, the experimental setup and the analysis results of efficiency are addressed. In Sect. 6, this paper is summarized and concluded.

2   Architecture of Search Advertising System

The popular architecture of search advertising system is shown in Fig. 1, in which, network users, advertising platforms and advertisers have the following interaction behaviors, and the involved key technique is to match the advertisements and the network users' information needs by the search engine to achieve the tripartite benefit. The advertisers submit the advertising information to the advertising platforms and buy the relevant bid phrases while bidding for desired display spaces. Subsequently, the advertising platforms update the advertising library with the submitted advertising information which will be used for choice and matching. Hereafter, the advertisers pay for the clicks of network users. The network users submit the interested query words to the search engine to express the certain information expectations. In terms of the submitted query words, the search engine retrieves the web corpus and the advertising corpus respectively, and returns the combination result of natural search and advertising search displayed in the web page. After proper screening the clicks of network users with the anti-cheating system filtering malicious clicks, the advertisers must pay the corresponding expenses for the clicks. Meanwhile, the displayed advertisements and the corresponding click-through rate should be logged.

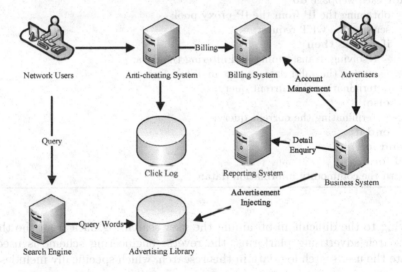

Fig. 1. The popular architecture of search advertising system.

3   Data Preparation

To investigate the basic process of search advertising recommendation, the data preparation including the advertising data and the user search log data should be firstly discussed. In this research, the advertising data collection is achieved using web crawler implemented by the Python standard library and some third-party libraries [9]. The implemented overall framework of crawler is depicted in

Algorithm 1. Specifically, the crawl request with customized *RowQuery* data is directed to the amazon.com to obtain the commodity information data which will be taken as the advertising data. The data format of *RowQuery* is defined as $< query\_condition, bidding, bidding\_id, query\_packet\_id >$. Owing to the anti-crawler measures employed in the amazon.com, multiple IP addresses effective supporting HTTPs and GET are needed to form the IP proxy pool. Such that, the commodity information data can be crawled with different IP addresses. If the GET request is successful with response data, the data should be resolved, transformed and filtered. For example, the crawled image path should be resolved to a local storage path, and the missing, invalid and nonstandard data fields should be transformed and filtered. After that, the valid data is stored as text in JavaScript Object Notation (JSON) format.

Algorithm 1. The implemented overall framework of crawler

Input: The *RowQuery* data.
Output: The commodity information data.
 1: searching loop in the *RowQuery* data;
 2: **for** each query **do**
 3:    **for** each webpage **do**
 4:       obtaining the IP from the IP proxy pool;
 5:       sending the GET request;
 6:       **if** Success **then**
 7:          resolving, transforming and filtering the data;
 8:          storing the valid data as text in JSON format;
 9:          terminating the current query;
10:       **else**
11:          terminating the current query;
12:       **end if**
13:    **end for**
14: **end for**
15: return the commodity information data;

Owing to the difficult in obtaining the user search log data from the third-party search advertising platforms, the reverse engineering scheme is used to generate the user search log data in this research, which specifically includes the following steps.

(1) Because different users have distinctive click preferences for search advertisements, the information of simulated network users should be firstly generated. In this research, ten thousand IP addresses are generated and five device IDs are correspondingly generated for each IP. Such that, a network user can be uniquely identified by the combination of a IP and a device ID.

(2) In this research, *query_group* indicates a group of queries having the same or similar characters. A *query_group* includes multiple biddings, and a

bidding includes multiple advertisements. Such that, the weight calculation involves calculating the weights for the advertisements and the biddings. Specifically. (i) The weight calculation for the advertisements and the biddings is determined by the advertisements and the user query, the relevance between the advertisements and the user query therefore should be calculated by matching the user query items and the corresponding keywords in the crawled advertisements, which can be represented by $Relevance = Match(query, keyworkds)/length(keywords)$. Where, $Match(query, keyworkds)$ is the number of matches between the user query items and the corresponding keywords in the crawled advertisements, and $length(keywords)$ is the length of advertising keywords. (ii) Calculating the weight for the advertisements, which can be represented by $Weight(ad) = Relevance/sum(Relevance)$. Where, $Relevance$ is the relevance between the current query and the advertisements, and $sum(Relevance)$ is the summation of the relevances between all the queries and the advertisements within the current bidding. (iii) Calculating the weight for the biddings, which can be represented by $Weight(bidding) = sum(Relevance)/SUM(Relevance)$. Where, $SUM(Relevance)$ is the summation of the relevances between all the queries and the advertisements within the current $query\_group$.

(3) Dividing the network users into different groups according to the click preferences, and then assigning the advertisements with different weights for different network users.

(4) With the calculated weights for the advertisements and the biddings, the random weight algorithm is employed in this research to achieve the overall advertising choices distributed according to the weights.

(5) The generated user search log data must include positive and negative samples in order to make a more reasonable classification of user click behaviors. For generating the positive samples, if the types of advertisement and the user query are matched and the user indeed clicks this advertisement, a positive sample is generated. The negative samples include four types, e.g., the types of advertisement and the user query are mismatched, the types of the user query and the bidding are mismatched, the advertisements and bidding have the lowest weights, and the types of advertisement and the user query are matched but the user does not click this advertisement.

4 Basic Process of Search Advertising Recommendation

Based on the data preparation, the basic process of search advertising recommendation including the specific operations is stated as follows, and the basic flow is shown in Fig. 2.

(1) Loading and preprocessing the advertising data, and converting the advertising keywords into $String$ format within the MapReduce framework [10].

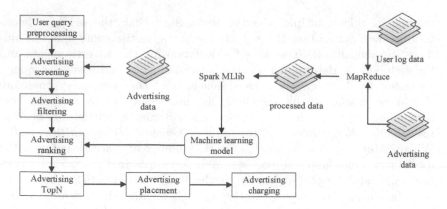

Fig. 2. The basic process of search advertising recommendation.

Subsequently, creating a reverse index of advertising keywords using Memcached caching system and loading the advertisers' bidding data [11]. After that, importing the processed data into the Spark MLlib [12].

(2) Once receiving the user query words, using the "Query Understanding" algorithm to cope with the user query words and build the corresponding *keywords* to complete the user query preprocessing operation [13]. Subsequently, the Memcached caching system uses the created reverse index to obtain and return the synonym data in terms of the *keywords*. After that, traversing the synonym data set and finding the corresponding advertising ID list for each synonym to achieve "Query Rewrite" with the Word2vector model in Spark MLlib [14], and screening the advertisements from the advertising data based on the advertising ID to complete the advertising screening operation.

(3) After the advertising screening operation, calculating the *Relevance* between the user query and the advertisements according to the method stated above and using the machine learning model, e.g., logistic regression, to estimate the click-through rate represented by CTR for the advertisements with the screened query characters [15]. In this research, the click event represented by *click* is taken as a random variable of binary variables and the probability of *click* $= 1$ is the click-through rate. Therefore, the distribution of the click event can be conducted as a binomial distribution shown as $P(click) = CTR^{click} \cdot (1 - CTR)^{1-click}$ with parameter CTR. The estimation of the click-through rate is to build a functional relationship between CTR and the triple of (A, U, C), which can be represented in formula (1) using logistic regression model [16]. Where, the three variables in the triple of (A, U, C) respectively represents *Advertisement*, *User* and *Content*, χ represents the eigenvector of (A, U, C), ω represents the weighting coefficient of each character, the output of the linear function $(2 \cdot click - 1) \cdot \omega^T \cdot \chi(A, U, C)$ is mapped into $(0, 1)$ through *sigmoid* function and $(2 \cdot click - 1)$ is used to transform the click variables within $\{0, 1\}$ into $\{-1, 1\}$.

$$P(click|(A, U, C)) = \sigma \cdot ((2 \cdot click - 1) \cdot \omega^T \cdot \chi(A, U, C))$$
$$= \{1 + e^{-(2 \cdot click - 1) \cdot \omega^T \cdot \chi(A, U, C)}\}^{-1} \qquad (1)$$

After that, configuring the thresholds for the relevance and the click-through rate, and filtering the screened advertisements based on the configured thresholds to complete the advertising filtering operation.

(4) In terms of the calculated relevance and click-through rate, the advertising quality can be calculated in formula (2), subsequently, the advertising ranking can be calculated as $Rank = Quality \cdot bidding$ with the advertising bidding data. After that, the advertising ranking operation can be completed in terms of the $Rank$.

$$Quality = \alpha \cdot CTR + (1 - \alpha) \cdot Relevance \quad (0 < \alpha < 1) \qquad (2)$$

(5) After the advertising ranking operation, selecting the TopN advertisements in terms of the configured threshold N and displaying the TopN advertisements at the proper placement in the webpage. Once the network user clicks the displayed advertisements, the anti-cheating system would filter the malicious clicks, and the advertisers should pay the corresponding expenses for the clicks.

5   Experiments and Analysis

To qualitatively analyze and evaluate the performance of the proposed recommendation scheme for e-commerce search advertisements addressing the issue of achieving high relevant recommendation for network users' searching behaviors and information needs, through adjusting and combining the Word2vector model parameters in "Query Rewrite", e.g., the size of synonym window (W), the size of vector (V), learning rate (R) and the number of model iterations (I), the elaborate experiments are conducted to evaluate the estimation of click-through rate from $Accucary$, AUC and $Logless$. The three estimation models, decision tree, random forest and gradient boosting decision tree (GBDT), are selected for comparison with logistic regression used in this research, and the comparison results are shown in Fig. 3.

Decision tree is a common prediction model. For binary classification problem, it wants to obtain a model from the given training data set to classify the new samples. In this research of estimating the advertisement click-through rate, it can be taken as a decision-making process for the problem of whether the current advertisement is clicked. Specially, a decision tree consists of a root node, a number of internal nodes and leaf nodes, where the root node contains the complete set of samples and the leaf node corresponds to the final decision result. Therefore, the model training is to build a complete decision tree through calculating the sample purity of each partitioned node. Random forest as an extension of decision tree is a kind of ensemble learning method. Through constructing multiple decision tree, it finally obtains the estimation result in the

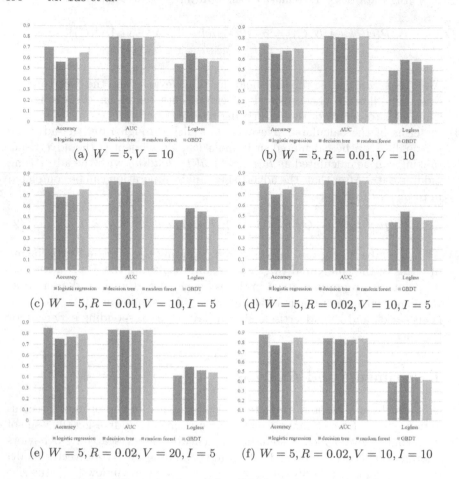

Fig. 3. The evaluation of the click-through rate estimation.

voting manner. Specifically, once the testing data enter into the random forest, each decision tree will do the classification, and the classification result is determined by the scores voted by the decision trees. Gradient boosting decision tree as an iterative decision tree consists of multiple decision trees as well, the final classification result however is the cumulative results of all decision trees. From Fig. 3, we can clearly see that the performance of estimating the click-through rate using logistic regression is totally better than that using the other three estimation models.

In addition, with the tuning of Word2vector model parameters in "Query Rewrite", the relevances between the synonyms and the submitted query words are enhanced. Once the system receiving the query words submitted by the network user, the advertisements better matching the network users' searching behaviors and information needs could be returned. Therefore, the performance of estimating the click-through rate improves gradually with the tuning of model parameters.

6   Conclusion

To address the issue of improving the recommendation efficiency of e-commerce search advertising in the increasingly complex internet ecosystem, a scheme of e-commerce search advertising recommendation using Spark based big data framework has been investigated in this paper through analyzing the popular treatment schemes of search advertising, which presents a solid solution to achieve high relevant recommendation for network users' searching behaviors and information needs while implementing the tripartite benefit of network users, advertising platforms and advertisers. In this context, the data preparation including the advertising data and the user search log data is firstly discussed, and the basic process of search advertising recommendation then is investigated on this basis. The conducted experiments finally have been shown to demonstrate the performance of estimating the click-through rate.

Acknowledgments. This work was supported in part by the Natural Science Foundation of Guangdong Province, China (Grant No. 2018A030313014); Guangdong University Scientific Innovation Project (Grant No. 2017KTSCX178).

References

1. Parkes, D.C., Wellman, M.P.: Economic reasoning and artificial intelligence. Science **349**(6245), 267–272 (2015)
2. Yang, Z., Shi, Y., Wang, B.: Search engine marketing, financing ability and firm performance in E-commerce. Procedia Comput. Sci. **55**, 1106–1112 (2015)
3. Tao, M., Wei, W.H., Huang, S.Q.: Location-based trustworthy services recommendation in cooperative-communication-enabled internet of vehicles. J. Netw. Comput. Appl. **126**, 1–11 (2019)
4. Rahman, M.M., Abdullah, N.A.: A personalized group-based recommendation approach for Web search in E-learning. IEEE Access **6**, 34166–34178 (2018)
5. Hwang, W.H., Chen, Y.S., Jiang, T.M.: Personalized internet advertisement recommendation service based on keyword similarity. In: IEEE 39th Annual Computer Software and Applications Conference, vol. 1, pp. 29–33. IEEE, Taichung (2015). https://doi.org/10.1109/COMPSAC.2015.202
6. Siriaraya, P., Yamaguchi, Y., Morishita, M., et al.: Using categorized web browsing history to estimate the user's latent interests for web advertisement recommendation. In: IEEE International Conference on Big Data (Big Data), pp. 4429–4434. IEEE, Boston (2017). https://doi.org/10.1109/BigData.2017.8258480
7. Gimenes, G., Cordeiro, R.L.F., Rodrigues-Jr, J.F.: ORFEL: efficient detection of defamation or illegitimate promotion in online recommendation. Inf. Sci. **379**, 274–287 (2017)
8. Youssef, Y., Aly, S.G.: Towards the integration of diverse context into advertisement recommendation on mobile devices. In: IEEE 13th International Wireless Communications and Mobile Computing Conference (IWCMC), 1734–1739. IEEE, Valencia, Spain (2017). https://doi.org/10.1109/IWCMC.2017.7986546
9. Zhao, F., Zhou, J., Nie, C., et al.: Smartcrawler: a two-stage crawler for efficiently harvesting deep-web interfaces. IEEE Trans. Serv. Comput. **9**(4), 608–620 (2016)

10. Dean, J., Ghemawat, S.: Mapreduce: a flexible data processing tool. Commun. ACM **53**(1), 72–77 (2010)
11. Cheng, W., Ren, F., Jiang, W., et al.: Modeling and Analyzing Latency in the Memcached system. In: IEEE 37th International Conference on Distributed Computing Systems (ICDCS), pp. 538–548. IEEE, Atlanta (2017). https://doi.org/10.1109/ICDCS.2017.122
12. Siegal, D., Guo, J., Agrawal, G.: Smart-MLlib: a high-performance machine-learning library. In: IEEE International Conference on Cluster Computing (CLUSTER), pp. 336–345. IEEE, Taipei (2016). https://doi.org/10.1109/CLUSTER.2016.49
13. Liu, J., Pasupat, P., Wamg, Y., et al.: Query understanding enhanced by hierarchical parsing structures. In: IEEE Workshop on Automatic Speech Recognition and Understanding, pp. 72–77. IEEE, Olomouc (2013). https://doi.org/10.1109/ASRU.2013.6707708
14. Jiang, M., Liu, R., Wang, F.: Word network topic model based on word2vector. In: IEEE Fourth International Conference on Big Data Computing Service and Applications (BigDataService), pp. 241–247. IEEE, Bamberg (2018). https://doi.org/10.1109/BigDataService.2018.00043
15. Gao, H., Kong, D., Lu, M., et al.: Attention convolutional neural network for advertiser-level click-through rate forecasting. In: ACM 2018 World Wide Web Conference (WWW), pp. 1855–1864. ACM, Lyon (2018). https://doi.org/10.1145/3178876.3186184
16. Edizel, B., Mantrach, A., Bai, X., et al.: Deep character-level click-through rate prediction for sponsored search. In: International ACM SIGIR Conference on Research and Development in Information Retrieval, pp. 305–314. ACM, Shinjuku (2017). https://doi.org/10.1145/3077136.3080811

File Recovery of High-Order Clearing First Cluster Based on FAT32

Xu Chang[1,2(✉)], Fanchang Hao[2,3], Jian Wu[1,2], and Guorui Feng[1,2]

[1] School of Cyber Security, Shandong University of Political Science and Law,
Jinan 250014, China
changxumail@163.com, jinanwujian@163.com,
fengguorui@163.com
[2] Key Laboratory of Evidence-Identifying in Universities of Shandong,
Shandong University of Political Science and Law, Jinan 250014, China
haofine@hotmail.com
[3] School of Computer Science and Technology, Shandong Jianzhu University,
Jinan 250101, China

Abstract. The core technical problems of file recovery are the first cluster number clearing of high-order two bytes and the fragmentation in the file. The algorithm proposed in this paper makes full use of file system information such as FAT, creation time, file identification and fragmentation characteristics, recover easy ones and the files difficult to recover which are recoverable at first, and then analyzes the status of remaining fragments after eliminating many interference of fragments. Experimental results show that the algorithm can significantly reduce the complexity of fragments and improve the accuracy of file recovery.

Keywords: FAT32 · File recovery · Fragmentation · File identification

1 Introduction

With the rapid development of information technology and intelligent equipment, electronic information storage equipment is rapidly popularized and has been continuously applied to various fields of human life and work. People got a great convenience in obtaining, storing and sharing data, which brought many challenges at the same time. Hackers, viruses, disoperation, storage medium quality defects and many other factors are threatening the security of data [1]. Once the data is lost, loss cannot be measured by money. On the other hand, in the process of cybercrime, with the enhancement of the criminal suspect's Anti-detection consciousness and the use of anti-forensics technology, especially the deletion of some sensitive and important data information, forensics becomes more difficult [2]. Data recovery is a technology to recover all or part of the data from the storage medium that has been destroyed or deleted. It has important application value and quickly becomes one of the key research areas to protect user data, fight computer crime and forensics.

For the convenience of use and management, most of the data is stored as files in specific file systems. Currently, the Windows operating system has a market share of

© Springer Nature Switzerland AG 2019
J. Vaidya et al. (Eds.): CSS 2019, LNCS 11982, pp. 467–476, 2019.
https://doi.org/10.1007/978-3-030-37337-5_38

over 92.6% [3], and its main application file systems are FAT32 and NTFS. In particular, the FAT32 file system is supported by numerous digital devices (NTFS has a lot of advantages, but is not suitable for portable storage). Since mainstream storage devices generally have large capacity, which make the probability of high-order zero clearing after file deletion is very high. Frequent file operations lead to more fragmentation on disk. After analyzing more than 350 hard disks including FAT, NTFS, UFS and other file systems, Garfikel [10] et al. found that probability of fragmentation is as high as 42%, the probability of MS word file was 17%, and JPEG file was 16% on the disk.

The main difficulty in file recovery is the high order clearing of the first cluster number after file deletion [4] and file fragmentation [10]. For file recovery, most existing tools (e.g. FTK, Encase, The Sleuth kit) are based on the assumption that the files stored sequentially in hard disks, Recover the file by extracting the block of data between the header and the footer, which caused them cannot handle the fragmented files [8]. The research on the zeroing of high order two bytes mainly focuses on creation time proximity, identification code comparison, time and feature code combination, etc., and the accuracy needs to be improved. However, recover the file correctly is impossible even if the first cluster is precisely located. This paper makes full use of the file system information such as FAT, creation time, file feature and shard feature to propose a data recovery method that can improve the precise location of the high-order clearing first cluster and deal with file fragments better.

The rest of this paper is organized as follows. Section 2 talks about related works. The theory of file deletion and recovery of FAT32 will be introduced in Sect. 3, followed by the proposed file recovery algorithm (Sect. 4). Section 5 shows the experimental results and Sect. 6 concludes the paper.

2   Related Work

Currently, file recovery can be divided into two major categories [6]: one is file recovery, and the other is file carving. File recovery is based on file system meta-information to recover Data. By scanning the file allocation table in the file system to locate the file start sector and the end of the sector to recover files, extract the data between header and footer mainly use the file system information or extract the size of data from header which can be acquired in FDT, The recovery efficiency is high for the files stored in the device continuously, but the accuracy of the data that cannot accurately locate the first cluster number or file header or fragment should be improved.

File carving works without using File system information. It attempts to recover and reconstruct files from the ostensibly unstructured original disk image (the binary data stream), without relying on the file system of the source disk image. Paper [1, 5] suggests that in view of the existence of the creation time of files that are completely deleted in FDT, the high order two bytes of files that are similar to the creation time of deleted files can be found to replace the high order two bytes of deleted files. In Paper [4], a rapid data recovery approach is proposed, which determines the storage space of the file according to the cluster number in the sector where the file header feature code is located and the file size in the remaining directory items. In addition, the method of extracting effective information from the compound document structure is also discussed. In paper [11], the author proposed a method to recover lost file data by comprehensive utilization of various feature information, that is, the information of the file itself was deleted and other information of the creation time or storage location adjacent to it was also used. The creation time was combined with the feature code of the file for correlation and comparison to determine the two bytes of high order. Paper [8] provides an algorithm based on CED which used to evaluate if two data blocks are consecutive in the same file. Paper [13] use CNNs proposed CNN-based detectors for aligned and nonaligned double JPEG compression detection and explored the capability of CNNs to capture DJPEG artifacts directly from images.

In summary, most of the current researches focus on the recovery of a certain type of files or separate the recovery and carving of files. Most researches on file recovery ignore the fragments and only consider the case of continuous storage, which has a very good effect on the continuous storage of files. However, the fragment of files leads to the failure to recover files correctly even if the first cluster is precisely located. On the other hand, most of the researches on file carving ignore the file system structure and only study the fragments of data. Many metadata can play an important reference role in duplication carving, like FAT. However, in reality, most storage devices are fragmented and also retain all or part of the metadata information of the file system. Making full use of this useful information can effectively improve the accuracy of file recovery.

3   Theory of File Deletion and Recovery of FAT32

3.1   FAT32 File System

FAT32 file system consists of DBR (DOS Boot Record and its reserved sectors, FAT (File Allocation Table), FDT (File Directory Table) and DATA [7], as shown in Fig. 1.

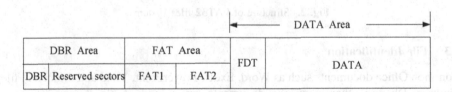

Fig. 1. FAT32 file system structure.

DBR. BPB in DBR is particularly important for data recovery, which records the file storage format of this partition, starting sector, hard disk media descriptor, end sector, FAT number, size of allocation unit and root directory size and other important information.

FAT. A registry of where files are stored on the hard disk, recording the different file clusters. The clusters occupied by files are stored in the FAT in the form of cluster chain. The previous cluster stores the serial number of the next cluster.

FDT. Also known as the DIR root area, all files and their subdirectories in the root directory directory table (FDT) have a "directory entry." Record the file name, extension, file creation date, creation time, access date, access time, last write date, last write time, file length, starting cluster of high and low bits and other information.

DATA. It is the FAT32 file system's true data storage area, occupying most of the hard disk space. When the file is deleted, the data in the data area corresponding to the file is still saved in the corresponding cluster, but this part of data is garbage data corresponding to the operating system. If new data is written, the cluster will be used as the idle cluster.

3.2 Fragmentation

Most files are stored sequentially on storage devices, but frequent file operations such as adding, deleting and modifying will lead to partial file fragmentation storage. File fragment is when a file is divided into several parts, scattered on a disk, but all parts are present and undamaged. These parts are called file shards. These fragments may be stored in order (as shown in file 1 in Fig. 2) or out of order (as shown in file 2 in Fig. 2). A complete continuous file is one where the data in the file is contiguous. The research in this paper is based on a continuous or ordered debris model with complete structure and no loss.

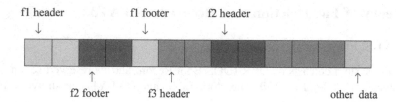

Fig. 2. Structure of FAT32 files system.

3.3 File Identification

Common Office documents such as Word, Excel, PowerPoint, Visio and thumbnail file Thumbs. Db and other composite documents are a kind of file storage structure. Composite documents have obvious file header and file footer characteristics, which can be used to identify file types. For example, in Word document format with the ".docx "extension, storage starts with hexadecimal keywords like" 0x504B030414." JPEG files start with "0xFFD8FFE0" or "0xFFD8FFE1" as the file header and end with "0xFFD9". The header and footer identifiers for some common files are shown in the following Table 1.

3.4 Analysis of File Deletion Operations

When deletes the file on disk, it does not really delete or overwrite the file data, but only modify some attributes of the file system. Just because the data still exists, it is not

Table 1. Identifications of common files.

File type	Header	Footer
Word2010	"0x504B030414"	
Word97 ~ 2007	"0xD0CF11E0A1"	
JPEG	"0xFFD8FFE0" or "0xFFD8FFE1"	"0xFFD9"
PDF	"0x25504446"	"0x2525454F46"
GIF	"0x47494687A" or "0x474689A"	"0x003B"
WMV	"0x3026B2758E66CF11"	
ZIP	"0x504B0304"	

completely deleted, which provides us with the possibility of data recovery. This is also the main reason to be able to restore deleted data. The deletion of files in FAT32 file system involves the following four situations [1, 4]. Changes of various parts of the file system before and after deletion by different deletion methods are analyzed as follows:

Shift+Delete. The FAT of the deleted file should be cleared, as shown in Fig. 3. The first byte of FDT is changed to "E5", and the top two bytes of the first cluster number are zeroed, as shown in Fig. 4. Therefore, the accurate location of the first cluster is not possible, which makes file recovery more difficult (Figs. 5 and 6).

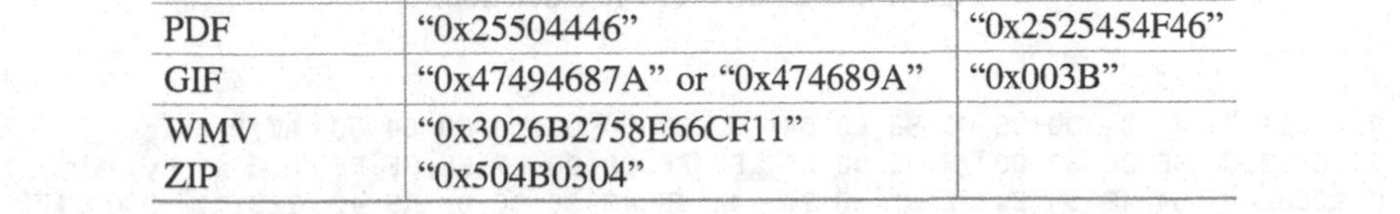

```
000533A80  A1 73 0D 00 A2 73 0D 00  FF FF FF 0F A4 73 0D 00   ¡s ¢s ÿÿÿ ¤s
000533A90  A5 73 0D 00 A6 73 0D 00  A7 73 0D 00 A8 73 0D 00   ¥s ¦s §s ¨s
000533AA0  A9 73 0D 00 AA 73 0D 00  AB 73 0D 00 AC 73 0D 00   ©s ªs «s ¬s
000533AB0  FF FF FF 0F AE 73 0D 00  AF 73 0D 00 B0 73 0D 00   ÿÿÿ ®s ¯s °s
000533AC0  B1 73 0D 00 B2 73 0D 00  B3 73 0D 00 B4 73 0D 00   ±s ²s ³s ´s
```

Fig. 3. Status of FAT before deletion.

Delete. Enter the recycle bin first, and empty the recycle bin. The FAT item of deleted file is cleared, the first byte of FDT is changed to "E5", the first cluster number has no change before and after deletion, the first cluster location of the file is accurate, and recovery is relatively easy to achieve.

Completely Delete the Subdirectory. The directory FAT empty, FDT the first byte to "E5", the first cluster number of two bytes clear; The FAT item of the file in the folder is cleared, the first byte of the FDT directory item is changed to "E5", the first cluster high position two bytes are not zero, you can locate the first cluster.

Format Disk. The FAT and FDT corresponding to the file are cleared, and the data still exists. The recovery of formatted files can only be achieved by reading binary data in storage devices. One method can be used to recover files by locating the start and end marks of files. However, for files that are stored discontinuously due to fragmentation, the recovery success rate is low. Another method can use data reconstruction technology [8–10] for recovery to identify, group, sort and reorganize file fragments.

```
000533A80  A1 73 0D 00 A2 73 0D 00  FF FF FF 0F 00 00 00 00   |s  ¢s  ÿÿÿ
000533A90  00 00 00 00 00 00 00 00  00 00 00 00 00 00 00 00
000533AA0  00 00 00 00 00 00 00 00  00 00 00 00 00 00 00 00
000533AB0  00 00 00 00 AE 73 0D 00  AF 73 0D 00 B0 73 0D 00   ®s  ¯s  °s
000533AC0  B1 73 0D 00 B2 73 0D 00  B3 73 0D 00 B4 73 0D 00   ±s  ²s  ³s  ´s
```

Fig. 4. Status of FAT after deletion.

```
001000220  41 54 00 45 00 53 00 54  00 2E 00 0F 00 F3 64 00   AT E S T .    ód
001000230  6F 00 63 00 78 00 00 00  FF FF 00 00 FF FF FF FF   o c x   ÿÿ  ÿÿÿÿ
001000240  54 45 53 54 7E 31 20 20  44 4F 43 20 00 8E A5 4C   TEST~1  DOC  I¥L
001000250  BC 4E BC 4E 0D 00 A4 4C  BC 4E A3 73 C8 91 00 00   ¼N¼N  ¤L ¼N£sÈ´
```

Fig. 5. Status of FDT before deletion.

```
001000220  E5 54 00 45 00 53 00 54  00 2E 00 0F 00 F3 64 00   åT E S T .    ód
001000230  6F 00 63 00 78 00 00 00  FF FF 00 00 FF FF FF FF   o c x   ÿÿ  ÿÿÿÿ
001000240  E5 45 53 54 7E 31 20 20  44 4F 43 20 00 8E A5 4C   åEST~1  DOC  I¥L
001000250  BC 4E BC 4E 00 00 A4 4C  BC 4E A3 73 C8 91 00 00   ¼N¼N  ¤L ¼N£sÈ´
```

Fig. 6. Status of FDT after deletion.

The deletion of removable devices such as U disk is slightly different from the above deletion analysis. For example, after the deletion and thorough deletion of flash drive and the deletion of files in folders, the high-order clearing first cluster, this makes it difficult to locate the first cluster accurately. This paper mainly focuses on the zero-clearing of the first cluster height by two bytes after file deletion, which makes it impossible to locate the first cluster accurately, and causes the recovered files to be unable to be opened or to be restored as garbled codes.

4   The Proposed Algorithm of High-Order Clearing First Cluster Based on FAT32

4.1   Recover Methods of High Level Clearing

According to the above analysis in Sect. 3, after the file is completely deleted, the first cluster number in FDT of the file directory entry is cleared to zero by two bytes, while the lower two bytes remain unchanged. To correctly locate the starting location of the file data, you need to recover the data exactly by getting two bytes high again by various means. The main methods include:

According to the Creation Time. The probability of starting cluster height being the same for files created at the same time is very high. Therefore, by looking for the files with the closest creation time in the same directory, we can refer to their height of two bytes.

Combined with the File Identification. The initial cluster address obtained by method above is used to locate the cluster, and the file identification is used to determine whether it is consistent with the file type of the file to be recovered in FDT.

When using the creation time to locate the first cluster number, if the storage device is fragmented, the address of the first cluster of different files with the same creation time varies greatly, so it is difficult to ensure the accuracy. Using the method of combining creation time with file identification, if more files of the same type are in the same directory or all files of the same type, it may cause miscalculation.

4.2   The Proposed Algorithm

In this paper, a more accurate method is proposed to determine whether the cluster's two bytes high are accurate or not, and to avoid the problem of low data recovery accuracy caused by fragmentation. From easy to difficult, the algorithm proposed by continuous data is divided into four modules, which are FAT idle state extraction, no high-order reset file recovery, high-order reset file recovery and fragments processing.

The algorithm first by the second, three modules will determine the correct documents to get rid of, again to the rest of the document analysis, a small amount of divided in this way can obviously reduce the complexity.

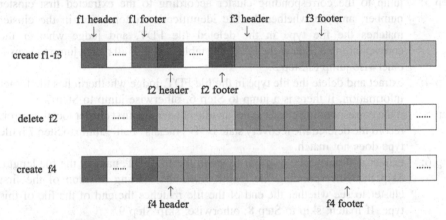

Fig. 7. f3 and f4 deleted at the same time, because of the head and footer with f3 to store data in a row, easy to restore, can restore its first, in the fourth module lamination processing algorithms to restore the f4, can eliminate interference of fragments, improve accuracy.

Idle State Extraction of FAT. Traverse the FAT, extract the state of the free cluster, mark the free cluster as "N", means none. In the data recovery process of the second and third modules, Successful recovery of cluster tags successful recovery marks, doubtful cluster mark file name, and file length and other information. In case the fourth module is called when analyzing fragmented data.

File Recovery with No High-Order Reset. Traverse the file directory, find deleted files in FDT, extract the deleted file's first cluster number, locate to the first cluster of files and match the file type, according to the length of the file to compare the end-of-file, if the head and footer, length is correct can be set for the first cluster to be successful, and the FAT to restore files occupy clusters are marked correctly. (for files without footer feature identification, footer data can be located and judged according to the file length. If there is data before the footer and no data after the footer, the deleted file can be determined. Otherwise, set the first cluster mark corresponding to the FAT, such file name, file type and length. The FAT status table has been prepared for reanalysis and use.

File Recovery with High-Order Reset. Traverse the file directory, delete files search, according to preliminary access creation time first cluster number and verification, by matching the same file type, compare the end-of-file, according to the length of the file on the file tag and without the file tag files for recovery, and FAT free cluster status table, use the same methods above. The specific algorithm of this step is as follows:

Step 1: traverse the root directory, extract the file directory items with deleted mark, analyze FDT, and extract the creation time of deleted files.

Step 2: according to the creation time of the extracted deleted file, find the existing disk file closest to the creation time of the deleted file, extract the two bytes high of the first cluster number, and merge the two bytes low in the deleted file FDT into the position of the first cluster number of the deleted file.

Step 3: jump to the corresponding cluster according to the extracted first cluster number, analyze whether the file identification information in the cluster matches the file type in the deleted file FDT, and judge whether the corresponding cluster in the FAT state table is idle. If all match jump to Step 4, otherwise jump to Step 5.

Step 4: extract and delete the file type in the file FDT, judge whether it has file footer information, if there is a jump to Step 6, otherwise jump to Step 7.

Step 5: if the corresponding cluster is not an idle cluster, the first cluster location error, record the deleted file recovery state is "F", means "Fail"; Jump to Step 7 if file type does not match.

Step 6: extract and delete the last four bytes in the file FDT, namely the file length. Skip the corresponding file length from the starting position of the first cluster to see whether the end of the file matches the end of the file of this type. If match, skip to Step 8; otherwise, skip Step 9.

Step 7: locate FAT. Locate to the end of the file according to the location of the first cluster extracted and the length of the file. If the data before the end exist (including the end), jump to Step 8 after no data. Otherwise jump to Step 9.

Step 8: extract the data of the deleted file according to the obtained first cluster number and file length, save it as the recovery success file, and mark the corresponding cluster as "V" and means "Victory" in the FAT idle state table.

Step 9: identify "FT" and means further treatment in the first cluster in the FAT status table, and delete the name, file length and file type information of the file, which has been prepared for the FAT status analysis of module four teams.

Fragmented Data Processing. After the processing of the first three steps, the remaining idle clusters are greatly reduced, which can improve the speed and accuracy of the analysis. Clusters with successful recovery, questionable clusters, and idle clusters in the FAT idle state table are identified. This module mainly analyzes the status of doubt cluster and idle cluster, and analyzes the data with fragments phenomenon when deleting files. If the file f4 in Fig. 7 is deleted, the nearest footer should be searched according to f4's header, and then the free cluster data directly from header and footer should be restored. The specific recovery algorithm is as follows:

Step 1:   scan FAT idle state table and read the clusters marked "FT" in sequence.

Step 2:   search for the nearest end tag matching the file type in the free cluster after the first cluster.

Step 3:   get the free cluster data between the first cluster and the end tag of the deleted file in the FAT free state table, and calculate the extracted data length.

Step 4:   compare the extracted data length with the file length in the FAT idle state table, if consistent, restore the file. And mark "V" in FAT idle state table. If the FAT state table is not modified in case of inconsistency, skip to Step 1 and continue to scan the next file

Step 5:   end of this round of scanning.

5   Experimental Results and Analysis

The test environment is: Intel(R) Pentium(R) CPU g3250 3.2 GHz, 4G memory, Windows7, ST1000DM 003-1er162. VHD (Microsoft Virtual Hard Disk format) technology was used to Virtual a Hard Disk with a size of 8G. After loading, DiskGenius was used to format it into FAT32 file system with the cluster size of 4096B (8 KB) cluster size of 4096 bytes (8 KB). In order to simulate real usage scenarios, common file types of different sizes, such as RMVB, GIF, PDF, BMP, ZIP, DOCX, TXT, etc. are randomly collected and written to them until they cannot be written, and then fragments are generated naturally by simulating the principle of fragmentation generation, with random fragment size and location. Fragmentation produces a simulation of the use of real storage devices, randomly deleting some files, and then writing files, 10 times. Finally, 100 files of different types were randomly deleted to complete the production of test data. The algorithm proposed in this paper is tested and compared with common recovery software. Experimental results are shown in Table 2:

Table 2. Analysis of experimental results.

Name	Number of success	Success rate
Foremost	168	84%
Scalpel	183	91.5%
Proposed algorithm	189	94.5%

The results show that the proposed algorithm is more accurate than the tools include foremost and scalpel, which improved the accuracy of file recovery.

6 Conclusion

In this paper, we analyzed two problems existing in data recovery and different file deletion methods. Through FAT32 file system analysis and the fragmentation model, we proposed a new method to recovery deleted files, using creation time combined with cluster idle state of FAT, characteristic of the high two bytes store by continuous and matching accuracy, through the analysis of the high two bytes and verify accurate correct deleting files for recovery, analysis of the rest FAT idle cluster state to avoid the interference of file fragments to restore to algorithm consists of four modules, respectively for the FAT idle state extraction, no high-order reset file recovery, high-order reset file recovery and fragments processing. Experimental results show that the proposed method can effectively improve the accuracy.

Acknowledgements. This work is supported by Projects of Shandong Province Higher Educational Science and Technology Program under Grant J18KA357, J16LN19, J18KA383; Doctoral Research Fund of Shandong Jianzhu University under GrantXNBS1810; Teaching Innovation project of Shandong University of Political Science and Law under Grant 2017JYB009; projects of Shandong University of Political Science and Law, Grant No. 2016Z03B, 2015Z03B; and also supported (in part) by the Key Research and Development Project of Shandong Province under Grant 2019GGX101068.

References

1. Liu, W.: In-Depth Disclosure of Data Recovery Technology, 2nd edn, pp. 248–257. Electronic Industry Press, Beijing (2016)
2. Guo, B., Youquan, M.: A computer forensics method based on FAT32 file system. Comput. Appl. Softw. **1**, 260–262 (2010)
3. Windows 10 Operating system version of the latest market share data released (2019). http://notebook.it168.com/a2019/0131/5155/000005155901.shtml
4. Yang, D.: Fast recovery method of effective data based on FAT32. J. Comput. Appl. **9**, 2500–2503 (2012)
5. Fan, H., Lipeng, W.: Research on data recovery technology of FAT32 file system. Sci. Technol. Inf. **36**, 55–57 (2013)
6. Hong, G.: Research on JPEG File Duplication Based on Thumbnail. Hangzhou Dianzi University (2012)
7. Dai, S., Tu, Y.: Data Recovery Technology (Classic Reproduction Version). Electronic Industry Press, Beijing (2014)
8. Tang, Y., et al.: Recovery of heavily fragmented JPEG files. Digit. Investig. **18**, 108–117 (2016)
9. Digital Assembly. Smart Carver (2015). http://digital-assembly.com/products/smartcarver-dc3/
10. Garfinkel, S.L.: Carving contiguous and fragmented files with fast object validation. Digit. Investig. **4**, 2–12 (2007)
11. Guangyu, G., Shujuan, Z.: A file recovery method in a FAT32 file system. Netw. New Media Technol. **2**, 36–41 (2016)

Mobile Recommendation Method for Fusing Item Features and User Trust Relationship

Shanguo Lv[✉]

Software School, East China Jiaotong University, Nanchang, China
42883824@qq.com

Abstract. User based collaborative filtering recommendation method does not consider the impact of user preferences on the user's similarity in the non-common score items, and the lack of traditional similarity measurement methods in sparse user score data. This paper proposed a hybrid recommendation method combining similar relationship and trust relationship of mobile users, using the EMD distance method of user preference on similar items to compute the preference similarity relation among the users, and fusing mobile user trust and similar user preferences for the target user's non-scoring items to be scored prediction. Experimental results on public data sets show that, compared to the traditional collaborative filtering recommendation algorithm based on users, this method has a lower MAE error value and higher P@N value, effectively alleviate the data sparsity and improve the performance of the recommendation system.

Keywords: Mobile recommendation · Collaborative filtering · Hybrid recommendation

1 Introduction

The rapid development of the Internet has caused the problem of information overload, and the recommendation system is an important means to solve the problem of information overload. Recommendation system is widely used in the field of electronic commerce [1, 2]. Mainly find the potential needs of users and the initiative to recommend to users to meet their needs of the project, the project will not be related to filter out to ease the user's information burden. At present, collaborative filtering algorithm is the most widely used recommendation algorithm in recommendation system. Collaborative filtering algorithm is mainly divided into two categories: memory based method and model based method [3]. However, there is a common problem in collaborative filtering recommendation system, namely user evaluation or view of the project is far less than the user has not been evaluated or not view the project [3]. As an effective means of information filtering, the recommendation system has been widely concerned in the mobile field. Because of the restriction of the mobile devices (such as small screen, input difficulties), the evaluation of mobile user feedback behavior becomes inconvenient, score sparse data in mobile recommendation system is still an important factor in the impact of mobile recommendation performance.

© Springer Nature Switzerland AG 2019
J. Vaidya et al. (Eds.): CSS 2019, LNCS 11982, pp. 477–488, 2019.
https://doi.org/10.1007/978-3-030-37337-5_39

Based on the users of the basic idea of collaborative filtering recommendation algorithm by computing the similarity between user preferences, to find with the similar users of other users, then use a similar user preferences for the current user preferences to predict and recommend. User-based collaborative filtering traditional algorithm using the user's score on the item, which uses the cosine, Pearson and other methods to calculate the similarity between users of different projects as different dimensions, by user score on the same dimensions to calculate its similarity. In order to make full use of the score of the mobile users on different items to calculate the similarity between the mobile users, in this paper, the EMD [4, 5] method of distance calculation in image retrieval, it is introduced into the mobile recommendation. The item features are integrated into the user's similarity calculation. To avoid sparse rating data to calculate user similarity, the researchers will be user social relations into the recommendation system [6, 7], recommended by the user's social relationships, in this paper, we will use the mobile user's mobile communication data mining to mining the trust relationship between users, and with the integration of the project characteristics of the mobile users to make a hybrid recommendation.

2 Related Research Work

Memory based collaborative filtering recommendation algorithm is mainly concerned with the similarity between users or projects. User based collaborative filtering recommendation algorithm first calculates the similarity between users according to the historical data of the user, such as user score data, browsing data, etc. Usually using the method of scoring data algorithm using cosine, Pearson and other methods to calculate the similarity between users [2, 6–8], then select the most similar according to the similarity of the user as a neighbor, and then predict with neighbors preferences. The cosine method uses vector space model to represent the user's preference, each item as a dimension of the vector, the user rating of the project indicates the user's preference for the item, user similarity using two users score on the same item to calculate. If there is no common score cannot calculate the similarity of users. Cosine method does not consider the user's own score criteria. In order to more accurately calculate the similarity between users, Pearson and the improved cosine method to consider the users own scoring criteria. The document [9] fusion of cosine, Pearson method and Jaccard coefficient, if the two user score on the 400 items, only 2 common rating items and score are 4, according to the cosine method of their similarity is 1. In fact, in the very small amount of items on the similarity cannot really reflect the similarity between users, the Jaccard coefficient to avoid high similarity between users of a small part of the common score. With the common score number as the user similarity factor, can accurately measure the similarity between users.

In order to alleviate the sparse effect on collaborative filtering algorithm, the researchers used other information outside of the rating data to mitigate the effects of sparse user similarity computing, but sometimes these are not easy to get information. Literature [10] introduced user demographic information, such as age, sex, education degree, the sparse user score of users using demographic information to calculate the similarity with other users and avoid the use of score data to calculate user similarity, in some degree alleviate score the effects of sparse data. In order to avoid the effects of sparse data on user similarity calculation, the researchers will introduce user social relations to the recommendation system [6, 7, 11–13], and makes use of the user's social relationship to recommend. Literature [7] combined with user's trust relationship and collaborative filtering recommendation, calculate the trust degree among users by using the trust relation and the transfer of trust relation, based on the strength of trust relationships to choose the nearest neighbors, the user similarity calculation in traditional collaborative filtering recommendation is avoided, and the effect of the sparse user score on the performance of the recommendation is alleviated. Literature [2] in the mobile service recommendation, based on the user's mobile communication data to analyze the trust relationship between the mobile user, a heuristic method based on social network and context awareness is proposed, mobile social network information and context information are introduced into the mobile service recommendation system. The study considered the impact of the user's social relationship on the recommendation, but did not take into account the impact of user similarity and item similarity on the recommendation. In this paper, considering the impact of project similarity and the social relationship of mobile users on mobile recommendation, this paper proposes a recommendation algorithm which combines the item feature and the trust relationship between the mobile users, EMD method is used to realize the similarity calculation of the mobile users of the fusion item, based on the mobile user's similar network and trust network to build a neighbor set and make recommendations.

3   Mobile Recommendation Algorithm Based on EMD

Definition 1: Mobile user-item score matrix $R = \{r_{u,i}\}$, R represents the score matrix of mobile user to the item, $r_{u,i}$ represents the mobile user U to item I score, scores usually an integer of 1–5.

Definition 2: Item set $I = \{i|i \in L\}$, I represents item set, wherein L is item set.

Definition 3: Mobile user set $= \{u_k|k \in M\}$, U represents mobile user set, wherein M represents ID set of the mobile user.

Definition 4: Item similarity matrix $S_I = \{s_{i,j}|i, j \in I\}$, S_I represents the similarity matrix between items, $s_{i,j}$ represents the similarity of item I and item j, 0 indicates no similarity between items, 1 represents exactly similar.

Definition 5: Item distance matrix $D_I = \{d_{i,j} = 1 - s_{i,j}|i, j \in I\}$, D_I represents item distance matrix, $d_{i,j}$ represents the distance between the item I and j, the range of values is [0, 1], larger values indicate large distances between items. 0 means that the items are completely similar, 1 means that the items are completely different.

Definition 6: Mobile user similarity matrix $S_U = \{sim(u_k, u_0)|u_k, u_0 \in U\}$, S_U represents mobile user similarity matrix, $sim(u_k, u_0)$ represents the similarity of mobile user u_k and u_0, the bigger the value indicates the higher the similarity between the mobile users.

3.1   Similarity Calculation of Mobile Users Based on EMD

User similarity calculation is the key of collaborative filtering recommendation algorithm based on user. In this paper, the EMD method combined with collaborative filtering recommendation system, change traditional collaborative filtering recommendation system to calculate the similarity of users based on the same score items.

Definition 7: MD distance of mobile user [4], assume that $D = \{d_{i,j}|i,j \in I\}$ represents the distance between the item i and j, the item score vector for the mobile user is
$V_{u_1} = \{(1, r_{u_1,1}), (2, r_{u_1,2}), \cdots, (i, r_{u_1,i})\}$, $V_{u_2} = \{(1, r_{u_2,1}), (2, r_{u_2,2}), \cdots, (i, r_{u_2,i}),$
$w_{u_1} = \sum_{i \in RI_{u_1}} r_{u_1,i}, w_{u_2} = \sum_{j \in RI_{u_2}} r_{u_2,j}$ preference flow $F = \{f_{i,j}\}$, $f_{i,j}$ represents the preference transfer between mobile user u_1 in item i and mobile user u_2 in item j, the computation needs to meet the constraints (1)–(4).

$$f_{i,j} \geq 0, i, j \in I \tag{1}$$

$$\sum_{j \in RI_{u_2}} f_{i,j} \leq w_{u_1,i}, i \in RI_{u_1} \tag{2}$$

$$\sum_{i \in RI_{u_1}} f_{i,j} \leq w_{u_2,j}, j \in RI_{u_2} \tag{3}$$

$$\sum_{i \in RI_{u_1}} \sum_{j \in RI_{u_2}} f_{i,j} = \min(w_{u_1}, w_{u_2}) \tag{4}$$

$$EMD(u_1, u_2) = \frac{1}{\sum_{i \in RI_{u_1}} \sum_{j \in RI_{u_2}} f_{i,j}} \sum_{i \in RI_{u_1}} \sum_{j \in RI_{u_2}} d_{i,j} \times f_{i,j} \tag{5}$$

Wherein, V_{u_1} and V_{u_2} represent score vector for a mobile user to item, $(i, r_{u_k,i})$ represents mobile user u_k score for item I is $r_{u_k,i}$, namely mobile user u_k preferences for item i, RI_{u_1} represents item set for score user u_1, RI_{u_2} represents item set for score user u_2, w_{u_1} and w_{u_2} represent the sum of the preference for the mobile user to item. Formula (1) indicates that the mobile user can selectively transfer preferences when calculating the EMD distance. Formula (2) indicates that mobile user u_1 can provide the total amount of preference transfer on item i can't exceed user u_1 preference for item i. Formula (3) indicates that mobile user u_2 can receive the total amount of preference transfer on item j can't exceed user u_2 preference for item j. Formula (4) indicates that mobile users u_1 and u_2 in all items the total amount of preference transfer is $\sum_{i \in RI_{u_1}} \sum_{j \in RI_{u_2}} f_{i,j}$, Its value is determined by user with a known small preference. Formula (5) indicates that the EMD distance between the mobile users, according to the calculation of the total and transfer cost. The calculation diagram of EMD method is shown in Fig. 1.

According to the difference of the total score between users, for example, the user u_1 project score vector $V_{u_1} = \{(1,2), (2,3), (3,2)\}$, the user u_2 project score vector $V_{u_1} = \{(1,2), (2,3), (3,2)\}$, using the EMD method to calculate the distance between the user U1 and U2 is 0, because the distance between the item and its own is 0, the optimal transport path will be transferred the user u_1 for 1, 2 and 3 preference to user u_2

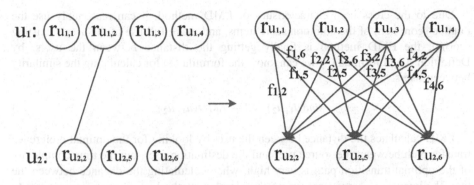

Fig. 1. EMD distance calculation illustration

corresponding 1, 2 and 3, its total transfer is 7, the transfer cost of the same item is 0, according to the formula (5), the distance between the two mobile users is 0, namely the similarity is 1, but in fact the score of the different items of mobile users is different, the similarity is not 1. In order to solve this problem, this paper constructs a virtual item in two users [5], a user with a small score, the user's score is the difference between the total score of two users. A user with a large score, the score is 0. Suppose the similarity between the virtual item and the other item is 0, namely, the distance between the system and the other item is 1. After a preprocessed two mobile users score, the number of items they score and the total score is equal, by Definition 5, the distance between the item by the similarity between the item calculating, using different similarity methods to calculate the similarity between items will affect the optimal path selection in the EMD method and the EMD distance between users. So we need to accurately measure the similarity between items, in collaborative filtering systems usually only know the user score matrix of the item, do not know the explicit characteristics of item, such as the type of film, film director, etc. Based on the user score for the item can heuristically compute similarity between items. Or using matrix decomposition mining the feature vector potential of item in a matrix scoring, we use the vector potential feature of item to calculate the similarity between items. We use matrix decomposition method to calculate the potential feature vector of item, and calculate the similarity between the items according to the feature vector potential of item using cosine method. Because the user score matrix is only part of the item of user score, when solving the potential feature vector used stochastic gradient descent method or alternating least squares method to minimize the formula (6), finally get the feature vector of user and item.

$$\min \sum\nolimits_{(u,i)\in P} \left(r_{u,i} - q_i^T p_u\right)^2 + \lambda(\|q_i\|^2 + \|p_u\|^2) \tag{6}$$

Wherein $r_{u,i}$ represents score of user u for item i, P represents the set of user and item, q_i represents the potential feature vector of item i, p_u represents the potential feature vector of the user U.

Due to the cross item characteristics of EMD method, it can reasonably use the outside score item of the common score items, and make full use of the user's existing scoring, the EMD method is finally getting the distance between the users, by Definition 4 and formula (5) we can know the formula (7) for calculating the similarity between users.

$$sim(u_1, u_2) = 1 - EMD(u_1, u_2) \tag{7}$$

EMD calculates the distance between the user by looking for the optimal preference transfer path between the source user and the destination user, but the time complexity of the optimal transition path is very high, when calculating the distance between the two N dimension score users, using the simplex method of linear programming to calculate, its time complexity is $O(N^3 logN)$ [4]. This paper is mainly to integrate the EMD method and the recommendation system, when using the simplex method to calculate the optimal transition path, the EMD method is not optimized.

3.2   The Trust Relation of Mobile Users

Because of the interaction between users of social relations, relationship with friends to choose the nearest neighbors, thereby avoiding score similarity calculation between mobile users can ease score data sparsity problem of collaborative filtering recommendation algorithm [7]. In people's daily communication behavior, the trust between the long talk time users will generally be greater than short talk time users, the trust between the high frequency of communications users will generally be greater than the trust between the low frequency communications users degree. Talk time and communication frequency can reflect the trust relationship between users [14]. Therefore, using the formula (8), according to the length of the call and communication times (including the number of calls and text messages) two aspects of the use of linear methods to calculate the degree of trust between mobile users.

$$trust(u_1, u_2) = \alpha \times \frac{time_{u_1,u_2}}{\max_{u \in C_{u_1}} time_{u_1,u}} + (1 - \alpha) \times \frac{f_{u_1,u_2}}{\max_{u \in C_{u_1}} f_{u_1,u}} \tag{8}$$

Wherein $trust(u_1, u_2)$ represents the trust of mobile users u_1 to u_2, C_{u_1} represents a mobile user set of communication behavior with mobile user u_1, $time_{u_1,u_2}$ represents the length of the call to the mobile user u_1 and u_2, $\max_{u \in C_{u_1}} time_{u_1,u}$ represents the maximum call length of a mobile user u_1 with other mobile users, α represents the weight of the call length in the calculation of trust, $1 - \alpha$ represents the weight of the number of calls in the calculation of trust. In the experiment the α value is 0.5.

3.3   Score Prediction

(a)   Score prediction based on similar items

Collaborative filtering algorithm based on the preference of similar users to predict, usually use the threshold, top-N and other strategies to select the most similar users as the nearest neighbor set, according to the nearest neighbor set use prediction formula (9) to predict the score [3].

$$r_{u,i}^n = \bar{r}_u + \frac{1}{\sum_{n \in N_u} sim(u,n)} \sum_{n \in N_u} sim(u,n) \times (r_{n,i} - \bar{r}_n) \qquad (9)$$

Wherein, N_u represents the neighbor users has been given a score for the item i in the user U nearest neighbor set, $sim(u,n)$ represents the similarity between user u and n, $\bar{r}_n$ represents average score of user n, $r_{u,i}^n$ represents prediction score of user u for item i. The traditional prediction formula, it is based on neighbor user score for the forecast item to predict. If all the neighbors do not have a score for forecast item, in this case, the traditional prediction formula will lose its effect, only according to the average score of mobile users u to predict, for example, predicting the score of the mobile user u_1 for the item i, mobile user u_1 nearest neighbors are mobile users u_2 and u_3, the mobile users u_2 and u_3 do not have a score for item i, the mobile users u_3 scored for item j, and the similarity of item i and j is 0.95, mobile users u_3 and u_1 similarity is very high, the item i and j similarity is also very high, based on the concept of similar users' score for similar items are similar, the score information of mobile user u_3 on the item j to predict the mobile user u_1 on the item i score is helpful, based on the above, this paper presents a formula (10) for scoring prediction based on similar items.

$$r_{u,i}^n = \bar{r}_u + \frac{1}{\sum_{s \in S} sim(u,s)} \sum_{s \in S} sim(u,s) \times (r_{s,i}' - \bar{r}_s) \qquad (10)$$

Formula (10) and formula (9) are basically similar, formula (9) directly ignores the nearest neighbor users without score for item i, formula (10) using the score these nearest neighbors in similar items with the item i to predict. When using the formula (10) to predict, need to identify items similar to item i. In this paper, we use the item potential feature vector obtained from the formula (7) and use the cosine method to calculate the similarity between the items. $r_{s,i}'$ in the Formula (10) can be calculated by the formula (11).

$$r_{s,i}' = \begin{cases} \frac{1}{\sum_{j \in S_{s,i}} S_{i,j}} \sum_{j \in S_{s,i}} r_{m,j} \times S_{i,j} & r_{s,i} = 0 \\ r_{s,i} & r_{s,i} \neq 0 \end{cases} \qquad (11)$$

$r_{s,i}'$ represents the score of mobile user s in the similar items with item i, when the mobile user S does not evaluate the item i, according to the similar items collection of the item I in the Mobile user S evaluation item to calculate the similar score. Wherein $S_{i,j}$ represents the similarity between item i and j, $S_{i,j}$ represents a collection of items that are similar to the item i and mobile users S on the item i has been scoring.

(b) Score prediction of fusion mobile user trust

The study of social network analysis shows that the interaction of users in social networks will become similar [15]. In the mobile communication network users, mobile users talk longer, more frequent communication, the greater the possibility of interaction between them. Due to the sparsity of the scored data, using scored data does not accurately measure the similarity between the user and the relationship of trust to some extent, also reflects the similarity between users, fusion of the preference prediction trust relationship between mobile user preference similarity with mobile users, in order to alleviate the score sparsity caused by calculating the similarity between mobile users accurately, which cannot accurately predict the user preference problem. In the heuristic fusion the similarity relation and trust relationship between users, literature [13] compared several fusion policy, according to the methods of literature [13], this paper choose the hybrid method to fuse user similarity and trust, because of the similarity and trust calculation between the mobile user using different methods, between them and the value cannot be compared directly, for example, the similarity between mobile users is 0.8, the trust between mobile users is 0.1, in the prediction score does not imply a similar affect users more influence than the user's trust. Therefore, this article will consider the impact of distinguishing two types of users of the prediction score of neighbors.

3.4   Recommended Process Description

Input: Mobile users - Project scoring matrix, mobile user communication data.
Output: Mobile users a list of items recommended.
Step 1: Calculate the item potential feature vector, using the gradient descent algorithm to obtain the formula (7) of the item potential feature vector.
Step 2: Calculate the similarity between items, based on the potential feature vectors of the project, the similarity between items is calculated using the cosine method. Obtain item similarity matrix S_I, And according to the Definition 5 calculation item distance matrix D_I.
Step 3: Calculate EMD distance between mobile users, according to the mobile user-item score matrix and item distance matrix D_I, according to the EMD method in the definition (7) using linear programming simple method to calculate the EMD distance between mobile users, get the similarity matrix S_u of mobile users.
Step 4: Calculate the trust weights between mobile users, according to the length of the user's call, the number of calls and text messages using formula (8) to calculate the weight of trust between mobile users.
Step 5: Choose the nearest neighbors for the target user, According to the nearest neighbor selection strategy of top-N, from similar users and trust users to select the appropriate user as the nearest neighbor.
Step 6: Predict target user preferences for unscored items, according to the nearest neighbor of the target user, the use of the score prediction formula (11) predicts the preference of the mobile user to the unscored item.
Step 7: Constructs recommendation list, according to the mobile user's preference for the prediction of the unscored items, select the predicted value of the top of the item as a recommendation to recommend the item to the mobile user.

Fusion item characteristics and recommendation method of mobile user trust relation, the difference between the recommended method of fusion item characteristics and mobile user trust relation and the traditional collaborative filtering recommendation method is mainly in the step 3 and step 6, using EMD method to calculate the similarity between mobile users and preference prediction method using fusion mobile user trust relation and item similarity relation.

4 Experiment and Analysis

4.1 Experimental Data Set

Currently there is no publicly available data set that includes both mobile user communication data and mobile user item score data. In order to simulate the item score of mobile users in mobile communication network. This article will use two public data sets: Mobile user communication data set of MIT [14] and film score data set of MovieLens, according to certain rules, the two data sets can be matched with the needed data sets.

Film score data set of MovieLens, it includes 6040 users on 3952 films about 1 million film score information, its score is 1 to 5, the film contains the film category, the name of the film the movie show times. This dataset sparsity score is 95.53%. MIT data set collected 94 users from September 2004 to July 2005 calls, SMS, Bluetooth interactive mobile user communication data, there are 9950 users and the 94 users have communication behavior. In this paper, according to the user's activity in the data set of MIT and MovieLens to match. In the MIT, user activity is the number of users to call and send text messages. In the MovieLens, user activity is the number of user score, because the number of users in the MovieLens is less than the number in the MIT, so select an equal number of users with the data set MovieLens from the data set MIT, and the two dataset by user activity from high to low matching. In order to verify the accuracy of the recommendation algorithm, the simulation data are divided into training set and test set, training set for learning or training related parameters in the recommended method, the test set is used to verify the accuracy of the recommendation. To ensure that mobile users in the training set and test set has a score data, by a certain percentage each mobile user ratings data were randomly divided into a training set and a test set. In the experiment, according to the proportion of 80:20, the score data of mobile users were randomly divided into training set and test set.

4.2 Evaluation

In order to verify the performance of the recommend system, using the MAE and P@N evaluation indicators. MAE is based on the user's prediction and the actual score to measure the accuracy of the prediction, Calculation formula (12) is as follows:

$$MAE = \frac{1}{|T|} \sum_{(u,j) \in T} \left| r_{uj} - r'_{uj} \right| \tag{12}$$

T represents the test set, $|T|$ represents the score number of users in the test set, r_{uj} represents the user U score on the item j, r'_{uj} represents the user U of Prediction based on the recommendation algorithm score on the item j.

4.3   Experimental Results and Analysis

The experiment is mainly to compare the accuracy of scoring prediction of the cosine, the Pearson method and the EMD method in collaborative filtering recommendation, using the formula (9) as the prediction formula. Experimental results are shown in Figs. 2 and 3.

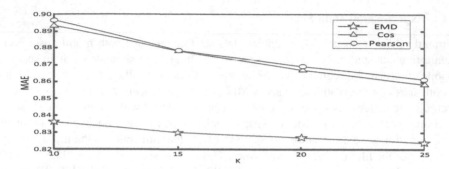

Fig. 2. MAE compare similarity calculation method

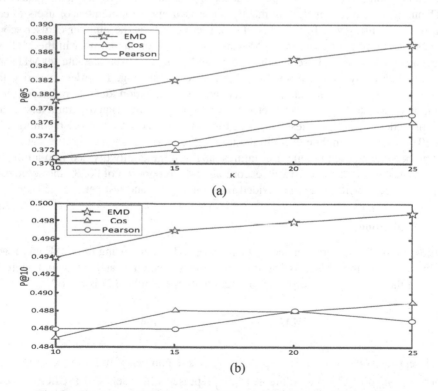

Fig. 3. The value (a) P@5 and (b) P@10 of similarity calculation method

Because each mobile user score prediction accuracy is not the same, so the experiment results are the mean scores for all mobile users. By Fig. 2, in the different number of nearest neighbor set, the EMD method is the best method of prediction accuracy in several ways. Compared with cosine and Pearson methods, when K = 10, the improvement in the accuracy rates were 5.4% and 5.7%.

Figure 3 shows, in a different number of nearest neighbors in the collection, accuracy of EMD is the highest at P@5 and P@10, compared with cosine and Pearson method, the accuracy increased by 1.2% and 1.1%. From the above analysis, EMD method can be more better recommendation results.

5 Conclusion

In this paper, we propose to calculate the similarity between mobile users by using the cross item EMD method. This method changes the user's score on the same item to calculate the user's similarity. EMD method can improve the accuracy of the prediction accuracy compared with the cosine, Pearson and other similarity calculation methods. The score in the prediction stage to make full use of existing score of mobile user and item similarity fusion to score prediction formula, the nearest neighbor to the similar project's score to predict, can effectively improve the prediction accuracy. At the same time, the method of fusing the mobile user's similarity and the communication and trust relationship of the mobile users is proposed, and the validity of the method is verified on the public data set.

Acknowledgment. The work of this paper were supported in part by East China Jiaotong university research fund under Grant No. 14RJ02 and Jiangxi provincial department of science and technology research found under Grant No. 20122BAB201040.

References

1. Wang, L.C., Meng, X.W., Zhang, Y.J.: A heuristic approach to social network-based and context-aware mobile services recommendation. J. Converg. Inf. Technol. 6(10), 339–346 (2011)
2. Meng, X.W., Hu, X., et al.: Mobile recommender systems and their applications. J. Softw. 24(1), 91–108 (2013)
3. Adomavicius, G., Tuzhilin, A.: Towards the next generation of recommender systems: a survey of the state-of-the-art and possible extensions. IEEE Trans. Knowl. Data Eng. 17(6), 734–749 (2005)
4. Rubner, Y., Tomasi, C., Guibas, L.J.: The earth mover's distance as a metric for image retrieval. Int. J. Comput. Vis. 40(2), 99–121 (2000). https://doi.org/10.1023/A: 1026543900054
5. Pele, O., Werman, M.: Fast and robust earth mover's distances. In: Proceedings of International Conference on Computer Vision, pp. 460–467 (2009)
6. Massa, P., Avesani, P.: Trust-aware collaborative filtering for recommender systems. In: Meersman, R., Tari, Z. (eds.) OTM 2004. LNCS, vol. 3290, pp. 492–508. Springer, Heidelberg (2004). https://doi.org/10.1007/978-3-540-30468-5_31

7. Massa, P., Avesani, P.: Trust-aware recommender systems. In: Proceedings of the ACM Recommender Systems Conference, pp. 17–24 (2007)
8. Deshpande, M., Karypis, G.: Item-based top-N recommendation algorithms. ACM Trans. Inf. Syst. **22**(1), 143–177 (2004)
9. Candillier, L., Meyer, F., Fessant, F.: Designing specific weighted similarity measures to improve collaborative filtering systems. In: Perner, P. (ed.) ICDM 2008. LNCS (LNAI), vol. 5077, pp. 242–255. Springer, Heidelberg (2008). https://doi.org/10.1007/978-3-540-70720-2_19
10. Pazzani, M.: A framework for collaborative, content-based, and demographic filtering. Artif. Intell. Rev. **3**, 393–408 (1999). https://doi.org/10.1023/A:1006544522159
11. Jatnali, M., Ester, M.: A matrix factorization technique with trust propagation for recommendation in social networks. In: Proceedings of the 4th ACM Conference on Recommender Systems, pp. 135–142 (2010)
12. Ma, H., King, I., Lyu, M.R.: Learning to recommend with social trust ensemble. In: Proceedings of 32nd Annual International ACM SIGIR Conference on Research and Development in Information Retrieval, pp. 203–210 (2009)
13. Liu, F., Lee, H.J.: Use of social network information to enhance collaborative filtering performance. Expert Syst. Appl. **37**(7), 4772–4778 (2010)
14. Eagle, N., Pentland, A., Lazer, D.: Inferring friendship network structure by using mobile phone data. Proc. Natl. Acad. Sci. **106**(36), 15274–15278 (2009)
15. Marsden, P.V., Friedkin, N.E.: Network studies of social influence. Sociol. Methods Res. **22**(1), 127–151 (1993)

Research on Collaborative Filtering Recommendation Method Based on Context and User Credibility

Hongli Chen[✉] and Shanguo Lv

Software School, East China Jiaotong University, Nanchang, China
44672154@qq.com

Abstract. In the traditional collaborative filtering recommendation, similarity measurement methods only consider the user rating and the credibility of user rating is not taken into account, user's contexts are considered inadequate in the mobile environment, and the scalability problem exists in the recommendation system. A parallel collaborative filtering model based on user context and credibility is proposed. This method firstly evaluates user rating credit degree. Secondly, the method builds the context vector of the user, calculates the context similarity between the target user and other users, and searches for similar nearest neighbors for the target user based on trust and context, and finally implements the parallel recommendation on the cloud computing Mapreduce. Experimental results show that this method achieved lower error values of MAE than the traditional recommendation method and higher recommendation accuracy, and effectively improved the performance of the recommendation system. This method could be applied in the contextual recommendation oriented the big data.

Keywords: Recommendation system · Collaborative filtering · User's credibility

1 Introduction

Collaborative filtering is one of the most successful recommendation techniques at present. It has been widely used in various types of electronic commerce recommendation systems, mobile applications, electronic travel, Internet advertising and so on [1]. Such as: Amazon, eBay, NetFlix and Dangdang. Collaborative filtering recommendation based on such an assumption: If the user scores on a number of projects are relatively similar, then they will be more similar to other items of the score. The basic idea of the algorithm is that the items not scored for the target user are approximated by the scores of the nearest neighbors to the items. In order to find out the nearest neighbor of the target user, the similarity between users needs to be measured. However, with the expansion of e-commerce system size, the number of users and projects has increased dramatically, user ratings become sparse, which reduce the recommendation quality of the algorithm. In order to solve this problem, some scholars have improved the traditional collaborative filtering method, which effectively improves the sparsity of user rating data by means of the project score prediction, the combination of the display and

© Springer Nature Switzerland AG 2019
J. Vaidya et al. (Eds.): CSS 2019, LNCS 11982, pp. 489–500, 2019.
https://doi.org/10.1007/978-3-030-37337-5_40

the implicit score and data dimension reduction. The similarity measure used in these studies assume that all users can be trusted, all ratings are real and reliable, but in fact the user's credibility is different, scoring matrix containing a certain amount of noise data, thereby greatly reducing the accuracy of the forecasts. In addition, just considering the evaluation information of the user and the project is not enough in mobile environment. It needs to take full account of the context information about a mobile user, such as time, the location, the season, the weather, the user's social role and historical preferences. With the exponential growth of the user behavior data in the mobile environment, simply introducing context information to the recommendation system for large data personalized recommendation, the effect is not good.

In view of the above problems, this paper proposes a collaborative filtering recommendation model based on context and user credibility. In order to ensure the reliability of the score in the forecast, the trust is introduced to measure the user's credibility in this model. At the same time, in order to make up for the deficiency of the traditional similarity measure methods which lead to the low accuracy of the score prediction, user's context interest is introduced to construct the user-item context model and the recommendation is based on the context similarity. It can further improve the quality of collaborative filtering recommendation. Then the MapReduce method is adopted to realize the collaborative filtering algorithm, which can enhance the scalability of the recommendation system. Experimental results show that the proposed method is of high recommendation accuracy and small mean absolute error. With the increase of the input data, the performance of the parallel recommendation algorithm is better.

2   Analysis of the Traditional Collaborative Filtering

2.1   The Description of Traditional Collaborative Filtering

Traditional collaborative filtering system analyzed the relationship between user and item by user-item rating data. Then use this relationship for the user to generate personalized recommendation. Assume that R is the user-item rating data set, $U = \{U_1, U_2, \ldots, U_s\}$ is user set, s is the number of users, and $I = \{I_1, I_2, \ldots, I_t\}$ is item set, t is the number of items. User-item rating matrix is represented as $R_{s \times t}$. The formal expression is shown in the formula (1).

$$R_{s \times t} = \begin{pmatrix} r_{U_1 I_1} & r_{U_1 I_2} & \cdots & r_{U_1 I_t} \\ r_{U_2 I_1} & r_{U_2 I_2} & \cdots & r_{U_2 I_t} \\ \cdots & \cdots & \cdots & \cdots \\ r_{U_s I_1} & r_{U_s I_2} & \cdots & r_{U_s I_t} \end{pmatrix}_{s \times t} \tag{1}$$

Wherein user u_i to item I_j rating is expressed as r_{u_i, I_j}, user u_i average rating and user u_j average rating are expressed as $\overline{r_{u_i}}$ and $\overline{r_{u_j}}$.

Collaborative filtering systems have adopted a variety of methods to calculate the similarity between users. The most commonly used measure of similarity is the Pearson correlation similarity and cosine-based similarity. The similarity between user u_i and user u_j is denoted as $sim(u_i, u_j)$, the items user u_i and u_j common rating constitute set I_{u_i, u_j}. The calculation method of the Pearson correlation similarity is shown in formula (2), and cosine-based similarity is shown in formula (3).

$$sim(u_i, u_j) = \frac{\sum_{I_k \in I_{u_i, u_j}} \left(r_{u_i, I_k} - \overline{r_{u_i}} \right) \left(r_{u_j, I_k} - \overline{r_{u_j}} \right)}{\sqrt{\sum_{I_k \in I_{u_i, u_j}} \left(r_{u_i, I_k} - \overline{r_{u_i}} \right)^2} \sqrt{\sum_{I_k \in I_{u_i, u_j}} \left(r_{u_j, I_k} - \overline{r_{u_j}} \right)^2}} \tag{2}$$

$$sim(u_i, u_j) = \frac{\sum_{I_k \in I_{u_i, u_j}} r_{u_i, I_k} \cdot r_{u_j, I_k}}{\sqrt{\sum_{I_k \in I_{u_i, u_j}} \left(r_{u_i, I_k} \right)^2} \sqrt{\sum_{I_k \in I_{u_i, u_j}} \left(r_{u_j, I_k} \right)^2}} \tag{3}$$

Collaborative filtering does not need to obtain the features of products or users, only depends on rating data and similarity measure method to predict the rating, and the more data, the higher the accuracy of the prediction accuracy.

2.2 Traditional Collaborative Filtering Problem Analysis

Traditional collaborative filtering based on user-item rating matrix to find the target user's nearest neighbor set can recommend user's interested items regardless of the representation form of the item. At the same time, there are some disadvantages in traditional collaborative filtering. (1) Just focus on analysis of user interest feature often lead to unreasonable recommendation due to sparse data, but in real life, not only the interest factors are considered, trust factors also affect the decision-making of the target users to a certain extent. (2) Only considering the user and item information to recommend is often not the most accurate, should also be further combined with the user's location information, season information, time information and social information comprehensive mining the potential interests of users. (3) Scalability is poor. With the increase of users and items, the system performance will be more and more low.

Considering the influence of trust on the recommendation results, trust is introduced into the recommendation system in the literature [2], trust aware recommender system framework was put forward, used the user's trust value to make the score prediction. The network trust model of P2P is proposed to solve the problem of trust between nodes in the network recommendation process in the literature [3] and [4]. Literature [5] combined with the recommendation based on trust and collaborative filtering recommendation based on the project, predicted the user's score on the target project by random walk.

To solve the above problems, proposed by foreign scholars Mallat knowledge to manage user-defined contextual information in the study, and based on the user's personalization scenarios in which to provide personalized service [6]. Adomavicius takes the user's buying time as a user's context variable, and then combining the traditional collaborative filtering method, to build an integrated multi-dimensional model recommended user context [7]. In order to make up for the deficiency of traditional collaborative filtering method, Zhang and Li [8] considered the impact of project classification on user rating in the prediction of scoring, and based on the recommendation model.

In addition, literature [9] combination of neural networks and collaborative filtering recommendation model. According to the user's information to measure the similarity between each item score to construct the similarity matrix score collaborate recommended in order to improve the quality of the system recommended. Zhou, Tao for mobile service scenario recommended, LBS AR + multilevel association rules "multi-level three-dimensional recommendation model is proposed, by introducing context aware computing to improve the precision and quality of recommender systems [10]. Yuan research also shows that mobile commerce scene information application in personalized recommendation system is the trend of the future research, and this is based on established learning resources based on user context recommendation model through user context information for learning resources sort [11].

In summary, the recommended model is based on user interest scenario has caused widespread concern of scholars, some scholars user profile introduction of mobile commerce recommendation system were discussed, but the current study is based on multi-user static information or item category score clustering to divide the users, by the lack of mobile commerce user's location, time, integrated mining business needs, based on different resource objects and scenes insight into mobile business users to potential interest and immediate interest in the research. In addition, user behavior data in a mobile environment exponential surge significantly increase the discovery of useful knowledge from massive data related to the difficulty of interest.

3   Collaborative Filtering Recommendation Model Based on Context and User Credibility

In view of the above problems, this paper proposes a collaborative filtering recommendation model based on context and user credibility. Based on the traditional collaborative filtering recommendation model, trust degree is introduced to measure the user's credibility in order to ensure reliability prediction rating. At the same time, context information is introduced to construct user-item context model and the recommendation is based on the context similarity. It can further improve the quality of collaborative filtering recommendation. Then the MapReduce method is adopted to realize the collaborative filtering algorithm, which can enhance the scalability of the recommendation system. Collaborative filtering recommendation process based on context and user context in cloud environment is shown in Fig. 1.

3.1   User Context Description

As mentioned above, only to consider the user and item information to recommend is often not the most accurate, but also should be further integrated the user's context to mine the user's potential interest. When the user scores on an item, we will be the location, time and social context as the scoring context. Firstly, the user's context is described. There are n kinds of context information in the recommendation system. This paper takes the form of vector to describe the rating context model: $IRContext = (Item, Context_1, Context_2, \cdots, Context_n)$.

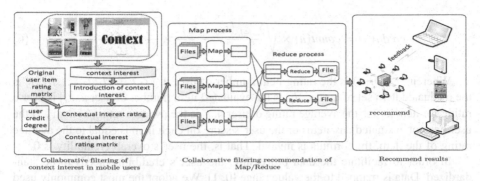

Fig. 1. Collaborative filtering recommendation process based on context and user credibility in cloud environment

Wherein, *Item* represents a specific score project, the component of a vector $Context_k(k = 1, 2, \cdots, n)$ represents a particular type of situation. The target user context information is represented by *IContext*. *IRContext* represents the user rating context that the user has experienced the item and made the rating. The similarity in the specific type i context between *IContext* and *IRContext* is $sim_i(IContext, IRContext)$. The similarity formula between *IContext* and *IRContext* is shown as formula (4).

$$sim(IContext, IRContext) = \frac{1}{n}\sum_{i=1}^{n} sim_i(IContext, IRContext) \tag{4}$$

When calculating the similarity between the target user and other users, the user rating context must be given full consideration. When the context similarity $sim(IContext, IRContext)$ between the target user and the scored user is larger, the scored user can get a higher recommendation value. The recommended weight is made as $k = sim(IContext, IRContext)$. The similarity measure formula (2) is modified and the formula (5) can be got.

$$sim'(u_i, u_j) = c \times sim(u_i, u_j) + (1 - c) \times k \times sim(u_i, u_j) \tag{5}$$

Wherein, the range of the adjustable coefficient C is subordinate to [0.8, 1], when c = 1, the recommendation algorithm here no longer consider the impact of user context factors.

3.2 User Credibility

Trust is introduced to measure the credibility of users. User credibility refers to the degree of credit in the evaluation of the overall resources. User credit degree is generally obtained by the user evaluation of the item collection. The credibility of user u is marked as $credit(u)$. The formula is shown as (6).

$$credit(u) = count(u) \times \sqrt{\frac{\sum_{j \in I_u} (r_{u,j} - \overline{r_u})^2}{|I_u|}} \times \frac{1}{\sum_{j \in I_u} (r_{u,j} - \overline{r_j})} \quad (6)$$

Wherein, $count(u)$ is the rating item number of user u, $j \in I = \{I_1, I_2, \ldots, I_t\}$, I_u is the evaluated item set of user u, $|I_u|$ is the evaluated item number of user u, $r_{u,j}$ is user u rating for item j, $\overline{r_u}$ is the average rating of user u, $\overline{r_j}$ is the average rating of item j. If the user has not evaluated any items or the user's score on each item is equal to the average rating of the item, the formula is invalid. That is, the user's overall credibility is 0.

In order to facilitate the data processing, the user's credibility needs to be standardized. Data is mapped to the value range [0, 1]. We adopt the most commonly used method min-max to deal with credit degree, the rule is as follows.

$$X' = \frac{X - Min(X)}{Max(X) - Min(X)} \quad (7)$$

The global credibility is standardized, the formula is shown as formula (8).

$$credit(u)' = \frac{credit(u) - Min(credit(u))}{Max(credit(u)) - Min(credit(u))} \quad (8)$$

When predicting the target user's score on the non-scoring items, use the modified formula $sim'(u_i, u_j)$ to select top N users with the largest similarity value as the similar user collection U', and user credibility is fully considered, weight similarity between the target user and similar users. According to the formula (9) to calculate the predictive value P_{u_i, I_j} of the target user u_i to item I_j.

$$P_{u_i, I_j} = \overline{r_{u_i}} + \frac{\sum_{u_j \in U'} \left(rs_{u_j, I_j} - \overline{r_{u_j}} \right) \times sim'(u_i, u_j) \times credit'(u_j)}{\sum_{u_j \in U'} sim'(u_i, u_j) \times credit'(u_j)} \quad (9)$$

3.3   Recommendation Algorithm

The collaborative filtering algorithm in this paper introduces the rating matrix combined item rating context and the user credit degree to predict the target user's score on the non-scoring items, ranks non-scoring items according to the prediction score, selects the top ranked N items to the target user as a recommended set. Algorithm process is described as follows.

Input: user-item rating matrix R, context vector $IRContext$, user set U, item set I;
Output: the prediction value P_{u_i, I_j} of user u_i to item I_j.
Step 1: according to the formula (6) to calculate $credit(u_j)$ of each user u_j, and use the formula (8) for the standardization.

Step 2: according to the formula (5) to calculate the similarity between the user u_i and each user of user set U.

Step 3: according to the formula (9) to calculate the predictive value of user u_i to the item I_j.

4 Collaborative Filtering Recommendation Method Based on MapReduce

MapReduce is a kind of parallel distributed computing model developed by Google, it has been widely used in the field of search and processing of massive data. Map is a decomposed process which assigned each data segment to a computer for processing. Reduce integrates separate data together and finally outputs the results. There are two core steps in the collaborative filtering recommendation process. One is the similarity calculation based on user-item score matrix, the other is score prediction of the non-scoring items based on similarity.

The above two steps are the two sequential steps, that can be regarded as two serial steps. Especially when calculating the similarity based on the user-item score matrix, the similarity calculation of any two score items is not coupled parallel process, this is compatible with the idea of distributed parallel processing in cloud computing environment, it can be implemented using MapReduce. The predictive scoring process of no-scored items can also be implemented in parallel with MapReduce. Therefore, we first calculate the similarity of user-item score matrix based on MapReduce workflow, and then predict the no-scored item scores.

According to the definition MapReduce programming model, a MapReduce process is actually the process of using the Input key pair to get the output key pair. In the process of calculating the similarity of the user-item score matrix, the input key pair is <null, (User, Item, Score)>, the output key pair is <(Item1, Item2), Sim>.

User-item score matrix calculation of similarity is mainly used 2 MapReduce processes to complete, the first MapReduce process is mainly used to collect user score for items, and sorted by user name; at this stage, Map function converts the input data to the corresponding key-value pair, and then use the Reduce function to merge items of the same user, the specific process is shown in Tables 1 and 2.

Table 1. The Map phase of the first MapReduce.

Map input	Map output
<null, (User 1, Item 1, Score)>	<User 1, (Item 1, Score)>
<null, (User 1, Item 2, Score)>	<User 1, (Item 2, Score)>
<null, (User 1, Item 3, Score)>	<User 1, (Item 3, Score)>
<null, (User 2, Item 1, Score)>	<User 2, (Item 1, Score)>
<null, (User 2, Item 2, Score)>	<User 2, (Item 2, Score)>
<null, (User 3, Item 2, Score)>	<User 3, (Item 2, Score)>
<null, (User 3, Item 3, Score)>	<User 3, (Item 3, Score)>

Table 2. The reduce phase of the first MapReduce.

Reduce input	Reduce output
\<User 1, (Item 1, Score)\> \<User 1, (Item 2, Score)\> \<User 1, (Item 3, Score)\>	\<User 1, ((Item 1, Score), (Item 2, Score), (Item 3, Score))\>
\<User 2, (Item 1, Score)\> \<User 2, (Item 2, Score)\>	\<User 2, ((Item 1, Score), (Item 2, Score))\>
\<User 3, (Item 2, Score)\> \<User 3, (Item 3, Score)\>	\<User 3, ((Item 2, Score), (Item 3, Score))\>

The second MapReduce process is to calculate the similarity between items, and convert key-value pairs of user-items into key-value pairs of item-item, Map function was used to obtain the same User of the same Item score comparison, while calculating the similarity between the items with the Reduce function.

The specific calculation process is shown in Tables 3 and 4.

Table 3. The map phase of the second MapReduce.

Map input	Map output
\<User 1, ((Item 1, Score), (Item 2, Score), (Item 3, Score))\>	\<(Item 1, Item 2), (Score, Score)\> \<(Item 2, Item 3), (Score, Score)\> \<(Item 1, Item 3), (Score, Score)\>
\<User 2, ((Item 1, Score), (Item 2, Score))\>	\<(Item 1, Item 2), (Score, Score)\>
\<User 3, ((Item 2, Score), (Item 3, Score))\>	\<(Item 2, Item 3), (Score, Score)\>

Table 4. The reduce phase of the second MapReduce.

Reduce input	Reduce output
\<(Item 1, Item 2), (Score, Score)\> \<(Item 1, Item 2), (Score, Score)\>	\<(Item 1, Item 2), Sim\>
\<(Item 1, Item 3), (Score, Score)\> \<(Item 2, Item 3), (Score, Score)\>	\<(Item 1, Item 3), Sim\>
\<(Item 2, Item 3), (Score, Score)\>	\<(Item 2, Item 3), Sim\>

After obtaining the similarity calculation results through two MapReduce processing, collect and collate the similarity list of each Item, as shown in Tables 5 and 6. According to the user's recommendation score similar list, use the Map function to predict, and finally use the Reduce output recommended results, as shown in Tables 7 and 8.

Table 5. The Map phase of the third MapReduce.

Map input	Map output
<(Item 1, Item 2), Sim>	<Item 1, (Item 2, Sim)> <Item 2, (Item 1, Sim)>
<(Item 1, Item 3), Sim>	<Item 1, (Item 3, Sim)> <Item 3, (Item 1, Sim)>
<(Item 2, Item 3), Sim>	<Item 2, (Item 3, Sim)> <Item 3, (Item 2, Sim)>

Table 6. The reduce phase of the third MapReduce.

Reduce input	Reduce output
<(Item 1, Item 2), Sim> <(Item 1, Item 3), Sim>	<Item 1, ((Item 2, Sim), (Item 3, Sim))>
<(Item 2, Item 1), Sim> <(Item 2, Item 3), Sim>	<Item 2, ((Item 1, Sim), (Item 3, Sim))>
<(Item 3, Item 1), Sim> <(Item 3, Item 2), Sim>	<Item 3, ((Item 1, Sim), (Item 2, Sim))>

Table 7. The Map phase of the fourth MapReduce.

Map input	Map output
<Item 1, ((Item 2, Sim), (Item 3, Sim))>	<null, (Item 1, PreScore)>
<Item 2, ((Item 1, Sim), (Item 3, Sim))>	<null, (Item 2, PreScore)>
<Item 3, ((Item 1, Sim), (Item 2, Sim))>	<null, (Item 3, PreScore)>

Table 8. The reduce phase of the fourth MapReduce.

Reduce input	Reduce output
<null, (Item 1, PreScore)> <null, (Item 2, PreScore)> <null, (Item 3, PreScore)>	<null, Recommended item sorting list>

From the above analysis, we can conclude that the collaborative filtering recommendation process based on MapReduce is shown in Fig. 2.

5 Experiment and Analysis

The validity of the model and method for verifying this recommendation, this section builds a distributed cloud computing environment, realize the parallel recommendation of the model and algorithm in distributed environment.

In the process of simulating the cloud computing environment, 9 servers use to build Hadoop environment, one of which as a NameNode, and the rest as DataNode, the specific construction process includes the following steps: Hadoop cloud environment system software installed in the VMware virtual machine system, Virtual machine Linux system using RedHat 5.5-x64, the version of jdx is jdx1.60, the version of Hadoop is Hadoop-0.21.0-0.21.0. 9 server hardware configuration of Hadoop cloud computing environment as follows: a Dell server, memory is 8G, hard disk capacity is 2T, the frequency of CPU is 2.8 GHz. The other 8 servers use personal computer instead, memory is 4G, hard disk capacity is 480G, the frequency of CPU is 2.6 GHz. NameNode of Hadoop cloud environment is the Lenovo server, named Hadoop; The remaining 8 servers as DataNode of Hadoop, named hadoop1, hadoop2, ..., hadoop8. After set up the basic Hadoop architecture, and then configure and install Hadoop, enabling users to access password-free between Hadoop nodes, access password-free between NameNode and DataNode nodes, and test configuration is successfully run.

In the testing process, the time period of the target user is used to pre filter the traditional context pre filtering method. Firstly, the number of the nearest neighbors is given different values, and then the influence of the number of the nearest neighbors on the MAE value of the two methods mentioned above is observed. In the test, the method is used to increase the number of neighbors nearest. Ten test ranges were selected, which were 5, 10, 15, 20, 25, 30, 35, 40, 45, 50, finally, the test results of different MAE values were summarized and compared, the specific results are shown in Fig. 3.

From Fig. 2, in a number of different nearest neighbors, compared with the traditional context filtering approach, the proposed algorithm has low MAE value, the improved algorithm proposed in this paper can obtain higher quality of recommendation.

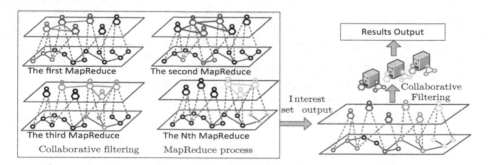

Fig. 2. The collaborative filtering recommender process based on MapReduce.

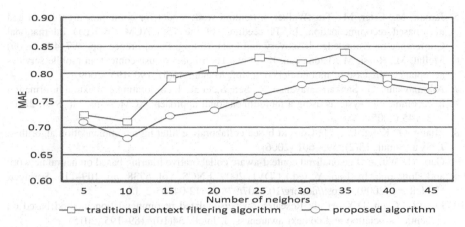

Fig. 3. Comparison of MAE between traditional context filtering and proposed algorithm

6 Conclusion

In view of the problems existing in the mobile commerce recommendation, this paper introduces the collaborative filtering recommendation process by introducing the context information of mobile commerce users, and proposes a collaborative filtering recommendation model based on the interest of mobile commerce users. The model first calculates the context similarity of the mobile commerce user, and constructs a set of similar context of target user current context, and establishes scoring matrix of item score context, finally, a collaborative filtering recommendation method based on MapReduce is proposed. Through the experiments on simulated data sets and public data sets show that compared with traditional recommendation algorithms. This algorithm obtains higher P(u)@N accuracy and lower MAE error value, so it can be used to forecast the situation of mobile commerce users in cloud environment.

Acknowledgment. The work of this paper were supported in part by East China Jiaotong university research fund under Grant No. 14RJ02 and Jiangxi provincial department of science and technology research found under Grant No. 20122BAB201040.

References

1. Zou, B.Y., Li, C.P., Tan, L.W., Chen, H., Wang, S.Q.: Social recommendations based on user trust and tensor factorization. Ruan Jian Xue Bao/J. Softw. **25**(12), 2852–2864 (2014)
2. Massa, P., Avesani, P.: Trust-aware collaborative filtering for recommender systems. In: Proceedings of the OTM Confederated International Conferences: CoopIS, DOA, and ODBASE, Agia Napa, Cyprus, pp. 492–508 (2004)
3. Wei, F., Li, J., Hu, J.: New trust model based on preference recommendation in P2P network. Appl. Res. Comput. **27**(6), 2271–2272, 2279 (2010)
4. Yu, Z., Shen, G., Liu, B., et al.: A trust model in P2P networks. Acta Electron. Sin. **38**(11), 2600–2605 (2010)

5. Jamali, M., Ester, M.: TrustWalker: a random walk model for combining trust-based and item-based recommendation. In: Proceedings of the 15th ACM SIGKDD International Conference on Knowledge Discovery and Data Mining, Paris, France, pp. 397–406 (2009)
6. Mallat, M., Rossi, M., Tuunainen, K., et al.: The impact of use context on mobile services acceptance: the case of mobile ticketing. Inf. Manag. 46(3), 190–195 (2009)
7. Adomavicius, G., Sankaranarayanan, R., Sen, S., et al.: Incorporating contextual information in recommender systems using a multidimensional approach. ACM Trans. Inf. Syst. 23(1), 103–145 (2005)
8. Zhang, G., Kang, J., et al.: Context based collaborative filtering recommendation algorithm. J. Syst. Simul. 18(2), 595–601 (2006)
9. Gao, M., Wu, Z.: Personalized context-aware collaborative filtering based on neural network and slope one. In: Luo, Y. (ed.) CDVE 2009. LNCS, vol. 5738, pp. 109–116. Springer, Heidelberg (2009). https://doi.org/10.1007/978-3-642-04265-2_15
10. Li, F.L., Chen, D.X., et al.: Research on personalized recommendation method based on semantic association and context awareness. J. Intell. 34(10), 189–195 (2015)
11. Jing, Y., Jiao, Y.: Personalized recommendation of learning resources based on contextual information. Inf. Stud. Theory Appl. 7, 116–119 (2009)
12. Wang, L., Meng, X., Zhang, Y.: Context-aware recommender systems. J. Softw. 23(1), 1–20 (2012)
13. Wang, L.C., Meng, X.W., Zhang, Y.J., et al.: New approaches to mood-based hybrid collaborative filtering. In: Proceeding of the Workshop on Context-Aware Movie Recommendation at the 4th ACM Conference on Recommender System, Barcelona, Spain, pp. 28–33 (2010)

Multi-watermarking Algorithm for Medical Image Based on NSCT-RDWT-DCT

Jingjun Zhou, Jingbing Li$^{(\boxtimes)}$, Hui Li, Jing Liu, Jialing Liu,
Qianning Dai, and Saqib Ali Nawaz

College of Information and Communication Engineering, Hainan University,
Haikou 570228, China
juingzhou@163.com, jialing_hainu@163.com,
dqn0526@163.com, jingbingli2008@hotmail.com,
jingliuhnu2016@hotmail.com, lihui@hainanu.edu.cn,
saqibsial20@gmail.com

Abstract. With the rapid development of medical imaging technology, digital information systems have become more and more important. However, medical images are vulnerable to be attacked or malicious tampered during transmission. Medical image watermarking algorithm using wavelet transform can solve the above problems and has been widely used in recent years. But due to its poor resistance to geometric attacks, the security of medical images cannot be guaranteed. In this work, a medical image multi-watermarking algorithm based on NSCT-RDWT-DCT is proposed. First, a more robust feature vector of medical image is extracted by combining non-subsampled contour transform (NSCT), redundant discrete wavelet transform (RDWT) and discrete cosine transform (DCT) to resist geometric attacks. Then, zero watermarking technology is adopted to embed and extract watermarks considering the capacity and invisibility of the medical image. Moreover, Arnold Cat Map is applied to enhance the security of the watermarks information. The experimental results show that the proposed algorithm can effectively extract the watermarked information. Compared with the existing algorithms, it has good performance against both conventional attacks and geometric attacks.

Keywords: Non subsampled contourlet transform · RDWT · Multi-watermarking · DCT · Arnold Cat Map

1 Introduction

Digitization plays an important role in our life today and has wide range of applications in the fields of medicine, science, engineering, entertainment, and communications. Especially in recent years, with the emergence of Internet technology, the popularization of mobile Internet and smartphones, in the context of the era of big data, there are various of data transmissions on the Internet every moment, such as images, text, audio, video, etc. Data security issues are becoming more and more serious, and their facing threats involve in theft, tampering and so on [1]. In the biomedical field, a large number of digital medical products are produced every day, including ultrasound, X-ray photographs, CT and MRI [2]. These medical images stored a large amount of

© Springer Nature Switzerland AG 2019
J. Vaidya et al. (Eds.): CSS 2019, LNCS 11982, pp. 501–515, 2019.
https://doi.org/10.1007/978-3-030-37337-5_41

patient ethical information, and are vulnerable to theft and tampering during their storage and transmission when they are attempted for inter-device access or cloud access through image archiving and communication systems such as PACS [3]. Therefore, the protection of these data is particularly important and urgent. There are many techniques to protect medical images, such as digital watermarking, image steganography, cryptography, etc. Digital watermarking technology is one of the most popular and widely used methods, which can be used for copyright, protection, content authentication, legal ownership, and communication security, etc. [4].

For digital watermarking, its robustness, imperceptibility, and watermark capacity are the most important features [5]. As for these three features are mutually exclusive, many digital watermarking algorithms are designed to balance them. [6]. Different from traditional digital images, in the biomedical field, medical imaging data for patients has extremely stringent quality specifications that do not allow storage or transmission to cause any visual quality changes [8]. The watermarking algorithm of medical images prohibits any modification of the original images and requires higher robustness against various attacks. Furthermore, the extraction and embedding of watermarks should be fast to satisfied telemedicine requirements [7]. Consequently, how to design a robust digital watermarking algorithm for medical images that can meet the above requirements becomes particularly important. In recent years, many scientists focus on spatial domain and transform domain in digital watermarking [9, 10]. The technique of spatial domain imbedding digital watermark directly by changing the pixel value of grayscale host image does not meet the special requirements of medical image [11, 12]. While the watermark algorithm based on the transform domain uses the asymmetry of the watermark information in the transform domain to embed the watermark information into the transformed host image, which has strong imperceptibility and robustness [13]. At present, digital watermarking has been proposed to be embedded in different medical images, such as X-ray, MRI, CT and so on. Such as the blind watermarking algorithm based on DWT and SVD proposed by Falgun et al. [14] embedded digital watermarking into the low-frequency sub-band of ROI (region of interest) of medical image for wavelet decomposition, and then made the singular value obtained by SVD to ensure the security of medical image. In this paper, many attacks are tested, but the watermark can only be embedded in ROI of the medical images, which resulted in high algorithm complexity. Al-Haj [15] proposed a blind digital watermarking algorithm combining DWT, DCT and PN sequence. The host image was decomposed twice by wavelet transform to select the second-order low-frequency sub-band carefully. Then the selected low-frequency sub-band was used by DCT. Finally, two PN sequences were embedded into its low-frequency sub-band to complete the watermarking embedding. Zhao et al. [16] proposed a blind watermarking algorithm for color images based on DWT and DCT. It has good robustness to conventional attacks, especially compression attacks. Also, the scheme used Logistic chaos to encrypt watermarks which improves the security. Dey et al. [17] proposed a blind watermarking algorithm based on Canny edge detection between ROI and RONI to get the edge of the medical image. After obtaining the edge of medical image, the watermarking can be embedded into the host image, and the embedded medical image can be obtained. Whereas the algorithms proposed in [15–17] are based on blind watermarking algorithms, the watermark embedding capacity is limited and the visual system quality is poor. But the medical images have extremely high requirements on the quality of the visual system. Then, the dual watermarking medical image algorithm proposed by Zhang et al. [18] firstly carried out use Laplacian space domain transformation to obtain a region of interest (ROI) and non-region of interest (RONI), embedded the watermarking into the ROI after Contourlet transformation and SVD, and obtained the entropy value of each block by using ROI and RONI to complete the watermarking embedding. The algorithm used Contourlet transformation without translation invariance, so the improved Contourlet transformation is used in our algorithm to make translation invariance. Singh et al. [19] proposed a digital image watermarking algorithm based on the DCT and genetic algorithm (GA). Ghafoor et al. [20] proposed a non-blind color image watermarking scheme based on the PCA, DWT, and SVD. They both robust but imperceptible to various signal attacks and the watermark is difficult to remove. Vafaei et al. [21] classified different sub-bands by three-level DWT, then used PCA to reduce the dimension, embedded the watermark, and used the feedforward neural network to repeatedly adjust the embedded watermark of the embedded intensity. It has good visual quality and improves the robustness of the watermark. Since the convolutional neural network has translation invariance, Nagai [22] proposed a digital watermarking algorithm based on convolutional neural network. But the convolutional neural network has a high degree of parameter sensitivity, once the model parameters are slightly changed, the performance is immediately Decline. Meanwhile, the translation invariance of convolutional neural networks is realized by a large amount of data and customized network structure, so the digital watermarking algorithm based on convolutional neural network has greater limitations. Gui et al. [23] proposed a zero-watermark text image algorithm based on improved DCT, which used zero watermark algorithm to embed watermark information without modifying the host image. It solved the problem of watermark capacity limitation and imperceptibility of blind watermark and non-blind watermarking algorithms. However, as for the algorithm used DCT, it has good resistance to conventional attacks and poor resistance to geometric attacks performance. Hence, we can use the advantages of DCT's excellent resistance to resist conventional attacks. Liu et al. [24] proposed a zero-watermark medical image encryption algorithm using DTCWT and DCT combined with chaotic encryption technology to solve the problem of remote transmission and storage medical image security. It is not necessary to manually extract the image information of the region of interest, which effectively solved the problem of watermark extraction and embedding. But the algorithm is a single watermarking algorithm, and the security performance needs to be improved.

Therefore, this paper designed a multi-watermarking algorithm to improve the security of the original medical image. It based on NSCT-RDWT-DCT, combined with Arnold Cat Map and the perceptual hash algorithm (p-Hash). The main features of medical images can be extracted by the low-frequency sub-bands of NSCT secondary scale decomposition and the low frequency of RDWT, DCT and p-Hash. Different initial values of the Arnold Cat Map were performed on the watermark information and XOR operation was applied to encrypt the watermark information. Finally, according to the universal image watermarking technology, combined with cryptography and third-party concepts and Arnold mapping, the problem of embedding and extracting medical image watermarking technology against geometric attacks and the visualization problem of medical images can be realized and solved.

2   Theoretical Background

2.1   Non-Subsampled Contourlet Transform (NSCT)

Although DWT is powerful, it has limitations for obtaining orientation information. NSCT is based on the Contourlet transform proposed by Minh N Do and Martin Vetterli in 2004. It abandoned the steps of sampling in image decomposition and reconstruction [27]. and has a better feature extraction ratio compared to the two-dimensional discrete wavelet transform. NSCT is a transformation based on Nonsubsampled Pyramid (NSP) and Nonsubsampled Directional Filter (NSDFB), in which NSP decomposes images into high-frequency and low-frequency to ensure multi-scale, NSDFB breaks down high-frequency self-banding into multiple. The sub-bands in different directions ensure multi-directionality, and the low-frequency part continues to be decomposed according to the tower model, so that the NSCT has good translation invariance, making the scheme can be well resisted against geometric attacks [25, 26]. Figure 1 shows the nonsubsampled pyramid which divided into two scales. Figure 2 is the segmentation diagram at two scales.

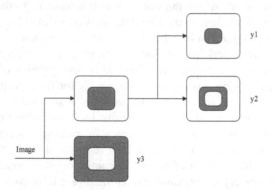

Fig. 1.   Nonsubsampled Pyramid (NSP)

2.2   Redundant Discrete Wavelet Transform (RDWT)

Subtle changes in the DWT coefficients can make the extraction of embedded watermark information incomplete, resulting in a decrease in the robustness of scheme [28]. To overcome this problem, Redundant Discrete Wavelet Transform (RDWT) was used by M. J. Shensa for signal detection and enhancement in 1992 which can maintain a uniform sampling rate in the time domain [29, 30]. RDWT ensures translation invariance by eliminating down-sampling. Due to the output image size remains the same, it results in a large amount of storage space, it can store more features for the next stage.

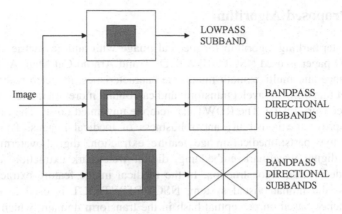

Fig. 2. The Nonsubsampled Directional Filter (NSDFB)

The forward transformation of RDWT is as follows:

$$\begin{cases} c_j[k] = (c_{j+1}[k] * h_j[-k]) \\ d_j[k] = (c_{j+1}[k] * g_j[-k]) \end{cases} \quad (1)$$

Where h[-k] and g[-k] represent the low- and high-pass filters via the RDWT forward transform; c_j and d_j denote low- and high- bands of j-order coefficients [31]. The LL part extracted after the RDWT forward transform the characteristics of the signal, the other three parts give the details or differences of the signal, and the LL subband is passed to the DCT transform (Fig. 3).

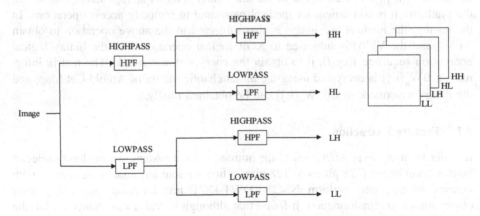

Fig. 3. RDWT transform

3 The Proposed Algorithm

A robust watermarking algorithm for medical image with anti-geometric attacks proposed in this paper is used NSCT, RDWT, DCT and Arnold Cat Map. As NSCT has shift invariance and multi-azimuth multiscale characteristics, its performance is better than wavelet transform. Wavelet transform and can obtain more orientation information and better recovery image. The RDWT can remove unwanted noise. The fusion of the two can improve the invisibility and robustness of medical images. The algorithm consists of five parts: medical image feature extraction, digital watermark image encryption, digital watermark embedding, digital watermark extraction, and digital watermark decryption reconstruction. In the medical image feature extraction stage, according to the human visual system, NSCT-RDWT-DCT is used to extract the feature sequence based on perceptual hash in the transform domain, which is used as the main feature of watermark embedding and extraction. Moreover, the algorithm design process is adopted. The traditional watermarking technology is combined with cryptography, Arnold Cat Map and the third-party concepts, which can improve the robustness and imperceptibility of the algorithm and enhance the security of the remote transmission process.

Figure 4 below is the entire algorithm flow. First, the NSCT-RDWT-DCT transform operation is performed on the host medical image, and the feature sequence conforming to the human's visual system is extracted in the transform domain. Implemented binary perceptual hashing to obtain the feature vector VF(j). Then the digital watermark image is binarized to get a image watermark matrix $W_n(i, j)$, and different chaotic matrices are initialized by Arnold Cat Map. After that, the binarized watermark image is encrypted to gain the encrypted watermark matrix $BW_n(i, j)$. Finally, the binary hash encryption sequence $Key_n(i, j)$ can be obtained by XOR operation with the perceptual hash feature vector VF(j) and the encrypted watermark matrix $BW_n(i, j)$, and then stored in the third-party Internet storage management. On the platform, it is convenient for medical personnel to remotely access operations. In the testing, the medical test image is also subjected to the above operation to obtain VF'(j), and the VF'(j) is subjected to XOR logical operation with the binary logical encryption sequence $Key_n(i, j)$ to obtain the encrypted watermark. The matrix information $BW'_n(i, j)$ is decrypted using the initial chaotic matrix of Arnold Cat Map, and the image watermark matrix $W'_n(i, j)$ can be obtained finally.

3.1 Feature Extraction

In order to meet the requirements of the human's visual system, we randomly select a human brain image (128 pixels × 128 pixels) first without any attacks, then resist with various attacks, and perform NSCT-RDWT-DCT transformation separately after observation and transformation. It found that although its value has changed a lot, the symbol has almost no changed. Table 1 shows the changes of NSCT-RDWT-DCT coefficients under different attacks for the original medical image. In this paper, 32 bit low-frequency data transformed by NSCT-RDWT-DCT is selected for p-Hash, that is, data greater than or equal to 0 is converted to 1, and others are converted to 0. For

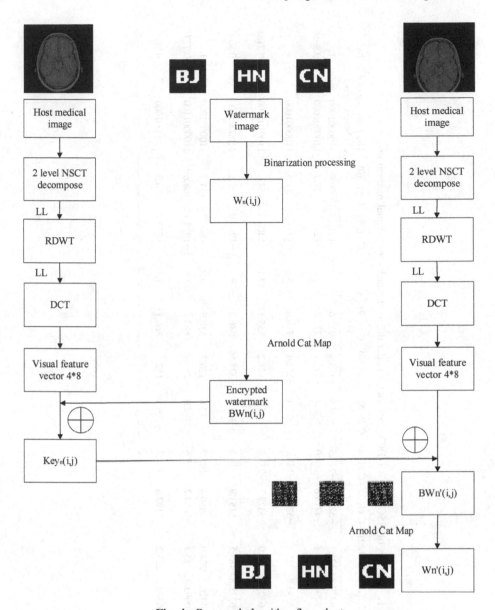

Fig. 4. Proposed algorithm flow chart

convenience, in the table, the first 10 data are listed so that we can get a set of characteristic binary symbol sequences "1 1 0 0 0 0 1 0 0 0" after the original image is transformed by NSCT-RDWT-DCT (Fig. 5).

Then based on the conclusion, the same test is randomly selected for multiple different medical images, and a 32 bit symbol feature sequence is extracted to verify the normalized correlation coefficient values between different medical images. Table 2

Table 1. Changes of NSCT-RDWT-DCT coefficients under different attacks for original medical image

Image processing	PSNR (dB)	C (1, 1)	C (1, 2)	C (1, 3)	C (1, 4)	C (1, 5)	C (1, 6)	C (1, 7)	C (1, 8)	C (1, 9)	C (1, 10)	The sequence of coefficient signs	NC
Original image	–	6329.8	324.5	–5253.9	–274.5	–38.9	–185.6	755.6	–5.2	–1216.3	–50.6	1100001000	1
Gaussian noise (3%)	20.4463	9294.4	194.4	–4719.6	–164.0	–30.4	–123.1	717.7	–71.8	–1247.3	–27.7	1100001000	0.8956
JPEG compression (30%)	33.5285	6383.8	225.3	–5267.0	–183.6	–72.1	–122.4	749.6	–23.6	–1314.3	–31.5	1100001000	1
Median filter [5 × 5] (10 times)	27.5227	6309.3	239.0	5378.3	–215.6	85.3	–141.2	855.1	19.1	–1406.3	–54.6	1100101100	0.7188
Rotation clockwise (10°)	22.7324	6329.8	485.5	5151.9	–319.6	–104.5	–324.56	686.8	–79.4	–1267.0	–459.5	1100001000	0.8043
Scaling (× 0.7)	–	4420.2	224.0	–3680.4	–191.7	–12.6	–126.2	530.9	–0.3	–846.9	–34.5	1100001000	1
Translation (6%, down)	21.5707	10093.8	85.7	–5664.2	–75.6	–3482.9	–252.9	1863.1	35.6	–1933.1	–408.6	1100001100	0.727
Cropping (6%, Y direction)	–	6346.2	223.2	–5192.8	–174.7	–206.99	–152.1	866.1	–7.1	–1829.7	–50.5	1100001000	0.8956

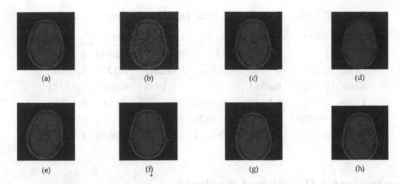

Fig. 5. Different attacks on the brain. (a) Original image; (b) Gaussian noise (3%); (c) JPEG compression (30%); (d) Median filter [5 × 5] (10 times); (e) Rotation clockwise (10°); (f) Scaling (×0.7); (g) Translation (6%, down); (h) Cropping (6%, Y direction).

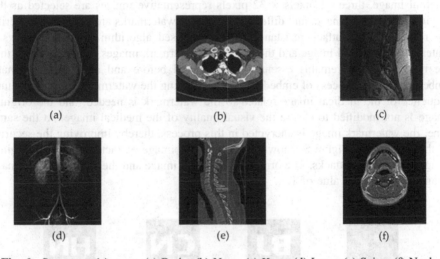

Fig. 6. Some tested images. (a) Brain; (b) Nose; (c) Knee; (d) Lung; (e) Spine; (f) Neck.

and Fig. 6 are different medical images and the NC values between them. From the data in Fig. 6, it can be shown that the feature symbol sequence extracted by our proposed algorithm has an NC value of less than 0.5 between different medical images and its own NC equal to 1. Therefore, it can be stated that the proposed algorithm is consistent. In the human visual system, the NSCT-RDWT-DCT transformed low-frequency data can be used as an effective symbol feature sequence to associate it with the digital watermark.

Table 2. Correlation coefficient value between different images (32 bit)

Image	Brain	Nose	Knee	Lung	Spine	Neck
Brain	1	0.071	0.0023	0.252	−0.0552	0.1972
Nose	0.071	1	0.4384	0.0626	−0.1294	0.1216
Knee	0.0023	0.4384	1	−0.1879	−0.0626	−0.3131
Lung	0.252	0.0626	−0.1879	1	0.3131	0.4384
Spine	−0.0552	−0.1294	−0.0626	0.3131	1	−0.0039
Neck	0.1972	0.1216	−0.3131	0.4384	−0.0039	1

4 Experimental Result and Analysis

Matlab2016b is selected as the test platform in this paper. In the experiment, the 128 pixels × 128 pixels gray human brain medical image is randomly selected as the original image, three 32 pixels × 32 pixels representative images are selected as the original watermark image, and different encryption watermarks are generated to verify the robustness and attack resistance of the proposed algorithm. Figure 7. shows a watermarked medical image and the encrypted watermark images. It can be noted that the medical image remains essentially unchanged before and after the watermark embedded. In the process of embedding and extracting the watermark, only the feature sequence of the medical image related to the watermark is needed, and the original image is not modified to ensure the visual quality of the medical image. At the same time, the watermark image is encrypted in this process, thereby improving the security of the watermark. Figure 8. shows the watermark image extracted from the original image without any attacks. The original watermark image and the extracted watermark image have an NC value of 1.

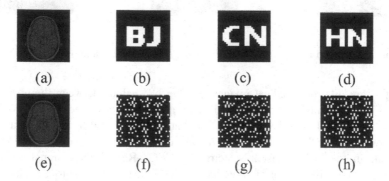

(a)   (b)   (c)   (d)

(e)   (f)   (g)   (h)

Fig. 7. Watermark medical image and encrypted watermark: (a) Host medical image; (b) Original binary watermark 'BJ'; (c) Original binary watermark 'CN'; (d) Original binary watermark 'HN'; (e) Watermarked medical image; (f) Encrypted watermark 'BJ'; (f) Encrypted watermark 'CN'; (h) Encrypted watermark 'HN'.

4.1 Attacks

(See Tables 3, 4, 5, 6, 7, 8 and 9).

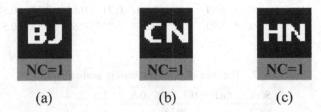

(a)   (b)   (c)

Fig. 8. Watermark extracted without attacks: (a) Extracted watermark 'BJ'; (b) Extracted watermark 'CN'; (c) Extracted watermark 'HN'.

Table 3. The data of different Gaussian noise attacks

Gaussian noise (%)	1	5	10	15	20	25
PSNR (dB)	21.2675	19.4272	17.116	14.9384	13.0365	11.4095
NC1	0.8900	0.8877	0.8924	0.8877	0.8005	0.7890
NC2	0.8931	0.8889	0.8889	0.8889	0.7998	0.7912
NC3	0.8929	0.8966	0.8966	0.8966	0.8027	0.8012

Table 4. The data of different JPEG compression

Compression intensity (%)	4	7	15	30	45
PSNR (dB)	26.8486	29.0990	31.2516	33.5285	34.7418
NC1	0.8924	1	0.8924	1	1
NC2	0.8899	1	0.8899	1	1
NC3	0.8956	1	0.8956	1	1

Table 5. The data of different median filtering attacks

Median filter	[3, 3]			[5, 5]			[7, 7]		
Repeat times	1	10	20	1	10	20	1	10	20
PSNR (dB)	33.76	31.09	30.54	29.68	27.52	26.98	27.65	26.23	26.16
NC1	1	0.80	0.80	0.80	0.79	0.80	0.72	0.64	0.64
NC2	1	0.80	0.80	0.79	0.80	0.79	0.70	0.63	0.63
NC3	1	0.79	0.80	0.80	0.80	0.80	0.72	0.65	0.64

Table 6. The data of different rotation angles

Rotation (Clockwise)	1°	5°	10°	15°	20°	30°	40°
PSNR (dB)	34.25	25.43	22.73	21.94	21.62	21.14	20.49
NC1	0.89	0.79	0.79	0.71	0.64	0.56	0.57
NC2	0.89	0.80	0.80	0.71	0.63	0.57	0.58
NC3	0.90	0.81	0.81	0.73	0.65	0.58	0.57

Table 7. The data of different scaling scale attacks

Scaling factor	0.3	0.5	0.8	1	1.4	2	4
NC1	0.79	1	1	1	1	1	1
NC2	0.80	1	1	1	1	1	1
NC3	0.80	1	1	1	1	1	1

Table 8. The data of different intensity downcast attacks

Down distance (%)	2	4	8	10	12	15
PSNR (dB)	24.57	21.83	21.20	20.93	20.55	20.07
NC1	1	0.80	0.70	0.70	0.70	0.50
NC2	1	0.79	0.72	0.72	0.72	0.51
NC3	1	0.80	0.73	0.73	0.73	0.51

Table 9. The data of different Cropping Scales Attacks

Cropping (%) Y direction	3	6	8	12	23	35
NC1	1	0.89	1	1	0.72	0.51
NC2	1	0.89	1	1	0.71	0.49
NC3	1	0.90	1	1	0.72	0.52

4.2 Algorithms Comparison

In order to verify the effectiveness and robustness of our proposed algorithm and reduce the difference between different test samples, we use 512*512 pixels "Lenna" grayscale image as the host image to compare with some existing watermarking algorithms [32–35]. The comparison results are shown in Table 10. Observing the data in Table 10, we found that the proposed algorithm is superior to the current watermarking algorithm, and we also use encryption technology to effectively improve the anti-theft ability of the algorithm. Accordingly, from the overall comparison of the proposed algorithm, it can be concluded that the proposed algorithm is Medical images, as well as ordinary images, provide a solution that is imperceptible, highly robust, and secure without regard to embedded capacity.

Table 10. Comparison data between different algorithms

Attacks	Intensity of attacks	Aditi Zear et al. [32] NC1	Rohit Thanki et al. [33] NC2	Seyyed Hossein Soleymani et al. [34] NC3	Vivek Singh Verma et al. [35] NC4	Proposed algorithm
Gaussian noise	1%	0.88	0.86	0.96	0.98	1.00
	10%	0.79	0.78	0.93	–	1.00
	25%	0.63	0.65	–	–	0.89
JPEG compression	4%	0.11	−0.02	–	–	1.00
	10%	–	–	0.71	0.92	1.00
	25%	0.91	0.47	0.84	–	1.00
Median filter (10 times)	[3, 3]	0.15	0.91	1.00	0.98	1.00
	[5, 5]	0.05	0.80	1.00	0.91	1.00
	[9, 9]	0.01	0.72	–	–	1.00
Scaling	×0.2	0.39	0.52	–	–	1.00
	×0.5	–	–	1.00	0.97	1.00
	×2.0	0.92	0.91	–	–	1.00
Rotation (clockwise)	0.25°	–	–	–	0.88	1.00
	0.3°	–	–	–	0.87	1.00
	10°	0.21	0.88	–	–	0.65
Translation (Down)	3%	0.73	0.80	–	–	0.89
Cropping (Y direction)	5%	0.76	0.89	0.81	–	0.89

5 Conclusions

In this paper, we proposed a multi-watermarking algorithm for medical image based on NSCT-RDWT-DCT and Arnold Cat Map, which also combines zero-watermarking concept. Due to the shift invariance of NSCT, a large amount of orientation information can be provided. Meanwhile, RDWT and DCT were combined to improve the noise suppression performance of the algorithm. We combined these three transforms to extract the feature vectors of original medical images. The proposed algorithm also used traditional watermarking technology and cryptography in the design process. The combination of Arnold Cat Map and the third-party concepts can improve the robustness, imperceptibility of the algorithm, and the security of the remote transmission process. It realized the embedding and extraction of watermarks information without selecting the region of interest in advance. The experimental results show that the proposed algorithm can effectively extract the watermark information and has stronger robust than the existing algorithm, which is enough to resist geometric attacks and conventional attacks. It can be applied to telemedicine, content authentication and communication security.

References

1. Kuyoro, S.O., Ibikunle, F., Awodele, O.: Cloud computing security issues and challenges. Int. J. Comput. Netw. (IJCN). **3**(5), 247–255 (2011)
2. Qasim, A.F., Meziane, F., Aspin, R.: Digital watermarking: applicability for developing trust in medical imaging workflows state of the art review. Comput. Sci. **27**, 45–60 (2018)
3. Rostrom, T.J.: Framework to secure cloud-based medical image storage and management system communications. All Theses and Dissertations. 2011,3124. https://scholarsarchive.byu.edu/etd/3124
4. Yu, X.Y., Wang, C.Y., Zhou, X.: A survey on robust video watermarking algorithms for copyright protection. Appl. Sci. **8**(10), 1891 (2018)
5. Hai, T., Li, C.M., Jasni, M.Z., Ahmed, N.A.: Robust image watermarking theory and techniques: a review. J. Appl. Res. Technol. **12**(1), 122–138 (2014)
6. Banitalebi-Dehkordi, A., Banitalebi-Dehkordi, M., Abouei, J., Nader-Esfahani, S.: An improvement technique based on structural similarity thresholding for digital watermarking. Adv. Comput. Eng. **2014**, 8 (2014)
7. Aldossary, S., Allen, W.: Data security, privacy, availability and integrity in cloud computing: issues and current solutions. Int. J. Adv. Comput. Sci. Appl. **7**(4), 485–498 (2016)
8. Mahmood, A., Hamed, T., Obimbo, C., Dony, R.: Improving the security of the medical images. Int. J. Adv. Comput. Sci. Appl. **4**(9), 130–136 (2013)
9. Ravisankar, K.: Robust medical image watermarking scheme based on RDWT- SVD. IJSRSET **5**, 132–135 (2018)
10. Sreenivas, K., Prasad, V.K.: Fragile watermarking schemes for image authentication: a survey. Int. J. Mach. Learn. Cybern. **9**, 1–26 (2017)
11. Su, Q., Niu, Y., Wang, Q., Sheng, G.: A blind color image watermarking based on DC component in the spatial domain. Int. J. Light Electron. Opt. **124**(23), 6255–6260 (2013)
12. Su, B., Chen, B.: Robust color image watermarking technique in the spatial domain. Soft. Comput. **22**, 1–16 (2017)
13. Soumitra, R., Arup, K.P.: A robust blind hybrid image watermarking scheme in RDWT-DCT domain using Arnold scrambling. Multimed. Tools Appl. **76**, 3577–3616 (2017)
14. Nagpal, S., Bhushan, S., Mahajan, M.: An enhanced digital image watermarking scheme for medical images using neural network, DWT and RSA. Int. J. Mod. Educ. Comput. Sci. **4**, 46–56 (2016)
15. Al-Haj, A.: Combined DWT-DCT digital image watermarking. J. Comput. Sci. **3**, 740–746 (2007)
16. Zhao, M., Dang, Y.: Color image copyright protection digital watermarking algorithm based on DWT, DCT. In: WiCOM 2008, pp. 1–4 (2008). https://doi.org/10.1109/wicom.2008.2913
17. Dey, N., Maji, P., Das, P., Das, A., Chaudhuri, S.S.: An edge based blind watermarking technique of medical images without devalorizing diagnostic parameters. In: ICATE 2013, pp. 1–5. IEEE (2013)
18. Zhang, Z., Wu, L., Li, H., Lai, H., Zheng, C.: Dual watermarking algorithm for medical image. J. Med. Imaging Health Inform. **7**, 607–622 (2017)
19. Singh, M., Saxena, A.: Image watermarking using discrete cosine transform [DCT] and genetic algorithm [GA]. Int. J. Innov. Eng. Res. Manag. **4**(3), 1–13 (2017)
20. Ghafoor, A., Imran, M.: A non-blind color image watermarking scheme resistent against geometric attacks. Radio Eng. **21**, 1246–1251 (2012)

21. Vafaei, M., Mahdavi-Nasab, H., Pourghassem, H.: A new robust blind watermarking method based on neural networks in wavelet transform domain. World Appl. Sci. J. **22**, 1572–1580 (2013)

22. Nagai, Y., Uchida, Y., Sakazawa, S., Satoh, S.: Digital watermarking for deep neural networks. Int. J. Multimed. Inf. Retrieval **7**, 3–16 (2018). https://doi.org/10.1007/s13735-018-0147-1

23. Feng, G., Huang, X.: An improved DCT based zero-watermarking algorithm for text image. In: Anti-counterfeiting, Security, Identification, pp. 1–4 (2012). https://doi.org/10.1109/icasid.2012.6325285

24. Liu, J., Li, J.B., Zhang, K., Bhatti, U., Ai, Y.: Zero-watermarking algorithm for medical images based on dual-tree complex wavelet transform and discrete cosine transform. J. Med. Imaging Health Inform. 188–194 (2019). https://doi.org/10.1166/jmihi.2019.2559

25. Elayan, M.A., Ahmad, M.O.: Digital watermarking scheme based on arnold and anti-arnold transforms. In: Mansouri, A., Nouboud, F., Chalifour, A., Mammass, D., Meunier, J., ElMoataz, A. (eds.) ICISP 2016. LNCS, vol. 9680, pp. 317–327. Springer, Cham (2016). https://doi.org/10.1007/978-3-319-33618-3_32

26. Agilandeeswari, L., Ganesan, K.: A robust color video watermarking scheme based on hybrid embedding techniques. Multimed. Tools Appl. **75**(14), 8745–8780 (2016). https://doi.org/10.1007/s11042-0152789-9

27. Dyson, F.J., Falk, H.: Period of a discrete cat mapping. Am. Math. Mon. **99**, 603–624 (1992). https://doi.org/10.1080/00029890.1992.11995900

28. Sachin, G., Vinay, K.S.: A RDWT and block-SVD based dual water-marking scheme for digital images. Int. J. Adv. Comput. Sci. Appl. **8**, 211–219 (2017)

29. Shensa, M.J.: The discrete wavelet transform: wedding the a trous and Mallat algorithms. IEEE Trans. Signal Process. 2464–2482 (1992). https://doi.org/10.1109/78.157290

30. Hien, T.D., Nakao, Z., Chen, Y.W.: RDWT domain watermarking based on independent component analysis extraction. Adv. Soft Comput. **34**, 401–414 (2006)

31. Ernawan, F., Kabir, M.N.: A block-based RDWT-SVD image watermarking method using human visual system characteristics. Vis. Comput. 1–19 (2018). https://doi.org/10.1007/s00371-018-1567-x

32. Zear, A., Singh, A.K., Kumar, P.: A proposed secure multiple watermarking technique based on DWT, DCT and SVD for application in medicine. Multimed. Tools Appl. **77**, 4863–4882 (2018)

33. Thanki, R., Borra, S., Dwivedi, V., Borisagar, K.: An efficient medical image watermarking scheme based on FDCuT-DCT. Eng. Sci. Technol. **20**, 1366 1379 (2017)

34. Soleymani, S.H., Taherinia, A.H., Mohajerzadeh, A.H.: A new blind robust watermarking method based on Arnold Cat map and amplified pseudo-noise strings with weak correlation. Multimed. Tools Appl. (2019). https://doi.org/10.1007/s11042-019-7282-4

35. Verma, V.S., Jha, R.K.: LWT-DSR based new robust framework for watermark extraction under intentional attack conditions. J. Franklin Inst. **354**(14), 6422–6449 (2017)

An Improved Container Scheduling Algorithm Based on PSO for Big Data Applications

Jiawei Li[1], Bo Liu[1], Weiwei Lin[2,3(✉)], Pengfei Li[1], and Qian Gao[1]

[1] School of Computer Science, South China Normal University,
Guangzhou 510000, China
[2] School of Computer Science and Engineering,
South China University of Technology, Guangzhou 510000, China
linww@scut.edu.cn
[3] Guangdong Luan Indusrty and Commerce Co., Ltd., Guangzhou 510520, China

Abstract. Existing big data computing and storage platforms are generally based on traditional virtual machine technology, which often results in low resource utilization, a long time for flexible scaling and expanding clusters. To deal with these problems, this paper proposes an improved container scheduling algorithm, Kubernetes-based Particle Swarm Optimization (K-PSO), for big data applications based on Particle Swarm Optimization (PSO). The K-PSO algorithm converges faster than the basic PSO algorithm, and the algorithm running time is reduced by about half. The K-PSO capacity for big data applications is implemented in the Kubernetes container cloud system. The experimental results show that the node resource utilization rate of the improved scheduling strategy based on K-PSO algorithm is about 20% higher than that of Kube-Scheduler default strategy, BalancedQosPriority strategy, ESS strategy, and PSO strategy while the average I/O performance and average computing performance of Hadoop cluster are not degraded.

Keywords: Docker · PSO · Container scheduling · Big data

1 Introduction

As an emerging virtualization technology, Docker container can be easily deployed to various IasS or PaaS platforms [1]. Besides, it has less resource overhead compared to traditional virtualization technologies [2] that can start/stop in seconds, continuous delivery and deployment as well as provide great support for the development of micro-services and DevOps [3]. As a result, Docker container technology is moving at an explosive rate [4].

Besides, the existing big data computing and storage platforms are generally based on traditional virtual machine technology (VM) [5]. However, this approach often results in low resource utilization, a long time for flexible scaling and cluster expansion, and tedious and repetitive work of a large number of

© Springer Nature Switzerland AG 2019
J. Vaidya et al. (Eds.): CSS 2019, LNCS 11982, pp. 516–530, 2019.
https://doi.org/10.1007/978-3-030-37337-5_42

nodes in a unified configuration [6]. As a fast-developing lightweight virtualization technology, Docker container technology provides a better solution to solve this problems [7]. Therefore, research on container-based big data technology has become hot in recent years.

To optimize the performance of the cloud computing center Docker container cluster, the container related to a certain service can be allocated as much as possible to the same node that has the suitable memory, CPU and other resources in the container scheduling process of the cloud computing center. Thereby that reduces network traffic consumption and improve service quality. The focus of this paper is on how to properly select a node when deploying a Docker container to optimize the service quality of the application in the container.

Based on the Docker container cluster scheduling tool, Kubernetes, this paper implements a PSO-based container scheduling algorithm for large data applications, K-PSO algorithm. The main contributions of the paper are: based on the PSO algorithm, an improved container scheduling algorithm is proposed. It converges faster than the basic PSO algorithm and has less running time when the final fitness value is consistent. Based on the proposed K-PSO algorithm, the Kubernetes scheduling strategy is improved. The node resource utilization rate of the improved scheduling strategy based on the K-PSO algorithm is about 20% higher than that of the Kube-Scheduler default strategy, BalancedQosPriority strategy [8], ESS strategy [9] and PSO strategy while the average I/O performance and average computing performance of Hadoop cluster are not degraded.

The paper is organized as follows: in Sect. 2 we discuss and summarize some existing container scheduling algorithms. In Sect. 3, the optimization stages of the Kubernetes scheduling process are improved for large data applications. A K-PSO algorithm based on the improved PSO algorithm is proposed. In Sect. 4 we compare the number of iterations and running time of the K-PSO algorithm and the basic PSO algorithm through experiments. In the Kubernetes container cloud system, we compare the scheduling strategy based on the K-PSO algorithm with the default scheduling strategy of Kube-Scheduler, BalancedQosPriority strategy, ESS strategy and PSO strategy for the utilization rate of node resources, then analysis the experimental results.

2   Related Work

In the past few years, there have been many pieces of research on the management and scheduling of cloud computing resources [10]. The task scheduling problem of the cloud computing center includes unified management of heterogeneous resources, rational scheduling, and allocation of resources, which has been proved to be an NP problem [11]. The container as a new cloud computing resource, its management and scheduling have become a very hot issue worthy of study. To solve this problem, Docker company developed the container cluster scheduling tool, Swarm; Google company gave the container resource scheduling tool, Kubernetes [12]; UC Berkeley gave the container resource orchestration solution, Mesos [13]. This paper focuses on the research and analysis of the container scheduling algorithm and intelligent PSO algorithm based on the Kubernetes container cloud system for big data applications.

Docker virtualization technology provides a great solution to the problems of large data computing and storage platform based on traditional virtual machine technology. [14] proposes an automated deployment scheme of the Hadoop distributed cluster using containers. The core idea is to encapsulate Ambari and its running environment into a Docker container image and start multiple containers based on this image, and finally, start the Hadoop cluster in the Docker container through Ambari and Bluprint. In the research of container scheduling algorithm and improvement of the Kubernetes container scheduling strategy, some scholars have proposed other solutions. [15] proposes a novel multi-objective optimization container scheduling, Multiopt, which is implemented based on Swarm. The Multiport algorithm combines advantages of the Spread algorithm, the Binpackalgorithm, the Random algorithm and then considers the time consumption transmitting images on the network, the association between containers and nodes and the clustering of containers so that the scheduling process of containers in a cluster is more efficient and meets the business needs better. [16] uses a genetic algorithm to search the global solution space, and a genetic algorithm is used to optimize the scheduling strategy of the Docker cluster to obtain the approximate optimal scheduling scheme. To combine the task load pattern, each task can set the runtime resource requirement parameters before scheduling; to support multi-task scheduling, multiple tasks will be scheduled in this paper. Tasks are merged into task groups, and the results of task group scheduling are taken as individuals, and the global approximate optimal solution is screened out by a genetic algorithm. To measure the load balance of cluster more accurately, the load of CPU, memory, hard disk I/O and network traffic is taken into account. [17] proposes a smart particle swarm optimization (SPSO) algorithm to obtain the optimal resource allocation plan for a given workflow, which reduces the number of iterations to less, thus reducing the execution time of the algorithm. To get rid of the local minimum problem, a variable neighborhood particle swarm optimization (VNPSO) algorithm is proposed. The VNPSO algorithm is based on repeated explorations of growing neighborhoods to identify better local optima using the so-called shaking strategy. [18] proposes an improved PSO algorithm for cloud computing task scheduling optimization is proposed. Unlike the PSO algorithm, the algorithm can dynamically adjust the inertia weight coefficient according to the number of iterations to improve the convergence rate. This algorithm improves the performance of the PSO algorithm and effectively solves the local optimal problem. However, experiments were conducted using the Cloudsim toolkit, and no further tests were conducted in the cluster. [19] proposes a new energy-saving container-based scheduling (EECS) strategy that uses accelerated particle swarm optimization (APSO) technology to find the appropriate container for each task with minimum delay. The main goal of EECS is to minimize the overall energy consumption and computing time of the task through effective resource utilization.

Although the above research has made some contributions to the field of large data application virtualization and container resource scheduling, there are also many shortcomings. In the following chapters of this paper, some corresponding algorithms and strategies are proposed to solve the problems and optimize the container scheduling for large data applications.

3 Improved Container Scheduling Algorithm Based on PSO Algorithm

3.1 Basic Definition

We define a set of nodes in a Kubernetes cluster as C, the j-th cluster is defined as C_j, and node is defined as no. The no_i indicates that the i-th node is used. There are multiple sets of Kubernetes clusters, thus the cluster with n sets of Kubernetes clusters is defined as $Cluster$:

$$Cluster = U_{j=1}^{n} C_j \tag{4.1}$$

$$c_j = U_{i=1}^{m} no_i \tag{4.2}$$

Define the set of mirrors required for the request Req_k to establish services from the k-th user $Client_k$ as $Image_k$. $Image_k$ contains m mirrors, expressed as

$$Image_k = \{l_1, l_2, l_3, ...l_y...l_m\}, y, m \in N \tag{4.3}$$

Let the collection of labels that play on the node no_i and contain n labels be $Labels_{no_i}$,

$$Labels_{no_i} = \{label_1, label_2, label_3...label_y...label_n\}, y, n \subset N \tag{4.4}$$

Let the first Pod to be established on the Kubernetes cluster be pod_l. Let the set of labels on the be $Labels_{pod_l}$,

$$Labels_{pod_l} = \{label_1, label_2, label_3...label_y...label_g\}, y, g \in N \tag{4.5}$$

3.2 Improvement of Kube-Scheduler Optimization Process

i. Cpu/Memory Factor. For a pending Pod pod_l, there is already a set of nodes that meet the scheduling criteria. But usually pod_l only need a specified number of nodes to complete the deployment, so it is necessary to optimize the node-set with the number more than pod_l deployment replicas.

When dispatching pod_i, it is often hoped that the resource utilization rate of node no_i will reach the minimum utilization rate desired by users as far as possible so that the resources can be fully utilized, so it should be satisfied as much as possible:

$$CPU_{no_i-t_x} = CPU_{no_i-t} + CPU_{pod_l-R} \geq CPU_{no_i-total} \times CPU^{PL} \tag{4.6}$$

$$MEM_{no_i-t_x} = MEM_{no_i-t} + MEM_{pod_l-R} \geq MEM_{no_i-total} \times MEM^{PL} \quad (4.7)$$

Among them, CPU^{PL} indicates the lowest CPU utilization rate of the node that the user wants. MEM^{PL} indicates the lowest memory utilization of the node that the user wants.

By matching the desired resources of pod_l with those of node no_i, we hope that the matching degree between the allocated resources can make full use of the resources. And we use the following formula to calculate the degree of agreement:

$$P_1(pod_l, no_i) = \frac{CPU_{pod_l-R} \times 10}{CPU_{nod_i-total} \times CPU^{PL} - CPU_{no_i-t}} + \frac{MEM_{pod_l-R} \times 10}{MEM_{nod_i-total} \times MEM^{PL} - MEM_{no_i-t}} \quad (4.8)$$

To keep the score of A and other factors in the same range as that of the latter, the result is enlarged by 10 times at a time.

ii. User Factor. Kubernetes' native dispatcher does not consider the user's usage characteristics, but in the actual production environment, the user's use characteristics are obvious. For example, some users are engaged in Hadoop/Spark big data development, and the characteristics of using Kubernetes cluster are obviously biased in high memory, high I/O; some users engaged in deep learning research, its use of Kubernetes cluster is biased towards high GPU; some users use Kubernetes cluster for Web services deployment, its use is biased towards High network usage. Therefore, according to these tags, the user's usage characteristics can be recorded and analyzed to classify users. When performing Pod scheduling, the nodes suitable for their use characteristics can be preferentially scheduled.

Assume that the set of m users using $Cluster$ is $USERS$ and the feature set of four feature count values for high i/o, high memory, high cpu, and high gpu of one of the users u_i is us_i:

$$us_i = \{io : 1, cpu : 1, gpu : 0, mem : 1\} \quad (4.9)$$

In the running process, the counting values of the four features of io/cpu/gpu /mem take the value in us obtained by the method that adding one when the user's request for resources reaches the threshold.

When the user u_i requests to create pod_l, pod_l inherit the feature set of user u on io/cpu/gpu/mem, add the collection of tags of us_i to the label collection $LabelS_{pod_l}$ of pod_l. For the label set of node no_i, if the label exists and the label is set to 1, it indicates the user u_i uses the feature to match the node to get a function that calculates the match value:

$$P_2(pod_l, no_i) = P_2(us, no_i) = \sum \frac{value_{us}}{value_{no_{i-1}}} \quad (4.10)$$

Among them, $value_{us} \epsilon Labels_{us}$, $value_{no_{i-1}} \epsilon Labels_{no_{i-1}}$, $Labels_{us}$ is user feature set us Collection of labels, $Labels_{no_{i-1}}$ for $Labela_{no_i}$ Corresponding user feature set us Label set.

iii. Affinity Factor. Affinity and AntiAffinity are the features of Kubernetes' native scheduler. The soft scheduling strategy for pods is realized by supporting In, NotIn, Exists, and DoesNotExist expressions.

Same as before calculation pod_l Tag set and node no_i The matching relationship of the tag set is the same, and the matching degree calculation function of the affinity and the anti-affinity can be defined. Since the four features of io/cpu/gpu/mem have been calculated before, the four features are eliminated here. The affinity matching function calculation function is

$$P_3(pod_l, no_i) = P_3(pod_{l\_0}, no_{i\_0}) = \sum \frac{value_{pod_{l\_0}}}{value_{no_{i\_0}}} \times weight \qquad (4.11)$$

among them, $value_{pod_{l\_0}} \epsilon Labels_{pod_{l\_0}}$, $value_{no_{i\_0}} \epsilon Labels_{no_{i\_0}}$, $weight$ The weight value set by the user when calculating a label, $Labels_{no_{i\_0}}$ for $Labels_{no_i}$ is Collection of labels Remove user feature set us.

$$Labels_{pod_{l\_0}} = Labels_{pod_l} - us \qquad (4.12)$$

$Labels_{no_{i\_0}}$ for $Labels_{no_i}$ is Collection of labels Remove user feature set us.

$$Labels_{no_{i\_0}} = Labels_{no_i} - us \qquad (4.13)$$

iv. Overall Rating. Through the discussion of cpu/memory factors, user factors, and affinity factors, these factors are comprehensively weighted and then obtained to be scheduled pod_l. For a node no_i Comprehensive scoring function

$$P(pod_l, no_i) = \sum_{i=1}^{3} P_i(pod_l, no_i) \times w_i \times 100 \qquad (4.14)$$

among them w_i is the weight value set by the rating item P_i for user, $w_t \times 100$ is for the convenience of operation.

3.3 Improvement Based on Particle Swarm Optimization

Particle Swarm Optimization (PSO) is an algorithm that mimics animal foraging, emphasizing the optimal solution by group coordination and coordination [20]. Each particle can be regarded as a partial solution to the problem. All particles use the optimal solution conditions as the guiding information, constantly change the running trajectory in space, and constantly update the global optimal solution to find the global optimal solution at the end of the algorithm.

The position of each particle in the particle swarm algorithm can be regarded as a feasible scheduling scheme. In the cloud computing task, a task is regarded as a particle. For the Kubernetes cluster after the pre-selected scheduling process, m nodes are selected and available. The position of the particle x is matrix $X_i = x_{ij}$ where x_{ij} represents the assignment of Pod_i to node $Node_j$

i. Fitness Function. The comprehensive scoring function for selecting the best node for a pod has been discussed above. Using this function, the fitness function of scheduling a set of tasks TASKS to m nodes is expressed as:

$$maxC_\sigma = \sum_{j=1}^{m} \sum_{i=1}^{m} P_{ij}, 1 \leq i \leq n, 1 \leq j \leq m \tag{4.15}$$

Where m indicates that there are m nodes in the cluster, and n indicates that a group of tasks TASKS needs to start n Pods to provide services after decomposition. $P_{ij} = P(pod_i, no_j)$, indicating that pod_i Scheduling to a node no_j, pod_i Pair of nodes no_j Comprehensive score function.

ii. Iteration of Particle Swarm Optimization. Suppose that in a multidimensional space, a particle swarm has n particles, and each particle runs at a certain speed. The running speed change function of particle i after the t-th iteration is as follows

$$v_i(t+1) = \omega \times v_i(t) + c_1 \times rand \times (pb_i(t) - x_i(t)) + c_2 \times rand \times (gb_i(t) - x_i(t)) \tag{4.16}$$

$$x_i(t+1) = x_i(t) + v_i(t) \tag{4.17}$$

In the above formula, t represents the number of iterations, ω indicates the inertia weight parameter, c_1 with c_2 is a learning factor, generally $c_1 = c_2 = 2$, $rand$ is a random number evenly distributed over $(0, 1)$, pb_i represents the local optimal solution obtained from the t-th iteration, gb_i represents the global optimal solution obtained from the t-th iteration.

iii. Improved Inertia Weight Parameter. As a parallel algorithm, particle swarm optimization is very efficient, but there are also some problems. Here we use inertia weight parameters. ω conduct key discussions and research.

Due to the parameters during iteration ω, the global optimal solution obtained when the linear decreasing trend changes is better, so consider $omega$ From linearly reduced from 0.9 to 0.4, the classical linear decrement formula is as follows [21]:

$$\omega(t+1) = \omega_{max} - \frac{\omega_{max} - \omega_{min}}{t_{max}} \times t \tag{4.18}$$

Among them, ω_{max} indicates the initial inertia weight and $\omega_{max} = 0.9$. ω_{min} indicates the termination of inertia weight and $\omega_{min} = 0.4$. t_{max} indicates the maximum number of iterations. t indicates the number of rounds for the current iteration.

This method is higher in the optimization accuracy than the basic particle swarm algorithm. But the inertia weight parameter is too large in the first few iterations, though the algorithm prematurely falls into the local optimal solution. Based on the research on improving inertial weight of [22] and [23], the nonlinear inertia weight parameter is proposed here. The parameter iteration formula is as follows:

$$\omega(t+1) = \omega_{min} + (\omega_{max} - \omega_{min})exp[-\frac{\theta \times t^2}{t_{max}^2}] \qquad (4.19)$$

Among them, θ is the control factor that controls the smoothness of the curve. In this experiment, when $\theta = 3.4$, the weight change effect is better, showing the characteristics of convex and concave. In the beginning, the weight acceleration is reduced, so that the particle swarm algorithm enters the local search faster. And then the change amplitude is smaller and gradually converges, thus avoiding the algorithm falling into the local optimal solution prematurely.

iv. Improved Learning Factor. This section focuses on the adjustment of learning factor c_1, c_2. When the algorithm is running, it is hoped that the particle's operating range will cover the entire space as much as possible at the beginning of the algorithm operation. And it is hoped to avoid falling into local extremum after the operation. [24] studies the factor c_1, c_2 and suggests $c_1 = c_2 = 2.5$. The setting of the proposed parameter is not very good in the experiment of this paper. So for this parameter, an improved method is proposed here which makes c_1 big first and then small, c_2 small first and then big. Set the formula as follows:

$$c_1 = c_{1-max} - \frac{c_{1-max} - c_{1-min}}{t_{max}^2} \times t^2 \qquad (4.20)$$

$$c_2 = c_{2-min} - \frac{c_{2-max} - c_{2-min}}{t_{max}^2} \times t^2 \qquad (4.21)$$

Among them, c_{1-max}, c_{2min} is the iteration initial valuefor of c_1, c_2.c_{1-min}, c_{2-max} is the iterative final value of c_1, c_2. t_{max} is the maximum number of iterations, t is the number of current iterations. In this way, the historical information of the particle itself is consulted in the initial stage of a particle's operation, and the group information is consulted in the later stage of its operation, and the later, the deeper the reference mechanism is. In this experiment, $c_{2-min} = 0.01$, $c_{1-min} = 0.01$, $c_{2-max} = 2.5$, $c_{1-max} = 2.5$.

v. Add Penalty. Although in the previous discussion, the inertia weight parameter setting and learning factor parameter setting of the basic particle swarm algorithm formula 4.26 have been improved, the algorithm may still have premature convergence of the particle cluster when solving the high dimensional optimization problem. In response to this problem, it is proposed to introduce a penalty term to adjust the running speed of the particle. By analyzing whether the particle swarm is trapped in the local extremum during the particle running process, it is determined whether or not to add a penalty term. The particle position update formula for item R is:

$$v_i(t+1) = \omega \times v_i(t) + c_1 \times rand \times (pb_i(t) - x_i(t)) + c_2 \times rand \times (gb_i(t) - x_i(t)) + R \qquad (4.22)$$

$$R = \begin{cases} 0, & s^2 < \gamma \\ \mu \times (\dfrac{s^2 - \gamma^2}{\gamma}), & s^2 > \gamma \end{cases} \tag{4.23}$$

Among them, R is the particle speed penalty, γ indicates the threshold indicating whether the particle running speed should be judged. The value is selected according to the specific situation (cluster size). In this paper, γ takes the logarithm of cluster size $logN$ to ensure that the penalty can be enabled when the size of the cluster is large. μ is the penalty factor that controls the extent to which the particle swarm is aggregated. The larger the value set by μ, the easier it is for the particle swarm to jump out of the local optimal solution, and the lower the efficiency of the particle swarm search. Through the experiment, 0.38 is better for μ in this paper. After adding the speed penalty, each iteration needs to calculate the fitness variance of the particle swarm s^2. After the particle has updated its local optimal solution and global optimal solution, s^2 needs to be judged to determine whether to add penalty items, to determine the running speed.

4   Experimental Environment and Results Analysis

4.1   Experimental Environment

In this paper, the virtual machine based on VirtualBox is used as the host operating system of the container on the physical server. The experiment uses Kubernetes 1.10 as the scheduling tool of the container cluster. In the experiment, the specific configuration of the Kubernetes node is shown in Table 1.

Table 1. Kubernetes node configuration

Node 1	Node name	node04
	Host-only network IP	192.168.56.104
	Node action	Master, Node, Etcd
	CPU	6 core
	RAM	12 GB
Node 2	Node name	node05
	Host-only network IP	192.168.56.105
	Node action	Master, Node, Etcd
	CPU	6 core
	RAM	16 GB
Node 3	Node name	node06
	Host-only network IP	192.168.56.106
	Node action	Master, Node, Etcd
	CPU	6 core
	RAM	12 GB

4.2   K-PSO and Basic PSO Algorithm Comparison Experiment

To verify the validity and execution efficiency of the K-PSO algorithm, the K-PSO algorithm formed by the improved basic PSO algorithm is compared with the basic PSO algorithm. By adding a new scheduling strategy to the source code of Kubernetes, the K-PSO algorithm and the basic PSO algorithm are applied to the scheduling process of Kubernetes.

To test the performance of the k-PSO algorithm and the basic PSO algorithm, we add 20 Kubernetes working nodes, and the configure of the working nodes is shown as Table 2.

We create 40 Hadoop low-load clusters with 1 master and 2 slaves at a time by script, that is, create 120 pod requests, set the number of particles in the particle swarm to 120, and set the maximum number of iterations to 100. Basic PSO algorithm set ω to 0.4, both c_1 and c_2 are set to 2.5. For the K-PSO algorithm, each parameter is set as Table 3. The basic PSO algorithm and the K-PSO algorithm both use the pod and node matching function of K-PSO-2 as the P_{ij} item in the fitness function.

Table 2. Work node configuration

Hard disk	100 GB
Operating system	CentOS7.5 Minimal
CPU	2 core
RAM	3 GB
Host-only network (manual)	192.168.56.0/24
Nat network (DHCP)	10.0.2.0/16
Docker version	18.03.1-ce

Table 3. K-PSO algorithm parameter configuration

θ	3.4	μ	0.38
ω_{max}	0.9	γ	log 23
ω_{max}	0.4	CPU^{PH}	0.95
c_{1-min}	0.01	MEM^{PH}	0.90
c_{1-max}	2.5	CPU^{PL}	0.75
c_{2-min}	0.01	MEM^{PL}	0.70
c_{2-max}	2.5	W^3	[0.4, 0.3, 0.3]
K	120	t_{max}	100

Under the condition that $t_{max} = 100$, the fitness curve of basic PSO algorithm and K-PSO algorithm is shown in Fig. 1. The fitness values of the two have been converged after several rounds of iteration and the fitness results are consistent. However, the K-PSO algorithm completes convergence in the

33rd iteration, and the basic PSO algorithm converges in the 66th iteration, so the K-PSO algorithm converges faster and performs better than the basic PSO algorithm.

The running time of the basic PSO algorithm and the K-PSO algorithm under different iteration rounds is as follows in Fig. 2. Before the 33rd iteration, since the calculation amount of the K-PSO algorithm is slightly larger than the basic PSO algorithm, the time consumption is more than the basic PSO algorithm. After the 33rd iteration, the K-PSO algorithm converges, and the algorithm ends. The basic PSO algorithm needs to go to the 66th iteration to complete the convergence. That is to say, in the actual scheduling process, to ensure that the algorithm must complete convergence to find the optimal solution, the K-PSO algorithm needs to perform at least 33 iterations, and the basic PSO algorithm needs to perform at least 66 iterations. Therefore, the actual running time that the basic PSO algorithm consumes is much more than the K-PSO algorithm. In the actual scheduling process, the K-PSO algorithm can save more scheduling time, thereby reducing the user's waiting time.

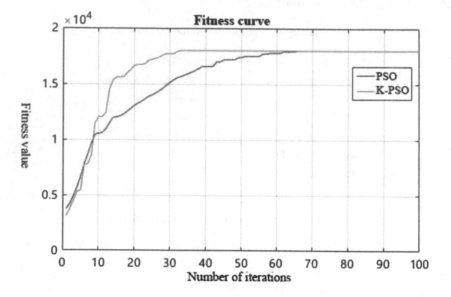

Fig. 1. Basic PSO algorithm and K-PSO algorithm fitness curve.

4.3 K-PSO Scheduling and Comparison of Existing Scheduling Strategies

To verify the feasibility and effectiveness of the K-PSO scheduling strategy, the K-PSO scheduling strategy is compared with the Kube-Scheduler default scheduling strategy, the BalancedQosPriority strategy, the ESS strategy, and the PSO strategy.

Under the above configuration conditions, 20 sets of repeated experiments are performed to test the Kube-Scheduler default policy, the BalancedQosPriority

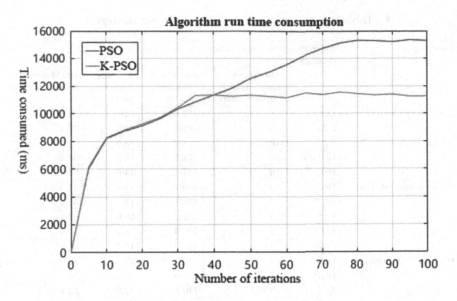

Fig. 2. Algorithm runtime consumption.

policy, the ESS policy, the K-PSO policy, and the PSO. The maximum number of Hadoop clusters that can be carried by the policy, the average I/O performance of the Hadoop cluster and the average computing performance of the Hadoop cluster are averaged as experimental results. Under various load Hadoop cluster tests, the performance of Kube-Scheduler default strategy, BalancedQosPriority strategy, ESS strategy, K-PSO strategy, and PSO strategy is shown as Table 4. From the performance of the Hadoop cluster, with the increase of memory and CPU resources configured for the Hadoop cluster, the Kube-Scheduler default policy, the BalancedQosPriority policy, the ESS policy, the K-PSO policy, and the PSO policy read and write the Hadoop cluster. Performance and computing performance have been greatly improved. In general, K-PSO has a slightly lower read/write performance and computational performance than the Kube-Scheduler default algorithm under various Hadoop loads, but the difference is very small.

From the number of Hadoop clusters accommodated by the Kubernetes cluster, the K-PSO has more Hadoop clusters than the Kube-Scheduler default strategy, the BalancedQosPriority strategy, the ESS strategy, and the PSO strategy. In general, the Kube-Scheduler default strategy and BalancedQosPriority strategy have similar performance for big data applications. ESS strategy, K-PSO strategy, and PSO strategy have similar performance for big data applications. But ESS strategy is a scheduling method that does not increase the new node when the node resource does not reach a certain threshold and does not consider other factors. As a result, the CPU/memory usage of some nodes under the ESS strategy is too high, even exceeding 95%. It may cause the node to lose its responsiveness. Therefore, in terms of resource utilization, the ESS policy,

Table 4. Comparison of various scheduling strategies

Load type	Algorithm strategy	Hadoop cluster test indicators			
		Maximum number of clusters carried	Average read rate (mb/s)	Average write rate (mb/s)	100 M data sorting average time(s)
Hadoop low load	Def	9	377.8	14.1	58.3
	BQP	9	375.3	14.6	58.1
	ESS	10	374.2	13.9	57.5
	K-PSO	12	374.5	14.0	58.0
	PSO	10	374.6	14.0	58.1
Hadoop medium load	Def	4	440.7	18.7	51.2
	BQP	4	438.1	18.1	51.9
	ESS	3	422.9	16.6	52.1
	K-PSO	5	440.9	18.2	51.3
	PSO	4	441.0	18.4	51.1
Hadoop high load	Def	3	466.3	25.8	12.3
	BQP	3	459.9	24.9	12.2
	ESS	3	440.1	22.9	13.1
	K-PSO	4	460.7	24.9	12.5
	PSO	3	462.7	25.8	12.2

K-PSO policy, and PSO policy are superior to the Kube-Scheduler default policy and the BalancedQosPriority policy. However, considering the impact on the normal responsiveness of the node, the K-PSO strategy is better than the ESS strategy. The K-PSO strategy optimizes the PSO parameters, so the K-PSO strategy performs better than the PSO strategy.

It can be determined that under the premise of not reducing the average I/O performance and average computing performance of the Hadoop cluster, the K-PSO algorithm uses the resource utilization rate of the node is about 20% higher than the Kube-Scheduler default policy, the BalancedQosPriority policy, the ESS policy, and the PSO strategy.

4.4   Analysis of Experimental Results

The K-PSO algorithm and the basic PSO algorithm are compared in our experiment. The experimental results show that the K-PSO algorithm converges faster than the basic PSO algorithm and the algorithm runs less time. Then we compared the Kubernetes default scheduling and the K-PSO algorithm. The experimental results show that under the premise of not reducing the average I/O performance and average computing performance of the Hadoop cluster, the resource utilization rate of the K-PSO algorithm is about 20% higher than the existing Kube-Scheduler default strategy, BalancedQosPriority strategy, and ESS strategy.

5   Conclusion

With the rapid development of cloud computing, big data and machine learning have made a great change in software architecture and the ideas for dealing with real problems. The main contribution of this paper is to propose an improved Kubernetes container scheduling algorithm K-PSO algorithm and change the inertia weight and learning factor of the PSO algorithm from static to nonlinear dynamic adjustment according to the operation of the algorithm while adding penalty terms to the particle running speed. The experimental results show that the K-PSO converges faster with the final fitness value. Based on the proposed K-PSO algorithm, the Kubernetes scheduling strategy is optimized and implemented on the Kubernetes platform. The experimental results show that the utilization of cluster CPU and memory resources is greatly improved.

Acknowledgment. This work is supported by National Natural Science Foundation of China (Grant Nos. 61772205, 61872084), Guangdong Science and Technology Department (Grant No. 2017B010126002), Guangzhou Science and Technology Program key projects (Grant Nos. 201802010010, 201807010052, 201902010040 and 201907010001), Nansha Science and Technology Projects (Grant No. 2017GJ001), Guangzhou Development Zone Science and Technology (Grant No. 2018GH17) and the Fundamental Research Funds for the Central Universities, SCUT (Grant No. 2019ZD26).

References

1. Felter, W, Ferreira, A, Rajamony, R, et al.: An updated performance comparison of virtual machines and linux containers. In: 2015 IEEE International Symposium on Performance Analysis of Systems and Software (ISPASS), pp. 171–172. IEEE (2015)
2. Alfonso, C.D., Calatrava, A., Moltó, G.: Container-based virtual elastic clusters. J. Syst. Softw. **127**, 1–11 (2017)
3. Li, Z., Zhang, Y., Liu, Y.: Towards a full-stack DevOps environment (platform-as-a-service) for cloud-hosted applications. Tsinghua Sci. Technol. **22**(1), 1–9 (2017)
4. Pahl, C., Brogi, A., Soldani, J., et al.: Cloud container technologies: a state-of-the-art review. IEEE Trans. Cloud Comput. **99**, 1–1 (2017)
5. Gandhi, A., Thota, S., Dube, P., et al.: Autoscaling for Hadoop clusters. In: 2016 IEEE International Conference on Cloud Engineering (IC2E). IEEE (2016)
6. Khan, M., Jin, Y., Li, M., et al.: Hadoop performance modeling for job estimation and resource provisioning. IEEE Trans. Parallel Distrib. Syst. 99, 441–454 (2015)
7. Naik, N.: Docker container-based big data processing system in multiple clouds for everyone. In: 2017 IEEE International Systems Engineering Symposium (ISSE), pp. 1–7. IEEE (2017)
8. Xu, Z., Yang, H.: Quality of service based on Kubernetes scheduler. Softw. Guide **17**(11), 77–80 (2018)
9. Zhang, K., Peng, L., Lu, X., et al.: Kubernetes elastic scheduling on open source cloud. Comput. Technol. Dev. **29**(02), 115–120 (2019)
10. Weiwei, L., Dejun, Q.: Review of cloud computing resource scheduling. Comput. Sci. **39**(10), 1–6 (2012)

11. Fernández-Baca, D.: Allocating modules to processors in a distributed system. IEEE Trans. Softw. Eng. **15**(11), 1427–1436 (1989)
12. Bernstein, D.: Containers and cloud: from LXC to Docker to Kubernetes. IEEE Cloud Comput. **1**(3), 81–84 (2014)
13. Hindman, B., Konwinski, A., Zaharia, M., et al.: Mesos: a platform for fine-grained resource sharing in the data center. In: NSDI, vol. 11, no. 2011, p. 22 (2011)
14. Jie, L., Guangzhong, L.: Research on automated container deployment of Hadoop distributed cluster. Comput. Appl. Res. **33**(11), 3404–3407 (2016)
15. Liu, B., Li, P., Lin, W., et al.: A new container scheduling algorithm based on multi-objective optimization. Soft Comput. **22**(23), 7741–7752 (2018)
16. Lin, W., Wang, Z.: Docker cluster scheduling strategy based on genetic algorithm. J. S. China Univ. Technol. (Nat. Sci. Ed.) **46**(3), 19 (2018)
17. Sujana, J.A.J., Revathi, T., Priya, T.S.S., et al.: Smart PSO-based secured scheduling approaches for scientific workflows in cloud computing. Soft Comput. **23**(5), 1745–1765 (2019)
18. Zhou, Z., Chang, J., Hu, Z., et al.: A modified PSO algorithm for task scheduling optimization in cloud computing. Concurr. Comput. Pract. Exp. **30**(24), e4970. 3404–3407 (2018)
19. Adhikari, M., Srirama, S.N.: Multi-objective accelerated particle swarm optimization with a container-based scheduling for Internet-of-Things in cloud environment. J. Netw. Comput. Appl. **137**, 35–61 (2019)
20. Zhang, L., Tang, Y., Hua, C., et al.: A new particle swarm optimization algorithm with adaptive inertia weight based on Bayesian techniques. Appl. Soft Comput. **28**, 138–149 (2015)
21. Nobile, M.S., Cazzaniga, P., Besozzi, D., et al.: Fuzzy self-tuning PSO: a settings-free algorithm for global optimization. Swarm Evol. Comput. **39**, 70–85 (2018)
22. Taherkhani, M., Safabakhsh, R.: A novel stability-based adaptive inertia weight for particle swarm optimization. Appl. Soft Comput. **38**, 281–295 (2016)
23. Deng, W., Yao, R., Zhao, H., et al.: A novel intelligent diagnosis method using optimal LS-SVM with improved PSO algorithm. Soft Comput. **23**(7), 2445–2462 (2019)
24. Clerc, M.: The swarm and the queen: towards a deterministic and adaptive particle swarm optimization. In: Proceedings of the 1999 Congress on Evolutionary Computation-CEC99 (Cat. No. 99TH8406). IEEE (2002)

Cloud and Security

A Secure Density Peaks Clustering Algorithm on Cloud Computing

Shang Ci[1,2], Liping Sun[1,2(✉)], Xiaoqing Liu[1,2], Tingli Du[1,2], and Xiaoyao Zheng[1,2]

[1] School of Computer and Information, Anhui Normal University, Wuhu, China
cs_xxy1994@163.com, slp620@163.com, xqliu7788@163.com,
2260436487@qq.com, zxiaoyao@ahnu.edu.cn
[2] Anhui Provincial Key Laboratory of Network and Information Security,
Wuhu 241002, China

Abstract. Cloud computing provides users with the convenience of data outsourcing computing at risk of privacy leakage, and clustering algorithms have high computational overhead when dealing with large datasets. Aiming at the above problems, this paper presents a security density peak clustering algorithm based on grid in hybrid cloud environment. First, the client uses the homomorphic encryption method to build the encrypted objects with user datasets. Second, the client uploads the encrypted objects to the cloud servers to implement the security protocols proposed in this paper. Finally, the cloud servers return the perturbation clustering results to the client to eliminate the disturbance. In the proposed scheme, only encryption and removing perturbation are performed on the client, ensuring that the client has lower computational complexity. Security analysis and experimental results show that the scheme proposed in this paper can improve the efficiency and accuracy of clustering algorithm under the premise of protecting user privacy.

Keywords: Cloud computing security · Density peaks clustering algorithm · Data mining · Privacy preserving · Homomorphic encryption

1 Introduction

With the rapid development of information technology, such as cloud computing, Internet of Things and social networks, industrial Internet of Things (IIoT) has led the era of intelligent enterprises and industries [1]. As an important research field of data mining, clustering aims at assigning objects to different junior high schools according to similarity. Big data usually contains a large number of samples and has very high dimensional attributes, which has high computational complexity in cluster analysis. Today, more and more enterprises are storing data in cloud servers, and their powerful computing power makes it easy to process big data [2, 3].

Because cloud service providers can be malicious, users' privacy may be compromised when sensitive data is outsourced directly to cloud servers for computation [4, 5]. In order to protect the security of user data in the cloud servers, the client encrypts the private data before outsourcing. That is, the client encrypts the data and

© Springer Nature Switzerland AG 2019
J. Vaidya et al. (Eds.): CSS 2019, LNCS 11982, pp. 533–541, 2019.
https://doi.org/10.1007/978-3-030-37337-5_43

outsourcing it to the cloud server. The cloud server calculates it directly on the ciphertext, and the cloud server returns it to the client, who decrypts it. During this process, the cloud server does not learn the middle of user sensitive data and computation, thus the security can be guaranteed. Zhang *et al.* [6] presented a privacy preserving HOCFS (PPHOCFS) method utilizing BGV encryption scheme. However, because some operations cannot be realized, such as comparison and division, only the similarity is computed on ciphertext, whereas CFS is still calculated on plaintext. To protect the original data stored in the cloud, Liu *et al.* [7] proposed a privacy-preserving K-means clustering algorithm using its own homomorphic cryptosystem for outsourced databases. It can preserve both data privacy and query privacy, but does not protect data access patterns. Rao *et al.* [8] proposed the privacy-preserving K-means clustering algorithm using the Paillier cryptosystem that can guarantee the confidentiality of the outsourced databases. However, it requires a high computation cost due to the usage of a bit array-based comparison.

Aiming at aforementioned challenges, a security density peak clustering algorithm (SDPC) based on grid in hybrid cloud environment is presented in this paper. The clustering centers are quickly found through the idea of grid, and the efficiency of density peak clustering algorithm is improved. At the same time, to ensure the security of user data, the client uses the homomorphic encryption scheme to encrypt the privacy data and upload it to the cloud server. Using public and private cloud operations reduces user computing overhead. Public and private clouds make up a hybrid cloud with public cloud computing capabilities and private cloud security. This paper uses the Paillier cryptosystem, the private cloud generates the public key *pk* and the private key *sk*, and publishes the *pk* to the users and the public cloud. Users use *pk* to encrypt private data, while the public cloud carries out secure clustering operations. In practical applications, public cloud providers are usually well-established IT companies like Microsoft and Google, whereas private cloud providers are usually special institutions under the government supervision. For the sake of reputation and commercial interests, a collusion between them is highly unlikely and they will not maliciously steal user information.

2 Preliminaries

The symbols used in this paper and their semantic meanings are as follows. n: number of samples; q: dimension of samples; a: original data; $[[a]]$: encrypted data; μ: edge length of grid; $[[\mu]]$: encrypted edge length of grid; ρ_i: local density of sample i; δ_i: distance from sample i to the local density is larger than its nearest sample j; $[[\rho_i]]$: encrypted local density of sample i; $[[\delta_i]]$: encrypted distance from sample i to the local density is larger than its nearest sample j; α: probability parameter; λ: magnification factor.

This paper used the Euclidean distance as the criterion for representing distance of sample points $a_i = (a_{i1}, a_{i2}, \ldots, a_{iq})$ and $a_j = (a_{j1}, a_{j2}, \ldots, a_{jq})$, where $1 \leq i \leq n$, $1 \leq j \leq n$.

$$d_{(i,j)} = [(a_{i1} - a_{j1})^2 + (a_{i2} - a_{j2})^2 + \ldots + (a_{iq} - a_{jq})^2]^{\frac{1}{2}}$$
$$= [\sum_{m=1}^{q} (a_{im} - a_{jm})^2]^{\frac{1}{2}} \tag{1}$$

Definition 1. Assume there is a dataset with size $n \times q$ and the data of the ith, mth dimension is a_{im}, where $1 \leq i \leq n$, $1 \leq m \leq q$. We partition the data space by dividing each dimension into equal and disjoint grid cells and the edge length μ of each grid is defined as follows:

$$\mu = \alpha \left(\prod_{m=1}^{q} \frac{a_{1m} + a_{2m} + \ldots + a_{nm}}{n} \right)^{\frac{1}{q}} \tag{2}$$

α is the parameter used to adjust the edge of each grid and n is the number of the data points in the dataset.

Definition 2. Assume there is a q-dimensional dataset $X = \{x_1, x_2, \ldots, x_n\}$ and the data space is divided into $\{\theta_1, \theta_2, \ldots, \theta_k\}$ grid cells according to **Definition 1**. Then the data points are mapped into corresponding grid cells, the density of the cell is:

$$\rho_{\theta_i} = count(G_{\theta_i}) \tag{3}$$

Where function count() represents the number of points in the gird cell whose grid number is G_{θ_i}.

3 Basic Security Primitives

3.1 Existing Security Protocol

The existing security protocols involved in SDPC are listed in Table 1, including secure multiplication (SM) [9], secure comparison (SC) [10], secure division 1 (SD1) [11] and secure sort (SSOAT$_k$) [12].

Table 1. Table of existing security protocol.

Protocol	Definition
Secure multiplication	$SM([[a]], [[b]]) \rightarrow [[a \cdot b]]$
Secure comparison	$SC([[a]], [[b]]) \rightarrow [[a \geq b]]$
Secure division 1	$SD1([[a]], b) \rightarrow [[qu_1]]$
Secure sort	$SSOAT_k([[a_1]], \ldots, [[a_n]], k) \rightarrow ([[a'_1]], \ldots, [[a'_k]])$

3.2   The Proposed Protocol

In order to implement the algorithm, a set of protocols is proposed as a standard. In addition, in order to control floating point precision, an amplification factor is added to the protocol. C_1 and C_2 denote the public cloud and private cloud, respectively.

(1) **SP Protocol:** As there is no homomorphic exponentiation operations in the Paillier cryptosystem, it can not directly support the secure computation between objects. In view of the above problems, this paper proposes a safe exponentiation method, the whole process is shown as Algorithm 1.

Algorithm 1: SP Protocol.

Input: C_1 has $[[\lambda_p a]]$ and b, C_2 has sk

Output: Encrypted exponential result $[[\lambda_p a^b]]$ only to C_1

C_1

1:   Select the top k maxima $m_1, m_2, ..., m_k$ from all possible values of b

2:   $i \leftarrow 1$

3:   **Repeat**

4:   Compute $[[\lambda_p a^{m_i}]]$, $[[\lambda_p m_i]]$

5:   $i \leftarrow i+1$

6:   **Until** $i > k$

C_1, C_2

7:   $i \leftarrow 1$

8:   **Repeat**

9:   $[[c_i]] \leftarrow SC([[\lambda_p b]], [[\lambda_p m_i]])$

10: $[[\lambda_p s_i]] \leftarrow SM([[c_i]], [[\lambda_p a^{m_i}]])$

11: $i \leftarrow i+1$

12: **Until** $i > k$

C_1

13: $[[\lambda_p a^b]] \leftarrow \prod_{i=1}^{k} [[\lambda_p s_i]]$

---

(2) **SED Protocol:** In order to safely calculate the distance between objects, SED protocol is proposed, the goal of which is to calculate $[[\lambda_0 d_{(i,j)}]]$ safely. The basic idea of SED is shown in Algorithm 2.

Algorithm 2: SED Protocol.

Input: C_1 has encrypted data $[[\lambda_0 a_{im}]]$ and $[[\lambda_0 a_{jm}]]$, where $1 \le m \le q$. C_2 has sk

Output: Encrypted distance result $[[\lambda_0 d_{(i,j)}]]$ only to C_1

C_1, C_2

1: $i \leftarrow 1$
2: **Repeat**
3: $j \leftarrow 1$
4: **Repeat**
5: $[[\lambda_0 (a_{im} - a_{jm})]] \leftarrow [[\lambda_0 a_{im}]] * [[\lambda_0 a_{jm}]]^{N-1}$
6: $[[\lambda_0^2 d_m]] \leftarrow SM([[\lambda_0 (a_{im} - a_{jm})]], [[\lambda_0 (a_{im} - a_{jm})]])$
7: $[[\lambda_0 d_m]] \leftarrow SD_1([[\lambda_0^2 d_m]], \lambda_0)$
8: $j \leftarrow j+1$
9: **Until** $j > n$
10: $i \leftarrow i+1$
11: **Until** $i > n$

C_1

12: $[[\lambda_0 d_{(i,j)}]] \leftarrow \sum_{m=1}^{q} [[\lambda_0 d_m]]$

---

4 Algorithm Description

4.1 Security Density Peak Clustering Algorithm Based on Grid

This section describes secure density peak clustering algorithm (SDPC) grid-based in hybrid clouds. By using the algorithm proposed in this paper, cloud computing is used to securely provide high quality clustering services without revealing any private information.

In this algorithm, C_1 holds private input $[[a_1]], \ldots, [[a_n]]$, and C_2 holds sk. The goal of the SDPC is to compute encrypted clustering result $[[cl]]$ without revealing any information about n objects to C_1 and C_2. At the end, only C_1 knows the final result $[[cl]]$.

Algorithm 3: SDPC.

Input: C_1 has encrypted data $[[a_1]],...,[[a_n]]$, C_2 has sk, the screening ratio: r.

Output: Encrypted clustering result $[[cl]]$ only to C_1.

C_1, C_2

1: Calculate the distance $[[d_{(i,j)}]]$ from all the encrypted data

2: Calculate the edge length μ of each grid

3: Map the encrypted data $[[a_1]],...,[[a_n]]$ into the corresponding grid cells which taken by **Definition 1**

4: Count the density ρ_{θ_i} for each grid cell accoring to formula (3) and sort them according to secure sort protocol

5: Screen the encrypted data in first $r\%$ 'dense' grids based on the screening ratio r, and remove the other encrypted data points to form a new encrypted dataset $A = \{A_1, A_2,..., A_t\}$ for finding cluster centers

6: Calculate the $[[\rho_i]]$ and $[[\delta_i]]$ for each data point in dataset A according to $[[d_{(i,j)}]]$

7: Select cluster centers with larger $[[\rho_i]]$ and $[[\delta_i]]$ based on decision graph

8: Assign the remaining data points in dataset A to the class of nearest point with equal or higher density

9: Assign the $n-t$ data points which removed in step 5 to the nearest classes according to the 'nearest neighbor' principle

10: Return the encrypted clustering result $[[cl]]$

4.2 Security Analysis

The security of the SDPC method can be proved by using the semi-honest model in secure two-party computation, and the users are not involved in the specific calculation of the algorithm. Both the public cloud C_1 and the private cloud C_2 in the algorithm follow the rules of each protocol, but they all try to infer the user's private information during the execution of the protocols. Since all intermediate and final results of the algorithm are protected using the formal Paillier cryptosystem, C_1 cannot obtain any private information. At the same time, the output of each protocol is a ciphertext that only C_1 knows. In addition, although C_2 can use the private key sk to decrypt intermediate results, it can only see random values or disturbed user data. Because each step of the protocols in this paper uses homomorphic encryption attribute or properly verified security classic protocols, it is claimed that the proposed SDPC method is completely secure based on the composition theorem [13].

4.3 Complexity Analysis

This section combines the characteristics of cloud computing cost and semi-integrity hybrid cloud security framework to theoretically analyze the computational and communication costs of the proposed scheme. Let the number of elements of a dataset be m, where the number of zero elements is m_0, while the number of nonzero elements is m_1, and the number of the object be n.

Computation Cost: The computational complexity of the client is $O(m_1 n)$.

According to the SDPC, the computation cost of the cloud T consists of the cost of secure computing SED and the cost of SDPC T_{SDPC}, which is defined as formula (4).

$$T = T_{SED} + T_{SDPC} \tag{4}$$

where time complexity T_{SED} is $O((m^2 - m_0^2)n^2)$, and time T_{SDPC} complexity is $O(rn^2 + k(n - t))$. Therefore, the total computation T is $O((m^2 - m_0^2)n^2 + rn^2 + k(n - t))$.

5   Performance Evaluation

For performance analysis, we do our experiment on Intel Xeon CPU E5 2620, 2.0 GHz and 4-GB physical memory. We considered the performance and time efficiency of the typical clustering algorithm and the comparability of this study, and compared and analysed the proposed SDPC algorithm with K-means algorithm [14] and DPC algorithm [15]. The datasets used for our experiment from the UCI machine learning library. The first Iris dataset consists of 150 records with 4 attributes. The second Adult dataset consists of 32561 records with 14 attributes.

In order to measure the influence of dataset size on running time, the client encrypts a quarter, half, three-fourth, and all of the samples of the datasets. The running time is shown in the Fig. 1. The running time of the SDPC algorithm is lower than K-means algorithms, and no significant increase is observed when compared with the original DPC algorithm.

For the two aforementioned datasets, the experimental results of SDPC algorithm and the comparison algorithm are shown in Table 2. As shown in Table 2, by using two evaluation metrics ACC and F-measure, to evaluate the clustering results, our proposed algorithm outperforms other algorithms on an average; this shows that SDPC algorithm produces more accurate clustering centers. For the Iris dataset, the ACC

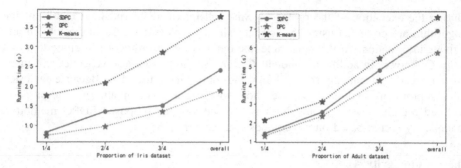

Fig. 1. Running times of comparison algorithms on two datasets.

index of SDPC algorithm is 52.6% higher than that of DPC algorithm. For the Adult dataset, the F-measure index of SDPC algorithm is 41.7% higher than that of *K*-means algorithm.

Table 2. Experimental results of different algorithms on datasets.

Datasets	Algorithms	ACC	F-measure
Iris	*K*-means	0.793	0.783
	DPC	0.576	0.712
	SDPC	0.879	0.867
Adult	*K*-means	0.653	0.521
	DPC	0.694	0.614
	SDPC	0.801	0.738

6   Conclusion

Aiming to provide clustering service for big data mining applications securely and efficiently, this paper proposes a secure density peak clustering algorithm grid-based in hybrid clouds. In this algorithm, all computing tasks are performed on the cloud without exposing or inferring any sensitive information, and clustering centers can be quickly found. This method not only improves efficiency, but also preserves user privacy. In the end, the performances of the proposed SDPC method are evaluated on two datasets in terms of clustering accuracy and efficiency. In our future studies, we will consider the secure method of other clustering algorithms and apply them to practical problems.

Acknowledgment. This work is supported by the National Natural Science Foundation of China under Grant 61602009 and Grant 61672039, and the Anhui Provincial Natural Science Foundation of China under Grant 1808085MF172.

References

1. Yin, S., Kaynak, O.: Big data for modern industry: challenge and trends. Proc. IEEE **103**(2), 143–146 (2015)
2. Armbrust, M., Fox, A., Griffith, R.: A view of cloud computing. Commun. ACM **53**(4), 50–58 (2010)
3. Fang, S.: An integrated approach to snowmelt flood forecasting in water resource management. IEEE Trans. Ind. Inform. **10**(1), 548–558 (2014)
4. Ma, M., He, D., Kumar, N., Choo, K.K., Chen, J.: Certificateless searchable public key encryption scheme for industrial internet of things. IEEE Trans. Ind. Inform. **14**(2), 759–767 (2018)
5. Esposito, C., Castiglione, A., Martini, B., Choo, K.K.: Cloud manufacturing: security, privacy, and forensic concerns. IEEE Cloud Comput. **3**(4), 16–22 (2016)
6. Zhang, Q., Yang, L.T., Chen, Z., Fan, Y.B.: PPHOCFS: privacy preserving high-order CFS algorithm on the cloud for clustering multimedia data. ACM Trans. Multimed. Comput. Commun. Appl. **12**(4), 66:1–66:15 (2016)
7. Liu, D., Bertino, E., Yi, X.: Privacy of outsourced k-means clustering. In: Proceedings of the 9th ACM Symposium on Information, Computer and Communications Security (ICCS), pp. 123–134 (2014)
8. Rao, F.-Y., Samanthula, B.K., Bertino, E., Yi, X., Liu, D.: Privacy-preserving and outsourced multi-user k-means clustering. In: IEEE Conference on Collaboration and Internet Computing (CIC), pp. 80–89 (2015)
9. Samanthula, B.K., Elmehdwi, Y., Jiang, W.: K-nearest neighbor classification over semantically secure encrypted relational data. IEEE Trans. Knowl. Data Eng. **27**(5), 1261–1273 (2015)
10. Bost, R., Popa, R.A., Tu, S., Goldwasser, S.: Machine learning classification over encrypt-ed data. In: Proceedings of 22nd Annual Network and Distributed System Security Symposium, pp. 8–11 (2015)
11. Veugen, T.: Encrypted integer division and secure comparison. Int. J. Appl. Crypt. **3**(2), 166–180 (2014)
12. Zhao, Y.L., Yang, L.T., Sun, J.Y.: A secure high-order CFS algorithm on clouds for industrial internet of things. IEEE Trans. Ind. Inform. **14**(8), 3766–3774 (2018)
13. Goldreich, O.: Foundations of Cryptography. Basic Applications. Cambridge University Press, Cambridge (2004)
14. Macqueen, J.: Some methods for classification and analysis of multivariate observations. In: Proceedings of the 5th Berkeley Symposium on Mathematical Statistics and Probability (BSMSP), pp. 281–297 (1967)
15. Rodriguez, A., Laio, A.: Clustering by fast search and find of density peaks. Science **344** (6191), 1492–1496 (2014)

Research on Cloud Computing Security Problems and Protection Countermeasures

Xiani Fan[1]($\boxtimes$), Jiayu Yao[1], and Ning Cao[2]

[1] School of Information, Beijing Wuzi University, Beijing, China
fxn0517@163.com, 1127893733@qq.com
[2] School of Internet of Things, Wuxi Commercial Vocational and Technical College,
Wuxi, China
ning.cao2008@hotmail.com

Abstract. In recent years, the Chinese government has attached great importance to the development and application of cloud computing industry, and issued a series of policies to encourage and regulate the development of cloud computing. The widespread use of cloud computing brings us both opportunities and challenges. This article will from the overview of cloud computing, the narrative model and characteristics, combined with the development of cloud computing and the basic structure, analysis of the main safety problems of cloud computing, it puts forward the model of elastic cloud security system, and puts forward some protective measures, so as to improve the security of cloud computing, cloud computing security applications, facilitating the orderly development of the role, in response to a cloud computing security issues and risks emerge in endlessly.

Keywords: Cloud computing security · Safety system · Protective countermeasures

1 Introduction

The emergence and development of cloud computing are profoundly changing the information construction mode and bringing opportunities to the innovation of technology application and service mode. The cloud computing industry is considered to be the fourth IT industry revolution after mainframe computers, personal computers and the Internet [1]. Cloud computing is a new computing model that integrates virtual technology, distributed computing, parallel computing and other technologies, aiming to realize the virtualization of cloud services and large-scale economic effects. With the gradual maturity of cloud computing technology, cloud computing technology has been adopted at home and abroad to reduce the investment scale of IT infrastructure and improve the utilization rate of resources.

Supported by organization x.

However, with the rapid development and promotion of cloud computing, while cloud computing brings convenience, its security issues bring great challenges to cloud service providers and users, and bring new security technology risks. In March 2018, for example, amazon experienced a storm-induced cloud outage that affected more than 240 online services [2]. In June 2018, aliyun experienced a massive failure due to a programmer disabling internal IP while performing an update operation. Frequent cloud security incidents sound alarm bells for cloud computing users. How to design the cloud computing security system and protection countermeasures and effectively improve the security protection ability is an important topic that urgently needs to be studied at present.

2   Overview of Cloud Computing

2.1   The Concept of Cloud Computing

Cloud computing is the pattern of increase, use, and interaction of internet-based related services, often involving the provision of dynamically scalable and often virtualized resources over the Internet. The cloud is a metaphor for the Internet. In the past, the cloud was often used to represent the telecommunications network in the figure, and later it was also used to represent the abstraction of the Internet and the underlying infrastructure [3]. As a result, cloud computing could even allow you to experience 10 trillion calculations per second, the kind of computing power that can simulate nuclear explosions, predict climate change and predict market trends. Users access the data center through computers, laptops, mobile phones and other means, and carry out calculations according to their own needs.

There are many definitions of cloud computing. There are at least 100 possible explanations for what cloud computing really is [4]. The widely accepted definition at this stage is the national institute of standards and technology (NIST): Cloud computing is a kind of pay by usage pattern, this pattern provides available, convenient, on-demand network access, enter the configurable computing resources Shared pool (resources including network, servers, storage, applications and services), these resources can be quick to provide, just in the management of the very few and or little interaction with service providers. In layman's terms, cloud computing is computing through a large number of computing resources in the cloud, such as: the user sends instructions to the cloud computing service provider through his computer, the "nuclear explosion" calculation through a large number of servers provided by the service provider, and then the results are returned to the user.

2.2   Cloud Computing Model

The Service Model. According to the service model, cloud computing can be divided into three types: software as a service (SaaS), platform as a service (PaaS) and infrastructure as a service (Iaas). SaaS: cloud computing users

(CSU), according to their own needs to apply for and deploy applications, users need only to simple configuration and the application does not need to know about and management program used by the software from where, where is the underlying hardware, thus reduces the users in such aspects as hardware purchase and maintenance, software development costs. PaaS: users according to their own requirements to apply for the corresponding computing platform to start and deploy their applications, they only need to manage your own application development process, without the need to understand and manage the hardware facilities and operation, the development platform of information, thus reducing the cost of the hardware and the operating platform, is effective for the development of complex software. IaaS: users can apply for storage, network bandwidth and other computing facilities in the cloud to run their own systems and programs according to their actual needs, without having to buy expensive hardware or find full-time personnel to manage and maintain these devices, which can greatly reduce the cost of enterprises [5].

Deployment Model. A private cloud is a cloud environment that is independently built and used by an organization/enterprise and does not share any resources with other enterprises or organizations; Public cloud is a cloud environment provided by cloud providers. Enterprises or users using public cloud share the resources owned by cloud providers. A community cloud is a cloud environment created by organizations that have similar needs and accept Shared infrastructure. Hybrid cloud refers to the cloud environment built by two or more cloud deployment modes, and the portability of data and applications is its key point of concern.

2.3   Six Characteristics of Cloud Computing

Compared with traditional computing models, cloud computing has the following six characteristics:

(1) Resource pooling: cloud computing service provider (CSP) USES virtualization technology to dynamically allocate a large number of computing resources to users in need.
(2) On-demand self-service: CSU can apply for and use applicable computing power and services at any time of need.
(3) Metered services: self-service on demand is metering, or billing. CSP realizes effective bill management by measuring the resource usage of CSU.
(4) Extensive network access: after cloud computing, the service capacity is provided through the network, and the service can be extended to different types of client platforms, such as mobile phones and tablet computers.
(5) Fast resiliency and scalability: CSU USES resources consistent with business requirements, avoiding degradation of service quality or waste of resources due to server performance overload or redundancy. For CSU, the required services, resources and infrastructure can be provided dynamically according to the changes of CSU requirements.

(6) Multi-tenancy: allows virtualized resources to be leased to multiple csus at the same time.

The six characteristics of cloud computing are interrelated and interactive. Resource pooling and multi-renting are the basis, self-service on demand is the driving force, fast elasticity is the guarantee, billing by quantity is the means, and extensive network access is the way (Fig. 1).

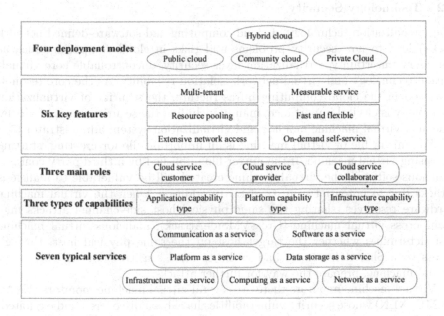

Fig. 1. Cloud computing model

3 Cloud Computing Security Analysis

3.1 Data Security

Cloud storage is one of the core services provided by cloud computing, the user's data is stored in the cloud service provider side, Shared with other users of cloud services provider of storage resources, data of the separation of ownership and control, users rely on cloud service providers to complete its organization, management and maintenance of the data, and security guarantees. First of all, the cloud data of users may include the core technical data, planning or personal privacy information of enterprises and other sensitive contents. In the whole life cycle, the user data includes storage, transmission, processing and destruction. Secondly, the cloud data may be maliciously attacked by other illegal users, or the cloud service provider may arbitrarily delete the data accessed by users with low frequency in violation of their service level agreement (SLA) for some purpose, thus damaging the integrity of the data. Finally, the cloud data of users are generally not backed up locally, and the availability of user data is damaged if the cloud service provider does not have the data redundancy backup and recovery capability after the occurrence of the node failure accidents such as application vulnerability or human error operation in the cloud computing environment [6].

3.2   Technology Security

The virtualization technology of cloud computing and software-defined network (SDN) lead to new security problems and risks in cloud computing, such as boundary uncertainty, virtualization layer security, uncontrollable core virtualization technology and virtual network isolation reliability. As the core technology used in the cloud computing infrastructure, the security of virtualization technology is of vital importance, mainly including the security issues of virtual machine, virtual machine monitor and virtualization system administrator [7].

The mirror file of virtual machine is an important file for creating, starting and using virtual machine. If the mirror file published by a third party contains malicious software, the virtual machine created will be vulnerable to malicious attacks due to potential security risks. In addition, when the virtual machine hardware resources, sharing the same physical host side-channel attacks may occur cross virtual machine (CrossVMSideAttack), malicious virtual machine first determines whether the target host on the same physical host, through access to a Shared hardware and cache to steal sensitive data in the target virtual machine, prepare the way for further attacks.

Virtual machine monitors there are several virtual machine monitors (KVM, QEMU, XEN) whose security vulnerabilities have been discovered and exploited, causing two major types of security problems. First, the right to attack. Ordinary users of virtual machines may obtain root privileges of virtual machines through this type of vulnerability. Further, it is possible to have virtual machine escapes, where an attacker can control the host to execute arbitrary code. Virtual machines in the virtualized environment can obtain higher permissions than themselves by taking advantage of the monitor vulnerability of virtual machines. For example, ordinary users of XEN virtual machines can use the vulnerability cve-2014-7155 to load their own interrupt descriptor table, causing virtual machines to go down and obtain root permissions. Second, denial of service attack. Physical resources are forcibly occupied by a virtual machine, and the host machine and the resident virtual machine cannot run normally. For example, KVM virtual machine can maintain high CPU utilization rate by taking advantage of vulnerability cve-2015-6815, resulting in virtual machine denial of service.

In the cloud computing environment of the virtualization system management platform, the cloud administrator manages the data center infrastructure (such as physical host, virtual machine, storage, etc.) through the virtualization system management platform. If there is no reasonable division of authority, the cloud administrator can use privileges to illegally invade the virtual machine or steal the user sensitive data. Public cloud computing environment according to the specifications, the network bandwidth or CPU usually total run time of the virtual machine as elastic computing charge indicators, such as an attacker can use virtualization layer scheduling mechanism of the defects, such as when the scheduler technology has not been successfully, make the system management platform testing the above fee index usage, wrongly, that implementation of service attacks.

3.3   Application Security

Security issues have become the main bottleneck restricting the rise of SaaS service model. SaaS provides users with various applications such as document editing software, web page operating system and content management system through the Internet. In addition to the above data security, the main security issues faced by cloud applications include vulnerabilities in the applications themselves, data isolation, and security attacks against cloud applications. Under the traditional computing mode, the software is deployed in the user's data center, and the physical resources, applications and data are managed and controlled by the user. However, in the SaaS service mode, the application used by users is deployed by the service provider, and whether the vulnerability existing in the application itself is handled timely depends on the service provider. In addition, the application data of users are stored in the database of the service provider, and the data of multiple tenants may be stored in the same data table, with poor data isolation. For example, in recent years, many cloud computing platforms such as Google application engine have witnessed botnet attacks, which have caused huge losses to both cloud service providers and tenants.

3.4   Other Safety Issues

CSU management issues: because internal users have access privileges to resources, malicious users are more destructive than external security attacks, causing more serious security problems. The access control policy of CSP determines the effectiveness of CSU management [8].

Authorization management problem: once authorization is successful, CSU becomes a legitimate authorized user. Failure of authorization management can directly lead to unauthorized access of cloud services and even confidential data.

SLA management issues: service level agreements (slas) are the basic security protocols that ensure that the CSU gets the right services. The SLA of cloud computing focuses on ensuring service availability, data integrity, confidentiality, and other aspects of security.

In addition to the above security issues, cloud computing also has a series of problems, such as unclear authority and responsibility between tenants and cloud service providers, imperfect audit system, and shifting responsibility due to the failure to quickly realize responsibility identification in the event of security incidents.

4   Research on Cloud Computing Security System and Protection Countermeasures

4.1   Establish Elastic Cloud Security System

Cloud computing due to its flexibility, extensibility, virtualization, virtual traffic safety fuzzy boundaries, invisible, and many other features, so in the cloud computing security architecture design is no longer in the traditional security defense is given priority to, but by Gartner proposed adaptive security architecture, according to the national laws and regulations and safety standards, combined with the safety characteristics of cloud computing and cloud security's actual needs, set up a dynamic positive cloud computing security system [9]. In order to cope with the real-time changing information security situation, we should maintain the information security elasticity, enhance the information security event response ability, and ensure that the cloud computing security system is forward-looking and advanced.

Build a Deep and Real-Time Scalable Cloud Security Defense System. Cloud computing environment contains both traditional physical resources and virtual resources, so cloud platform security and system security on the cloud need to be guaranteed at the same time. The security system of cloud computing realizes three layers of defense through the security defense system in depth: the first layer of defense realizes the physical boundary of the cloud platform and the security protection in the north-south direction through the traditional security equipment and appropriate regional division. The second layer of defense is to isolate and control the resources in the cloud through the cloud computing platform's own security mechanism, VPC and security group firewall. Layer 3 defense: through SDN service chain arrangement and east-west security resource pool, east-west security enhancement protection within the cloud is realized. Meanwhile, the dynamic active security system realizes the ability of cooperative defense through the linkage of predictive perception system and continuous monitoring system with the defense system in depth.

Establish a Comprehensive and Continuous Cloud Security Monitoring System. Cloud computing security system based on multiple data sources (including the syslog logs, audit log, security logs, network traffic), a variety of types (including the log and monitoring of the physical resources and virtual resources, and monitoring) of the monitoring data and the audit data for centralized collection, analysis, and continue to find security problems, and can carry on the tracking and traceability of security issues, and will find security problems and security response linkage system, security defense system, in a timely manner to prevent further damage of events, to achieve dynamic positive effect.

Establish a Quick and Timely Emergency Response System. Response is a process in which security risks and threats are discovered, and corresponding security measures are quickly taken to avoid, suppress, remove and recover. The ultimate purpose of the response is to stop the loss, so the response is required to be as fast and effective as possible. In the cloud computing security system, the emergency response system takes the predictive perception system as the foundation, the security defense system and the security monitoring system as the means, and combines the vulnerability scanning equipment and patch management system to respond to and deal with the discovered security events in a timely manner.

Establish a Data-Driven Predictive Perception System. The establishment of the predictive perception system requires the establishment of an internal and external threat intelligence system, which can be used to analyze the development trend of events and conduct situational awareness according to the current situation in the cloud. At the same time, big data technology is used for data analysis and threat tracing, so as to realize the security prediction and perception before the occurrence of security incidents, constantly adjust the security protection strategy according to the security situation, link with the security defense system and security monitoring system, and shut out the security incidents.

4.2   Security Countermeasures for Cloud Computing

Combining the advantages of the cloud computing security architecture based on trusted roots, the cloud computing security architecture based on isolation and the SOA architecture, a manageability, controllable and measurable security architecture based on the evaluation of cloud computing security model is proposed, as shown in Fig. 2. According to the above safety framework and related standard requirements, the following protection points are proposed.

(1) Authentication and permission allocation

Effective authentication and permission allocation is one of the means to avoid security threats such as service hijacking and service abuse. In the specific authentication authorization process, each tenant is usually composed of multiple users. The principal of authentication authorization needs to be applied to a single user level and the object to a single application level.

(2) Isolation and recovery

The isolation mechanism of computing, storage, network and other resources enables tenants not to interfere with each other when using services. More importantly, it ensures the security of tenant data. It is important to note that the cloud service provider should provide the ability to clear the contents of physical resources such as memory and disk when reallocating them to ensure that the data information of the previous tenant cannot be recovered. The recovery mechanism enables users to provide tenants with continuously high availability services in case of failure or attack.

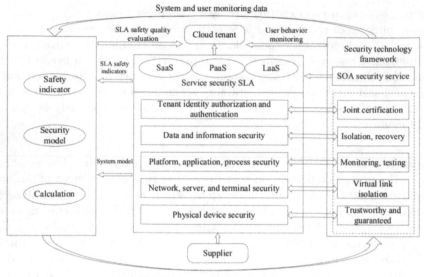

System and user monitoring data

Fig. 2. Cloud computing security architecture

(3) Safety monitoring

In the virtual environment, the administrator through the system security monitoring function to understand the use of physical resources and virtual resources, to ensure the safe operation of the system. Furthermore, dynamic monitoring technology based on virtualization technology can detect intrusion and check malicious code by tracking the information flow between the processes of the virtual machine operating system. In addition, the integrity of system critical files is monitored.

(4) Data protection

In addition to the residual information protection mentioned in the above isolation mechanism, data transmission shall adopt technologies such as data encryption and VPN to ensure the confidentiality of communication behaviors, support encrypted storage services during storage, support data backup and recovery, and provide fine-grained data access control policy Settings.

5   Conclusion

With the rapid development of network technology and 5G, cloud computing is a complex and developing technology in both academic and business circles, and security has always been the biggest threat that affects and restricts the development of cloud computing. In the face of growing complex cloud computing security issues, this article will from the overview of cloud computing, the narrative model and characteristics, combined with the development of cloud computing and the basic structure, analysis of the current main safety problems of cloud computing, it puts forward the model of elastic cloud security system, and puts forward some protective measures, aimed at improving the safety in cloud computing, to promote cloud computing security applications and orderly development.

Acknowledgement. This work was supported in part by the Beijing Great Wall Scholars' Program under Grant CIT and TCD20170317, in part by the Beijing Tongzhou Canal Plan "Leading Talent Plan", in part by the Beijing Collaborative Innovation Center and in part by the Management Science and Engineering High-precision Project.

References

1. Congdong, L., Gang, Q., Tao, C.: A cloud computing security model based on noninterference. Wuhan Univ. J. Nat. Sci. **03**, 1–7 (2019)
2. Hafiz Gulfam, A., Zeeshan, A.: Current cloud computing security concerns from consumer perspective. Mach. Tools Hydraul. **41**(24), 1–5 (2013)
3. Chunming, W., Qianjun, L., Yuwei, L., Qiumei, C., Haifeng, Z.: A survey on cloud security. ZTE Commun. **15**(02), 42–47 (2017)
4. Shengli, Z., Lifa, W., Canghong, J.: A privacy-based SLA violation detection model for the security of cloud computing. Chin. Commun. **14**(09), 155–165 (2017)
5. Xiaoming, Y., et al.: An anomalous behavior detection model in cloud computing. Tsinghua Sci. Technol. **21**(03), 322–332 (2016)
6. Wen-Lung, S.: An evolution, present, and future changes of cloud computing services. J. Electron. Sci. Technol. **13**(01), 54–59 (2015)
7. Chuanlong, L., Jing, G.: Model of security evaluation of infrastructure as a service layer of cloud computing system. J. Donghua Univ. (Engl. Ed.) **32**(02), 323–327 (2015)
8. Wen-Lung, S., Chao-Ming, H.: A unified framework of the cloud computing service model. J. Electron. Sci. Technol. **11**(02), 150–160 (2013)
9. Feng, D., Zhang, M., Zhang, Y., Xu, Z.: Cloud computing security research. J. Softw. **22**, 71–82 (2011)

Research on Logistics Distribution Vehicle Scheduling Algorithm Based on Cloud Computing

Huwei Liu[1]([⊠]), Yan Zhao[1], and Ning Cao[2]

[1] School of Information, Beijing Wuzi University, Beijing, China
liuhuwei@outlook.com, 605671232@qq.com
[2] School of Internet of Things, Wuxi Commercial Vocational
and Technical College, Wuxi, China
ning.cao2008@hotmail.com

Abstract. A logistics distribution vehicle scheduling model under cloud computing environment is established based on the analysis of factors affecting resource scheduling. The order information and logistics distribution vehicle information processing are completed under the framework of cloud computing, so as to obtain the most reasonable logistics distribution plan. To solve the problem of vehicle allocation in logistics distribution, a distribution path algorithm model and a minimum delivery cost algorithm model are established to provide the best strategy for logistics distribution scheme.

Keywords: Cloud computing · Logistics · Vehicle scheduling

1 Introduction

Urban logistics is a necessity for the modern city's normal operation and people's daily life. It is mainly to transport goods within the city to achieve the transfer of goods, meet the needs of the development of the city, and it also brings a series of problems, such as urban road congestion, environmental pollution, etc. Along with the development of e-commerce, low inventory production mode, timely delivery requirements, trends of delivery business to small and complex have brought the unprecedented low efficiency. In daily it needs the help of various aspects to guarantee the normal operation of logistics in developed city. This is a question that needs to be explored, which not only to reduce the bad influence to logistics, but also to raise their working efficiency.

Cloud computing is a derivative of grid computing, distributed computing, and parallel computing, which provides another service that the data in data center will be packaged into a resource available to any customer who needs it. No matter who needs it, it can be purchased. And any customer can seek out their own needs from any cloud computing by following the principle of self-selection. This relatively commercialized operation can achieve a rational allocation of resources and meet various requirements. Customers can also get corresponding services and their satisfaction is generally high. In this process, an algorithm is needed, and what used more commonly are resource allocation strategies and operation scheduling algorithms. Although the traditional

© Springer Nature Switzerland AG 2019
J. Vaidya et al. (Eds.): CSS 2019, LNCS 11982, pp. 552–561, 2019.
https://doi.org/10.1007/978-3-030-37337-5_45

algorithm can meet the needs of customers, it consumes too much resources in this process, which makes the utilization rate and the cost performance not very high.

To solve the problems, we propose a logistics operation scheduling algorithm based on the combination of cloud computing and neural networks. The algorithm, which considers the service quality of the scheduling and user satisfaction, establishes a parameterized processing model to calculates the user's overall satisfaction on various resources and then allocates tasks and system resources to satisfy users' needs and achieve resource balance by fully using improved neural network to optimize vehicle scheduling. The customer's requirements for arrival time and the operating costs of logistics companies must also be considered in the actual distribution process in addition to considering the classification of items and the generation of distribution plans. The expansion of information scale will cause a large amount of calculation, and it is difficult to meet the requirements of rapid response. Therefore, the use of multi-constraint methods combined with heuristic algorithms to optimize the distribution scheduling program in logistics vehicle distribution center can be a very good solution to these problems.

2 Literature Review

Researches on logistics and distribution by domestic and foreign experts and scholars are summarized as follows:

He [1] combined with the status of e-commerce logistics in China, established an intensive logistics distribution system for logistics centers, distribution centers and delivery stations at all levels, and proposed corresponding central-level, regional-level and sub-regional virtual distribution centers. The three-level virtual distribution system of the distribution center eventually established a three-tiered physical distribution network in cities, counties, and rural areas. Yang et al. [2] described the self-operating distribution model. He believed that the self-operating logistics model refers to e-commerce enterprises establishing logistics distribution centers that require their own companies. This is mainly conducive to the company's internal control, and that the products ordered by consumers are sent to the required locations according to the specified time and method. Zhang [3] took e-commerce logistics and the supply and demand of community as the research object, analyzed various forms of the terminal logistics distribution model and proposed various possible cooperation models. He also presented a decision-making strategy for distribution based on three factors of supply and demand and vertical integration. Gu et al. [4] used the vehicle routing problem of large-scale retail stores as the object of research. Firstly, the work balance volume was used as a determinant for the distribution area and a cluster-based two-phase distribution area planning method was used to integrate the multi-vehicle market. The distribution vehicle path optimization problem was transformed into a single-vehicle distribution vehicle path optimization problem, and a hybrid heuristic algorithm was used to solve the vehicle routing problem. The validity and feasibility of the algorithm were verified by case studies. Guan [5] analyzed the existing problems of China's current joint distribution activities, such as resource information, distribution of benefits, etc., and proposed suggestions for the development of e-commerce logistics and joint distribution through such means as government participation and the establishment of a fair interest distribution mechanism.

Wei et al. [6] conducted a specific analysis of which logistics distribution model the company selected, and concluded that the choice of logistics distribution model mainly depended on two factors: One is whether the company has the ability to distribute for itself, and the other is the importance of the logistics and distribution link to the company. Enterprises could choose the logistics distribution model based on the combination of these two factors. Zhang and Li [7] studied how B2C e-commerce companies chose the logistics and distribution model to solve the "last kilometer" distribution problem. Based on the Ballow logistics two-dimension decision model, they established a selection model of the logistics distribution model to solve the logistics matching model through the decision matrix, and proposed a third-party logistics supplier hierarchy model with considering the logistics characteristics in the B2C e-commerce environment. Zhu et al. [8] built a service-oriented vehicle resource collaboration super-network structure model between production and retail. Targeted with the highest profits and minimum carbon emissions, a multi-objective optimization model was established and variational inequalities were given. The solution method, through the case of A and B companies, proved the feasibility and effectiveness of the model and discussed the related influencing factors. Han et al. [9] proposed to solve the "last kilometer" problem through the smart community logistics distribution mode. In the research, the smart community logistics distribution model and the centralized logistics distribution model were established based on intellectual property.

There are more studies on vehicle routing issues. Ding [10] studied the vehicle routing problem of emergency logistics, defined the emergency logistics vehicle routing problem by comparing the emergency logistics with the traditional logistics. He also established a model and gave a genetic algorithm to solve the model. Ma and Li [11] established and solved an end-distribution vehicle path model with limited vehicle capacity, which designed a genetic algorithm with local search capabilities by using the minimum distribution cost as the objective function in order to solve the distribution center's problem of distribution to multiple customers. Yang [12] summed up the characteristics of urban express delivery, taking into account the delivery vehicle model factors and delivery time factors, with the minimum vehicle transportation costs and time penalty costs as the objective function to construct multi-objective vehicle path optimization model with time windows and design genetic algorithm to solve. Zhang [13] mainly focused on self-operated logistics e-commerce companies and considered the traveling salesman problems with profits and stochastic customers (TSPPSC) under consideration of the random probability of customer demand. And she established corresponding mathematical models respectively by dividing it into three types of sub-problems, and provided solving methods to solve the "last mile" distribution problem of e-commerce and logistics enterprises. Zhou et al. [14] set up a two-stage model of site selection-distribution-multi-model vehicle distribution problem based on the last-mile distribution problem of online shopping flow. It was solved based on the simulated annealing algorithm and verified the validity and feasibility of the model by comparison and example simulation.

3 The Model and Its Analysis

3.1 Logistics Resources Scheduling Problem

The Influencing Factors of Logistics Scheduling. With the developing trend of e-commerce and trade globalization, the core goal of logistics service is to meet the customer's needs with the minimum comprehensive cost in the process of logistics distribution, so the logistics dispatch information will grow on a large scale. For a logistics company, generally there are many distribution outlets in various parts of the country. For distribution orders assigned by logistics centers, designated personnel of designated vehicles are required to assign the goods on the distribution list to the designated delivery point. After the vehicle leaves the distribution point, it is necessary to make each distribution point have one and only one vehicle for one visit, and finally return to the distribution point to arrange the number of vehicles and the vehicle route rationally so that the delivery route can be used in a minimum time and resource in a high utilization.

The classification and dispatching of goods, as well as the arrangement of vehicles and line programs directly affect the distribution costs and service quality. The factors affecting the volume of logistics dispatch information include: vehicle scheduling, personnel scheduling, allocation of distribution orders, distribution route program, and delay time. The logistics and distribution plan must first satisfy the vehicle arrangement of the big waybill, then divide the distribution area and time, use the larger delivery volume for the distribution of the remote customer group, and the closer customer group use the general vehicle for distribution. Designate a certain number of vehicles to be responsible for the temporary demand. In route arrangement, the general method is to divide the customer into several regions according to geographical location, and then sort the delivery time according to the customer's request from small to large. The priority is to meet the customers who require to delivery early, and if there is any problem, it will be adjusted again.

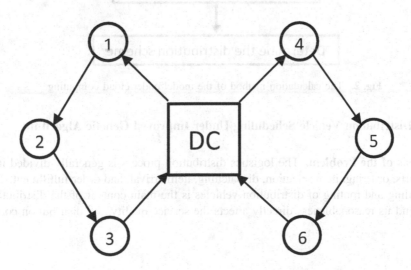

Fig. 1. The plan of distribution route

As shown in Fig. 1, 1 to 6 are distribution points. All vehicle routes start and end at the distribution center. Each distribution point is served by only one car. Each car can serve multiple distribution points. The sum of the quantities does not exceed the maximum load of the vehicle. The total time spent on each vehicle's driving route does not exceed the specified value to meet the customer's request for delivery time. The arrival time of a vehicle at a customer site is limited to a certain time period.

Logistics Scheduling Under Cloud Computing. Because the cloud computing has the ability to deal with massive data, the response speed is faster and the price is low, it is widely used by many industries. Due to the number of vehicles involved in the logistics and distribution process in logistics industry, the distribution time problem and the routing problem involve more complicated algorithms. The complex algorithm puts forward higher requirements for the computer hardware and operation mode. Because of the slow time response, traditional calculation methods often fail to meet the real-time requirements of logistics companies. Taking the cloud computing approach to deal with the massive data in the logistics distribution process can not only get the minimum cost of real-time logistics distribution but also get the delivery method that meets the customer's needs [15] (Fig. 2).

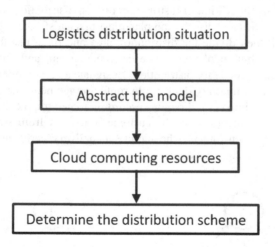

Fig. 2. The calculation method of the model under cloud computing

3.2   Distribution Vehicle Scheduling Under Improved Genetic Algorithm

Analysis of the Problem. The logistics distribution process is generally divided into five parts, ordering, item selection, dispatching, item arrival, and order fulfillment. The scheduling and routing of distribution vehicles is the main content of the distribution plan, and its reasonableness directly affects the service quality and distribution costs.

The scheduling of logistics vehicles belongs to the problem of multi constraint conditions, so the constraints of the problem are analyzed first.

Constraint 1: The logistics distribution route is divided into several major routes. Each delivery vehicle only delivers along one large route, that is, only one visit to each distribution node;

Constraint 2: The branch path is where the delivery vehicle departs from the distribution point and returns to the distribution node sequence or a single distribution node after passing through other delivery points;

Constraint 3: A reasonable path does not include the sequence of several branch paths of duplicate sites;

Constraint 4: The branch path satisfies the major route of the constraint condition;

Constraint 5: The total demand for goods on the delivery route cannot be greater than the maximum load of the delivery vehicle;

Constraint 6: The total delivery time on the distribution path cannot be greater than the agreed time in order to achieve maximum customer satisfaction.

Vehicle Dispatching Model. According to the above model constraints, we suppose that there are N distribution points and M vehicles to dispatch. $d(x, y)$ represents the running distance between the demand point x and the demand point y. $R(x)$ represents the total amount of goods delivered to the demand point x, Q represents the maximum load of the delivery vehicle, and D indicates the maximum distance of the delivery vehicle. The selection of distribution path needs to meet all distribution orders, and cannot exceed the maximum driving distance of the distribution vehicle. The shortest delivery path $f(x)$ of the distribution scheme can be described as:

$$f(x) = \sum_{i=0}^{N+M-2} d(x_i, x_{i+1}, d(x_0, x_N + M - 1)) \tag{1}$$

The objective function of the minimum distribution cost is established by the mixed integer programming method with the constraint conditions analyzed:

$$F = \min\left(\sum_{i,j,k} c_{ij} y_{ijk} + \sum_{i=1}^{n} P_i(T_i)\right) \tag{2}$$

To ensure that each waybill can be processed in a timely manner, distribution vehicles and delivery personnel can start from the distribution center, we must meet:

$$\sum_{i=1}^{m} x_{ik} = \begin{cases} m, i = 0 \\ 1, i = 1, \cdots, n \end{cases} \tag{3}$$

To make the sum of the demand for the goods delivered by each delivery vehicle not exceed the maximum load of the vehicle, then:

$$\sum Q_i x_{ik} \leq Qk, \forall k \in K \tag{4}$$

For any delivery point j delivered by the delivery vehicle k, there must be another delivery point i delivered by k. The delivery vehicle k arrives at the delivery point j from the delivery point i. Similarly, for the delivery point i delivered by the vehicle k, there is also another distribution point delivered by k. The delivery vehicle arrives from the delivery point to the delivery point i, and so on:

$$\sum y_{ijk} = x_{jk}, \forall j \in G_0, k \in K \tag{5}$$

$$\sum y_{ijk} = x_{ik}, \forall j \in G_0, k \in K \tag{6}$$

In order to ensure that the total delivery time of the route for each delivery vehicle does not exceed the specified delivery time, then:

$$T_0^k + \sum\sum y_{ijk}(T_{ij} + S_i) \leq T_R^k, k \in K \tag{7}$$

If the arrival time of a delivery vehicle for a distribution point is limited to a certain time period, then:

$$T_j + S_i + T_{ij} - M(1 - y_{ijk}) \leq T_j, \forall i, j \in G, k \in K \tag{8}$$

In this model, K is a set of all schedulable delivery vehicles, $K = \{1, 2, \cdots, m\}$; G is a set of all demand nodes, $G = \{1, 2, \cdots, n\}$; G_0 is $G \cup \{0\}$, where $\{0\}$ represents a distribution center and G_k is a set of all demand points delivered by delivery vehicle k; T_i is the time when the delivery vehicle reaches the demand point I; C_{ij} is the transportation cost of the vehicle from the demand point i to the demand point j; T_{ij} is the travel time of the vehicle from the demand point i to the demand point j; Q_i is the total demand for goods of demand node i; Q_k is the maximum load of delivery vehicle k; S_i is the residence time of delivery vehicle at demand point i; T_0^k is the departure time of delivery vehicle k; T_R^k is the time required to return for delivery vehicle k; M is positive. The variable x_{ik} represents the distribution plan of the logistics delivery vehicle, which can be represented by a Boolean matrix; if is the demand point i is served by the delivery vehicle k, then x_{ik} is 1, otherwise it is 0; the variable y_{ijk} represents the route arrangement of the logistics delivery vehicle, if the delivery vehicle passes through the distribution point i to j, then y_{ijk} is 1, otherwise it is 0.

3.3   Algorithm Analysis of the Model

The goal of the logistics resource scheduling model algorithm is to find the delivery plan x_{ik} and the delivery route y_{ijk} under the condition that the logistics operation cost F is the minimum. In the absence of special conditional constraints, the distribution vehicle k has $\left(P_n^1 + P_n^2 + \cdots + P_n^n\right)$ schemes for the distribution route, and the calculation amount of the logistics information scheduling scheme is $\left(P_n^1 + P_n^2 + \cdots + P_n^n\right)^m$. Under the constraint of the above model conditions, the maximum value of i for delivery vehicle k that satisfies $\sum Q_i x_{ik} \leq Q_k$ is I_k, the maximum value of i that satisfies $T_j + S_i + T_{ij} - M(1 - y_{ijk}) \leq T_j$ is J_k, the maximum value of i that satisfies $T_0^k + \sum\sum y_{ijk}(T_{ij} + S_i) \leq T_R^k$ is H_k, and if $L_k = min(I_k, J_k, H_k)$, each delivery vehicle k has $\sum_{u=1}^{L_k} P_{L_k}^u$ choices for the delivery plan in total. Then, the information volume of the logistic scheduling of m freight bills is $\prod_{k=1}^{m} \left(\sum_{u=1}^{L_k} P_{L_k}^u \right)$. With the increase of n and m, the amount of information calculated by logistics dispatching plans will increase exponentially both in space and in time.

3.4 Algorithm Flow Under Cloud Computing

All logistics scheduling information is sorted by priority, and then classified, and according to the classification, cloud computing algorithm is used to implement distribution scheduling of distribution vehicles and distribution personnel to bind tasks and resources and run tasks. The algorithm flow in the cloud computing environment is shown in Fig. 3.

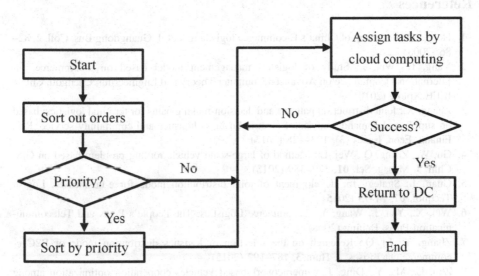

Fig. 3. Algorithm flow under cloud computing

4 Conclusions

The time required to implement the distribution scheduling algorithm in the cloud computing mode is much less than that of artificial, and it is also relatively more accurate. The use of cloud computing technology can greatly shorten the time for determining delivery plans and improve the efficiency of distribution. The global logistics industry has developed rapidly and has played an important role in the fields of trade, commerce, and services. Reliable and efficient logistics and distribution system is an important part of e-commerce application research. Faced with the problem of scheduling information processing under large-mode logistics orders, the optimization model algorithm based on cloud computing environment can realize rapid and reasonable arrangement of logistics distribution program. The logistics resource scheduling problem is represented by a mathematical model, and the vehicle scheduling and route allocation in the algorithm are divided into two stages to solve the problem, which reduces the constraints of the problem, shortens the calculation time, and can meet the solution requirements of large-scale logistics distribution problems. The optimization algorithm is obviously superior to the traditional method in dealing with the total amount of logistics scheduling information and overall efficiency. Of course, this algorithm needs further improvement and in-depth research.

Acknowledgement. This work was supported in part by the Beijing Great Wall Scholars' Program under Grant CIT and TCD20170317, in part by the Beijing Tongzhou Canal Plan "Leading Talent Plan", in part by the Beijing Collaborative Innovation Center and in part by the Management Science and Engineering High-precision Project.

References

1. He, S.: On designing of China's E-commerce logistic model. J. Guangdong Bus. Coll. **2**, 82–86 (2003)
2. Yang, L., Wu, S.: Study of logistics management model based on e-commerce. In: International Conference on Advanced Computer Theory and Engineering, Chengdu, China. IEEE Xplore (2010)
3. Zhang, X.: Joint distribution patterns and decision-making paths for terminal logistics: based on supply and demand analysis of electric business logistics and community service. Res. Financ. Econ. Issues (3), 123–128 (2013)
4. Gu, W., Zhang, Q., Wei, L.: Method of large-scale vehicle routing problem based on GIS. Chin. J. Manag. Sci. **01**, 379–389 (2013)
5. Guan, J.: Strategy for development of joint distribution mode for e-businesses. Logist. Technol. **07**, 74–75 (2015)
6. Wei, X., Yan, J., Wang, Y.: E-commerce Logistics. The People's Posts and Telecommunication Press, Beijing (2008)
7. Zhang, Y., Li, Q.: Research on the selection of logistics distribution mode of B2C e-commerce enterprises. J. Hum **3**, 187–192 (2015)
8. Zhu, L., Ma, Y., Ding, J.: Supernetwork-based vehicles cooperation optimization among logistics enterprises under low-carbon concept. Sci. Technol. Manag. Res. **36**(24), 260–266 (2016)
9. Han, M., Wang, H.: Study of community E-commerce logistic distribution model based on intelligent community property. In: Li, X., Xu, X. (eds.) Proceedings of the Fourth International Forum on Decision Sciences. UOR, pp. 645–650. Springer, Singapore (2017). https://doi.org/10.1007/978-981-10-2920-2_55
10. Ding, W.: Solving of emergency logistics vehicle routing problem with genetic algorithm under capacity constraints. Huazhong University of Science and Technology, Wuhan, pp. 61–76 (2013)

11. Ma, X., Li, H.: A new genetic algorithm for the capacity constraints vehicle routing problem. Adv. Appl. Math. **03**, 222–230 (2014)
12. Yang, Z.: Research on the multi-objective vehicle routing optimization in urban express distribution. Harbin Institute of Technology, Harbin, pp. 66–82 (2015)
13. Zhang, M.: Vehicle routing problems with uncertain factors. University of Science and Technology of China, Hefei, pp. 71–85 (2016)
14. Zhou, L., Lin, Y., Wang, X.: Integrated optimization for multiclass terminal location-heterogeneous vehicle routing of urban distribution under online shopping. Comput. Integr. Manuf. Syst. **22**(4), 1139–1147 (2016)
15. Liu, Z.: The application of cloud computing in marine transportation logistics electronic management system. Ship Sci. Technol. **38**(18), 103–105 (2016)

Cloud Security Solution Based on Software Defined Network

Shengli Zhao[1]([⊠]), Zhaochan Li[1], and Ning Cao[2]

[1] School of Information, Beijing Wuzi University, Beijing, China
13624843806@163.com, zhaochanlibwz@126.com
[2] School of Internet of Things, Wuxi Commercial Vocational and Technical College,
Wuxi, China
ning.cao2008@hotmail.com

Abstract. With the rapid development of cloud computing, the Internet of Things, mobile Internet, big data, and smart cities, enterprise data centers are becoming more and more complex. How to protect information security in the era of Internet big data has become a hot topic in various fields. By analyzing the software-defined network and related technologies, a cloud security solution model based on software-defined network is proposed. The three levels of the reference model and the security service framework are described in detail. The model mobilizes the components of the entire security system to synergize in a software-defined manner according to demand. It can not only adapt to the flexible and flexible environment of cloud computing, but also enhance the security and reliability of the network. At the same time, a more granular classification management of network applications has been implemented, providing cloud users with on-demand, accurate, and reliable security service capabilities.

Keywords: Cloud security · Security services · Software-defined networks · Virtualization

1 Introduction

With the advent of the Internet age, data is being generated at an absolutely alarming rate, and this situation will not change. How to protect information security in the era of internet big data has become a hot topic. A large amount of sensitive data is leaked or damaged due to improper handling, and it will inevitably cause incalculable losses to the involved parties. In recent years, there have been a number of major data breaches, such as Turkey's major data breaches; the leaking of World Check which is the world's largest counter-terrorism database in the United Kingdom; the disclosure of Net Ease's billions of emails were suspected. The entire world is facing eager data security and confidentiality problems. The impact of leaked incidents is deeply thought-provoking [1].

© Springer Nature Switzerland AG 2019
J. Vaidya et al. (Eds.): CSS 2019, LNCS 11982, pp. 562–574, 2019.
https://doi.org/10.1007/978-3-030-37337-5_46

The development of cloud storage for the majority of users in the Internet is also extremely rapid in recent years, but it is still facing security threats. The first thing that the current users think of when they talk about cloud storage is whether the data is safe. The security issue has attracted the attention of researchers. A recent security summary report pointed out that as high as 95% of security breaches were motivated by material benefits or commercial espionage, enterprises and organizations spent a lot of money to prevent external network attacks and internal hidden threats. In the network environment, the goal of protecting data security is to prevent data in the data from being accidentally or maliciously deleted, inserted, tampered with, or damaged.

This paper proposes a cloud-based security solution based on software-defined network, gives a reference model for the solution and analyzes its working mechanism, and then analyzes the advantages of the solution. In the software-defined framework, the security resources are integrated in a resource pool and the security capabilities are serviced. The model can adapt to the flexible and flexible environment of cloud computing, enhance the security and reliability of the network, and achieve a more fine-grained classification management of network applications, providing cloud users with a better security service experience.

2   Software-Defined Networks and Related Technologies

2.1   Software-Defined Network

Definition and Development Process. Software-defined network (SDN) is a new type of network architecture. Its design concept is to separate the control plane of the network from the data forwarding plane, so as to achieve programmable control of the underlying hardware through the software platform in the centralized controller, and to achieve flexible on-demand deployment of network resources. In an SDN network, a network device is only responsible for simple data forwarding and can use general-purpose hardware. The original operating system responsible for control is refined into an independent network operating system and is responsible for adapting different service features. Moreover, the communication between the network operating system and service features and hardware devices can be programmed. SDN essentially has three major features: control and forwarding separation, device resource virtualization, and general hardware and software programmability.

Although the history of SDN can be traced back to earlier, but strictly speaking, the explosive development of SDN began in 2010 OpenFlow 1.0 released by Stanford University [2]. Before 2010, network equipment vendors occupied most of the network market share, of which Cisco is the most representative. Starting in 2011, companies began to invest in SDN, including the traditional companies Cisco, HP, and IBM, as well as start-up companies, Contrail and others. In 2015, Google confirmed the use of SDN in its Jupiter & Andromeda project to manage large-scale environments. Google pointed out that its SDN is based on three elements: white box switch, SDN controller and Clos architecture design. In 2017,

VMware announced that its NSX has more than 2,400 customers, bringing in $1 billion in sales [3].

Comparison Between SDN and Traditional Networks. In the traditional network, the logic control function and data forwarding function are tightly coupled to the network device. That is, the control layer and the data forwarding layer are all configured in the switch, this makes the management of the network control plane extremely complex. In addition, due to tight coupling, new technologies and new developments at the network control level are difficult to directly deploy on existing networks and lack flexibility and scalability. In the traditional network age, people-centricity responds passively to the needs of business online, change, and troubleshooting, and solves various network problems based on experience.

Since the birth of OpenFlow, the idea of flow table control has given fine-grained control over network data, and it has brought the idea of global control. After the traffic transmitted by each network device, any traffic flowing through the network can be defined by the flow table. The actions of each flow of each packet can be finely set and controlled. SDN gives network data new vitality.

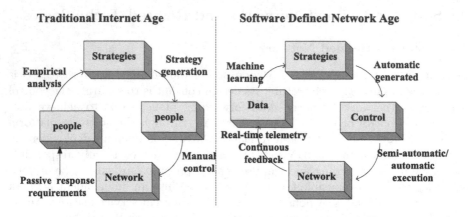

Fig. 1. Comparison between traditional and software-defined networking ages.

The data is not only data packets, but also data flow, device data, environment data, tenant data, cloud resource data, dynamic behavior data, etc. A real-time network data platform is constructed through real-time telemetry and continuous feedback. Algorithms, big data systems, and cloud computing provide a natural platform for data processing, analysis, and machine learning. The global controller provides a central processor for the semi-automatic and automatic execution of the strategy. Its control antennae can reach any part of the network. As shown in Fig. 1.

The advantages of SDN over traditional networks are: Simplify the complex network composed of different manufacturers' equipment so that the network can be controlled centrally; Reduce the complexity of network maintenance; Enhancing the security and reliability of the network; Realize more fine-grained classification management of network applications; Subvert business development methods and simplify business deployment methods; Reduce the time and cost of network management and development; The new network architecture provides a better user experience.

SDN Network Architecture. An SDN network consists of three abstraction layers: physical device layer, SDN control layer, and SDN application layer, as shown in Fig. 2. Figure 3 is a complete set of SDN solutions.

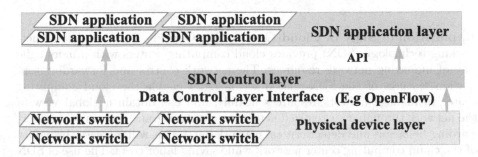

Fig. 2. The SDN network architecture.

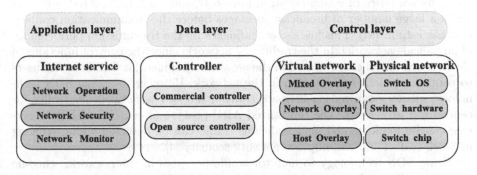

Fig. 3. A complete SDN solution consists of.

Physical device layer consists of all physical devices in the entire IT infrastructure network and is the lowest layer of the network. Generally include the physical switch and the virtual switch, but here the control processing function of the switch has been stripped, it only has the underlying function of data traffic forwarding, like a channel, only responsible for the flow of traffic. At this point the OpenFlow protocol is used to control the interface of this switched network.

SDN control layer is the key to the entire architecture, which is equivalent to the "middleware" in the architecture. The responsibility is to integrate all physical and virtual devices in the network. When the control layer abstracts various physical devices, it is achieved by the SDN software corresponding to the physical network devices. The control layer is highly integrated with the network devices and closely cooperates with all network tasks. The control layer communicates with the switch relying on the OpenFlow protocol and the NET-CONF protocol. The SDN application layer is an organic "vitality" component of the entire SDN environment. Users can freely write, develop, and customize the functions of the "switch" (network). Because these APIs are open, users can freely control the network according to their own needs for further innovative research.

Application of SDN in Cloud Computing Center. Software-defined networking technology (SDN) provides cloud computing centers with a more agile way of managing network resources. The network control and forwarding separation features of the SDN-related technologies enable the cloud computing center to manage network resources flexibly, and can obtain a global view of the network through a customized network control program, customize data forwarding behavior, and detect critical network data. This will increase the agility of the cloud computing center network while saving labor costs. The use of SDN technology to give the network a flexible scheduling management features, there have been a lot of innovative research.

Using centralized control of SDN technology, broadcast packets are processed centrally. In order to communicate with other terminals, the communication terminal uses a series of communication protocols, such as DHCP, ARP, etc., and sends a large number of broadcast messages before the communication connection has established. This has a great influence on the transmission performance of large-scale networks. In the traditional network, since the control functions of the network are all concentrated in the network equipment, it is difficult for users to control the data transmission in the network. However, by using SDN technology, all unrecognized packets are transmitted to the network controller for centralized processing. The centralized ARP proxy and centralized DHCP service can be implemented, and malicious traffic can be detected while reducing network traffic, and can improve network security [4].

Using SDN technology to monitor traffic hotspots in the network, schedule hotspot traffic, reduce network congestion, and achieve network load balancing [5]. Before the SDN technology was applied to the cloud computing center, the network was a black box for the cloud computing center and could not obtain the detailed information of the traffic, load, etc. in the network. As a result, there are few changes to the network and only the limited functionality that network equipment vendors can provide. Using the SDN technology, the cloud computing center can detect the load condition of the network in real time, discover the hotspot of the traffic, and schedule the hotspot traffic. E.g. Tencent uses SDN to

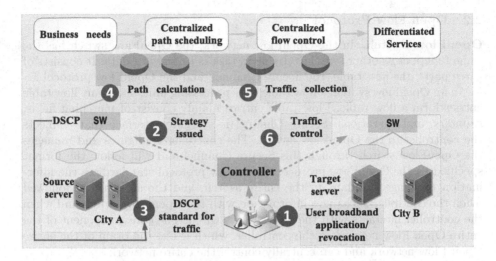

Fig. 4. A example of using SDN to implement differentiated services.

implement differentiated path calculations, flow control, and services to provide users with a better experience, as shown in Fig. 4.

Network automation management. The management of traditional switching and routing devices is done through the network administrator directly controlling the command line interface of each device or through the Web management page provided by the SNMP protocol. Because of the complexity of control commands, network administrators are prone to errors when operating network devices. To this end, it is possible to use SDN centralized control and underlying abstraction to simplify network management. Through the control plane, the network control function is stripped from each discrete network device, and the controller provides a global view of the underlying network. Network administrators can flexibly write network control programs based on the abstract view of the network and provide the open programming interface provided by the upper layer of the controller to complete the control and management of the entire network. In addition, through network automation management, different network control functions can be arranged together with IT resources to realize the automatic management of the entire infrastructure resources [6].

Network virtualization [7]. With the widespread application of virtualization technologies such as desktops, applications, and storage, network virtualization has become an urgent need for cloud computing and data center technology development. The purpose of network virtualization is to draw up a logically independent network on the same shared physical network resource to meet the application trend of multi-tenancy, traffic isolation, and logical network free management and control [8]. The centralized control of SDN makes it easier to implement network virtualization.

2.2   Open Flow Protocol

OpenFlow Switch. In the OpenFlow network, the OpenFlow switch has the same functions as other switches. Its main task is to forward data. It consists of three parts: the flow table, the Secure Channel, and the OpenFlow protocol.

In an OpenFlow switch, a flow table is its processing unit, and many flow table entries form a flow table. Flow table entries mainly consist of matching fields, counters, and operations. Secure Channel is a secure interface that connects the controller to the OpenFlow switch. The controller configures and manages the OpenFlow switch through this Secure Channel and will follow the format specified by the OpenFlow protocol. OpenFlow protocol standardizes the information exchange standard in the entire switch, and the standard is followed when the controller exchanges information with the OpenFlow switch and when the controller interacts with the Open Flow switch. The core component of the entire Open Flow network is the controller, which is like the brain of the entire Open-Flow network and can centrally control the entire network.

Network Architecture. The OpenFlow switch, Flow Visor and controller form the OpenFlow network architecture. Among them, the OpenFlow switch is different from other switches, although it is also responsible for data forwarding, when data is forwarded, the data flow is determined by the flow table; Network virtualization is indispensable in the OpenFlow network architecture and is implemented by Flow Visor; The controller will implement the functions of the control layer. The control plane is represented by its control logic, when it works, it will implement centralized control of the network through the entire network view. The OpenFlow switch, Flow Visor and controller form the Open-Flow network architecture. Among them, the OpenFlow switch is different from other switches, although it is also responsible for data forwarding, when data is forwarded, the data flow is determined by the flow table; Network virtualization is indispensable in the OpenFlow network architecture and is implemented by Flow Visor; The controller will implement the functions of the control layer. The control plane is represented by its control logic, when it works, it will implement centralized control of the network through the entire network view.

2.3   Software Defined Security Services

The intelligent and dynamic control of network flows provided by SDN not only provides sufficient flexibility in the deployment of the topology, but also allows the physical security products to obtain the required network flows through simple access on SDN-enabled switches. Moreover through the fine-grained control of the network flow load, the on-demand distribution of network security service load is realized. This provides the possibility for software-defined network security services.

The core issue addressed by the Software Defined Data Center (SDDC) is to allow customers to obtain more flexible and rapid business deployment, management, and implementation at a lower cost. Software-defined data centers can

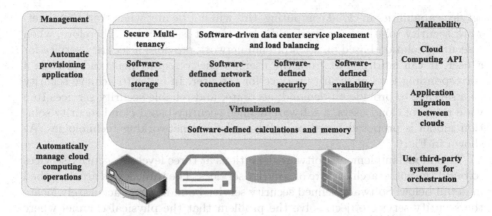

Fig. 5. List of cloud computing components defined by software.

extend the benefits of virtualization to all areas of the data center, including computing, storage, networking and security services. This creates a cloud computing environment that supports flexible, flexible, efficient, and reliable IT services. The list of cloud computing components under software definitions is shown in Fig. 5.

Software-driven data centers simplify the process of defining applications and all the resources they need. Through software, the abstraction, pooling, deployment, and management of infrastructure resources within the entire data center can be realized, and customized and differentiated applications and business requirements can be met at the same time, effectively delivering cloud services. In a software-defined cloud environment, virtualized objects are protected. This will result in the virtualization protection boundary of the cloud computing, that is, it can be flexibly expanded and dynamically adjusted. In this environment, abstracted and pooled resources can reduce dedicated hardware as much as possible, thereby improving utilization; A logical network can be created according to the user's needs to speed up the deployment of applications and further simplify the user's operations; According to their own needs, they can add corresponding services to conduct integrated management of devices in the cloud environment. In addition, they can also extend third-party services; Provides support for policy-based automation, dynamic scheduling and adjustment, and full use of efficiency and agility.

3 Cloud Security Solution Model Based on Software-Defined Network

3.1 The Three Dimensions of the Model

When relying on virtualization technology to build a public cloud or private cloud service system, because of the need to provide elastically scalable on-demand service capabilities in cloud computing, this will not be met when traditional network security solutions are used and multi-tenant issues arise. Therefore, when a security solution based on a traditional network provides a security service for a user, it can hardly start from the user's security requirement and provide a corresponding level of security service for the user. In order to achieve security as a service, to provide on-demand, accurate, and reliable security services to a wide range of cloud users, a software-defined security-based cloud security solution model is proposed based on software-defined networking technologies. As shown in Fig. 6.

This model implements software definitions at three levels of security services to build the entire architecture of security services. The three levels are described in detail below. Software-defined security service boundary can accurately locate the security service object, solve the problem that the physical channel where the protected host traffic is caused by network physical boundary miscellaneous and virtual host drift in the virtualized network is not fixed.

Software-defined security service items can dynamically and selectively configure security services for protected objects according to their business needs, and configure intrusion detection and audit services for business system servers. It is not necessary for all unrelated traffic belonging to a network to pass through each security product successively, thereby greatly improving the detection efficiency of security products and reducing the false alarm rate.

Software-defined security service resources can realize the measurement of service resources and the reasonable allocation according to performance requirements, this is a necessary prerequisite for the security service, and it is also a noticeable characteristic of the elastic computing of cloud computing. In this model, a software-defined security service system is constructed using the separation of management layer, data layer, and service layer. Through such a layered decoupling architecture, software-defined control logic is implemented at different levels to realize the serviceability of security capabilities. Through the in-depth analysis interface, according to the strategy to import traffic into the big data security analysis platform on demand, the data that requires in-depth analysis is stored and mined based on big data technology. Through the continuous correlation analysis of a large amount of data in a time window and space range, deep security issues such as advanced persistent threat attacks that are difficult to detect by a single point of detection are detected.

3.2   Security Service Framework

The entire security service framework can be divided into four layers: security service presentation layer, security service management layer, network traffic diversion and diversion layer, security service resource pool module.

Security Service Presentation Layer. The security service presentation layer mainly solves the problem of service visualization and provides users with human-computer interaction interfaces for software-defined security services.

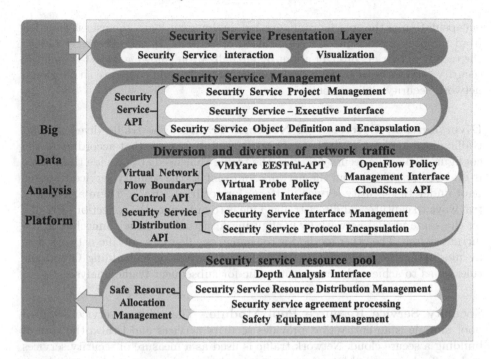

Fig. 6. Software-defined network security services framework.

In a software-defined data center environment, neither the user's infrastructure nor the security service device is a simple single hardware device, but exists in the entire data center as software, hardware, or a combination of software and hardware, providing users with on-demand services. However, it is difficult for users to intuitively feel the physical presence of these devices, and it also makes it difficult for users to understand the reliability and effectiveness of the security services. Therefore, the security service presentation layer is mainly responsible for resolving the problem of service visualization, masking the changes brought about by virtualization to the data center, visually reducing the user's difficulty in understanding the deployment of security services, and visually displaying the security posture of the network. The interaction interface of the security service provides users with the choice and customization of the service.

Security Service Management. The security service management layer implements the encapsulation and management of the security service content. Once the security service is customized, it will be issued and configured by the security service management. The security service management layer provides an encapsulated service configuration interface to the interaction layer. When the interface is invoked, the management layer invokes the execution interface of the security service to implement a series of service logic operation sequences to complete the configuration of the entire service. Through such abstraction and encapsulation of the specific configuration deployment logic, the user is shielded from unnecessary details of virtualization operations. It can effectively reduce the technical barriers brought about by virtualization, allowing users to configure security services in their cloud environment as they would configure a traditional network security environment.

Diversion and Diversion of Network Traffic. The traffic diversion and traffic diversion layer of the network traffic mainly realizes that according to the configuration of the security service, the traffic that needs to provide the service is grabbed or guided from the network and sent to the security service resource pool under the security service platform for security service. There are mainly two ways to capture and direct traffic: One is to automate the collection of traffic on the same virtual network by configuring a virtual machine connected to the virtual switch. The other method is to change the flow of a specific network flow by modifying the configuration of the virtual switch or embedding OpenFlow rules so as to achieve the export of traffic for subsequent traffic analysis.

Security Service Resource Pool Module. The security service resource pool module is an entity that provides security services and is also the core of building a secure cloud. Network traffic is used as a measure of security services and traffic is imported into the resource pool through traffic capture and boot. In the end, traditional physical security devices are used to implement security functions. Therefore, the SDN switch supporting the OpenFlow rule is used to construct the service bearer channel of the security resource pool.

In this way, the entire security service consists of the service object, the bearer channel, and the service implementation end. Among them, the service object is a software-defined security domain, and the virtual probes or diversion products deployed in the network capture or guide traffic belonging to a security domain to a bearer channel according to the division of the security domain. The bearer channel is implemented in the SDN switch in a flow manner. Through the control of the OpenFlow rules that are converted from the security policy, the network flow that meets specific rules is guided to the corresponding network interface. At the same time, this interface is connected to physical security devices such as IDS, UTM, etc. The security devices on the service implementation side include all physical network security products with bypass access and serial access. For security devices that do not support their own virtualization, a set of lightweight devices such as 10M or 100M devices is used to form a resource pool. The load of the access port is controlled based on the OpenFlow protocol to implement the on-demand security service scalability. For self-virtualized security products, a more granular on-demand service distribution can be implemented by the security device itself.

3.3   The Advantages of a Cloud Security Model Based on Software Definitions

This solution body differs from other solutions in that it embodies the four major advantages of software definition, on-demand, focus, and panorama. As a service, security is no longer a fantasy, and it has the feasibility of landing.

Software definition. During the entire life cycle of the above-mentioned cloud security solution, flexible configuration is supported in a software-defined manner, from the planning of the solution to the implementation and deployment of the solution, to the operation and maintenance of the operation process, and security planning and deployment, all of them provide users with dynamic and flexible management capabilities in a software-defined manner.

On-demand. After the resource pooling, network traffic is used according to demand. For security, the protected objects are more flexible and flexible to use after resource pooling. This also requires that the security protection scheme can also change with the demand. The "needs" here include multiple dimensions such as time, resources, and security granularity. For example, if a user generates a business virtual machine, corresponding security protection functions need to be assigned to it at this time. If the user destroys a virtual machine, the corresponding security resources should be released. After the network intrusion detection through the peripheral discovers that a virtual machine may be invaded, on-demand security services such as anti-virus scanning, fine granularity, and high resource consumption are enabled for in-depth detection and protection.

Focus. To help users simplify the operation and maintenance of cloud computing security, through the implementation details of the encapsulation virtualization technology, users are presented with an easy-to-use interface. And by helping different businesses focus on different planes, users can help clarify the management of assets, services, and security in the cloud computing environment.

Panorama. Corresponding to the next-generation security defense system, the cloud security solution will no longer be achieved through a single point of equipment. Instead, it establishes a defense-in-depth system from the boundary of the cloud to the virtual machine, and obtains panoramic security knowledge through a unified cloud security management platform. In a software-defined manner, components in the entire security system are mobilized according to the needs for collaboration to achieve a powerful and complete security solution.

4   Summary

With the rapid development of cloud computing, the Internet of Things, and big data, enterprise data centers are becoming more and more complex. Various applications are emerging in an endless stream. These applications require different requirements for back-end computing, storage, and networking. Secondly, IT hardware technology has also witnessed diversified development. For example, the number of CPU cores is increasing, and the use of virtual machines and cloud computing is becoming more and more popular. These new challenges to the user's heterogeneous resource management and IT application resource matching is urgently needed to be resolved through management software. Therefore, the "software definition" has attracted widespread attention.

The occurrence of multiple major data leak incidents has caused people to pay constant attention to the protection of information security. This article first introduces software-defined networking and related technologies, and then proposes a cloud-based security solution based on software-defined networking. It describes in detail the three dimensions of the reference model. The security service framework was analyzed from four aspects: the security service presentation layer, security service management layer, network traffic diversion and flow distribution, and security service resource pool module. The model can adapt to the flexible and flexible environment of cloud computing, enhance the security and reliability of the network, and realize more fine-grained classification management of network applications, providing cloud users with a better security service experience.

Acknowledgements. This work was supported in part by the Beijing Great Wall Scholars' Program under Grant CIT and TCD20170317, in part by the Beijing Tongzhou Canal Plan "Leading Talent Plan", in part by the Beijing Collaborative Innovation Center and in part by the Management Science and Engineering High-precision Project.

References

1. Li, Y.: Difficulty and attribution of the U.S. in dealing with the problem of unauthorized information leakage-an analysis based on typical secret leakage events. Arch. Manag. **2**, 59–61 (2016)
2. The McKeown Group. http://yuba.stanford.edu/derickso/openflow-spec-v1.0.0-cookieenhancements.pdf. Accessed 26 Feb 2018
3. Blog Beat Homepage Page. https://blogs.vmware.com/networkvirtualization/2017/01/nsx-growth-success-2016.html/. Accessed 26 Feb 2018
4. Hu, Z., Wang, M., Yan, X.: A comprehensive security architecture for SDN. In 18th International Conference on Intelligence in Next Generation Networks. IEEE, pp. 30–37 (2015)
5. Li, H., Wang, M.: Research and implementation of traffic management applications based on software-defined network. Comput. Appl. Softw. **32**(5), 17–19 (2015)
6. Vilalta, R., Mayoral, A.: The SDN/NFV cloud computing platform and transport network of the ADRENALINE testbed. In: 1st IEEE Conference on Network Softwarization. IEEE, pp. 1–5 (2015)
7. Jiang, Y., Lan, J.: Mapping algorithm for service aggregation in network virtualization environment. J. Softw. **25**(6), 1328–1338 (2014)
8. Koponen, T., Amidon, K., Balland, P.: Nework virtualization in multi-tenant data-centers. In: The 11th USENIX Conference on Networked Systems Design and Implementation on Proceedings, pp. 203–216. USENIX Association (2014)

An Optimized Multi-Paxos Consensus Protocol for Practical Cloud Storage Applications

Wenmin Lin[1,2,3($\boxtimes$)], Xuan Sheng[1,2], and Lianyong Qi[4]

[1] Department of Computer Science,
Hangzhou Dianzi University, Hangzhou, China
linwenmin@hdu.edu.cn, upxuans@163.com
[2] State Key Laboratory of Complex System Modeling and Simulation,
Hangzhou, China
[3] State Key Laboratory for Novel Software Technology, Nanjing University,
Nanjing, China
[4] School of Information Science and Engineering, Qufu Normal University,
Jining, China
lianyongqi@gmail.com

Abstract. For cloud storage applications running typical Multi-Paxos protocol, the processing of a client command normally consists of two steps, i.e., commit and apply. Commit step is to guarantee a client command achieves identical sequence number among all storage replicas; apply step is to execute a committed client commands one by one in sequence and return back the execution result to client. In practice, committed client commands are not necessarily be applied after all its previous commands get applied. In view of this observation, an optimization for Multi-Paxos protocol is proposed to improve system performance for cloud storage applications in this paper. Compared with typical Multi-Paxos protocol, we allow out-of-order applying of committed client commands. And a committed client command can be applied as long as it has no dependency on its previous commands or all dependencies are resolved. Comparison between two protocols is implemented and analyzed to prove the feasibility of our proposal.

Keywords: Optimized Multi-Paxos · Consensus protocol · Out-of-order apply

1 Introduction

Nowadays, increasing amount of applications are deployed in cloud, due to the convenience of "pay as you go" manner of using IT infrastructure. Among those applications, cloud storage application is one of the most popular one. Cloud storage applications enable users to store data of their applications on cloud, instead of building their own storage infrastructures [1, 2]. As a typical distributed computing application, cloud storage systems take advantage of replica technique to achieve fault tolerance and high availability, by storing user's data on multiple disks over the network, so as to make sure the data won't be lost as long as majority disks working probably [3].

As a distributed computing application, a cloud storage system can be treated as a set of distributed servers belonging to one cluster. The servers work as a whole to

© Springer Nature Switzerland AG 2019
J. Vaidya et al. (Eds.): CSS 2019, LNCS 11982, pp. 575–584, 2019.
https://doi.org/10.1007/978-3-030-37337-5_47

process client commands (i.e., write or read operations to store data and read stored data) [4]. Each sever can be described as a deterministic state machine that performs client commands in sequence. The state machine has a current state, and it performs a step by taking as input a client command and producing an output and a new state. The core implementation of a cloud storage system is the consensus module to guarantee all servers execute the same sequence of client commands [5]. As a result, every cloud storage server can be modeled as a replicated state machine as shown in Fig. 1.

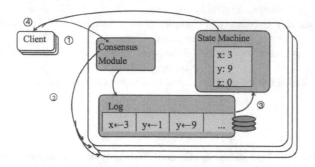

Fig. 1. Replicated state machine architecture [5].

Replicated state machines are typically implemented using a replicated log [4, 5]. Each server stores a log containing a series of client commands, from which its state machine executes in sequence. Each log contains the same commands in the same sequence, so each state machine processes the same sequence of commands. Since the state machines are deterministic, each computes the same state and produces the same sequence of outputs. Keeping the replicated log consistent is the job of the consensus algorithm. The consensus module on a server receives commands from clients and adds them to its log. It communicates with the consensus modules on other servers to ensure that every log eventually contains the same requests in the same sequence, even if some servers fail. Once commands are properly replicated, each server's state machine processes them in log order, and the outputs are returned to clients. As a result, the servers appear to form a single, highly reliable state machine.

There have been numerous researches on the consensus algorithm for replicated state machines. Among which Paxos is the dominated one over last decades: most implementations of consensus are based on Paxos or influenced by it. Representative algorithms include Multi-Paxos [4], E-Paxos [6], as well as Raft [5]. The difference between Paxos and its variants Raft is: Raft is strongly based on leadership mechanism, all client commands are handled by leader replica and other replicas work as followers; while for Multi-Paxos, leader is not necessarily required, but it always employs a distinguished leader to guarantee liveness of the algorithm; Moreover, E-paxos is totally leaderless to guarantee client latency for handling client commands in wide area environment. In this paper, we mainly focus on the optimization of Multi-Paxos regarding its performance optimization.

For cloud storage applications running typical Multi-Paxos protocol, the processing of a client command normally consists of two steps, commit and apply. Commit step is to guarantee a client command achieves identical sequence number among all storage replicas; apply step is to execute committed client commands one by one and return back the execution result to client. In practice, client commands could be distributed to all replica servers concurrently. Therefore, commands could be committed in an out-of-order manner due to factors such as network delay. In original design, commands should be applied strictly in sequence after they are committed [1, 7, 8]. That means, any committed command C_i and C_j, $(Seq(C_i) < Seq(C_j)$, C_j must be applied after C_i is applied even C_j is committed before C_i. In practice, this is not necessary if C_j has no dependency on C_i. By allowing out-of-order apply, we can reduce client latency by improving the system's I/O throughput of each storage replica node.

In view of this observation, we propose an optimized Multi-Paxos protocol in this paper, where client commands could be applied in out-of-order manner after they get committed. The reminder of this paper is organized as follows: Sect. 2 discusses related work on consensus algorithm for cloud storage applications. Section 3 highlights the problem of typical Multi-Paxos protocol. The details of the optimization of Multi-Paxos protocol is presented in Sect. 4. Section 5 evaluates the performance of optimized Multi-Paxos protocol and typical Multi-Paxos protocol in terms of commit throughput. And Sect. 6 concludes the paper.

2   Related Work

As a distributed computing system, the core component of cloud storage applications is the consensus module, which is to guarantee each replica server executes client commands in the same sequence [10–12]. There have been numerous researches on consensus algorithms of distributed systems over last decades [13, 14], from which Paxos is the dominated one. Most implementations of consensus are based on Paxos or influenced by it. Among those consensus algorithms, they can be categorized as follows: (1) Lamport's Paxos [4, 8, 9], and its variants such as Multi-Paxos, Elaborations Paxos (E-Paxos) [6]; (2) Raft protocol [5], which is based on strong leadership mechanism.

Paxos protocol is a two-phase protocol, which contains prepare phase and accept phase [15, 16]. For a given command C_i, prepare phase is to make sure majority replicas agree to append C_i as the i-th command in its local log; and accept phase is to double confirm C_i has been appended as the i-th command in majority replica servers. Since majority replicas (more than half members) reach consistency regarding the sequence of C_i, all replicas will finally learn such information according to pigeonhole principle. As a result, Paxos protocol could guarantee that each replica sever will reach consistency regarding the sequence of each client command. A single Paxos instance is to determine the sequence of a single client command. Multi-Paxos is a variant of Paxos protocol, which enables handling multiple client commands concurrently with multiple Paxos instances. Moreover, in Multi-Paxos protocol, a leader could be elected to nominate sequence for each client command. As a result, the prepare phase could be omitted to improve system latency, so as to guarantee the liveness of the protocol.

E-Paxos is also a variant of Paxos protocol, which is to optimize system performance of client latency in wide-area applications, especially when there are nodes fail during consensus process. RAFT is a strong leader-based consensus protocol, where all determinations regarding the sequence of each command is made by the leader, and all other replica servers works as follower of the leader replica.

The main difference between those consensus algorithms is the leadership mechanism: (1) Multi-Paxos does not necessarily requires a leader; and when there's no leader in a replica group, Multi-Paxos degrades to the basic two-phase protocol. (2) E-Paxos is totally leaderless, which is designed to reduce client latency in wide-area scenario. (3) Moreover, Raft uses a strong leadership mechanism compared with other two consensus algorithms. Without a leader, the system running Raft protocol will become unavailable.

In this paper, we focus on optimization for Multi-Paxos protocol. As mentioned in aforementioned section, a cloud storage application running Multi-Paxos protocol normally consists of commit phase and apply phase. Commit phase is to guarantee a client command achieves identical sequence number among all storage replicas; apply phase is to execute a committed client commands one by one and return back the execution result to client. In practice, committed client commands are not necessarily be applied after all its previous commands get applied. In view of this observation, an optimization for Multi-Paxos protocol to improve system performance of cloud storage applications is proposed in this paper. By enabling out-of-order apply client commands, we can improve system's throughput, so as to reduce client latency to read committed commands.

3 Preliminary Knowledge

3.1 How Multi-Paxos Protocol Works

A typical Multi-Paxos protocol is similar to two-phase commit protocol (i.e., the two phases are prepare phase and accept phase, respectively). When a replica R_i within a replica group receives a client command C_k, the two-phase Multi-Paxos protocol works as follows:

Prepare Phase: R_i first record C_k as the k-th client command in its local log, then broadcast $prepare\_C_k$ requests with proposal number R_i-k within the replica group. On receiving the $prepare\_C_k$ request for each replica R_j, it will send back $prepare\_C_k\_OK$ response to R_i after checking it's ok to log C_k as the k-th log entry locally. If R_i receives $prepare\_C_k\_OK$ response from majority replicas, it will enter Accept phase to make C_k as the k-th log entry in majority replicas.

Accept Phase: R_i initiates $Accept\_C_k$ requests and broadcast it within the replica group. On receiving $Accept\_C_k$ requests for each replica R_j, it will record C_k as the k-th log entry, and send back $Accept\_C_k\_OK$ response after it checks there's no proposal number larger than R_i-k for the k-th log entry. Similarly, when R_i receives $Accept\_C_k\_OK$ responses from majority replicas, it will mark C_k as committed; and broadcast *Commit_C_k* requests. Once R_j receives *Commit_C_k* request, it will mark C_k as committed if it has recorded C_k as the k-th log entry as well.

After a command get committed, it can be applied to state machine as long as it has no dependency on other commands, or all its dependency are resolved probably. Therefore, a response will be send back to client to indicate the success of executing C_k by the cloud storage application.

An issue with Multi-Paxos protocol is when there are multiple replicas raising prepare requests simultaneously, it is with great possibility that none replica's proposal will be accepted. For example, when R_i raises (*Prepare_C_k*, R_i-k), there is another replica R_j raises (*Prepare_C_k'*, R_j-k') with R_j-k' > R_i-k simultaneously. R_j will win majority votes in prepare phase since R_j-k' is the largest proposal number. Before R_j's accept requests reaches majority replicas, R_i will initiate a new prepare request with a new proposal number R_i-m > R_j-k' to win majority votes in prepare phase. As a result, R_j's accept request will be ignored by majority replicas since R_i-m is the largest proposal. This scenario is called "mutual-tread" and will cause live lock of the protocol [4]. For the cloud storage applications, the live lock issue means for a same log entry (e.g., the k-th log entry), more than one replica issues *Prepare_C_k* requests within the replica group and none replica wins the right to write to the k-th log entry. To address this problem, a distinguished replica could be elected as leader to determine the sequence for each client command. Therefore, the two-phase protocol is reduced to one-phase protocol by omitting the prepare phase, so as to improve system's performance and avoid the liveness issue. The difference between the two-phase Multi-paxos protocol and the one-phase Multi-paxos protocol is depicted in Fig. 2.

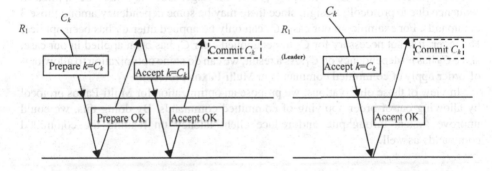

Fig. 2. Two-phase Multi-Paxos protocol vs. One-phase Multi-Paxos protocol

Let's take the scenario in Fig. 3 to describe how Multi-Paxos protocol works. A client sends three commands C_1, C_2 and C_3 at the same time to the leader replica R_1, i.e., {C_1: "$x = v_1$", C_2: "$y = v_2$", C_3 = "$x*$ = v_3"}. C_1 and C_3 are updating the same key x; while C_2 is updating key y. Then R_1 will log C_1, C_2, and C_3 in sequence at its local log firstly, then broadcast *Accept_C_k* messages regarding each command to each follower in the replica group. On receiving the *Accept_C_1* request from R_1, R_2 and R_3 will record the C_1 in its local log; then send back *Accept_C_1_OK* message to R_1. Once R_1 receives Accept OK messages from at least follower replica, it will mark C_1 as committed, and broadcast *Commit_C*$_1$ request to all followers. And on receiving a *Commit_C*$_1$ message, a follower replica will mark C_1 as committed if it has already record C_1 in its local log. Once C_1 is committed, it can be applied to the state machine and sends back to client that C_1 has already been recorded correctly. For C_2 and C_3, the workflow is similar to C_1.

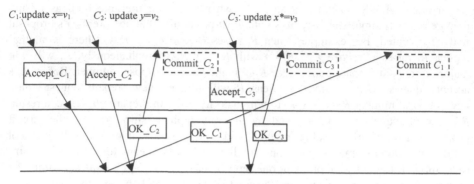

Fig. 3. A Multi-Paxos workflow example

3.2 Problem Statement

In the example depicted in Fig. 3, C_1, C_2 and C_3 may get committed in out-of-order manner, since the network delay may results the "*Accept_C*$_2$*_OK*" and "*Accept_C*$_3$*_OK*" messages arrives R_1 before "*Accept_C*$_1$*_OK*" message. But they must be applied in sequence due to protocol's design, since there may be some dependency among those 3 commands. For example, in our case, C_3 can only be applied after C_1 has been applied. However, it is not necessary for C_2 to get applied after C_1 has been applied in our case, since C_2 has no dependency on C_1. As a result, we can do some optimization to allow out-of-order apply of committed commands in Multi-Paxos protocol.

In view of those observations, we propose an optimization for Multi-Paxos protocol by allowing out-of-order applying of committed commands. By doing this, we could improve system throughput, and reduce client latency on reading the committed commands as well.

4 Our Solution: An Optimized Multi-paxos Protocol

Motivated by the problem discussed in Sect. 3, the optimized Multi-Paxos protocol is discussed in details in this section. In our proposal, we introduce a concept named dependency window for each client command. And a committed command could be applied as long as it's dependency window is empty or all the dependent commands are getting applied.

Definition 1 (dependency window). For a command C_k, its dependency window Dep_k is a data structure recording the m former keys close to command C_k in the whole log entry, i.e., $Dep_k = \{x_{k-m}, x_{k-(m-1)}, \dots x_{k-1}\}$. For each x_i in Dep_k, if C_k depends on its corresponding command C_i, C_k can only be applied after C_i get applied.

Compared with original design of Multi-paxos protocol, dependency window is added for each client command, to help a replica judge whether a client command can be applied or not. When a client command C_k arrives the leader replica R_i, an Accept message for C_k will be broadcast to all followers, with the dependency window information (i.e., Dep_k) attached. With Dep_k, a follower replica R_j can extract the dependent keys on which C_k relies on. And R_j will intuitively check whether C_k can be applied once it get committed.

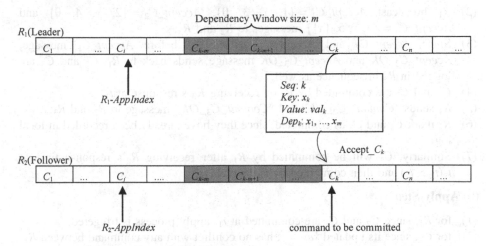

Fig. 4. The workflow of optimized Multi-Paxos protocol to commit a command

Step 1: Commit client commands

Figure 4 demonstrates the workflow to commit a client command C_k in our proposed optimized Multi-Paxos protocol. For a given client command C_k sent to Leader R_i, the commit protocol works as follows: (1) R_i records C_k in its local log as the k-th command in sequence; (2) R_i broadcasts "$Accept\_C_k$" message to all follower replicas in the cluster; (3) On receiving a "$Accept\_C_k$" message, a follower replica will first log C_k locally and sends back R_i the "$Accept\_C_k\_OK$" message; (4) Once R_i receives "$Accept\_C_k\_OK$" message from the majority in the cluster, it will identify C_k as committed; then broadcasts "$Commit\_C_k\_OK$" message to all followers in the cluster; (5) On receiving a "$Commit\_C_k\_OK$" message, a follower replica will mark C_k as committed if it has C_k in local log; otherwise it will mark C_k as committed after "$Accept\_C_k\_OK$" message arrives.

Step 2: Apply committed commands

Definition 7 (Apply index R_i-$AppIndex$). R_i-$AppIndex$ is the index of a replica R_i evolves in a Multi-Paxos protocol. It indicates that commands C_1, C_2, ... $C_{Ri\text{-}AppIndex}$ are already applied from local log to the state machine.

Concretely, for a command C_k to be applied, 2 conditions should be satisfied. (1) C_k must be committed: for leader, it means it receives "$Accept\_C_k\_OK$" message from the majority of peers in the system. For a follower replica, it must receive both "$Accept\_C_k$" and "$Commit\_C_k\_OK$" from leader; (2) C_k's key has no dependency on the command keys between R_i-$AppIndex$ and the command C_k itself.

Taking Fig. 3 for example, the optimized multi-paxos protocol works as follows:

(a) Commit Step

(1) On receiving client request C_1, C_2, C_3, R_1 records C_1, C_2, C_3 in sequence to local log;
(2) R_1 broadcast $Accept\_C_1 = \{1,\ x,\ 3,\ \theta\}$, $Accept\_C_2 = \{2,\ y,\ 4,\ \theta\}$ and $Accept\_C_3 = \{3, x, 5, \{x\}\}$ messages to R_2 and R_3;
(3) Since $Accept\_C_2$ and $Accept\_C_3$ arrives R_3 before $Accept\_C_1$ message, $Accept\_C_2\_OK$ and $Accept\_C_3\_OK$ message sends back to R_1, C_2 and C_3 are logged in R_3 in sequence as well;
(4) C_2 and C_3 are committed by R_1 on receiving R_3's response at t_1;
(5) R_1 sends "$Commit\_C_2\_OK$" and "$Commit\_C_3\_OK$" message to R_2 and R_3;
(6) R_3 mark C_2 and C_3 as committed, since they have already been recorded in local log;
(7) Similarly, C_1 will be committed by R_1 after receiving R_2's response time at $t_2(t_2 > t_1)$ and then committed by R_2 as well.

(b) Apply Step

(1) for R_1, since C_2 and C_3 are committed at t_1, apply process is triggered;
(2) for C_2, since its updated $key = y$, has no conflict with any command between R_1-$AppIndex = 0$ and C_1, it get applied immediately;
(3) while for C_3, since its updated $key = x$, is interfering with C_1 which also updates key x, so it won't be applied immediately at t_1. And it will only be applied after C_1 get applied;
(4) After t_2, C_1 get committed, and R_1-$AppIndex$ is updated to 2 as well;
(5) C_3 get applied since it has no dependency on commands between C_2 and C_3.

5   Evaluation

We evaluated the optimized Multi-Paxos protocol against typical Multi-Paxos protocol, using three replicas for each replicated state machine. The protocols are implemented with Golang and running on Mac OS 10.13.16.

According to [3], in practice, dependency among commands is rare cases for cloud storage applications with statistics around 1%. We did this comparison just to highlight that dependency among commands does have impact on distributed system's performance. In our scenario, we assume there is 20% probability a command depends on another command.

The size of client commands sent by each client is 100, 000; and for each command, the key is a random integer with 64bits; while the value is a random string with fixed size (i.e., 4 KB). The size of dependency window for each Accept message is set to 4. We compare the difference of throughput between the two protocols.

As shown in Fig. 5, with the increase of number of clients, the throughput is increasing linearly. And the optimized Multi-Paxos protocol increases faster than the typical one. This is because it's unnecessary for each replica to wait until all previous commands get applied before applying a committed command. Moreover, from Fig. 5, we can find that when the number of clients reaches 6, the throughput does not change anymore in optimized Multi-Paxos protocol. The reason for this is when client number reaches 5, the storage I/O is fully utilized to process client commands.

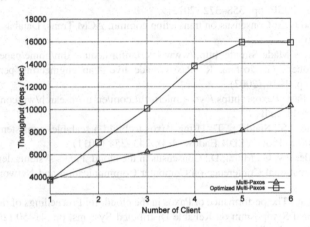

Fig. 5. Throughput performance comparison with no dependency among commands

6 Conclusion

In this paper, we proposed an optimization for Multi Paxos protocol by allowing out-of-order applying client commands. Compared with original design of typical Multi-Paxos protocol, a committed client command could be applied to state machine, as long as it has no dependency on its previous commands or all dependencies are resolved. By doing this, we could improve the system throughput of cloud storage applications. Finally, comparison between two protocols is analyzed to prove the feasibility of our proposal.

Acknowledgments. This paper is supported by The National Key Research and Development Program of China (No. 2017YFB1400601), National Natural Science Foundation of China (No. 61872119), Natural Science Foundation of Zhejiang Province (No. LY12F02003).

References

1. Wenying, Z., et al.: Research on cloud storage architecture and key technologies. In: Proceedings of the 2nd International Conference on Interaction Sciences: Information Technology, Culture and Human, pp. 1044–1048. ACM, Korea (2009)
2. Arokia, R., Shanmugapriyaa, S.: Evolution of cloud storage as cloud computing infrastructure service. IOSR J. Comput. Eng. 1(1), 38–45 (2012)
3. Ousterhout, J., Agrawal, P., Erickson, D., et al.: The case for RAM Cloud. Commun. ACM 54, 121–130 (2011)
4. Lamport, L.: Paxos made simple. ACM SIGACT News 32(4), 18–25 (2001)
5. Ongaro, D., Ousterhout, J.: In search of an understandable consensus algorithm. In: Proceedings of ATC 2014, Usenix Annual Technical Conference, pp. 1–18 (2014)
6. Moraru, I., Andersen, D.G., Kaminsky, M.: There is more consensus in Egalitarian parliaments. In: SOSP, pp. 358–372 (2013)
7. Gray, J., Lamport, L.: Consensus on transaction commit. ACM Trans. Database Syst. 31(1), 133–160 (2006)
8. David, M.: Paxos Made Simple. http://www.scs.stanford.edu/~dm/home/papers/paxos.pdf
9. Tushar, C., Robert, G., Joshua, R.: Paxos made live - an engineering perspective. In: ACM PODC, pp. 1–16 (2007)
10. Lamport, L.: Fast Paxos. https://www.microsoft.com/en-us/research/wp-content/uploads/2016/02/tr-2005-112.pdf
11. Jun, R., Eugene, J.S., Sandeep, T.: Using Paxos to build a scalable, consistent, and highly available datastore. Proc. VLDB Endow. 4(4), 243–254 (2011)
12. Ailidani, A., Aleksey, C., Murat, D.: Consensus in the cloud: Paxos systems demystified. In: 2016 25th International Conference on Computer Communication and Networks, pp. 1–10 (2016)
13. Parisa, J.M., et al.: The performance of Paxos in the cloud. In: Proceedings of the 2014 IEEE 33rd International Symposium on Reliable Distributed Systems, pp. 41–50 (2014)
14. Jonathan, K., Yair, A.: Paxos for system builders: an overview. In: Proceedings of the 2nd Workshop on Large-Scale Distributed Systems and Middleware, pp. 1–5 (2008)
15. Wang, C., Jiang, J., Chen, X., Yi, N., Cui, H.: Apus: fast and scalable Paxos on RDMA. In: Proceedings of the 2017 Symposium on Cloud Computing, pp. 94–107 (2017)
16. Lamport, L., Malkhi, D., Zhou, L.: Reconfiguring a state machine. SIGACT News 41(1), 63–73 (2010)
17. GoLang. https://github.com/golang/go

A Blockchain Based Searchable Encryption Scheme for Multiple Cloud Storage

Chao Zhang[1], Shaojing Fu[1,2(✉)], and Weijun Ao[1]

[1] College of Computer, National University of Defense Technology, Changsha, China
fusj_nudt@163.com.com
[2] State Key Laboratory of Cryptology, Beijing, China

Abstract. Searchable encryption is a necessary and important service for cloud storage since it can realize the function of information retrieval on encrypted cloud data while protecting privacy. However, the typical searchable encryption models consisting of only a single cloud service provider can not prevent malicious behavior. In this paper, a new searchable encryption scheme in multi-cloud was proposed based on blockchain. We first define a system model based blockchain in multiple clouds and combine multiple cloud service providers together to store data together through a consortium chain. And then we store the encrypted document and document index in the IPFS, at the same time the hash value of the documents and the IPFS address of the document are stored in blockchains. Our scheme can provide a sorting retrieval scheme based on multi-keywords over the outsourced encrypted data and a validation scheme to detect file integrity. The theoretical analysis and experiments on real-world data show the security and high performance of our scheme.

Keywords: Cloud storage · Multi-cloud · Blockchain · Searchable encryption

1 Introduction

As a convenient basic service of cloud computing, cloud storage can provide users with flexible storage environment, saving the cost of physical devices. User access to data is no longer limited by geographical restrictions, only through the network identity authentication can obtain data. Our outsourcing of data means we lose direct control over the data. The following three limitations are obvious, especially in the case of a single CSP [7]:

- **Access instability:** Once the centralized service facilities are shutdown, users will fall into a state of unaccessibility. In 2017, amazon's cloud service product AWS status was abnormal, and the network in North America could not be accessed.

© Springer Nature Switzerland AG 2019
J. Vaidya et al. (Eds.): CSS 2019, LNCS 11982, pp. 585–600, 2019.
https://doi.org/10.1007/978-3-030-37337-5_48

- **Data Intrusion:** It's not uncommon for hackers to hack into the CSP. Apple's cloud service, iCloud, often suffers from user's privacy breaches.
- **Data integrity:** Data corruption can occur once a single cloud server crashes. In this case, the data is difficult to recover.

In order to prevent illegal access of the data by the server or unauthorized users, data encryption is usually used to make it impossible for an unauthorized entity to recover the original data from the encrypted data. However, data encryption will cause a decrease in data availability, making it difficult to perform operations such as information retrieval on ciphertext. How to search over the outsourced encrypted data effectively on the cloud server has becomes a topic worth studying. Song et al. [16] proposed a practical searchable encryption mechanism based on SWP algorithm, which realized the precedent of keyword search on ciphertext. But this method requiring to scan all documents is inefficient. Cao et al. [21] used KNN technology to establish index and trap door and proposed a multi-keyword searchable encryption technology based on vector space model. In this scheme, a key word dictionary is established previously to generate a file index vector for each file. Each dimension of the file index vector corresponds to a key word in the key word dictionary. The product of query vector and file index vector is used to get the correlation score of query and file. [5] modifies [21] to make it more efficient and add personalization factors in the scheme. The searchable encryption have gotten rapid developments and a line of studies have been done on security issues such as security analysis [11,12], fuzzy search [6,19], verification [3,17,18] and data privacy protection in other scenarios [13,23].

In response to the limitations of the single cloud server model, many scholars have begun to propose a cloudy server model for research [2,7,20]. [24] first proposed a searchable encryption model in multiple clouds and extend two security protocols with shamir's secret schemes to achieve better availability and robustness.

In recent years, there have been many works based on blockchain applied to the field of searchable encryption. Li [10] proposed a cloud storage encrypted data search model based on bitcoin, and proposed two different solutions for data set size, but this model is only suitable for lightweight documents, and is not suitable for dynamic data. In [4], data is stored in segments, and a distributed hash table (DHT) that stores data on a blockchain does not store all of the data. Huang et al. [9] used the payment characteristics of Bitcoin to construct a new type of outsourced data payment model, which ensures that the honest peers get paid after completing the calculation task. However, this solution lacks more functionality and flexibility due to the limitations of the bitcoin script. In [8], a distributed storage architecture is proposed, which supports keyword query function and uses blockchain technology to ensure data integrity. In addition, client verification and search result verification are implemented by designing a secure keyword search protocol. Guo et al. [15] applied blockchain technology to medical data to provide reliable data services for patients and key management was not assigned by a central server. By sharing the secret pseudorandom function seeds among authorities, this protocol resists collusion attack out of N from N − 1 corrupted authorities. This scheme builds distributed storage based on the blockchain instead of the central server, which reduces the control of the data by the server, thereby reducing the threat of data being damaged by the malicious server. In the scheme of Zhang [25], a server-side verification is implemented to protect the honest server from malicious attacks by malicious data owners during the data storage phase and a trusted query fee transaction mode that does not rely on a third party is proposed.

To address security issues in multiple clouds, we propose firstly a system model based blockchain in multiple clouds and combine multiple cloud service providers together to store data together through a consortium chain. This scheme supports multiple keywords search and a verification for detecting file integrity. Meanwhile, there is an incentive to maintain the CSP alliance.

2 Preliminaries

2.1 Blockchain and Smart Contract

The blockchain is derived from a chain structure composed of blocks proposed by Nakamoto [14]. Under the support of cryptographic techniques such as hash and asymmetric encryption, the peers in the trading system take the transactions as an input and run through a hashing algorithm which gives an output of a fixed length. The operation of the hash competition is to gain the mastership of the system. The traditional trading system needs a trusted third party as the center to maintain the transaction, but the blockchain system is different from the traditional trading mode. The Bitcoin system has no central node. Every peer follows the blockchain consensus protocol and establishes a point-to-point communication. The consensus mechanism can synchronize the transaction status of the entire system without relying on any third-party trust organization. All transaction information will be written into the chain structure. The more peers participating in the consensus, the more difficult it is to change the information on the chain.

According to the size of the blockchain network, the blockchain can be divided into public blockchain, consortium blockchain and private blockchain:

(1) The public blockchain is a network that is completely open to the outside world and it is not subject to identity restrictions. Anyone can be involved in mining, transaction transfer and other operations of the network. The public chain system relies on pre-agreed protocols to ensure the normal operation of the network and is not subject to any third party management. Public chain systems generally have a certain incentive mechanism to encourage miners to deal with transactions, aiming at maintaining the normal operation of the entire network system. Typical public chain representatives are Bitcoin and Ethereum [22].

(2) The consortium blockchain is different from the public blockchain. There is a certain access mechanism. The peers in the network are determined by the organizer of the consortium chain. It doesn't have the concept of token. The process of transaction doesn't require tokens to execute. Consortium blockchain has a higher speed to deal with transaction per second than public blockchain. In our model, it can store data quickly, cheaply and securely.

(3) The private blockchain is a multi-center or centralized weakly network. Unlike the public blockchain, the control of the network is completely determined by an institution. Whether the network is open to the outside world depends on the pre-regulation of the institution. Private blockchain handles transactions faster with less resource consumption.

Smart contract is the trusted shared program code which deployed on a blockchain. Participants who sign the contract agree on the content of the contract. Once the smart contract is deployed, it will automatically execute the program without relying on any central authority.

2.2 InterPlanetary File System

IPFS (The Interplanetary File System) [1] is a point-to-point distributed file system designed to create persistent and distributed storage and shared files. Nodes in IPFS will form a distributed file system with content addressed hyper links. The core of PFS is MerkleDAG, a directed acyclic graph. All content searches are based on its multihash checksum. In our scheme, IPFS provides the storage of encrypted data. IPFS interacts with clients and servers. The interactive part consists of three phase:

- **Data storage phase:** The encrypted document set and encrypted index will be uploaded to the IPFS by the user. IPFS will return the hash value of each file after storing the document set.
- **Index pullback phase:** Before computing scalar product of encrypted index and trapdoor, the CSP need to pullback the encrypted index from IPFS according to index's mutlihash checksum.
- **Document pullback phase:** The result returned by the CSP is not the document set but the mutlihash checksum set. The user can search for documents based on multihash checksum.

2.3   Notations

Notation	Meaning
N	The number of documents
n	The number of keywords
D	A document collection $D = (D_1, D_2, D_3, \cdots, D_N)$
C	A encrypted document collection $C = (C_1, C_2, C_3, \cdots, C_N)$
T	The trapdoor
I	The encrypted index of D
$Root_{multi-sig}$	The multi-signature of the Merkle tree root value
(pub_{key}, pri_{key})	A RSA public and secret key pair
$CAddr_D$	A Content Address set of document collection D

2.4   System Model and Threat Model

We organize a CSP alliance to build a multi-CSP storage platform. A multi-CSP storage platform has significant advantages over a single CSP platform:

– Provide more stable service.
– Provide more powerful computing resources.
– Provide a more secure service platform.

The blockchain-based searchable encryption system consists of four parts: user, multi-CSP, blockchain and IPFS. Users can be divided into data owners and data consumers. Data owners in this system can upload documents in the data storage phase. The key can be delivered to other authorized users over a secure channel and the authorized user can also retrieve over the encrypted document. Data consumers construct search request with multiple keywords in data search phase. The encrypted document and document index are stored in the IPFS. The hash value of the documents and the IPFS address of the document are stored in blockchains. The multi-CSP constitute consortium chain and does not save any encrypted documents. Only accept user requests and calculate the product of the trapdoor and the index. We assume that both data owner and data consumer are trusted, But the CSP alliance can be malicious. Specifically, the majority of CSP alliance members may work together to tamper with data or cause data corruption. Some members may be curious about the contents of the file. In addition, Some data stored in IPFS that has not been accessed for a long time may be lost (Fig. 1).

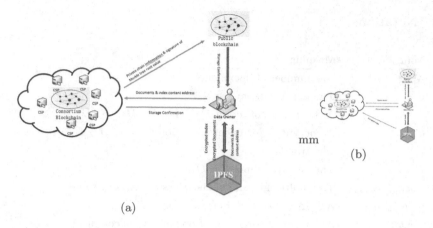

mm

(b)

(a)

Fig. 1. System model. (a) Data storage phase. (b) Documents search phase.

3   The Proposed Scheme

3.1   Detailed Design of Ciphertext Retrieval System Based on Blockchain

The design is described in detail as follows:

- **Key generation phase:** $sk \leftarrow Gen(n)$, set parameter n and generate two $(n+d+1) \times (n+d+1)$ invertible matrices M_1, M_2 and a split indication vector S of length $(n+d+1)$ bits. The three elements constitute the master key $sk = \{S, M_1, M_2\}$.
- **Index generation phase:** The user selects the document collection D to be uploaded and performs the following processing:
  - Document collections keyword analysis: extract keywords using the potter stems to form a keyword dictionary. In order to evaluate the impact of keywords on the document collection better, we choose to use statistical methods TF-IDF to count keywords.

$$S_{t,Dd} = \frac{ln(1 + f_{d,t}) \times ln(1 + \frac{m}{f_t}))}{\sqrt[2]{\sum_{t \epsilon D_d}(ln(1 + f_{d,t}) \times ln(1 + \frac{m}{f_t}))^2}} \tag{1}$$

  $f_{d,t}$ represents the occurrence times of the word t in the document D_d. f_t represents the number of the word t in document D. m represents the number of documents in the collection D.
  - Construct an index vector $p_i = (s_{t1,D_d}, s_{t2,D_d}, s_{t3,D_d}, s_{t4p,D_d}, \cdots\cdots, s_{tn,D_d})$ for the document Di according to s_{t,D_d}. We extend n-dimensional vector p_i to a $(n+d+1)$-dimensional vector $\boldsymbol{p}_i$ using a extension scheme in security KNN. After the splitting process, we can split $\boldsymbol{p}_i$ into two random vectors $\boldsymbol{p}_i'$ and $\boldsymbol{p}_i''$. Finally, the two vectors are encrypted with

two reversible matrices in the key sk to generate the encrypted index $I_i = \{M_1^T \boldsymbol{p}_i', M_2^T \boldsymbol{p}_i''\}$.

$$\boldsymbol{p}_i' = \{\boldsymbol{p}_{ij}'\} = \begin{cases} \boldsymbol{p}_{ij}, & \text{if } S_j = 1 \\ \boldsymbol{p}_{ij} + r, & \text{otherwise} \end{cases} \quad (2)$$

$$\boldsymbol{p}_i'' = \{\boldsymbol{p}_{ij}''\} = \begin{cases} \boldsymbol{p}_{ij} & \text{if } S_j = 1 \\ \boldsymbol{p}_{ij} - r & \text{otherwise} \end{cases} \quad (3)$$

- **Interaction with IPFS:** In our scheme, cloud servers are no longer used to store encrypted data for three reasons:
  - Prevent the CSP alliance from modifying the data. We need a storage method that doesn't require any third party control.
  - Although alliance chains are more efficient than public chains, there are only a few thousand TPS at most.
  - Weaken the CSP alliance in the system. In previous models, CSP has always been dominant, so it is a big threat.

  Client uploads the ciphertext collection C which is encrypted with symmetric encryption algorithm AES to the IPFS. There are two kinds of stored data: one is the index, the second is the encrypted document collection. After the data is stored on IPFS, IPFS will send back the multihash checksum of the document collection $CAddr_D = \{CAddr_{D_1}, CAddr_{D_2}, CAddr_{D_3}, \cdots, CAddr_{D_N}\}$ to client. Match the content address to the document number to build the data structure $MapAddr = \{Addr_i\}$, $Addr_i = CAddr_{D_i} \| Doc_i^{Num}$, $i\epsilon(0 - N)$.

- **CSP Alliance:** CSP alliance is based on existing consortium chain technology HyperLedger fabric. The entire structure is shown in Fig. 3. The construction of the consortium chain aims to solve two problems:
  - IPFS is a distributed file system with content addressed hyper links. We need a secure storage environment that store mapping of content addresses to plaintext.
  - We need an incentive to encourage CSP to help users calculate the product query vector and index. We can build a blockchain-based incentive to solve this problem

  There are four types of peers in the CSP alliance framework network: Membership Service Provider (MSP), Endorsing Peer, Ordering Peer, Committing Peer.
  - **MSP:** MSP is composed of multiple CSP through negotiation. This organization manages the authorization, join and delete of other peers throughout the network. The peers played by CSP may assume multiple responsibilities.
  - **Endorsing Peer:** Some CSP accept transaction requests as ep and are responsible for verifying transactions. The endorsing peer then signs the transaction and returns it to the proposer.

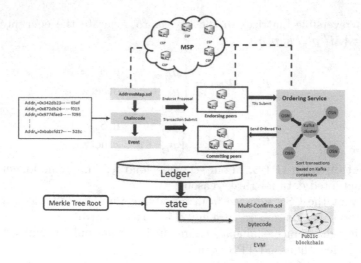

Fig. 2. Blockchain state lock

- **Ordering Peer:** The CSP Alliance will select some service providers as ordering peer and such peers are responsible for sorting transactions based on consensus. Finally, The ordering peers will return result to committing peers.
- **Committing Peer:** CSP as committing peer will verify the correctness of the transaction and record the transaction information on the ledger.

– **Content address storage:** The CSP alliance server will receive $hash_D$ and document number set Num =from the client by the client. In order to facilitate the subsequent work, we store the content address on the consortium blockchain through the smart contract. The consortium chain is open to users, and the user can access data stored in the chain at any time. Although the consortium chain is only controlled by one cloud service provider currently, it has good scalability to accommodate other cloud service providers to maintain together (Fig. 2).

– **State lock:** Due to the consortium blockchain controlled by multi-CSP, We are convinced that there is a very low probability of the majority of CSPs becoming adversaries together. We need a method to guarantee the information security of consortium blockchain. The specific method is as follows: We are convinced that the data on the public block chain is credible. We use the public blockchain to lock the consortium blockchain's state. A Merkle tree T is built by cloud server, where the leaf nodes is made up of $CAddr_D$. ($Root$ is used for integrity verification as a crucial information which is recorded on the public blockchain. In addition, we record the consortium blockchain height H and transaction id Tx_{id} when we updated the smart contract last. The three elements constitute a message stored on the public blockchain for locking the consortium blockchain's state $state = (Root||H||Tx_{id})$. Let all CSPs sign the

---

Algorithm 1: Smart contract: Content address update

Input: content address set $MapAddr$, the user id $User_{addr}$
Output: state T

1 addressMap : unit32 $\rightarrow$ string ;
2 require (dataonwer $== User_{addr}$);
3 **for** $i = 0, 1, 2, \cdots, N$ **do**
4 | **if** $isvalid(Addr_{D_i}) == true$ **then**
5 | | addressMap[i] $= (Addr_{D_i})$;
6 | **else**
7 | | return false;
8 | **end**
9 **end**
10 set Boolean $T = $ true;
11 **return** T;

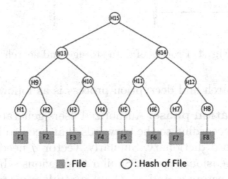

■ : File   **○ : Hash of File**

Fig. 3. The construction of Merkle tree

state credibly and automatically through smart contracts, before uploading *state*. See the Algorithm 2 for the specific signature scheme.

Algorithm 2: Smart contract: Multi-signature of state

Input: state *state*, Minimum confirmation number *threshold*
Output: signature of state $state_{multi-sig}$

1 confirm[] = false;
2 $state_t = state$;
3 require($CSPs.size >= threshold\&\&threshold! = 0$);
4 **for** $i = 0, 1, 2, \cdots, CSPs.size$ **do**
5 | confirm[CSP_i] = true;
6 | $state_t = $ signature($state_t$);
7 | last-confirm $= CSP_i$;
8 **end**
9 $state_{multi-sig} = state_t$;
10 **return** $state_{multi-sig}$;

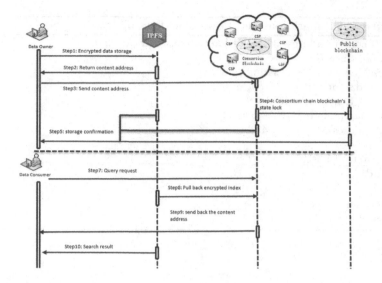

Fig. 4. Process of data storage and search

The document search and decryption process is as follows:

- **Trapdoor generation phase:** Authorized users generate vector $q = (q_1, q_2, q_3, q_4, \cdots, q_n)$ according to the keywords that need to be searched and the constructed keyword dictionary. Similarly, vector q need to be extended to an $(n+d+1)$-dimensional vector. Similar to previous scheme, we also split q into two random vectors q' and q''. the two random vector are encrypted by the two inverse matrices to get $T = \{M_1^{-1}q', M_2^{-1}q'\}$ (Fig. 4).

Algorithm 3: Build Trapdoor: $T \leftarrow GenTraodoor(w, sk)$

Input: secret key $sk = \{S, M_1, M_2\}$, the search keywords w
Output: Trapdoor T

1 build the (n+d+1)-dimensional vector q according w;
2 **Vector splitting phase:**
3 **for** $i = 0, 1, 2, \cdots, (n+d+1)$ **do**
4 $\quad$ **if** $S_i == 0$ **then**
5 $\quad\quad q_i' = q_i'' = q_i$;
6 $\quad$ **else**
7 $\quad\quad q_i' = q_i + r$;
8 $\quad\quad q_i'' = q_i'' - r$;
9 $\quad$ **end**
10 **end**
11 **Vector encryption phase:**
12 $T = \{M_1^{-1} \cdot q', M_2^{-1} \cdot q'\}$;
13 **return** T;

– **Search phase:** in this phase, the cloud server only provides computing power. It will interact with IPFS in the process.
  - IPFS: Receiving the request, cloud server will pullback the index from IPFS in the case where there is no index copy locally.
  - Calculate the product: Cloud server will compute the scalar product of encrypted index I and trapdoor T to capture the relevance of data documents.
  - Find the Mapping on the ledger. Cloud server only select top-k documents based on the relevance score. Since the cloud server does not store encrypted documents at all, only send back the hash corresponding to the encrypted documents. This process involves mapping the files on the consortium chain to find the corresponding content address.

$$I_i \cdot Q = \{M_1^T \cdot p_i', M^T \cdot p_i''\}\{M_1^{-1} \cdot q', M_2^{-1} \cdot q''\}$$
$$= p_i' \cdot q' + p_i'' \cdot q''$$
$$= p_i. \tag{4}$$

– **Incentive mechanism:** CSP Alliance needs an incentive mechanism to encourage CSP to provide computing power. In order to prevent malicious CSPs from providing erroneous results, this incentive mechanism needs to cooperate with the verification. Good behavior needs to be rewarded and bad behavior will be punished.
  - When the user verifies that the result is correct, the user will send a record to the alliance chain. After the alliance link is subject to this record, it is saved on the ledger after a consensus. This record includes the user id $User_{id}$, the CSP id CSP_id and the signature of the returned result $Sig(result)$.
  - When the user discovers that the validation result is an error, the keyword Bad is added to the record header field.

– **Verification phase:** There may be a case where the server maliciously sends back the erroneous data. The documents downloaded from IPFS maybe are different from the one previously stored or the documents are already damaged. Based on the above state locking method, we verify the integrity and blockchain's state. Authorized users execute the following steps: As shown in Fig. 3, user sends a request $H_D = (H_2, H_7)$ to verify integrity of file 2 and file 7. Before sending the request, user can download $state$ from public blockchain to check if H_D exists. After receiving the request, the cloud server returns the H_D-related index path $H_{path} = \{H_1, H_{10}, H_8, H_{11}\}$ as evidence form the Merkel tree saved locally to the user for verification. User can calculate the value of the Merkel root quickly based on according to H_{path}. Let's compare the root value which you recovered based $state_{multi-sig}$ with the root value you compute locally (Fig. 5).

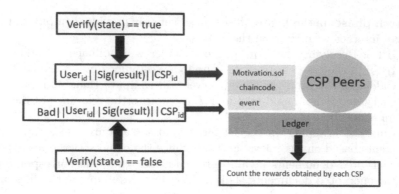

Fig. 5. Incentive mechanism

Algorithm 4: Verification

Input: $l = 2^n$, H_{path}, H_D, pub_{key}, $state_{multi-sig}$
Output: Validation results $flag$(boolean)

1 $H_{input} = H_D$, $H_{output} = Null$, $H_{temp} = Null$;
2 **for** $i = 1, 2, 3, \cdots, n$ **do**
3   **while** $H_{input}! = Null$ **do**
4   select a element H_j from H_{input};
5   **if** $j\%2 == 1$ **then**
6   select H_{j+1} from H_{path};
7              $H_{j+n/i} = Hash(H_j||H_{j+1})$;
8   add $H_{j+n/i}$ to the set H_{temp};
9   remove H_j from the set H_{input};
10   **else**
11   select H_j from the set H_{j-1};
12             $H_{j-1+n/i} = Hash(H_{j-1}||H_j)$;
13   add $H_{j-1+n/i}$ to the set H_{temp};
14   remove H_j from the set H_{input};
15   **end**
16   **end**
17     $H_{input} = H_{temp}$;
18 **end**
19 $H_{output} = H_{input}$;
20 **return** $flag = Verfiy(H_{output}, state_{multi-sig}, pub_{key})$;

---

4 Security and Performance Analysis

In order to verify the correctness and efficiency of the proposed scheme, we implement our scheme on real-world data set: the Enron Email Data Set using java language. We use the VMware software to install the virtual machine to

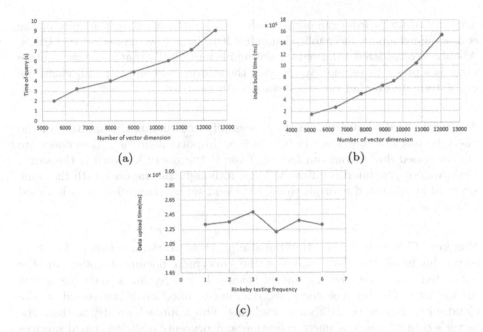

Fig. 6. The time cost in the experiment. (a) For the different number of vector dimension in the process of building an index. (b) For the different number of vector dimension in the process of building an query. (c) For data upload to Rinkeby

build an IPFS local cluster. Virtual machine configuration: CPU Intel (R) Core i5-7500, 4G RAM. We build four peers in the cloud used to play a role of the consortium chain. The configuration: 8-core processor, 100 GB, 16G RAM. The test chain Rinkeby was used instead of the public chain for simulation. The test document set contains 12063 keywords. The data stored in the test chain is 520 bits. After several tests, the average time required for data to be uploaded to the chain is 23289 ms. It takes an average of 125632 ms for each 1000 uploads of content addresses to the consortium chain (Fig. 6).

4.1 Security Analysis

Data Privacy: In our scheme, encrypting the document collection using the traditional symmetric encryption algorithm AES is adopted to assure security, before the documents are sent to the IPFS. AES is secure enough that it ensures that adversary can not get any information of the documents without key. The document index is encrypted with a secure KNN. [21] has theoretically proved that in the absence of a key SK, the cloud service cannot restore the encrypted index.

Data Verifiable: Tamper-proof is a prominent feature of blockchain. In our scheme, we adopt a double-chain mode to verify the data. To prevent the majority of CSPs from tampering with data jointly, we store the state of the consortium chain on the public chain after it is signed by the majority of CSPs. A state is considered valid only if the number of CSP's that recognize a state exceeds a preset threshold. By verifying the information on the public chain, we can determine whether the union state is trustworthy.

Trapdoor Unlinkability: In the process of constructing the splitting of the query vector, randomization factors have an important impact. Trap doors are always varied due to random factors. Even if the query keyword is the same, the trapdoor generated is different. Thus, although the trapdoor with the same keyword is submitted multiple times, the cloud server cannot learn the keyword information.

Weaken Control: In the traditional ciphertext retrieval scheme, the cloud server holds all the data including the encrypted document collection, the encrypted index and the documents hashes. It is easy for a malicious server to corrupt data. But, the encrypted document collection is not stored on the cloud server but on the IPFS in our scheme. This approach greatly weakens the server's control over document collection and prevents malicious cloud services from damaging the data.

4.2   Storage Performance Analysis

In the blockchain-based application scenarios, system performance limited by throughput capacity. The lower the throughput is, the fewer transactions generated in per unit of time is. The efficiency of the system is affected by the number of transactions. In the scheme of [10], the data is stored on the opcode OP_RETURN in bitcoin. The maximum capacity OP_RETURN can save is 40kB. Suppose there are n documents containing n_k keywords. [10] generates $n + n_{k/2}$ transactions during the data storage phase. At least two transactions occur during the user search phase. considering the performance and storage problems of the system, [25] generate only one transaction in the data storage phase. Scheme [25] has solved the system congestion problem caused by too many transactions, but the schemes have also weakened the status of blockchain in the system. As for our scheme, smart contract is adopted to store data, and the upper limit of data storage is no longer limited by OP_RETURN. in the data storage phase, only $n + 1$ transactions are generated where n transactions are stored on the Consortium chain. We can improve system throughput by adjusting the difficulty of mining. This scheme is Effectively compatible with low overhead and blockchain security.

Scheme	Privacy	Trapdoor unlinkablity	Weaken control	Low storage on the chain
[10]	✓	✓	✓	✗
[25]	✓	✓	✗	✓
Our scheme	✓	✓	✓	✓

5 Conclusion

This paper proposes a searchable encryption scheme in multi-cloud based on blockchain, aiming at the enormous storage cost in current blockchain-based ciphertext retrieval schemes. We organize a CSP alliance to build a multi-CSP storage platform. There is an effective incentive mechanism within the alliance to maintain the CSP's initiative to provide services. It combine low overhead with blockchain security Effectively. The data is stored in the IPFS instead of the cloud server. It reduces the server control of encrypted document collection. Meanwhile, this solution has the ability to verify file integrity.

For the further work, We will focus on how to increase the throughput of the blockchain to accommodate a large amount of data storage and information extraction.

Acknowledgments. This work is supported by the National Nature Science Foundation of China (NSFC) under grant 61572026, 61672195, Open Foundation of State Key Laboratory of Cryptology (No: MMKFKT201617).

References

1. Benet, J.: IPFS-content addressed, versioned, P2P file system. arXiv preprint arXiv:1407.3561 (2014)
2. Bessani, A., Correia, M., Quaresma, B., André, F., Sousa, P.: DEPSKY: dependable and secure storage in a cloud-of-clouds. ACM Trans. Storage (TOS) 9(4), 12 (2013)
3. Chai, Q., Gong, G.: Verifiable symmetric searchable encryption for semi-honest-but-curious cloud servers. In: 2012 IEEE International Conference on Communications (ICC), pp. 917–922. IEEE (2012)
4. Do, H.G., Ng, W.K.: Blockchain-based system for secure data storage with private keyword search. In: 2017 IEEE World Congress on Services (SERVICES), pp. 90–93. IEEE (2017)
5. Fu, Z., Ren, K., Shu, J., Sun, X., Huang, F.: Enabling personalized search over encrypted outsourced data with efficiency improvement. IEEE Trans. Parallel Distrib. Syst. 27(9), 2546–2559 (2016)
6. Fu, Z., Wu, X., Guan, C., Sun, X., Ren, K.: Towards efficient multi-keyword fuzzy search over encrypted outsourced data with accuracy improvement. IEEE Trans. Inf. Forensics Secur. 11(12), 2706–2716 (2017)

7. Gunasundari, R.: Cloud computing security from single to multi-clouds. In: Hawaii International Conference on System Sciences (2012)

8. Guo, R., Shi, H., Zhao, Q., Zheng, D.: Secure attribute-based signature scheme with multiple authorities for blockchain in electronic health records systems. IEEE Access **6**, 11676–11686 (2018)

9. Huang, H., Chen, X., Wu, Q., Huang, X., Shen, J.: Bitcoin-based fair payments for outsourcing computations of fog devices. Future Gener. Comput. Syst. **78**, 850–858 (2018)

10. Li, H., Zhang, F., He, J., Tian, H.: A searchable symmetric encryption scheme using blockchain. arXiv preprint arXiv:1711.01030 (2017)

11. Li, J., Huang, Y., Wei, Y., Lv, S., Lou, W.: Searchable symmetric encryption with forward search privacy. IEEE Trans. Dependable Secur. Comput. **PP**(99), 1 (2019)

12. Lin, W., Wang, K., Zhang, Z., Chen, H.: Revisiting security risks of asymmetric scalar product preserving encryption and its variants. In: IEEE International Conference on Distributed Computing Systems, pp. 1116–1125 (2017)

13. Luo, Y., Jia, X., Fu, S., Xu, M.: pRide: privacy-preserving ride-matching over road networks for online ride hailing service. IEEE Transactions on Information Forensics and Security, p. 1 (2018). https://doi.org/10.1109/TIFS.2018.2885282

14. Nakamoto, S., et al.: Bitcoin: a peer-to-peer electronic cash system (2008)

15. Peng, J., Guo, F., Liang, K., Lai, J., Wen, Q.: Searchain: blockchain-based private keyword search in decentralized storage. Future Gener. Comput. Syst. S0167739X17318630 (2017)

16. Song, D., Wagner, D., Perrig, A.: Practical techniques for searches on encrypted data. In: Proceeding of 2000 IEEE Symposium on Security and Privacy, S P 2000, pp. 44–55 (2000). https://doi.org/10.1109/SECPRI.2000.848445

17. Sun, W., et al.: Verifiable privacy-preserving multi-keyword text search in the cloud supporting similarity-based ranking. IEEE Trans. Parallel Distrib. Syst. **25**(11), 3025–3035 (2013)

18. Wan, Z., Deng, R.H.: VPSearch: achieving verifiability for privacy-preserving multi-keyword search over encrypted cloud data. IEEE Trans. Dependable Secur. Comput. **6**, 1083–1095 (2018)

19. Wang, C., Ren, K., Yu, S., Urs, K.M.R.: Achieving usable and privacy-assured similarity search over outsourced cloud data. In: IEEE INFOCOM, pp. 451–459 (2012)

20. Wang, H.: Identity-based distributed provable data possession in multicloud storage. IEEE Trans. Serv. Comput. **8**(2), 328–340 (2015)

21. Wong, W.K., Cheung, D.W.l., Kao, B., Mamoulis, N.: Secure KNN computation on encrypted databases. In: Proceedings of the 2009 ACM SIGMOD International Conference on Management of Data, pp. 139–152. ACM (2009)

22. Wood, G., et al.: Ethereum: a secure decentralised generalised transaction ledger. Ethereum Project Yellow Paper **151**, pp. 1–32 (2014)

23. Xue, K., Li, S., Hong, J., Xue, Y., Yu, N., Hong, P.: Two-cloud secure database for numeric-related SQL range queries with privacy preserving. IEEE Trans. Inf. Forensics Secur. **12**(7), 1596–1608 (2017)

24. Zhang, W., Lin, Y., Xiao, S., Liu, Q., Zhou, T.: Secure distributed keyword search in multiple clouds. In: 2014 IEEE 22nd International Symposium of Quality of Service (IWQoS), pp. 370–379. IEEE (2014)

25. Zhang, Y., Deng, R.H., Shu, J., Yang, K., Zheng, D.: TKSE: trustworthy keyword search over encrypted data with two-side verifiability via blockchain. IEEE Access **6**, 31077–31087 (2018)

Correction to: Efficient and Secure Three-Factor User Authentication and Key Agreement Using Chaotic Maps

Jiaxi Hu, Zhiqiang Xu, Debiao He, Sherali Zeadally,
and Kim-Kwang Raymond Choo

Correction to:
Chapter "Efficient and Secure Three-Factor User Authentication and Key Agreement Using Chaotic Maps" in: J. Vaidya et al. (Eds.): *Cyberspace Safety and Security*, LNCS 11982, https://doi.org/10.1007/978-3-030-37337-5_15

The original version of this chapter was revised. The affiliation of Sherali Zeadally was corrected to "College of Communication and Information, University of Kentucky, Lexington, USA."

The updated version of this chapter can be found at
https://doi.org/10.1007/978-3-030-37337-5_15

Author Index

Printed in the United States
By Bookmasters